50.00

PREACHING GOD'S TRANSFORMING JUSTICE

A Lectionary Commentary, Year B

Edited by
Ronald J. Allen
Dale P. Andrews
Dawn Ottoni-Wilhelm

WJK WESTMINSTER
JOHN KNOX PRESS
LOUISVILLE • KENTUCKY

© 2011 Westminster John Knox Press

First edition
Published by Westminster John Knox Press
Louisville, Kentucky

11 12 13 14 15 16 17 18 19 20—10 9 8 7 6 5 4 3 2 1

Book design by Sharon Adams
Cover design by Eric Walljasper, Minneapolis, MN
Cover artwork by Dr. He Qi titled Mary and Martha, *www.heqigallery.com*

Library of Congress Cataloging-in-Publication Data

Preaching God's transforming justice : a lectionary commentary, year B / edited by Ronald J. Allen, Dale P. Andrews, Dawn Ottoni-Wilhelm. — 1st ed.
    p. cm.
    Includes indexes.
    ISBN 978-0-664-23454-6 (alk. paper)
    1. Social justice—Sermons. 2. Social justice—Biblical teaching. 3. Church year sermons. 4. Common lectionary (1992) I. Allen, Ronald J. (Ronald James), 1949– II. Andrews, Dale P., 1961– III. Wilhelm, Dawn Ottoni.
    BS680.J8P74 2011
    261.8—dc23

2011021422

Contents

Contents

Preface

The editors are grateful to the members of our households—spouses and children—not only for love and understanding during the preparation of these volumes but also for conversation, child care, and running to the store for necessary supplies of chocolate, coffee, and other things important to editorial work. We recognize our Presidents, Deans, and colleagues for encouragement, questions, and suggestions. The editors particularly thank the ninety persons who wrote for this series. To their already overflowing lives as activists, ministers, and scholars, they added responsibility for preparing the articles for these volumes. We honor Jon Berquist for his formative role in this project and for multiple forms of support. We thank Amy-Jill Levine of the Divinity School, Vanderbilt University, who graciously read the manuscript with a discerning eye. The editors express appreciation to J. B. Blue and Song Bok Jon, graduate students at Boston University School of Theology, who sacrificed time from their own academic responsibilities to engage in research on the Holy Days for Justice. The editors and contributors are responsible for limitations that result from not following the suggestions of these learned colleagues.

We send this book forward with the prayer that God will use it to help re-create the world as a community of love, peace, freedom, mutuality, respect, security, and abundance. May it be a resource for preaching that, under the influence of the Holy Spirit, empowers social transformation.

Introduction

Many people today yearn to live in a world of love, peace, freedom, mutuality, respect, security, and abundance for all. The Bible calls this combination of qualities justice. The best of the Bible and Christian tradition envision the heart of God's own mission as re-creating the world as a realm of love and justice. Joining God in this mission is at the heart of the calling of the preacher and the congregation. The aim of this three-volume series is to empower sermons as active agents in God's mission.

Ninety preachers and scholars contribute to this work. These writers are known for their insight into social dimensions of the divine purposes as well as for their capacity to interpret the social vision boldly and sensitively. Approximately half of the writers are women and half are men; about 40 percent of them are African American, Hispanic, Asian American, or Native American.

Preaching for Justice: A World of Love, Peace, Freedom, Mutuality, Respect, Security, and Abundance

This commentary is a resource for preaching for a world of justice from the deepest theological convictions of biblical texts. *Preaching God's Transforming Justice* is distinctive in two ways. First, while other aids for preaching from the lectionary sometimes discuss matters of social justice, this series is the first commentary on the Revised Common Lectionary to highlight God's life-giving intentions for the social world from start to finish.[1] *Preaching God's Transforming Justice* is not simply a mirror of other lectionary commentaries (such as the impressive *Feasting on the Word: Preaching the Revised Common Lectionary*) but concentrates on how the lectionary readings can help the preacher identify and reflect theologically and ethically on the social implications of the biblical readings. Second, this series introduces twenty-two Holy Days for Justice. Explained further below, these days are intended to enlarge the church's awareness of the depth and insistence of God's call for justice and of the many ways that call comes to the church and world today.

The comments on the biblical texts are intended to be more than notes on contemporary social issues. The comments are designed to help preachers and congregations develop a deep and broad theological vision out of which to interpret the social world. Furthermore, this book aims to provide practical guidance for living more justly as individuals and communities.

Special Feature: Twenty-Two Holy Days for Justice

This commentary augments the traditional liturgical calendar by providing resources for twenty-two special Holy Days for Justice. The title for these noteworthy days, suggested by Professor Amy-Jill Levine of Vanderbilt University, requires explanation. God's mission for justice is holy. Consequently, the church's commitment to justice is holy. Some of the events, however, that call forth these special days are not holy. Indeed, some days—such as Yom haShoah (which remembers the murder of six million Jewish people by the Nazis)—are occasions for mourning. However, at the same time these days also call the church to take bold and powerful actions to join the holy work

---

1. The Revised Common Lectionary (RCL) was developed by the Consultation on Common Texts, an ecumenical consultation of liturgical scholars and denominational representatives from the United States and Canada. The RCL provides a collection of readings from Scripture to be used during worship in a schedule that follows the seasons of the church year: Advent, Christmas, Epiphany Day, Lent, Easter, Day of Pentecost, Ordinary Time. In addition, the RCL provides for a uniform set of readings to be used across denominations or other church bodies.

The RCL provides a reading from the Hebrew Bible, a Psalm response to that reading, a Gospel, and an Epistle for each preaching occasion of the year. It is presented in a three-year cycle, with each year centered around one of the Synoptic Gospels. Year A largely follows the Gospel of Matthew, Year B largely follows Mark, and Year C largely follows Luke. Selections from John are also read each year, especially during Advent, Lent, and Easter.

The RCL offers two tracks of Hebrew Bible texts for the Season after Pentecost or Ordinary Time: a semicontinuous track, which moves through stories and characters in the Hebrew Bible, and a complementary track, which ties the Hebrew Bible texts to the theme of the Gospel texts for that day. Both tracks are included in this volume.

For more information about the Revised Common Lectionary, visit the official RCL Web site at http://lectionary.library.vanderbilt.edu/ or see *The Revised Common Lectionary: The Consultation on Common Texts* (Nashville: Abingdon Press, 1992).

of God in attempting to transform the circumstances that led to lamentation. We can never undo pain and suffering, but we can try to reshape the world to minimize the danger of such things recurring, and to encourage possibilities for people and nature to live together in justice.

Each Holy Day for Justice derives from either a person or an event that helps the contemporary community become aware of arenas in the world that cry for justice. These Holy Days bridge significant phenomena in our history and present culture that do not receive adequate attention in the church's liturgical calendar or may not otherwise be noted in the congregation. They draw our attention to circumstances in need of social transformation.

Each Holy Day for Justice has a different focus. In *Preaching God's Transforming Justice* these days are placed close to the Sunday on which they occur in the Christian year and the ordinary calendar. When reaching a Holy Day for Justice in the lectionary, the preacher can choose whether to follow the readings from the Revised Common Lectionary or to work instead with the readings and themes of the Holy Day for Justice.[2] The concerns highlighted in these special days may also inspire preachers to bring those concerns to the fore in sermons prepared in conversation with the traditional lectionary readings.

In the list of Holy Days for Justice below, the editors place in parentheses a date or season when the congregation might naturally observe a Holy Day for Justice. The dates for many of the Holy Days for Justice are already widely accepted, such as the dates for World AIDS Day, the Universal Declaration of Human Rights, Martin Luther King Jr. Day, Salt March, Earth Day, Yom haShoah, and the Fourth of July. The editors assigned the dates for other Holy Days for Justice in conversation with scholars who work closely with the concerns of those days and with communities closely related to the origin of the person or concern at the center of the day. Of course, preachers and worship planners are free to observe the Holy Days for Justice on other dates that fit more naturally into the congregation's local calendar.

The Holy Days for Justice are:

1. World AIDS Day (December 1)
2. Universal Declaration of Human Rights (December 10)
3. Martin Luther King Jr. Day (January 15)
4. Asian American Heritage Day (February 19)
5. International Women's Day (March 8)

---

2. In addition, the Revised Common Lectionary already sets aside possible readings for All Saints' Day and Thanksgiving. The specific dates of some of the Holy Days for Justice change from year to year. These days are placed in the commentary in the season of the lectionary year when they typically occur.

6. Salt March Day: Marching with the Poor (March 12)
7. Oscar Romero of the Americas Day (March 24)
8. César Chávez Day (March 31)
9. Earth Day (April 22)
10. Holocaust Remembrance Day: Yom haShoah (27th of Nissan, usually from early April to early May)
11. Peace in the Home (second Sunday in May)
12. Juneteenth: Let Freedom Ring (June 19)
13. Gifts of Sexuality and Gender (June 29)
14. Fourth of July: Seeking Liberty and Justice for All
15. Sojourner Truth Day (August 18)
16. Simchat Torah: Joy of the Torah (mid-September to early October)
17. International Day of Prayer and Witness for Peace (September 21)
18. Peoples Native to the Americas Day (fourth Friday in September)
19. World Communion Sunday (first Sunday in October)
20. Night of Power (27th Night of Ramadan: From 2011 through 2020 the date moves from September to August, July, June, May, and April)
21. World Food Day (October 16)
22. Children's Sabbath (third weekend in October or another date that works for the congregation)

The discussions of these days in the commentary are distinctive in three ways. (1) In the case of almost every special day (with the exception of Simchat Torah: The Joy of the Torah), the editors selected four biblical texts that relate to these special emphases, including a reading from the Torah, Prophets, and Writings, a reading from a Psalm, a reading from a Gospel, and another from an Epistle. The editors chose the texts for each day in the hope that the passages can become good conversation partners in helping the congregation reflect on how the day enlarges the congregation's vision and practice of justice. Most of the texts were chosen because they support potential emphases in the day, but some were chosen because they give the preacher the opportunity to enter into critical dialogue with the text or with the way the biblical text has been used in the church or the culture. While a few of the biblical texts for the Holy Days for Justice duplicate passages in the Revised Common Lectionary, most of the texts for the Holy Days for Justice are not found in the lectionary. (2) Each day is introduced by a brief paragraph offering a perspective on why that day is included. We repeat the same introductory paragraph in all three volumes. (3) Each day also includes a quote from a figure or document in the past or the present that voices a provocative perspective on the concerns represented by that day. For example, in Year A on Martin Luther King Jr. Day, the preacher is presented with an excerpt from the "Letter from Birmingham City Jail."

Some readers may initially be put off by some of these selections, especially days that also appear in the civic calendar in the United States, such as Fourth of July: Seeking Liberty and Justice for All. These days are not intended to promote uncritical celebration of present culture. On the contrary, the appearance of these days can become the occasion for the preacher to reflect critically with the congregation on the themes of those days. Some of the motifs associated in popular culture with Fourth of July, for instance, run against the grain of God's best hopes for the human family. In the name of being faithful, some preachers studiously avoid speaking about days suggested by the civic calendar. However, the congregation may too easily construe such silence as the preacher's consent to the culture's prevailing mind-set. The sermon can attempt to redress the prevailing cultural mind-set that either neglects attention to questions of justice or actively promotes injustice.

The Holy Days for Justice address the criticism that the Revised Common Lectionary does not adequately represent biblical texts that deal with matters of justice as fully as those texts are represented in the Bible. Such special days might also enlarge the vision of the preacher and the congregation while offering preachers a venue for addressing matters that are sometimes hard to reach when following the lectionary. For the congregation that may be hesitant to consider such matters, the appearance of these emphases in a formal lectionary commentary might add to the preacher's authority for speaking about them.

God's Vision for the Social World

The purposes of this commentary series are rooted in the core of God's vision for the social world. To be sure, the Bible is a diverse document in the sense that its parts were written at different times and places, in different cultural settings, and from different theological and ethical points of view—for example, Priestly, Deuteronomic, Wisdom, and apocalyptic. Nevertheless, the different materials in the Bible share the common perspective that God intends for all individuals and communities (including the world of nature) to live together in justice.

The Priestly theologians begin the Bible with the vision in Genesis 1 by picturing God creating a world in which each and every entity has a particular place and purpose and in which all entities—the ecosphere, animals, and human beings—live together in covenantal community. The role of the human being is to help the different entities live together in the mutual support that God envisions. The aim of the Ten Commandments and Israel's other laws is to create a social community that embodies how God wants people to live together in blessing. The Priestly theologians show special concern for ensuring that the poor and marginalized experience providence through care practiced by the community. Israel is to model how God wants all peoples to live together in blessing (Gen. 12:1–3). Israel is to be a light to the nations in these regards (Isa. 42:6). The church later understands its message to be grafted onto that of Israel (e.g., the church shares in the mission of being a light to the world, Matt. 5:13–14).

The Deuteronomic thinkers envisioned Israel not only as a community in covenant with God, but also as a community whose members were in covenant with one another so that all could live in love, peace, and security. Deuteronomy 15:7–8 epitomizes this attitude. "If there is among you anyone in need . . . do not be hard-hearted or tight-fisted toward your needy neighbor. You should rather open your hand, willingly lending enough to meet the need, whatever it may be." The Deuteronomic monarch is to rule with a copy of the Torah present at all times and is not to be "above other members of the community nor turning aside from the commandment" (Deut. 17:19–20). The monarch is responsible to God and to the community for seeing that justice is enacted in all aspects of Jewish life. The covenant includes nature such that when the people are faithful, nature blesses them, but when they are unfaithful, nature itself curses them (Deut. 28:1–45).

The Wisdom literature encourages practices that not only provide for individual and household prosperity but build up the community. The wise life shows respect for the poor as full members of the community (Sir. 4:1–10). The Wisdom literature cautions the prosperous not to become self-absorbed by their possessions but to use their resources to strengthen the community. Indeed, the wise are to "speak out for those who cannot speak, for the rights of all the destitute . . . [to] defend the rights of the poor and needy" (Prov. 31:8–9). Moreover, the sages thought that God charged the natural order with wisdom so that by paying attention to the way in which the elements of nature work together, human beings can learn how God wants human beings to live as individuals and in community, as we can see in the case of the ant modeling wisdom (Prov. 6:6).

The apocalyptic theologians believed that the present world—both the social sphere and nature—is so broken, unjust, and violent that God must replace it with a new world, often called the realm of God. The apocalyptic book of 4 Ezra (2 Esdras) vividly expresses this hope:

> It is for you that Paradise is opened, the tree of life is planted, the age to come is revealed, plenty is provided, a city is built, rest is appointed, goodness is established and wisdom perfected beforehand. The root of evil is sealed up from you, illness is banished from you, and death is hidden; hell has fled and corruption has been forgotten; sorrows

have passed away, and in the end the treasure of immortality is made manifest.[3] (4 Ezra 8:52–56)

In this new world all relationships and situations manifest God's purpose. Those who defy God's desires through idolatry, exploitation of the poor, and violence are condemned.

Paul, Mark, Matthew, Luke, and most other early Christian writers share this general viewpoint (e.g., Rom. 8:18–25; Mark 13:24–27). These first-century theologians believed that the life, ministry, death, and resurrection of Jesus signaled that the final and complete manifestation of the realm of God had begun in a limited way in the ministry of Jesus and would come in its fullness with the return of Jesus. The ministry of Jesus both points to that realm and embodies it. Jesus' disciples are to alert others to the presence and coming of the realm and to live in the present as if the realm is fully here. The church is to embody the transformed world.

From the perspective of the Bible, God's vision for the interrelated communities of humankind and nature is, through and through, a social vision. It involves the intertwining relationships of God with humankind and nature, of human communities with one another, and of human communities with nature. Marjorie Suchocki, a major contemporary theologian, uses the evocative phrase "inclusive well-being" to sum up God's desire for every created entity to live in love, peace, justice, dignity, freedom, and abundance in a framework of mutually supportive community.[4] Anything that threatens the well-being of any entity in the created world goes against the purposes of God.

Individual Bible Readings and Implications for Social Justice and Transformation

Every passage in the Bible has social implications. In connection with each text in the lectionary, the commentators in this series help the congregation envision God's purposes for human community. Some texts are quite direct in this way. For example, Amos exhorts, "Let justice roll down like waters, and righteousness like an ever-flowing stream" (Amos 5:24). The prophet wants the people to practice justice. Other texts are less direct but are still potent in their implications. According to the book of Acts, Priscilla was a teacher of the gospel alongside her spouse Aquila (Acts 18:24–28). From this and

3. "The Fourth Book of Ezra," trans. Bruce M. Metzger, in *The Old Testament Pseudepigrapha: Apocalyptic Literature and Testaments*, ed. James H. Charlesworth (Garden City, NY: Doubleday & Co., 1983), 1:544. Fourth Ezra was written in the late first century CE and is sometimes known as 2 Esdras.

4. Marjorie Suchocki, *The Fall to Violence: Original Sin in Relational Theology* (New York: Continuum, 1994), 66.

many other texts, we glimpse the vital role of women in the leadership of the earliest churches (e.g., Mark 16:1–8; Luke 8:1–3; Acts 9:36–42; 16:11–15; Rom. 16:1–3, 6, 7, 12; 1 Cor. 1:11; Phil. 4:2–4).

The contributors to these volumes articulate what the biblical writers hoped would happen in the social world of those who heard these texts in their original settings and point to ways in which interaction with the biblical texts helps today's congregations more fully embrace and enact God's intent for all to experience inclusive well-being. The following are among the questions the writers consider:

- What are God's life-giving intentions in each text?
- What does a particular text (in the context of its larger theological world) envision as a community that embodies God's social vision, a vision in which all live in inclusive well-being?
- What are the benefits of that vision for humankind and (as appropriate) nature?
- How do human beings and nature fall short of God's possibilities when they do not follow or sustain that vision?
- Do individuals or communities get hurt in the world of the text or in the way that text has been interpreted?
- What needs to happen for justice, healing, re-creation, and inclusive well-being?

At the same time, writers sometimes criticize aspects of the occasional biblical text whose social vision does not measure up to the fullness of God's intentions. For example, according to Ezekiel, God ordered marks placed on faithful people who lamented abominations that took place in Israel. God then commanded some of the faithful to murder the unfaithful: "Pass through the city . . . and kill; your eye shall not spare, and you shall show no pity. Cut down old men, young men and young women, little children and women, but touch no one who has the mark" (Ezek. 9:5–6). This passage invites the reader to believe that God commanded murder. The first letter of Peter asserts, "Slaves, accept the authority of your masters with all deference, not only those who are kind and gentle but also those who are harsh. For it is a credit to you if, being aware of God, you endure pain while suffering unjustly" (1 Pet. 2:18–19). This passage assumes the validity of slavery and encourages recipients to accept being abused.

Texts such as these do not measure up to the Bible's highest vision of God's desire for a just world; hence, many preachers cannot commend such barbed texts as positive guidance for today's community. Instead, such a preacher critiques the passage. However, even when the preacher cannot fully endorse what a text invites the congregation to believe and do, the appearance of theologically and ethically problematic texts in the lectionary can open an important door for a conversation among preacher and congregation regarding what they most truly believe concerning God's social vision. The text may not be directly instructive, but the congregation's encounter with the text can be an important occasion of theological and ethical reflection.

Naming and Confronting Systems That Frustrate God's Purposes

Individuals acting alone and with others can defy God's purposes for humankind and nature. But beyond individual and small-group actions, a key insight to emerge in recent generations is that systemic forces distort God's purposes for humankind and the larger created world. Ethicists often refer to such phenomena as systemic evil.

A system is a transpersonal network of attitudes, values, and behaviors that shape the lives of individuals and communities. Systemic evil creates force fields that push individuals and communities to distort God's purposes in the social world. Systems can affect communities as small as the Wednesday-night prayer group and as large as nations and transnational associations. Examples of systemic evils that subvert God's life-giving purposes are racism, sexism, neocolonialism, ageism, nationalism, classism, heterosexism, and ecological destruction.

Preachers need to recognize and name systemic distortions of God's purposes for the social community. While this analysis is important, it sometimes leaves individuals and congregations feeling impotent in the face of massive structural forces. When possible, the writers in this series urge preachers to give these concerns a human face and to offer specific insights and stories that help congregations envision practical steps that they can take to join God in seeking to transform the social world. What attitudes and actions can individuals and congregations take to become agents of transformation? These writers want congregations to feel empowered to make a difference. We hope that each comment will offer a horizon of hope for the preacher and the congregation.

The Preacher Speaks from, to, and beyond the Local Context

The importance of taking account of the context of the congregation is a permeating emphasis in preaching—and more broadly in theological scholarship—today. The preacher is called to understand the congregation as a culture in its own right. The preacher should conduct an exegesis of the congregation that reveals the events, memories, values, practices, attitudes, feelings, patterns of relationship (especially power relationships), physical spaces, and larger systems that combine to make the congregation a distinct culture.

This commentary does not intend to provide the minister with prepackaged ideas for sermons but urges ministers to begin their approach to preaching on matters of justice from inside the culture of the congregation. The local pastor who has a thick understanding of the local community knows much better than a scholar in a far-off city how the life of that congregation needs to develop in order to witness more fully to God's purposes.

The preacher should typically speak *from* and *to* the local context. Rather than impose a social vision that the preacher has found in a book of theological ethics, on the Internet, or at the latest clergy network for peace and justice, the preacher can approach matters of social justice from inside the worldview of the congregation. Hence, one can usually identify points of contact between the world of the congregation and the need for transformation. The preacher can then use the base of identification and trust between the pulpit and the pew to speak *to* the congregation. To help the congregation participate more fully in God's transformative movement, the preacher will typically need to help the congregation think beyond itself.

From this point of view, the contributors to *Preaching God's Transforming Justice* intend to be conversation partners in helping preachers identify particular areas in which the congregation might reinforce patterns of thought and behavior that manifest their deepest theological convictions. We hope the book will help congregations to grow in the direction of God's social vision and to find steps they can take to become agents of justice.

Recent literature in preaching leads preachers to think of the congregation not just as a collection of individuals but as a *community*, the *body* of Christ. While sermons should help individuals imagine their particular social witnesses, sermons should also be addressed to the congregation as community and its corporate social witness.

Moreover, the congregation is itself a social world. While the larger goal of the book is to help preachers move the congregation toward reflection and mission in the larger social arena, some texts may lead the preacher to help the listeners reflect on how the internal life of the congregation can more fully witness to God's life-giving purposes.

Prophetic Preaching with a Pastoral Goal

In the broad sense this book calls for prophetic preaching. We think of prophetic preaching in contrast to two common notions. From one common perspective, prophetic preaching predicts specific future events, especially those that point to the return of Jesus. This way of thinking does not catch the fullness of prophetic preaching in the Bible itself. A second common viewpoint associates prophetic preaching with condemnation. In this view, the prophetic preacher identifies what the text is against and what is wrong in the social world, sometimes denouncing the congregation and others. These sermons can chastise the congregation without providing a word of grace and empowerment. This perspective is also incomplete.

The editors of *Preaching God's Transforming Justice* regard the purpose of all preaching as helping the congregation and others interpret the world from the standpoint of God's life-giving purposes. Preaching seeks to build up the congregation as a community of witness and to help the world embody the divine realm. The goal of all preaching is pastoral in the root sense of building up the flock so that the congregation can fulfill God's purposes. The word "pastoral" derives from the world of flocks and shepherds, in which the shepherd (the pastor) did whatever was necessary to maintain the health of the flock.

From the perspective of the Bible, the prophet is a kind of ombudsperson who compares the actual behavior of the community with God's purposes of inclusive blessing. The special call of the prophet is to help the community recognize where it falls short of those purposes and what the community needs to do to return to them. On the one hand, a prophet such as Amos concentrated on how the community had departed from God's purposes by exploiting the poor and, consequently, faced judgment. On the other hand, a prophet such as Second Isaiah called attention to the fact that the community in exile did not trust in the promise of God to return them to their homeland. In both cases, the community was not living up to the fullness of God's purposes. While the prophet may need to confront the congregation, the prophet's goal is to prompt the congregation to take steps toward restoration. Prophetic preaching ultimately aims at helping the congregation name *for* what they can be.

Representative Social Phenomena

Preaching God's Transforming Justice urges preachers and communities toward conscious and critical theological reflection on things that are happening in the contemporary social world from the perspective of God's purpose to re-create the world as a realm of love, peace, freedom, mutuality, abundance, and respect for all. Nevertheless, some preachers refer to a limited number of social phenomena in their sermons. A preacher's hermeneutical imagination is sometimes enlarged by pondering a panorama of representative social phenomena that call for theological and ethical interpretation, such as the following:

Abortion	Gender orientation	Police brutality
Absent fathers	LGBTQA	Pollution
Addictions	Geneva Convention	Pornography
Affirmative action	Genocide	Postcolonialism
Aging	Gentrification	Poverty
Animal rights	Glass ceiling	Prisons
Anti-Semitism	Greed	Public schools/private
Arms sales	Gun control	schools
Church and nation	Health care	Racism
Civil religion	Homelessness	Repression
Classism	Housing	Reproductive rights
Colonialism	Human rights	Sexism
Consumerism	Hunger	Socialism
Death penalty	Idols (contemporary)	Stranger
Disability perspectives	Immigration	Systemic perspectives
Diversity	Islam and Christianity	Terrorism
Domestic violence	Islamophobia	Torture
Drugs	Judaism and	Transnational
Ecological issues	Christianity	corporations
Economic exploitation	Language (inclusive,	Tribalism
Education	repressive)	Unemployment
Empire	Margins of society	Uninsured people
Energy	Militarism	U.S. having no single
Eurocentrism	Multiculturalism	racial/ethnic major-
Exclusivism	Nationalism	ity by 2040
Flight to the suburbs	Native American rights	Violence
Foster care	Neocolonialism	White privilege
Gambling	Peace movements	Xenophobia
	Pluralism	

This catalog is not suggested as a checklist of social issues that a preacher should cover in a given preaching cycle. Returning to an earlier theme, the minister who is in touch with the local culture can have a sense of where God's vision for justice interacts with particular social phenomena. Nonetheless, such a list may help some ministers think more broadly about possible points of contact between the core theological convictions of the church and the social world.[5]

---

5. A preacher might find it useful to review regularly the social forces that are current in the sphere of the congregation and in the larger world. Preachers can easily slip into thinking about social perspectives from limited and dated points of view. Preachers may find it helpful

Index of Passages in the Order
of Books of the Bible

For preachers who do not regularly preach from the lectionary, and for preachers who want to look up a particular passage but do not know where it is located in the lectionary, an index of passages discussed in the commentary is located at the end of the volume. This index lists biblical texts in the order in which they are found in the Bible.

The contributors typically discuss the biblical texts in the following order: first lesson(s) from the Torah, Prophets, and Writings; the Psalm(s); the Epistle; and the Gospel. However, a writer will occasionally take up the texts in a different sequence as a part of his or her interpretive strategy for the day.

Inclusive Language, Expansive Language

This series uses inclusive language when referring to humankind. In other words, when contributors refer to people in general, they use language that includes all of their intended audience (e.g., humankind, humanity, people). When a writer refers to a particular gender (female or male), the gender-specific referent is used.

We seek to use expansive language when referring to God. In other words, the contributors draw on various names, attributes, and images of God known to us in Scripture and in our individual and corporate encounter of God in worship. We avoid using exclusively masculine references to God. When a Scripture passage repeatedly uses language for God that is male, we have sought more gender-inclusive emendations that are consistent with the intent of the original. Readers searching for an entire inclusive-language translation might try *The Inclusive Bible: The First Egalitarian Translation*.[6]

The Bible and Christian tradition use the term "Lord" to speak of both God and Jesus. The word "lord" is masculine. The English word "Lord" derives from a time when much of the European social world was hierarchical with the lord and lady at the top and with human beings arranged in a pyramid of descending social power with the upper classes at the top and other classes below, and with males having authority over women. People in the upper reaches of the pyramid are authorized to dominate those below them. While we try to minimize the occurrence of the title "Lord," occasional writers in this book use the term

---

to interview members of the congregation regarding the social phenomena that are most in the consciousness of the congregation.

6. Priests for Equality, *The Inclusive Bible: The First Egalitarian Translation* (Lanham, MD: Rowman & Littlefield, 2007).

"Lord" for God to call attention to God's absolute sovereignty; these writers do not intend for the use of the expression "Lord" to authorize masculine superiority or the detailed social pyramid implied in the history of the word. Indeed, this book sees the purposes of God pointing toward a human community in which hierarchical domination is dismantled and power is shared.

Although the historical Jesus was a male, he announced the coming of the realm of God, a social world that is egalitarian with respect to gender and social power. In the hope of evoking these latter associations (and minimizing the pyramidal associations with "Lord") we have shifted the designations of some historic days in the Christian Year that highlight aspects of the ministry of Jesus from lordship language to the language of "Jesus" and "Christ": Nativity of Jesus, Baptism of Jesus, Resurrection of Jesus, and Reign of Christ (in place of Nativity of the Lord, Baptism of the Lord, Resurrection of the Lord, and Christ the King).

We have also tried to speak expansively of the realm of God (NRSV: kingdom of God) by using terms such as realm, reign, rule, dominion, kin-dom, and holy commonwealth. The word "kingdom" appears where the author has specifically requested it.

Language for the Parts of the Bible

The contemporary world is a time of critical reflection and experimentation regarding how to refer to the parts of the Bible that many Christian generations have referred to as the Old and New Testaments. The discussion arises because in much contemporary usage the word "old" suggests worn out and outdated, while "new" often implies "better" and "improved." Many Christians believe that the unexplained use of the phrases Old Testament and New Testament can contribute to supersessionism: the conviction that new and improved Christianity has taken the place of old and outdated Judaism. The old covenant is no longer in force, but has been replaced by the new covenant. When used without interpretation, this way of speaking contributes to injustice by supporting anti-Judaism and anti-Semitism. In an attempt to use language that is more just, many people today are exploring several ways forward.

As a part of the contemporary exploration, the writers in this series use a variety of expressions for these parts of the Bible. There is no fully satisfactory way of speaking. We note now the most common expressions in this series and invite the reader to remember the strengths and weaknesses of each approach.

Some leaders think that today's community can use the expressions Old and New Testaments if the church explains what that language does and does not mean.[7] In antiquity old things were often valued and honored. Moreover, the words "old" and "new" can imply nothing more than chronology: The literature of the Old Testament is older than that of the new. The church would then use the terms Old and New Testaments without casting aspersion on Judaism and without suggesting that God has made Christianity a much purer and truer religion. Occasional writers in the series use the phrases Old and New Testaments in this way. However, a growing number of speakers and writers think that the words Old Testament and New Testament are so deeply associated with negative pictures of Jewish people, writings, institutions, and practices that, even when carefully defined, the language feeds negative perceptions.

The words "Hebrew Bible" and "Hebrew Scriptures" are a popular way of referring to the first part of the Bible. These titles came about because English versions are not based primarily on the Septuagint (the translation of the Hebrew Scriptures into Greek in the third and second centuries BCE) but are translated from Hebrew (and Aramaic) manuscripts in consultation with the Septuagint. However, the designation "Hebrew Bible" raises the question of what to call the twenty-seven books that make up the other part of the Bible. We cannot call the other books the "Greek Scriptures" or the "Greek Bible" because the Septuagint is also in Greek. We cannot call them the "Christian Scriptures" or the "Christian Bible" since the church honors the entire Bible.

Occasional Christians refer to the Old Testament as the "Jewish Bible." This nomenclature is unsatisfactory because people could understand it to mean that the first part of the Bible belongs only to the Jewish community and is not constitutive for the church. Furthermore, the Christian version differs from the Jewish Tanakh in the way that some of the books are ordered, named, and divided.

The designations "First and Second Testaments" are increasingly popular because many people see them as setting out a chronological relationship between the two bodies of literature—the First Testament came prior to the Second. However, in competitive North American culture, especially in the United States, "first" can imply first in value, while "second" can imply something not as good as the first. The winner receives first place; second place is often a disappointment. Moreover, "second" can imply second best or secondhand.

Seeking a way of referring to the Bible that respects its diversity but suggests its continuities, and that promotes respect for Judaism, writers in this

7. On this discussion, see further Ronald J. Allen, "Torah, Prophets, Writings, Gospels, Letters: A New Name for the Old Book," *Encounter* 68 (2007): 53–63.

series sometimes refer to the parts of the Bible as Torah, Prophets, Writings, Gospels, and Letters. This latter practice adapts a Jewish way of speaking of the Scriptures as TANAKH, an acronym derived from the Hebrew words for Torah, Prophets, and Writings (*torah, neviim, ketuviim*), and adds the categories of Gospels and Letters.[8] To be sure, the books in TANAKII are divided and arranged differently than in the Christian Bible. Furthermore, while some may object that the books of Acts, Hebrews, and Revelation do not fall into these categories, we note that Acts is less a separate genre and more a continuation of the Gospel of Luke. In the strict sense, Revelation has the form of letter. Although scholars today recognize that Hebrews is an early Christian sermon, it likely circulated much like a letter.

All designations for the parts of the Bible are vexed by the fact that different churches include different books. We should really speak of a Roman Catholic canon, several Orthodox canons, and a Protestant canon. As a concession to our inability to distinguish every permutation, we ask the reader to receive these designations with a generous but critical elasticity of mind and usage.

The designation "son of man" is challenging in a different way, especially when it is used of or by Jesus. Interpreters disagree as to whether the phrase "son of man" is simply a way of saying "child of a human being" or "son of humanity" (or, more colloquially, simply "human being"), or whether it has a specialized theological content, such as "apocalyptic redeemer" (as in Dan. 7:13–14). Since individual contributors interpret this phrase in different ways, we sometimes leave the expression "son of man" in the text of the commentary, with individual contributors explaining how they use it.

Diverse Points of View in the Commentary

The many writers in this commentary series are diverse not only in gender, race, and ethnicity, but also in exegetical, theological, and ethical viewpoints. Turning the page from one entry to the next, the reader may encounter a liberation theologian, a neo-orthodox thinker, an ethnic theologian, a process thinker, a socialist, or a postliberal. Moreover, the writers are often individually creative in the ways in which they see the forward movement of their texts in calling for social transformation today. While all authors share the deep conviction that God is even now seeking to lead the world toward more inclusive, just community, the nuances with which they approach the biblical material and even the social world can be quite different.

---

8. For further discussion, see Allen, "Torah, Prophets, Writings, Gospels, Letters."

Rather than enforce a party line with respect to matters of exegesis, theology, and ethical vision, the individual writers bring their own voices to clear expression. The editors' hope is that each week the preacher can have a significant conversation with a writer who is an other and that the preacher's social vision will be broadened and deepened by such exposure.

Diversity also characterizes the process by which this book came into being. The editorial team itself is diverse, as it includes an African American man from the African Methodist Episcopal Zion Church; a woman of European origin from the Church of the Brethren, a historic peace church; and a man of European origin from the Christian Church (Disciples of Christ). While the editors share many common convictions, their vision has been impacted deeply by insights from preachers and scholars from many other churches, movements, communities, and cultures. Dawn took the lead in editing Year A, Ron for Year B, and Dale for Year C. While the editors regarded one of their core tasks as helping the individual writers bring out their own voices forcefully, each has inevitably edited in light of her or his theological and ethical commitments.

Ultimately the goal of *Preaching God's Transforming Justice* is not simply to give preachers resources for talking about social issues, but to empower congregations to develop a theological life perspective that issues in practices of justice and to participate with God in working toward a time when all created entities—every human being and every animal and plant and element of nature—can live together as a community of love through mutual support with abundance for all.

First Sunday of Advent

Leonora Tubbs Tisdale

ISAIAH 64:1–9
PSALM 80:1–7, 17–19
1 CORINTHIANS 1:3–9
MARK 13:24–37

The lections from the Hebrew Scriptures begin not on a note of joyous expectation, but in despair and longing for a world shaped by the presence and values of God. Both Isaiah and the psalmist give voice to Israel's existential yearning for a God who once seemed so close but now seems distant and silent. The Gospel and Letter point toward the hope that is ours as sinful believers in Christ (1 Cor. 1:3–9), and to our call to live in the time between Christ's first and second comings in watchful faithfulness (Mark 13:24–37).

Isaiah 64:1–9

This passage begins with a plea for God to rip open the heavens, to come down to earth, and to make God's presence known among the nations (vv. 1–2). The prophet makes this cry on behalf of the Israelites because they are (a) beleaguered by their enemies (and longing for God's vindication of them) and (b) aware that their own sinfulness that has landed them in this mess. They have broken covenant with God, and have not dealt justly or lived in harmonious community with one another. Consequently, the God who once drew near now seems distant and remote.

As a result, the people are miserable. They know that without God, their lives are not only precarious and vulnerable; they are also devoid of meaning and purpose and goodness. So they draw on their memories of God in the past—God as their creator/potter (v. 8b) and God as their compassionate parent (v. 8a)—as they urge God to intervene in their future.

One of the challenges this text poses for contemporary hearers is that often we do not see ourselves as being sinful and cut off from God. Furthermore,

1

even when we do acknowledge our sinfulness, the focus is often more on personal and individual sins than on the corporate sins of church or community or nation.

In his book *The Road to Daybreak*, Henri Nouwen writes of returning to his homeland of Holland one Christmas season, and marveling that in one short generation the country had changed from being a very pious nation to becoming a very secular one. He writes:

> Many reasons can be given. But it seems to me, from just looking around and meeting and speaking to people, that their captivating prosperity is one of the more obvious reasons. People are just very busy—eating, drinking, and going places. . . . The Dutch have become a distracted people—very good, kind, and good-natured but caught in too much of everything.[1]

I suspect the same could be said of many prosperous nations today, including the United States. We are an affluent and self-sufficient people. Our lives are busy and distracted. As a result, many in our culture have lost a deep sense of connection with God and with one another. We are afraid to slow down for fear that all we will find inside is emptiness and a chasm of unfulfilled longing.

Robert Putnam uses the haunting phrase "bowling alone" to describe our culture. In earlier generations, we bowled together in leagues, but now we bowl alone, that is, we live in affluence but in isolation.[2] Bowling alone is a symbol for the loss of responsibility for one another, similar to the loss of responsibility for one another that characterized Isaiah's day.

The prophet voices the deep yearnings of a people who are "bowling alone," a people who know that their only hope for individual and communal restoration rests in the God who first formed and fashioned them. "O that you would tear open the heavens and come down," the prophet cries (v. 1). Israel experienced an answer to this prayer when God came down (so to speak) and liberated the community from exile. The church glimpses an answer to that prayer in the birth of the Incarnate One, the child who in his very being bridges the great chasm between heaven and earth.

Psalm 80:1–7, 17–19

Psalm 80 is a communal lament. But unlike Isaiah, the psalmist does not claim that the suffering of God's people is the result of their own sin. Indeed, the

---

1. Henri J. M. Nouwen, *The Road to Daybreak: A Spiritual Journey* (New York: Doubleday, 1988), 108.
2. Robert D. Putnam, *Bowling Alone* (New York: Touchstone Books, 2000), 414.

theological source of suffering here is a mystery. We know only that Israel is oppressed by the hands of their enemies (v. 6). While they are befuddled as to why God—the one whom they know to be both Shepherd and sovereign ruler—is silent in the face of their suffering, they are confident that God will restore their life. Indeed, the fact that the community can raise the question of God's relationship to oppression is itself a sign of theological health.

As if giving God a pep talk, the psalmist urges God to be true to whom the Israelites know God to be. "Stir up your might!" (v. 2b) the psalmist says to the ruler of the universe. "Restore us!" (v. 3a) the psalmist says to the Shepherd of Israel. "Let your face shine, that we may be saved" (vv. 3b, 19b), pleads the psalmist—calling to mind both the shining face of Moses after encountering God on Sinai (Exod. 34:29–35) and the Aaronic blessing (Num. 6:24–26).

This psalm gives a voice especially to those who suffer injustice at the hands of others: who know oppression and persecution at the hands of ruthless enemies, who experience economic exploitation and unfair treatment in the workplace, who know the indignity of systems that do not treat them equitably, and who are ravaged by the atrocities of war. The sermon can bring these voices into the worshiping community.

Beyond voicing frustration and pain, the psalmist points to a practical means by which God can act to restore and to let God's face shine: God can work through "the one at [God's] right hand," that is, the monarch (v. 17). The monarchy in Israel was to promote policies and ways of living together that would bring peace, justice, and abundance to all (Ps. 72). The psalm thus implicitly invites those who have the power to shape life systems to cooperate with God in bringing wholeness to the whole broken fabric of the current social order.

The psalm implies that, for renewal to take place, our communities need leaders who are genuinely committed to the good of all. And members of the community are important here. Robert Putnam notes that "if decision makers expect citizens to hold them politically accountable, they are more inclined to temper their worst impulses rather than face public protests."[3] In Advent, a preacher can encourage the congregation to make public officials accountable for policies and behaviors that are truly just.

1 Corinthians 1:3–9

It is both astonishing and puzzling that the apostle Paul begins the letter to the Corinthians with thanksgiving for "the grace of God that has been given you in Christ Jesus" (v. 4b), with affirmation for their many spiritual gifts

3. Ibid., 346.

(v. 7) and with confidence that Christ will "strengthen you to the end, so that you may be blameless on the day of our Lord Jesus Christ" (v. 8).

The Corinthians? Full of the grace of God and the gifts of the Spirit? Blameless on the day that Christ returns?

At Corinth the church fought so bitterly over whose spiritual gifts are the greatest that Paul reminded them that love is the greatest gift (1 Cor. 13). This church was so fractious that Paul reminded them they were to work harmoniously together like parts of the body (1 Cor. 12). In this church the rich gobbled up the best food when they gathered for their potluck celebrations of the Lord's Supper, so that nothing was left for the poor (1 Cor. 11). Why would Paul begin this letter with such uplifting words about them?

Perhaps the real question is, why does God care so much for them? Indeed, Paul is not simply expressing his own sentiments about the Corinthians but emphasizes what God is doing. *God* gave this church grace through Jesus Christ. *God* equipped them with every spiritual gift. *God* strengthens them to the end, so that they may be blameless when Christ returns. Indeed, Paul's last line brings this theme to a climax by stressing God's absolute faithfulness (v. 9).

Paul's uplifting tone in this passage reminds us of a temptation in preaching social justice: to leave people with a clear vision of how far short we have fallen in doing what God requires (hence, with a lot of guilt), but without much encouragement or grace to move toward God's vision. The encouragement and grace in this text is a theological antidote. Yes, we fall short. Yes, we fail. Yes, we are afraid. Yes, we worry more about what the congregation will think than about what God needs for us to say. Yes, we get more entangled in our own internal church fights than in the quest to bring God's justice to a hurting world. Yes, we are paralyzed by fear. But that is not the last word.

God is faithful! The One who has called us and has equipped us with all the gifts needful for our ministries, will also strengthen us to the end, so that we too may be found in faithful witness on the day of Christ's return.

In the rest of 1 Corinthians, Paul points the congregation to ways they can more fully respond and live out this grace. In so doing, Paul writes to the Corinthians as a community. For Paul, the church is a corporate body intended to demonstrate the life of the coming realm in the present, through the way members relate with one another. Preaching in Advent often focuses on personal, individual preparation for the coming of Christ, but Paul reminds us to prepare as community.

Mark 13:24–37

This text can strike terror in the heart of the most seasoned preacher. The distance between our contemporary world and that of the early Christians, who expected Jesus' imminent return, is nowhere more evident than here. What do we do with this apocalyptic language: the sun being darkened, the moon not giving light, the stars falling, and the Son of Man coming? How do we bring a word from this text that makes sense to people today—many of whom have ceased expecting Christ to come again in glory? The closing verses (vv. 32–37) set out the goal of this baffling language. According to Mark, the purpose of this text is motivate us to be watchful. What does it mean to be watchful in the sense that Mark intends?

Since no one knows the day or hour when Christ will return (not even the angels!), we are not to spend our time trying to figure out when or how it will happen. That is not our concern. Rather, our charge is to "keep alert" (v. 33) and "keep awake" (v. 37), lest Christ return and find us napping. In the apocalyptic worldview, to be alert and awake is to engage in faithful witness. In the Gospel of Mark, this means to continue doing what Jesus said: to grow in discipleship, to announce the coming of the realm of God, to cast out demons (3:13–15), and to carry this ministry to the Gentiles (nations) (13:10). The congregation is to continue these activities even when suffering (13:7–13).

In Mark's world, these acts of witness all point toward social justice, for they point toward the realm of God as a social world in which all circumstances and relationships fully manifest God's purposes of love, justice, peace, mutual support, and abundance. The preacher can help the congregation identify how it can carry out similar missions today.

This text, then, is not so much about what will happen in the end time as it is about how to live between Christ's first and second coming. Christ has given us a mission. At the same time, this text is a warning. Some of us—individuals and congregations—have become complacent, and lackadaisical, thinking we have all the time in the world to do what Christ asks of us. Not so, says the Gospel writer. We are dealing with an urgent situation here. Life is short. So live in a way that makes a difference. Keep awake!

World AIDS Day (December 1)

Chris Glaser

ZEPHANIAH 3:14–20
PSALM 103:6–18
1 THESSALONIANS 5:1–11
MATTHEW 22:34–39

World AIDS Day began in 1988 to heighten awareness of the ways the HIV/AIDS pandemic ravages the human family and to take steps to deal with this disease. This day opens the door for the preacher to help the congregation learn how many people are affected by this disease and to provide reliable information about the disease in order to reduce the mystery and fear that still surround it in some corners. The preacher can help the congregation claim what they can do to end HIV/AIDS and to ease the suffering of those directly afflicted by HIV/AIDS and their families and friends.

> As always, children and women carry the burden of abandonment, vulnerability, stigma, shame, poverty and desperation. They constitute, for you, the cause you must lead. You constitute, for them, the meaning of salvation in terms both spiritual and practical. . . . The sacred texts, from which all religion flows, demand a higher level of morality. And if ever there was an issue which bristles with moral questions and moral imperatives it's HIV/AIDS.
>
> *Stephen Lewis*[1]

One of the first films about AIDS, *Longtime Companion*, concluded with a euphoric reunion on the shore of survivors with their friends, partners, and

1. Stephen Lewis, UN Special Envoy for HIV/AIDS in Africa, speaking at the African Religious Leaders Assembly on Children and HIV/AIDS, Nairobi, Kenya, June 10, 2002. http://data.unaids.org/Media/Speeches01/sp_lewis_african-religious-leaders_10jun02_en.pdf. (accessed March 23, 2010).

6

family members lost to AIDS, with smiles and hugs abounding. [2] As I watched it through tears when it was released in 1990, I glimpsed the "day of the Lord" (1 Thess. 5:2), when Christ would return to uplift the living and the dead, a vision that helped the early Christians withstand their persecution and suffering. When I think back on those years, it amazes me that we were not overwhelmed. It's hard to think that what we experienced then is being experienced again by those in developing countries, those in poorer populations, and those of younger generations. [3]

We held "celebrations" of those who died—of their humor, their gifts, their love—and found a way to celebrate them in panels assembled as the Names Project AIDS Quilt, providing comfort and catharsis. Gray tombstones were not for us. Colorful fabrics and photos and mementoes better represented the vibrancy of our friends, our partners, our family members. These were our shrouds, our icons, our sacramental items that represented their sacred worth.

World AIDS Day observed as a Holy Day for Justice gives occasion to join in such celebrations with panels from the AIDS Quilt and worship that is hopeful, uplifting, and re-creational. It is about a vision of reunion with those we've lost to God's eternal realm. A friend whose partner died in his arms told me a week later, on Easter, "I felt him leave his body. That's why I know I will see him again." What faith!

Zephaniah 3:14–20

Zephaniah's ministry is believed to date from 630 BCE. The prophet was concerned with God's judgment on spiritual complacency and religious malpractice. Our particular text speaks of deliverance from all this, but may have been added to the original.

Nonetheless, its hopeful tone gives a much needed reprieve from the doleful tone of Zephaniah's concerns. Decades ago, the National Conference on Christians and Jews (now the National Conference for Community and Justice) recommended that for Holocaust Remembrance Day, positive instances of courage and faithfulness be highlighted and celebrated, including the actions of Christians who hid Jews from the Nazis at great risk to themselves. World AIDS Sunday could follow this lead of positive reinforcement by celebrating stories of faith in the midst of AIDS.

---

2. Visit www.worldaidsday.org for the theme of World AIDS Day for the current year.
3. I have discussed this topic more fully in the chapter "Death by Plague" in my book *The Final Deadline: What Death Has Taught Me about Life* (New York: Morehouse, 2010). For further resources, see www.chrisglaser.com.

"Sing aloud, O daughter Zion; shout, O Israel! Rejoice and exult with all your heart, O daughter Jerusalem! The LORD . . . is in your midst; you shall fear disaster no more" (vv. 14–15). No explication can substitute for the boundless joy leaping from these words. Though well-meaning Christians might want to beat their breasts and say, "Mea culpa," to those the church initially abandoned or ignored in the AIDS crisis, that may prove self-indulgent when those living and dying with HIV and AIDS now need uplifting spiritual practices.

In the communities initially touched by AIDS, I believe many people flocked to New Age spirituality meetings, not only because of their distrust of the church, but to hear affirmations rather than confessions. That's why this Scripture from Zephaniah works; it lends its vision of a day when true religion is restored in Zion and, for us in the church, when God is the friend we were taught God was in Jesus: "The LORD, your God, is in your midst; . . . [God] will rejoice over you with gladness, [God] will renew you in love; [God] will exult over you with loud singing, as on a day of festival" (vv. 17–18). How marginalized people, how people with a life-threatening illness, long to hear such words!

The verses that follow speak of removing disaster and oppressors, and changing shame to praise, even as God gathers the physically impaired and the outcast to bring them home. I think of the T-shirts with letters writ large: "HIV-POSITIVE"—surely an antidote to the ostracism once experienced by the AIDS community. A social-service worker counseling a homeless man with AIDS said she tried "every trick in the therapeutic book" to get him to turn from suicidal thoughts and take his medications. Finally, she decided to use the "F-word—Faith," and, by getting him to talk about his Christian faith, this Jewish therapist helped him to find a way home. The good news of faith has been vastly underestimated as a restorer for those cast out of family homes, church homes, and hometowns.

Psalm 103:6–18

Though there are things in our lives worthy of judgment, the psalmist declares, God's anger is slow to rise and quick to dissipate (v. 9). God's mercy, grace, love, and justice are eternal (vv. 6, 8). God is not a cosmic clerk who pays tit for tat (v. 10), but compassionately divorces our transgressions "as far as the east is from the west" (v. 12) from our identity as beloved children (v. 13). God "remembers that we are dust," mere mortals, whose days are brief on earth, like flowers and grass, while God's love and righteousness last eternally for those who hold God in awe and extend for generations to those who keep God's covenant and commandments.

I witnessed the Midwestern parents of a young man dying of AIDS who embodied this love for their son. But the church had ingrained in him more about God's judgment than God's love, and he died believing AIDS was God's judgment of his own love. Given the level of his pain, discomfort, and self-loathing, death proved a kind of healing, an opportunity to at last rest in peace in the everlasting arms of God's love. The psalmist, in singing thanksgiving for healing from disease, may just as well have been singing of this healing from the dis-ease of believing one's self beyond God's love.

Houses of worship have begun to offer AIDS healing services, but perhaps the best purpose of such gatherings is to provide a healing balm to those who have suffered toxic religion and spiritual abuse.

Matthew 22:34–39

Mark puts this summary of the law on Jesus' lips, but both Matthew and Luke suggest Jesus used a rabbinic teaching method of eliciting the summary from others, a summary current among rabbis of the time. Spiritual guides and directors know the value of helping seekers discern their own answers to questions of faith. This very action from Jesus suggests a way of being with those facing questions of faith as they deal with fear, suffering, and mortality. Though our temptation as preachers and pastors and caregivers may be to offer our own answers, our best first response is to help people remember or discern what they already know.

A Pharisee had asked Jesus which commandment is the greatest. In Luke's version, the lawyer is trying to justify himself, and Jesus tells the parable of the Good Samaritan. In Matthew, the motive may be "to entrap him" (v. 15). Jesus tells him to love God "with all your heart, and with all your soul, and with all your mind" (v. 37), quoting Deuteronomy 6:5. Jesus adds, "You shall love your neighbor as yourself" (v. 39), quoting Leviticus 19:18, which assumes we love ourselves, an assumption not necessarily true for the marginalized groups affected by HIV/AIDS, who have been taught to hate themselves because of their color, gender, sexuality, or poverty. To teach this verse sufficiently, we need to proclaim that Jesus expanded the definition of "neighbor" that included both fellow Hebrews and resident aliens (Lev. 19:33–34) to anyone in need. For Jesus, "neighbor" was anyone, even the enemy (e.g., Luke 6:27, 35). Ministry among people living with HIV/AIDS is not optional, but a duty inextricably bound to loving God absolutely, for "those who say, 'I love God,' and hate their brothers or sisters, are liars" (1 John 4:20). A person with AIDS whose family had disowned him when he came out as gay rediscovered their love for him only as they surrounded him on his deathbed. His final observation to a chaplain was, "Love heals."

1 Thessalonians 5:1–11

In this letter, believed to be the earliest writing in the New Testament, circa 50 CE, the apostle Paul addresses the concerns of the church at Thessalonica about "the day of the Lord" (v. 2) that early Christians awaited, the Parousia, or coming of Christ. Church members are concerned for those who have "fallen asleep" (4:14, translated in the NRSV as "died"), their metaphor for death, and Paul wants to assure them that those who have fallen asleep "will rise first. Then we who are alive, who are left, will be caught up in the clouds together with them to meet the Lord in the air; and so we will be with the Lord forever" (4:16c–17).

The text that follows could be read with foreboding: "the day of the Lord will come like a thief in the night" (v. 2), "then sudden destruction will come" and "there will be no escape!" (v. 3). But Paul's purpose is to suggest the suddenness of Christ's victory and its serendipitous nature for those who are "children of light and children of the day" (v. 5). Thus the Thessalonian Christians have nothing to worry about, though they must remain prepared: "since we belong to the day, let us be sober, and put on the breastplate of faith and love, and for a helmet the hope of salvation" (v. 8).

Unprovidentially, however, many who discover themselves infected with HIV cope with multiple stigmas, being part of marginalized groups and now associated with illness, contagion, and death. So when they hear Paul's contrasting the plight of the saved with the unsaved, they may fear they themselves are perceived as those children "of the night or of darkness," "drunk," and destined for the "wrath" to come (vv. 5, 7, 9). Preachers on this text need to tread carefully in its use on World AIDS Day. A minister told me that a person he had been assigned as an AIDS buddy told him over the phone that he didn't want any "religious garbage" dumped on him, but the first words out of his mouth when they met was, "Do you think my having AIDS is some kind of punishment from God?"

It is better to focus on Paul's intent of assuring those concerned for their departed loved ones that they will be reunited on the day of the Lord. This is what carried the early church in its own fears, sufferings, and deaths. As the passage concludes, "Therefore encourage one another and build up each other, as indeed you are doing" (v. 11).

Pollyanna challenged her dour preacher to discover there are more blessings than curses in the Bible. To those who already feel cursed by HIV and AIDS, God's blessings are all the more dear and necessary. Zephaniah's celebration of the Lord's return to Zion is a tonic in the midst of our own spiritual complacency and religious malpractice as a church and a people. The psalmist's rejoicing at a God of compassion who readily forgives shortcomings and works for justice for the oppressed surely inspires us to do the same. Jesus' explanation that all the law and the prophets are applications of the commandment to love God and neighbor gets to the heart of what matters both spiritually and in regard to how we live in the world every day. Paul's uplifting vision in 1 Thessalonians of the day of the Lord, when we will be reunited not only with Christ but with all our departed loved ones, serves as a taste of God's commonwealth to come.

Second Sunday of Advent

Marvin A. McMickle

ISAIAH 40:1–11
PSALM 85:1–2, 8–13
2 PETER 3:8–15A
MARK 1:1–8

Advent is a time of waiting for the realm of God. But Advent waiting is not sitting silently with folded hands while God magically establishes the realm. Advent waiting is active: we not only join God in the movement toward the realm, but, as much as possible, we live as if the realm is already here. Today's readings call attention to different aspects of active waiting. Isaiah urges us to be patient, even if we suffer for our sins. The psalm reminds us that God will bless a nation that puts justice for all into action, and God will punish a nation that privileges a few at the expense of the many. The passage from 2 Peter encourages us toward holy living as our means of holy waiting. John the Baptist calls us to repent of our complicity with injustice as we wait for the coming realm. Taken together, these passages urge us to work as we wait for the realm of God.

Isaiah 40:1–11

In *The Pursuit of God*, A. W. Tozer says that before God can bless a person, God often hurts that person deeply.[1] This idea is out of step with much contemporary preaching, but it is at home in the preaching of Isaiah. People today prefer a religion that would keep them from suffering. The nation of Judah operated from such an assumption, but the Babylonian exile proved them wrong. The people of Judah violated the covenant through idolatry, exploitation, injustice, and false alliances. As a consequence, God hurt them not as an end, but to chasten them for better service. The unthinkable occurred when

1. A. W. Tozer, *The Pursuit of God* (Camp Hill, PA: Christian Publications, 1969), 5.

the chosen people were exiled from the promised land. Their monarch was carried away in chains. The temple of Solomon was in ruins.

They had been stripped of everything that had become an obstruction in their relationship with God. By the time of Isaiah 40, the exiles were poised to return home and to serve God. "Comfort my people. . . . she has served her turn . . . her penalty is paid . . . she has received from the LORD's hand double for all her sins" (Isa. 40:1–2).

What are the obstructions in our relationship with God that lead to judgment? How do we violate our covenantal responsibilities? Perhaps we value our political party and its principles more than we value God. Maybe we prefer to sing "God Bless America," rather than "[God's] Got the Whole World in [God's] Hands." Perhaps we prefer the precise observance of church rituals over the diligent pursuit of justice in behalf of the poor and oppressed. According to Isaiah, God punishes such violations. For example, despite the many sacrificial deaths of so many people in the armed services, the fact that our country has been in a constant state of war overseas for a decade, with thousands of deaths, international tension, and a cost of more than one trillion dollars, may be God's judgment on the fact that the United States continues to turn to violence as a means to peace. The constant racial tension in the United States may be God's judgment on more than three hundred years of racism, violence, and legalized discrimination.

Whatever our sin, Isaiah 40 reminds us of God's love and grace. After repenting, the sinful nation is allowed to return. The community will build a highway in the wilderness to lead them from Babylon to Jerusalem. Here is the message of Isaiah 40:1–11: God will punish us for our sins, but if we repent, God will forgive us and give another chance. Nations rise and fall, both tiny Israel and great Babylon. One hundred years ago, England was the mightiest nation in the world. Today, the United States fits that description. One hundred years from now, China may be spoken of in those terms until they too are eclipsed. Nations rise and fall, but the promise of God's wrath and God's mercy stands forever.

Preachers should "bring good tidings to Zion." We must preach about both God's anger at injustice and God's faithfulness, which comes from God's grace. Sadly, some preachers never talk about sin, because that topic leaves people unhappy and uncomfortable. Preachers think, "God forbid that preaching should ever leave God's people unhappy and uncomfortable." Yet if we fail to preach about sin, God holds us accountable for the blood of those we failed to warn (Ezek. 3:18). Meanwhile, the people we failed to warn in our preaching end up unhappy and uncomfortable as they suffer the consequences of those actions we should have warned them to avoid.

The people of Israel sat by the rivers of Babylon for many years. During that time they developed essential spiritual resources that would serve them well upon their return to Judah: patience and perseverance. Moreover, they developed practices for sanctifying the body, the community, and the world. They became proactive in developing patterns that would sustain them in the future. Patience is on display while God is working out the divine purpose in our lives and in the world. Perseverance is our determination to remain faithful, no matter what temptations get in our way, even when the hope of God's reign on earth seems wholly unattainable. There will always be obstacles and obstructions. The challenge is to persevere in the face of all resistance and opposition.

Evil has not yet surrendered, so we must persevere. Injustice still occurs, so we must persevere. Human suffering and cruelty are still all too frequent, but God is patiently at work, so we must persevere. As James Russell Lowell said:

> Though the cause of evil prosper,
> Yet the truth alone is strong.
> Though her portion be the scaffold
> And upon the throne the wrong.
> Yet that scaffold sways the future,
> And behind the dim unknown
> Standeth God within the shadows
> Keeping watch above [God's] own.[2]

Psalm 85:1–2, 8–13

This psalm reinforces the message of Isaiah 40. The nation of Israel has suffered greatly because of sin. However, God has restored the fortunes of the people and forgiven their sins. They have seen God's fierce anger (v. 3), but now the cry is for God's "steadfast love" (v. 7). God gives a second chance to those who do "not turn back to folly" (v. 8). God's mercy and grace are available to "those who fear [God]" (v. 9).

Has Israel learned anything as a result of having been exiled in Babylon for so long? Will they return to a life of faithfulness and obedience to God? Will they abandon the idolatry and injustice that earned God's displeasure? All of that is to be determined, but for the moment God is set once again to pour out blessings upon the land that has recently been punished: "The LORD will give what is good, and our land will yield its increase" (v. 12).

What remains is for the people of God to understand that they had been chosen not for special treatment but for special service. God had chosen Israel

---

2. James Russell Lowell, "Once to Every Man and Nation," in *The Singing Church* (Carol Stream, IL: Hope Pub. Co., 1985), 450.

not only to bless them but also to demonstrate what can happen when any nation keeps faith with God by showing justice, mercy, and love toward all, especially the most needy and vulnerable. God has shown love and faithfulness to Israel. If the people show those same traits to one another, "The LORD will give what is good, and our land will yield its increase."

This psalm applies to the contemporary United States as much as it did to ancient Israel. We are at a crossroads. The greed of a few brought about the massive economic collapse that began in 2008 and has caused suffering for people of every income level, race, and ethnicity. This is God's judgment on a nation that has not only tolerated but celebrated greed. But now, the nation has a choice: We can repeat the mistakes of our past, or we can create a new economy that is based on managing the nation's wealth for the good of all. If we simply rebuild what we have had, we can expect this cycle of suffering to go on and on and on. If we create an economic system that brings abundance and security to all, we can expect "what is good, and a land that will yield its increase."

2 Peter 3:8–15a

When I was growing up in Chicago in the 1950s and '60s there was a man who stood every day on a street corner holding up a sign, "The end is near." I do not know how old that man was, but his message got old to me as the years went by and nothing happened. I saw that man at least once a week for ten years, but the end did not come. It has been more than forty years since I last saw that man, but the end he seemed to be forecasting has not come. After a while that man became more of a side show to be observed than a spiritual messenger to be heeded.

That is the tension present in this passage. People had been hearing about the coming of the Day of the Lord for years—a day when evil people and their practices would be destroyed and the reign of God would be established on the earth. By the time of the writing of 2 Peter, many Christians had turned skeptical about such an idea. Peter's call to live holy and godly lives so as to avoid the fire that would soon consume the world was falling on deaf ears. Peter encouraged them to be patient, but to wait actively by leading lives of holiness. To live such a life was not to hold a sign on a street corner, but to be holy as God is holy, that is, by showing the love, peace, and justice God wants for all people.

We have always waited. Israel waited in Egypt for 430 years. Moses waited on Sinai for forty days, and the Hebrews waited forty years before entering their promised land. They waited for the exile to end. The waiting did not end with the coming of Jesus. Indeed, the waiting goes on: waiting for God's eschatological reign of justice and peace. God is not late; we are anxious. We need not be. God has promised.

Mark 1:1–8

What is the right way to establish a relationship with Jesus? Do we join the church one Sunday morning and suddenly number ourselves among the company of the believers? Do we come to Christ as we come to any secular organization—fill out an application, be initiated, and maintain our dues? That is what some Christians today believe. We need to hear the message proclaimed by John the Baptist: God welcomes those who come by way of the baptism of the repentance of sin. The call was not merely for baptism, but for a baptism of the repentance of sin.

Only God can accomplish our salvation. Once we repent of our sins, the same God who provided a way for Israel to return from Babylon has already provided a way for us. John said, "The one who is more powerful than I is coming after me" (v. 7). Our hope for salvation is in that person, Jesus Christ. We need to follow the example of the people who came out to be baptized by John and repent of our sins. In ancient Judaism, repentance was a "turning" (*tshuva*) away from the bad and toward the good. Repentance needs to lead to action. To come out to John is to come out from the old complacency to new life; to be baptized by John is to be baptized in public, and so to attest to the community that we are starting again and that the community should hold us responsible.

In this Advent season, of what sins does your congregation need to repent? Many congregations are segregated according to race, ethnicity, and economic class, rather than reflecting the rich human diversity of the realm of God. Many congregations gladly receive stock dividends, never noticing that they come from international arms sales. Many congregations are outspoken on why women cannot be ministers while they remain silent while people are tortured. John's message is simple: repent.

Universal Declaration
of Human Rights (December 10)

Christine Marie Smith

DEUTERONOMY 16:18–22
PSALM 10:10–18
REVELATION 18:1–8
LUKE 18:1–8

In the shadow of World War II, the United Nations set forth the Universal Declaration of Human Rights on December 10, 1948. This document asserts that all human beings are free, equal, and entitled to dignity, safety, peace, and security regardless of nationality, gender, race, ethnicity, or religion. It prohibits actions that deny these values (such as slavery, torture, or discrimination). Commemorating it in Advent, the preacher could help the congregation to repent of violations of these rights and to recognize that living by them can be an important component in preparing for the Advent of Christ.

> The peoples of the United Nations have in the Charter reaffirmed their faith in fundamental human rights, in the dignity and worth of the human person, and in the equal rights of men and women.
> *Preamble, Universal Declaration of Human Rights*

> Everyone, as a member of society, has the right to social security and is entitled to realization . . . of the economic, social, and cultural rights indispensable . . . for dignity and the free development of . . . personality.
> *Article 22, Universal Declaration of Human Rights*

In the aftermath of World War II, with the realization of the violence of which human beings are capable and the horror of the Shoah, the visionary creation of the Universal Declaration of Human Rights was a crucial historical act. In our time, in which human rights violations continue at an inhumane level

17

and genocide takes place with impunity, the global community (including the church) desperately needs to remember the Universal Declaration of Human Rights. This declaration, now available in 360 languages, is one of the most translated documents in the world. Although it originated as a hope-filled document, the human community today is far from realizing it (except for the privileged elite). Indeed, before preachers move too quickly to the biblical texts for today, it would be good to print the whole document, to read slowly the preamble and the thirty articles, and then to reread the entire document through the eyes of the most poor and oppressed.[1]

When reading the declaration through the lens of the poor and oppressed, the preacher is confronted with the privileged assumptions that gave rise to it, privileges that many preachers of Eurocentric background enjoy: that everyone has the right to own property; that everyone has the right to rest and leisure and periodic holidays with pay; that no one shall be subjected to arbitrary arrest, detention, or exile; that everyone has the right to education, and to a standard of living adequate for their health and well-being; that everyone has the right to form and to join trade unions; and that everyone has the right to seek asylum from persecution.[2]

If the most oppressed were to write a Declaration of Human Rights today, it would likely be no less visionary, but shocking for many middle- and upper-class preachers. I imagine they would write articles like this: the right to have enough to eat to sustain one's self and one's family; the right to potable water; the right to a plot of land to farm; the right to health care that keeps members of one's community from dying of things that are easily preventable; the right not to be forced to fight against one's own family members in wars that serve international corporations and the elite in one's country; the right to maintain and express one's indigenous culture and religious beliefs; the right to vote; the right to be treated as a human being who has inalienable rights.

Christians who take Advent seriously do not only await the incarnation of God among us in Christ; we also long for the coming of the realm of God's justice on earth. Many preachers need to reclaim the eschatological nature of Advent as a season in which we remember that we are God's hope for even a taste of that reign of God to be realized for most of the world's people. Because of this truth, a major element of this holy day might be to deepen and broaden our understanding of Advent in ways that connect us to the whole of God's creation and to all those who still suffer dehumanization and poverty and live under circumstances in which universal human rights

1. United Nations Web Services section, Department of Public Information, United Nations, 2007, http://www.un.org/events/humanrights/2007 (accessed July 5, 2010).
2. These occurrences of the words "right" and "rights" actually appear in the declaration itself.

can be assumed by only a very few. The creators of this visionary document would surely expect the world community, and particularly the privileged who enjoy these rights, to work tirelessly until the rights become reality for all God's people.

Revelation 18:1–8

The Roman Empire (likened to Babylon, the destroyer of the temple in 586 BCE) is falling, for God's judgment is imminent. Christians, no matter where they live, are to "come out of" (v. 5) the kind of oppressive luxury and power the Roman merchants and elites have accumulated. John calls all Christians to "come out of" all forms of idolatry that have replaced the ultimate power and goodness of God and of living in covenant with one another. Judgment is coming and they/we still have a chance to "not take part in [the] sins" (v. 4) of oppressive powers. John is saying, turn now, and say no to all forms of injustice and death. John calls for what Latin American liberation theologians describe as denouncement.[3] You must say no to every kind of injustice and disengage in every way possible from further wrongdoing.

In the absence of so many basic human rights for so many people, why is so little denouncing heard in our Christian churches? Isn't it time to denounce the fact that the vast majority of God's people live in abject poverty and suffering? Isn't it time to denounce the exploitation of the poor by the rich?

In allowing this text to inform what we say about universal human rights, it would be easy to linger on the injustices of the Roman Empire, rather than turn our sights to the injustices perpetrated by the United States Empire. Maybe it is time for a little judgment closer to home. In our wealthy nation, there are people who actually starve and freeze to death. In our wealthy nation, there are thousands of people who have no health care. In our wealthy nation, some people act like demons in the way that they keep robbing others of basic human rights.

A sensitized preacher must face the fact that once again evil is equated with a *woman*. Here, fornication is the act that has polluted all who are associated with *her*, and for *her* sins *she* will be tormented, plagued, burned, and judged by the God of justice. To preach that God will ultimately overthrow injustice, a preacher does not have to perpetuate the metaphor of Rome as a woman. Rather, a truthful preacher, concerned to not undermine the dignity of women, will properly name the Roman officials, the Roman officers, the

---

3. Leonardo Boff, *When Theology Listens to the Poor* (San Francisco: Harper & Row, 1988), 39. Boff writes about the two primary tasks of any prophet: to denounce and to proclaim. The theme of denouncement is a primary one in Latin American liberation theology and is a challenging concept to most preachers of privilege.

Roman elite, and the emperor as the perpetrators of injustice, and properly name the powerful and elite of our day, as well as the primary perpetrators of injustice, even when we are they.

Luke 18:1–8

A simple reading of this parable delights and supports our human sensibilities: Those treated unjustly will triumph if they are persistent. If you are suffering some kind of injustice, the right strategies and constant prayer can actually persuade the powerful to grant you justice. While Luke in this parable dramatizes for the disciples and us the conviction that God never delays in helping those who are treated unjustly, we are left in our contemporary world with the truth that many powerful "judges" have dealt with so many people unjustly. If we look and do not turn away, we can see an entire world full of persistent widows who have the human courage to keep struggling for justice for their families and communities but who have yet to experience justice. A radical parabolic turn comes when we, the privileged, realize that we are the judge, not the widow. It is painful to admit that many in our world "bother" us or are reduced to "begging us" for the justice they deserve. The Declaration of Human Rights, when truly realized, will release people from having to beg for the basic resources that sustain life, and it will guide the privileged to share in mutual, not exploitive, existence.

Psalm 10:10–18

The Declaration of Human Rights was created so "that those from earth may strike terror no more" (v. 18). The preacher listens to the psalmist to be reminded to proclaim God's comfort as well as God's ultimate justice. The psalmist reminds people who continue to experience injustice and suffering that God only "seems" to be silent and distant. The psalmist rehearses for the oppressed that God has always judged the unjust and heard the cries of the grieving and orphaned. While other texts today urge human beings to denounce injustice and to seek justice, this psalm leaves us wondering how, in the face of so much injustice, we can proclaim that God is close and that there are universal human rights. Indeed, are we willing to admit that the arms of the wicked and evildoers have not been broken, that the nations who inflict suffering have not been held accountable?

If proclaiming that God is not far away is to be more than a pious, empty reassurance, then we must take action to alleviate all forms of suffering. How does God come near for those who are starving, except through the work of those who provide food? How does God keep so many innocent people in our world from falling to the might of the powerful, except through those who stand in solidarity with the innocent? How does God draw near to a community massacred while praying for peace, except through those who say no to the continued use of violence?[4] If we are not the face and hands of God's abiding love, expressed in solidarity and some level of accompaniment with people who are oppressed, then these words will ring empty.

Deuteronomy 16:18–22

In a world filled with endless partiality, bribes across national and international lines, and the distortions of justice serving the elite, this text is good news in its unwavering clarity. This short passage points immediately to what it will take to realize a Universal Declaration of Human Rights. Justice must be the one and only standard of human life together. No one will have the resources to bribe another person, community, or country at the expense of those who are without those resources. No one can show partiality (whether for self, community, or country), and no one can distort justice. However, until God's people become a massive force to organize human life for justice, we will keep planting trees of greed, and setting up stones of disparity that will never become a true altar to God. The original Universal Declaration of Human Rights can help us create a new set of rights closer to what most of God's people need, not just those rights that protect the privileged. We might thus come closer to erecting the one true altar of justice to our God and on behalf of all God's created family.

---

4. Teresa Ortiz, *Never Again a World without Us: Voices Of Mayan Women in Chiapas, Mexico* (Washington, DC: EPICA, 2001), 167–95. This section of the book describes the massacre of Las Abejas of Acteal, Chiapas, who were killed while praying for peace in their own chapel.

Third Sunday in Advent

Monica A. Coleman

ISAIAH 61:1–4, 8–11
PSALM 126 OR LUKE 1:46B–55
1 THESSALONIANS 5:16–24
JOHN 1:6–8, 19–28

Like a hand lifted with fingers pointing outward and inward, this week's lectionary readings help the church think about the mission and life of prophets in the context of Advent. Isaiah describes the Suffering Servant's call to preach justice; Mary sings praise for the conception of Jesus. The Fourth Gospel describes John the Baptist as a prophet who joins Isaiah and Mary in shining light upon the larger work of God. The Psalm and Epistle remind us that the spiritual life of the prophets sustains them in living out the divine call. Moving attention away from the charisma of the prophet, these texts remind today's witnesses for justice that the work is really about God and justice (and not about the prophets), but the worker must be sustained through spiritual reflection.

Isaiah 61:1–4, 8–11

Isaiah 61 is an inspiring call to justice. Written after the Israelites returned from the exile, it describes the holistic salvation of God's people. The use of the word "anointed" indicates that God called the prophet. Thus Isaiah's work is aligned with God's desires for Israel and also for the world: "Nations shall come to your light" (Isa. 60:3). As such, the prophet is called to work for justice for the disenfranchised. When Jesus invokes this passage in Luke 4:18–19, he places his ministry in the same stream as Isaiah.

Part of the call for justice is spiritual and emotional. Prophets are called to bring good news to the oppressed, to bind up the brokenhearted, and to comfort those who mourn. These themes remind us not only of the physical repression under which Israel suffered then (and under which many people suffer today), but also of the nihilism and despair that typify the disenfranchised.

Those working for justice cannot be so preoccupied with systems and structures that we forget to encourage and inspire the hearts of those ground down by social oppression.

The call to justice is also physical and communal. Isaiah connects the proclamation of liberty to the captives and release of the prisoners with "the year of the LORD's favor" (v. 2). This is a reference to the jubilee year in ancient Hebrew society, which releases individuals of all debts, all slaves of their servitude, all foreigners to their families (Lev. 25:10). It is also a year of rest for the land, when people do not work the land, and the land can rest and renew itself. The need for jubilee persists in contemporary society. Many less developed or small nations are in paralyzing debt to powerful first-world nations. Indeed, through the International Monetary Fund and the World Bank, developed nations, largely in Europe and North America, are essentially economic terrorists from the perspective of developing nations. Misuse and overuse of the earth causes unnecessary poverty and drought. The philosophy and practice of the United States' prison industrial complex is more concerned with punishment than with redemption. In the last decade, the move toward privately operated prisons exacerbates this trend in the name of capitalist gain. In each of these situations, and many others, an Isaianic jubilee would mean a new beginning: forgiveness of debt, restoration of the earth, release not only from prison but for a renewed life.

Unfortunately, the lectionary skips verses 5–7, which indicate that strangers and foreigners from all nations will contribute to the restoration of Israel and righteousness. However, that theme recurs in the final verses of this passage, which anticipate the inclusion of foreigners within the covenant of God's people. This is an especially relevant word. Isaiah envisions strangers gathering with Israel in a new multicultural community in the realm of God. By contrast, Eurocentric society today often views immigrants as lecherous outsiders, rather than as faithful, integral, and full members of society whose gifts enrich North American cultures. By turning away from newcomers, people of European origin turn away from Isaiah's vision.

The fulfillment of justice causes the prophet to rejoice (v. 10). Thus, there is a joy that comes from relationship with God and the call toward justice—whatever the challenges of the work. Think of how this joy could be multiplied in the human community through jubilee practices and by creating a new multicultural world that welcomes and celebrates all.

Luke 1:46b–55

This passage in Luke is one of the best-known praises in the Bible. Echoing Miriam's praise in Exodus for the deliverance of the Hebrews from the oppressing Egyptians, Mary praises God for using her to deliver God's promises to a new generation (see Exod. 15:20–21 and Hannah's song in 1 Sam. 2:1–10).

Mary is at the home of her cousin Elizabeth, celebrating Elizabeth's pregnancy and God's help in effecting the seemingly impossible birth of John the Baptist, much as God created life within Sarah in Genesis 18:1–15. Having been told by Gabriel that she will bear "the Son of God," Mary thanks God in this praise-poem known as the Magnificat.

When we can see Mary as a prophet—one who works with God to bring good news and justice to the world—we remember that we should not overlook anyone as the embodiment of God's activity. Mary is much like today's single mother, especially a single mother in poverty. When society would ordinarily judge and ostracize her, God not only has compassion for her but moves through her as an active agent of justice. Mary recognizes that she is considered "lowly" (v. 48) by those around her, but she is confident that God is working through her to fulfill God's promises. Others may not immediately recognize her, but in time she will be called blessed. At the most basic level, this passage calls the church to honor and support single mothers and all the people they represent (those at the bottom of the social pyramid and those who are vulnerable and struggling). At another level, Mary's song reminds the church to pay attention to the ways that single mothers can be active agents in pointing the church toward ministries of justice. The preacher might help the congregation see the world through the eyes of the single mother. The church needs to help single mothers see themselves not simply as the world sees them (vulnerable and struggling), but as God sees them: as instruments of God's promises. As Mary praises God, contemporary readers are reminded that when God brings justice to the world, it may come in the ways we least expect, through the individuals and communities that society eschews.

John 1:6–8, 19–28

This passage follows the prologue in John's Gospel that lyrically asserts the preexistence and creating and redeeming activity of the Word, the *logos*. Variously interpreted as Plato's Demiurge, Sophia (Wisdom), and the second person of the Trinity, this Word is the central focus and undergirding force of John's understanding of God's activity in Jesus. Jesus is the embodied Word at work in the world.

The selected scriptures focus on John the Baptist's explanation of his ministry. Using the metaphor of light, John the Baptist explains that his role is to point to God. His care to articulate the difference between himself as the messenger and Jesus as the source of life and the message is instructive for contemporary prophets who understand their justice work to be inspired by God. This passage reminds them that they are not the point in and of themselves; their work, like that of John, is to point to the work of God. This passage is also instructive for the church as we contemplate contemporary prophets. It is easy for the church to focus on charismatic leaders who are able to rally the masses, navigate politics, alter structures toward equity, and secure measures of justice for the underclass, rather than to focus on the message and mission of the prophet. This passage guards against idolatrous focus on the prophet. Our work for justice is a testimony of God's goad for justice.

John the Baptist clearly states that he is not the Messiah or the returned Elijah. In verse 23, John invokes the words of Isaiah by saying that he is one who "prepares the way of the Lord" (Isa. 40:3). John thus connects himself to that which will be salvific for God's people. Again, John makes it clear that he is not the salvation himself.

As in Mary's Magnificat, there is an unexpected element in the prophet. John the Baptist's unauthorized baptism rings of the "priesthood of all believers," to which Peter will later refer. John does not wait for authorization from others. He takes the authority given to him by God to welcome all to the salvation that God offers. Verse 28 indicates that John the Baptist's ministry took place outside of Israel. This text thus encourages the church to recognize that justice work often takes place outside the church. Indeed, the church is sometimes one of the last communities to recognize and embrace initiatives toward justice. The church needs to learn to recognize prophets who are not connected to any religious community.

1 Thessalonians 5:16–24

At the conclusion of his first letter to the Thessalonians, Paul turns to spiritual issues. This passage speaks powerfully to those who are actively engaged in the struggle for social justice in two ways.

First, justice workers are reminded to maintain their inner spiritual lives. There is so much work to do to realize justice. Yet the work must be undergirded by a living relationship with God. Paul encourages people to develop internal resources through prayer, gratitude, and rejoicing. We are encouraged to nourish our awareness of the Holy Spirit. The Spirit can operate both in the individual life and in the wider community. While the Spirit can work anytime on any day, people who work for justice often find that regular spiritual practices—such as Bible reading, small-group Bible studies, prayer, and partaking of the loaf and the cup—help them respond to the Spirit.

Second, this text reminds justice workers to rely on God for their inner and outer strength. The prayer at the end of this passage asks that God sanctify the

Christian community and asserts that God is faithful and will maintain believers in a holistic manner (vv. 23–24). In Paul's context, sanctification means to be holy, and to be holy means to live in community according to the covenant. Thus the prayer for sanctification itself is a prayer for social justice.

Psalm 126

This liturgical psalm was part of public worship for the ancient Israelites. The psalm celebrates God's fulfillment of promises and unabashedly rejoices. This psalm has two justice implications. The first verse indicates that when the Israelites were released from exile, they "were like those who dream." In one sense, their dreams could not have come true if they had never dreamed! The lesson for justice workers is in the importance of dreaming. Part of working for justice is envisioning justice. This Scripture implies, "Dream big!" Imagine the kin-dom of God on earth. Imagine it in your local area. The language of dreaming conjures images of Martin Luther King's "I Have a Dream" speech. Although not King's most radical vision for justice, this oration speaks to the importance of imagining a world that one cannot yet see. God partners with those who dream for justice.

Second, the psalm points to the joy of restoration. There may be sorrow when one looks around at the injustice in our midst and the everyday struggles of the oppressed. Surely our hearts break. Yet this psalm assures justice workers that this is not the end of the story. There will be joy and shouts of harvest. Those who trust that the end will result in justice for the world, do not have to wait until "their fortunes are restored." A song phrases it thusly: "Don't wait till the battle is over to shout now!"[1] There can be joy in the journey.

---

1. Walter Hawkins, "When the Battle Is Over," http://www.lyrics007.com/Walter%20Hawkins%20Lyrics/When%20The%20Battle%20Is%20Over%20Lyrics.html (accessed March 27, 2010).

Fourth Sunday of Advent

John M. Buchanan

2 SAMUEL 7:1–11, 16
PSALM 89:1–4, 19–26
ROMANS 16:25–27
LUKE 1:47–55
LUKE 1:26–38

The Fourth Sunday of Advent is one of the most important, and most challenging, preaching Sundays of the year. For months, many in North America have been waiting for this week. Retail merchants are holding their corporate breath to see whether holiday shopping will result in year-end profitability, and the economists watch to see how the market will react. People in the pews are preoccupied with finishing last-minute shopping, making travel arrangements, and attending parties. Congregations and preachers, caught up in this frenzy, are understandably exhausted. And just at this moment, the preacher's assignment is to announce the coming of good news that will be for all people, in all situations, including those sitting in a pew, worn to a frazzle, preparing for Christmas.

2 Samuel 7:1–11, 16

This text contains three ideas with enormous social and political implications.

1. David wants to build a house for God in the worst way. His theological and spiritual advisor, Nathan, agrees at first, then, after a dream, pronounces God's verdict on the plans for a temple: "No . . . No house . . . Not now." God's response to David's building project is theologically and socially loaded. God's presence with the people along their journey from slavery in Egypt to freedom has been portable, movable. Their God, unlike other deities, does not live in a building, or in a heavenly palace, but among the people, in the midst of all the complexities of their life together, that is to say, in their economic, political, and social relationships.

27

2. A different, but related, direction is the homelessness of God, suggesting the church's responsibility to be with the homeless who walk our streets and turn to the church for support and who, in large measure, are victims of a market economy that does not see them. Look for the homeless: God is among them.

3. The passage also contains the promise of the land, an idea which could not be more relevant as the modern state of Israel struggles to establish itself securely and justly. The text promises that in the land the people will be disturbed no more; evildoers shall not afflict them. This promise is dear to a people afflicted as no one else in history. This may not be the Sunday to discuss the biblical promise of land in the context of the struggle for peace and justice in the Middle East, but the preacher might remember that Jews, Muslims, Israelis, and Palestinians share with Christians the hope for lasting peace.

Psalm 89:1–4, 19–26

The psalm returns to the Davidic promise and consequent monarchy. The psalmist describes it in extravagant, political/military terms: enemies will be overcome, foes will be crushed. Even nature will acknowledge God's chosen one. David's throne will be built for all generations. In fact, the Davidic experiment did not last very long, and ultimately the monarchy disappeared. One foe after another rolled over the people, defeated their armies, exiled the leaders, scattered them over the earth, and finally nearly exterminated them. The opening promise of that psalm (God's "faithfulness is as firm as the heavens" [v. 2]) and the grateful response ("I will sing of your stead-fast love forever" [v. 1]) have indeed lived down through the centuries. One thinks of God's enslaved people singing "Swing Low, Sweet Chariot" or trying to observe Sabbath in concentration camps. God's promise, finally, is fulfilled not in a powerful monarchy or political operation, but in a steadfast love that will never abandon God's people regardless of their circumstances. This love became incarnate and appeared in the most marginalized, vulnerable, powerless scenario imaginable: incarnation in an infant's birth in a Bethlehem stable.

Romans 16:25–27

This short text is a virtual cascade of words. I imagine Paul dictating so fast that his secretary can't keep up—the words flow down in layers of doxology—as the apostle concludes this letter that many biblical interpreters regard as his climactic work. The themes return: unlikely chosenness, surprising revelation, secrets unveiled, and the unchanging, always present and available power of God to strengthen God's chosen. Paul has struggled with and resolved the questions of God's chosen people, Paul's own people, the Jews. They are still partners in the covenant and recipients of God's promise. Nothing will ever change that. There is no supersessionism here. This is an expanded vision of covenant, picking up on Israel's long-standing tradition that the Gentiles were also part of God's people. Through the testimony of the prophets, all peoples are now included. In Christ, God's steadfast love comes to all.

The preacher should remember who is in the pews this Sunday. Sitting beside exhausted shoppers, weary parents, and excited, starry-eyed children will be the brokenhearted ones, the lonely ones whose loneliness is exacerbated by the festive holiday season, the grieving ones whose recent loss is unbearably painful at the first Christmas without their dear one: all in need of the promise of God's steadfast love.

Luke 1:47–55

An alternate reading to the psalm today is Mary's song (in response to the angel's announcement), right after Elizabeth's blessing ("Blessed are you among women, and blessed is the fruit of your womb" [v. 42]). William Willimon observes that when Mary hears the momentous announcement and receives her older relative's blessing, she "hums a little tune of liberation."[1]

Luke understands that the birth of Jesus will recover and reframe ancient Jewish ways of thinking and behaving offered by the prophets and Deuteronomy. While Jesus' message is not original (being rooted in tradition), it is so different from the way things are ordinarily that "revolutionary" is an appropriate way to describe it. It privileges the hungry, vulnerable, and marginal. It is a reminder that Jesus spent his life among those kinds of people—not exclusively, to be sure. Jesus seems never to have rejected men or women because of their relative wealth, but Jesus did emphasize as God's order of things a world in which the proud are scattered, the powerful brought low, the lowly lifted up, and the hungry fed.

On a day when our abundance will be either on display or on everyone's mind, the preacher can remind listeners that we live in an economy of shameful disparity; that Jesus' followers, as they celebrate his birth, also celebrate his radical rule; and that the work of the church, year-round, includes addressing social, economic, and political symptoms that produce poverty, injustice, and

1. William H. Willimon, *On a Wild and Windy Mountain and 25 Other Meditations for the Christian Year* (Nashville: Abingdon Press, 1984), 21.

suffering. This probably is not the Sunday to focus exclusively on it, but the preacher could remind the congregation that young Mary does not hesitate to mix religion and politics and economics as she waits for her son to be born. The preacher can also remember that the hungry and lowly are not just outside the church. They are also in the pews at Christmas: inside every proud and prosperous soul, there is also a soul lowly and hungry for hope and love and peace.

Luke 1:26–38

She is perhaps the most recognizable woman in human history. She stands sentinel on thousands of dashboards and is the subject of some of the most sublime Western art. The Italian Renaissance was obsessed with her. Fra Angelico's *The Annunciation* portrays the moment when the angel appears to a young Jewish girl and says, "Hail, Mary. The Lord is with you." Mary, startled, afraid, says, "Here am I, the servant of the Lord; let it be with me according to your word" (v. 38). The original is a fresco painted on the wall of the monastery of San Marco in Florence, at the head of a stairway. The colors are delicate pastels. The angel and Mary sit across from each other and are leaning slightly, the angel toward Mary and Mary drawing back gently. It is a mysterious moment when heaven and earth momentarily meet and God chooses an ordinary young woman as instrument of God's mercy and love and grace, a moment for which words and concepts and intellectual propositions are hopelessly inadequate, and which art and music come much closer to expressing.

Mary speaks to people, regardless of their religious faith or lack of it. She resonates deeply in the human soul.

She is, after all, central to the whole story. She was there at the birth of Jesus and his death and many days in between. We first meet her in the nativity story: already betrothed to Joseph, not yet married—and pregnant.

The late Morton Kelsey imagines the gossip:

> Most people are more comfortable with violence than unconventional sexual behavior and Mary's neighbors were no exception. The villagers could count and they talked about the impropriety of Mary's pregnancy. They smiled knowingly as Mary passed them to draw water from the village well. When the story of a heavenly visitor leaked out they snickered openly.[2]

2. See Morton T. Kelsey, *The Drama of Christmas* (Louisville, KY: Westminster John Knox Press, 1994), 20.

Author Reynolds Price imagines Mary as the object of lifelong scorn because of her problem pregnancy. "Bastard, Bastard, Mary's Bastard boy! God's big baby!" he imagines her neighbors taunting her and her son.[3]

It's a long journey from Nazareth to Bethlehem, ninety miles. It took a week traveling on foot and by donkey along winding roads. When they finally arrived, she had her baby son, in a stable behind an inn, and she and Joseph wrapped him in the bands of cloth they brought with them and laid him in the manger.

Mary is a reminder of how grounded in life this faith of ours is. We often think about our faith in terms of ideas and propositions and truth claims. We often measure faith in terms of doctrinal statements and creeds and whether or not we can subscribe to them. Mary reminds us that our faith is a response to a love that was expressed not in a carefully reasoned treatise but in a human life, in the everyday drama and passion of betrothal and marriage and pregnancy and birth and death.

Mary reminds us that God cares deeply about the human condition. God chose a modest, nondescript young woman. God chooses to be with the modest and marginal, the poor and weak, the humble and forgotten. Mary reminds us that God can use modest men and women who do not seem to have much to commend them, not much that the world recognizes as important and powerful. Sometimes young human beings do the most important work.

Mary reminds us that we should expect God to show up, not only in inspired worship, beautiful art, and elegant theology, but where the poor people are forgotten, vulnerable people oppressed, weak people overlooked. Mary is part of a movement that is more than a political agenda advocating for human rights, equal justice, and the excruciatingly difficult work of peacemaking.

Mary is a reminder of the most distinctive characteristic of biblical faith, namely, the profound compassion of God. Many Christians picture God as all-powerful, omnipotent, omniscient, "in light inaccessible, hid from our eyes."[4] Our God can be a little intimidating actually, but for centuries Mary has reminded the faithful that God is also infinite compassion and infinite love.

For centuries Mary has reminded people whose needs were urgent and who needed something more than a well-reasoned theology—suffering people, oppressed people, sick people, dying people—of an accessible side of God, a feminine side, a maternal side, a God who comes to us in the midst of suffering and oppression.

3. See Reynolds Price, "Jesus of Nazareth Then and Now," *Time*, vol. 154, no. 23 (December 6, 1999).
4. Walter Chalmers Smith, "Immortal, Invisible, God Only Wise," in *The Chalice Hymnal* (St. Louis: Chalice Press, 1995), 66.

So let Mary—who, at the end, held the lifeless body of her son in her arms—be a reminder to the mother whose son was killed in Afghanistan, or on the streets of Chicago, of the mercy and compassion and nearness of God.

Let Mary be a reminder that—whatever fear or loss or anxiety or uncertainty, whatever joy or anticipation or eager love lies ahead—love came down at Christmas, to be with us and to keep us, and all creation, always and forever.

Christmas Day

Elizabeth Conde-Frazier

ISAIAH 62:6–12
PSALM 97
TITUS 3:4–7
LUKE 2:(1–7) 8–20

Today's texts prompt us to think about the appearing of Christ in connection with righteousness and salvation. Are we aligned with the birth of Jesus that ushers in the reign of God? Evaluating our relationships and disconnections helps us reflect on this theme.

Isaiah 62:6–12

This passage belongs to Third Isaiah, which scholars believe was written after Judah's exile to Babylon (the exile took place 587–539 BCE). The early part of Isaiah contains oracles of judgment. Chapters 40–55 of Isaiah (Second Isaiah) balance the judgment with consolation. Soon the power of Babylon as empire will subside. God has used Babylon as an instrument of judgment to punish Judah, but Babylon will be brought to its knees and its shame exposed (Isa. 47:1–9).

The imagery of Third Isaiah (chaps. 56–66) also changes. Political and historical monarchs are displaced in favor of God's sovereignty.[1] This gives the book a theological focus where God is the ideal cosmic ruler. Third Isaiah is concerned with what will happen to the community in exile, now that judgment has taken place. It is a time to seek out the hope of a future. God is referred to as savior, and the city of Zion is the city of those who emerge after the judgment as righteous, the "Holy People" (vv. 11–12).

---

1. See Marvin A. Sweeney, "The Reconceptualization of the Davidic Covenant in Isaiah," in *Studies in the Book of Isaiah: Festchrift Willem A. M. Beuken*, Bibliotheca Ephemeridum Theologicarum Lovaniensium, ed. J. Van Ruiten and M. Vervenne (Louvain: Leuven University Press, 1997).

As a text of consolation, the prophet's message is that God is present to the people in the suffering and oppression of their exile. Sentinels at the walls of the city remind God to establish Jerusalem and to vindicate the city before other nations (vv. 6–7). The next verses give shape to God's promise. The enemies will no longer take their grain or wine (vv. 8–9).

As I read these verses, I am reminded of my trip to El Salvador before the civil war there. In their prayers the people petitioned God for justice and vindication from those who exploited their labor and failed to pay them fair wages. Later, Oscar Romero consoled the people on Christmas Day, "One day Prophets will sing not only the return from Babylon but our full liberation."[2] This is the prayer and hope of the oppressed. Israel suffered judgment because they had been oppressors and now, they were the oppressed whom God consoled with promises of liberation.

Whose lands do we use today for our own nourishing, taking the fruit of their lands and paying the workers so little they cannot afford to buy the fruit of their own labor? To whom is God promising today that they will be able to harvest and enjoy that which they have labored to plant? When we go to the supermarket, from whose lands does our produce come? Who picked it? Do their wages afford them the fruit of their own labor?

Whom do the next verses address: "See your salvation comes. . . . They shall be called, . . . The Redeemed of the LORD, . . . A City Not Forsaken" (vv. 11–12)? The foreign policies of the United States have brought oppression to others. Is God promising salvation to them and judgment to us? Can we listen to the news and always believe that salvation will come to us and not to others?

When we worship with another congregation with whom we share our facilities, what are their supplications? What does salvation look like to them? Do we hear in their prayers God's calling to us that we might become "The Holy People," a priestly people who bear the eternal covenant of righteousness and justice, because we belong to a cosmic ruler whose rule brings righteousness and salvation?

Psalm 97

Scholars categorize this as a psalm of enthronement that responds to the consequences of exile. In exile the people lost their connection to the land, the temple, and the monarch. The people's identity was related to their land. The monarch was tied to God's promises to the people. In an agrarian

---

2. Oscar Romero, *The Violence of Love* (Farmington, PA: Plough Publishing House, 2007), 39. See www.plough.com.

society the land and religious rituals are closely linked. The picture is one in which the main foundations of the people's identity were deeply shaken.

As a response to such a crisis, the psalm is a part of developing a religious framework outside of their land. It presents a different monarch, who reigns even when the people have no earthly monarch. The difference between this God-monarch and the other earthly monarchs is that God's rule is cosmic in scope. All honor and majesty are due to this ruler. All the nations (the coast-lands), the earth and the heavens, the sea and mountains are depicted as being affected by God's presence (vv. 2–6). These images have their origins at Sinai, where the people of Israel first experienced the elements of creation respond-ing to the presence of God.[3]

The poet now contrasts God, the sovereign, to the other gods. The word used to speak of gods other than God is *'elilim*, a word that means powerless, useless, weak, and vain.[4] This focuses on the foolishness and shame of wor-shiping such a god.

The implication of such an exaltation of a sovereign ruler is that no one would go against this monarch's rule. God's rule is characterized as righ-teous. Because of this, those who are evil or who do not exercise righteousness receive judgment, while the faithful are rescued from the effects of those who oppress them (v. 10). This is good news not only for the people in exile but for us today, as economic globalization is producing new forms of oppression and great discontent.

For example, the North American Free Trade Agreement (NAFTA) is a free trade agreement between Mexico, Canada, and the United States to reduce trading costs, increase business investment, and help North America become more competitive in the global marketplace. NAFTA made it pos-sible for many U.S. manufacturers to move jobs to lower-cost Mexico. The manufacturers that remained lowered wages to compete in those industries. Many of Mexico's farmers were put out of business by U.S.-subsidized farm products.

President Obama has mentioned that he would like to renegotiate the agreement by adding provisions relating to workers and to the environment. How could we become involved in a constructive dialogue with our legislators to make this a more just agreement?

A rural congregation seeks such dialogue by holding midweek worship where they have soup followed by a discussion of issues that affect their community. They write letters to their legislators. Children seven years old

---

3. Sandra L. Richter, "Psalm 97," in *Psalms for Preaching and Worship: A Lectionary Commen-tary*, ed. Roger E. Van Harn and Brent A. Strawn (Grand Rapids: Eerdmans, 2009), 256.
4. Ibid.

receive a pen to join in the letter writing. This advocacy is a beam of the light dawning for the righteous.

Titus 3:4–7

This passage is possibly a baptismal hymn.[5] Baptism is the beginning of an eschatological hope. Titus speaks of the theme of the saving appearance of Jesus. In this pericope the appearance of our Savior-God is because of God's goodness and benevolence. Goodness and benevolence were often used together to speak of the attentive care of rulers. This care was considered the "quintessential quality of a good [ruler]," who extended it even to the conquered expressed in the form of clemency.[6]

In antiquity, these qualities were connected to the reign of peace and harmony in sovereign rule. Rulers would receive petitions appealing to their benevolence as people asked them to intervene in a situation on their behalf. Monarchs expected a reciprocal benevolence on the part of those who received it. Other epistles speak of baptism as the beginning of a new life expressed through the vocation of service, of good works. These could be the reciprocal goodness for the benevolence we have received.

Finally, upon the coming of a governor to a city, benevolence was expected. If indeed a governor demonstrated benevolence to the people, that person was considered a savior.

At Christmas, we remember by telling and reenacting the appearing of our Savior; it is time to tell of our Savior's benevolence and saving grace. As we reflect about this, we may ask ourselves, in what ways have we reciprocated in like manner toward those around us?

The petitioning of the subjects for intervention reminds me of the invitations that groups of pastors sometimes make to the mayor and other political officials to meet with the clergy. When the political figures arrive, they sit at a table with the clergy, who may petition them for laws that will protect them from guns and the violence they bring or for quality education even when it means voting to balance the powers of teachers' unions. Their petitions may include just laws for the immigrants and the passing of health care bills that cover the poor. Clergy petition for creative solutions to provide the fundamental needs of housing and jobs. The meetings are not about promises but honest problem solving on behalf of the oppressed, that is, salvation appearing for all. We are both humbled and empowered by these meetings, in

5. See Raymond F. Collins, *1 and 2 Timothy and Titus: A Commentary*, New Testament Library (Louisville, KY: Westminster John Knox Press, 2002).
6. Ibid., 362.

which we participate in imparting benevolence and goodness—the appearing of salvation in our neighborhoods as an ongoing, eschatological event.

Luke 2:(1–7) 8–20

Luke depicts the poor and Jesus' interactions with them. Luke declares God's vindication of the poor and God's judgment upon the wealthy. Luke prominently displays God's coming in the form of humanity. Tradition has it that Jesus' parents were poor (though it must be admitted that the text does not directly say this). God chooses to identify with this community of poverty.

This narrative has been portrayed in numerous pageants. Each time, it is dressed up in the culture of the community that interprets it. The Mexican *posadas* invite every person to enter into the reality of the poverty of Jesus' community. They do not take the role of spectators. *Posada* participants walk from house to house searching for shelter, meeting with repeated rejection and homelessness, as tradition depicts Joseph and Mary. They return to the experience of "identification with," and it becomes a sacramental experience.

A sacrament is an outward sign that mediates, embodies, and reveals the grace of God. God comes as a babe in poverty, and the poor become the sacrament. This invites us to reflect on how we love God through our love for the poor. Our manger scenes may imply that Joseph and Mary were the only ones who could not find shelter that evening, but many in that time were on the edge of survival, as are many more today. We often see the poor not as individuals but as an aggregate, "the poor," in which the distinctiveness and dignity of individuality is lost. The birth of a child on that evening must have brought out the women of the community, particularly a midwife. The birth of a son came with celebratory traditions. The shepherds were invited to this celebration by the angels. They represented another kind of poor.

In southern California, because of home foreclosures many families have found themselves homeless. Some gather in a makeshift camp on a patch of waste ground, Tent City, with no electricity, plumbing, or drainage. The poor are in community because we wish to keep them contained. Containment means isolated from the rest of us, disconnected.

Identification stands in direct contrast to disconnection. In many Latino and African cultures, personhood is defined by one's relationship to others. Our identity is given to us by the others to whom we are related—parents, community, nation, and land.[7] To give Jesus his identity, God chose Joseph and Mary in Bethlehem, along with those without shelter and the despised shepherds. The Lukan story is a narrative about the embodiment of God as identity;

---

7. In many homes of Asian and European descent, people are also defined relationally.

therefore it is about connections. God is wrapped in "bands of cloth and laid . . . in a manger, because there was no place for them in the inn" (v. 7).

This causes us to reflect on our relationships and what informs these ties. Jesus' birth announces the reign of God, a reign of connectedness to those disconnected from us, an idea already present in the corporate culture of Judaism. This interconnectedness grounds the ethical political imperative to love others and the creation. Reconnecting to the disconnected "others"—immigrants, prisoners, peoples of other cultures and sexual orientations—is the sacrament of this season.

First Sunday after Christmas

Ruthanna B. Hooke

ISAIAH 61:10–62:3
PSALM 148
GALATIANS 4:4–7
LUKE 2:22–40

It is astonishing how quickly the shadow of the cross falls over the glory and merriment of Christmas. In Year A of the lectionary, the First Sunday after Christmas brings the horrific story of the massacre of the children ages two and under in Bethlehem. The readings today offer Luke's account of Jesus' presentation in the temple, a joyous occasion that nevertheless has ominous overtones. While Simeon rejoices that he has lived to see the Messiah, he also predicts that this child will cause opposition among the people of Israel, leading to the falling and rising of many. Jesus' coming means that everyone is faced with a choice: whether they believe in him or reject him. This theme of division, with the necessity of choice, runs through the passage from Galatians as well. Here too the coming of Christ has led to a decisive parting of the ways between old and new ways of being. From the perspective of apocalypticism, this difference is not between Judaism (old) and Christianity (new), but between ways of living that are complicit with the old age of sin and death and ways of living that seek to be aligned with the present and coming realm of God. Readers are compelled to choose which way they will go. Only Isaiah and Psalm 148 retain the tones of pure rejoicing.

Luke 2:22–40

In Luke's Gospel, Jesus is presented as a Messiah whose mission in many ways follows that of the Hebrew prophets. One way in which Jesus' course parallels that of the prophets is that his coming divides people. Simeon first announces this future path, and his pronouncement is programmatic for the entirety of Luke–Acts. Throughout these books, those who encounter Jesus

39

are divided: some receive him, and some reject him. Two reasons explain this mixed response, both related to Jesus' behavior as a prophetic Messiah.

First, the prophet proclaims—and, in Jesus' case, also brings about—the divine reversal, in which, as Mary proclaims in her Magnificat, the powerful are cast down from their thrones and the lowly raised up (Luke 1:46–55). This program causes division. On the one hand, many people, including the poor, sinners, tax collectors, women, people with leprosy, and some of the wealthy, accept this promise. Significantly, Mary, a woman, first announces God's program of transformation, and Anna welcomes Jesus when he is presented in the temple. On the other hand, many of the rich, the members of the establishment, are threatened by this promised reversal. They reject and ultimately kill Jesus.

Second, Jesus' offer of salvation is offensive to some because it includes not only sinners and others within his own people, but also Gentiles. Simeon predicts that the child will be a light to the nations. In his sermon in the synagogue at Nazareth, Jesus draws on the prophets to assert that Gentiles have a place in salvation and that through Jesus' ministry God is inviting Gentiles to participate in the fullness of salvation in the present and future (Luke 4:25–27; see 1 Kgs. 17:1–16; 2 Kgs. 5:1–14). The church in the book of Acts extends Jesus' mission by reaching out to Gentiles. For Luke, Jesus' messiahship is a means whereby the Gentiles are included in the promises of God. As we see in Luke 4:25–30, this offends the residents of Jesus' hometown enough that they are prepared to throw him off a cliff.

The social justice implications of this text are evident: the coming of Jesus that we celebrate at Christmas presents us with a clear choice as to which side we are on and which God we serve. Are we on the side of justice for poor people, women, and sinners? Or are we on the side of the rich and powerful, those who "have received [their] consolation" (Luke 6:24)? Do we stand with the God of Israel on the side of radical inclusion?

Galatians 4:4–7

This lection poses the preceding question in a stark way. In this letter Paul argues against other Christian Jewish missionaries who are telling the Galatian Gentile converts that, having come to believe in Jesus as the Messiah, they should now undergo circumcision as a sign of their entry into covenant with God. Paul's argument is not with Judaism as such, but with those who maintain that converts to the way of Jesus Christ should adopt signs of Jewish identity. While such signs are appropriate for Jewish people, Paul believes God has justified Gentiles through the death and resurrection of Jesus Christ, so that they are now fully in covenant with God. Indeed, in Paul's apocalyptic theology, the ministry of Christ has already begun to bring about a new creation in which previous social divisions, such as those between "Jew [and] Greek . . . slave [and] free . . . male and female" (Gal. 3:28), no longer determine standing with God or one's place in God's community. Paul's concern here is not to diminish the law but to assure believing Gentiles that they are included in the promises of God, both now and at the apocalypse, when the realm will become fully manifest.

Paul's message parallels Luke's in important ways. Both proclaim that Jesus Christ's birth, death, and resurrection have created a stark choice for Gentiles between two conflicting ways of living, compelling all to choose between these two ways. Furthermore, it is clear that the way offered by Jesus is the way of radical inclusiveness, such that social divisions are leveled, lifting up the lowly and casting down the proud. Finally, Gentiles who reject the way of Jesus opt for a life of slavery to the principalities and powers that Jesus' life, death, and resurrection have rendered powerless. It is notable that Simeon, when he sees the baby Jesus, says, "Lord, you now have set your servant free," using language referring to the manumission of a slave (Luke 2:29); he too experiences the coming of the Messiah as a release from bondage to the brokenness of the old age.

There are several social justice implications of Galatians' message of freedom. The freedom that Christ offers is first of all a release from social barriers and hierarchies based on race, class, gender, and sexual orientation. To live as a child of God is to renounce these divisions and to build communities in which such forms of discrimination do not exist. Likewise, Galatians proclaims that the saving work of Christ is available to all, even to those outside our habitual communal boundaries.

Moreover, those who are other are to be received into the community without requiring them to become "like us" in ways that are not appropriate or essential. Rather, those aspects of their identities that are consistent with God's purposes are to be honored and incorporated into the Christian community. To do otherwise is nothing less than to repudiate Christ's saving work.

Finally, Galatians and Simeon's words of freedom challenge us to examine in what ways we are enslaved to the "powers of this age." Are we enslaved to our possessions, to patterns of overwork, to addictions, to overconsumption, to ways of life that exploit others? These ways of being are not simply personal failings, but are the results of systemic forces that hold us captive. Christ offers freedom from these patterns of existence. This freedom takes the form, first, of recognizing our captivity, and second, of recognizing that in Christ the power of these forces is broken. As we accept freedom, we begin to find ways to live in greater freedom from these captivating powers, while recognizing that our power to live in this new way comes not from our own efforts, but from God's gracious initiative.

Isaiah 61:10–62:3

Isaiah 61:10–62:3 is a fitting ode to the salvation Luke and Paul celebrate. As a part of Third Isaiah (chaps. 56–66 of Isaiah), this section is set after the return from exile. Third Isaiah registers that this return was less glorious than had been expected in Second Isaiah and that those returning encountered hardships: the temple still in ruins, a return to pagan practices, instances of economic oppression of the poor. Into this troubled situation, the prophet announces that "the spirit of the Lord GOD is upon me, because the LORD has anointed me; [God] has sent me to bring good news to the oppressed . . . to proclaim liberty to the captives" (Isa. 61:1). The Lord promises that the people will rebuild their ruined cities, and live in them amid abundance. Jerusalem will be a city in which "righteousness" reigns: the people live in right relationship with God. As in Galatians and Luke, this "right relationship" is a society in which the poor and oppressed are lifted up and in which there is release from captivity. When these conditions are met, the city dons the "robe of righteousness" and the "garments of salvation" (61:10), festive attire suitable for weddings. When these conditions are met, Jerusalem's "vindication shines out like the dawn" (62:1), becoming a light to the nations, just as Simeon prophesied that Jesus would be. If the people wish to realize the splendid vision of return to Zion prophesied in Second Isaiah, they need to establish just social relationships, for only thus will rebuilt Jerusalem become truly glorious.

Reading Isaiah 61:10–62:3 in the Christmas season reminds us to rejoice that in Jesus' birth salvation has come to us. The context of the Isaiah passage reminds us that salvation is accomplished not only in our innermost beings, but still more in the social arrangements by which we live. Righteousness looks like a society in which the oppressed are lifted up and honored, in which captives are set at liberty. Perhaps living out this vision means looking at our prison justice system and asking why our prisons are overwhelmingly populated with people who are poor and people of color. Salvation looks like a city where no one lives among the ruins. Perhaps living out this vision means working toward ensuring adequate housing for all.

Psalm 148

This psalm also sounds an inclusive vision of salvation. Just as Luke and Paul describe God's salvation as offered to all, irrespective of social status or nationality, the psalmist offers the flip side of this expansive promise of salvation, calling on all that is to respond to the promise by praising God. The psalmist calls for praise of God "from the heavens," from sun, moon, stars, and "the highest heavens," and "from the earth"—not only from humans, animals, and plants, but even from inanimate objects such as mountains and hills. In relation to Luke and Paul, we can say that Psalm 148 calls for an appropriate response from those who have been granted the gift of God's salvation. We are all invited to praise God because all of us—male and female, Jew and Greek, slave and free, gay and straight—have been included in God's new creation and brought into a new covenant with God through the incarnation of God in Jesus Christ. This new reality is worthy of praise and is worthy of our action to make the new creation a social reality.

As we embark on this new way of living, it is important to remember Galatians' message about the primacy of God's grace in our salvation. Our work for social justice must never devolve into "works of the law," such that we wrongly believe that our work for social transformation earns us God's grace. Rather, because God has inaugurated a new creation in Jesus Christ, and because we are already children of God, we can live differently in God's new creation. Our work for social justice must flow from our rejoicing over what God has already accomplished. This is why the tone of merriment and joy that Christmas brings, and that Isaiah and the psalmist capture so poetically, needs to be seen not as antithetical to the work of bringing about God's justice, but precisely as the foundation for all such work.

Holy Name of Jesus

Dianne Bergant, CSA

NUMBERS 6:22–27
PSALM 8
PHILIPPIANS 2:5–11
LUKE 2:15–21

Ancient people had a great respect for names. They believed that a portion of the personality of the individual resided in the name: the more powerful the person, the more powerful the name. Two readings for today's feast, Psalm 8 and Philippians 2:5–11, demonstrate the power of the divine name. The psalm describes the power of God's name in effecting creation; the passage from Paul's letter to the Philippians reports the dignity that God bestowed on the name of Jesus. While Christians may not immediately associate the feast of the Holy Name with social justice, the readings for today contain implications in that direction.

Psalm 8

The psalm praises the name of God because of the wonders of creation. The psalmist is depicted as gazing at the night sky, spellbound by its magnificence, marveling first at the splendor of the universe and then at the extraordinary role played by humankind within that universe. Though the wonders of creation overwhelm the psalmist, it is really the name of God that is praised, for creation gives witness to the awesomeness of that name.

The psalmist's musings begin with a comparison of the immeasurable scope of the heavens and the very limited condition of humankind. There is no comparison between the magnificent bodies in the night sky and puny, short-lived human beings. Yet God is mindful of them and cares for them. What is often translated "angels" is really the Hebrew plural for "gods" (*'elohim*). The psalmist claims that human beings have been created just a little less than heavenly beings and in that capacity are given the authority to rule over creation (cf. Gen. 1:26–28). This language paints a picture of royalty. Human beings are crowned as royalty is crowned. They are endowed with honor and glory, two characteristics closely associated with ancient Near Eastern monarchy. As comprehensive as the control of ancient Israel's monarchy might have been, it was all delegated rule. Furthermore, the monarch was answerable to God for the exercise of that rule. The kings and queens were merely vice-regents, agents of God's will, exercising dominion in God's stead, according to God's plan.

The weak and fragile human beings, who were given control over the sheep and the oxen and the beasts of the field, over the birds and the fish and whatever swims in the seas, do not rule autonomously. The realm that was put in their charge is not theirs; it is God's. While their choice by God is an incalculable honor, it is also a tremendous responsibility. Still, regardless of the honor conferred on humankind, it is God's name that is proclaimed in both the opening and the closing of this psalm.

The similarities found in Psalm 8 and the creation account in Genesis 1 suggest that these two passages belong to the same theological tradition. The passages not only report the creation of various elements that comprise the cosmos—the heavens, the moon, and the stars—but they also clearly mention the responsibility that humans have with regard to "the beasts of the field, the birds of the air, and the fish of the sea, whatever passes along the paths of the seas" (Ps. 8:7–8; Gen. 1:26, 28).

With respect to social justice, the psalm and Genesis 1 depict the role of the human being in the same way: having dominion over other creatures. Dominion here does not mean having arbitrary power over others; it means serving God's purposes of helping all members of the created world live together in peace.

Most people are familiar with the idea of God creating by word, as found in Genesis 1. This is probably because it is repeated again and again: "And God said" (Gen. 1:3, 6, 9, 14, 20, 24, 26). It is easy to overlook this same concept in the psalm because of the psalm's emphasis on creation itself rather than on the activity of God in creating. However, Psalm 8 begins and ends with the same exclamation of praise: "O LORD, our Sovereign, how majestic is your name in all the earth" (vv. 1, 9). The power of the word and the power of the name are clear.

Though Genesis 1 does not use the personal name of God (Yahweh), Psalm 8 does. Like many traditional people, the ancient Israelites believed that knowledge of the name of an individual gave one a certain power over that individual. For this reason, they were careful not to allow the personal name of their God to fall into the hands of their enemies, lest those enemies presume to have power over their God. Indeed, the Jewish community

believes that the divine name is holy and should not be pronounced; the practice of not saying the divine name comes from the sanctity of the name. The
practice of never speaking God's name is still observed by contemporary Jews.
Out of reverence for the sacred name, most Bible translations today do not
print it in full. Some versions only print the consonants, YHWH. The more
common practice is to substitute LORD in place of the name itself, as found in
the citation from Psalm 8 that appears above.

The Exodus story of God's self-revelation to Moses in the midst of the
burning bush (Exod. 3:4–15) includes the disclosure of the sacred name: "God
said to Moses, 'I AM WHO I AM.' . . . Thus you shall say to the Israelites, 'I
AM has sent me to you'" (v. 14). This name is some form of the verb "to be."
However, it is a very unusual form, and we are not sure how to translate it.
The translation stated above is the most common rendering. It is a present
tense form of the verb and reflects belief in God's enduring presence now and
into the future. Some translators choose the future form of the verb: "I WILL
BE WHO I WILL BE." This rendition emphasizes God's freedom from human
manipulation.

In either case, the name stresses God's absolute sovereignty: God purposes
for all people (and all creation) to live together in the harmony of Genesis 1.
Moreover, the context in Exodus 3 in which the name is revealed—the divine
call to Moses to confront Pharaoh with God's desire to free the Hebrew people from slavery—forever associates this name with liberation from all that
denies God's purposes.

Numbers 6:22–27

This passage may be one of the oldest passages in the Bible. As presented in
Numbers, Moses receives the blessing from God and then delivers it to Aaron
and his children (vv. 22–23). Moses, Aaron, and other priests pronounce the
blessing in God's name.

YHWH, the personal name of God, is repeated three times in the blessing
(vv. 24–26). The priests are told to put God's name over the Israelites. This is
an unambiguous example of the power of the personal name of God. In this
name the people are blessed. God looks upon them and grants them peace.

The blessing itself is crisp and direct. Each line invokes a personal action
from God, but there is very little difference in the petitions. They all ask for
the same reality, that is, peace: the condition of absolute well-being. When
this blessing is pronounced over the congregation today, it not only wishes
peace for individuals in the community. It also wishes for the congregation
to be a community of peace, and it commissions the congregation to be an
agency of peace.

Philippians 2:5–11

This christological reflection can be divided into two parts. In the first (vv. 6–8), Jesus is the subject of the action; in the second (vv. 9–11), God is. The first part describes Jesus' humiliation; the second recounts his subsequent exaltation by God.

Christ Jesus did not cling to the dignity that was rightfully his. Christ was in the form of God, equal to God. Christ did not merely set aside his Godlike state, but actually emptied himself of it. Though in the form of God, Christ chose the form of a servant or slave. Without losing his Godlike being, Christ took on the form of a slave, becoming vulnerable to all of the circumstances of that station in life. As God, he could elicit obedience from others; he voluntarily binds himself to others as part of his own obedience.

The exaltation of Christ is as glorious as his humiliation was debasing. While Christ was the subject of his self-emptying, his superexaltation is attributed to God. Just as form and appearance denote being, so name contains part of the essence of the individual. In exalting Jesus, God accords his human name (Jesus) a dignity that raises it above every other name. It now elicits the same reverence that the title Lord (*kyrios*) does. In ancient Rome, "Lord" was the title often ascribed to the emperor. Because of his exalted state, the title is now bestowed on Jesus. Furthermore, *kyrios* is the word used in the Septuagint (the Greek version of the Old Testament) as the substitution for YHWH, the personal name of God. This explains why Paul insists that "at the name of Jesus" every creature shall do him homage and every tongue shall proclaim his sovereignty (vv. 10–11).

Luke 2:15–21

This passage has two distinct parts: the visit of the shepherds, and the circumcision and naming of Jesus. The shepherds were ordinary folk whose lives were hard, as they were often isolated and had to be with the sheep in all kinds of weather. That shepherds would leave their flocks in the hills and go into Bethlehem in search of a newborn was extraordinary. Even if they left their sheep in pens, if anything happened to the sheep while they were gone, they would suffer a financial setback if the flock belonged to them, or they would be liable to the owner. This risk did not deter them. Instead, they promptly responded to divine revelation.

When the shepherds saw Mary and Joseph and the baby, they understood what the angel had said. Convinced of the arrival of the long-anticipated Messiah, they set out to proclaim this to all they met. Such behavior must have compounded the jeopardy into which they had placed themselves. They had not only abandoned their responsibilities and put their own futures at risk; they were now praising God for the birth of the Savior in Bethlehem. What would people think of them and their message?

In accord with Jewish custom, eight days after his birth Jesus was circumcised. This ritual initiated the males into the community of Israel. It was enjoined by God on Abraham and his descendants, and from that time forward, it was considered a sign of the covenant (Gen. 17:9–12). This ritual affirms what Paul declares about Jesus in Philippians: "being born in human likeness, and being found in human form" (Phil. 2:7).

The name given Jesus is both common and extraordinary. It is an Aramaic form of Joshua, a common Jewish name. It means "God saves."

Holy Name has important social dimensions. By saying that the name of Jesus is "above every name," Philippians 2:5–11 asserts that the name of Jesus is more powerful than any other name by which individuals and communities are named. Paul assumes there are many other names (beings) in the universe who have power. Many other entities, such as the elemental spirits of the universe (Gal. 4:3), ravage human life. While these entities may be hurtful, their power is temporary and limited. Human experience in the present may be named by distortions of God's purposes, such as addiction, poverty, racism, and war. However, such names are penultimate. They do not finally define us. The presence of the name of Jesus means that God through Jesus is ultimately sovereign over all things that destroy the divine purposes. The power of God is at work to reshape all personal and social circumstances. Those in covenant with God through Jesus will ultimately be free of the forces that distort God's intentions. This perspective helps the congregation (a) to name these lesser entities as undermining God's purposes and (b) to live toward the final coming by living in servant community in the pattern of Jesus.

Second Sunday after Christmas

Alyce M. McKenzie

JEREMIAH 31:7–14
PSALM 147:12–20
EPHESIANS 1:3–14
JOHN 1:1–18

These texts show up like old friends the Second Sunday after Christmas in Years A, B, and C. Like conversations with old friends, our dialogues, while always enriching, are not the same every year. In Year A our conversation focuses on the question, "What is the gift God is offering us through these texts?" In Year B: "What are the obstacles in the way of receiving those gifts from God?" And in Year C: "What kind of life results when we live by these gifts of God?" God's gifts to us in these passages are wisdom in a world of folly (John 1:1–18), a vision of unity in a world of division (Eph. 1:3–14), a "foregleam" of a hopeful future of restoration amid a dismal present (Jer. 31:7–14), and a moment of clarity about who and whose we are in the midst of confusion (Ps. 147).

John 1:1–18

John's Gospel was probably written around 90 CE to a community in conflict with the followers of John the Baptist and Jewish authorities. The community experienced a tension related to a split between the Johannine community and the parent synagogue (9:22; 12:42; 16:2). John's members may have been excommunicated from the synagogue for affirming that Jesus was the Messiah.[1] This would explain the Gospel's focus on the internal life of the community

---

1. J. Louis Martyn, *History and Theology in the Fourth Gospel*, revised and expanded, New Testament Library (1968; repr., Louisville, KY: Westminster John Knox Press, 2003). For arguments against this hypothesis, see Adele Reinhartz, *Befriending the Beloved Disciple: A Jewish Reading of the Gospel of John* (New York: Continuum, 2002), and Raimo Hakola, *Identity Matters: John, the Jews and Jewishness*, Supplements to Novum Testamentum 118 (Leiden: E. J. Brill, 2005).

rather than on reaching beyond it in mission. It would account for the Gospel's primary portrayal of Jesus as source of comfort, healing, and support.

John sought to counter two forms of "wisdom" in his milieu. One said that Jesus was Messiah and Son of God but not fully human. The other said that Jesus was a human teacher, but not the Messiah and Son of God. From John's point of view, believing one or the other but not both is the chief obstacle to receiving the gift of the fullness of Jesus' gifts. The prologue warns against living by half-truths. John is at pains to emphasize that Jesus is both fully divine (the Word present at the beginning of creation) and fully human (the Word that "became flesh and lived among us," v. 14). Believing that Jesus is fully divine but not human can absolve us of ethical accountability. We think, "We could never live like Jesus: He was the Word of God!" Believing that Jesus is fully human but not divine can lead us to follow him as a moral teacher but can also allow us to distort his teachings.

A current version of these distortions is the self-help philosophies that paint a veneer of Jesus' teaching about "abundant life" onto a self-centered prosperity gospel. These philosophies teach that God wants the best for you. Think positive thoughts, and wealth and happiness and harmony will be yours. Such philosophies can perpetuate the belief that people are in poverty because they have not thought the right thoughts. Jesus, the Word made flesh, calls us to a life that like his own is full of grace and truth: a life in which we overcome our desire for convenience and comfort and are willing to love others as Jesus loves us (13:34–35).

Ephesians 1:3–14

From the themes in Ephesians we infer that conflicts were bubbling up in the congregation. Often conflicts in faith communities, then and now, take the form of one group trying to block another's reception of the good news. These efforts were evident in Ephesus. The first several verses of Ephesians paint a broad canvas of God's saving plan for all humankind. God chose the church for adoption as God's children through Jesus Christ. God provided redemption, the forgiveness of our trespasses, and God made known these plans and gifts. God is the protagonist of the story of salvation, and God desires reconciliation and salvation for us. Paul tells us in Romans 8:39 that nothing can separate us from God's love in Christ.

Except ourselves. We can put blockades in the path of God's grace. We create blockades in at least two ways: by denying God's blessing to others, and by attempting to hoard it. In Ephesians, Gentile and Jewish Christians both denied that God wanted to bless the other. When we deny that God wants to bless someone else, we become stumbling blocks to God's plan of salvation.

Recounting a tragic event in her community involving the death of a young gay man, a pastor remarked that, in the aftermath of the tragedy, a small group of gay men from the community came to church on two occasions: the funeral and Christmas Eve (which came shortly afterwards). She said they came to church on those two occasions because "their need was greater than their discomfort" at entering a church that had rejected them and excluded them from God's saving plan. The church is an obstacle to God's salvation when it creates an uncomfortable, judgmental atmosphere instead of a welcoming one.

Another way we become obstacles to God's blessing is by hoarding the blessing for our private use as did the gnostics. Gnosticism was the name for a variety of cults in the first few centuries of the Common Era that emphasized secret saving knowledge, dualism, and salvation as escape. In contrast to the gnostics, Ephesians insists that, for Christians, the mystery of salvation is an *open* secret. "With all wisdom and insight [God] has made known to us the mystery of [God's] will" (1:8–9). The view of salvation in Ephesians is diametrically opposed to a gnostic, elitist understanding that limits salvation to a few who are "in the know." Salvation means the inclusion of Gentiles: a mystery, but not a secret.

I am reminded of a quote attributed to John Wesley: "Whatever religion can be concealed is not Christianity." This is probably a condensation of Wesley's Sermon 24: "Upon Our Lord's Sermon on the Mount." Wesley begins the sermon by setting out his plan to explicate the words of the Sermon on the Mount: "I shall endeavour to show, first, that Christianity is essentially a social religion; and that to turn it into a solitary one is to destroy it; secondly, that to conceal this religion is impossible, as well as utterly contrary to the design of its author."[2]

Jeremiah 31:7–14

Often called the "weeping prophet," Jeremiah was also a prophet of hope. Our passage is part of the Book of Consolation (chaps. 30–33), which comes in the middle of a collection of Jeremiah's oracles, largely of doom and coming judgment. God and Jeremiah want the same thing: for the people to repent and return to God for a joyful homecoming (31:14). Jeremiah faces two obstacles to achieving this task: his own reluctance to speak, and the people's resistance to hearing.

---

2. *The Works of John Wesley: The Bicentennial Edition*, Sermons 1–33 (Nashville: Abingdon Press, 1984), 1:533.

R. E. O. White describes Jeremiah as having a "nervous temperament, craving peace, inwardly insecure and outwardly lacking confidence, yet driven by an inescapable sense of duty. Not only was he denied the comfort of a wife and family, but he also faced imprisonments and ridicule." All of this, says White, combined to cause Jeremiah intense suffering in his later years.[3]

Not only did Jeremiah face internal opposition to his calling, but the prophet faced opposition among his audience. His early prophecies did not seem to pan out. The people to whom he was called to take his message would not believe him. Their attention was distracted by the temptations and brutalities of their day. Two ravenous would-be world dominators (Assyria and Babylonia) vied for power in a plot that makes the latest Hollywood blockbuster seem tame. This story has it all: assassination (Amon is killed by zealous priests), cultic sex (Assyrian kings allow cultic prostitution), human sacrifice (to the god Molech), murder (Zedekiah's sons are executed by Nebuchadnezzar), torture, and kidnapping (Zedekiah is blinded and taken in chains to Babylon).

God speaks of God's desire to gather the people, to guide them as a shepherd, to guard them out of a parental love (Jer. 31:10). That's beautiful, but not everybody is willing to be gathered. Some have become comfortable in Babylon. Others are in too much pain to move. It is not enough to tell people, in the midst of their misery and despite all experiences to the contrary, that a promising future awaits them, that they have but to repent and turn toward God. Words from the pulpit are not enough. If I am lame and blind, pregnant, or in labor, I am not going to set out alone on a journey. But if someone will go with me on the journey home, hold me up when I fall, feed me when I'm hungry, then I might set off toward home. Words are not enough from the church to an unjust, pain-filled world. People need companionship on the way. Are we as a church offering companionship, or only charity?

Despite our unwillingness as church to offer the invitation and people's unwillingness to receive it, God continues to offer the invitation to repentance, return, and restoration. God continues to empower people to answer it. All obstacles will be overcome. That's a message reluctant prophets need to hear in every age.

Psalm 147:12–20

Denise Hopkins's *Journey through the Psalms* includes a chapter on praise psalms entitled "Your Hallelujahs Don't Have to Be Hollow Anymore."[4]

---

3. R. E. O. White, *The Indomitable Prophet* (Grand Rapids: Eerdmans, 1992), 7.
4. Denise Dombowski Hopkins, *Journey through the Psalms* (St. Louis: Chalice Press, 2002), 32–58.

Psalm 147 offers us a gift, a moment of clarity amid our confusion, in which we are reminded of who and whose we are: chosen children of a Creator whose power takes the shape of tender compassion for the poor. There are three attitudes that can make our hallelujahs hollow and that prevent us from receiving the full gift of Psalm 147. First, our hallelujahs become hollow when we recite the psalm as a superficial thanks to God because things are pretty good for us right now. We recite snippets of the psalm during the call to worship to butter up God early in the service, so we can ask for stuff later on.

Second, our hallelujahs become hollow when we forget that, just as every lament psalm implies praise, every praise psalm implies lament. Samuel Terrien points to harsh realities that lie behind the positive praise of Psalm 147. Verses 16 and 17 praise God for the beautiful landscapes that snow and frost paint in the winter season, but such cold conditions are hard on poor people (v. 17b). God melts the snow and hail and thus provides water crucial to human well-being, while also causing floods in the narrow canyons of the region.[5] God's choice of Israel is reason for praise (v. 20). Yet we need to be wary of superficial praise when everything is going well for us, praise that is not sturdy enough to look at the whole of life, bad and good. The praise psalms, when seen in the context of the whole Psalter, allow us to affirm God's loving presence as a reality deeper than material prosperity and physical protection.

Third, our hallelujahs become hollow when we forget that praise psalms do not only describe how things are; they anticipate how things will be. They speak, not just about creation, but about eschatology. They affirm the goodness of God's creation, but they also anticipate an ordered life. Praise psalms, says Denise Hopkins, "tap us as co-creators in that order in the making."[6] When we praise these psalms, we agree to join God in ordering all of life.

5. Samuel Terrien, *The Psalms: Strophic Structure and Theological Commentary* (Grand Rapids: Eerdmans, 2003), 916.
6. Hopkins, *Journey through the Psalms*, 36.

Epiphany of Jesus

Terriel R. Byrd

ISAIAH 60:1–6
PSALM 72:1–7, 10–14
EPHESIANS 3:1–12
MATTHEW 2:1–12

In today's readings, God's enlightening and liberating presence bursts forth like a budding flower in the springtime breeze. Paul, as spiritual director, helps us see the riches of God's grace and mercy shown to both Jew and Gentile. Likewise, the psalmist ascends to the heights of jubilation that accompany the quiet assurance that justice and righteousness have no social, cultural, or class barriers: True liberation must begin with the least among us, which ultimately makes all of us truly whole. Matthew announces the visitors from the East (*magoi*) with their wonder, enthusiasm, and excitement over the birth of the liberating Ruler. They, like many, longed to behold the very embodiment of the good news of salvation, the bright and morning star. Isaiah echoed in tone and texture those prophetic utterances that he envisioned would bring emancipation from darkness by the overwhelming presence of God's glory.

Ephesians 3:1–12

Paul writes this letter from jail, where he is imprisoned by Nero, the Roman emperor; yet he calls himself a prisoner of the Lord. How ironic. On the other hand, how amazingly ordinary that Paul is less concerned about who has him in physical bonds than about who has him in spiritual accord. He writes, "This is the reason that I Paul am a prisoner for Christ Jesus for the sake of you Gentiles" (v. 1). For those who understand what it means to be sold out, both to and for a cause greater than themselves, this is not an unusual concept. Paul's faith and his understanding of the revelation of God's grace and mercy made his imprisonment seem small to him in comparison to the cause of hope he has in the liberating Messiah. Martin Luther King

Jr., gives a similar rationale for being in jail in his famous "Letter from the Birmingham Jail":

> I am in Birmingham because injustice is here. Just as the prophets of the eighth century B.C. left their villages and carried their "thus saith the Lord" far beyond the boundaries of their home towns, and just as the Apostle Paul left his village of Tarsus and carried the gospel of Jesus Christ to the far corners of the Greco-Roman world, so am I compelled to carry the gospel of freedom beyond my own home town. Like Paul, I must constantly respond to the Macedonian call for aid.[1]

In 1943, Dietrich Bonhoeffer, the great freedom fighter, was imprisoned in Berlin for his role in the resistance movement against Nazism. Bonhoeffer wrote in his famous essay "Costly Grace:" "Costly grace is the gospel which must be *sought* again and again, the gift which must be *asked* for, the door at which a [person] must *knock*. Such grace is *costly* because it calls us to follow, and it is *grace* because it calls us to follow *Jesus Christ*."[2] Both King and Bonhoeffer endured imprisonment in the struggle for human liberation and causes bigger than themselves.

Conversely, Paul says, "For surely you have already heard of the commission of God's grace that was given me for you" (v. 2). The cause of liberation is a just cause! The desire to bring others out of the darkness of oppression, rejection, and condemnation is a just cause. Liberation is a great prophetic theme. Isaiah affirms his prophetic call: "The spirit of the Lord GOD is upon me, because the LORD has anointed me; [God] has sent me to bring good news to the oppressed, to bind up the brokenhearted, to proclaim liberty to the captives, and release to the prisoners" (Isa. 61:1). In the same spirit, Paul became nothing less than the mouthpiece of God in bringing forth the mystery of the liberating gospel of Christ; in so doing he stands in the prophetic tradition.

Isaiah 60:1–6

Isaiah 60–62 comprise one long prophetic oracle of salvation and liberation. As we reflect on the words found in Isaiah 60:1–6, we observe two events taking place that will make Jerusalem radiant and prosperous once again. In verse 4, Jerusalem's sons and daughters will return from exile. The exile is one of

---

1. Martin Luther King Jr., "Letter from Birmingham City Jail," in *A Testament of Hope:The Essential Writings of Martin Luther King, Jr.*, ed. James M. Washington (San Francisco: Harper & Row, 1986), 290.
2. Dietrich Bonhoeffer, *The Cost of Discipleship*, trans. R. H. Fuller (1963; repr., New York: Touchstone Books, 1995), 45.

the most important events recounted in Jewish tradition. From the exodus, to the period of the judges, the divided nation of Israel, and the subsequent fall of Judah to Babylon, exile has been a recurring experience in the life of the Hebrew people. Yet the prophet Isaiah with hope conveys to the people that the long night of dejection and rejection will come to an end.

Emancipation awaits those who struggle without relief. The spiritual mystic Howard Thurman speaks of those "whose backs are against the wall."[3] Thurman says, "There is one overmastering problem the socially and politically disinherited always face: Under what terms is survival possible?"[4] Isaiah sees more than simply the possibility of survival: "Then you shall see and be radiant; your heart shall thrill and rejoice, because the abundance of the sea shall be brought to you, the wealth of the nations shall come to you" (v. 5). The wealth of the nations will begin to flow into Jerusalem to beautify and enrich the new temple (vv. 7, 13). The temple, like the church, has always been a refuge from the hostilities, the harsh realities of an indifferent, often unkind, uncaring society. In spite of the plight of the downtrodden, those who have been battered and bruised by the vicissitudes of life, there is a measure of solace in knowing that there is a Word of hope for those who have suffered injustices.

Psalm 72:1–7, 10–14

With spiritual precision, the psalmist acknowledges the monarch's responsibility to administer justice and righteousness to all. "Give the [ruler] your justice, O God, and your righteousness to a [ruler's child]" (v. 1). At the heart of the psalmist's prayer, there seems a reversal of fortunes. There is hope for the hopeless, a way of escape for those locked behind the doors of poverty, oppression, and despair. The psalmist declares, "May the mountains yield prosperity for the people, and the hills, in righteousness. May [God] defend the cause of the poor of the people, give deliverance to the needy, and crush the oppressor" (vv. 3–4). Martin Luther King echoed a similar hope for the poor and oppressed of his day in his "I Have a Dream" speech. After pointing out that America made a promissory note that every American would be guaranteed "the unalienable rights of life, liberty, and the pursuit of happiness," King declares that America "has defaulted on this promissory note." Yet he asserts, "We refuse to believe that there are insufficient funds in the great vaults of opportunity of this nation. So we've come to cash this check,

3. Howard Thurman, *Jesus and the Disinherited* (1949; repr., Boston: Beacon Press, 1996), 9.
4. Ibid., 20.

a check that will give us upon demand the riches of freedom and the security of Justice."[5]

We live in a time when our nation, indeed our world, is faced with unparalleled challenges. Our world is faced with social and economic injustice and downright exploitation of the poor and needy, who often find themselves disenfranchised from opportunities within their rights of citizenship. Class distinctions and differing spiritual values create their own schisms, and in King's call for justice, these distinctions are made clear and have made a lasting impact on our society.

The psalmist speaks with amazing compassion for the poor and oppressed of his age. Today, by contrast, in our uncivil discourse, voices of reason, compassion, and sound judgment that advocate for the poor and underserved are drowned out. A comparable salient concern of our day is to see that those who are denied or lack health insurance have the opportunity to obtain adequate medical services when needed. Those who oppose this idea often deem the poor, or working poor, unworthy of what should be the right of every American—to see a medical professional when ill. Legislation to help the jobless maintain a subsistence existence is filibustered in our Senate for days. These positions are difficult to understand in a nation as wealthy as America; but, the psalmist gives us the road map: "For [God] delivers the needy when they call, the poor and those who have no helper. [God] has pity on the weak and the needy, and saves the lives of the needy" (vv. 12–13). May we pray as the psalmist prayed, that justice and righteousness be given to all who are poor. And may we join our prayers with actions.

Matthew 2:1–12

Matthew depicts the wonder and majesty of Jesus as the great liberator. When the visitors from the East asked, "Where is the child who has been born king of the Jews? For we observed his star at its rising, and have come to pay him homage" (v. 2), they were affirming the divine nature of the Liberator. The response of the earthly ruler, Herod, was different: "When King Herod heard this, he was frightened, and all Jerusalem with him; and calling together all the chief priests and scribes of the people, he inquired of them where the Messiah was to be born" (v. 3). Oppressors and tyrants are always threatened by proponents of truth and justice. Later we catch a glimpse of the cruelty and vicious nature of Herod the Great. "When Herod saw that he had been tricked by the wise men, he was infuriated, and he sent and killed all the children in

---

5. Martin Luther King Jr., "I Have a Dream," in *Testament of Hope*, 217.

and around Bethlehem who were two years old or under, according to the time that he had learned from the wise men" (v. 16).

Darkness and light cannot dwell together. Truth dispels the darkness of evil. The visitors from the East recognized the light from the star that rested above the place where the baby Jesus lay as cause to be filled with joy, and they worshiped the newborn child (vv. 10–11). Luke's Gospel parallels this idea of light: "the dawn from on high will break upon us, to give light to those who sit in darkness and in the shadow of death, to guide our feet into the way of peace" (Luke 1:78–79). As Liberator, Jesus, unlike Herod, brought forth light and life, not death and destruction. Jesus gave guidance to those in trouble. Jesus tried in every way to relieve the burdens of those already heavily oppressed. The Light still shines: this is the message to all who feel darkness has overtaken them. The radiant majesty of God's mercy and grace will minister to our greatest needs. Jesus comes to all as the Liberating One. Jesus came to dispel gloom. He came to heal our wounds. He came to exchange our nagging guilt for the quiet assurance of forgiveness. Jesus came to give us something to live for. He came to restore all that we have lost. In a world of unrest and restlessness, we can rejoice in the liberty and light of God's love. May this Epiphany season be a time when we rest in the spirit of liberty that abides within us, with us, and around us.

First Sunday after the Epiphany (Baptism of Jesus)

Joseph Evans

GENESIS 1:1–5
PSALM 29
ACTS 19:1–7
MARK 1:4–11

I cannot recount how many times I have read *The Souls of Black Folk*.[1] I was introduced to W. E. B. Du Bois's classic by my grandmother, along with Booker Taliaferro Washington's *Up from Slavery*.[2] She instructed my reading to prevent what Carter G. Woodson called "the mis-education of the Negro."[3] Currently, people are rediscovering an appreciation for social and political significances found in Du Bois's *Souls of Black Folk*. I read *Souls* as a book of fourteen civic sermons.[4] In "Of Our Spiritual Strivings," Du Bois masterfully demonstrates his double consciousness, namely, interpreting the majority culture's Eurocentric traditions and values without abandoning the minority culture's interpretive critique of those traditions and values, and adding some of their indigenous experiences that have been shaped by oppression.

Evans Crawford, for many years dean of the chapel at Howard University, makes use of this double consciousness as part of a process that he refers to as biformation in *The Hum: Call and Response in African American Preaching*. Biformation is "a shaping of identity, perspective and expression that flows

---

1. W. E. B. Du Bois, *The Souls of Black Folk* (New York: Bantam Books, 1989). This edition includes an insightful introduction by Henry Louis Gates Jr.
2. Booker T. Washington, *Up from Slavery*, ed. William L. Andrews (London: W. W. Norton & Co., 1996).
3. Carter G. Woodson, *The Mis-education of the Negro* (1933; repr., New York: Africa World Press, 1990).
4. See Jonathon S. Kahn, *Divine Discontent: Religious Imagination of W. E. B. Du Bois* (Oxford: Oxford University Press, 2009). Also see Edward J. Blum, *W. E. B. Du Bois: American Prophet* (Philadelphia: University of Pennsylvania Press, 2007). Kahn and Blum substantiate my claims that Du Bois writes *Souls* with religious language.

from being both African and American."[5] In this important book, Crawford turns to the well-known preacher Howard Thurman to illustrate the biformation process, suggesting that Thurman would have evolved toward his biformation theory:

> The biformative process and its consequent creative marginality would have been an inevitable part of Howard Thurman's spiritual development as a black man in America. That is why I prefer to call the process of preparation for preaching that I observed in Thurman and that I am exploring . . . "spiritual biformation." That term keeps before us the particular legacy of being black in America and its impact upon the homiletical musicality of African American preaching traditions.[6]

Echoing Du Bois, Crawford points out that the African American preacher has a "felt twoness" that is partly African and partly American. One lens for both Du Bois and Crawford is the majority cultural lens, a lens that affirms Western traditions and values. The other lens is the African American lens, a marginalized cultural lens that critiques Western traditions and values from the margins. The preacher who responds with "dogged persistence" to these two "warring tendencies" comes to a consciousness that "makes for 'creative marginality.'"[7]

In *The Souls of Black Folk*, Du Bois mainly focuses on the second lens. His objective is to orient his primary readers toward oppression as a means to understand the African American experience. Du Bois creates a new space for his readers to hear a new voice. Du Bois wants to abolish racial inequality and social barriers. He seeks to do so by exposing the inequities of racial and social castes, particularly by highlighting the experience of oppression (epitomized by the sorrow songs).

In doing so, Du Bois makes use of the motif of tricksters, found in both African and African American lore.[8] These tricksters act to create a space in which listeners or readers can come to fresh understanding of text or a tradition. Du Bois employs this approach by beginning each essay with a well-

---

5. Evans Crawford with Thomas H. Troeger, *The Hum: Call and Response African American Preaching* (Nashville: Abingdon Press, 1995), 19.

6. Ibid.

7. Cleophus J. LaRue, *The Heart of Black Preaching* (Louisville, KY: Westminster John Knox Press, 2000), 9. When discussing African American preaching, LaRue contends, "At first glance, the very breadth, diversity and complexity of this tradition would seem to hamper the search for identity, common methods and dynamics. On closer inspection, however, one can detect an integrative force, a common thread running throughout this style of proclamation that clearly provides its spirit and raison d'être, namely, a distinctive biblical hermeneutic."

8. On the trickster motif, see Henry Louis Gates Jr., *Signifying Monkey: A Theory of African American Literary Criticism* (Oxford: Oxford University Press, 1988), xx–xxi.

known literary passage and then a bar of music from a spiritual. Thus Du Bois begins his first essay, "Of Our Spiritual Strivings," by quoting from the poet Arthur Symons.

> O water, voice of my heart, crying in the sand,
> All night long crying with a mournful cry,
> As I lie and listen, and cannot understand
> The voice of my heart in my side or the voice of the sea,
> O water, crying for rest, is it I, is it I?
> All night long the water is crying to me.
>
> Unresting water, there shall never be rest
> Till the last mood droop and the last tide fail,
> And the fire of the end begin to burn in the west;
> And the heart shall be weary and wonder and cry like the sea,
> All of life crying without avail,
> As the water all night long is crying to me.[9]

The musical bar that follows is from the spiritual "Nobody Knows the Trouble I've Seen." These ideas set out a leading motif of *The Souls of Black Folk*: suffering and struggle as the contexts in which to understand the experience of the African American community.

The baptism of Jesus is an epiphany, not only in revealing Jesus, but in modeling what should happen to all who are baptized: we should all have an epiphany of God's purposes. My purpose now is to use motifs inspired by *The Souls of Black Folk* in the mode of biformation to help preachers recognize how biblical themes for today in support of the baptism of Jesus call for the inclusive social world for which Du Bois longed.

Genesis 1:1–5

The opening words of the Hebrew Bible, "In the beginning when God created the heavens and the earth" (v. 1), communicate an intelligent design, a world that has final approval of order. The text assumes a Sovereign Actor who controls all things. According to verse 2, the world before God began to create was dark, without form and void. The world was chaos. In the first essay in *The Souls of Black Folk*, "Of Our Spiritual Strivings," W. E. B. Du Bois writes with shades of dark melancholy:

> Between Me and the other world there is ever an unasked question: unasked by some through feelings of delicacy: by others through the

---

9. Du Bois, *The Souls of Black Folk*, 1.

difficulty of rightly framing it. All, nevertheless, flutter around it. They approach me in a half-hesitant sort of way, eye me curiously or compassionately and then, instead of saying directly, "How does it feel to be a problem?" they say, "I know an excellent colored man in my town; or, I fought at Mechanicsville; or, Do not these Southern outrages make your blood boil?" At these I smile, or am interested, or reduce the boiling to a simmer, as the occasion may require. To the real question, "How does it feel to be a problem," I answer seldom a word.[10]

In the haunting question, "How does it feel to be a problem?" the preacher can recognize experience similar to that of the universe before God began to create. The experience of people of color is often that of chaos.

Yet, as the narrative of creation unfolds, order emerges from chaos. When we reach the climax of creation, the creation of the first human beings, there is no suggestion of racial or ethnic inequity. Clearly racial inequality is inconsistent with the Sovereign Actor's master plan of order. Inequality leaves us formless and void, effectively returning the social world for all peoples to a time of chaos.

However, the preacher has good news today! The Sovereign Actor is still working to bring shape to all relationships according to Genesis 1:3–2:4. With respect to race and ethnicity, God seeks to move the human family from chaos to community. When we are baptized, we turn away from chaos and commit ourselves to work with God for a world in which no people are seen—or see themselves—as problems.

Psalm 29

The psalmist describes a Sovereign Actor who is revealed through nature. In the introduction (vv. 1–2), the writer ascribes to God glory, strength, and holiness. For the psalmist, these attributes are cause for people to worship God alone. These attributes, glory and strength, are disclosed through the holy beauty in heaven's storms.

Verses 3–11 describe natural phenomena that God alone can create. Notice that in verses 3–9 the psalmist repeats that the voice of God speaks through natural events. These observations are existential musings about God. The psalmist is not investigating scientific motifs. Instead, the writer chooses poetry to disclose his or her feelings about the nature of God and how people and nature are shaped by the Sovereign Actor.

10. Ibid., 1.

In the same way that God speaks to nature and through nature in this psalm, God speaks to and through us. Indeed, God gives us voice. In the storm of life W. E. B. Du Bois seeks to give marginalized people a voice:

> So [has] dawned the time of *Sturm und Drang:* storm and stress to-day rocks our little boat on the mad waters of the world-sea; there is within and without the sound of conflict, the burning of body and rending of soul; inspiration strives with doubt and faith with vain question. The power of the ballot we need in sheer self-defense, else what shall save us from a second slavery?[11]

Du Bois sees the condition of people of color as a stressful storm. But within the storm, the voice of God speaks and gives us voice.

Acts 19:1–7

The Holy Spirit is the subject of this passage. The setting is Ephesus.[12] At Ephesus, the apostle Paul seeks ways to evangelize the Ephesians.[13] Accordingly, the apostle Paul asks people, "Did you receive the Holy Spirit when you became believers?" They reply, "No, we have not even heard that there is a Holy Spirit" (v. 2). They knew only the baptism of John for repentance. Paul proclaims Jesus. Afterward, the people are baptized. The new Christians immediately prophesy in Jesus' name.[14]

People cannot always see God's purpose when they are not transformed. Writing of the conditions of African Americans in the South, Du Bois says this in his essay "Of the Dawn of Freedom":

> The opposition to Negro education in the South was first bitter, and showed itself in ashes, insult, and blood; for the South believed an educated Negro to be a dangerous Negro. And the South was not wholly wrong; for education among all kinds of men always has had, and always will have, an element of danger and revolution, of dissatisfaction and discontent. Nevertheless, men strive to know.[15]

---

11. Ibid., 8.
12. F. F. Bruce, *New Testament History* (Garden City, NY: Doubleday, 1969), 303. Bruce writes of Paul and Ephesus, "Paul had been hard at work for two years, with a number of colleagues, evangelizing Ephesus and other cities of Asia to such good effect that for centuries that province was one of the strongest citadels of Christianity in the world."
13. Ephesus was one of the most important cities in Asia Minor, as assumed in Acts 18:19.
14. See Acts 8:17. It expresses a similar experience in Samaria. Contextually, Samaria had been enslaved to spiritual strongholds. They had been exposed to sorcery. See Acts 19:13, where Paul confronts Jewish exorcists who attempt to misuse the power in the name of Jesus for selfish greed.
15. Du Bois, *The Souls of Black Folk*, 24.

The implication of Acts 19:1–7 is clear: under the leading of the Holy Spirit, European Americans will put aside racism and seek a transformed community in which all people can live together in opportunity, dignity, respect, and abundance.

Mark 1:4–11

F. F. Bruce writes, "Of all the religious movements in Palestine on the eve of Christianity none is more directly relevant to Christianity itself than the ministry of John the Baptist."[16] John the Baptist played a significant role in helping form the sociopolitical movement called Christianity.

Verse 4 describes a place, person, and proclamation. John the Baptist was in the desert preaching forgiveness of sins. In verses 5–6, Mark says that John's proclamation had power; and people came from Jerusalem, Judea, and the vicinity of the Jordan River to hear his message. John wore a garment of camel hair and a leather belt around his waist. He ate locusts and wild honey.

John was an eschatological prophet; that is, he announced that God was about to end the present evil age, marked by injustice, exploitation, violence, and death, and would complete the manifestation of the realm of God as a world of justice, mutual respect, sharing, and eternal life.[17] John saw Jesus as the one who would bring this age. John's mission was to prepare people for the coming world by inviting them to repent and to be baptized. However, while John prepared the way, Jesus would be the one to begin the transformation (vv. 7–8).

Furthermore, John baptized Jesus. The opening of the heavens and the descent of the Spirit like a dove upon Jesus are symbols confirming that Jesus was the one who would bring the realm. Double confirmation comes from the voice out of the heavens: "You are my Son, the Beloved; with you I am well pleased" (v. 11).

Du Bois introduces us to John, first an unprepared boy, and then a man prepared to join the social movement toward the realm. We meet John in Du Bois's essay "Of the Coming of John." Du Bois describes a change of consciousness that took place:

> He had left his queer thought-world and come back to a world of motion and of men. He looked now for the first time sharply about him, and wondered he had seen so little before. He grew slowly to feel almost for the first time the Veil that lay between him and the white world; he first noticed now the oppression that had not

16. F. F. Bruce, *New Testament History*, 152.
17. Ibid., 154.

seemed oppression before, differences that erstwhile seemed natural, restraints and slights that in his boyhood days had gone unnoticed or been greeted with a laugh.[18]

In effect, Du Bois describes an epiphany that took place over time.

The preacher who develops a sermon along the lines of John's preaching can hope for a similar transformation in the congregation today. Many Euro-centric people are hardly aware of racism and its destructive effects on the entire community. Such people can acknowledge their complicity in racism, can repent, and can join the movement to a more just society. The preacher might help people of color develop more nuanced understandings of the oppression in which they live and point them toward liberative action. In both cases, the preacher hopes to bring about an epiphany, a growing aware-ness of God's purposes.

18. Du Bois, *The Souls of Black Folk*, 173.

Second Sunday after the Epiphany

Lincoln E. Galloway

1 SAMUEL 3:1–10 (11–20)
PSALM 139:1–6, 13–18
1 CORINTHIANS 6:12–20
JOHN 1:43–51

Today's texts invite faithful listening to God, whose all-encompassing knowledge cannot be fathomed. The texts encourage us to speak truth to power through trust in God, as well as to show proper reverence to our bodies, to engage in the unrelenting search for truth and revelation, and to respond with committed witness.

1 Samuel 3:1–10 (11–20)

This text provides us with a glimpse of a new beginning, even a new era. Samuel represents hope for a religious landscape bereft of any sign of spiritual vitality. "The word of the LORD was rare in those days; visions were not widespread" (v. 1). The old, depleted era is represented by Eli, whose "eyesight had begun to grow dim so that he could not see" (v. 2). Samuel, however, is surrounded by symbols of divine presence; "the lamp of God had not yet gone out," and Samuel's place of rest was in the temple, "where the ark of God was" (v. 3). Samuel seems to be well positioned to hear the voice, to see the work, and to experience the presence of God.

Yet Samuel does not come to this moment alone. He stands on his mother's prayers, vows, and confidence in God, who exalts and brings low, and who "raises up the poor from the dust" (2:1, 7–8). He stands on the faithful actions of his parents (1:28; 2:11; 3:1), and with each passing year (2:18–19) he grows "both in stature and in favor with [God] and with the people" (2:26). Samuel's prophetic work and understanding are quite likely influenced by parents who witness faithfully to a God whose justice embraces the poor. It may also be that our responsiveness to issues of justice is cultivated by the stories, cries, and prayers of those who shape our lives.

In the first part of the chapter, Samuel hears the voice of God call to him in the night (vv. 1–10). This is a new beginning for Samuel, since the word of God had not yet been revealed to him (v. 7). In the second part (vv. 11–20) Samuel understands that in his ministry he must not only listen, but speak. In both of these assignments, Eli the priest gives him direction and encouragement to prepare him for listening (v. 9) and to speak truthfully and courageously the message from God (vv. 15–17). Finally, Eli affirms that the word of God has indeed been revealed to Samuel (v. 18). Samuel continues to mature and grow in his speaking ministry (v. 19) until he is established as a trustworthy prophet in all of Israel (3:20; 4:1).

Samuel's ministry unfolds in the context of family, he grows in favor with people (2:26), he is guided by a priest. He learns that justice is the prayer and the faithful work of a community. He learns how to be open to instruction. He accepts that a prophetic ministry that proclaims truth, even to religious or political powers, must be anchored in a life of devotion and fidelity to God's call to listen and to speak, because, ultimately, the work of justice is initiated and supported by God. This was the case of Dr. Martin Luther King Jr., who, whether in silent reflection in jail or soaring oratory in the nation's capital, interpreted his life's work as that of a drum major of justice, peace, and righteousness.[1] As we receive affirmation for our prophetic ministry from family or faith community, we proclaim with assurance that God is with us and will not let our "words fall to the ground" (v. 19).

Psalm 139:1–6, 13–18

This psalm reflects an amazing intimacy between God and the psalmist. God's all-encompassing knowledge is unfathomable. Such knowledge includes thoughts (v. 2), words (v. 4), and actions (v. 2). The fullness of God's knowledge is the heart of the psalmist's direct address, "O LORD, you have searched me and known me" (v. 1). The psalmist's testimony (vv. 5–6, 7) permits us to wonder if God's all-encompassing love is a source of complaint and resistance or of gratitude and acceptance of God. The answer comes in the final request: "Search me, O God, and know my heart; test me and know my thoughts" (v. 23).

---

1. Martin Luther King Jr., "The Drum Major Instinct," in *A Testament of Hope: The Essential Writings of Martin Luther King Jr.*, ed. James M. Washington (San Francisco: Harper & Row, 1986), 267.

One is immediately drawn to the intensely intimate relationship reflected in the psalm between God and the psalmist, God and the individual, God and each living being. Our personal piety calls attention to our thoughts, words, and actions in our home, business, or civic life, and also to the widespread personal addictions of pornography, drugs, gambling, and consumerism that plague society today. Yet the personal cannot be divorced from its social consequences; personal addiction to gambling jeopardizes family resources and contributes to economic collapse; addiction to pornography contributes to obsession with the physical body and the objectification of the person within the wider culture. Facing these challenges, each person stands with the psalmist naked and vulnerable in the presence of God, often feeling hemmed in "behind and before" (v. 5), in both private and public spaces.

The psalmist knows "very well" (v. 14) that God's wonderful works extend from being "knit . . . together in my mother's womb" (v. 13) through the end of life (v. 18). God's wonderful works call forth in us greater compassion for every created being and greater commitment to the stewardship of God's creation, even to vulnerable wildlife threatened with extinction. God's wonderful works invite wonder and reverence for the sanctity of life as we honor and protect all forms of life: from the womb, to the disenfranchised, to the inmate on death row, to the enemy combatant or terrorist. Awesome, intimate, and personal knowledge of God leads to social commitments and conversations about abortion or reproductive rights, animal rights, arms sales, pollution, and the proliferation of nuclear weapons, among other things. Only when we share such awareness and investment will we be able to say with the psalmist, "Wonderful are your works; that I know very well" (v. 14).

1 Corinthians 6:12–20

How is freedom to be understood? During the opening exchange, certain philosophical differences related to this question immediately come to the forefront. The perspective expressed in this text is that freedom cannot be interpreted in ways that enslave or oppress. Freedom cannot be defined or expressed in theoretical constructs that engage the intellect with no ramifications for our own bodies or those of others. Freedom has implications, not just for the individual, but for that individual's participation in a faith community. Indeed, we are reminded of the adage: none is free until all are free.

Paul indicates that freedom cannot include men engaging their sexual fantasies at the expense of women, even if these women are in shackles as slaves or live as prostitutes. Freedom has to be defined in terms that honor and respect human bodies. The body is not a morally neutral zone. According to Paul, the physical body provides a home and full expression for human intimacy and sexuality, the delights of eating good foods, and also a home for divine presence and activity.

In our own time, have we found ways to define Christian freedom so broadly that we no longer care about persons who struggle with issues directly related to their bodies, such as abortion, drug abuse, hunger, pornography, and poverty? Issues that find expression in our bodies are of utmost importance for our spiritual lives. In reflecting on the journey toward justice through direct action, Dr. King remarked, "We would present our very bodies as a means of laying our case before the conscience of the local and national community."[2]

Paul wants the Corinthians to see that how we treat the body is a central matter of Christian faith and ethics. God does not redeem the self from the body; God redeems the self as embodied (v. 20). From this point of view, the text also provides a reminder of a painful world of buying and selling of human bodies for the slave trade. One is reminded of the plunder of the African continent for its resources and people—bodies on an auction block, bodies bloodied, whipped, and lynched. Human bodies cannot be viewed as property or chattel or collateral damage. To enslave a person is to violate the temple of God. While chattel slavery is no longer as common as it was prior to the twentieth century, the passage calls the church to stand against contemporary forms of forced labor or sexual slavery (with its child prostitution and human trafficking).

John 1:43–51

John's disciples hear him testify concerning "the Lamb of God who takes away the sin of the world" (John 1:29, 36). Two of John's disciples follow Jesus in response to John's testimony. The disciples receive from Jesus an invitation to discipleship, and their commitment to him is evidenced by their willingness to invite others to "come and see" (John 1:39; cf. 1:43, 46). These first disciples contextualized their message about Jesus by engaging and interpreting him through different forms of address. Jesus could be understood as "rabbi" (vv. 38, 49), "Messiah" (v. 41), the one "about whom Moses in the law and also the prophets wrote" (v. 45), "Jesus son of Joseph from Nazareth" (v. 45), "Son of God" (v. 49), "King of Israel" (v. 49), and "Son of Man" (v. 51).

The Fourth Gospel interprets God for the world (John 1:29; 3:16). In our increasingly pluralistic contexts, we learn how to respect the multiple ways that others seek to be in relationship with or interpret God. Discipleship cannot be built on principles that promote disrespect for other religious

2. Martin Luther King Jr., "Letter from Birmingham City Jail," in *A Testament of Hope*, 291.

traditions. By honoring the humanity of all people, we learn how to be disciples without creating negative stereotypes of others. The diverse titles that the disciples use may be a constant reminder that confession of faith and discipleship require fresh, ongoing, creative acts of interpreting and contextualizing our faith story. How will we invite others to come and see without adopting an insulting and demeaning posture toward their own spiritual pathway? How do we respond to those who choose not to follow or confess Jesus? Will our discipleship reflect bigotry and hatred, like the anti-Jewish or anti-Muslim sentiment that leads to violence against synagogues and mosques? Our discipleship must be for the world the reality of love, justice, peace, and compassion for all.

The Fourth Gospel reveals Jesus to us and invites us to see and to follow him. We see through our various lenses what Jesus means for the world. From one perspective: "What has come into being in him was life, and the life was the light of all people" (1:3b–4). From another perspective: "Here is the Lamb of God who takes away the sin of the world" (1:29). In our faith communities, we can proclaim Jesus who sees the intimate details of our beings. He sees the individual who says, Teacher (rabbi), teach me; Messiah, deliver me; fulfillment of the sacred Scriptures, reveal yourself to me. In our proclamation and discipleship we continue to say, "Come and see God's love for the world as the hungry are fed, undocumented workers are given water for their thirst, homes are built for the victims of natural disasters, and justice is demanded on behalf of the voiceless. Come and see God's love, not just for some but for the world."

Martin Luther King Jr. Day
(January 15)

Dale P. Andrews

HABAKKUK 2:1–4
PSALM 77
HEBREWS 10:32–39
MARK 4:1–20

Racism is the one of the most pernicious and permeating realities of life in North America. If left unchecked, racism will destroy both people of color and people of European origin. The Gospel insists that the church be anti-racist and pro-reconciling. The birthday of Martin Luther King Jr. (1929–68) offers to preachers the opportunity not only to honor the life of this prophetic leader, not only to name the abiding oppression of marginalized racial/ethnic communities and the duplicitous dominating effects on European communities, but also to help congregations recognize practical ways that the community can join the struggle for justice.

Nonviolent direct action seeks to create such a crisis and foster such a tension that a community which has constantly refused to negotiate is forced to confront the issue. It seeks to dramatize the issue that it can no longer be ignored. My citing the creation of tension as part of the work of the nonviolent resister may sound rather shocking. But I confess that I am not afraid of the word "tension." I have earnestly opposed violent tension, but there is a type of constructive, nonviolent tension which is necessary for growth.[1]

Martin Luther King Jr.

1. Martin Luther King Jr., "Letter from Birmingham City Jail," in *A Testament of Hope: The Essential Writings of Martin Luther King, Jr.*, ed. James M. Washington (San Francisco: Harper & Row, 1986), 290.

We learned anew from Martin Luther King Jr. that prophetic ministry wrestles under the strain of theological questions, perhaps because the few answers that we may actually discern are not free from internal theological challenges, never mind the tortured navigation through our political terrain. The biblical texts today raise such questions and challenges for our preaching ministries regarding the very character of God and the character of lived faith facing oppression, suffering, and the day-to-day struggles of life. The prophet invites us into the dialogue of complaint and prayer before God, while the psalm lifts lament into a communal encounter. The ancient sermon to the Hebrews calls for us to partner with God and people, while Mark speaks of the faithful toil of the sower and soil in the reign of God.

Habakkuk 2:1–4

Much has been made of the recurring role of Habakkuk 2:4b in Second Testament texts like Hebrews 10:38. Prevailing interpretations center in how people of faith understand their own covenantal identity and the plight of other peoples, particularly in situations of oppression or struggle.[2] The preceding chapter, Habakkuk 1, outlines the prophet's complaints over how God allows another people, who are seemingly less righteous than the troubled covenant people, to hold power over them. What does it mean, then, to be a people of a sovereign God, if not freedom from oppression of any kind? Disturbing theological arguments of God's judgment emerge in such texts and our preaching. Violent actions between nations become twisted rationales of God's wrath and will. This troubled reasoning stirs behind the prophet's own depictions of God's judgment in direct complaint to God that this kind of divine action or theological reckoning makes no sense in view of God's word and relation (1:4).

The complaints feel unresolved, though God does assure the prophet that all creation, even the "wicked," shall learn and know the sovereignty of God. God calls upon the "righteous" to "live by their faith" (2:4b). Preachers ponder, "What does righteous faith look like?" Do we seek the ruin of our oppressors because of their unrighteousness? King wrestled with these questions continuously. His answers would always return to nonviolence and the struggle of *agapē* love to seek the careful liberation of the oppressor along

---

2. Alice Ogden Bellis, "Habakkuk 2:4b: Intertextuality and Hermeneutics," in *Jews, Christians, and the Theology of the Hebrew Scriptures*, ed. Alice Ogden Bellis and Joel S. Kaminsky (Atlanta: Society of Biblical Literature, 2000), 369–85. See also Rom. 1:17 and Gal. 3:11 for other reiterations of Hab. 2:4b.

with the liberating care for the oppressed.[3] Certainly we must consider how the unrighteous who oppress in whatever form—racial, gendered, economic, or militaristic—incur God's judgment. This prophetic dialogue reveals that God expects righteous faithfulness in our resistance to oppression, even when we cannot not yet see how or if God is at work in our behalf. Though the problems of suffering contending with God's sovereignty remain alarming, we learn from the prophet that the character of God becomes the source and object of the prophet's prayer: "in wrath may you remember mercy" (3:2).

Psalm 77

How do we deal with the unrelenting assault that life seems to wage upon our hopes and faith? This psalm asks some unfathomable and yet very real questions that challenge the character of God. Has God's steadfast love run out? Has God actually lost sight of grace? Verses 8–9 speak for us in our cry for mercy while we are under the dominance of suffering. "Domination" does feel like the right word when we face injustice that will not relent. Some persons might charge that it is too simple-minded to regard all suffering as domination. For those suffering, however, the word hardly does justice to the experience. Our public debates over "if" we share public responsibility for social and personal healing only add to the experience of relentless domination. We debate the public responsibility for health care, for poverty, and other things perhaps because we too feel overwhelmed by the feared domination of suffering upon our resources, if not our privilege. Injustice is difficult to fight when the "enemy" is us—our wants, or even our fears. Our fears are never very far removed from our wants.

King found fear deeply entrenched in both violent and passive resistance to justice. He distinguished between two predominant kinds of fear—one that "protects" us and one that "paralyzes" us. Yet the spaces between them often become distorted. King saw the fears that protect sometimes become fears that hate. Even the perceived needs for protection become fearful lies to deceive our communal conscience. Fear becomes the "misuse of the imagination" when communal conscience implodes and negates life, even if by neglect or avoidance, not to mention denial or assault. King saw that fear could be managed only through the virtues of courage, love, and faith that God is involved within the life of humanity.[4]

Though the psalm's lament is spoken through an individual voice, it relies heavily on communal experience and outcry. The Israelite exodus figures

3. For example, see Martin Luther King Jr., "Love Your Enemies," in *Strength to Love* (1963; repr., Philadelphia: Fortress Press, 1981), 49–57.

4. Martin Luther King Jr., "Antidotes for Fear," in *Strength to Love*, 115–26.

prominently, of course, in the communal memory of verses 11–20. The fulcrum of lament itself, however, in verses 8–9, reflects back upon Exodus 34, particularly regarding the character of God. This juxtaposition calls upon our covenantal life of faith and care.[5] That God moves in sociopolitical life is no small factor in biblical literature; God's actions indicate not only God's character but God's desires for humanity and communal life.

Hebrews 10:32–39

Hebrews calls us into a life of worship amid the mess we make in living. The letter calls us to become a community of faith with endurance. Chapter 10 begins with the impetus behind this charge to endure: the enduring quality of Christ's sacrifice. Christ accomplishes what no offerings for sin could (vv. 5–10). Yet the role of sacrifice in Christology presents some difficulties. Does God's abhorrence for sin require blood for the covenant of forgiveness? Hebrews 9 sets up the sacrificial teaching of Hebrews 10 with that assumption. Preachers will have to wrestle carefully here with how to translate sacrifice and divine justice within the exigencies to resist social sin. Does divine justice call for shedding blood? Unfortunately this is a common misreading.

Instead, the nature of Christ's own divine sacrifice was to endure against the assault of sin, in the love of God for humanity, despite his own loss of blood and breath. Wrestling with Hebrews requires us to reevaluate the call of sacrifice in how we preach atonement and enduring faith. Social transformation does not seek blood sacrifice in the name of divine righteousness or divine indignation. We endure with faith in the transformation of life wrought by Christ's sacrifice. The atonement is in Christ's faithfulness to endure in love.

As Hebrews 10 speaks of an enduring life of faith, memory empowers us in our struggles and daily walk (v. 32). We draw strength from remembering God's faithfulness (Ps. 77:11–12). This is a recurring biblical theme when dealing with trials and suffering that seemingly press us beyond our capacity to resist or overcome. Sometimes persevering against social sin is sustained only in solidarity with those who suffer relentless injustice (v. 33). Partnering with those who suffer was the brilliance of the Civil Rights Movement and the theology of nonviolent resistance espoused by King. The "call to partner" drove King to expand his work on racism into an analysis of global capitalism and militarism. How then will our sermons partner with those who suffer without becoming saccharine tolerance of our own felt impotence?

5. Gregory M. Stevenson, "Communal Imagery and the Individual Lament: Exodus Typology in Psalm 77," *Restoration Quarterly* 39 (1997): 215–29.

The perseverance to partner with those who suffer for their sake reflects the perseverance of Christ so central to this chapter and before. We may partner with those who suffer in kind with us, but our partnership with Christ and humanity does not mete out compassion, mercy, or justice with a strainer or a stopwatch. Indeed, we pause to recover, to lift thanksgiving and joy for the gifts of life. But the very joy and the very need of God's faithfulness impel us into partnership with those yet to discover such gifts and joy in life, especially when our thriving has been at their expense.

Mark 4:1–20

One of the more perplexing aspects of this parable is its lack of direct challenge. The only immediate expectation created by the parable is to listen closely. It feels rather difficult to extract a meaningful challenge for justice from a confusing parable about God sowing seeds, many of which will perish or be carried off. The initial focus is upon the generosity of the sower to spread seed without restraint. Many scholars report that sowing so widely reflects typical agricultural practices of the age. One first sows freely and then tills the soil. Such generous seeding therefore appears somewhat practical. The idea that some seed then will perish amid different soil is assumed— hence the practice to sow bountifully. Still, as the parable proper ends (v. 9), we wonder, to what lesson or reversal are we charged to listen?

We are granted a substantial interpretation of the parable at the plea of the disciples (v. 10). God is the sower; but are we the seed, the soil, or the fruit to be harvested? We gain some insight into the seed from verse 14. The word is sown. Misinterpretation of this parable often occurs when deciphering the seed. Some of us might mistake the language of verses 15, 16, and 18: "these are the ones who . . ." and "others are . . ." The temptation is to associate this language with us, the recipients of the message, and therefore attempt an apocalyptic interpretation pointing to some destruction of the unfaithful (the inadequate soils) and vindication of the faithful (the good soil). To the contrary, this parable is focused on overturning simple apocalyptic expectations of the reign of God.[6] Instead of promising violent victory or the destruction of worldly opponents, the parable promises bountiful harvest in spite of the harsh elements and opportunistic consumption of ravenous scavengers.

It would be misguided to preach an adversarial message from this parable. The victory is not ours but the power of God's word. Justice is not secured with the Sower withholding the seed of God's favor; nor does transformation

---

6. Theodore J. Weeden Sr., "Recovering the Parabolic Intent in the Parable of the Sower," *Journal of the American Academy of Religion* 47 (1979): 97–120.

occur via the imposition of harsh seasons. Harvest results from bountiful grace in sowing without relent or measure.

To discern our lesson in the parable of the Sower, perhaps a more accurate tagline would be the parable of the Soil. Scholars point out that the four types of soil are all passive even in such argument.[7] Soil is not an agent of action. While this perspective can complicate discernment of social transformation, the condition of the soil may reflect how we view the natural world and humanity. The natural elements along with the soil hold destructive capacities. Yet this parable holds the promise of God's fruitful faithfulness through the seed. Despite the facts that we can be caustic and our world can be threatening, the crux here is not that an evil other is against us. Rather, the crux is that God's word of grace will be fruitful. The parable implicitly admonishes us to be "good" soil.

This parable does not teach us how to become good soil. But the parable has become a message to the church of God's promise to nurture God's reign, even in the face of destructive forces. We are charged to listen to that reassurance. When we detect little evidence of transformation in our world or in our own lives, the *promise* of harvest can empower us to remain faithful, even fertile soil. Responding with justice to the word of God's grace in Christ can hold little reward or promise if we expect only an immediate harvest. We rejoice in the good news, both revealed and promised. The dominated and the dominant then join with the Sower to be relentless in sowing unsparingly the grace of redemption, justice, reconciliation; that is soil transformed, yet it still seeks transformation.

7. Donald H. Juel, "Encountering the Sower," *Interpretation* 56 (2002): 273–83.

Third Sunday after the Epiphany

Melinda A. Quivik

JONAH 3:1–5, 10
PSALM 62:5–12
1 CORINTHIANS 7:29–31
MARK 1:14–20

On this Third Sunday after the Epiphany, the preacher is confronted with command, reversal, promise, Jesus' enabling call, and life in the subjunctive mood. These prophets call out a new possiblity, a "what if" sense. Anyone who introduces a whole new way of thinking is bound to a difficult task. The people of Nineveh can hardly be expected to hear Jonah, let alone heed him. And yet they do. Jesus' announcement—that "the realm of God has come near"—can hardly be expected to be understood among a people who are focused on making their livelihoods. Yet they drop their nets and leave their boats and coworkers to follow. Both Jonah and Jesus cry out, "Repent," to people who, in fact, accept the messages of these prophets.

On this Sunday, named according to the "epiphany" through which Jesus' identity was revealed, Jesus can be readily distinguished from Jonah. Despite their common callings as prophets of the God who makes promises (in these texts, both negative and positive!), Jonah announces God's plan; Jesus announces his own. Therein lies the significance of the Epiphany and the way in which the texts of this time *after* the Epiphany draw out Jesus' import. I draw out the social implications of the Third Sunday after the Epiphany at the end of this commentary.

Jonah 3:1–5, 10

The great reversal that occurs for the Ninevites cannot be said to equate with the change that comes upon Simon, Andrew, James, and John. The people of Nineveh are not in the same situation in which the story finds Jesus' would-be followers.

Unlike the fishing shores of the Sea of Galilee, Nineveh is a place of power. Ninevites are not used to hearing that their ways deserve their destruction. In the time of Jonah, Nineveh (in the twenty-first century, the Iraqi city of Mosul) was capital of a superpower, built by King Sennacherib with thick walls, huge buildings, and fountains, among other wonders. In Jonah's story, Nineveh is amply fortified and has no need to listen to the cries of a street prophet come to pronounce judgment. One would suppose a prophet with a good sense of justice would relish announcing condemnation against Nineveh, and yet there is something in God's command to Jonah that sets the prophet on edge. Jonah does not want to go to Nineveh. When he cries out, the people believe God. The promised desolation is reversed with a startling turn: "God changed [God's] mind" (v. 10). We know from the rest of the Jonah story that the Ninevites' repentance infuriates the prophet. In his pouting, Jonah castigates God for doing what Jonah knew God would do: Refrain from giving to the people of Nineveh what they deserved. They did not deserve to be released from calamity.

But in this Sunday's lection, we do not see *that* part of the story, and there is value in disallowing its introduction into the preaching for this day. The epiphany for Jonah is that the word of the Lord in Jonah's mouth was effectual for the purposes for which God intended it. This is not always the case, but Jonah has to see that "God changed God's mind" and therefore that God is vulnerable.

It isn't necessary at this juncture to inquire about that theological change. Scholars might call it process theology or co-creation. We do not need to label it as a theology in order to note the fact that, in Jonah's story, God's relationship with humanity takes a decided turn when human beings hear the word of God and believe it. The prophet is needed in order that the will of God be named. Afterwards, the people are free to attend to their lives, weighing whether the prophet's words are an accurate description of them and whether a change in their ways is appropriate or whether to ignore the matter entirely. Clearly, for the Ninevites, *something* in Jonah's cry has gotten through.

It would be a mistake for contemporary prophets to assume that Jonah's experience of proclaiming impending doom will always render the same response in contemporary society. After all, Jonah made a preposterous statement: In forty days, you'll all be captured by your enemies or you'll be dead (or so we can imagine that is what "overthrown" might mean). Why would anyone believe him? This sounds crazy. We would demand evidence.

Human beings like to think we base our prospects on choices that are rational. We look at national relationships, the economy, our military power, the relative stability of our people, and on the basis of that data either heed the prophetic voice or brush it aside. This is evident in the environmental, economic, and sociopolitical threats in our own time, as it would have been in Jonah's. Some who cry out warnings are taken seriously; others are not. Whatever the reason, the Ninevites reckoned that Jonah's vision of their future was possible, if not accurate, and they chose to take a new direction.

Note that Jonah does not tell the people what will happen if they repent. They simply do it. We do not know—and should not guess—whether their motivation was fear, self-preservation, or a desire for the good. All such causes might play a role, which is perhaps one of the reasons Jonah's story has been preserved. In its openness to ambiguity, it incorporates the range of human interpretations.

Psalm 62:5–12

The congregation has great reason to respond to the reading from Jonah by singing from Psalm 62. At its heart, it reminds us of "God alone" who is rock, salvation, and stronghold. In contrast, we have no weight at all. "Those of low estate are but a breath; those of high estate are a delusion; in the balances they go up; they are together lighter than a breath" (v. 9). When the mighty and the poor are set together to be measured, even a mere breath is heavier. This is a sobering word that places the arrogance of the powerful against the power that judges their (our) lack of compassion. What has weight is what prevails. On this day, the assembly would do well to sing this song together, in order to weigh the fleeting nature of temporal gain against God's eternal strength.

Mark 1:14–20

We see some stark differences between Jonah's story and Jesus calling the disciples. Both speak a word from God, but unlike the prophet, Jesus does not spell out the significance of the realm of God. In Jonah's story, God's power means to destroy; in Jesus' story, God's powerful realm is called "good news." Unlike the Ninevites, the fishers do not turn away from expected destruction, but like the Ninevites, they move into an unknown future. The one promise Jesus makes is not destruction but community: the fishers will catch people who will *follow* him into a new future.

What is the purpose of this growing community of caught people? Ched Myers locates the root of the fishing metaphor (v. 17) in Jeremiah 16:16.[1] There, God sends for those who fish to catch the people of Judah to bring the

---

1. Ched Myers, *Binding the Strong Man: A Political Reading of Mark's Story of Jesus* (Maryknoll, NY: Orbis Press, 1997), 132.

people back to the land God has given them.[2] As in Jonah's story, in Mark it is not merely a warm homecoming that is in store for those who are caught. The people who have turned away from God must be *found* in order to repent and once again become a people that knows God's name. Jesus therefore calls his disciples to a new way of fishing, a new catch, a new purpose. No longer does their work have to do with the food of daily living; they will be about the realm of God that has come near. This new future is one that does not send people into exile but gathers people together. Community becomes more important than individual acquisition. What some consider the inevitable sacrifice of families, neighborhoods, cities—even nations—comes to seem ridiculous. The greater call—Jesus' invitation—is inclusion.

1 Corinthians 7:29–31

Especially in festival time (such as the Sundays after the Epiphany), the Epistle reading carries a strong complementary relationship to the First Testament and Gospel readings. In this case, the relationship is, as with the Ninevites and fishers, a visceral turning to a new life. The Corinthians are told by Paul to live in the subjunctive mood: as if . . . ("those who have wives be as though . . . those who mourn as though . . . those who rejoice as though . . . ," vv. 29–30). In other words, whatever the situation, the people of God should undergo a full reversal of their situations. Why? "For the present form of this world is passing away" (v. 31).

This Third Sunday after the Epiphany urges us to embrace life in the subjunctive as a call from God. The Epistle's command pulls together all of today's texts. The subjunctive mode would mean living *as if* other people mattered and *as if* we ourselves are beloved of God, instead of condemned for self-absorption or the myriad other faults we so easily pour down upon our own heads. Life in the subjunctive means that even if we don't believe we ourselves are loved or that others are deserving of more _____ [fill in the blank with peace, justice, food, security, appreciation, a home, health care, freedom, good government, joy, blessing, community, education, meaningful work, etc.], God is holding out a vision to help us imagine such a world and to shape our lives on the possibilities.

One outcome of such a life is that, instead of coming up with reasons meant to explain why we ought to help the poor get jobs, safe homes, or good medical care, we would be unable to envision a world in which doing so would be merely a matter of choice. Care for our neighbors would be simply a matter

2. Walter Brueggemann, *To Pluck Up, To Tear Down: Jeremiah 1–25*, International Theological Commentary (Grand Rapids: Eerdmans, 1988), 148–49.

of course. Living *as if* makes certain assumptions, chief of which is that God's desire for all humanity, and in fact all of creation, is wholeness and health in all manner of things. In an *as if* world, we would not question whether we ought to create a society in which all children can thrive, whatever their family background or neighborhood.

Under a subjunctive orientation to life, the foundation of political, economic, and social issues is the unquestionable well-being of all people. Pundits and politicians would no longer sway us with the consequences of leaving anyone outside of the benefits that the powerful accrue. Rather, the orientation of all decision makers, all citizens—fueled by people of faith who hear God's call to life *as if*—would be one of making choices that have at their heart a posture of repentance. We all would live embraced by sackcloth on account of the pain of those in our midst who do not have enough—be they mammals without enough land to roam, trees without enough community within which to thrive, or human beings without enough support for livelihood.

The fishers will collect the people in order that the sackcloth can be handed out. But the gathering will include celebration, for the realm comes near. The present unfair form of this world is always passing away, wherever the people hear, see, turn, and follow—and even when they do not, for the coming of the realm is God's doing.

Fourth Sunday after the Epiphany

Kenyatta R. Gilbert

DEUTERONOMY 18:15–20
PSALM 111
1 CORINTHIANS 8:1–13
MARK 1:21–28

While the themes in the readings for today are quite different, they all cohere around dynamics that make for faithful—and unfaithful—community. Deuteronomy assures the community that God will provide them with a prophetic leader in the tradition of Moses. Our encounter with the psalm reminds us to praise God for no reason other than God's own being and self-giving. Paul exhorts the established and mature members of the community to respect newcomers whose faith is still maturing. Mark reminds us that while following Jesus can create opposition even within the community of the church, Jesus' authority ultimately prevails.

Deuteronomy 18:15–20

According to Patrick D. Miller, for many years on the faculty at Princeton Theological Seminary, the book of Deuteronomy is a book of "preached law"—contextually applied law or "torah."[1] Deuteronomy offers instructions for road-weary Hebrews on the edge of the land that God promised the patriarch Abraham and matriarch Sarah. Moses is the giver of the law. His portrait is mosaic. From the reed basket set afloat in the Nile River to an upbringing in palatial quarters in Egypt, Moses increasingly becomes an iconic figure who has great stature in the eyes of God and who is venerated by the people. Moses was a leading aristocrat and partner in Pharaoh's enterprises, but ultimately Moses made a radical break from this secure life.

1. Patrick D. Miller, *Deuteronomy*, Interpretation series (Louisville, KY: John Knox Press, 1990), 12.

82

When the Hebrews, Egypt's principal labor force, were subjected to increased harshness, an awakened Moses remembered his heritage. Unlike many African Americans or members of other racial-ethnic groups today who have a long history of pain and suffering but who have now obtained a significant measure of material success, this prophet did not abandon his kin, but fought against injustices perpetrated against his enslaved kinspeople. Moses killed a person when he saw an Egyptian beating a Hebrew. Moses cried out with stutter and stick, "Let, my people, go!" and initiated the dismantling of Egypt's stronghold on his people. Moses was God's prophetic instrument. Moses critiqued those who protected the interests of the powerful elite and spoke truth to the power of an oppressive and dehumanizing world system.

Despite these things, it is painfully evident in today's text that Moses' leadership has now run its course. God promises new leadership. But what does this mean? The preacher might hear a number of things when approaching this text. The text promises God's loyalty to God's own people in a violent society. Or it might be a useful passage to help congregants reflect on the character of a leader, with Moses being the prophetic exemplar. Such reflection may spur hearers to ask what gives certain individuals the right to address the community in God's name. Further, this passage notes that seeking God's guidance in anticipating a leadership transition is the best succession plan.

This text points to God's commitment to provide continuity of care for Israel. Furthermore, as Moses fades from the picture, God provides the people with some measurements to determine who speaks to them under divine authorization. Unfortunately, God appears short on details regarding this matter. This passage encourages hearers to look beyond the puzzling picture of a daunting present in a strange land, toward a hopeful view of their future based on two unmistakable promises: (1) God will raise up a prophetic successor to Moses, and (2) that prophet will speak in God's name and be held accountable for what is spoken.

The major implication of this Scripture passage is this: God takes full responsibility for the community's provisions. In Deuteronomy God provides laws to be obeyed, privileges to be enjoyed, commandments to be kept, regulations to be followed, and prescriptions for right practice. These are what God sets forth for the good of the people. But what might these promises from Scripture of an all-providing Sovereign mean for the church today, as church membership rapidly drops off in the historic churches, and alarming reports of immoral and unethical conduct of religious leaders abound? This passage encourages the preacher to stand with the congregation to inquire about God's provision for the community.

The prophet's most basic task is to hear and communicate God's instruction.[2] This text is fascinating, because it declares that "the only proper medium for revelation for Israel is the prophet."[3] However, as this passage suggests, the prophet who speaks with God's tongue may not be immediately recognizable to the assembly. One thing seems clear: when promise finds fulfillment, the prophet God raises will be of the Moses tradition.

Psalm 111

This hymn begins exuberantly. The grateful psalmist announces God's praiseworthiness and rehearses God's mighty deeds. Moreover, the psalmist spares no mention of God's virtuous attributes: God is "full of honor and majesty . . . gracious and merciful . . . mindful . . . powerful and giving . . . faithful and just . . . holy and awesome."

The preacher may focus on verse 7, "The works of [God's] hands are faithful and just; all [God's] precepts are trustworthy." The preacher asking how this hymn might speak again to a contemporary community of sufferers first realizes that beneath this hymn is a person's hunger to acknowledge the "givenness of God." Howard Thurman declares that the "givenness of God" as expressed in the hunger of the heart is prayer at its highest. The heart yearns for encounter. However, the irony about this hunger, Thurman continues, is that "the hunger itself is God, calling to God."[4]

What makes us grateful? This psalm brings to mind a kesha (prayer service) in which I participated during a summer ministry internship in Machakos, Kenya. I was profoundly changed by this sacred worship. Heartfelt singing, dancing, praying, and the manifestation of glossolalia (speaking in tongues) incited an emotional frenzy. The experience was majestic. The exuberant spirit of kesha participants helped me to appreciate the renewing and spiritual power of unscripted prayer, testimony, and song.

This worship practice was an offering—gifts returned to a gracious God. Despite the economic impoverishment of my Kenyan brothers and sisters and the craggy worship quarters, the hunger of the people's hearts signified freedom, a demonstration of embodied worship. Liberty in the presence of an almighty God is what the psalmist conveys. What occurred that night in a blighted Kenyan township was, as theologian Geoffrey Wainwright says,

---

2. Gene Tucker, "Prophetic Speech," in *Interpreting the Prophets*, ed. James L. Mays and Paul Achtemeier (Philadelphia: Fortress Press, 1987), 39; Patrick D. Miller, *Israelite Religion and Biblical Theology: Collected Essays* (Sheffield: Sheffield Academic Press, 2000), 430.

3. Cf. Richard D. Nelson, "Deuteronomy," in *Harper's Bible Commentary*, ed. James L. Mays (San Francisco: HarperCollins, 1988), 189–214.

4. Howard Thurman, *Disciplines of the Spirit* (New York: Harper & Row, 1963), 87.

adoration for the transcendent for no other reason than the fact that doxology is made possible because God is self-giving.[5]

What lessons in gratitude might this psalm teach developed nations, who have mostly unearned privileges and access to available goods and services? The miraculous revelation for me was that in the deprived Kenyan setting, one's offering can be an act of indolence when one's petition obstructs the worship acts of prayer and praise to God. At the kesha, the people gave thanks to almighty God for being the one who is "beside none other," as the elder saints used to say in my home church. God is majestic. God provides. God gives a heritage. The psalmist makes no requests but simply speaks out of a deep hunger for God. This psalm promises wisdom and understanding as the fruit of reverence. To pray this hymn is to pray with a thankful heart for God's own sake.

1 Corinthians 8:1–13

The person who loves God discovers a truth: knowledge corrupts if not chastened with humility. This passage stands on the heels of Paul's instructions to the unmarried Corinthians. For the never-before-married and widows, guidelines are established concerning moral conduct (7:25–40). In 1 Corinthians 8, the pragmatic apostle lays down a code of ethics for uniting Christian brothers and sisters around the food table. Paul reminds the elite Christians— the seasoned bureaucrats and church elders who had privileged seating—to scrutinize their dining practices and to reconsider their obligation to be disciplined, wise, and humble before new converts.

The apostle assures these more knowledgeable Christians that they are right in thinking that food offered to idols is not unworthy because of its previous use in pagan rituals. Paul agrees that eating food offered to idols bears no effect on one's relationship with God. However, the apostle perceives that their thinking creates division because some in the community do believe that eating food offered to idols is wrong. The weak in conscience feel defiled.

"No idol in the world really exists," exclaims Paul (v. 4). The way to righteousness is to have consideration for new converts who take offense because veteran Christians participate in eating practices that undermine community. While eating food offered to idols is lawful, it is not always wise to exercise certain liberties in the context of those who have not learned to demystify religious doctrine. Thus, to possess knowledge with a lack of concern for the less knowledgeable infants of the faith is detrimental to Christian unity.

---

5. Geoffrey Wainwright, *Doxology: The Praise of God in Worship, Doctrine and Life; A Systematic Theology* (New York: Oxford University Press, 1980), 37.

Such a message seems appropriate for the pulpit when the church appears overtaken by new members. An example of this phenomenon occurred during the Great Migration of the early twentieth century, when the African American religious landscape was remade as Black southern migrants swarmed into Black urban churches in the industrial North. But instead of the Old Settlers extending Christian hospitality, most northern Black churches were unwelcoming and unwilling to embrace the New Settlers. Such inhospitable behavior instigated the proliferation of storefront churches. The elitists' disregard for their southern siblings is hugely responsible for internal strife among African Americans. The preacher-interpreter must wrestle with this text and find examples of intellectual arrogance and name them sin, because arrogance is always antithetical to the gospel in the culture, because it eschews Christian unity and genuine hospitality.

Mark 1:21–28

"Have you come to destroy us?" This question (v. 24) comes from an unreliable spirit that confronts the protagonist (Jesus) in this passage. Aside from the wilderness temptation (1:12–15), Mark here records the first challenge to Jesus' ministry. An unclean spirit cries from the crowd. I struggle with whether the man with the unclean spirit is speaking in its own right as community member or as one designated to speak on behalf of the community. In either case, the man blatantly opposes Jesus' gospel of the coming of the reign of God.

This text is instructive for believers. It affirms that Jesus has the authority to cast out demons. Brian Blount describes the exorcism as a pocket-moment or inbreaking of divine intervention that achieves victory over demonic forces.[6] It is important for the reader to see that Jesus has such authority, since Jesus soon confers such power upon the disciples (3:14). For Mark, the church is to continue the ministry of exorcism. Jesus is present in the church to exorcise our demons and empowers the church to engage in the ministry of exorcism.

Dawn Ottoni-Wilhelm argues that to consider Jesus' rebuke of the unclean spirit is to notice how the speaking of Jesus reveals who Jesus is. According to Ottoni-Wilhelm, the significance of Jesus' self-revelatory speaking makes evident his decisive authority over demonic forces; it is a clear demarcation between what is demonic and what is holy. Here the people respond to Jesus'

---

6. Brian K. Blount, *Go Preach! Mark's Kingdom Message and the Black Church Today* (Maryknoll, NY: Orbis Press, 1998), 88.

teaching with amazement, though it is unclear that this amazement provides stimulus for faith.[7]

This text provides fodder for discussing how to understand demon possession today, as well as how possession might relate to spiritual warfare, mental illness, and New Age spirituality. Does the preacher see in these phenomena forces analogous to the demons in the text? In discussing such topics, the preacher should guard against promoting a negative view of Judaism and thereby encouraging a form of Christian triumphalism. That would, perhaps inadvertently, only reinforce the anti-Jewish demon that has long occupied many in the Christian house.

7. Dawn Ottoni-Wilhelm, *Preaching the Gospel of Mark: Proclaiming the Power of God* (Louisville, KY: Westminster John Knox Press, 2008), 24–25.

Fifth Sunday after the Epiphany

Chandra Taylor Smith

ISAIAH 40:21–31
PSALM 147:1–11, 20C
1 CORINTHIANS 9:16–23
MARK 1:29–39

A powerful message emerges from the passages today that speaks boldly both to those who fight for God's social vision and to those who experience earthly social injustices. Those who are hopeless because of social injustice require a deep and courageous faith. Those who seek to achieve God's righteous and equitable social ends for every human, animal, and plant in the universe need an obedient and selfless faith. Isaiah 40:21–31 reminds victims of social injustices and fighters for social justice alike that only God supplies the patience and strength to endure suffering, and only God is capable of the life-giving ability to transform unjust situations. God's loving and gracious actions in Psalm 147:1–11 illuminate the unparalleled and praiseworthy benefits of God's social vision for both humankind and nature. Paul's willing self-denial to preach the gospel in 1 Corinthians 9:16–23 exemplifies a God-centered (not self-centered) model for intentions and actions essential for achieving God's social vision. Mark 1:29–39 narrates Jesus' selfless acts of healing and then his vital act of self-care that sustains his desire and ability to rectify the social conditions of those who seek him and believe in him.

Isaiah 40:21–31

African Americans have faithfully turned to Isaiah 40 because of its awesome vision of liberation and hope in the face of oppression and hopelessness. In African American church services across North America, gospel choirs regularly sing a moving rendition of a song titled "They That Wait on the Lord." The melodic blending of alto, soprano, tenor, and bass voices intones the graphic lyrics of Isaiah 40:29–31, instructing anguishing congregants that

88

"those who wait on the Lord shall renew their strength, they shall mount up with wings like an eagle, they shall run and not be weary, they shall walk and not faint." Thus, like Israel during Isaiah's time, African Americans welcome and embrace God's liberating social vision of freedom, vigor, and endurance symbolized by the soaring eagle.

Visualizing the imposing wingspan of this regal bird of prey, hovering unfettered and confident above the earth, inspires the awe-inspired down-trodden to look up toward the heavens. This view incites invigorating images of being swooped up in the powerful and protective clutches of the eagle or gliding along the air streams, straddling the expanse of its sturdy wings. These are assuring visions that symbolize God's lifting up and steadying the broken and weak, and empowering them to take flight and soar by themselves. Every Sunday morning, as prayerful faces tilt toward the rafters, warmed by stream-ing light through stained-glass windows, the congregation is comforted, forti-fied, and motivated by God's deliverance portrayed in the lilting rhythm of Isaiah 40:31. Central to Isaiah's message is the placing of one's faith in God's deliverance and grace alone.

Isaiah contrasts aerial and earthly imagery in verses 22–26 to remind and refocus Israel to look to the only source of irrefutable power to liberate and transform. Uncertainty, from being vulnerable and disillusioned, conspires to make the powerless believe that those who impose oppression and injustice have absolute power over them. To repudiate any pretense that anyone other than God has all authority and power, Isaiah depicts the fragility and diminu-tive weight of humanity as grasshoppers. Grasshoppers can easily be stepped on (v. 22). God makes powerless those who would have royal influence and are abusive and corruptive in their authority (v. 23). Moreover, humanity's persistent attempts to claim lasting authority are groundless and unsustain-able (v. 24). The prophet cautions that even the young falter when they put their total faith in their agility and youthfulness, which are fleeting and can-not supersede God's power (v. 30). This Scripture reminds us that human authority is fundamentally powerless before God, and there are no grounds for putting one's faith in human sources of authority.

In stark contrast to this depiction of humanity, Isaiah paints lofty, hover-ing images of God sitting "above the circle of the earth" (v. 22a), stretching out "the heavens like a curtain" and spreading "them like a tent to live in" (v. 22b). Isaiah depicts God not as passive but as dynamically active in cre-ation. Isaiah directs Israel to "lift up your eyes on high and see: Who created" the stars? (v. 26a). Because of God's unmatched strength and power, God created, numbered, and named all the stars (v. 26). "The LORD is the everlast-ing God, the Creator of the ends of the earth" (v. 28), reiterates Isaiah. God asks, "To whom then will you compare me, or who is my equal?" (v. 25).

Isaiah's fundamental message is that absolutely nothing can be compared to or is equal to God the creator. This fact, Isaiah indicates, has been known "from the beginning" and has been "understood from the foundations of the earth" (v. 21). Both victims of social injustices and fighters for social justice fall short of God's possibilities when they do not put their faith in God's life-giving intentions to transform human injustices.

Psalm 147:1–11, 20c

In exaltation of God's ultimate power of the kind portrayed in Isaiah, the psalmist implores Israel to sing a hymn of praise that elucidates God's gracious and righteous practices for transforming oppressed people and community (v. 1). Renovating the city (v. 2), bringing back together the inhabitants, especially those who have been marginalized and driven out (v. 2), and healing their spirits and physical bodies (v. 3) are all dynamic actions of God's loving justice and grace. In the same venerating illustration used by Isaiah (40:26b) to demonstrate God's unmatched strength and power, the psalmist also emphasizes that God "determines the number of the stars" and "gives to all of them their names" (v. 4). Moreover, the psalm highlights God's power to lift up the powerless and to hold responsible those who oppress (v. 6).

The gratitude that the psalmist implores Israel to sing about (v. 7) expands beyond God's social vision for humankind. The entire planet must benefit and flourish. God's loving justice and grace are embodied in the clouds that provide rain for the earth and make the grass grow (v. 8). God provides for animals, even the baby birds (v. 9). Human beings fall short of God's righteous possibilities when they venerate physical force and speed as ultimate power (v. 10). God is pleased only by those who are in awe of the ultimate power of God's love, grace, and mercy to heal and transform the world (v. 11). In the praiseworthy manifestation of God's awesome transformative power, all people and creatures on the planet flourish in an equitable, healthy, and harmonious balance.

1 Corinthians 9:16–23

Paul's message in 1 Corinthians 9:16–23 calls the reader to have the right intentions to achieve God's just social vision. Paul's actions model a righteous approach to preaching the gospel and the resulting unfolding of justice that is generated and sustained only by God. First, Paul explains that he is driven to proclaim the gospel by an obligation to God (v. 16). Even though the customs of his time allow him to receive payment for his preaching services, Paul chooses to proclaim the gospel without recompense (v. 17). Without the obligation associated with monetary compensation, Paul is free to challenge social injustices and is not fettered to special interests that may be abusive and exploitative of the powerless and oppressed (v. 18).

Furthermore, Paul's freedom compels him to be reliant solely upon his faith, which sustains him in his practice of self-denial of personal liberties for the sake of helping others to accept and be blessed by the gospel (v. 19). In other words, Paul does not spread the gospel for his own sake. His preaching is not about him or a personal need for recognition from those he seeks to liberate. Paul sheds his external identity and social privileges to assure that the focus of his practice is on those to whom he proclaims the gospel.

Discarding social, economic, and even gender and ethnic/racial advantages afforded to one at the expense of social injustices is not easy. It is especially challenging for churches today with wealthy, predominately white con-gregants, who must go well beyond the altruistic outreach of their social-justice committees to achieve the selflessness realized by Paul. It requires a deeper and deliberate acceptance of material discomfort in order to experi-ence the full, transformative power of God's spiritual comfort. Only then is one fully equipped to fight for social justice.

In his selfless and gospel-centered approach, Paul concentrates on what separates people from God. The practical outcome of the social vision in the gospel is the reconciliation of humans with God. Paul is willing to accept dis-approval so that people may recognize through him the embodiment of God's vision under Christ (v. 21). Thus, he does not approach the weak or oppressed from a place of privilege and judgment, but he meets all people where they are in life, to identify with their alienation from God and then reunite them to God by proclaiming the gospel through his life (v. 22).

Many individuals and churches that work toward social justice today fall short of Paul's attitude and approach the poor with a "charity mentality," presuming that their privileged identity is the measure of God's social-justice outcomes. This sanctimonious expectation of God's social vision belies the reality that those who may be white, male, and rich can be as alienated from God as those who are poor, female, and black. God's social-justice vision tran-scends the limits of the human condition and does not replicate the perceived benefits of the present world. Those who are reconciled through the gospel and those who strip themselves of their privileges in order to proclaim the gospel are transformed by a greater impartial social good that God manifests for everyone (v. 23).

Mark 1:29–39

In this first chapter of his Gospel, Mark captures a dramatic series of events that illuminates the way Jesus begins to seed his vision of social justice among those whose daily lives were continuous experiences of oppression. Jesus starts with the individual and is drawn to those who are compromised by diseases and demons (v. 34). In the just and loving society that Jesus desires to achieve through his life, all people are healthy, strong, liberated, and whole in their mind, body, and spirit. Jesus is uncompromising in his impartiality and does not discriminate by gender, age, social or economic status, or creed when he touches those who seek to be healed. When Jesus touches and transforms one individual, others are inspired to be touched and healed by him. Thus Mark tells how the whole city gathers around the door to be healed (v. 33).

The hallmark of Jesus' approach to social justice is to love and care for everyone, which includes taking care of himself. After healing so many people, Jesus deliberately takes time to steal away and pray (v. 35). This speaks directly to the need for those in social justice ministries to sustain a devotional practice that nurtures their mind, body, and spirit. People active in social ministries sometimes both literally and figuratively bleed on behalf of those they seek to help. Healers must embody the health they seek to help others achieve. In Jesus' self-loving practice, he is cleansed and strengthened by God to continue to face the challenges of ministry. A persistent devotional practice is vital for all who seek to carry on Jesus' work today.

Asian American Heritage Day (February 19)

Fumitaka Matsuoka

PROVERBS 3:5–18
PSALM 18
REVELATION 5:1–10
JOHN 16:16–24

This Day of Remembrance is honored on a Sunday near February 19, the day in 1942 on which Japanese American citizens were locked into U.S. concentration camps for the duration of World War II. Asian American Heritage Day celebrates the distinctive qualities of Asian cultures and provides a venue for non-Asians to become more acquainted with those cultures. The preacher can lift up the contributions that people of Asia have made to North America and the world at large and can call the congregation to repent of the injustices inflicted upon people of Asian origin in the United States (e.g., exploitation during the building of the first transcontinental railway, Japanese internment following the Pearl Harbor attack). Preachers may also celebrate Asian Pacific American Heritage Month in May, which was recognized by a congressional and presidential act in 1979.

Plate in hand,
I stand in line,
Losing my resolve,
To hide my tears.
I see my mother
In the aged woman who comes.
And I yield to her
My place in line.
Four months have passed.
And at last I learn

To call this horse stall
my family's home.
                    Yukari[1]

The readings for today open windows of interpretation that help the church
enlarge its understanding of people of Asian origin in North America.
Through Proverbs, we see the importance of wisdom in both the Asian American and larger communities. Psalm 18 implies that being faithful in difficulty
can mean being honest about uncertainty, questions, and doubts. John 16
provides a venue to think about the church as an alternative culture, even
within the Asian community. Revelation 5:1–10 helps us see that while the
Asian American community may sometimes appear to be powerless according
to conventional standards, that community can be powerful.

Proverbs 3:5–18

In Proverbs, wisdom is the most valuable possession (3:13–18). Having wisdom
does not mean merely having information. Rather, wisdom both originates
from God and involves "an active love of God seeking a deeper knowledge of
God," as Anselm of Canterbury (1033–1109) said.[2] In other words, wisdom
is "faith seeking understanding." Christians seek a deeper knowledge of God
because we are first loved by God in Jesus Christ who reveals God's wisdom.
Wisdom can both derive from revelation and be a source of revelation, which,
according to H. Richard Niebuhr, is "that special occasion which provides us
with an image by means of which all the occasions of personal and communal
life become intelligible." Revelation "illuminates other events and enables us
to understand them."[3] Asian Americans draw on wisdom, and honoring their
experience can help people of other cultures live wisely.

   Wisdom was embodied in Japanese American pastors in the concentration
(internment) camps during World War II. During the internment of Japanese
Americans, Christian pastors, Buddhist priests, and other religious leaders—
often young and inexperienced—provided wisdom (including a sense of comfort, stability, and hope) to those in the camps. One couple who married in
the Poston concentration camp in the wilderness of Arizona recall a prominent Baptist pastor who officiated at their wedding. It was the pastor's first

---

   1. Yukari is the pen name of the mother of Yoshiko Uchida, author of *Desert Exile, The Uprooting of a Japanese American Family* (Seattle: University of Washington Press, 1984). This poem is
quoted on p. 83.
   2. See Thomas Williams, "Anselm of Canterbury," in *Stanford Encyclopedia of Philosophy*, ed.
Edward N. Zalta; http://plato.stanford.edu/entries/anselm/ (accessed February 28, 2010).
   3. H. Richard Niebuhr, *The Meaning of Revelation*, 3rd ed. (New York: Macmillan Publishers,
1964), 80.

experience of conducting a wedding. His hands shook during the ceremony, but by helping the community see that God was present and active in the lives of the young couple even in the stark, cold, and inhumane environment of the concentration camp, the minister brought joy to the couple, their family, and friends.

The love of God was incarnate in the ministry of such pastors and thereby became an impetus for the deepening of faith of those who received the love of God in the camps. The ministers practiced faith seeking understanding by helping those in the camps seek a deeper knowledge of God in their situation. By acting in wisdom, the ministers were thus agents of justice for those in the camps. Those ministers are still models for Christians in situations of difficulty.

Psalm 18

This text is a royal psalm of thanksgiving attributed to David. The community had been in a time of distress, and God had delivered them. When the Israelites were actually experiencing their difficulties, the only thing the community could do was cry to God (v. 6a). We do not know whether David had a solid trust in God's power to deliver the Israelites from their sufferings. What we do know is that David turned to God in the midst of trouble. David's thanksgiving took place after the fact, not amid the trouble. Therefore, we notice that David's faithfulness included his willingness to turn to God even in the midst of uncertainty about the outcome of the distress.

In the midst of the uncertainty faced by Japanese Americans in concentration camps during World War II, there were signs of faithfulness among many people. Included in the faithfulness expressed by Christians was questioning God's relationship to suffering. "No one was accused of any crime, and yet no one was able to call upon the protection guaranteed us by our country's constitution."[4]

Many people find it spiritually comforting to say that God has a plan to save the righteous. But the reality is that life is full of many unanswerable questions. Why did Japanese American citizens suffer the humiliation of being placed in a concentration camp in a desert when the United States guaranteed certain "unalienable" rights to its citizens, such as "life, liberty, and the pursuit of happiness"? If God had a plan, why wouldn't God tell the innocent people what the plan was? Believing that God has a plan for such circumstances is too easy.

---

4. Florence Date Smith, "Days of Infamy," *Messenger* (November 1988), 11.

In such circumstances, we need to know that a part of being faithful is questioning God. One of the hardest things about the concentration camp for Japanese Americans was the spiritual crisis created by internment. Among the questions that came to the internees were these: Do you believe in anything now? Do you care about anything? Where does meaning come from? Is love stronger than death? Is there any resurrection? One question was especially important to those who had young adult children in the U.S. Army who were killed in Europe. Will the person I love—who was plucked out of the camp, sent to the European theatre of war, killed for saving fellow American solders—will that person be saved? How can I bear what that person has suffered? Was God with him? Was God not with him?

David must have asked similar questions when the Israelites faced their crisis. Even in the midst of uncertainty and doubt David surely prayed to God, "Hear, O Israel, the LORD our God, the LORD is one" (Deut. 6:4). Since God is one, everything is connected. Japanese Americans said something like, "I don't know what is going on here, but this I know: I am connected with my community and I am connected with God."

The psalm as interpreted in connection with the Japanese American experience in World War II is thus a powerful model for all who experience injustice. The psalm authorizes those who suffer injustice to question God in the midst of their agony. Furthermore, as a survival strategy, those who suffer injustice can remember that they are connected with one another and to God. By joining into communities of solidarity, like the Japanese Americans in the camps, they can develop strength to survive.

John 16:16–24

The Gospel of John offers a vision of a radically alternative world. This out-of-the-box message is that of hope against hope. In the text for today, the image of a woman in labor and the new life she brings into the world (v. 21) point to the significance of Jesus' death and resurrection. The anguish of the disciples will turn to gladness, because Jesus who left them in death will meet them in resurrection life. The world causes the disciples to suffer, but Jesus is with them and will eventually bring them joy. The disciples are to hope, even when they cannot see immediate reason for hope.

Martin Luther King Jr. rearticulated this message of hope against hope at the height of the civil rights struggle in 1967. "To be a Negro in America is to hope against hope," he explained.

> Darkness cannot drive out darkness; only light can do that. Hate cannot drive out hate; only love can do that. Hate multiplies hate,

violence multiplies violence, and toughness multiplies toughness in a descending spiral of destruction. . . . The chain reaction of evil—hate begetting hate, wars producing more wars—must be broken, or we shall be plunged into the dark abyss of annihilation.[5]

Civil rights struggles continue in our era, especially the struggle for the rights of lesbian, gay, bisexual, transgendered, questioning, and asexual people. Asian American lesbians and gays and their parents and allies have been largely invisible in Christian churches. Some Asian American churches avoid the issue for fear of conflict. Other Asian American church leaders have condemned homosexuality and publicly protested against same-sex marriage. The LGBTQA community must thus hope against hope.

There are many gay and lesbian Asian American Christians and their families, quiet and invisible, in churches across the country. An honest and thought-provoking film invites us to hear personal stories that have long been unheard. *In God's House: Asian American Lesbian and Gay Families in the Church* tells the story of Oneida Chi, a young adult Chinese American, who speaks of her struggle with the discovery of her own sexual orientation and her search for self-acceptance and for acceptance in the religious community. Harold and Ellen Kameya, the parents of another lesbian, tell the story of their shock and confusion when their beloved daughter first came out, of the isolation and alienation they felt in their congregation, and of the importance of a church community in their Christian journey to grow in understanding, courage, and love.

A gay Episcopal priest, Rev. Leng, who married his husband Hung Ngugen in San Francisco, says: "We'll move forward in fits and starts. There's the way of compassionate learning, where we have our hearts open to those we don't agree with. That's the way of Jesus and Confucius, who said, in their different ways: Do (not do) to others, what you would (not) have others do to you. I never intended to get married, because I thought it wasn't possible. I had so accommodated myself to being second-class, just like so many immigrants in their own ways. But when I did [get married], the most amazing words to our ears, was to hear from the Officer of the Peace, an ex-Roman Catholic priest, gay, of course, say to us: 'The State of California and the People of California proclaim you spouses for life.' I felt like a full citizen. That was wonderful."[6] Rev. Leng lived with hope against hope.

5. Martin Luther King Jr., *Strength to Love* (New York: Pocket Books, 1963), 51.
6. Leng Lim, quoted in Kwok Pui-lan, "Gay Activism in Asian and Asian American Churches," *Witness Magazine*, May 19, 2004; www.thewitness.org/article.php?id=12 (accessed February 28, 2010).

Revelation 5:1–10

In this passage, the author of the book of Revelation (John) expects to see a
Lion, but sees a Lamb instead. The Lamb is presented in a way sympathetic
and powerful; the Lamb is living but still has the marks of previous death
upon it. In the place of the conventional symbol of power (the Lion), the
representative of the realm of God is a Lamb, evoking humility, gentleness,
powerlessness, and sacrificial love.

Former president of the Czech Republic Vaclav Havel said in his essay
"The Power of the Powerless" that "an examination of the potential of the
'powerless,' can only begin with an examination of the nature of power in the
circumstances in which these powerless people operate."[7] Christ's death on
the cross, the symbol of the power of the powerless, is the ultimate referential
point of Christian faith. This is the message of Revelation 5:1–10.

The power of the powerless reminds Asian Americans of the story of the
442nd Infantry of the U.S. Army during World War II. This unit was composed of mostly Japanese Americans who fought in Europe. Remarkably, the
families of many of the soldiers in this unit were interned. Fighting in Italy,
southern France, and Germany, this group became the most highly deco-
rated regiment in the history of the United States armed forces, including
twenty-one Medal of Honor recipients. Battle reports show the casualty rate,
combining KIA (killed) with MIA (missing) and WIA (wounded and removed
from action), was 93 percent, uncommonly high.

However, the unit's exemplary service and many decorations did not
change the attitudes of the general U.S. population to people of Japanese
descent after World War II. Veterans of the 442nd were received home by
signs that read "No Japs Allowed" and "No Japs Wanted." Many veterans
were denied service in shops and restaurants, and had their homes and property vandalized. Anti-Japanese sentiment remained strong into the 1960s, and
only gradually faded (and has not faded yet in certain circles).

The Lamb in the book of Revelation has been slain. However, God has
brought it back to life. In Revelation 6, God condemns the Roman Empire and
others who reject God's values and visions for human community. On the one
hand, the story of the 442nd is an inspiration to people who are like the Lamb:
powerless and suffering injustice. God is with them, even as God was with the
Lamb. On the other hand, the story of the 442nd after its return to the United
States is a warning. A culture that does not accept and honor all its members is
under the judgment of God as surely as the world in Revelation 6.

7. Vaclav Havel, "The Power of the Powerless"; excerpts from the original electronic text
provided by Bob Moeller, University of California, Irvine (1978); http://history.hanover.edu/
courses/excerpts/165havel.html (accessed on March 3, 2010).

Sixth Sunday after the Epiphany

Charles L. Campbell

2 KINGS 5:1–14
PSALM 30
1 CORINTHIANS 9:24–27
MARK 1:40–45

Radical Christian and theologian William Stringfellow argues that the healings in the Bible should be construed as involving not just individual, physical healings, but also political resistance to the powers of death:

> Healing, seemingly, is a most intimate event, distinct and distant from politics. Yet the healing episodes reported in the New Testament are very much implicated in politics. . . .
> In raising Lazarus, . . . Jesus reveals what is implicit, but hidden, in all of the healing episodes, that is, his authority over death, his conclusive power over death, his triumph over death and all that death can do and all that death means. To so surpass death is utterly threatening politically; it shakes and shatters the very foundation of political reality because death is, as has been said, the only moral and practical sanction of the State.[1]

Psalm 30

This psalm confirms Stringfellow's point. In the psalm physical illness is connected with the powers of death. The ill person proclaims that his or her soul has actually been in Sheol, the place of death (vv. 3, 9). Moreover, the healing involves restoration to life, as the person is actually brought back from "those [who have] gone down to the Pit" (v. 3). Finally, the celebration following the healing is phrased in terms of a return from death: "You have turned my mourning into dancing" (v. 11). Here death is not simply the cessation of

---

1. William Stringfellow, *An Ethic for Christians and Other Aliens in a Strange Land* (Waco, TX: Word Books, 1973; repr., Eugene, OR: Wipf & Stock, 2004), 148–49.

99

physical life, but is actively present in illness, encroaching upon the one who longs for healing. Consequently, Stringfellow notes, the healings in Scripture play a much more significant role than simply being "medical" events. They are victories over the powers of death at work in the world.[2]

Moreover, as the texts for this Sunday make clear, healings do not only deal with the encroachment of death upon individuals but are also a challenge to social forces of death. Healings have a social as well as a personal dimension. Preaching on healing should never become narrowly medical or individualistic, but should also explore the social forces that create illness and death, and the challenge the gospel presents to them.

Mark 1:40–45

The cleansing of the leper in Mark 1:40–45 assumes the social dimensions of death that Jesus engages in his healings. The leper is not simply physically ill. He is socially dead. As a leper, he is religiously unclean; he must live outside the community, and he cannot have physical contact with anyone, because that would make them unclean. Indeed, he must shout, "Unclean! Unclean!" wherever he goes, so that people can avoid interaction. He is "untouchable," an outsider, a shamed person. He is a victim of both the physical ailment and the social and religious system based upon distinctions of clean and unclean, insider and outsider, honored and shamed—and he is on the losing end of all the dichotomies. As such, he is dead. In a time prior to individualism, a time when community and life are inseparable, the leper is isolated. Like the speaker in Psalm 30, he is for all practical purposes in "Sheol." In his body, he carries the burden not only of his illness but of an oppressive social order.

When Jesus touches the leper, he interrupts the entire social and religious order. In healing the leper, Jesus not only restores him to physical health, but he restores this unclean, shamed outsider to community and social standing. When Jesus touches the leper, he challenges a system of exclusion that created a living death for countless people, not just lepers, by isolating them from community. In fact, in touching the leper, Jesus figuratively reaches down into the depths of Sheol and the Pit, the deepest places of death, to which both society and the church condemn the "other" through categories and systems of exclusion.

In touching the leper, Jesus shatters all our artificial categories of clean and unclean, insider and outsider. He grants citizenship to the illegal alien. He

---

2. Editor's note: In dialogue with Stringfellow and others, Charles L. Campbell offers a bold approach to preaching about and to the powers in *The Word before the Powers: An Ethic of Preaching* (Louisville, KY: Westminster John Knox Press, 2002).

welcomes gay, lesbian, bisexual, and transgender persons into the fellowship of the church, including the ordained ministry. He steps across all the barriers dividing race and class, and he reconfigures the exclusive, deathly social order as one of hospitality, community, and life.

Moreover, this healing does not simply benefit those who are considered "unclean" or "outsiders"; it offers life to those who are viewed as "clean" or "insiders" by dismantling their privilege. The entire social order, Jesus reveals, participates in death. Those who cast out the leper also suffer from death—the death of conscience that prevents their full participation in community. As Mary Elizabeth Hobgood says in relation to racism, the deadly ways of such exclusivism "infect" even the privileged, by destroying the essential relationships necessary for community and life:

> Because white status depends on denying the deepest parts of the relational self, our humanity is impoverished, and our capacity to be moral—in right relationship with others—is diminished. White supremacy produces trauma, pain, fear, ignorance, mistrust, and unshared vulnerability, and for this reason, white moral character is warped and undermined. Our integrity is necessarily damaged in environments that systematically promote discrimination, harassment, exploitation, and misery. Our integrity is damaged when, as participants in white culture, we are divorced from our deepest longings and capacities for creativity, and when we do not know how to intervene.[3]

Those privileged by being "clean" suffer the same death as those who benefit from and reinforce white status and privilege. Jesus offers new life to them as well as to the leper. Jesus' healing is socially radical indeed!

Like all those who seek to change the social order, Jesus pays the price. Despite Jesus' warning to tell no one, the person who has been healed shares the good news—no longer shouting "Unclean," but, rather, "spreading the word" (v. 45). The leper becomes the preacher. Consequently, "Jesus could no longer go into a town openly, but stayed out in the country; and people came to him from every quarter" (v. 45). Jesus himself, having touched the leper, himself becomes figuratively "unclean"—no longer able openly to enter the city. Jesus takes upon himself the identity of the "other": Jesus embodies solidarity with all who are the victims of deathly systems and institutions that exclude. Indeed, Jesus' action foreshadows his death on the cross—outside the city in the "unclean" space. In his crucifixion, this story suggests, Jesus does not simply forgive individual sins, but publicly and graphically exposes the

3. Mary Elizabeth Hobgood, *Dismantling Privilege: An Ethics of Accountability* (Cleveland: Pilgrim Press, 2000), 58.

"powers that be," whose exclusive ways are death. In this sense, Mark 1:40–45 is the gospel in miniature, with all of its unsettling social implications.

2 Kings 5:1–14

The healing of Naaman likewise crosses boundaries—the boundaries of ethnic and religious separation. Elisha reaches across the boundaries that divide Israel and the Gentiles to heal the very general who led the army of Israel's enemy. Moreover, in one of the most extraordinary moments in the story, a young servant girl, a social nobody who had been taken captive from the land of Israel and served Naaman's wife, is the first to witness to the mighty, boundary-crossing God of Israel (vv. 2–4). The powerful soldier, Naaman, hears and believes the servant girl from Israel, goes to the monarch of Israel, and requests healing at the hands of the prophet Elisha. And Elisha heals him. It is a remarkable story in which various characters—the servant girl, Naaman, and Elisha—look beyond the social, ethnic, and religious boundaries that divide them and work together to enable the healing.

In his "Nazareth Manifesto," Jesus takes up this radical hermeneutical trajectory for preaching from this story. He draws on the story of Naaman to subvert all notions of religious or ethnic superiority that hold people captive and cause them to denigrate and oppress "outsiders" (Luke 4:27). In telling Naaman's story (along with the story about the widow at Zarephath) Jesus invites the congregation at Nazareth to see the mercy of God at work in the "other"—even the enemy. He undercuts one of the main sources of domination and violence in the world—ethnic and religious superiority—which continues to wreak its havoc through contemporary movements for ethnic cleansing and acts of religious violence, from Iraq to Palestine to Rwanda and Sudan. As with Jesus' healing of the leper in Mark 1:40–45, the healing of Naaman is not simply about the healing of a single individual, but about the challenge to the powers of death.

1 Corinthians 9:24–27

In many ways, Paul is a version of Elisha, crossing religious boundaries to bring good news to Gentiles and to welcome them into the people of God. It is difficult to imagine the radical change in Paul from one who violently persecuted the followers of Christ to one whose mission was to preach the gospel to both Jews and Gentiles. Paul had been freed from the powers of death that hold people captive in their sense of social, ethnic, and religious superiority. It is difficult to imagine a more radical witness to Paul's boundary-crossing Jesus than his baptismal confession in Galatians: In Christ, "there is no longer

Jew or Greek, there is no longer slave or free, there is no longer male and female" (Gal. 3:28).

This boundary-crossing, gospel race is the one Paul runs in 1 Corinthians 9:24–27. The character of this race is made clear in the preceding verses, in which Paul relates the various ways his life and witness have crossed multiple boundaries for the sake of the gospel. Indeed, the character of the gospel compels and creates this kind of boundary-crossing witness and community.

> For though I am free with respect to all, I have made myself a slave to all, so that I might win more of them. To the Jews I became as a Jew, in order to win Jews. To those under the law I became as one under the law (though I myself am not under the law) so that I might win those under the law. To those outside the law I became as one outside the law (though I am not free from God's law but am under Christ's law). . . . To the weak I became weak, so that I might win the weak. I have become all things to all people, that I might by all means save some. I do it all for the sake of the gospel, so that I may share in its blessings. (1 Cor. 9:19–23)

At one level, Paul might sound like a chamelion who will gladly change colors, depending on whom he is addressing. However, at a deeper level, Paul simply lives out a gospel that does not stand on religious or ethnic superiority, but crosses those boundaries to serve the "other," just as Jesus touched the leper and Elisha healed the enemy. As Richard Hays notes, "Paul represents himself as a conciliator, seeking to overcome cultural and ethnic divisions in order to bring people of all sorts into the one community of faith."[4] Indeed, Paul suggests, only by serving Christ in this way can he himself share in the gospel's blessings (v. 23). The race he runs, the discipline he endures, is all for the purpose of "proclaiming to others," so that, along with them, he too might enjoy the prize. For the imperishable wreath of "victory" belongs to the one whose freedom in Christ paradoxically empowers service to the "other." Paul runs that race and calls the church to run it too.[5]

4. Richard B. Hays, *First Corinthans*, Interpretation series (Louisville, KY: John Knox Press, 1997), 153.

5. Editor's note: For examples of people who have been profoundly affected by boundary crossing, see the stories of seminary students and others who have worked with the homeless in Atlanta and engaged in street preaching and in public acts of resistance, in Stanley P. Saunders and Charles L. Campbell, *The Word on the Street: Performing the Scriptures in the Urban Context* (Eugene, OR: Wipf & Stock, 2000).

Seventh Sunday after the Epiphany

Stephen G. Ray Jr.

ISAIAH 43:18–25
PSALM 41
2 CORINTHIANS 1:18–22
MARK 2:1–12

Today's texts weave together the simple ideas that God holds in special favor both the weak and those who have regard for the weak and that this preference for weakness expresses something of God's wisdom and power. This common theme, which runs throughout Scripture—that God, Godself, has a special and unequivocal regard for the weak, the outsider, those who are on the margins—is given a multidimensional interpretation in today's texts. These dimensions show how God through Christ says "Yes" to those to whom the world so often says "No." God's inclination and that of the followers of God are thus explicitly rendered as being contrary to the reigning common sense of the world. Divine power is revealed unambiguously in and on behalf of seeming weakness.

Isaiah 43:18–25

This portion of the book of Isaiah is generally attributed to that part of the text that the two-text theory labels as Second Isaiah, and that the three-author text theory attributes to the second author of the book of Isaiah. All commentators, however, agree that the text is a part of the corpus that ostensibly deals with the prophecy of deliverance for the people of Israel in the midst of their Babylonian captivity. Read canonically—as the text of Scripture, and not primarily a historical document—this text highlights God's renewing faithfulness toward God's people, even when they are suffering the punishment for their own unfaithfulness (exile and captivity). More precisely, the text speaks of God's wish that people not re-member themselves to this past unfaithfulness but, rather, look to the new future that God is preparing for them, when

104

they will declare God's praise and be witness to this bountiful forgiveness and renewing work of God.

Poignantly, the writer describes this living into the vocation of witnesses to God's renewal and forgiveness as seeing clearly the natural order of things. When read in the midst of captivity, these words do more than provide a promise of redemption; they remind the community that the world of captivity is *not* the natural order of things or God's desire for God's people. The witness of many who have lived in the midst of generational oppression and suffered genocidal assault is that the most pernicious dimension of their plight was the reigning cultural common sense that their condition *was* the natural order of things—or worse, the will of God. In contexts such as these, the words of Isaiah carry new meaning: God's restoration of the natural order of things will mean their liberation to express their full humanity as human beings and children of God—not a continuation of their suffering.

Given the way the prophets in general, and Isaiah in particular, interpreted both Israel's setbacks and Israel's victories as coming immediately from the hand of God, this text reiterates the sense that any future they might have would come from honoring God. More importantly, this honoring of God would not only lead to a future, but would also simultaneously expose the false claims of their captors that their captivity was the natural order of things. In place of this false ideological claim, the wisdom that turns them toward God allows the people to see in that turning the new thing that God has for them, their redemption.

Psalm 41

While canonically the book of Psalms presents something of a journey of revelation by David, many of the psalms seek simply to provide wisdom and insight into ways of living that invite God's favor. Psalm 41 is one such example. The psalm begins by linking God's power and deliverance to the inclination toward the weak. What is being proffered is a more general admonition continually to have regard for the weak. What follows is an account of the specific ways in which God protects and delivers the faithful person who interprets this divine activity as a response to the prior benevolence of the one now in peril. This deliverance is grounded in the conviction that God's inclination, made evident throughout Scripture, makes itself materially known in God's protection and oversight of the weak. Given God's history with Israel, this inclination is understood by the people as a part of God's very nature.

This inclination on the part of God toward the weak and those who would be their allies is far from the logic of human history. This is made clear as the psalmist assures that God has already protected him from the ways of defamation, conspiracy, and betrayal. This protection came as God's good pleasure in response to the psalmist's regard for the poor. There is no language of righteousness or simple personal piety. Rather, there is a reflection on the rewards of dealing in the world in the same way that God deals with creation, namely, demonstrating power through the visible display of mercy. This is another dimension of God's power displayed in ways other than the logic of the world.

2 Corinthians 1:18–22

A significant dimension of Paul's understanding of God's power and preference seen in the world is that it expresses God's love and acceptance of those who are weak that is neither ambiguous nor tentative. Paul gives poignant expression to this understanding in his regret at the need for this letter to come in his stead. It is clearly done to show the Corinthians that he has neither forgotten nor forsaken them. While this will be important in giving gravity to the remonstrance which follows, Paul feels the pressing need to give assurance to the faithful at Corinth that they are still important to him and to God. Although the letter may point to a measure of material privilege that some in the church at Corinth enjoy, on the whole they are still a marginal community, always on the precipice of persecution and privation (1 Cor. 1:26).

A common dimension of this experience of marginalization is ambiguous devotion on the part of those in religious and social privilege. It is the constant witness of the oppressed that, when difficult times descend, they are easily forgotten and relegated to the corners of memory. A particularly pernicious rendering of God's will by those in power is that the oppressed have simply been forgotten by God in their suffering, because they bear no claim on God's faithfulness. I say pernicious because, even in the rendering of God's will repudiated by the previous text from Isaiah, the marginalized are given some notice by God—treated as subjects, even if that notice is desultory. In this case, they are not even worthy of a second thought.

This is precisely the type of thinking that Paul is concerned to expose as a lie; thus, we have his strong admonition to the church at Corinth that neither he nor God has forgotten them. The logic of the world understands God to be concerned exclusively with those in power—emperors and kings—leaving the weak and marginalized forgotten in their trials. But in the incarnation and passion God is revealed precisely in one who was condemned, executed, and quickly forgotten by such rulers. In that revelation God has overthrown the wisdom and frames of understanding from which these rulers draw their power, namely, that they are the only ones with whom God is truly concerned.

Mark 2:1–12

Understanding Christ to be the bearer of the new order of things brings freedom. This is made exquisitely manifest in the story of a man who has borne not only the burden of physical affliction, but also the social approbation that came with it. In the context in which this story unfolds, physical affliction was linked to sin of either the individual or the individual's parents. This is reiterated by the words Jesus uses to bring about the healing. Jesus' forgiveness of the man's sins is the gesture that seems to heal the man. It is not at all clear, however, that this gesture was exclusively toward the afflicted man; it also involved those in authority, whose power rested upon the system of religious ideas that caused the man's exclusion in the first place. Rather, the power of healing had little to do with a public forgiveness of sins, and more to do with the power of God in Christ to heal the brokenness in both body and social life that the man experienced.

Without seeming to be ahistorical and somewhat idiosyncratic, it would not be inappropriate to read this story canonically as one in which Jesus embodies and exemplifies the very inclination toward the weak identified in the previous texts. This inclination expresses itself in Jesus' materially changing the circumstances in which the marginalized man finds himself. Once he picks up the pallet, the natural order of things in which he is an object of public rendering has changed forever. Through the healing and blessing of Jesus, Immanuel, the one who was once weak, becomes a subject in his own power and in God's unfolding history of new things.

Why is God's power most often interpreted in Scripture as predominantly displayed on behalf of the weak and in ways contrary to the wisdom of the world? One way to answer the question might be to recognize that God called into being a community who were suffering in oppressive slavery, and this memory conditioned their self-identity forever. While this answer helps us get at the historical and sociological dimensions of the faith of the people of Israel, it is not adequate to express the theological insight that conditions the faith given witness in these passages. Nor is it fully adequate to the task of understanding why peoples across time whose experiences were very different from that of the people of Israel still find this interpretation compelling and formative.

The interpretation of God's power found in today's text remains compelling because these passages give voice to a powerful insight about the workings of goodness and evil: power—social, political, economic, or otherwise—when utilized by the powerful against the weak, is always prone to become a display of evil. I do not mean those who feign a type of powerlessness as a way of masking their own privilege. I mean those who are materially weak and made so by the workings of systemic evil. We may ask, why is Scripture clear on this connection between privilege and the use of oppressive power? Perhaps because human history is so clear on this matter.

The witness and testimony of marginalized and lethally oppressed peoples throughout human history has been that evil displays itself most visibly in the broken bodies and communities of the weak. Stories that emerge from the Shoah, the Rwandan genocide, American chattel slavery, and the decimation of indigenous peoples in Meso-America all share the insight that the brutal use of power exercised in each instance could most fittingly be described as evil—not misguided, not time conditioned, not unfortunate, but evil! According to Scripture, it is precisely in those instances when the poor are ground to dust (Amos 2:7) and the weakest in society (widows and orphans, Isa. 10:2) are made the prey and spoil of power that evil is most exquisitely displayed.

Herein lies the significance of the texts for today. They remind us that God's power is displayed precisely in the midst of the wicked use of power. God's wisdom is exactly counter to those ideological formations that deem the destruction of the weak as the natural and therefore necessary order of things. God's natural order is a new and different way that brings about well-being for the powerful and the weak alike. This is goodness in the world, and the first step toward living in its midst is regard for the weak.

Eighth Sunday after the Epiphany

Jeffery L. Tribble Sr.

HOSEA 2:14–20
PSALM 103:1–13, 22
2 CORINTHIANS 3:1–6
MARK 2:13–22

In these passages, we find an abundance of biblical themes that bear witness to the manifestation of God in the ministry of Jesus. Prophetic images from the First Testament direct us to engage in risk-taking mission to bring hope to troubled communities. Our work of social justice should be balanced by our commitment to praise and worship God with all of our being. In the Epistle, we are challenged that our "letter of commendation" to the world is the efficacy of our work among the poor. As we follow Jesus, we learn to deal creatively with controversy, conflict, and change.

Hosea 2:14–20

Hosea 2:14–20 may be interpreted as an invitation to the people of God to return to their covenant relationship with God by engaging in the risk-taking mission of bearing God's will of shalom in troubled communities. People in communities torn by violence face a "valley of trouble" (v. 15; see Josh. 7:22–26) while religious people often retreat behind the false security of self-righteousness, ingrown habits, and elaborate security systems. Our vision has narrowed to that of seeking personal salvation, church growth, and comfort in our private sanctuaries. Meanwhile, outside our doors, residents lack public safety. They are under siege by drug dealers who control their neighborhoods. They distrust law-enforcement officers, who not only appear unable to protect them, but are also perceived as allies with crime figures. Individuals who would "blow the whistle" face severe sanctions, risking their very lives. In such a setting, who can be trusted? Who will take a risk? Do religious

109

leaders foster "prophetic imagination" to shepherd persons from the "valley of trouble" through "doors of hope"? (v. 15)

In this passage, God speaks tenderly to lure the people of God into the wild. Inner-city churches will not be saved through church growth strategies that lack prophetic involvement in troubled communities. Paradoxically, the church is restored to fruitfulness through engagement in the wilderness of social-justice ministries. A change of name ('*emeq 'akor*, the Valley of Achor, meaning "valley of trouble," to *petakh tiqvah*, meaning "door of hope") signals a radically changed relationship. The Valley of Achor refers to the broad plain near Jericho where Achan stole plunder devoted to God from the conquest of Jericho (Josh. 7). Only after Achan (and his whole household) was stoned to death for his transgression were the Israelites able to defeat their enemies (Josh. 7:25). Only when the community was mobilized to stand up against the transgressor was the trouble eliminated.

God's people cannot tolerate injustice within their own camp; neither can residents tolerate the unjust acts of a few errant members of their communities. If they do, there is a consequent loss of moral authority and power. To be sure, we should not stone people to death; but when the community organizes to stand up to the false elements within themselves and within the broader world, "a "door of hope" is offered.

The people of God are called to remember the terms of the relationship with God that they have forgotten. We are called to be God's spouse in righteousness, in justice, in steadfast love, in mercy, and in faithfulness. When God's people remember this, they risk their personal safety and venture into the "wilderness" of ministry, where we are divinely commissioned to work for justice, peace, prosperity, and human fulfillment.

Psalm 103:1–13, 22

This psalm reminds us of the interdependence of dynamic praise and our works of justice. The work of social justice is most complete when it is related to authentic evangelical witness and worship.[1] This psalm comprehensively calls on the entire universe to give praise to God—from the individual (vv. 1–15) to the hosts who surround the throne (vv. 19–22a) back to the individual (v. 22b). The praise of God should be intimate in its personal expression and vibrant in its corporate expression. This praise is focused on God's "holy name." In focusing on the name of God, worship is integrally connected to the acts of God and God's people in history. Recollection of

---

1. Richard J. Foster, *Streams of Living Water: Celebrating the Great Traditions of Christian Faith* (New York: HarperCollins Publishers, 1998), 187.

God's name brings to mind the benefits to the covenant community and the mighty acts of God throughout the history of redemption: liberation from Egypt, sustenance in the wilderness, giving of land, and the fulfillment of promises.

Among those benefits, we know God, who forgives, heals, redeems, crowns, and satisfies. The "allure" of these benefits should help to bind Israel to her covenant-making "husband" (cf. Hos. 2:14–20). Notwithstanding the specific and personal "benefits" bestowed on the individual, the worshiper sees God's concern for the establishment of righteousness and justice for the oppressed: God does not tolerate injustice in the world, but reigns such that God will right that which is wrong. "Righteousness" relates to two aspects of divine activity: "salvation" and "justice," that is, vindication for the oppressed. The benefits of knowing God must be extended to those who are poor in spirit as well as those who are materially poor.

Verses 7–10 are an extended commentary on the character of God as revealed to Moses: God is "merciful and gracious, slow to anger and abounding in steadfast love." Though God may be justly angry because of sin and injustice, God does not keep on criticizing or maintain divine anger for long (v. 9b). God does not respond in kind to human infidelity. God's covenant and rule are characterized by grace and divine fidelity to the people of God.

The love of God is not indiscriminate, for love is extended to those "who fear him" (vv. 11, 13). Though God expects godliness, God also understands the frailty of humanity. All creatures are but dust (v. 14) and must be sustained by acts of divine grace and mercy.

2 Corinthians 3:1–6

The congregation at Corinth apparently reflected the socioeconomic and religious makeup of the city and of much of the Greco-Roman world. In this social world, there were few wealthy people and practically no middle class as we know it; hence, many were poor. Paul acknowledges this, saying in 1 Corinthians 1:26 that "not many of you were wise by human standards, not many were powerful, not many were of noble birth." Hence it is primarily to the poor that Paul speaks in today's passage.

Behind the questions in verse 1 ("Are we beginning to commend ourselves again?" and Do we need "letters of recommendation to you or from you?") is a background in which the Corinthians must have requested letters of commendation from some missionaries. Paul does not have a written letter that recommends him to others; rather, the Corinthian community itself is the demonstration of the efficacy and competence of his ministry. Paul does not disparage the use of letters of introduction; however, the most eloquent letter was their very lives as men and women in Christ—the result of the grace of God operating in Paul's ministry.

Paul's work among the poor is his letter of commendation to be known and read by all. Likewise, our work among the poor and disadvantaged of society ("the least of these") or our failure to work among the poor and disadvantaged is "our letter of introduction" to the world. Ultimately, no other credential really matters. Any church can serve those who will, in turn, benefit the institution. However, when we are divinely commissioned, we are also divinely equipped as "ministers of a new covenant." The new covenant does not replace the old, but promises God's dynamic life-giving Spirit to Gentiles who come to know God through Jesus Christ. We need God's life-giving Spirit to infuse our words as well as our work of charity and justice with transforming power. Our mission among the poor is sustained only as we are spiritually formed and sustained as ministers of justice, mercy, and faith (Matt. 23:23).

Mark 2:13–22

What does it mean to follow Jesus? Does it not mean that we are willing to learn to manage the controversy and conflict that inevitably arises in the pursuit of justice and righteousness? Followers of Jesus are on a journey of transformation that requires us to be the change that we want to see in others. We must struggle to confront our own hypocrisy, religious formality, conflict avoidance, and rigidity of habits.

In this passage, we see Jesus as subject of two controversies: (1) Jesus' companions in sharing meals (vv. 15–17), and (2) the observance of ritual practices in general (vv. 21–22), with fasting being a prominent example (vv. 18–20). Jesus taught those who followed him (v. 13) not only with his words, but with his deeds, "as he was walking along" (v. 14a). In "walking the talk of justice" we can be guided and inspired by his example.

In response to the controversy arising from table fellowship with the tax collectors, Jesus said, "Those who are well have no need of a physician, but those who are sick; I have come to call not the righteous but sinners" (v. 17). We see here a magnificent truth: that God loves and saves persons *as sinners*. Self-righteous persons may not see their own needs, but "sinners" can, when they recognize both their alienation from God and their need. Tax collectors were despised because they were seen as agents of extortion working on behalf of the Roman government. These individuals were actors in the broader social, economic, and political systems of oppression. Nonetheless, many of these "sinners" followed Jesus. Jesus' hospitality reminds us that stereotypical profiling of persons is unjust and cannot be tolerated. Those "in need of a physician" are not made whole by being kept at arm's length.

In the book *Congregations in America*, Mark Chaves analyzes the charitable activities of congregations. Arguing against the assumption that religious organizations are well suited to holistic service delivery that fosters personal transformation, he states that "their activities, however well intentioned, are shaped and constrained by the same social inequalities that shape and constrain other organizations' activities and their operations are governed by the same pressures toward social homophily [love of the same, the tendency of people to relate to other people who are similar] that operate in the rest of society."[2] In other words, without critical reflection and discernment of how we have been socially formed and culturally conditioned, we will not be transformed to foster personal transformation with the marginalized. Ministries of social change must not neglect the change that needs to occur within our own lives.

Conflicts, controversy, and disruption in being change agents are envisioned in the metaphors of sewing a piece of new cloth on an old garment and putting new wine into an old wineskin (vv. 21–22). Old garments and old wineskins do not have sufficient elasticity to accommodate the new. Putting new wine in old wineskins and patching an old coat with new cloth are as inappropriate as fasting at a wedding feast. New situations demand new rituals and forms. In one sense, the metaphor of wineskins is incomplete. An old wineskin does lose its elasticity, whereas human beings have the potential to change. Historic practices can become fresh and powerful when they are enlivened by a sense of God's presence and leading. Of course, the act of enlivening can create tensions within community.

Some dilemmas in ministry require leadership where there are no easy answers. The newness that the coming of Jesus brings cannot be confined in old forms. The reign of God calls us to develop habits and new forms of ministry that are fresh and give life while managing the messiness of conflict and change.

---

2. Mark Chaves, *Congregations in America* (Cambridge, MA: Harvard University Press, 2004), 65–66.

Ninth Sunday after the Epiphany

Sharon H. Ringe

DEUTERONOMY 5:12–15
PSALM 81:1–10
2 CORINTHIANS 4:5–12
MARK 2:23–3:6

The readings on this Ninth Sunday of Epiphany bring to a conclusion the time of the manifestation of Jesus' divine nature (Epiphany) and prepare us to enter a time of penitential preparation in the season of Lent. This moment on the cusp bids us to focus on what it means to live in covenant with God in both of those seasons of life. The Gospel and Torah face us with the meaning of keeping a day holy to God. Paul reminds us of the vulnerability of our physical body as the vessel that carries "the light of the knowledge of the glory of God in the face of Jesus Christ." The psalmist sketches a "covenant lawsuit" in which God is pulled between demands for our obedience and the desire to reward a faithful people. God's holiness and God's vision of a just social order intertwine in all of these texts, in defiance of our self-protective efforts to keep them separate.

Deuteronomy 5:12–15

This foundation for the week's lections is part of the Decalogue. We are told not just to "remember" the Sabbath day (as in Exod. 20:8–11), but to do something, to conform our behavior to the holiness of the day. Although we tend to emphasize the rest or "not-working" that marks the day, the text emphasizes two other dimensions of that observance. First is the inclusiveness of the commandment to keep Sabbath. *All* people in the society are to be granted a day free from work, from the heads of households and their children to male and female slaves and resident aliens living among them. This is especially striking, since it raises to the status of free people groups that would not normally be accorded such dignity, but that would often be treated as mere property and not as human beings at all. And, in a glimpse of ecological justice as part of keeping the Sabbath, even their cattle and livestock are to have the day off!

Second, the passage in Deuteronomy emphasizes the reason for the commandment to keep Sabbath: "Remember that you were a slave in the land of Egypt, and the LORD your God brought you out from there with a mighty hand and an outstretched arm; therefore the LORD your God commanded you to keep the sabbath day" (v. 15). God's own liberating act on behalf of Israel is held as the norm for their behavior to keep the day holy.

The inclusiveness of the Sabbath law challenges us as well, given the assumption that retail establishments and the service sector of our economy will remain open seven days a week. What provision do we make for those earning minimum wage to be able to afford a time when they do not work? Conversely, what does it mean to keep Sabbath when so many people are unemployed or underemployed, and when the ability to work and earn a living appears as a great blessing that would honor both God and God's vision of justice and dignity seen in Israel's liberation from slavery in Egypt?

Mark 2:23–3:6

The commandment to keep the Sabbath is sketched in general terms. Exactly what it would mean in practice would require long and careful interpretation through Israel's history, and even today, as social and economic systems continue to change. Jesus lived in a time when the Jewish people had a long period of that interpretation under their belts, but the meaning was still a matter of contention in the context of their captivity under the Roman Empire. This reading in Mark presents two occasions when Jesus is shown stretching the boundaries of Sabbath interpretation.

The first story, Mark 2:23–28, depicts Jesus being asked to account for his disciples' apparent transgression of Sabbath law by casually plucking and eating grain as they walked through a field. Such gleaning would be permitted if the person was hungry, but no such circumstance is cited here. Nevertheless, the explanation attributed to Jesus does refer to an action by David and his followers when they were hungry. Jewish law and practice provided that not just holy time (the Sabbath), but also a holy substance (the bread of the Presence), could be put to a common use in a crisis of life or death. The concluding statement in verses 27–28 changes the question, from what can be permitted on the Sabbath, to which takes priority, humankind or the Sabbath? The answer of Jesus gives priority to human well-being: "The sabbath was made for humankind, and not humankind for the sabbath"—a point that is also made in Jewish sources. The final point is even more surprising, for not even the Decalogue has greater authority than "the Son of Man," who is called "[ruler] even of the sabbath."

Christian usage has accustomed us to hearing "the Son of Man" as one of the titles of Jesus; so we barely blink an eye at the declaration that that figure is sovereign over the Sabbath. In the Hebrew Bible, in addition to using the expression "son of man" as a way of speaking about a human being, two figures are referred to more specifically as "son of man." One is the prophet Ezekiel, whom God addresses by that title when the prophet receives a new commission to bring a word from God to the people.[1] The second reference in the Hebrew Bible is in Daniel 7:13–14, where "one like a son of man" (rendered "one like a human being" in the NRSV) is given an everlasting dominion over all the peoples of the earth, in the presence of the Ancient One. In both cases, the ones referred to by this title are charged with mediating God's justice to the people. By extension, then, the issue in Mark 2:23–28 is not obedience to religious rules for their own sake, or even the authority of God's anointed, but rather whether those rules and the Anointed One truly bring God's justice to expression in the life of the community.

A similar theme continues in Mark 3:1–6, where the Sabbath rule in question is the prohibition of work in the form of healing. The story is set in a synagogue on the Sabbath, and people are watching to see what Jesus will do when a man with a withered hand approaches. Were this a matter of life or death, even that of an animal, there would be no question but that intervention would be permitted and even required (Matt. 12:9–14; Luke 13:15). Clearly this condition was not life threatening, and furthermore, since it was the Sabbath, the man would not have been able to do any work with that hand anyway until after the Sabbath had ended. Jesus could easily have told the man to wait until sunset, when the Sabbath was over, and then have healed his hand. The question is reframed, however, from what is permitted (and, by implication, what is forbidden) on the Sabbath, to what actions and purposes make this a holy time. Failing to do the good that would clearly hallow the day is equated with doing harm (v. 4), and acting on behalf of healing and wholeness of life is equated with saving life, which is always appropriate to the Sabbath.

In an ironic conclusion to the story, the Pharisees who have been concerned about Jesus' actions on the Sabbath enter into a death plot against him on the Sabbath (v. 6). So much, from Mark's point of view, for God's day being about God's justice!

---

1. In the NRSV of Ezekiel, the Hebrew is rendered "O mortal" instead of the more literal "Son of Man" found in earlier translations. See Ezek. 2:1; 3:1; etc.

Each of these examples raises the relationship of justice to quality of life as a standard for Sabbath keeping. The same concern meets us as we consider examples of justice issues confronting us today. Being able to obtain food beyond the basics necessary for survival would allow people to fathom an economy of abundance and generosity, instead of the economy of scarcity that currently shapes our decisions. We would learn to move to a broad consideration of what is possible, rather than a tense calculation of what is allowed. And in matters of health care, what promotes fullness of life—instead of a judgment about what constitutes a "real" emergency—would govern decisions that permit "business as usual" to be set aside in the allocation of medical resources.

2 Corinthians 4:5–12

If the previous two readings focused on how ordinary time becomes holy time, Paul leads us to think about the common material of human life itself as the place where God's glory shines. In particular, this passage conveys words of encouragement to those whom life has treated harshly.

Paul uses himself as a counterexample to the powerful and apparently successful "super-apostles" (11:5) who are making inroads on the Corinthian congregation. His suffering and weakness have been occasions for God's power to shine through. A danger in such an argument, however, is that it can be used as an excuse not to change the circumstances that impose suffering on others. Clearly that is not Paul's intent here. Rather, this stands as an example of God's bias in favor of those who are weaker over those who are stronger. In God's economy, justice is not blind or impartial, but instead God tips the balance in favor of those whom the world has disdained. Those crumbly and common "clay jars" of ordinary human life carry a content more splendid than the most luxurious vessels of the temple, palace, or church.

We too are challenged to see treasure in simple human beings. Current battles over immigration legislation and whether education and health care should be available to undocumented workers pit one definition of a worthy person against an affirmation that all persons are treasures, regardless of their status. We have so elevated Paul in our esteem that it is hard to get his point about his lack of prestige or status. Substitute for him one of the people gathered in the parking lots of convenience stores, hoping to be hired for a lawn service or painting crew for a few dollars a day. Then listen to their accounts of employers who disappear at the end of the day without paying them. God's justice with, so to speak, a finger on the scale in favor of the "leasts, lasts, and losts" of our society demonstrates the richest of God's gifts.

Psalm 81:1–10

This psalm contains one of the many "covenant lawsuits" found in the Hebrew Bible. God is putting the people on trial for their violations of the covenant with God and unfolds the case against them, in the midst of reminders of all God has done for them.

The psalm begins with a hymn of praise (vv. 1–5a). In verse 5b they hear a voice not previously known that recites God's great work of deliverance done for them (vv. 6–7). Those liberating deeds carry expectations for the people to remain loyal to their God, who has done these things for them (vv. 8–10), but they ignore God's rules, and God's response is simply to abandon the people to their own ways (vv. 11–12). Note that this is not a matter of God's punishing the people, but of simply letting them live with the consequences of their actions.

God's yearning for the people's well-being persists in the final verses of the psalm (vv. 13–16). The banquet God dreams of preparing for them includes the finest wheat and sweet "honey from the rock" (v. 16)—a meal that is lavish, luscious, and celebratory. It would be a holy meal, the transformation of ordinary foods into blessings for everyone, like the ordinary day that becomes the holy time of the Sabbath, and like fragile and common human flesh that can bear "the light of the knowledge of the glory of God in the face of Jesus Christ" (2 Cor. 4:6).

Transfiguration Sunday (Last Sunday after the Epiphany)

Ched Myers

2 KINGS 2:1–12
PSALM 50:1–6
2 CORINTHIANS 4:3–6
MARK 9:2–9

The Feast of the Transfiguration probably dates to the late Roman period. A major feast in the Eastern Church, it was not widely practiced by the Western Church until the ninth century. August 6 was designated as the feast day for the whole church in 1456. The Roman Catholic Church today also commemorates the transfiguration on the Second Sunday in Lent, but the Revised Common Lectionary puts the story at the Last Sunday of Epiphany. The latter position, which recognizes the transfiguration's close relationship to Jesus' journey toward the cross in the Gospel narratives, is my focus here.

Mark 9:2–9 and 2 Kings 2:1–12

The Markan narrative section in which the transfiguration appears revolves around Jesus' "turn to Jerusalem," a sequence faithfully preserved by both Matthew and Luke:

1. This section commences with what I call the "confessional crisis" at Caesarea Philippi, in which Jesus begins trying to reorient his disciples' perception of his identity from triumphal Messiah to suffering Servant (Mark 8:27–30; see Matt. 16:13–20//Luke 9:18–21).
2. This is followed by Jesus' first passion "portent," as Jesus talks plainly about the political consequences of his public practice (Mark 8:31–33; see Matt. 16:21–23//Luke 9:22). Jesus invites his followers to take up the cross, Mark's "second" call to follow (the first coming in 1:16–20), and the defining metaphor for the cost of discipleship in this story (Mark 8:34–9:1; see Matt. 16:24–28//Luke 9:23–27).
3. In the middle of this sequence, like a fulcrum, is the transfiguration story. This "summit" meeting functions both to give Jesus courage for the road

119

ahead and to lend divine legitimacy to his way (Mark 9:2–10; see Matt. 17:1–9//Luke 9:28–36).

4. The mountaintop experience is followed by a highly symbolic healing. A young boy suffering from a disabling spirit confounds the disciples, whose impotence reveals that they may be possessed by the very demons they are trying to cast out (Mark 9:14–29; see Matt. 17:14–21//Luke 9:37–43a).

5. Jesus then reiterates his conviction that his imminent showdown with the powers in Jerusalem will result in his execution and resurrection (Mark 9:30–32; see Matt. 17:22–23//Luke 9:43b–45).[1]

The transfiguration stands in the middle of this sequence, with the disciples sharply instructed to "listen" to Jesus so that they might truly reckon with the *via crucis* (Mark 9:7). But Mark's wider narrative segment—framed by the healing of two blind men (8:22–26 and 10:46–52)—emphasizes the disciples' inability (indeed, unwillingness) to grasp this crucial point.

The "high mountain" setting of the transfiguration vision calls to mind foundational stories of Israel (discussed in my forthcoming comments on Transfiguration Sunday, Year A). This is the second of three "apocalyptic moments" in Mark's story—"openings" between earth and heaven—that serve as structural pillars around which the overall narrative is organized. The first comes at Jesus' baptism, when a "voice from heaven" declares the Nazarene "My Child, the Beloved" (1:11). That affirmation is repeated here on the mount of transfiguration. The third apocalyptic moment comes at the cross and stands in stark contrast to the first two: instead of a descending dove or a bright cloud, there is darkness over the land, and Jesus' appeal to heaven is met with silence (15:33–37).

The "special effects" surrounding the transfiguration allude to the book of Daniel, in which Daniel's visions are explained by a man in glorified clothing (Dan. 10:5ff.; see also 7:9). The affinity is important: Daniel is a Hellenistic-era tract of nonviolent resistance to empire, and Jesus is about to begin his fateful march to face down the imperial authorities in Jerusalem. Moreover, Jesus appears in shining white clothes, an apocalyptic costume symbolizing martyrdom that reappears at the end of Mark's story (Mark 16:5).[2]

Jesus confers with the two greatest heroes of Israel (9:4), who we can imagine would have had profound empathy for the dilemmas facing Jesus at this

---

1. For more on Mark's narrative strategy in this sequence, see my *Binding the Strong Man: A Political Reading of Mark's Story of Jesus* (Maryknoll, NY: Orbis Books, 2008), chapter 8.

2. The young man at Jesus' empty tomb is so clothed. White-clothed martyrs also appear in the apocalyptic book of Revelation (Rev. 3:5; 4:4; 6:11; 7:9, 13; see Wes Howard-Brook and Anthony Gwyther, *Unveiling Empire: Reading Revelation Then and Now* [Maryknoll, NY: Orbis Books, 1999]). For more on Daniel as resistance literature, see John J. Collins, *The Apocalyptic Imagination: An Introduction to the Jewish Matrix of Christianity* (New York: Crossroad, 1992), chapter 3.

point in the story. Moses, the archetypal mediator of Torah, was rejected by his people, and had to ascend Sinai a second time, returning with tablets and his face transfigured (Exod. 34:29–35). Elijah, the archetypal prophet, was hunted by authorities he had challenged, and then instructed, "Go out and stand on the mountain before God," where he returned to face the powers (1 Kgs. 19). Similarly, Jesus struggles with disciples who do not comprehend his mission and leaders who are already plotting his demise (Mark 3:6); he has come to summon strength and clarity from his ancestors.

All of this is lost on Peter, however, who broadcasts his ignorance for the second time in this sequence (9:5; see 8:31–33). Still operating from a framework of messianic triumphalism, Peter offers to commemorate the epiphany by establishing "tabernacles" (cf. the booths of Lev. 23:4ff.). Institutionalizing cults of religious admiration may be an age-old human religious impulse, but Mark disapproves (v. 6). Peter is again rebuked, this time not by Jesus but by the divine voice itself (v. 7). The vision then terminates abruptly, and Jesus warns his companions that they will not understand what they have just witnessed until after the "Human One" (NRSV "Son of Man") has been raised from the dead (v. 9). But the ambiguous ending of Mark's Gospel offers the resurrection not as an "answer" to the disciples' perplexity, but as a *third* call to discipleship (16:6–7). There is no rescue from the difficult vocation of the cross to which we are all summoned.

Today's reading from 2 Kings 2 resonates with these themes, narrating the last moments of Elisha and Elijah before the latter's "ascension" into heaven. Three times Elijah tries to withdraw from Elisha, and each time his disciple begs to accompany him (vv. 1–6). This is echoed in Mark's story of Jesus' looming "departure": three times he anticipates his fate at the hands of the Jerusalem authorities, and each time his disciples react cluelessly (Mark 8:31–33; 9:31–37; 10:32–45). The Elijah cycle stands in the background throughout Mark's narrative, beginning with his portrait of John the Baptist as Elijah redivivus (Mark starts where the Elijah story ends—at the Jordan river, Mark 1:4–6).[3] Elijah's appearance at the transfiguration underlines Jesus' intent to speak truth to power, to face the consequences, and to be "received into glory."

Disciples who would take up the mantle of such leaders *should* understand the cost of the prophetic vocation, yet today's reading suggests otherwise. Elijah's question to Elisha—"Tell me what I may do for you" (2 Kgs. 2:9)—is repeated by Jesus to James and John on the heels of his third passion portent

---

3. For example, Jesus' call of the disciples is patterned after Elijah's call of Elisha (Mark 1:16–20; cf. 1 Kgs. 19:19–21), while Jesus' distribution of bread and fish to the poor in the wilderness is clearly predicated upon Elisha's feeding miracle (Mark 6:35–44; cf. 2 Kgs. 4:42–44). King Herod mistakes Jesus for Elijah (Mark 6:15), as do others (Mark 8:28), while Jesus affirms the Baptist as Elijah returned (9:11–13). And at the end of Mark, Jesus' psalmic cry is mistaken for an appeal to Elijah for rescue (Mark 15:34–35).

(Mark 10:36). Their respective requests indicate that both Elisha and Jesus' followers are more focused on increasing personal power than upon the difficult way of nonviolent struggle modeled by their mentors. This is a "hard thing" (2 Kgs. 2:10) and a poignant theme for preaching.

Psalm 50:1–6, 2 Corinthians 4:3–6

Today's psalm hears YHWH's thundering voice that refuses to keep silent in the face of injustice. This motif invites the listener to imagine the "tone" of the voice from heaven at the transfiguration. Was it commanding, as heard by Moses on Sinai, or "still and small" as experienced by Elijah on Mt. Horeb? Is it surrounded by "fire and tempest" as in the psalm, or plaintive in its plea to the disciples (and the reader) to embrace fully the way of Jesus (Mark 9:7)? No doubt all these modalities are necessary in the long biblical saga of YHWH's appeals to a wayward people to be faithful to the vocation of *tikkun olam*—repairing the world. The cosmos may share the divine passion for justice (Ps. 50:6), but too often we in the churches do not, because we (like disciples in both testaments) are preoccupied with personal anxieties, distracted by spectacle, and fixated on ladder climbing.

Today's epistle speaks to this conundrum. To those "blinded" by "the god of this world," Paul warns, the gospel is "veiled" (2 Cor. 4:3–4). It is crucial to understand that Paul is not speaking here about those "outside" the church (much less categorically about Jews). Rather, he is addressing the struggle for truth *within* the Christian community, which includes those who disingenuously "cheapen God's word" (NRSV "falsify," v. 2).[4] In Corinth the apostle addresses a community not unlike our churches in the United States: stubbornly self-focused, largely domesticated under empire, and thus gullible to preachers who identify faith in Christ with personal gain.[5] For Paul, those who are unable or unwilling to embrace the way of servanthood and the cross have not *truly* seen "the glory of God in the face of Jesus Christ" (v. 6)—the very blindness exhibited by the disciples on the mount of transfiguration!

The challenge to our churches is to nurture the psalmist's thundering passion for justice that "does not keep silence" (Ps. 50:3), on one hand, and to be clear that this carries a cost, on the other. There is no more widely prevalent or negatively consequential "cheapening" of the gospel in North America than the notion that following Jesus will improve our personal prospects and

---

4. See my forthcoming comments on 2 Cor. 3:12–4:2, the epistle for Transfiguration Sunday, Year C.

5. For a concise portrait of Paul's context in Corinth, see Ched Myers and Elaine Enns, *Ambassadors of Reconciliation*, vol. I: *New Testament Reflections on Restorative Justice and Peacemaking* (Maryknoll, NY: Orbis Books, 2009), chapter 1.

guarantee happiness and success. Such "hucksters of the word of God" (NRSV "peddlers," 2 Cor. 2:17) are building tabernacles to the glorified Christ without *listening* to his call to a discipleship of the cross. Mark's Gospel is the best corrective to those so blinded by the gods of entitlement and privilege that they proclaim Jesus as a patron rather than a victim of empire, and think that justice can wait until the next world.

At the same time, there is no quick or painless way to achieve social and economic sustainability for everyone, or racial or gender equity, or an end to exploitation or war making. This work requires patient and committed organizing and action, and the ability to persist in the face of discouraging results. Martin Luther King Jr. remains the most exemplary advocate of this sort of discipleship. His insistence that "we shall overcome because the arc of the moral universe is long, but it bends toward justice" echoes Psalm 5.[6] But King was a follower of Mark's Jesus who embraced his own Calvary in Memphis because of his unwavering commitment to the poor and to nonviolence, which he placed above the political calculus of popularity polls and favorable press.

King was America's greatest public prophet, yet, as a devotee of Howard Thurman, maintained a mystical relationship with the Divine. Such dialectical faith characterized other great saints in the struggle for justice and peace in the modern church as well, both the famous (e.g., Dorothy Day, César Chávez, and Dietrich Bonhoeffer) and the forgotten (e.g., Fannie Lou Hamer, Tom Fox, and Julia Esquivel). This balance of engagement and contemplation is both demanded and nurtured by a Gospel story that embeds the experience of transfiguration at the heart of a journey toward the cross. King dramatically bore witness to such faith in his deservedly famous last words on the eve of his assassination, in which he invoked Moses, Elijah, and Jesus on the mount:

> We've got some difficult days ahead. But it doesn't matter with me now. Because I've been to the mountaintop. . . . I just want to do God's will. And He's allowed me to go up to the mountain. And I've looked over. And I've seen the promised land. I may not get there with you. But I want you to know tonight, that we, as a people, will get to the promised land. . . . Mine eyes have seen the glory of the coming of the Lord.[7]

6. This quote appears in several of King's speeches, the latest being the final sermon he delivered before his assassination in 1968, "Remaining Awake through a Great Revolution" (in James M. Washington, ed., *A Testament of Hope: The Essential Writings and Speeches of Martin Luther King, Jr.* [San Francisco: HarperSanFrancisco, 1986], 277). The thought dates back to Rev. Theodore Parker in 1853.

7. These words closed his "I See the Promised Land" address at Mason Temple, Memphis, TN, April 3, 1968; found in Washington, *A Testament of Hope*, 286.

Ash Wednesday

Peter J. Paris

ISAIAH 58:1–12
PSALM 51:1–17
2 CORINTHIANS 5:20B–6:10
MATTHEW 6:1–6, 16–21

A major purpose of the forty days of Lent is to prepare for Good Friday and Easter. The congregation should not think of those events as having taken place only in the past, but should ponder the degree to which the realities they represent are still a part of the world—violence generated by injustice, and resurrection that restores God's purposes for life. Ash Wednesday begins the season of Lent by calling the congregation to a sober and realistic examination of its faithfulness. Where the preacher and congregation discern they are violating God's purposes for all to live together in covenantal support, the community should repent.

The biblical passages for Ash Wednesday help the preacher and the congregation to reflect on the faithfulness of the community, to name points for correction, and to identify ways to do so (especially through repentance). Isaiah invites the church to compare what it says in worship with the way it lives in the everyday world. Psalm 51 calls the community to repent of its offenses against God and other people. Paul urges the congregation to consider the degree to which they have imported conflicts from the larger society into the church. Making use of the ancient idea that one stores up treasures in heaven by expressing solidarity with the poor, Matthew prompts the church to consider the degree to which we are doing that very thing.

Isaiah 58:1–12

In this text Second Isaiah calls upon the people to discern the difference between true and false worship. The former not only involves proper ceremonies in the house of worship but also implies doing justice in solidarity with

124

the most vulnerable people in the community, through such things as sharing one's resources with the hungry, the homeless, and the naked. What happens in liturgy is supposed to shape how the community lives. In other words, true worship results in ethical practices that embody God's purposes. False worship is a self-serving enterprise that appears to seek the righteousness of God while contradicting that righteousness in the community's own practices toward others. By doing justice, the people cooperate with God's activity of restoring God's damaged creation.

Isaiah uses the practice of fasting as a case in point. In Jewish tradition, fasting was to have a double purpose. The feeling of hunger caused by fasting is supposed to awaken the self to the profound need for God and to alert the self to the hunger of the neighbor. In covenantal community, becoming aware of the hunger of another should motivate community members to alleviate that hunger. In Isaiah's day, however, people were fasting (and engaging in other rites of worship) only to garner social prestige and social power. They did not consider the ethical responsibilities to others that are inherent in the act of worship.

Reading this text in the aftermath of the horrific 9/11 tragedy raises a number of theological and moral questions related to these themes. Prior to 9/11, many citizens of the United States were like the people of Isaiah's day: moving through life in self-satisfied, self-secure ways. Airliners commandeered by terrorists destroyed the World Trade Center in New York, plunged into the Pentagon, and might have hit a third target, had that plane not been forced to crash by the actions of the passengers themselves. This day of horror has been indelibly written into the memory of the United States. Deceived by its own sense of moral goodness, our nation could not imagine that any others in the world would act with such hatred toward us. Countless moral questions continue to puzzle our people. Two such questions are the following: (1) Is our nation willing to perceive 9/11 as a wake-up call to the fact that in the world scene we have often been self-centered and acted in many other unjust ways? It is small wonder that people in other nations are resentful. (2) Are the so-called terrorists demonic beings undeserving of humane treatment?

One of the most redeeming acts following the 9/11 attack was an event at the Riverside Church in New York City, called "A Time for Healing," This event sought to loose the bonds of injustice and to offer true worship by coming together in supportive community. It was an interfaith gathering of Christians, Jews, Muslims, Buddhists, Sikhs, and others, who drew upon the resources of their respective traditions as offerings for the healing of the city and the nation. The people at this event were united in their grief and fright, and the service, by honoring and drawing sustenance from the different worship traditions, helped them to draw closer to one another and to demonstrate the solidarity that God desires among all peoples.

Psalm 51:1–17

This text manifests a theme important in Jewish religion, namely, deep anguish over sin against God, the creator and judge, which is also sin against humankind. This psalm has been associated with David's sin of adultery with Bathsheba. Here we have the repentance of Israel's greatest leader, in whose lineage Jesus of Nazareth was born. The prayer presupposes God's forgiving and redemptive spirit and has been a sign of hope for countless peoples ever since. Without forgiveness, troubled souls would despair and indulge themselves in many self-destructive activities as signs of hopelessness and meaninglessness. Instead, the God of David and Jesus is merciful and willing to forgive all who sin, if they sincerely repent and diligently resolve with the help of God to live new lives of faithfulness.

Repentance means not only turning away from offenses to God, but also turning toward covenantal living. The point of repentance is not simply to feel badly about one's sin, but to take the dynamic step of moving toward a better future in partnership with God.

Here is an example of this positive aspect of repentance. For several decades New York Theological Seminary has offered a master's degree in theological studies at the Sing Sing Correctional Facility in New York. When this text and similar psalms are read in that context, one can easily discern the spirit of repentance in those prisoners who have turned away from a style of life that resulted in their incarceration. Though they must remain in prison for some indefinite period of time, they now have hope, as they prepare themselves for ministry in the prison and perhaps outside of prison one day. These men have prayed incessantly for clean hearts, steadfast spirits, and the joy of salvation. Most important, all who work with these men know the importance of strong communities of support that are needed to sustain them in their ongoing journey through life, whether inside or outside the prison walls.

2 Corinthians 5:20b–6:10

Clearly, members of any church are also members of the larger society outside the church. Thus, many of the values and practices they embrace outside the church are transmitted by them into the church. These values include distrust, biases, hatreds, and other vices. This had happened in the church in Corinth, and Paul himself became the target of such fractious practices. After all, he was an outsider, who had organized the church in the busy commercial city of Corinth, which had been rebuilt recently under Roman colonial rule. Further, the city had a reputation of being altogether morally decadent. Though Paul's feelings had been hurt by the accusations made against him both during and after his visit, this second letter was written in a very pastoral manner that does not dwell on his own previous hurt, except for placing it in the context of his struggle to be a faithful witness to Christ. Indeed, Paul sought to be an ambassador of reconciliation. For Paul, reconciliation meant not only reconciliation with God but reconciliation with the other members of the community.

The majority of black churches are composed mostly of people who are relatively poor and who live in the midst of considerable social and economic turmoil. Many of those contexts are characterized by negative forces such as the illegal sale of drugs, prostitution, homicide, and other criminal activities. Thus one should expect to experience the impact of such experiences on the congregations in those contexts. Paul's response to the conflicts in Corinth exemplifies his method of pastoral ministry, which is not to individuals alone but to the church as a whole. Though his reference to his own personal suffering might be viewed by some as self-serving, it fits the aim of the letter nonetheless. That purpose is to remind the church of its mission to represent Christ, and hence the necessity for the church to be reconciled to God through the life, death, and resurrection of Christ and for the members of the congregation to live in reconciliation with one another and with him. In any case, Paul's pastoral strategy is useful even today: he focuses attention on the church's primary mission rather than becoming bogged down in the dispute itself.

Matthew 6:1–6, 16–21

The so-called Sermon on the Mount contains many of Jesus' principle teachings. According to many scholars, Matthew presents Jesus as a prophet whose message within the Gospel is intended to speak to Matthew's own congregation, to help the community toward authentic expression of a right relationship with God and with one another. Thus, this passage of Scripture points to that right relationship by a critical assessment of the way in which many people of that time carried out three important religious rituals: almsgiving, prayer, and fasting. According to the Matthean Jesus, many people—including many in the Matthean community—carried out these practices mainly to be praised by others (and thus to gain social standing and power).

In our passage, Matthew puts forward a prophetic challenge to "store up for yourselves treasures in heaven" (v. 20). When using that expression, Matthew invokes a tradition that one laid up treasure in heaven by contributing alms for the care of the poor (e.g., Sir. 29:11–12; Tob. 4:9–11). By giving alms in secret, the members of the community fulfill the true purpose of almsgiving, which is to embody solidarity with the poor. Sirach continues, "Help the poor for the commandment's sake, and in their need do not send them away empty-handed" (Sir. 29:9). The faithful are to put their silver (money) in the service of the poor and are not to let it "rust under a stone and be lost" (Sir. 29:10).

When this Scripture is read in an African American context, it should evoke memories of three prophetic challenges by African American prophets who sought to lead their people to an alternative piety. First, Martin Luther King Jr. challenged the churches of his day to resist the prevailing ethos of racial segregation and discrimination, to which they had become adapted for a very long while. Second, black liberation theology challenged the theological ethos of seminaries and churches that rendered the African American religious tradition invisible and thus trained black seminarians and all others in a theology bent on preserving the status quo in race relations. Third, Jesus' teaching about "stor[ing] up for yourselves treasures" (vv. 19–21) provides an opportunity for a critical assessment of the so-called prosperity gospel that has gained prominent expression in America and elsewhere in our day: a gospel that emphasizes wealth as a result of Christian piety. Such an orientation corrupts Jesus' teaching about materiality in relation to authentic spirituality. Without a proper understanding of that relationship, the former is likely to compete with the latter for supremacy and become the worship of mammon instead of the worship of God.

First Sunday in Lent

Nicole L. Johnson

GENESIS 9:8–17
PSALM 25:1–10
1 PETER 3:18–22
MARK 1:9–15

On this First Sunday in Lent, the Scripture readings present some important themes as we ponder the journey toward Easter. From the hope symbolized by the rainbow in the Genesis flood narrative, to the psalmist's trust in God and Peter's emphasis on suffering in solidarity with the oppressed, to Jesus' preaching of the good news following his baptism, the readings call the community of Christ not only to renewed hope but also to a renewed witness for social justice.

Genesis 9:8–17

This reading takes us to the denouement of the flood story; the waters have receded, the dove has returned with the olive leaf, Noah and his family have disembarked from the ark and have made burnt offerings, and now God makes a promise never similarly to destroy "all flesh" again.

God makes a covenant with Noah and his family, the representatives of the rest of humankind, but that covenant extends beyond humanity: "I am establishing my covenant with you . . . and with every living creature that is with you, the birds, the domestic animals, and every animal of the earth with you" (vv. 9–10) and, in fact, with "the earth" itself (v. 13). The implications of this covenant toward ecological justice are hard to miss; God's promise to protect the *entire* creation calls the faith community to see its own existence and well-being as tied together with the existence and well-being of the rest of the created order, so loved and protected by its creator. Humans are in covenant not only with one another and God but with the natural world as well. The flip side of this relationship is that humankind's destruction is also tied

129

to environmental destruction caused by irresponsible use of limited natural resources. Christianity's sense of environmental justice must be strengthened by God's promise to "remember my covenant that is between me and you and every living creature of all flesh" (v. 15).

The sign of this covenant is, of course, the rainbow "set . . . in the clouds" (v. 13) by God. The rainbow, like the dove carrying the olive leaf in Genesis 8, is a symbol of both peace and hope. The rainbow symbolizes the peace God grants to humans and the promise not to destroy life again using the waters of a flood. As a symbol of peace, the rainbow serves as a symbol and sign of hope. To "hope" means "to desire with expectation of obtainment" or "to expect with confidence."[1] Hope, the *expectation* that things will get better, not only gets us through the difficult times but also gives us strength to work proactively in the interest of a just and peaceful world. Hope helps communities to rebuild after a deathly and devastating natural disaster. Hope moves an addict through to the next day without succumbing to the desire to feed the addiction. Hope encourages the faith community to seek justice for all *now*, while waiting expectantly for the reign of Christ that will usher in pure justice. In a world that sometimes seems so lacking in hope, the Christian community is called to live that hope for others.

Psalm 25:1–10

The theme of hope continues in this psalm of lament, in which the psalmist expresses trust in God and in God's protection from enemies. Here the psalmist cries to God for help in the present troubled circumstances and asks that God not remember past sins and transgressions. Rather, the psalmist implores God—in God's mercy and love—to come quickly to the psalmist's rescue.

The lection raises some issues when viewed through the lens of social justice. First, is this not the yearning of those who suffer injustice at the hands of enemies? The claim of hope and trust in God's protection springs from the mouths of those who have no hope or trust in systems of oppression, violence, and injustice. History is replete with stories of people and communities who are capable of radical hope, trust, and faith in the face of the worst experiences of powerlessness; in fact, one often finds the most profound manifestations of hope within the poorest communities.

Second, the psalmist speaks of enemies, asking God not to let the enemies "exult over" the psalmist (v. 2) and to "let them be ashamed who are wantonly treacherous" (v. 3). We get an impression that these enemies seek to harm

---

1. "Hope," *Merriam-Webster Online Dictionary* 2010, Merriam-Webster Online; http://www.merriam-webster.com/dictionary/hope (accessed February 27, 2010).

the psalmist. In the broader scheme, who or what are the enemies of justice? This question is not just about ill-meaning individuals but about attitudes, systems, and "isms" that threaten justice and peace. Greed, abuse of power, elitism, oppression, poverty, fear, actual or threatened violence, concern for oneself or one's own community over the well-being of others—all of these are enemies of authentic justice. But the psalmist lists the attitudes and characteristics that *do* make for authentic justice: humility (vv. 8–9), mercy, love, goodness (vv. 6–7), and faithfulness (v. 10). These are the things of God and therefore make for genuine social justice.

1 Peter 3:18–22

The Epistle reading carries us back to the Hebrew Scripture's reading about the flood. Whereas God once used water to blot out the evil and wickedness in the world, now water is sign and symbol of God's grace; it is the life-giving stuff of baptism, the water that "now saves you" (v. 21). Hope continues to abound through today's readings!

However, these verses from 1 Peter also take us in a new direction in asserting Christ as the example to be followed: Christ who "suffered for sins once for all, the righteous for the unrighteous, in order to bring you to God" (v. 18). The meaning of this notion becomes clearer when we take into consideration the verse prior to it: "For it is better to suffer for doing good, if suffering should be God's will, than to suffer for doing evil" (v. 17). Christ, the righteous, did good for us, the unrighteous, in suffering for our salvation; the call is clear for those who follow Christ to do the right thing despite the possibility of suffering.

It can be tremendously difficult to choose the good. When we choose the good of acting justly—which includes aligning ourselves with those who suffer at the hands of the enemies of justice and otherwise standing up for what is good and right—we ourselves may suffer as the victims of injustice. Some of history's great heroes of social justice—Martin Luther King Jr., Archbishop Oscar Romero, Mohandas Gandhi—knew this all too well.

Jesus too knew this. The Epistle says that Jesus suffered for the sins of the unrighteous. His suffering to bring about salvation was at the hands of the very "authorities and powers" who were "subject to him" (v. 22). How can this be? How can Jesus be in charge of the very systems that crucified him? In his book *The Powers That Be: Theology for a New Millennium*, Walter Wink addresses this situation poetically:

> Jesus died like all the others who have challenged the world-dominating Powers. Something went awry in Jesus' case, however.

The Powers scourged him with whips, but each stroke of the lash unveiled their own illegitimacy. They mocked him with a robe and a crown of thorns, spitting on him and striking him on the head with a reed, ridiculing him with the ironic ovation, "Hail, King of the Jews!"—not knowing how their acclamation would echo down the centuries. They stripped him naked and crucified him in humiliation, all unaware that this very act had stripped the Powers of the last covering that disguised the towering wrongness of the whole way of life that their violence defended. They nailed him to a cross, not realizing that with each hammer's blow they were nailing up, for the whole world to see, the affidavit by which the Domination System would be condemned (Col. 2:13–15).[2]

Through being resurrected, "made alive in the spirit," Christ exercises power over these unjust authorities and powers "in order to bring [us] to God" (v. 18). Thus, in overcoming death, Christ achieves for us the salvation that we cannot achieve for ourselves and shows the "authorities and powers" that Christ's reign is one of goodness, righteousness, and justice.

Mark 1:9–15

Today's Gospel reading picks up on the Epistle reading's mention of baptism by iterating the story of Jesus' own baptism. As Mark describes it, Jesus descends into the water to be baptized by John and, after Jesus comes out of the water, the Spirit of God alights "like a dove" on him. The "voice from heaven" confirms Jesus' identity as the "Son" and the "Beloved" and says of Jesus, "With you I am well pleased" (v. 11). Then follows Jesus' temptation by Satan in the wilderness, of which Mark tells us almost nothing (vv. 12–13). Finally, we find Jesus coming to Galilee and "proclaiming the good news of God" and preaching about the realm of God (vv. 14–15).

Mark is reticent to fill in what this "good news" is, other than to link it to the nearness of the rule of God. Within American culture, too many Christians tend to think the good news is limited to the gift of individual salvation and eternal life. While salvation is part of the story, the good news extends beyond such a me-based interpretation to include the social world of the realm of God. The Gospel according to Luke puts the same theme more vividly. In Luke's rendering of the inauguration of Jesus' ministry, Jesus stands in the synagogue to read from the scroll of Isaiah and says that he has been anointed to "bring good news to the poor," "proclaim release to the captives" and "sight to the blind," and to "let the oppressed go free" (Luke 4:18).

---

2. Walter Wink, *The Powers That Be: Theology for a New Millennium* (New York: Random House, 1998), 82–83.

These are the signs that the realm of God is present, and for Mark that *is* the good news: "The time is fulfilled, and the [realm] of God has come near" (v. 15). Evidence of God's sovereignty is, in some ways, already present. Where there is justice and peace, there is the realm of God. Where those who suffer in poverty are made glad, where people are liberated and captivity to injustice ends, where new vision is given to those who have never experienced freedom from oppression—there is the realm of God in the here and now. The faithful still wait in hope and expectation for the reign of God to be *fully* present, that is, for there to exist pure and unadulterated freedom, peace, justice, and harmony. Until that time, the community can point to such sign-posts of an alternative way of life and say, "There it is."

Here, again, is hope! In preaching the "good news," Jesus preaches hope. The good news is not only the salvation available to those who accept the free gift, but the promise of something new and different *in this life* for those who are most victimized by systems of injustice and oppression. The Christian community is called to this social dimension of the good news; the call to work for justice is thus a way of participating in our own salvation. In working for justice *now* and in our present context—in helping to bring the "good news" to those who need it—we point with hope to the coming reign of Jesus.

Second Sunday in Lent

Alejandro F. Botta

GENESIS 17:1–7, 15–16
PSALM 22:23–31
ROMANS 4:13–25
MARK 8:31–38

The texts for this week emphasize several core theological topics in the Bible: the promise to Abraham and how Gentiles benefit from it, the hope for the realm of God to be established on earth, and the faith and trust of the community of believers in God's promise. Either directly or indirectly, each text calls today's community to a life of justice.

Genesis 17:1–7, 15–16

Genesis 17 describes the P (Priestly) version of the covenant between God and Abraham (of which the J [Yahwist] version appears in Gen. 15). The covenant that God establishes with Abram in Genesis 17 has several preconditions: being "blameless" (v. 1); a commitment on God's part to make Abram the ancestor of a multitude of nations; the promise of the land ("all the land of Canaan, for a perpetual holding," v. 8); a sign: circumcision (vv. 10–11); and the promise of a continuous relationship between God and Abraham's descendants (v. 7). Although the J account of the covenant between God and Abraham (Gen. 15) did not include Sarah in the process, the P account makes her an essential component of God's promise.

Abram is required to *hitthallek lephanay* (NRSV: "walk before me," v. 1). This expression is also used in many other places.[1] The reflexive meaning of the Hebrew verb is better conveyed in English by "to walk about," "to behave," that is, "to conduct yourself before me." A more accurate translation

---

1. Gen. 17:1; 24:40; 48:15; 1 Sam. 2:30, 35; 2 Kgs. 20:3; Isa. 38:3; Ezek. 28:14; Pss. 56:13; 116:9.

is provided by JPS, "walk in my ways," which fits the following command: "be blameless." Being blameless before God is an achievable goal in the Hebrew Bible; there is no such thing as "original sin" anywhere in the Hebrew Scriptures. Genesis 6:9 tells us that Noah was blameless before God (even when he was caught naked under the influence, Gen. 9:21). In the book of Job, God states in very clear terms that Job was blameless (Job 1:8; 2:3).

Abraham is to walk in God's ways, to live a blameless life, to recognize the covenant, the promise, the blessing of a numerous and prosperous progeny (Gen. 12:2; 13:16; 15:5; 18:18) and the land in which they will live (Gen. 12:1, 7; 13:14, 15, 17; 15:18–21; 17:8). To behave in a blameless way before God is "to know God." In the Hebrew Bible "to know" God is practically the same as to fear God (1 Kgs. 8:43; Ps. 119:79; Prov. 1:7; Isa. 11:2; et passim), to serve God (1 Chr. 28:9), to believe in God (Isa. 43:10), to trust God (Ps. 9:10), and to cleave to God (Ps. 91:14). The most positive definition of the knowledge of God is clearly stated in Jeremiah 22:15–16 and relates directly to the core theme of these commentaries. Speaking to Shallum, the son of Josiah, the prophet declares: "Your father ate and drank and dispensed justice and equity—Then all went well with him. He upheld the rights of the poor and needy—Then all was well. That is truly knowing me—declares the Lord" (JPS). To promote justice and equity, to uphold the rights of the poor and the needy: that is the key element of the life of those who know God, of those who walk blameless in God's ways.

Contrary to common opinion, an "everlasting covenant" (Heb.: *berit 'olam*) in the Hebrew Bible is not a covenant that lasts forever but a covenant that is not a priori limited by time, whose blessing and continuity are indeed limited by the *behavior* of the parties or, at least, when we are dealing with a covenant between a human and a deity, by the behavior of the human party.[2] As Isaiah states: "The earth lies polluted under its inhabitants; for they have transgressed laws, violated the statutes, broken the everlasting covenant" (Isa. 24:5). This is perhaps the core component of any covenantal relationship with God and the one that communities of faith seem to forget very easily. To stay in the covenantal relationship, both Abraham and the communities of faith that trace their origins to him should walk in God's ways and be blameless before God. To be blameless includes acting justly for all members of the community.

Psalm 22:23–31

Psalm 22 is an individual complaint that also includes expressions of confidence, petition, and thanksgiving. The lectionary reading omits the first

---

2. For a different perspective, see http://www.theonion.com/articles/israelites-sue-god-for -breach-of-covenant,423/ (accessed May 7, 2010).

section (vv. 1–22), which deals with the distress of the psalmist facing abandonment by God. We cannot forget that verses 1–22 have been appropriated by the writers of the New Testament to describe the experience of Jesus (cf. 22:1 with Matt. 27:46; 22:7 with Matt. 27:39; 22:8 with Matt. 27:43; 22:15 with Matt. 27:48; 22:16 and 22:18 with Matt. 27:35). "My God, my God, why have you forsaken me?" were the words of Jesus on the cross. The statement has fueled theological debates for millennia, but its deepest meaning is to refute the mythological hopes of external divine intervention in human affairs. Writing from his prison cell, less than a year before being executed by the Nazis, the German pastor and theologian Dietrich Bonhoeffer reflected:

> We cannot be honest unless we recognize that we have to live in the world *etsi deus non daretur* [even if there were no God]. And this is just what we do recognize—before God! God . . . compels us to recognize it. So our coming of age leads us to a true recognition of our situation before God. God would have us know that we must live as [people] who manage our lives without him. The God who is with us is the God who forsakes us (Mark 15:34). The God who lets us live in the world without the working hypothesis of God is the God before whom we stand continually. Before God and with God we live without God.[3]

The implications might be, sometimes, unbearable. But we should bear them: for our sake, for the sake of God, and for the sake of our human species. The dominion of God that is described and hoped for in verses 23–31 will not come as a result of external divine intervention, but by divine inspiration put to work in our quest and struggles for peace and justice. A world where the afflicted are not despised (v. 24) and where "the poor shall eat and be satisfied" (v. 26) and deliverance will be declared even to the people yet unborn (v. 31) is at hand.

Romans 4:13–25

The letter to the Romans is one of the most important documents for our understanding of Paul's theology. Paul's understanding of the role of Israel's Torah for Israel and for the emerging community of Gentile believers is still a debated issue.[4] Was Paul proclaiming that because the messianic era had begun, the Torah was no longer valid? The Babylonian Talmud (*Sanhedrin* 97a) quotes Eliyyahu, who taught that "The world is to exist six thousand years. In the first two thousand there was desolation; two thousand years the Torah flourished;

---

3. Letter to Eberhard Bethge, July 16, 1944; in Dietrich Bonhoeffer, *Letters and Papers from Prison*, ed. E. Bethge (New York: Macmillan, and London: SCM Press, 1971), 359–61.
4. See John Gager, "Paul's Contradictions: Can They Be Resolved?" *Bible Review* 14 (1998): 32–38.

and the next two thousand years is the Messianic era."[5] Was Paul following a similar line of Jewish theology? Was Paul proclaiming that Torah was the salvation for Israel and the gospel the salvation for the *goyyim* (the Gentiles)?

According to Paul, those whom God promised will inherit the world to come are not only the adherents of the law, but also those who share the faith of Abraham (v. 16). Let us emphasize this: Paul, the Jew, is not in any way suggesting that God has disinherited the Jewish people, but that there is another way to benefit from the promise. Paul states in clear terms that by no means has God rejected the Jewish people (Rom. 11:1)—and that the advantage of the Jews, including circumcision, is "much in every way" (Rom. 3:1–2). "The law is holy, and the commandment is holy and just and good" (Rom. 7:12). Paul emphasizes that his notion of faith does not overthrow the law in any way; "on the contrary, we uphold the law" (Rom. 3:31).

But, in addition to adhering to the Torah (as do the Jewish people), one can inherit the promise also by faith (the way for Gentiles), that is, being faithful as Abraham was and trusting in God's promise. "God shows God's righteousness, faithfulness to the promise, in a new act, apart from the Sinai covenant but not contradictory to it (Rom. 3:21)."[6] In this new way, Paul proclaims, the promise to Abraham is fulfilled (Gen. 17).

This reading of Paul has an important justice implication, for Christians have often claimed that faith in Jesus has superseded Torah, and that Christianity has replaced Judaism. These attitudes early developed into anti-Judaism and ultimately anti-Semitism,[7] which led to the continuous persecution and oppression of Jews in Christian nations and the murder of 6,000,000 Jewish people by the Nazis in World War II. The wild olive shoot that was grafted onto the olive tree to share its rich root has become so arrogant as to forget that "it is not you that support the root but the root that supports you" (Rom. 11:18).

Mark 8:31–38

The words that the author of the Gospel attributed to Jesus reflected the beliefs of the early Jesus movement. They asserted Jesus' death and resurrection as fulfilling the Scriptures, as Paul proclaimed in 1 Corinthians 15:3–5. The expression "son of man" is used in the Hebrew Bible both to refer in general to the human condition (NRSV "mortal"; Job 25:4–6; Ps. 8:3–6), but

5. See Leo Baeck, "The Faith of Paul," in his *Judaism and Christianity* (Philadelphia: Jewish Publication Society, 1960), 139–68.

6. Lloyd Gaston, *Paul and the Torah* (Vancouver: University of British Columbia Press, 1987), 32.

7. The term "anti-Semitism," coined by Wilhelm Marr in 1879, was aimed *only* against Jewish people. He founded the Antisemiten-Liga (Antisemitic League) and advocated the removal of all the Jews from Germany.

also in reference to an apocalyptic figure that would come to rule the Jewish people and the earth (Dan. 7:13–14). In my view, in the authentic sayings of Jesus, the reference to the apocalyptic "Son of man" should be understood not as a self-reference but as pointing to a different figure. The book of *Enoch* (considered canonical by the Orthodox Church and sometimes known as *1 Enoch*) proclaimed that "the sum of judgment was given unto the son of man, and he caused the sinners to pass away and be destroyed from off the face of the earth" (*Enoch* 69:27).

The Gospel of Mark clearly proclaimed, in the words of Jesus, that the coming of the son of man to establish God's rule on earth was going to happen soon, during the lifetime of some of the believers (9:1). The setting of this passage in Mark is found in the early persecution suffered by the early Jesus movement. The hope of that eschatological irruption fed their faithfulness. Mark's generation passed and no eschatological event took place, and—it is time to come to terms with this fact—it never will. What is going to empower contemporary faith communities today in a similar powerful way?

Faith communities in the Western world today are faced with very different challenges from those of the early Jesus movement. Poverty, persecutions, and marginality have been replaced by social acceptance, political power, and affluence. Practically speaking, only a few expect a figure like the "son of man" to appear in the sky accompanied by angels to impose God's rule on earth. What kind of hope, based on the biblical tradition, can we articulate today to feed the faithfulness of contemporary communities of faith?

God's imperial control on earth is an image anchored in monarchic and imperial understandings of government. However, even though monarchs and emperors are not heads of many states in the West, imperialism (in its European, Middle Eastern, or Far Eastern expressions) is still a reality in our world. How does the hope for God's imperium challenge the non–godly imperialistic aspirations of today's national and multinational world powers? What is our role in the revitalization of the biblical hope for justice and equality embedded in the biblical concept of the "realm of God"?

Rabbi Robert Levine wrote in the provocative book *There Is No Messiah and You Are It,*

> We realize that no one is going to come along and hand us truth, justice. We get that only in comics and in the movies, not in the real world. The real world is a messy, complicated place, where there are many hard questions, no easy answers, and lots of work to do. But inside of all of us there is the capacity to live up to the potential given

to us as human beings created in God's image. . . . We can make the world a better place. Bring the dream of redemption a little closer.[8]

If that dream of redemption, of justice, is not the dream of the communities of faith . . . they are "no longer good for anything" (Matt. 5:13).

---

8. Robert N. Levine, *There Is No Messiah and You Are It: The Stunning Transformation of Judaism's Most Provocative Idea* (Woodstock, VT: Jewish Lights, 2003), 166–67.

International Women's Day (March 8)

Dawn Ottoni-Wilhelm

EXODUS 4:21–26
PSALM 78:1–4
1 CORINTHIANS 14:1–12
LUKE 2:36–38

This Holy Day for Justice recognizes the extraordinary acts of courage and determination by ordinary women around the world. In 1908, National Women's Day was established in honor of the garment workers' strike in New York. Thereafter, women in the United States and Europe held rallies to express solidarity with other activists and the Russian women's peace movement during World War I. International Women's Day was first celebrated by the United Nations in 1975 and has continued its global connections. In worship and daily living, Christians are called to greater support of women's rights and their full participation in political and economic arenas of life.

> As truly as God is our Father, so truly is God our Mother, and God revealed that in everything. . . . I understand three ways of contemplating motherhood in God. The first is the foundation of our nature's creation; the second is his taking of our nature, where the motherhood of grace begins; and the third is the motherhood at work. . . . The mother can give her child to suck of her milk, but our precious Mother Jesus can feed us with himself . . . with the blessed sacrament, which is the precious food of true life.[1]
>
> *Julian of Norwich*

It can be difficult to discern the voices of women in Scripture but they are there, moving in, through, and beyond the written text. It is important that

---

1. Quoted in Joan Chittister, *A Passion for Life: Fragments of the Face of God* (Maryknoll, NY: Orbis Books, 2001), 99.

people of faith learn to listen to and speak in support of women whose voices have been silenced, denied, or ignored by the church and world. It is also essential that women hear themselves speak, and that they do so know-ing that God—the source of life and giver of voice to all creation—speaks through them.

All of the texts for this holy day have to do with speaking. Two of them, Exodus 4:21–26 and Luke 2:36–38, record the names and voices of women who encounter the powerful presence of God and speak out of their experi-ences. Their words and deeds proclaim anew God's life-giving intentions for themselves, their kindred, and others. For these women, to give voice is to give life: Zipporah's words and actions avert God's will to kill Moses; Anna sees the baby Jesus, praises God, and proclaims God's redemptive purposes at work through him. Both of these women embody what Psalm 78:1–4 and 1 Corinthians 14:1–12 tell us: the importance of announcing God's activities and purposes among us, and that women do so with clarity and the courage of their convictions. In word and deed, women participate in the fulfillment of God's promises by pronouncing them anew.

Exodus 4:21–26

The passage from the Torah designated for this holy day includes two parts. In the first, 4:21–23, God directs Moses to confront Pharaoh, demand that the Israelites be freed, and perform various wonders that demonstrate God's resolve. However, Moses is told not to expect a favorable outcome: God will harden Pharaoh's heart, and Pharaoh will refuse to free the Hebrew slaves. God alone speaks; Moses is a passive recipient of divine instructions and the terrifying announcement that God intends to kill Pharaoh's firstborn son. The horror of impending events may distract us from noticing that familial language is used to describe God's relationship to Israel, God's "firstborn son." God is both father and mother to the people of Israel, who are the privi-leged heirs of divine promises.

The second part, 4:24–26, includes one of the most enigmatic and trouble-some episodes in the Exodus account. It is also among the most remarkable, as Zipporah acts and speaks decisively to save Moses' life. Like the midwives who refused to kill the newborn sons of their kinswomen, Moses' mother who set him afloat on the Nile, the maid who retrieved him, and the Egyptian princess who created a safe haven for him, Zipporah is one of many women who are vigorous and assertive in acting to save Moses' life. But whereas the others protected Moses from Pharaoh, Zipporah saves him from God. Ear-lier, God assured Moses that those seeking his life were dead (4:19), but now God is on the attack.

The text does not tell us God's motives. But Zipporah, as wife and mother, is not interested in a theological argument. Her actions are swift and her words definitive. She takes a stone flint and cuts off her son's foreskin. The expression "bridegroom of blood" is puzzling; neither is it clear to whom it refers or at whose feet she places the bloody tissue. While Moses neither speaks nor acts, Zipporah responds boldly in word and deed. Unlike her spouse, who earlier voiced his fears and weighed his inadequacies (Exod. 3:11, 13; 4:1, 10), Zipporah has no such opportunity and does not ask for one. She protects her loved ones through the ritual of circumcision, pronouncing Moses' new relationship to her as "a bridegroom of blood by circumcision" (v. 26).

As is the case with many other women in the Bible, we know little about Zipporah. She endures separation from her husband (Exod. 18:2), and her life-saving role is noted only briefly in Scripture. Her name, which means "bird," reminds us of eagles and hawks, who are ferocious in protecting their own. Like many other women who endure hardship, dislocation, and little recognition, Zipporah is somehow able to reach beyond her circumstances. What enables women like Zipporah to speak and act as she did? In her commentary on this passage, Tikva-Frymer Kensky speaks of the "habitual disempowerment" of women who have "learned the skills of indirection, wits, and deception—skills well adapted to conditions of subjugation."[2]

In addition to these skills, women have also known the importance of following personal imperatives for the sake of those they love. This includes speaking on behalf of women who are irrevocably beaten down, denied opportunities to speak, and have little means of securing their own safety or the well-being of loved ones. In Yabelo, Ethiopia, a woman named Godana broke tribal tradition by attending the meeting of male elders and courageously speaking of topics that had long been neglected: reproductive health, family planning, and HIV/AIDS prevention. As the mother of nine children, she insisted that the all-male council consider the injustices suffered by the women in their tribe. Godana spoke of the importance of educating young women, not only for their own sake, but to improve the lives of those around them.[3] Her story, like Zipporah's, encourages women to speak and act in life-giving ways as they seek the well-being of all God's children.

---

2. Tikva Frymer-Kensky, *Reading the Women of the Bible* (New York: Schocken Books, 2002), 32–33.
3. Phil Borges, *Women Empowered: Inspiring Change in the Emerging World* (New York: Rizzoli Books, 2007), 73–75.

Psalm 78:1–4

If women like Zipporah and Godana have stories to tell, the psalmist urges us to tell them—and many other stories as well.

This festival psalm (and others, such as Pss. 105, 106, 135, 136) is intended for public recitation in worship. Its historical focus lends itself to teaching (v. 1), but it has an even more distinctive function. Psalm 78 is an extended parable (*mashal*) that includes riddles (*hidot*, translated as "dark sayings" in the NRSV, v. 2). Israel's past deeds of faithlessness are recounted, and God's extraordinary acts of mercy are remembered. As the opening verses indicate, there are stories worth telling that must not be hidden from our children or the coming generation (v. 4).

The stories we tell of sin and hope, the characters we include or exclude, the songs we sing, the prayers we raise—all of these shape the lives of listeners in powerful ways. When we exclude women's stories, prayers, songs, and voices from worship, we deny God's voice speaking through them. Are women's concerns remembered in public prayers? Do we include the stories of women from other countries and/or ethnic groups in our sermons? What are the "dark sayings" and parables of God's grace and human fortitude that have not been told because they perplex, astonish, or frighten us? What of the old women and young girls, the sex slaves and concubines, those abused by spouses and overlooked by society, women who feed their families with minimum resources, give birth, and sometimes die while doing so?

In *Reading Lolita in Tehran*, Professor Azar Nafisi speaks of gathering seven of her best students to study several forbidden Western novels when fundamentalists seized control of the universities. Her goal was simple: to discuss literature and see how "these great works of imagination could help us in our present trapped situation as women."[4] She also hoped that their encounter with characters in the novels they studied would inspire their own courage. Prior to leaving the University of Tehran, Nafisi led a classroom discussion about the characters in Henry James's novel *The Ambassadors*. In them, "we find several different kinds of courage, but the most courageous characters here are those with imagination, those who, through their imaginative faculty, can empathize with others."[5] To inspire our faithful imagination and the courage needed to envision God's world anew, the stories of women must be told.

---

4. Azar Nafisi, *Reading Lolita in Tehran: A Memoir in Books* (New York: Random House, 2003), 19.
5. Ibid., 249.

Luke 2:36–38

As a prophet, Anna is endowed with God's Spirit. As a widow, she is among those whom Luke upheld as exemplars of faith (see 21:1–4). As a woman of great age, she may, according to biblical scholar Joel Green, be as old as 105 years (married at age 14, plus 7 years of marriage, followed by 84 years as a widow).[6] In addition to earthly endurance, Anna also cultivated divine insight. Beyond noting her ancestral heritage, Luke's description focuses primarily on her piety as someone who worshiped at the temple night and day. Through prayer she regularly communed with God, and through fasting she embodied deep longing for the restoration of her people. When she met Jesus, Anna's prayers and fasting were answered. She could not help but speak of Jesus to all others in search of Jerusalem's redemption.

Given her amazing gifts for recognizing and proclaiming God's mysterious presence, it is extraordinary that Anna's story is scarcely acknowledged during Advent and rarely noted at other times. For that matter, why are older women among us so often ignored and so rarely extolled? Why are they seldom portrayed as positive role models in films or literature?

Well into the sixth decade of her life, Maya Angelou recalled her grandmother, "Mamma." As a single black woman, Mamma tended her crippled son and two grandchildren while managing the general store in Stamps, Arkansas, during the Great Depression. One of Angelou's earliest memories of Mamma was of "a tall cinnamon-colored woman with a deep, soft voice. . . . Mamma drew herself up to her full six feet, clasped her hands behind her back, looked up into a distant sky, and said, 'I will step out on the word of God.'"[7] Visualizing her grandmother "flung into space, moons at her feet and stars at her head, comets swirling around her," Angelou "grew up knowing that the word of God had power." Her grandmother's life bore the fruit of countless decisions and courageous actions reflecting spiritual insight and the farsightedness of love. Like Anna, such seasoned sisters of faith help us to recognize God's presence in the world and to proclaim this marvelous gift to others.

1 Corinthians 14:1–12

Any woman who has been interrupted during discussions or denied the opportunity to speak in public knows that speech can either build up or tear down; both speaking and limiting speech can be sources of blessing to many

---

6. Joel B. Green, *The Gospel of Luke*, New International Commentary on the New Testament (Grand Rapids: Eerdmans, 1997), 151.
7. Maya Angelou, *Wouldn't Take Nothing for My Journey Now* (New York: Bantam Books, 1994), 73–74.

or means of control by a few. Beneath Paul's advice to the congregation in 1 Corinthians 14 is his underlying concern that, while speaking in tongues may edify one person who speaks, it does little to better all who are listening. Instead, he prefers the gift of prophecy, because it is intended to upbuild, encourage, and console the entire community (vv. 3–4). However, what Paul does *not* say in these verses is even more amazing than what he says: there is no indication that the gift of prophecy—that is, the public edification of the community through divinely inspired speech—is limited to men or subject to hierarchical approval. When these verses are taken alongside Paul's other letters, it is evident that women played an active role in leading, preaching, teaching, and prophesying in the early church (e.g., Phoebe and Prisca in Rom. 16:1–4; Junia in Rom. 16:7; Euodia and Syntyche in Phil. 4:2–3). For this and other reasons, the troublesome admonition in 1 Corinthians 14:34–35 for women to be silent in the churches is believed by many scholars to be a later interpolation by subsequent Christians, reflecting tension in the early church about the role of women in bearing public witness to the gospel.[8] This later addition to the text stands in marked contrast to Paul's overarching concern to upbuild the church by recognizing the gifts and participation of all members. Through words of encouragement and consolation, all God's people are called to minister to others.

Studies of women's ways of speaking (including those related to women's preaching) have long identified patterns of relationality in women's communication. Women more often than men speak in terms of "we" rather than "I"; they are more likely to name connections between people rather than differences that divide; women's frequent use of personal stories and self-disclosure is more likely to invite others into a shared sense of common experience than to highlight any one woman's exceptional accomplishments. In her book *The Power to Speak: Feminism, Language, God*, Rebecca Chopp speaks of the solidarity (i.e., the linguistic equivalent to values and norms) that guides feminist discourse.[9] Because many churches deny the ordination of women and many others resist listening to women's stories and their vocal ministry, it is time to listen anew to women like Zipporah, Anna, and other prophets who speak God-given words for the sake of the church and world.

8. See Elisabeth Schüssler Fiorenza, *In Memory of Her: A Feminist Theological Reconstruction of Christian Origins* (New York: Crossroad, 1983), 160–84.

9. Rebecca Chopp, *The Power to Speak: Feminism, Language, God* (Eugene, OR: Wipf & Stock, 2002), 35.

Third Sunday in Lent

Nyasha Junior

EXODUS 20:1–17
PSALM 19
1 CORINTHIANS 1:18–25
JOHN 2:13–22

Dum-dum. That familiar sound heralds the start of another *Law and Order* episode and tells me to hurry and get comfortable on the couch. I have seen nearly all of the episodes of the original series, and usually I can identify the episode by simply watching the opening scene. I enjoy courtroom drama and the provocative questions that it raises about the criminal justice system, including its laws and its enforcement. Like *Law and Order*, this week's lectionary texts offer us the opportunity to reflect on the law and living according to the law. The Ten Commandments are part of the law, and Psalm 19 celebrates the law. John 2:13–22 raises questions regarding the observance of the law. The law is equated with wisdom (*chokma*) in Jewish tradition (Sir. 24:23–34), and 1 Corinthians contrasts human wisdom and the wisdom of God.

Because the notion of law plays a central role in these readings, it is important to remember that the Hebrew word *torah*, which is usually translated as "law," is more accurately rendered "instruction." In Judaism, a law is not simply a legal statute to regulate behavior but a guide for life.

Exodus 20:1–17

This reading is usually called the Ten Commandments or the Decalogue (Gk. *deka logoi*, Eng. "ten words"). Similar texts appear at Deuteronomy 5:6–21 and Exodus 34:11–27. Yet the term "ten commandments," or more precisely, "ten words" (Heb. *'aseret haddebarim*) appears only in Exodus 34:28 and Deuteronomy 4:13. While Christians focus on the Ten Commandments, within

146

Jewish tradition there are not simply 10 commandments, but 613 *mitzvot* or commandments, including 248 positive commandments and 365 negative ones. While Christians rightly see the Ten Commandments as important to Judaism, it is important to remember that they are only part of Torah. In addition to specific guidelines, Torah is intended to form patterns of respect and relationship that can shape all of life.

In 2001, Roy Moore, chief justice of the Alabama Supreme Court, sparked a huge controversy when he installed a monument to the Ten Commandments at the State Judicial Building in Montgomery, Alabama. Previously, he had put up a smaller wooden plaque of the Ten Commandments in his courtroom. The new granite monument weighed more than two tons. Eventually, Moore was removed from office, and the monument was removed from the building. During this controversy, passionate crowds gathered to support Moore and what they regarded as a tribute to America's fundamental values. Many others objected to Moore's action, and the controversy ignited a national discussion regarding religion and public life in the United States.

As in the case of Justice Moore, Christians sometimes elevate the Ten Commandments above other laws in the Old Testament and treat them as a summation of Old Testament law. The Ten Commandments are printed on T-shirts and plaques or even tattooed on skin. Yet, within Exodus, this text is not set apart from other legal texts. Selective emphasis on these laws points to a "canon within a canon" perspective, in which particular texts within the canon are elevated above others. While *Law and Order* wraps up neatly in one-hour episodes, something as complex as the anthology that is called the Bible cannot be reduced to one simple list.

The commandments provide instruction regarding relationships with God, family, and other people. The covenant relationship between God and God's people undergirds the law. Jewish tradition emphasizes the importance of this exclusive relationship by treating Exodus 20:1–2 as the First Commandment and separating it from the prohibitions against polytheism and idolatry. God declares, "I am the LORD your God, who brought you out of the land of Egypt, out of the house of slavery." Thus, recognizing God as God is the first step in following the commandments. Also, the commandments emphasize the importance of our relationships to other people and provide guidance on how to live together in community. Deuteronomy 5:14 accentuates this notion by extending the observation of the Sabbath to resident aliens, slaves, and livestock. It reminds the Israelites of their enslavement and deliverance from Egypt and requires them to include others in Sabbath rest.

Psalm 19

In 1927, African American scholar and writer James Weldon Johnson published a book of poetry, *God's Trombones: Seven Negro Sermons in Verse*. Here is the first stanza of one of the most famous poems, "The Creation":

> God stepped out on space,
> And he looked around and said,
> "I'm lonely—
> I'll make me a world."[1]

For Johnson, God's loneliness serves as the catalyst for the creation of the universe.

In Psalm 19, God's creation speaks back in praise to God. The first section of the psalm, verses 1–6, is a hymn to God as creator. This part of the psalm reflects an ancient cosmology in which a dome (*rāqîa*) or "firmament" holds back the water in the sky. This barrier divides the sky and the waters above the sky. In the creation story, God creates this dome on the second day (Gen. 1:6–8).

The second section of the psalm, verse 7–14, praises God for the revelation of the law. This psalm connects with Exodus 20 through its emphasis on the law. The psalm praises the law and then includes warnings regarding the importance of keeping the law. This law is not the same as the legal statutes of the American legal system. Instead, it is more desirable than gold and sweeter than honey (v. 10). The law of the Lord is a life-giving gift.

Verse 14 closes the psalm with a petition to the Lord to accept the "words of my mouth and the meditation of my heart." Many preachers recite verse 14 before delivering a sermon (cf. Ps. 104:34), but in its immediate literary context, the psalmist's petition is linked to the verses immediately preceding, in which the psalmist desires to be "blameless" and "innocent of great transgression" (v. 13). Jewish tradition includes recitation of this verse at the conclusion of the Amidah (also known as the Eighteen Benedictions or Shemoneh Esreh), a Jewish daily prayer.

1 Corinthians 1:18–25

In his first letter to the church at Corinth, Paul stresses the importance of not relying on human wisdom but, instead, relying on divine wisdom. He constructs a series of contrasting parallels to illustrate the simple message of faith.

---

1. James Weldon Johnson, *God's Trombones: Seven Negro Sermons in Verse* (New York: Penguin Books, 1990), 17.

In verse 19, he quotes Isaiah 29:14: "I will destroy the wisdom of the wise, and the discernment of the discerning I will thwart." While Isaiah is speaking to the Judeans, Paul is addressing those who do not accept the "message about the cross" (v. 18). Those who accept it are being saved, while those who do not are "perishing." Those who believe are saved simply through grace.

Paul is not arguing against clear thinking. As is evident from the subsequent verses, he is against the elitism of the "powerful" and those of "of noble birth" (1:26). Yet texts like this are often used to promote anti-intellectualism. As a divinity school professor, I spend most of my time trying to convince my students that God would not have given them brains if She/He did not want them to use them. The home pastors of the students, Bible study teachers, and others have told them that matters of faith are not to be questioned. Many of my students are bivocational, older students. Despite their educations and the significant accomplishments in their lives and careers, when it comes to matters of faith, some have accepted being silenced. They were told, "Just believe!" Some of my students become angry when they learn more about the historical and literary context of biblical texts. They feel that their seminary-educated pastors have been keeping this knowledge from congregants, as if the knowledge were a secret. Some pastors practice a type of paternalistic elitism in not sharing their knowledge of biblical scholarship.

Paul is calling for humans not to use human wisdom against each other. His message encourages belief, but not at the expense of education or critical thinking. "Just believe" is a wonderful summary of how to respond to the gospel of Jesus Christ and the gift of Christianity. No prerequisites. No entrance exam. No literacy test. No physical examination. No admission fee. No blood test. "Just believe!" Nevertheless, this message becomes distorted when it is used to support an abuse of power. "Just believe what I say" is not Paul's message. Moving toward transformative ministry involves not shutting down minds but opening hearts to receiving this deceptively simple message of belief.

We must be able to think critically in order to discover how biblical texts may be appropriated for contemporary social situations. For example, New Testament scholar Mary Ann Tolbert relates a classroom experience in which an African American male pastor argued that the household codes in Colossians 3–4 were not relevant to contemporary society, while at the same time interpreting Genesis 2–3 as supporting women's subordination.[2] Biblical texts can be used for social transformation, but such use requires critical engagement with the text.

2. Mary Ann Tolbert, "A New Teaching with Authority: A Re-evaluation of the Authority of the Bible," in *Teaching the Bible: The Discourses and Politics of Biblical Pedagogy*, ed. Fernando F. Segovia and Mary Ann Tolbert (Maryknoll, NY: Orbis Books, 1998), 189 n40.

John 2:13–22

"Jesus Flips Out!" "Jesus Loses It!" "Jesus Blows a Gasket!" These could all be subheadings for this week's lectionary Gospel text, John 2:13–22, and all of them would be much more appropriate than its typical heading, "Jesus Cleanses the Temple." This episode appears in all four Gospels (cf. Matt. 21:12–17; Mark 11:15–19; Luke 19:45–48), and "cleansing" does not appear in any of them. Unfortunately, the notion of cleansing can be used to support anti-Jewish sentiments.[3] In fact, the text does not explicitly define what it is that offends Jesus.

In the Synoptic Gospels, Jesus seems to be concerned with the lack of respect that some show for the temple as a place of worship. John's account is more dramatic than the others, with Jesus making a "whip of cords" and driving out the money changers, along with the sheep and the cattle (v. 15). Also, Jesus exclaims, "Take these things out of here! Stop making my Father's house a marketplace!" (v. 16). Because these animals were needed for sacrifice, the temple merchants were providing a needed service and probably would not have regarded their behavior as inappropriate. In any event, the Johannine Jesus finds the current conditions unacceptable, and this prompts a question for the preacher today: What are the current conditions in our lives, our congregations, or our communities that we should find unacceptable?

In a 1962 article, "As Much Truth as One Can Bear," James Baldwin contends that the writer is the instrument of change. He writes, "Not everything that can be faced can be changed; but nothing can be changed until it is faced."[4] Baldwin also explains, "Societies are never able to examine, to overhaul themselves: this effort must be made by that yeast which every society cunningly and unfailingly secretes. This ferment, this disturbance is the responsibility, and the necessity of writers."[5] In what ways can contemporary faith communities be part of the force that works to face issues, if not to change them? For Baldwin, the writer is the solution. Can churches also be part of the solution? Jesus' actions in the temple got attention. Like the writer described by Baldwin, Jesus helps people to face the things that they may prefer not to face.

---

3. On anti-Judaism, see *Jesus, Judaism, and Christian Anti-Judaism: Reading the New Testament after the Holocaust*, ed. Paula Fredriksen and Adele Reinhartz (Louisville, KY: Westminster John Knox Press, 2002). For a commentary series from the perspective of combating anti-Judaism, see Ronald J. Allen and Clark M. Williamson, Preaching without Prejudice, *Preaching the Gospels without Blaming the Jews, Preaching the Letters without Dismissing the Law*, and *Preaching the Old Testament* (Louisville, KY: Westminster John Knox Press, 2004, 2006, 2007).

4. James Baldwin, "As Much Truth as One Can Bear," *New York Times Book Review* (January 14, 1962), 38.

5. Ibid.

Salt March Day: Marching with the Poor (March 12)

Rebecca Todd Peters

DEUTERONOMY 15:7–11
PSALM 33
JAMES 5:1–6
LUKE 12:13–21

During their occupation of India, the British had a monopoly on the sale of salt and taxed its purchase. This arrangement burdened the poor. Moreover, Indians viewed the salt tax as a symbol of oppression. On March 12, 1930, Mohandas K. Gandhi (1869–1948) led a march to protest the tax and to call for Indian independence. Such nonviolent resistance in India inspired similar nonviolent civil disobedience in other places (including the civil rights movement in the United States).

> The mystery of the poor is this: that they are Jesus, and what you do for them you do for Him. It is the only way we have of knowing and believing in our love. The mystery of poverty is that by sharing in it, making ourselves poor in giving to others, we increase our knowledge of and belief in love.[1]
>
> *Dorothy Day*

Three texts for today share a common purpose of pressing us toward a proper orientation toward wealth. The Gospel and Letter, in particular, represent some of the most difficult and challenging themes in the Bible for people of privilege and means. For those of us who live in first-world countries and who enjoy remarkable privileges vis-à-vis the majority of the world's population, these texts offer a disquieting message of caution and even judgment. The harsh condemnation of their rhetoric reminds us why prophets are often

---

1. Dorothy Day, "The Mystery of the Poor," *Catholic Worker*, April 1964, as quoted in *Houston Catholic Worker*, vol. 26, no. 3 (May–June 2006).

despised and rejected by their contemporaries, given that prophets' words are often aimed at challenging and dismantling the status quo. The difficulty of disrupting the status quo is often simply the difficulty of calling people away from what they know toward an as-yet-unrealized vision of the possible. Human nature tends toward stasis, and many people are content to accept the "devil that they know" rather than to take the risks necessary to challenge injustice. Making such challenges can be even more difficult when we are implicated as beneficiaries of an unjust economic system. Nevertheless, these texts call us toward Gandhi-like solidarity with the poor in the march toward a world of justice.

Deuteronomy 15:7–11

This text from Deuteronomy is a classic articulation of the principles of social justice in Mosaic law. The author instructs the community, clearly and specifically, in the habits and attitudes that one should practice toward neighbors in need. The admonition to care for your neighbor is broadly defined as "anyone in need among you," including any member of the community in any towns in the land. This is quite a tall order! Imagine if Christians were to take seriously the call of Deuteronomy in our own time. What would it look like if we were to open our hands willingly to meet the needs of our poor neighbors, whoever those may be? Few of us are prepared for the realities of such radical social behavior. Does God really expect us to give liberally *and* to be ungrudging when we do? Wouldn't we all end up bankrupt? What exactly does God expect of us?

This passage is part of the Deuteronomic code compiled over a period of years and "found" in the temple during Josiah's reform. This law code is intended to guide and shape Jewish and Christian expectations about social ethics and political and economic structures. The vision of a just community presented in Deuteronomy 15:7–11 is how the wealthy and privileged *ought* to live; the vision puts forward a positive ethic of compassion and solidarity with our neighbors that envisions justice and righteousness as people share joyfully out of our abundance, because this is what it means to live in covenant relationship with God.

Luke 12:13–21

The behavior of the rich fool in Luke's parable, on the other hand, stands in stark contrast to the social ethic promoted in Deuteronomy. In this parable, we see the behavior of a wealthy landowner (the Gk. *chōra*, "land," v. 16, indicates an extensive estate or even a district) who does not embody the covenant responsibilities of caring for neighbors or sharing the bounty of his good fortune and wealth.[2] In fact, in the midst of an unexpectedly productive harvest, the rich person in this parable is self-obsessed and thinking only in terms of personal well-being and satisfaction.

This parable is striking to modern ears for obvious connections to the contemporary problems of capitalistic greed and the dangers of individualism. The covenantal ethic includes mutual responsibility to one's neighbors and recognition that the abundance of God's creation (as well as our souls!) belongs to God. Eschewing this wisdom, this person exhibits a very twenty-first-century interpretation of his relationship to wealth. The landowner's emphasis on *my* barns, *my* grain, *my* goods, and *my* soul echoes the way in which many contemporary Christians think about possessions: *my* house, *my* car, *my* toys, and *my* salary. Our proprietary orientation toward the material aspects of our lives undermines our ability to live in right relation with God and with our neighbors by reinforcing subtle, but vicious assumptions about our own "deservedness."

As we contemplate how to handle the bounty of our own lives, don't we often respond like the rich person, engaging in our own internal dialogue about what to do with our riches? Rather than heeding Deuteronomy and the broader Jewish social-justice tradition to share with those in need, or following the example of Joseph, who saved the abundant crops to help the people make it through the lean years of the famine, the rich fool can think only in self-serving terms. Ignoring the simplest response to build additional barns to hold his crops, the selfish landowner flaunts success by tearing down the existing barns and replacing them with larger ones that will better reflect (and perhaps enhance) his social status.

The self-centered landowner exemplifies the very life that Jesus warns against when telling the crowd that they must "be on guard against all kinds of greed; for one's life does not consist in the abundance of possessions" (v. 15). Our rich fool is unable to see that the experience of a life well lived must consist of more than relaxation, good food, drink, and merriment.[3]

James 5:1–6

For those made uncomfortable by Luke's parable of the Rich Fool, the words of James offer little succor. Luke highlights the fact that wealth, possessions, and a lack of recognition of our collective well-being as the people of God

2. Bernard Brandon Scott, *Hear Then the Parable: A Commentary on the Parables of Jesus* (Minneapolis: Fortress Press, 1989), 132.
3. See Douglas A. Hicks, *Money Enough* (San Francisco: Jossey-Bass, 2010), 21–33, esp. 24, on this point of the parable and reorienting our values from econocentrism to theocentrism.

can displace an authentic understanding of our own humanity and proper relationship with God. James goes one step further, by intimating both that wealth itself is evidence that testifies against the righteousness of the rich and that possessions will ultimately "eat your flesh like fire" (v. 3, a not-so-veiled reference to the fate of the wealthy in the afterlife).

While this text stands in a long tradition of "prophetic oracles of doom," the immediacy of the language may cut closer to the bone of contemporary Christians than the rhetoric of the First Testament prophets.[4] While Amos's denunciation of the wealthy is just as trenchant as James's, the language of "buying the poor for silver and the needy for a pair of sandals" (Amos 8:6) is somehow easier for many people today to hear than the direct statements from James, who does not mince words. As we read the opening lines of the text, "Come now, you rich people, weep and wail for the miseries that are coming to you," many people in our pews begin to squirm. For even those of us in the first world who count ourselves among the middle class rather than the "rich" recognize our relative wealth in the context of the larger human population. As we consider the fact that the quarter of the world's population who live in the developed world account for 86 percent of total private consumption, our relative wealth as the "rich people" of the world comes into stark relief, making the words of James more and more disquieting.

The Epistle of James, which is largely a collection of moral exhortations, is often classified as Wisdom literature, which has the purpose of instructing communities in the "practical wisdom of right behavior."[5] James's instructions were aimed at helping newly formed and forming Christian communities understand how moral responsibilities ought to shape their behavior and life in the world. In this passage, we see a strong moral indictment of the abusive behavior and lifestyles of the first-century wealthy members of the community who were obsessed with their own possessions (represented by the references to riches, clothes, gold, and silver). Their greed and desire for building up their stores of treasure even caused them to cheat the laborers who worked their fields. Like the rich fool in Luke, the wealthy oppressors in James forgot their right relationship with God and God's call to righteousness and justice, found in Psalm 33, "For the word of [God] is upright, and all [God's] work is done in faithfulness. [God] loves righteousness and justice; the earth is full of the steadfast love of [God]" (Ps. 33:4–5). Not only did the wealthy fail to share with the poor out of their abundance; their wealth was gained through the exploitation and oppression of their workers.

4. Bo Reicke, *The Epistles of James, Peter, and Jude*, Anchor Bible (Garden City, NY: Doubleday, 1964), 50.

5. Luke Timothy Johnson, "The Letter of James," in *The New Interpreter's Bible*, ed. Leander Keck et al. (Nashville: Abingdon Press, 1998), 12:179.

The words of Luke and James, in concert with the life and message of Gandhi, offer a distinct challenge to the consumptive and acquisitive lifestyles of people living in the midst of a system of global capitalism. Consumerism has become our status quo; desire for consumer goods is synonymous with development and, in even more insidious ways, with success. The logos of Coca-Cola, McDonald's, and Nike are ubiquitous, as the globalization of our world economy has opened up consumer markets in the developing world. Sugary soft drinks, fatty foods, and overpriced footwear have become symbols of wealth and success in communities where malnutrition is still a real threat, while the wealth and success of many people in the United States is often measured by ever larger homes (or second homes), luxury cars, and other possessions intended to distract, divert, and entertain. Rather than asking ourselves, "How much is enough?" too many of us share the desire of the rich fool to "relax, eat, drink, [and] be merry" (Luke 12:19).

While the harsh words of the Gospel and Epistle texts may offer a haunting condemnation of contemporary attitudes toward wealth and consumerism, the prophetic tradition is not focused on condemnation as an end in itself. The redemptive message of these texts for our contemporary world lies in the power that they have to hold up a mirror to us and to allow us to examine our participation and complicity in the unjust and unequal distributions of social and economic power in our world. The covenant obligations presented in Deuteronomy are apt guidelines as we consider what it means to "march with the poor" in today's society.

These texts offer an opportunity for those of us who have been socialized into thinking of shopping not only as entertainment but as a patriotic duty, to remember Jesus' call to "Take care!" and to be on guard against greed. These texts challenge us to think differently about wealth and to remember it is not a reward for our behavior, as the concepts of exceptionalism (we are better, smarter, stronger, more qualified, etc., than others, and therefore deserve our rewards) and blessing (God has given this abundance to me as a sign of God's favor) mislead us to believe. Nor should our wealth be seen as a possession that belongs only to us. Like the rest of God's good creation, our wealth comes from God, and we have been invited to share in the abundance of God's bounty. Wealth is a resource that can be used for good or ill. When it is entrusted to any of us, we have a covenant obligation to God and to our neighbor to share what we have with others.

Fourth Sunday in Lent

Randall K. Bush

NUMBERS 21:4–9
PSALM 107:1–3, 17–22
EPHESIANS 2:1–10
JOHN 3:14–21

By exploring one passage each Sunday of the year, preachers can discover how that reading illuminates important themes at the heart of Christian faith. But when we take all four lectionary passages together, they have the possibility to move sequentially into deeper territories of historical perspectives and foundational truth. Such an in-depth comparative study can be critical when seeking to glean messages about justice and social ethics from Scripture.

For the Fourth Sunday in Lent, the Gospel lesson from John speaks about eternal life and judgment, while building upon an illustration from prior material in Numbers 21. Likewise, the Numbers 21 rescue of the people through God's intervention is enhanced by the companion language of Psalm 107, with its vocabulary of God's "steadfast love" enduring forever. Finally, the Ephesians passage brings the conversation back full circle, for now there is a richer context available for discussing what it means to be "dead through trespasses and sins" but alive again, thanks to the great love of God, "who is rich in mercy."

John 3:14–21

In examining this Gospel lesson, it is important to remember two basic guides for sound exegesis. First, just because the passage offers its own interpretative illustration does not mean that this is the only interpretation available to preachers. There would be very meager fare for sermons on the parable of the Sower if preachers could only repeat the verbatim interpretative summaries appended to it in the Synoptic Gospels (Matt. 13:18–23, Mark 4:13–20, Luke

8:11–15). Likewise, linking the serpent in the wilderness event with the Son of Man being "lifted up" was done to provide a historical point of reference for appreciating Christ's passion, not to limit the fullness of Jesus' crucifixion, death, and resurrection to one analogy from the book of Numbers.

Second, abbreviating passages and reading verses in isolation from their context always vastly changes the tone and meaning of the Scripture being cited. For example, the frequent recitation of John 3:16 without the inclusion of verse 17 risks narrowing the focus to one of condemnation instead of salvation. Likewise, reading verse 18 without continuing through verse 21 allows the emphasis to shift to popular-piety understandings of a future day of judgment, instead of hearing how the entire passage offers strong warnings about present ethical behavior and acts of darkness.

The power of John 3:14–21 rests in the inherent message of hope and salvation captured in the phrase "for God so loved the world." Motivated by forgiving love, God provided the healing serpent for the repentant Israelites in the wilderness. From a similar motivation of life-giving love, God acted in Christ, not to condemn the world, but to save the world. John is offering words of solace to a persecuted community, but the comfort is neither for them alone nor restricted to people of the light (especially when defined as baptized congregants in privileged denominations). It is a love for the "world" expressed through an act directed at all the world. Later in John 3, the inclusiveness of this vision is evident in the multiple times Jesus is referred to as the one who "is above all" and in whose hands God "has placed all things" (vv. 31, 35). Thus, it is important not to allow either John's occasional polemics or present-day denominational discord to distract us from the overarching precedent of God's embrace of all people and all creation.

One helpful option in maintaining this broader focus is to recognize that the Greek term used in verse 19 for judgment (*krisis*) is not referring to a point in time when a verdict is handed down by a divine Judge. Rather it describes an ongoing process of judging, in which deeds are continually evaluated as relating to light or relating to darkness, being righteous or being oppressive, sustaining life or diminishing life. Christians are too often prone to see the life of faith as an examination for which we hope to receive a passing grade, rather than as a continuum of daily acts done to glorify and enjoy God forever (see Westminster Shorter Catechism). The message of John's Gospel is that the good news in Christ extends to all and lasts for all our days, a message echoed well by the philosopher Cicero: "While there's life, there's hope."[1]

---

1. Marcus Tullius Cicero, *Letters to Atticus: Books VII–XI*, trans. O. E. Windstedt, Loeb Classical Library (Cambridge: Harvard University Press, 1929), 9.10.4.

Numbers 21:4–9

In most situations of conflict, there is a presenting issue that deflects attention from a deeper issue that is the real source of tension and discord. The Israelites' presenting issue was that they were afraid of starving in the wilderness (v. 5: "There is no food and no water"). But that could not have been a serious concern, because they were being sustained by heaven-sent manna, whether they liked it or not (v. 5 "We detest this miserable food"). The real issue was named in verse 4: "the people became impatient on the way" as they made their detour while traveling to the promised land. This impatience was more than just bad behavior while on a long road trip. It involved accusations against God and Moses, and more than likely this impatience can be read as indicative of the people's self-centered spirits that led them to reject God's providential care.

The biggest hurdle to living as a covenantal community is that each people invariably view reality from their own perspectives and based on their understanding of their own needs. God is commonly defined as the one who provides whatever is needed in life; however, we are prone to prioritize what is needed on the basis of our personal tastes instead of the tastes of our neighbor. While the writer of Numbers 21 did not delineate the offenses that provoked the plague of poisonous snakes, they could be characterized as sins of impiety and rebellion. In succinct terms, the people demonstrated a vexing spirit of ingratitude. The inability to give thanks and recognize the God-given blessings all around was a serious sin during the time of the exodus, and it remains so today. It is present in doctrines of "might makes right," whether implemented in military acts or business models. It is manifest when environmental desecration is both tolerated and promoted through wasteful habits of energy consumption. It is intrinsic to our spirits of chronic busyness, our being unable to disengage from electronic stimulation and communication devices long enough to reengage with either God or the world God created.

The sin of idolatry has remained a risk for people of faith down through the ages. We are daily tempted to allow something other than God to be our "ultimate concern" (Tillich), whether that relates to race, economic privilege, or simply getting our own way over others through any and all means necessary. In the end, this means that we have grown impatient with God's providential care. God transformed the evil of live serpents into a lifeless, bronze sculpture lifted up on high, visibly to remind the people where their true help comes from. God's diversion of their gaze from their own sinful preoccupations helped set the people free from the thralldom of idolatry. That same God-focused, upward-diverted gaze prompted the writer of the Gospel of John to see in this isolated event a foreshadowing of Christ's elevation on the cross, the ultimate conquest of the sin of idolatry and the source of true healing for all.

Psalm 107:1–3, 17–22 and Ephesians 2:1–10

Along with John's language about true life and the Numbers passage about the restoration of the divine-human covenant, now comes the psalmist's worshipful proclamation about the steadfast love at the heart of God's nature. Six times in Psalm 107 the author uses the rich word *hesed*, which has been variously translated as God's mercy, steadfast compassion, loving-kindness, and covenantal loyalty. The psalm describes an ingathering of the redeemed who will come from east, west, north, and south. There are countless ways to interpret this image effectively; one can speak of people rescued from an enforced diaspora, refugees finally able to return home safely, or the powerless at last given a voice and vote and economic means to shape their own destiny.

The second set of selected verses from Psalm 107 again expounds on the connection between broken covenants and their consequences of sickness, dissatisfaction, and personal distress. As in the two prior passages, God again is the one who saves (v. 19). God's word offers healing, and in a time of possible destruction God opens a pathway of deliverance. Although the core of the psalm is not included in the lectionary, the selected verses accentuate the symmetry of verses 1–2 and 21–22, thereby reinforcing the fundamental affirmation about God's *hesed*. The community's response is, appropriately, one of gratitude ("offer thanksgiving sacrifices") and proclamation ("tell of [God's] deeds with songs of joy," v. 22).

Added to the psalmist's language of God's steadfast love finally comes the Pauline emphasis on God's unmerited grace. Again the contrast is drawn between the path of death and the path of life, and how we are, by nature, "children of wrath" (v. 3), quick to grow impatient on life's detours (cf. Num. 21) or hide our deeds of injustice and vanity in the dark shadows of secrecy (cf. John 3). But resolution is offered in this description of God who loves us "even when we were dead through our trespasses" (v. 5) and who offers us "the immeasurable riches of [God's] grace in kindness toward us in Christ Jesus" (v. 7).

If John 3:16 has earned a well-loved and oft-recited status in the church, then Ephesians 2:8 merits similar prominence and fame. By grace we are saved, something not of our own doing but a gift of God. This divine beneficence is captured in the Greek word *eleos* (translated "mercy"), which is the parallel to the Hebrew word *hesed*. Much should be made of the virtue of mercy today, with its sense of empathy, compassion, and mutual concern. Mercy calls us to stand beside those in need and in solidarity with those oppressed. Mercy is not a work of faith, lest anyone boast; nor is it an attitude of condescension, lest anyone fall prey to vanity. Rather, it is a demeanor of humility and grace that finds expression in sincere kindness shown to others.

From my own experience in congregational ministry, mercy in the sense of *hesed* is the difference between church volunteers doing an impersonal, weekend renovation project on a run-down home and programs where churches partner with first-time homeowners for at least a year, helping them clean up their credit history, renovate a house, and stay in faithful contact with them over the months to make sure they succeed as new homeowners. Mercy is the qualitative difference between having an African American choir visit a congregation one Sunday a year and having an ongoing relationship between two ethnically different congregations that is of such a depth that congregation members attend each others' funeral services or church fellowship events.

The closing verse of this passage from Ephesians asserts that mercy is intrinsic to our true nature: we have been "created in Christ Jesus for good works" (v. 10). According to Scripture, whatever unity held us together in the sorry fellowship of trespasses and sins is now replaced by a truer fellowship, prepared long ago by God, of lives that are shaped by grace, nurtured through faith, and renewed in salvation.

Oscar Romero of the Americas Day (March 24)

Ada María Isasi-Díaz

MALACHI 2:1–9
PSALM 27:7–14
1 CORINTHIANS 15:51–58
MATTHEW 10:16–42

Oscar Romero (1917–1980), Roman Catholic archbishop of El Salvador, was a powerful leader in the struggle for human rights, especially among the poor. Romero opposed military regimes and the brutal methods (including torture and assassination) by which dictators maintained power, and he called for economic, social, and legal justice. On March 24, 1980, Romero was assassinated while lifting the consecrated host during Mass. The preacher could join countries in Central and South America in observing Oscar Romero Day on March 24 (or the Sunday nearest that date) as a sign of respect for this martyr and as an act of commitment to continue the struggle for justice. The fate of Oscar Romero gives haunting testimony to the Lenten theme of taking up the cross.

In our preaching to rich and poor, it is not that we pander to the sins of the poor and ignore the virtues of the rich. Both have sins and both need conversion. But the poor, in their condition of need, are more disposed to conversion. They are more conscious of their need of God. All of us, if we really want to know the meaning of conversion and faith and confidence in another, must become poor, or at least make the cause of the poor our inner motivation. That is, when one begins to experience faith and conversion, when one has the heart of the poor, when one knows that financial capital, political influence, and power are worthless, and that without God we are nothing. To feel that need of God is faith and conversion.[1]

Oscar Romero

---

1. Oscar Romero, *The Church Is All of You: Thoughts of Archbishop Oscar A. Romero*, ed. James R. Brockman, SJ (Minneapolis: Winston Press, 1984), 61.

The lectionary readings for this feast celebrate Romero's life and condemn those who murdered him. Romero's commitment to justice has to loom large in this celebration for the texts to become fully alive, challenging and encouraging the community of believers.

Malachi 2:1–9

Malachi reminds the people of Israel that God will always help them and honor their faithfulness, while holding them accountable and urging them to repent. God's love is unswerving, but that does not mean that God ignores failures in the community's life. The first three verses of today's reading are addressed to leaders who were not listening to God. Their condemnation continues in verse 7–9, condemnation they earned because they caused "many to stumble." Punishment is heaped on them not only by God but also by the people who see them as "despised and abased" (v. 9). The accused in this text are priests, those in charge and those in power. Their main function is to guard divine knowledge and to teach God's ways to the people. Since they have not fulfilled their duties, they will be ineligible to serve in the temple (cf. 1 Sam. 2:30–31).

In contrast to the lashing out against those who are not faithful and are evil, verses 5–6 praise Levi and, by extension, all those who truly fear and stand in awe of God and who faithfully communicate God's message. Through faithful messengers, the people will find what they need to live according to the covenant. In Malachi the covenant is two sided: It offers God's *shalom* to the people of Israel, while requiring from the people reverence for God's law.

Psalm 27:7–14

This psalm probably originated as a prayer at the time of David's conflict with Saul. Verses 1–6, not included in this reading, consider God a "stronghold" for the supplicant, and are a song of trust. In the verses included in this reading, the supplicant once again speaks out to make sure that God is listening, will always be present, will not be angry, and will never forsake the petitioner. Knowing that enemies are always present and that "false witnesses" plot destruction, the supplicant asks not to be abandoned. The trust expressed in the first part of the psalm continues as an undertone in verses 7–14. Faced with trials, the supplicant nonetheless needs to implore God. Entreaty with trust and faith as a backdrop is a needed reassurance in times of distress. Verse 13 is a strong statement of belief not only in God's goodness but in a goodness that will be specifically enjoyed by the supplicant "in the land of the living." In verse 14, the supplicant whispers internal words of encouragement to be stouthearted and to wait for God, regardless of the perils being confronted.

In the celebration of Oscar Romero of the Americas, this psalm is a prayer on the lips of Romero. He believed staunchly and unfailingly that God would not forsake him. That is why he could speak truth to power, convinced that, whatever the consequences, God would take him in, as verse 10 exclaims. The psalm epitomizes the belief of martyrs that they must stand for what they believe, and that they do so not alone but with God's support, being embraced by God just as a father and a mother embrace their child.

1 Corinthians 15:51–58

In chapter 15 of 1 Corinthians, the author constructs an argument to convince those who believe in the resurrection of Christ to believe in their own resurrections. Paul wants the community to believe that resurrection awaits them at the end of life. In verses 51–58, Paul brings the argument to an emotional conclusion: "Where, O death, is your victory? Where, O death, is your sting?" (v. 55). This closing argument assures believers that resurrection is the reward for their labor and that they do not labor in vain. This closing remark grounds resurrection in a belief that is not apart from and cannot exist without devoting oneself to the work of God. The glorious picture of believers rising from death at the sound of the "last trumpet," clothed "with imperishability," is the destiny of those who do God's work.

One needs this background to read and understand Romero's claim that, if he were killed, he would "rise again in the Salvadoran people. I say it without boasting, with the greatest of humility. . . . A Bishop will die, but the Church of God, which is the people, will never perish." For Romero, we live and move and have our being in community. His claim was a simple "testimony of hope in the future." [2] His humble claim finds echoes in the often-quoted poem "Threatened with Resurrection," by Julia Esquivel, Guatemalan poet and activist, who encourages those "in this marathon of Hope" to know there "are always others to relieve us / who carry the strength to reach the finish line which lies beyond death." Esquivel invites all to accompany her people so as to know "how marvelous it is / to live threatened with Resurrection!" How marvelous it is, "to live while dying / and to already know ourselves already resurrected!" [3]

Matthew 10:16–42

This text is part of the "mission discourse." The previous chapter concludes with Jesus' observation that there is much work to do but few to do it. On the

2. My own translations. María López Vigil, *Monseñor Romero—Piezas para un retrato* (La Habana: Editorial Caminos, 2002), 310.
3. Julia Esquivel, *Threatened with Resurrection: Prayers and Poems from an Exiled Guatemalan* (Elgin, IL: Brethren Press, 1994), 61, 63.

heels of that statement he sends his disciples to do the work that will usher the unfolding of the kin-dom of God—the family of God that Jesus' followers are called to become (Matt. 10:5–42). Jesus sends the disciples to do what Jesus has been doing: to carry on the work, the mission, for which Jesus is willing to die.

The initial injunction, verse 16, calls the disciples to be wise, *phronimos* in Greek. The word is at times translated as "shrewd," since the connotation is that of the wisdom of common sense, as indicated by the use of the word in Matthew 7:24 regarding the man who builds his house upon a rock. *Phronimos* refers to the wisdom of grassroot folk who have learned through experience and the struggle for justice and survival to be perceptive in practical matters, that is, in *lo cotidiano*—the everyday life where the unfolding of the kin-dom of God takes place. This commonsense wisdom is paired with the innocence of doves. When people combine these qualities, they are to be single-hearted and focused and proceeding at all times with integrity.

Verses 17–20 catalog what had happened to Jesus. Those for whom this Gospel was written knew well the tragic ending he had. Here they are told that the same will happen to them. Why would one expect anything different as a follower of Jesus, an *alter Christus* ("another Christ"), as the early Christians communities believed they were called to be? These verses not only spell out the attitude of speaking truth to power, but also indicate that in doing so, the Spirit of God speaks through us.

The situation escalates because the disciples of Jesus will not only be scourged by religious and governmental leaders, but will also suffer at the hands of those whom they love. Verses 21 and 34–37 make it clear that being in the family of God requires thinking of family in a new way. Belief in justice and peace, the central message of the gospel, is thicker than flesh and blood! But if we are indeed part of the kin-dom of God, if we are hated because we believe in justice, we will be saved.

Verse 23 speaks of the need to keep on keeping on. We always have work to do. If not here, then there; if not anymore today, then again tomorrow; if not among those I know, then among those I have just met or am about to meet. There is no excuse for not being in mission, for not thinking of oneself as one who is sent by Jesus to do what he did, and acting accordingly.

Verses 24 and 25 give the disciples a different perspective on the difficulties and sufferings they will face because of the gospel. Trials and tribulations confirm them as disciples; they are not to expect any better than, or any different from, what Jesus had to endure.

Verses 26–31 continue to exhort the disciples to look at what happens to them from the perspective of God. This perspective will comfort them. In these verses Jesus tells the disciples three times not to be afraid and assures them that God is in control of the present (vv. 29–31) and of the future (v. 28).

Verses 32 and 33 reflect on the mutuality of the relationship between Jesus and the disciples. Those who acknowledge Jesus will be acknowledged by him, but the opposite is also true. It is not a matter of Jesus wanting to get even; rather, true relationships require mutuality: the core of intimacy. The intimacy between master and disciple is such that, as verses 40–42 make very clear, there is an identification between the two: whoever receives the disciple receives Jesus, what is done to the disciple is done to Jesus, and what is done to Jesus is done to the one who sent him.

Verse 38 is one of the most demanding verses in the all of the Gospels. It might not seem so today, because, when we think of the cross, we think of Jesus. However, for the early Christians living in the Roman Empire, the cross brought thoughts of shame, humiliation, social rejection, marginalization, and unbearable pain. The cross meant dying in a terrifying way. The call of Jesus to take up the cross is a call to martyrdom, not for the sake of suffering and dying, but for the sake of establishing the kin-dom of God, that family of God that all are called to become.

This discourse in Matthew is most disturbing. The verses that offer encouragement—assuring the disciples that the Spirit will help, insisting that they need not be afraid, and pledging that Jesus will acknowledge them in heaven—do not balance out the terribly negative reality that awaits the disciples of Jesus. Monseñor Oscar Romero woke up many mornings knowing that he would be flogged, that he would "be dragged before governors and kings," that he would "be hated," that those to whom he proclaimed peace would answer with the sword, and that this could very well be the day when he would "lose his life." He humbly told those around him he was afraid.

How did he face such terrifying reality? Was it his commitment to the gospel message? Yes, a commitment with a face, the faces of the Salvadoran people. He could confront death every day because he had been given such wise and single-hearted people to pastor: "With this people," he said, "it is not hard to be a good shepherd. They are a people that impel you to service." His commitment to God and his commitment to the people were one and the same thing. Eight days before he was murdered, speaking about this very discourse in Matthew, Monseñor Romero said, "Nothing is more important . . . [than] human life, [than] the human person, above all, the person of the poor and the oppressed, who, besides being human beings, are also divine beings, since Jesus said that whatever is done to them he takes as done to him."[4]

4. Oscar Romero, *The Violence of Love: The Pastoral Wisdom of Oscar Romero*, trans. and compiled by James R. Brockman, SJ (San Francisco: Harper and Row, 1988), 236.

Fifth Sunday in Lent

Lee H. Butler Jr.

JEREMIAH 31:31–34
PSALM 51:1–12
HEBREWS 5:5–10
JOHN 12:20–33

The readings for the Fifth Sunday in Lent gather around the theme of faithfulness in covenant. Life expands in goodness when we commit to relationships defined by covenant. Jeremiah helps us to reflect on the differences between covenant and contract and the importance of being in covenant with God and one another. The psalm reminds us that while God is forgiving, we must be clear about the importance of being committed to the process of forgiveness. The lessons from Hebrews and John call attention to the fact that faithfulness sometimes requires suffering.

Jeremiah 31:31–34

Lent is a time of new beginning through reflection. The Spirit of God and the human spirit always desire new life. We can contrast the old life and the new life in this passage by thinking of the difference between covenant and contract. A contract is a business arrangement between two parties that can be cancelled when one party does not fulfill its obligation. By contrast, a covenant is a promise of commitment of two parties to one another; even when one party violates the terms of the covenant, the covenant goes on. Remedial action may need to take place, but the relationship continues.

According to Jeremiah, the people of Israel treated the old covenant like a contract. Many people today think of marriage more as a contract than as a covenant. Hence, it is easier for them to walk away from the responsibilities of marriage. As a contract, the marriage can be disputed and dissolved for reasons small and large. Many marriages are guided by principles of contract, when they should be guided by principles of covenant. The principles of contract are more attentive to dealing with financial and legal questions than to sheltering commitments of the heart.

By contrast, the prophet emphasizes covenant, a promise and law written on the heart. God's covenant is intended to create a social world in which people are committed from the heart to the welfare of one another and of the community. We may have drifted from the covenant, but God is still at work to freshen the relationship so that the promises are written on our hearts and so that we obey the covenant from our hearts. Within the Hebraic understanding, the heart is the center of the emotions and thoughts, the center of the self within the core of one's identity. The new relationship, then, includes not just behavior but also the entire self, directed toward God and others in intimate relationships.

People living in covenant should acknowledge the broken relationship of the past and declare forgiveness. A common adage is, Forgive and forget. Hence, for most of us, forgiveness is a matter of forgetting how we have been wronged. Unfortunately, this is often a one-sided approach. We are encouraged to release our pain, regardless of what the perpetrator has done. But without a heartfelt apology, can we truly forgive?

Moreover, history and memory are grounded in remembering, not forgetting. Those who forget their history often repeat it with the same negative consequences. Consequently, when the prophet declares that God will forgive and not remember, the prophet is not declaring that God will forget but, rather, that God will not hold our failings over us. This should be true in our individual relationships. When someone has violated me, and that person seeks forgiveness, the violation ceases to have power over my living, even as the violator consciously seeks never to repeat the violation in our relationship. This can also be true in social relationships. When one people has systematically violated another people, but then repents and apologizes, the two peoples should not forget the past, but should work together toward creating a new covenantal future.

For example, people of European origin in the United States must repent of the racism of the past five hundred years, apologize to African Americans and other people of color, and seek forgiveness. On the basis of such repentance, present-day peoples can take steps—albeit slowly and painfully—toward a new covenant with one another and with God.

Psalm 51:1–12

The meaning of this very familiar psalm of David should never be separated from its context. David spoke because his wrongdoings had been exposed. Actions he hid from human eyes, he could not hide from God. Only after

David's offense was exposed did he go before God. David asked for mercy, restoration, and cleansing. But, he never asked God for forgiveness. Although we often read this text as a confession of sin (and interpret it from our various theological positions on human depravity), it is important that we see this text as the words of a person who desires his wrongdoings to be overlooked. A person unable to accept the consequences of her or his behavior will not be able to honor restitution, reparation, or restoration. David never considered giving compensation to those he had wronged. He was self-centered almost to the point of narcissism.

Thinking of David's attitude, people today should not be surprised when big business or government does not respond to the cries of people who have been offended, abused, and wronged. Just as David did not consider his actions as having any negative consequences, many people who occupy the seats of power today do not see themselves accountable to other people. They declare, "Against you and you alone, O God, have I sinned and done what is evil in your sight." To suffering people whose lives they shatter, the powerful respond, "It is not personal. It is business." For instance, when Eurocentric corporations pour industrial waste into a racial-ethnic community, that is not only an act against creation; it is industrial racism.

Hebrews 5:5–10

The suffering at the center of this text is not suffering in general but the specific suffering that results from being faithful to God. The writer raises the question, Are we saved from suffering, or saved by suffering? The writer is clear that Christ did not glory *in* his suffering but was glorified *by* being faithful in suffering. There is a big difference between seeking the praises of the world and being seen as praiseworthy due to being faithful in tribulation. Too many people choose to place emphasis upon suffering as though God is a punitive parent who abuses, in order that we might learn to appreciate joy in this life. We must remain clear: the suffering of Christ was the result of the actions of people who were intent on doing harm and not good.

We can always learn a lesson about relationships from every positive and negative life experience. We can emphasize that Jesus "learned obedience through what he suffered" without believing that God deliberately intended for him to suffer. Jesus resisted evil and advocated for the weak who were unable to fight against the powers of wickedness. Those powers responded by causing him to suffer. Jesus learned that, as he was faithful when others were cruel to him, so God was faithful to him.

This text brings a hard reality to our attention: God did not deliberately cause Jesus to suffer. But when Jesus stood up for God's ways, the world rejected those ways and caused him to suffer. Similarly, God does not deliberately cause us to suffer. But when we stand up for God's values and God's ways in this world—especially when the social implications would cause us to rearrange parts of our comfortable social worlds—the reaction sometimes causes us to suffer. The claim of this text is that, just as God did not desert Jesus in his suffering but used that suffering for redemption, so God is continuously with us when we suffer for justice, and God attempts to work through our suffering to help create a social world that reflects God's values.

John 12:20–33

John helps us to reflect on what it means to be alive, and he helps us choose to live our highest spiritual values. Jesus captured the imagination of many in the ancient world. The impact of his ministry was far and wide, so that in this text some Greeks wish to see him. According to John, his ministry called to the faithful from every culture.

Jesus declares this time to be his time, and timing is everything. In this text, Jesus sees the time for his glorification at hand (v. 23), a glorification that, ironically, takes place when he dies; only then does God raise him. The disciples must follow a similar path. Indeed, says Jesus, if you love your life, you lose it, whereas if you hate your present existence, you will find real life. That seems counterintuitive. Earlier in John, we find the familiar words of Jesus that "God so loved the world that God gave [God's] only [Child]" (John 3:16). Through believing in Jesus, God offers eternal life.

A better way of understanding these concepts is this: if you lust after life, you lose it; if you recognize the limitations of your present existence and follow God's way revealed through Jesus, you will find eternal life. Lust involves being selfish and self-centered in relationship with others. Lustful people are interested only in their own gratification. As a result, those persons who are driven by lust lose their lives, because they live without compassion for others.

We tend to consider hate the opposite of love. We think of love as the deep sharing of the self with and for another, and typically think of hate as a deep disdain of one for another. Such disdain for one's life may be self-hatred, or it may become a motivating energy to pursue change. If it is self-hatred, we regularly redirect people who are consumed by self-hatred with a message to love God, self, and others. Too often, people who hate themselves find no value in this life, and they become suicidal. Jesus' message is exactly the opposite. When Jesus advocates "hating your life," he means for you to recognize where your present existence departs from God's ways, to have a deep disdain for your situation, and then to let that recognition motivate you to redirect your energy toward real love for God, self, and others. It is as if you state, "I repent of my current circumstances, and I determine to strive for a life defined not by the values of this world but by those of God and the world to come."

Consequently, when Jesus prayed, "Father, save me from this hour," and concluded that the glorification of God's name was what brought him to the hour, he turned away from this world and turned toward the path that leads to life. In the sense above, Jesus hated the values of this world, even while loving the world in the sense of giving himself so that the world could know God and God's values more fully. He acted because of love so that we all might experience a good that transcends this present life, might retain the best of what God intends for human relationships, and ultimately might obtain eternal life.

This thinking applies to the social world. Many individuals, groups, corporations, and nations lust for control, recognition, and glory. Such entities can become self-serving, thinking that by holding power to themselves they can secure their own worlds. John is clear that pursuing this path leads to death. Today's text reminds us that true glorification takes place only when we turn away from lust (self-centered grabs for power at the expense of others) and follow the example of Jesus in love: giving ourselves for the good of all in the community. In this way, we find not only continued physical existence but life.

César Chávez Day (March 31)

Frederick John Dalton

MALACHI 3:13–4:3
PSALM 135
1 PETER 4:7–11
LUKE 9:1–6

César Chávez Day, March 31, commemorates the birthday of César Chávez (1927–1993), a Mexican American who was moved by the poor working conditions, exploitative wages, and other injustices of Latino and Latina farm workers in the United States. Chávez organized the United Farm Workers, which led to upgrading the quality of life for such workers. In addition to honoring Chávez, this day calls attention to the solidarity needed to correct injustice, especially when injustice is inflicted upon workers. César Chávez Day further celebrates the ways in which Hispanic peoples enrich and strengthen the larger life of North America.

> Our union was born out of our common suffering, our common hopes for our children, and our common love for each other. Brothers and sisters, that love is still strong in our hearts. . . . We all must know that to let outsiders come in and destroy that love we have for each other is to destroy what we can make tomorrow mean for our children and our loved ones. We came as far as we are today through sticking together. We will go even further tomorrow if we remember that under everything else our strength is love and respect for each other.[1]
>
> *César Chávez*

1. Quoted in Mario T. García, ed., *The Gospel of César Chávez: My Faith in Action* (New York: Sheed & Ward, 2007), 115–16.

171

The first reading today raises a fundamental question: who serves God in our society and who does not? This question is uncomfortable, divisive, contentious, and seemingly judgmental. Malachi judges society in light of God's word. If we cannot judge sinful reality, we are incapable of faithfully announcing salvation. Today's psalm praises God's judgment and salvation in Israel. God's goodness and power are revealed by God's compassionate action in liberating slaves from oppression. The Gospel reading emphasizes the Christian mission to witness against evil and to heal broken humanity. Luke reminds us that sin is a reality that must be confronted and that suffering and death are expressions of demonic powers. Christians are to share Jesus' mission of reconciliation and to testify against evil. Today's final reading identifies hospitality, service, and constant love as characteristics of those who authentically serve God, even in the midst of suffering.[2]

Malachi 3:13–4:3

Malachi describes a society that has lost its way and a religious community that has lost its insight. The nation is plagued with pathetic religious leaders, careless spiritual practices, and immoral lifestyles. The priesthood and the people are weary and demoralized. They are unable to discern God's presence and action in their lives and in the world. Even while critiquing the nation, the prophetic word assures the people of God's love. There are six prophetic oracles in the book of Malachi, and each has three elements: a word from God, the people's response, and the prophetic message.

Today's reading is from the final oracle. In 3:13–15 the people question why some people prosper and others suffer, especially why some evildoers prosper and some righteous persons suffer. The people speak harshly against God because things are not what the people expect them to be. They see service to God in terms of personal benefit; they think it is a waste of time to serve God if they fail to prosper. The people are bitter; the arrogant prosper, and God will not or cannot do anything about it. God indicts the people for lack of faith. The people then respond by reaffirming their faith in God in

---

2. In researching the readings of the day, I am indebted to the following scholars: Aelred Cody, "Haggai, Zechariah, Malachi," in *The New Jerome Biblical Commentary*, ed. Raymond E. Brown, Joseph A. Fitzmyer, and Roland E. Murphy (Englewood Cliffs, NJ: Prentice Hall, 1990); Mary Margaret Pazdan, "Malachi," in *The Collegeville Bible Commentary*, ed. Dianne Bergant and Robert J. Karris (Collegeville, MN: Liturgical Press, 1989); John S. Kselman and Michael L. Barré, "Psalms," in *New Jerome Biblical Commentary*; Richard A. Clifford, "Psalms," in *Collegeville Bible Commentary*; Robert J. Karris, "The Gospel according to Luke," in *New Jerome Biblical Commentary*; Jerome Kodell, "Luke," in *Collegeville Bible Commentary*; William J. Dalton, "The First Epistle of Peter," in *New Jerome Biblical Commentary*; Jerome H. Neyrey, "1 Peter," in *Collegeville Bible Commentary*.

a renewal described in the imagery of a "book of remembrance" (v. 16), a record of the names of the just and righteous.

The prophetic message at the end of the reading is a word of salvation for the righteous and of judgment for evildoers. God reaffirms the covenant relationship and promises compassion for those who serve God (3:17). Evildoers will be brought down, an event described in strong language: burning, stubble, and ashes (4:1). The righteous and reverent will leap for joy (4:2). God's decisive action will reveal who serves God and who does not.

In a similar spirit, Chávez organized the United Farm Workers as a community of service dedicated to confronting injustice. In 1969 the union was fighting on five fronts: a grape strike in California vineyards, a table grape boycott in supermarkets across the country, legal battles against ordinances, injunctions and mass arrests of striking workers aimed at breaking the union, and a public relations campaign to counter the political and economic power of agricultural interests. On Good Friday in April 1969 César wrote the "Letter from Delano," in which he explained the farm worker movement.

> You must understand . . . that our membership and the hopes and aspirations of the hundreds of thousands of the poor and dispossessed that have been raised on our account are, above all, human beings, no better and no worse than any other cross section of human society; we are not saints because we are poor, but by the same measures neither are we immoral. We are men and women who have suffered and endured much, and not only because of our abject poverty but because we have been kept poor. The color of our skin, the language of our cultural and native origins, the lack of formal education, the exclusion from the democratic process, the numbers of our slain in recent wars—all these burdens—generation after generation have sought to demoralize us, to break our human spirit. But God knows that we are not beasts of burden, agricultural implements or rented slaves; we are men locked in a death struggle against man's inhumanity to man. . . . And this struggle itself gives meaning to our life and ennobles our dying.[3]

Denouncing injustice and announcing liberation is prophetic work that can be divisive. It demands judging society in light of the word of God, so that society may be saved. Chávez and the farm workers spoke a word of judgment and liberation for the sake of the righteous who suffer unjustly.

Psalm 135

This psalm of praise recounts God's gracious acts in the history of Israel. Verses 1–4 praise God's election of Israel and celebrate God's covenant of

---

3. Quoted in García, ed., *The Gospel of César Chávez*, 36.

faithful love. Verses 5–7 sing the greatness of God, with nature revealing the power and goodness of God. God's everlasting compassion is revealed in the liberation of God's people from affliction and oppression in Egypt, as well as deliverance of the nation from its enemies (vv. 8–14). Israel responds by rejecting powerless idols (vv. 15–18) and blessing and praising God alone (vv. 19–21).

It is difficult to bless and praise God amid the daunting challenges of the contemporary world. Global poverty and hunger stalk billions. Pollution and environmental degradation lay waste to the natural world. War, terror, and violence claim innocent lives and inflict destruction in every corner of the globe. Human rights are violated with impunity, and human dignity is assaulted without shame. In a world of suffering it is imperative to confront reality and not hide in this uplifting hymn.

Today's psalm must be understood in ways that reveal reality and do not conceal it. Praise for God's covenant reveals the need to be a covenanted people. Praise for creation reveals the need to take responsibility for this good planet. Praise for God's compassion and liberative action reveals the moral demand for us to liberate others. Praise for God reveals the need to destroy idols that render us powerless. Today's psalm is not a quiet interlude but a call to action. The antidote for spiritual malaise and moral confusion is commitment to justice.

Luke 9:1–6

Jesus' ministry of salvation is meant for all people, and in this passage Jesus commissions the apostles to go to villages to proclaim the realm of God and to heal (v. 2). Simplicity of means and trust in God are essential for proclaiming the gospel. Jesus tells the apostles to take nothing for the journey and to depend on the people they encounter (v. 3). Some people will welcome them and some will not (vv. 4–5). The apostles do what Jesus instructs (v. 6). Today's passage completes a section within Luke's Gospel that begins at 7:1 and ends at 9:6. This section reveals that the realm preached by Jesus embraces all: women and men, Gentiles and Jews, lowly and important. Jesus has the power to forgive and to heal, the power of creation and life itself. Jesus manifests God's power and makes the realm a reality. Jesus confers upon the apostles the power of the word of God so that they will go out into the world to heal and forgive.

Following the lead of Jesus, César Chávez embraced the poorest workers in America by denouncing their unjust suffering and announcing their liberation to live and labor in dignity. The union community empowered otherwise powerless field workers to solve their problems. In its early years the union offered its members a credit union, cooperative store, auto repair shop, gasoline station, and funeral insurance. The union helped workers' families obtain medical care, enroll in local schools, and register to vote or work out immigration issues. Chávez's goal was an independent farm labor union that would bargain collectively with growers and negotiate contracts guaranteeing decent wages, safe and humane working conditions, medical insurance, and old-age pensions. In 1970, after years of struggle, the United Farm Workers became the first farm workers' union in American history to achieve these goals. For a moment, the justice of the realm of God was manifest.

1 Peter 4:7–11

Today's reading is part of a larger section, beginning at 1 Peter 3:13, that addresses Christian life in the face of suffering and persecution. Christians should not be fearful or intimidated in the face of suffering for doing right. Christ suffered for the sins of others, and Christ's followers will also suffer. Verse 7 places the reading in the context of the risen Christ, who is expected to return at the end of time. As followers of the risen One, Christians should be confident in the face of suffering, a quality that requires prayerful discipline. The Christian community is not perfect (v. 8), but faithful stewardship of God's grace is manifest through constant love, hospitality, service, and authentic preaching of God's word (vv. 8–11). The end of Christian life is to glorify and praise God through Jesus Christ.

Despite the sacrifice of so many people and the gains farm workers made in the 1960s and 1970s, Chávez's beloved union entered a period of increasing difficulties, disappearing contracts, and diminishing membership during the 1980s. In 1988 César Chávez, an aging prophet of justice and follower of Christ, fasted as a sign of penance and purification and as a declaration of noncooperation with the injustices field laborers continued to experience. In a statement explaining his prophetic action, Chávez said,

> The solution to this deadly crisis will not be found in the arrogance of the powerful but in solidarity with the weak and the helpless. I pray to God that this fast will be a preparation for a multitude of simple deeds for justice, carried out by men and women whose hearts are focused on the suffering of the poor and who yearn, with us, for a better world. Together, all things are possible.[4]

4. Quoted in Frederick John Dalton, *The Moral Vision of César Chávez* (Maryknoll, NY: Orbis Books, 2003), 136.

In a world of daunting challenges for farm workers and others who suffer, the words of César Chávez announce a day of salvation. All we need to do is take the suffering of the poor to heart, perform a simple deed for justice, and the world will be transformed. Indeed, the transformation is already underway, for the realm of God is already present among those who yearn for justice and righteousness.

Sixth Sunday in Lent (The Liturgy of the Palms)

Teresa Lockhart Stricklen

PSALM 118:1–2, 19–29
MARK 11:1–11
JOHN 12:12–16

For many Christians, Palm Sunday recalls ecclesial parades of children confused about why they're walking around waving flimsy palm branches. But they look so cute, marching as we sing, "Hosanna, loud hosanna!" and it's all so wonderful—except that we can miss the subversive power of the Gospel.

Psalm 118:1–2, 19–29

When those following Jesus shouted, "Hosanna! Blessed is the one who comes in the name of the Lord!" from Psalm 118:26, they were evoking the associations that gathered around *all* of that psalm. We thus need to understand Psalm 118 in its ancient usage so that we can see how these allusions illumine Mark's telling of Jesus' entry into Jerusalem.

Psalm 118 is a premier enthronement psalm that reads as a script of a dramatic liturgy used at various festivals through Israel's history. The liturgy was for a procession in which the people moved from outside the temple into the presence of God symbolized upon the altar. The first part of the psalm functions like cheerleaders calling forth shouts of acclamation from the crowd (vv. 1–4): "Let the people say!" (response) "Now let the priests say!" (response) "Altogether now!" (response). After this, an individual, usually the monarch, recalls God's deliverance in times past (vv. 5–7). Verses 8–9 seem to be the people's response, which functions like the commentary of the chorus in a Greek drama. The monarch continues in verses 10–14, perhaps enacting a humiliation unto death. The people again comment. Verse 17 begins the ruler's deliverance and exaltation with his assurance that he will not die but instead live to testify to God's deliverance. On death's doorstep, the priest may have dramatically crawled to the threshold of the temple gate perhaps known as the Gate of Righteousness (v. 19). The people comment on the meaning of the gate in verse 20. The gate then opens with the ruler's thanksgiving in verse 21, and a joyful procession into the temple with the presentation of the monarch as the stone once rejected now being the keystone (NRSV "chief cornerstone"). The people then break into praise and petition: "Save us" (v. 25), which is the meaning of "Hosanna." They call upon the sovereign as liberator. Like Moses leading forth the captives, the monarch then leads the liberated people to the altar in a procession of light and branches, amid thanksgiving for God's eternal *hesed* (covenant loyalty, steadfast love, loving-kindness).

This ritual likely draws its inspiration from the Festival of Booths or Tabernacles (Sukkot). Like Passover, Sukkot had its origin in ancient Middle Eastern agricultural festivals. It seems that the ritual of thanksgiving for the harvest's abundant vegetation included water offerings, wine offerings, and torch-lit processions petitioning heaven for an abundance of rain and sunlight for a good vintage in the months ahead.[1] Israel later reinterpreted these ritual actions as prayers for God to create life (water), shalom (wine), and salvation (light).

Sukkot, or the Feast of the Tabernacles, became the primary holiday of Israel's preexilic monarchy, commemorating life in the wilderness during the exodus, when people lived in temporary shelters, or booths, that reminded the people that they were sojourners on the way to the promised land. These booths were often roofed with branches, and worshipers waved branches, perhaps, as is now the custom, not only in the four directions of the earth but also up and down as a way of drawing the Spirit of God unto them.

Sukkot was the festival chosen for the dedications of the first and second temples (1 Kgs. 8; 2 Chr. 7; Ezra 3:2–4), perhaps because it had also been used to commemorate David's procession of the ark into Jerusalem. In the Maccabean period, after priests who had been bought and installed for political purposes were routed by Judas Maccabeus, the water offering of the ancient agricultural ritual served as a cleansing of the temple during Sukkot.

By the time of Jesus, Sukkot was one of three great festivals during which pilgrims poured into Jerusalem. Psalm 118 and its Sukkot associations embodied eschatological longings for the restoration of the Davidic monarchy. The light mentioned in verse 27 had become an elaborate ceremony with modern Olympic-like bowls of oil that lit up the entire temple at night to remind the community of the presence of God in their midst, so that even the night is as

---

1. Sigmund Mowinckel, *The Psalms in Israel's Worship*, trans. A. R. Ap-Thomas (Grand Rapids: Eerdmans, 1962), 128.

day. They poured water libations with words anticipating the Day of the Lord when the Spirit would be poured out on all people, and a wine libation was also poured into a bowl in such a way that it mingled and flowed down with the water onto the altar.[2]

Thus, all of Psalm 118 and its ritual symbolic contexts down through history were evoked when Jesus' followers waved branches and cried out, "Hosanna! Blessed is the one who comes in the name of the Lord!" upon approaching Jerusalem. The crowd proclaimed Jesus as the anticipated Messiah who was coming to cleanse the temple, judge the nations, rout evil, and dwell with humanity as the divine presence. Like the ark of the covenant carried on a beast of burden, God-with-us has arrived, but the Sovereign will suffer humiliation unto death and be poured out as an offering upon the altar with prayers for the manifestation of God's Holy Spirit.

Mark 11:1–11

Mark's Gospel underscores the unsettling nature of proclaiming Christ as Sovereign, for Jesus' "triumphal" entry into Jerusalem is a bit off all around. It is hardly a Roman triumphal entry, and it deliberately reinterprets one of Israel's messianic expectations.

People in Jesus' day might have viewed his triumphal entry as a satire of Pilate's own entry into Jerusalem just days before, when the prefect may have entered Jerusalem with a parade meant to announce that Rome ruled over Passover. Unlike other triumphal entries in the Greco-Roman world, though, Jesus rides not a grand steed, but a little donkey, hardly a symbol of power. In this regard, Zechariah 9:9 whispers in the background, an allusion that would not be lost on those who knew the Scripture. No political or religious dignitaries meet Jesus with flowery speeches, as was customary. When he is later met by political leaders, they do not praise Jesus, but take steps to bury him. His devotees are not dressed in their best, nor do they wear wreaths of palm branches on their heads. Instead, they throw down and trample ordinary clothes and branches in the street. No cultic action in the temple follows.

There were none of the requirements for Roman triumphal military parades: no imperial authorization confirmed by the people for a past battle in which the blood of many had been shed, no liberated captives, no prisoners, no soldiers who had fought valiantly in the battle.[3] Jesus' offensive parade had

---

2. Jeffrey Rubenstein, "The Sukkot Wine Libation," in *Ki Baruch Hu: Ancient Near Eastern Biblical and Judaic Studies in Honor of Baruch Levine*, ed. Robert Chazan, William W. Hallo, and Lawrence H. Schiffman (Winona Lake, IN: Eisenbrauns, 1999), 575–92, 575.

3. Brent Kinman, *Jesus' Entry into Jerusalem*, Arbeiten zur Geschichte des Antiken Judentums und des Urchristentums 28 (Leiden: E. J. Brill, 1995), 27–47.

no Roman authority behind it; Rome didn't even notice it, though the authorities were on alert for potential problems during the Passover. The people did not confirm his power, but ignored, betrayed, and denied it. The victorious battle was not behind him in the past, but ahead of him in the future, a battle in which the blood of One would liberate many captives and take no prisoners. Jesus' soldiers (the disciples) are comic *milites gloriosi* [boastful soldiers] figures in Mark, deserters who are chastised for drawing swords (Mark 14:47–50), called not to military action, but to deeds of healing, love, and mercy.

To add insult to injury, Jesus does not fulfill many popular expectations. Yes, Mark depicts Jesus as both royal and priestly. Only a monarch can conscript something for royal use, as Jesus does with the colt. Similarly, the fact that the donkey has never been ridden points to two different meanings: no one but the sovereign ruler can ride the royal horse, and things set aside for holy use cannot be used for secular activities.[4] Yes, Jesus' followers lay down their cloaks and branches from the fields on his pathway, perhaps alluding to 2 Kings 9:13, when Jehu (known for his maniacally fast chariot driving!) is crowned, but Jehu is hardly a messianic figure. The crowd shouts acclamations from Psalm 118, but they are not saying, "Blessed be the monarch!" but "Blessed is the coming *dominion* of our ancestor David" (v. 10). They shout, "Blessed is the one who comes in the name of the Lord!" but these words were used for any pilgrim entering Jerusalem. Mark thus leaves Jesus' status as the anticipated Sovereign ambiguous. Moreover, instead of cleansing the temple like Judas Maccabeus, Jesus goes into the temple, looks "around at everything," and leaves because it is "already late" (v. 11). Mark seems intent to picture a dud Messiah. Mark's picture of Jesus thwarts some messianic expectations of his day.

John 12:12–16

John is more explicit about Jesus' royal rule, clearly stating that he is "the Sovereign of Israel" (v. 13). However, Jesus does not deliberately conscript the donkey but simply finds it. The Fourth Gospel alone specifies *palm* branches (cf. Rev. 7:9), but there is ambiguity here too, as John tells us that the disciples were as clueless about Jesus' entry as they are depicted throughout Mark's Gospel (v. 16).

Both Gospel writers make it clear, though, that power of the realm of God flows through Jesus. At the entry into Jerusalem, the process leading

4. See Douglas R. A. Hare, *Mark*, Westminster Bible Companion (Louisville, KY: Westminster John Knox Press, 1996), 138; and R. T. France, *The Gospel of Mark* (Grand Rapids: Eerdmans, 2002), 431.

to salvation takes an important turn. The coming of the realm will not be accomplished by military political power or institutional power, as it all too often gets played out on the human stage. God's power is twisted according to our way of thinking—not grandly glorious, but invisible, accomplished through obedient servanthood. What is twisted, though, as we will see in the passion of Jesus, is not God, but humankind, bent by the sin of using power to crucify. Christ's ironic crowning on a cross displays the end result of sinful human power and gives birth to God's new reign. The psalm thus foreshadows what is to come—the humiliation of the Sovereign of the universe who enters the gate of righteousness (Ps. 118:19) to become the condemned, humiliated Gate of Righteousness through which all may freely enter.

A youth looking at the Gulf Coast oil spill that took place in 2010 asks, "Why bother protesting injustice when it all seems too big to effect any real change?" Many feel that the personal sacrifices required are too great for too little. A Jewish nobody from Podunk who was devoted to God changed the course of history—this is the power of God unto salvation.

Ordinary people doing small, ordinary things—like women in the Women's Political Council in Montgomery talking on the telephone, printing flyers, and visiting door to door to organize a one-day bus boycott—can turn into big things like a national civil rights movement. Children marching peacefully in the streets of Birmingham exposed the abuse of power as water cannons and dogs tried to stop the power of divine justice. Here was no triumphant parade, yet God turned this travesty into triumph as this turning point garnered momentum for the movement. Microloans of $200 or less are empowering women to own their own businesses in Africa, and these small loans are proving more successful in solving poverty than huge amounts of national aid. It seems insignificant to send bees, bunnies, or heifers halfway across the world with vacation Bible school offerings, yet Heifer Project transforms whole communities.

Our protests against injustice often seem like a drop in the bucket, yet an ocean is just many drops. Through these small, almost imperceptible, and seemingly insignificant acts, God's reign continues to grow like a beatific spill of goodness that eventually, but surely, is spreading to encompass the world with blessing. Hosanna!

Sixth Sunday in Lent (The Liturgy of the Passion)

Teresa Lockhart Stricklen

ISAIAH 50:4–9A
PSALM 31:9–16
PHILIPPIANS 2:5–11
MARK 14:1–15:47

A candidate for the ministry once confessed, "Politics has nothing to do with Christianity, so I'm apolitical." While we may wish this were so, until God's new age is fully present on earth, wherever two or three are gathered, politics will be there. Providentially, however, what ultimately prevails over death-dealing politics is the sovereignty of God in Christ, where two or three gather in his name and seek to live his way until God's full reign comes.

Mark 14:1–15:47

Mark is clear that politics prompts Jesus' ministry from beginning to end. During Jesus' baptism by John, the heavens open and the Spirit descends upon Jesus, identified with Isaiah's Suffering Servant, who alleviates Israel's political oppression (Isa. 50:4–9). Returning from his own exodus experience in the desert, Jesus, like Moses, begins proclaiming: "God's reign is at hand; repent and believe" (Mark 1:14). His preaching is accompanied by signs of God's new age—a new community (calling the disciples, 1:16–20); healing, exorcism and casting out of Satan (3:22–27); forgiveness of sins; Messianic feasting (2:18–20; 6:41–43; 8:1–9), resurrection (5:41–42), and the arrival of the ruler of the Sabbath (2:23–28) whose teaching authority surpasses that of established ecclesial leaders. Such preaching and its embodiment in Jesus lead to a clash with both religious and sociopolitical leaders and to a cross.

Besides the people who receive messianic blessings, it's Herod who first wonders who Jesus is (6:14–16); then the scribes and the Pharisees follow

182

suit (7:1–13). After Peter confesses Jesus as Messiah (8:27–30), Jesus discusses his impending death. He goes to Jerusalem, overturns the money changers' tables, "and when the chief priests and the scribes heard it, they kept looking for a way to kill him; for they were afraid of him, because the whole crowd was spellbound by his teaching" (11:18). All of Mark, then, is about whose politics, whose standards, will prevail—human traditions' or God's (7:8).

Jesus is a wanted man by the time the passion narrative begins. The chief priests and the scribes seek to arrest Jesus by stealth, before Passover so that there will be no riot (14:1–2)—a common strategy yet today for leaders, who do things quietly so that they go unnoticed by the populace, lest there be an uprising.

Preparations for Jesus' death are made with his anointing at the house of Simon, a person afflicted with leprosy. Jesus's anointing is extravagant.[1] A woman understands the *kairos* moment by giving what was probably a prized possession to anoint Jesus. Despite Jesus saying that "wherever the good news is proclaimed in the whole world, what she has done will be told in remembrance of her" (14:9), the woman ironically remains unnamed.

Judas betrays Jesus, they celebrate the Last Supper, and Jesus is arrested in Gethsemane. Then he is deserted by his followers and denied by "rock solid" Peter. After a night of abuse by religious authorities and their guards, Jesus is bound and led to Pilate, who alone has the power to execute. Whereas Jesus has been condemned to death for blasphemy by the religious council, blasphemy is not a Roman cause for death; so the priests and elders tell Pilate that Jesus calls himself the ruler of the Jews. When Pilate asks him if this is so, Jesus sidesteps the issue: "You say so" (15:2). Then, as the spiritual sings, "He never said a mumblin' word" until he speaks the cry of dereliction.

Mark pictures the priests continuing their politics by influencing a crowd to ask Pilate to release a prisoner. Mark depicts such a request as customary during Passover. However, Pilate asks if the crowd wants him to release Jesus; for, though Jesus is arrested like "a bandit" (14:48), Pilate sees him as a rabbi who has roused the religious leaders' jealousy (15:10). But the crowd asks for Barabbas, an insurrectionist (15:7). Pilate then asks what the people want done with Jesus, a ludicrous question in actuality, for, though his job did require their compliance, he did not need their permission. "Crucify him!" Again, Pilate hesitates, but when the people look as if they are ready to riot, Pilate orders Jesus scourged and crucified (15:15).

---

1. Craig A. Evans, *Mark 8:27–16:20*, Word Biblical Commentary (Nashville: Thomas Nelson Publishers, 2001), 359.

Barabbas, whose name means "son of the father," is a foil highlighting the fact that the nameless face of humanity has chosen the wrong son of the wrong father. "The crowd has a choice between two kinds of salvation," Douglas Hare observes, "the do-it-yourself 'salvation' of human violence, represented by Barabbas, and the salvation effected by God through Jesus" (Mark 10:45; 14:24).[2] Humanity chooses violence, the result of humanity's desire for power and control apart from God.

Crucifixion involved horrendous torture before death's mercy. Jesus is scourged, meaning he was stripped and beaten with a whip that had bone or lead on the end, to flay the flesh to the bone. Many died of this treatment before being crucified. Weak and bloody, Jesus is then subjected to the mockery of a cohort (600–1,000 soldiers) of military police. He is costumed, hailed as king, batted around like a piñata. They put his own clothes on him, a tattered robe of his divine royalty, to lead him to Golgotha. Jesus is so weak that Simon of Cyrene is conscripted to carry the cross to which Jesus will be nailed and left to die between two bandits, under a sign that carries his charge: "The King of the Jews." It is a picture of utter degradation.

Birds of prey gather. Passersby taunt (15:29–30). The chief priests and scribes deride, "We will believe you are the Christ if you save yourself." But no other sign is given. The whole world is plunged into darkness, as on the anticipated Day of the Lord (cf. Amos 5:18, 20; 8:9–10). Jesus gives up his spirit with a mighty cry, unlike most who simply slipped into unconsciousness. Jesus' cry of dereliction comes from Psalm 22, which ends with assurance that "future generations will be told about the Lord, and proclaim his deliverance to a people yet unborn" (Ps. 22:30–31). Thus, Jesus' cry of dereliction could be a shout of victory, even as it is a desolate cry of human agony. Jesus' deepest weakness, dying on a cross, thus becomes the sign of the most exalted divine strength, as Philippians 2:5–11 sings.

As Jesus breathes out his last breath, the veil of the temple is torn in two by a heavenly force that rends it from top to bottom, as opposed to human power, which could have torn it only from the bottom to the top. With this divine act, even a hardened centurion believes what God pronounces at the beginning of the Gospel when the heavens are torn open and the Spirit descends upon Jesus: This is God's Son (1:11; 15:39). Jesus is buried like a pauper, dependent upon the kindness of a stranger (15:43). Usually the crucified remained unburied, eaten by birds of prey and dogs until finally burned. Jesus' body was at least spared this. Even so, in the end he lies hurriedly disposed of in a borrowed tomb, stone-cold dead in darkness.

2. Douglas Hare, *Mark*, Westminster Bible Companion (Louisville, KY: Westminster John Knox Press, 1996), 208.

Philippians 2:5–11

This early hymn to Christ indicates what kind of power the early church understood Jesus, the Christ, to have: the power of good for all, even at the expense of oneself. The language is of power flowing like water to the lowest place, which can then be flooded with the glory of divine exaltation. This lowest place is the degradation of the cross, which is simultaneously Christ's throne. To confess Jesus as Lord is thus to live in his way, seeking the common good in our individual choices and our social policies.

Isaiah 50:4–9a

The third of the four Suffering Servant Songs from Isaiah comments on the meaning of the Servant's suffering.[3] Though the lection begins at verse 4, the larger context is significant. God asks an unfaithful Israel that is complaining under exilic suffering, "Is my hand shortened, that it cannot redeem? Or have I no power to deliver?" (50:2). The Servant enters. Under the sackcloth cover of heaven-sent blackness, he speaks a poem that indicates that the one who has been taught by God is the one who teaches to sustain the weary with a word. With a face set like flint, a rock associated with Israel's covenant, the Servant faces abuse without objecting. He does not hide his face from insult or spitting—two details chronicled in the crucifixion account. He faces them confident that the God who is near helps him. What can mere mortals do to him? Only the eternal God can declare him guilty (v. 9); his adversaries will die like wool before moths and will be judged, for, in their own darkness, they kindle their own fires, refusing to walk in the light of the Lord (v. 11).

In the context of Isaiah, the Servant is almost certainly the community of Israel. The work of the Servant Israel is to demonstrate God's ways to the other peoples of the world. The Servant community in exile appears to be weak and defeated. However, the power of the unseen God is at work to reconstitute that community and thereby to reveal the power and purposes of the God of Israel. Consequently, it is no wonder that Christianity looked to Isaiah's Suffering Servant to help explain Jesus' life and death. Jesus on the cross, like Israel in exile, appeared to be weak and defeated, but God raised Jesus from the dead, thus again affirming God's power and life-giving purposes. The community that follows Jesus, the church, thus joins Israel in the Servant role: witnessing in the world to God's power and purposes.

---

3. The other three Servant Songs are found in Isaiah 42:1–9; 49:1–7; and 52:13–53:12.

Psalm 31:9–16

Psalm 31 is an individual lament whose central section, verses 9–16, poignantly describes a person in profound distress. Although the psalmist does not specifically name the circumstances that created the distress, verses 11, 14, and 15 imply that the psalmist has enemies who brought about this suffering. Psalm 31:9–16 has a number of thematic and verbal links to Jer. 20:7–13 (see also Jer. 11:18–20; 20:3), in which Jeremiah too was beset by enemies who sought to end his prophetic ministry. If the psalmist intentionally echoes Jeremiah, then the psalmist, too, is persecuted for prophetically calling the community to faithful, covenantal life. Yet, as is characteristic of the individual lament, even in the midst of the violence inflicted by enemies, the psalmist trusts that God will ultimately bring about a community marked by goodness, steadfast love, and blessing (Ps. 31:9a, 15–16; cf. vv. 19–24). The psalm thus has an implicit political dimension. In the context of Passion Sunday, the words of the psalm help interpret the experience of Jesus, whose crucifixion occurs at the hands of those who oppose God's purposes of love and justice. According to the psalm, God ultimately vindicates faithful witnesses.

It is easy to see why Christians might want to be apolitical, given what ecclesial and secular politics did to Jesus. But God's reign, which Christ commissions us to preach, challenges human authorities, confronting all with a *kairos* decision as to whose rule will prevail, not just over individual lives, but over social customs as well (see Mark 10:1, 14:12, 15:8). Without attention to the social dimension of life, crucifixions of other innocents embodying God's way will continue. If we juxtapose news accounts with the Passion narrative and other lections, we can readily see the ways in which we continue to torture God's goodness by our complicity in sin. This can lead to repentance and belief that God's sovereign rule for the common good is the better way.

The powers that oppose God's rule may continue to cause distress for those who work for social justice. Mark, Paul, Isaiah, and the psalmist empathize with this while also being honest: when we work for a just society under God's rule, we too may suffer. However, even in their deepest despair, the biblical authors trusted that God's purposes of love and justice will ultimately prevail, and they assure us that we can share that trust.

Maundy Thursday

Rhashell Hunter

EXODUS 12:1–4 (5–10), 11–14
PSALM 116:1–2, 12–19
1 CORINTHIANS 11:23–26
JOHN 13:1–17, 31B–35

Maundy Thursday is characterized by communion and community. We share liturgy, bread and cup, and we eat together. The texts for today emphasize diversity and inclusion. Some people are welcomed to tables, and some are not. Some are enslaved, and some are free. And in the midst of suffering and even death, there is gratitude to the God who hears and cares for God's people.

In the Exodus passage (12:1–14), the first Passover is instituted, and 1 Corinthians 11:23–26 reports the institution of the Lord's Supper. Both the Passover and the Lord's Supper are festivals of remembrance and empowerment. Psalm 116 expresses thanksgiving and praise to God for God's good gifts and care. And in John 13:1–17, 31–35, Jesus washes the disciples' feet and gives a new commandment to love one another just as Christ loves us.

Exodus 12:1–4 (5–10), 11–14

This passage records the institution of the first Passover, God's "passing over" Israelite houses during the plague of the firstborn. Pharaoh refused to free the enslaved Israelites, so God brought ten plagues to Egypt: blood, frogs, gnats, flies, livestock disease, boils, hail, locusts, darkness, and death to the firstborn of Egypt. The intent of the tenth plague, and thus of the Passover observance, was to appeal to Pharaoh to let the people of Israel go out of his land. Eventually, Moses led the Israelites out of the land of bondage toward freedom.

The passage records strict guidelines for securing a lamb and slaughtering it at midnight. Some of the blood of the lamb was to be placed on two doorposts of the houses in which the lambs were eaten. There are specific instructions on preparing and even eating the lamb.

This text challenges our contemporary sensitivities. Most challenging is the killing of every firstborn in Egypt. This is particularly difficult as it comes from the mouth of God. As the Bible has a historical context, it is helpful to discover what ancient participants of the Passover would have understood after reading or hearing this text. The specific instruction of placing blood on the doorposts was a protection against the destroyer. The people who followed the blood ritual did so at the instruction of God, through Moses and Aaron. When they did this, they knew God was protecting them.

In the Passover haggadah (or "telling") used in Passover observances, a child asks, "What does this observance mean?" Exodus 12:27 gives us the answer: "You shall say, 'It is the passover sacrifice to [God], for [God] passed over the houses of the Israelites in Egypt, when [God] struck down the Egyptians but spared our houses.'" Thus the Passover festival marks the beginning of freedom for people who were enslaved.

The story of the Israelites' exodus reminds us that one of God's purposes is to free us from those things that enslave. The passage is a reminder to oppressed people that freedom is possible, and it is an invitation to all—including oppressors—to join with God in pursuing freedom.

Psalm 116:1–2, 12–19

This psalm is a song of thanksgiving and faithfulness and is attributed to one who has been ill or has faced death and has recovered. Verses 1–2 express love of God, because God heard the psalmist's voice and acknowledged the psalmist's suffering. Even in suffering, the writer of the psalm gives thanks and praise to the God who hears. The psalmist is filled with gratitude for God's care.

Verse 12 of the psalm provides the first line of an old hymn, "What shall I render to the Lord?"[1] Of course the answer is nothing. There is nothing that we can give to God that God does not already have. We do, however, give gifts to God as symbols of surrendering or giving ourselves to God, in gratitude for God's good gifts to us (vv. 12, 17).

Lifting the cup of salvation refers to a libation, perhaps in the context of a sacred meal, in praise of God's goodness (v. 13). The vows that we fulfill

---

1. Wilhelm A. F. Schulthes, "What Shall I Render to the Lord?" 1871; http://www.cyberhymnal .org/htm/w/h/whatshal.htm (accessed August 19, 2010). See a similar hymn by Charles Wesley, "What Shall I Render to My God?" 1868; http://www.jumbojimbo.com/lyrics.php?songid=6050; (accessed August 19, 2010). Contemporary Christian songs have also been produced with this title.

are what our vocational callings are all about, fulfilling our vows and calls through our ministry and service among God's people (vv. 14 and 18). Death does not bring fear to the psalmist, because the death of the faithful is precious to God (v. 15).

By repeating the sentence, "I am your servant. I am your servant" (v. 16), the psalmist emphasizes that serving God is the core of the psalmist's identity. Just like my mother before me, I am your servant, the child of your servant-maid.

1 Corinthians 11:23–26

The Lord's Supper in Corinth took place in what we might call today a new church development. The community of faith in Corinth was multicultural, and like many multicultural new church developments today, it was exciting and also messy. The church included Jews, Gentiles, slaves, slave owners, homeowners, and those who were homeless. Women, such as Priscilla, who trained Apollos (Acts 18:26, 1 Cor. 16:19), and Chloe, whose people reported to Paul that there were quarrels among them (1 Cor. 1:11), were in positions of leadership. The people of the church met in members' houses, and the Lord's Supper was indeed an Agape, a love feast. We sometimes forget the "supper" part of the Lord's Supper.

In Corinth, there were problems, though, in that those who brought food for the Lord's Supper sat down and ate, while those who had nothing to contribute were not invited to share in the meal. They must have forgotten that the supper was a church gathering. When the Corinthian Christians received Paul's letter, it said, "I do not commend you, because when you come together it is not for the better but for the worse. For, to begin with, when you come together as a church, I hear that there are divisions among you; and to some extent I believe it. . . . When you come together, it is not really to eat the Lord's supper. For when the time comes to eat, each of you goes ahead with your own supper, and one goes hungry and another becomes drunk" (11:17b–18, 20–21).

The Lord's Supper is much more than eating and drinking. Like the Passover meal, the Lord's Supper is a ritual of remembrance that empowers the community to live faithfully as God's servants in the world. Christian communities of faith remember Jesus and proclaim his life, death, resurrection, and promised return. When Jesus ate his last meal with the disciples, even though he was the honored guest and host, he served them. He took bread and broke it, and offered thanksgiving to God. Then he said, "This is my body that is for you. Do this in remembrance of me" (v. 24b). They all shared in the meal, and it was a time of koinonia or communion. After they had their fill and finished supper, Jesus took the cup. And just as he had done with the bread before the meal, he gave thanks to God and said, " 'This cup is the new covenant in my blood. Do this, as often as you drink it, in remembrance of me.' For as often as you eat this bread and drink the cup, you proclaim the Lord's death until he comes" (vv. 25b–26).

While all the divisions in the church have not gone away, we share this meal proclaiming unity in Christ, hopeful that one day the lines will be erased, and we will commune together as sisters and brothers in the beloved community of God.

John 13:1–17, 31b–35

This is a day characterized by love. Jesus said, "I give you a new commandment, that you love one another" (v. 34). Humility is also an overarching theme, as on Maundy Thursday Jesus, the Holy One, models service by washing the feet of his friends. "Maundy," which is from the Latin word *mandatum*, means "mandate" or "commandment." We have a commandment given by Jesus to love one another just as Christ loves us.

This commandment is instructive for us today. Loving and valuing others is not easy. We live in a society in which people constantly assign value to others, and we operate according to social hierarchies. Some people are seen as more important than others. Women, children, persons of color, those with disabilities, seniors, and others are not always looked upon with honor but are often overlooked or disdained. But on this day almost 2,000 years ago, Jesus upset the hierarchical structure of his time: this leader became a servant, when he knelt at the feet of his disciples and washed their feet.

We have opportunities every day to love others by reassigning value and giving it back to those from whom we have arbitrary removed value and worthiness. As we are products of a society in which racism, sexism, and other isms are prevalent, we have adopted a system that places more or less value on arbitrary human distinctions such as skin color, hair texture, or food preferences. These categories limit us, define our relationships, and even determine with whom we will worship. This arbitrary human system of valuing or devaluing others is a function of sin, though many of us are unaware of its insidiousness.

Many years ago, a biracial child was with his mother. The mother was European American. You can almost see the minds of people who encountered them working overtime, as they tried to figure out what the circumstances were for this mixed-race mother and child. This mother certainly wanted her child to be everything that he could be. She did not want him to be limited by lower or double standards that others imposed upon him. She surely wanted her son to believe that, one day, he could become the president of the United

States. And he did. President Barack Obama was inaugurated on January 20, 2009, as the forty-fourth president of the United States of America.

We habitually prejudge other people, and in doing so, we often limit them, not knowing how significant they may be in our lives or in human history. President Obama learned from his mother, Ann Dunham, values of inclusion and appreciation for diversity. For some years they lived in Indonesia, where Ms. Dunham's table was a gathering place for leaders in human rights, women's issues, and grass-roots development.

These values embody the social values of today's Scriptures. The Exodus and 1 Corinthians passages show us that God wants to free us from those things that enslave. Creating tables of diversity that welcome others allows us to live as freed and empowered people. God's love, as exhibited in the psalm and the Gospel, is more powerful than sideways glances or double standards, which often hurt or limit others. We are encouraged to welcome others and to feast at the table with Christ.

Maundy Thursday provides us with an opportunity to expand our tables, to welcome and empower others, just as Christ did. As we sit at our potlucks and Communion services, notice who is sitting around the table. More importantly, notice who is not there. Who is not welcomed to worship? Holy Week is an opportunity to recommit ourselves to become communities of love and humility, even getting on our knees, literally or figuratively, and washing the feet of others. By doing so, we will embody the new commandment to love one another just as Christ loves us.

Good Friday

Charles G. Adams

ISAIAH 52:13–53:12
PSALM 22
HEBREWS 10:16–25 OR 4:14–16; 5:7–9
JOHN 18:1–19:42

Good Friday is a wonderful day, when the church unites across all geographical divisions and religious differences to praise the crucified Christ, whose death manifests salvation, restores the cosmos, redeems all nations, and reconciles all races and ethnic groups. The Russian anthem "Salvation Is Created" represents the spirit and universal significance of the incarnation, crucifixion, and resurrection of Jesus. This beautiful anthem starts in a minor key but ends in a major chord of a positive outcome that is inclusive of all nations.[1] Similarly, John's Gospel represents unity between the humiliation and glorification of Christ on Good Friday.

Yet the critics of this union between tragedy and triumph, humiliation and glorification, sometimes fear that followers of Christ are so celebrative on Good Friday that they do not take human suffering seriously enough. We in the Western world are so success oriented and pleasure prone we must plead guilty when charged with being insensitive to the pains, problems, and agonies of most of the people in the world. We consume 80 percent of the earth's resources, but we are less than 20 percent of the earth's people. We must not be so sealed in our success and comfort that we fail to feel the agonies of the many who suffer needlessly because of our abuses. Lord help us!

So we come to Good Friday to weep and to rejoice in the death of a good person for the salvation of all persons and the peace of all nations. This universal significance of the crucifixion and resurrection of Jesus is the startling theme of the Hebrews pericope, which cannot escape the eschatological spirit

---

1. For the history of the anthem, its text, and a recording of a performance, see http://songs forpraise.com/SalvationIsCreated.html (accessed July 9, 2010).

of its belief that the hand of God is at work in all of human history, to make and keep human life more human. God wills for all people to be liberated, nourished, and sustained, in eternal wisdom, perfect justice, deathless hope, and steadfast love.

Isaiah 52:13–53:12

The Suffering Servant sings of glorious triumph in this concluding song of the four Servant Songs. Song one (Isa. 42:1–4) tells of God's call to the Servant and the outpouring of the spirit, and the ethics and character of the Servant.

The second Servant Song (Isa. 49:1–6) affirms the universal reach of the Servant's suffering and triumph. It is "too light a thing" for the Servant to die vicariously only for Israel. The second Song calls the Servant of God to be a "light to the nations, that God's salvation may reach to the end of the earth" (Isa. 49:6). The theme of universality and total human and cosmic inclusiveness is not strange in the Hebrew Bible. The people of Israel and the church of the Messiah are blessed, not for private enjoyment, but for their public and universal responsibility to all (see Gen. 12:1–3 and the many parallel references to Israel's responsible mission to transmit the blessings of God to all the families of the earth). Paul D. Hanson finds this to be the chief theological characteristic of Second Isaiah.[2]

In the third Servant song (Isa. 50:4–9), the Servant is insulted and assaulted. Nevertheless, the Servant sings, "The Lord GOD helps me; . . . I shall not be put to shame" (Isa. 50:7). This song leads to Isaiah 52:13–53:12. This passage is the climatic meditation for today because of its reciprocal relationship to the way Jesus understood his life and mission and the way writers of the New Testament interpreted Jesus. The fourth Servant Song provides a lens to interpret the sufferings of Jesus, who as a Jew was believed by his followers to be the incarnation of God and the replication of the Suffering Servant. His followers used Isaiah's poetic words to interpret his agony in Gethsemane, his trials, floggings, taunts, and curses. The vicarious redeemer of the whole earth is believed by Christians to be the Lord Jesus. Do not miss the jagged, riveting pounding of the Lord's Suffering Servant as depicted in the Second Part of Handel's *Messiah*, with the percussion and screaming strings and expressive voices singing, "Surely he hath borne our griefs and carried our sorrows."

The passion of the Servant in Isaiah gives way to the saving sovereignty of God, who delivers the meek but courageous one who suffered to redeem

---

2. Paul D. Hanson, *Isaiah 40–66*, Interpretation series (Louisville, KY: Westminster John Knox Press, 1995), 5–11.

others and who was ingloriously buried with the wicked. The Suffering Servant was marvelously delivered to see his offspring and prolong his days.

Although Isaiah's fourth Servant Song does not necessitate a New Testament reference to explain its meaning, this ancient song serves in the Christian era to pose an imaginatively poetic Christology, soteriology, and liberation theology. Without Isaiah's music and words, the passion narratives in the New Testament could never have been conceived. We must never forget that Jesus was a believing and practicing Jew who never apologized for or renounced Judaism. He remained committed to the Hebrew rock from which he was hewn.

Psalm 22

This lesson is read primarily because Jesus is said to have quoted the first verse while he was dying on the cross. In the passion narrative of the two earliest Gospels, Mark and Matthew, this is the only statement that Jesus is reported to have spoken from the cross. Psalm 22 is one of the most misunderstood Scriptures in the biblical tradition, because it is judged by its first verse to be full of despair. Only by pressing beyond verse 1 do we reach the positive testimony of God's deliverance and of restoration of communion with God and community. Psalm 22 is actually a song of triumph and praise. It begins in the weakness of suffering and ends in thanksgiving attesting to liberation and restoration. In the Bible, lamentation is the flip side of thanksgiving and praise. If God is sovereign, one must in the pathos of lamentation simultaneously recognize the ultimate triumph of God and steadfast love through and beyond all suffering and despair. A believer's despair is never bereft of the glory and honor of God, who transforms the pain of those who suffer into vindication, justification, sanctification, and praise.

Hebrews 10:16–25; 4:14–16; 5:7–9

Many great scholars see the most highly developed Christology in the New Testament in Hebrews. The saving Messiah who died on the cross is not so much the Suffering Servant as the High Priest whose offering to God (the high priest's own life) is a sacrifice for sin to redeem all creatures. Like the Suffering Servant, the great High Priest is God's anointed and divinely appointed agent to redeem the human race. Hebrews 10:16–25 proclaims that Jesus as High Priest has offered a perfect sacrifice to end all sacrifices. "For by a single offering [of the God-Human] he has perfected for all time those who are sanctified" (Heb. 10:14). The sanctified are those whom the Holy Spirit claims as people of the new covenant (Jer. 31:31–34). In that covenant, the action of sacrifice is moved from the altar in the temple to the heart of the believer. The internal re-creation of the heart is the place where the transaction of restoration and re-creation occurs. The new covenant will be written, not on tablets of stone, but on the hearts of the justified and sanctified by the blood of the meek, humble, and obedient High Priest. Though he is the incarnation of God, he does not arrogate authority to himself, but obeys the will of God, learns obedience from his suffering, endures the cross and social shame, and is now seated at the right hand of God.

Hebrews is a complicated sermon that draws major lessons for Christians from the High Priest who was human in order to relate to humanity, yet also divine in order to have the power to save. The preacher-theologian of Hebrews exhorts his dispirited congregation to press forward to perfection, following the example of Jesus and the prophets and martyrs of ancient Israel.

John 18:1–19:42

John's passion narrative makes several compelling changes to the passion stories told by the Synoptic Gospels. John assigns a greater role for women, including Mary, the mother of Jesus, who stood faithfully near the cross. The male disciples had all fled, with the exception of one whom the Lord loved. When noticing several people who had enough courage to be faithful to the end, John cites last sentences not found in Synoptic record. Jesus addresses his mother, "Woman, here is your son" (19:26). He says to the disciple, "Here is your mother" (19:27). This Scripture honors women and expands the concept of family beyond the boundaries of physical or genetic affinity to universal human acceptance of all people as relatives in Christ.

Jesus identifies further with human suffering when the Christ, who made all things, utters, "I am thirsty" (19:28). Jesus, the sacrificed Lamb of God who takes away the sins of the world, says triumphantly, "It is finished" (19:30). John does not count this death as martyrdom, but as the glory of the Word made flesh saving the world.

John's Christology is as sophisticated as the well-developed Christology in Hebrews. Indeed, is there a higher Christology than the "Word made flesh"? The confidence that God became a human being to save human life perennially captures the attention. The Fourth Gospel has a higher sense of universal redemption than Hebrews, which is more localized than John's conception of Jesus as the *logos*, the divine Word that is the nucleus and centering reality of creation. The *logos* is the person, power, and presence of God that enlivens and redeems the whole of humankind. John sees Christ as the Word, at creation. That this "Word became flesh," a human being, "and lived among us" (John 1:14) is the heart and nerve center of the Gospel of John.

When God was ready to convert old creation into new creation, when God was ready to speak the word of truth that sets captives free, when God was ready to release abundant life among all, God opened God's mouth, and the Word was a child, a person, living, loving, lifting, teaching, blessing, healing, forgiving, hurting, dying, and rising again. The speech became a human being who continues to live among us, full of grace and truth.

The Word is far more than a speech or a book. Speech, language, talk, teachings, writings—none is sufficient, because they assume that people have within themselves the capacity to hear, to understand, to accept, and to live up to the standard of the speech. But what of the blind, who cannot see to read, or the deaf, who cannot hear the words, or the dull of spirit or the slow of heart, who will not respond to verbal truth? Verbal truth is invisible sound waves in the air. It has no hands, no feet, no flesh. It cannot rescue those in danger.

If I am caught in a house on fire, I need more than someone to tell me where the door is located, or write me some directions to the nearest window, or preach me a great sermon describing the route to the fire hydrant. I need more than someone to give me a set of directions to be applied in case of an emergency. I do not need a speech at that time. My lungs are filled with poisonous vapors. My eyes are irritated and red with smoke. My body is sick. My legs are weak. My consciousness is fading fast. I need human hands to reach me and pull me out of the fire. I need human hands to carry me when I cannot walk. I need human flesh to lift me when I cannot help myself. I need not a creed, but a Christ. I need not a plan of salvation, but a savior. I need not an announcement of liberation, but a liberator. I need somebody not to point the way, but to be the way. That is what we have. And Jesus said, "It is finished!"

Easter Day (Resurrection of Jesus)

Randall C. Bailey

ACTS 10:34–43
PSALM 118:1–2, 14–24
1 CORINTHIANS 15:1–11
JOHN 20:1–18

Easter is the heart of Christian faith. It celebrates the resurrection of our Lord and Savior, Jesus the Christ, and gives us hope that our lives will be better in days to come. It grounds hope with the conviction that the saying "Truth crushed to the ground will rise again"[1] is not just a proverb, but a truth that we can all experience and hold on to. Today's readings give us glimpses of how the early followers of the way understood the meaning and importance of this holy event. While we note that at times today's texts speak to justice concerns, more often the biblical writers minimize and even depoliticize those concerns. A guiding question will be, "What have they done to my Lord?"

Acts 10:34–43

In the first passage, Peter speaks to Cornelius. This passage parallels the story in Acts 8:26–40, which tells of the conversion of the Ethiopian official, the finance manager of the Candace (the queen who ruled Ethiopia). In that narrative, which fulfills the statement of the risen Christ in Acts 1:8 that the gospel will be spread from Jerusalem to Judea to Samaria and to the ends of the earth, the text tells us only that Philip "began to speak, and starting with this scripture, he proclaimed to him the good news about Jesus" (Acts 8:35). Thus, we are left to speculate what parts of the narrative of the life and ministry of Jesus were important.

---

1. This saying derives from Dan. 8:12.

197

In Acts 10:34–44, however, Peter's speech gives the reader information as to what the early believers understood to be the significant acts of Jesus. Peter begins by making a universal claim that God is interested in all people who fear God and do what is right (vv. 34–35).[2] Peter continues that Jesus was sent to Israel to preach "peace" (v. 36). This designation of the centrality of Jesus' preaching seems strange, given Jesus' statement, "Do you think that I have come to bring peace to the earth? No, I tell you, but rather division!" (Luke 12:51). While the angels make the claim that his birth signals "on earth peace" (Luke 2:14), peace is only for those whom God "favors." The other times Jesus uses the word "peace" are either to greet an individual or group (Luke 10:5; 24:36) or to dismiss an individual after a miracle (Luke 7:50; 8:48). Thus, this characterization of Jesus' preaching appears to be ironic, especially since in Acts 10:34–44 Peter is talking to a Roman soldier, a representative of the group that pressed imperial peace/*Pax Romana*[3] by terrorizing the people in the colonies through acts such as crucifixion, an ancient equivalent of lynching.[4]

In verses 37–38 Peter summarizes the life and ministry of Jesus. He cites Jesus' baptism by John, where the Holy Spirit gave Jesus power to perform miracles for those who were "oppressed by the devil." This reference to the devil is surprising, since the devil is mentioned only in Luke 4:2, 3, 13 and Luke 8:12, and neither reference is to a miracle story. This designation seems to remove the miracle stories from their sociopolitical realm to a spiritual realm. By the same token to use the term "oppressed" alongside the "devil" removes the term oppressed from the sociopolitical sense it held in Isaiah 61:1–2 (quoted in Luke 4:18). From these things we see Luke depoliticizing the life and ministry of Jesus and spiritualizing it.

In verse 39 we get the claim that "they put him to death by hanging him on a tree." This is most troubling, since the antecedent to "they" is not clear. Are "they" the ones whom Jesus had healed? Why doesn't Peter say to Cornelius, "Your government killed him"? Why doesn't he say "crucified" as opposed to "hung him on a tree"? This description seems to exonerate the Romans and to depoliticize the events that ended Jesus' life. Similarly, Peter's description of the charge from the postresurrection Jesus to proclaim him as "the one ordained by God as judge of the living and the dead" (v. 42) also deradicalizes

2. Demetrius Williams sees this as the central focus of the sermon of Peter and the inclusion of the story in the book. See his "The Acts of the Apostles," in *True to Our Native Land: An African American New Testament Commentary*, ed. Brian K. Blount (Minneapolis: Fortress Press, 2007), 230–31.

3. Klaus Wengst, *Pax Romana and the Peace of Jesus Christ*, trans. John Bowen (Philadelphia: Fortress Press, 1987).

4. Richard A. Horsley, *Jesus and Empire: The Kingdom of God and the New World Disorder* (Minneapolis: Fortress Press, 2003), 29–30.

Jesus the political revolutionary who was killed by the Romans for trying to liberate his people from Roman oppression and whose resurrection promises that the revolution will continue.[5] This speech contrasts with the story in Acts 8:26–40, where the social justice proclamation of Isaiah 53 interests the Ethiopian in the story of Jesus. Similarly, Acts 10 begins the story of the gospel traveling to Europe and away from Africa (the focus of Act 8). What has Peter done to my Lord in this portrayal?

Psalm 118:1–2, 14–24

This psalm is chosen for Easter because of verses 17 and 22, which claim that the psalmist will not die but will live, and that the rejected stone will become the cornerstone. Some writers in the Gospels and letters apply these concepts to Jesus (e.g., Matt. 21:42; Mark 12:10; Luke 20:17; Acts 4:11; 1 Pet. 2:7). What is surprising is that the speaker in the psalm is the monarch of Israel, who is talking about a war situation: In the war he will not be killed but will live, and he claims survival as the work of God. In the Gospels Jesus does die but is raised from death, contrary to the movement of this psalm. Finally, Psalm 118 provides the liturgy for the monarch coming to the temple during a war, seeking God's help for the nation and support from the priesthood. This text is the literary backdrop of the triumphal entry into Jerusalem. So its use on Easter is ironic, to say the least. The positive side is that the sociopolitical situation of the psalm does fit the revolutionary Jesus and what happened to him in that revolution.

1 Corinthians 15:1–11

In this passage Paul gives his interpretation of the importance of the Jesus events. The life of Jesus is not important to his theology. Thus, in contrast to Peter's telling of the story in Acts 10, Paul begins with the crucifixion of Jesus. Or does he? Paul states "Christ died for our sins" (v. 3). But Paul does not say Jesus was killed or by whom. He also does not say what "sins" caused Jesus' death. And who is the "our"? The Corinthians? Paul totally takes the crucifixion out of its sociopolitical context and spiritualizes it. The crucifixion is no longer a "lynching of the revolutionary." Paul's statement merely interprets the death of Jesus as a death for sin, thereby depoliticizing Jesus and his mission.

5. Randall C. Bailey, "The Biblical Basis for a Political Theology of Liberation," in *Blow the Trumpet in Zion: Global Vision and Action for the 21st Century Black Church*, ed. Iva E. Carruthers, Frederick D. Haynes III, and Jeremiah A. Wright Jr. (Minneapolis: Fortress Press, 2005), 91–96.

In verses 5–11 Paul speaks of the resurrection of Jesus in terms of listing those *men* to whom Jesus appeared,[6] but he does not speak to any social justice charge that Jesus gives to the audience at these appearances. Instead, Paul uses this passage to confess that he, Paul, oppressed the followers of Jesus after the crucifixion and resurrection and that in spite of this behavior Paul was chosen to interpret these events. In this way the stage is set to say that resisting political persecution and addressing social oppression are not at the base of the gospel imperative. What has Paul done to my Lord?

John 20:1–18

In the above passages we have heard only the voices of males talking to males about the male Jesus. In this Gospel lesson, we encounter a woman as the key actor. We must remember that in Paul's recounting above, Jesus only appeared to males.[7] In this text, however, the main focus is Jesus' appearance to Mary.

When Mary sees the stone has been rolled away, she immediately returns to the community to warn them. Peter and the disciple whom Jesus loved do not bring the news to the community. Instead, they start a footrace to the tomb, and when they get there, they both look in and see that the linen is out of place. The text says that the beloved disciple believed. Presumably Peter did as well. This scene is almost comical in its portrayal of males who go to a gravesite and are concerned primarily about the location of linen, not about what has happened to the body.

Mary returns to the tomb, looks in, and sees angels. Were the angels there when the men looked? Did they miss this apparition? She stays and struggles to find out what has happened. Is this emblematic of the differences between male and female spirituality? As Peter and Paul tell the story of Jesus in Acts 10 and 1 Corinthians 11, we see the suggestions of competitiveness, depoliticizing, and stressing the role of males. The males in those passages do not manifest the communal care that Mary exhibits.[8]

In Mary's persistence, both with the angels and the resurrected Jesus (vv. 13–17), she even moves Jesus, from referring to her with the term *gynē*, "woman" (v. 15), to calling her by name, "Mary!" (v. 16). While Jerena Lee and Maria Stewart used this passage to justify their right to preach, Jesus

---

6. Boykin Sanders sees that the central part of this unit shows how widespread the gospel is in his "1 Corinthians," in *True to Our Native Land*, 299.

7. Sanders follows the NRSV's rendition of *adelphoi*, to be "brothers and sisters" (299), but the preponderance of males named in the unit testifies against this translation.

8. Cf. Allen Dwight Callahan, "John," in *True to Our Native Land*, 206–7.

instructs Mary to go tell his "boys" that he has risen. Thus, the inclusive nature they claim is still imbedded in patriarchal discourse.

Mary's question, "What have they done to my Lord?" (vv. 13, 15), becomes the justice entrée into preaching all of the passages for today. On the one hand, the preacher needs to critique the depoliticizing that has taken place in these biblical texts. On the other hand, the preacher must preach a revolutionary gospel that goes beyond the content of these specific texts. The resurrection of the revolutionary Jesus, concerned about the freedom of his people under Roman occupation, needs to be proclaimed, and the congregation needs to see how these texts point us away from this understanding of both the crucifixion and resurrection. We can then inspire each other to enter the struggles of our day for justice and liberation with the assurance that, even if we get vamped on by the government and other oppressive forces, this will not be the end of the resistance movement. Rather, the story of the resurrection moves us to keep on struggling.

These portrayals of the resurrection are similar to the ways that Martin Luther King Jr. has been stereotyped as the dreamer of 1963, and not as the revolutionary who came to understand the interlocking of the war in Vietnam with the struggle of garbage workers in Memphis and the poor people's campaign, which had to go beyond race to include all poor people. Just as Martin has been tamed in our day, Jesus was tamed by these texts in his time. But we can resist this taming and proclaim the resurrection of Jesus, which shows us that the struggles must continue.

Second Sunday of Easter

Olive Elaine Hinnant

ACTS 4:32–35
PSALM 133
1 JOHN 1:1–2:2
JOHN 20:19–31

The texts for the Second Sunday of Easter tell stories about living in human community, with the desired outcome being a world of peace, unity, and harmony. A community committed to *shalom* is based upon mutually supportive relationships with each other and with God. While having unity is good, more often than not, life is a striving for unity *en la lucha*, "in the struggle." Beginning with the local level, do we have peace in our families? Then what about our churches, our society, and our nation? How does the resurrected One, the Prince of Peace, make a difference in our world? The path of *shalom* requires more than we imagine. At the same time, it already exists; William Sloane Coffin has written, "Am I my brother's keeper? No, I am my brother's brother or sister. Human unity is not something we are called upon to create, only to recognize."[1] Is it too hard to let go of our beliefs, our possessions, our rights, and our religion for the sake of peace, harmony, and unity?

Acts 4:32–35

Wow, what a great idea! Everybody pitch in, give what they have, and no one will be in need. As Deuteronomy 15:4 says, "There will be no one in need among you." To understand what is taking place in Acts with the early believers and their possessions, it is important to know two of Israel's economic principles. First, the Israelites who had written the creation stories about all the animals, land, and heavens given to them, and who had been freed from slavery

1. William Sloane Coffin, *Credo* (Louisville, KY: Westminster John Knox Press, 2004), 33.

202

into a land flowing with milk and honey, believed God was a God of abundance. As long as this abundance was shared, there were no poor people among them. But the community got out of balance: some would take more than they needed, and poverty occurred. Second, Israel developed practices to maintain equitable distribution of resources: the sabbatical year and the jubilee. Once every seven years, the sabbatical year required three things to happen: the land to lie fallow, so that it might renew itself and not be overfarmed (Exod. 23:10–11); debts between Hebrews to be canceled (Deut. 15:1–11); and all slaves to be set free and paid for their work (Deut. 15:12–18). Jubilee included these stipulations and added another. At jubilee, celebrated every forty-nine years, every family would take possession of their ancestral land (Lev. 25:13–34). In this way, no family could permanently hold on to an increasing amount of land and become wealthier than others. Otherwise, if left unchecked, the economy could become out of balance, with a few monopolizing wealth and the majority living in poverty. If practiced, jubilee was a reversal of fortune, a chance to start over again.

Jesus came proclaiming the jubilee (Luke 4:18–19). By the first century, poverty was widespread, and neither jubilee nor sabbatical year had been practiced fully for 400 years (though people had let the land lie fallow from time to time). Jesus with all of his emphasis on the poor must have known that getting people to share through certain practices (jubilee or sabbath year) was practically impossible, especially for the wealthy. They needed another chance. Jesus came preaching forgiveness of sin and the opportunity to practice sharing every day. In Acts 4:32–35 we have a glimpse of the early church practicing jubilee and the sabbath year. Though the early church encountered problems with this practice later, the community's life in Acts acknowledged that all we have is not really ours.

The type of sharing in Acts 4:32–35 may not be the ideal way to share what we have with others, but it is helpful to return to such examples when our economic way of living has crashed. Education activist Parker Palmer illustrates: "The collapse of the U.S. housing market at the heart of the recent financial crisis is also the collapse of a series of long-held illusions in American society: that housing prices will always rise, that Americans can live beyond their means forever, and that the growing gap between rich and poor doesn't matter."[2] The church needs to lead the way toward an economic order based not on self-accumulation but on the sharing depicted in Acts 4.

2. Parker Palmer, http://www.pbs.org/moyers/journal/02202009/profile2.html (accessed February 20, 2010).

Psalm 133

If we were to search for places of unity on Earth today, how many do you think we would find? What if the United Nations was about locating and celebrating harmony among nations, rather than trying to prevent wars? Psalm 133 instructs the search for peace.

This psalm is the fourteenth of fifteen Songs of Ascents used by the pilgrims as they went to and from the temple in Jerusalem. The psalm joyfully declares the hopes of kindred and nations. It moves from the familial (kindred), to the priestly (Aaron), to the political (Hermon and Zion). As families journey to Jerusalem to worship God in the temple, they move out of their local and private lives into the public and communal life in which the priest mediates for the whole people. The psalm reminds the entire community, including families, of the true source of life—God's presence. Psalm 133, read during the season of Easter, when we have just experienced the life-giving power of the resurrection, can remind us that "to profess the resurrection is to take our place in *God's family*, and thus to receive an identity that prevents our making an idol of human familial reality in all of its various cultural forms."[3] Family values are important, and family is a crucial institution, but the family cannot be the most important or only source of support.

This psalm is also a prayer that the two countries can find peace. The northern nation, represented by Hermon, and the southern nation, represented by Zion, are divided politically. The psalmist points out that in God's realm the dew falling (snow melting) from Hermon will run down upon the mountains of Zion, and *both* will receive nourishment. God does not show partiality.

1 John 1:1–2:2

First John uses language reminiscent of the Fourth Gospel, such as "from the beginning," "word of life," "eternal life," "that your joy may be complete," and "light" and "darkness." This author gives testimony to salvation through Jesus' resurrection and the continuing forgiveness of sin through an advocate. In addressing the current fellowship, the author uses "declare," a strong and confident word, once in each of the first three verses. Other verbs are active, bodily, engaging actions: see, hear, look, touch, and testify. Each of these implies a sensory way of experiencing the world; only taste and smell are left out of the list. What might it be like to taste and smell the good news of resurrection and forgiveness? This testimony is not about creeds of belief or a

3. J. Clinton McCann, "Psalms," in *New Interpreter's Bible: A Commentary in Twelve Volumes*, ed. Leander Keck et al. (Nashville: Abingdon Press, 2002), 4:1216.

certain path to heaven, but about humanly actions, ways of knowing what one knows in the world. The author of 1 John is an eyewitness to Jesus' resurrection from the dead and wants everyone to know it is true!

In his testimony, there are keys to *shalom* in human community: "if we say that we have no sin, we deceive ourselves" (1:8); "if we say that we have not sinned, we make him [Jesus or God] a liar, and his word is not in us" (1:10). The amazing thing is that when we sin, we have an advocate (1:9; 2:1); we have forgiveness in Jesus, we have a second chance. And not only for "us": this experience is for everyone. These are not instructions for budget management, program development, preaching, administration, or even mission. This is the foundation for the church.

Sara Miles was a journalist and a chef who wandered into an Episcopal church in San Francisco one Sunday, had Communion, and kept coming back. She had not been raised in the church, but she was transformed by Communion and the words, "Take and eat, this is my body given for you." Miles's spiritual transformation led her to start a food pantry that now feeds 600 families a week. Her first book, *Take This Bread*, details her spiritual awaking within Christianity as an outsider and how she felt called to offer food to others.[4] "Religion Dispatches," an online magazine, talked with her recently about her *Jesus Freak: Feeding, Healing, Raising the Dead*.[5] She said:

> Well, we feed everybody. We feed the undeserving poor. That to me is one of the great gifts the church can offer. And again, it gets expressed in what people believe. Do people believe that God's grace is for the people who deserve it? Do people believe that in my tradition, communion is for the people who deserve it? Do people believe that the sacramental rite of marriage is for the people who deserve it? Or do you just think: God's grace is everywhere. It's out of control. You actually cannot manage it. God rains on the deserving and undeserving alike.[6]

John 20:19–31

Death is final for almost everyone. That could be the reason that Jesus' return from death was so frightening to the disciples. They didn't know what to make of it. The powers exerted to put him to death had lost, and Jesus lived! Who then held power over death? Frightened and uncertain, the disciples

---

4. Sara Miles, *Take This Bread: A Radical Conversion* (New York: Ballantine Books, 2008).
5. Sara Miles, *Jesus Freak: Feeding, Healing, Raising the Dead* (San Francisco: Jossey-Bass Publishers, 2010).
6. http://www.religiondispatches.org/archive/mediaculture/2283/ (accessed May 30, 2010).

locked themselves away, hoping their lives were safe and sound.[7] But Jesus broke through their presumed security and offered them a different kind of peace. He uttered "Peace be with you," twice, in his first visit and again later to Thomas. In so doing, Jesus fulfills the promise of John 14:27.

The words "Peace be with you" (20:19b) are a blessing of *shalom*, the Hebrew word for peace that means wholeness—body, mind, and soul, well-being for all. Offering this peace at his resurrection appearance, Jesus was saying, in effect, that God's power is not, will not, and cannot be killed or silenced. No matter what violence, oppression, or injustice is done to another person, that is not the final word. "Peace be with you" is. God's power is always present. Humanity, like the disciples, may not be able to see this, but the resurrection holds this ultimate promise of God's transforming work among us.

Then Jesus breathed the Holy Spirit on them (20:22). This fulfilled another promise from the Farewell Discourse (14:26; 15:26–27). They would have God's help to return to the world and continue Jesus' work. They were not left alone.

The next message the resurrected Jesus offered is one of forgiveness: "If you forgive the sins of any, they are forgiven them; if you retain the sins of any, they are retained" (20:23). Jesus does not tell them how to organize the church, or how to baptize or serve Communion or do building campaigns. He does not discuss the doctrine of resurrection with them. He instructs them to forgive.

Our world is in desperate need of this Easter message of forgiveness. Daily we struggle with the powers and principalities that do not make for *shalom*: injustice, racism, poverty, betrayal, greed, torture, lies, war, and the list goes on. To forgive is to give someone a second chance, to start over, to have new life. This is true not only among individuals but also among communities and even among nations. For example, think of what it would mean for nations in the third world to have their monetary debts forgiven. It would mean a chance to start over in rebuilding their economies.

The act of forgiveness has the possibility of creating harmony, unity, and peace in our lives and society. Jesus gives us the power to forgive, because God has forgiven us. On the Second Week of Easter, before we move too quickly from the cross, may we begin the practice of forgiveness in personal and communal ways, so that we are bearers of new life and peace in our world.

---

7. The Fourth Gospel says that the disciples had locked the doors of the house "for fear of the Jews." The expression "the Jews" here refers, as it does throughout this Gospel, not to the entire Jewish people but to select Jewish leaders with whom the Johannine community was in tension. The remark that the disciples locked the doors "for fear of the Jews" is likely not a historical reminiscence. The Gospel writer probably added it as part of the Fourth Gospel's ongoing polemic against "the Jews" as just described. The preacher could explain the historical background of this reference and caution the congregation not to repeat the historical and theological error of the writer of the Fourth Gospel of negatively caricaturing some within the Jewish community or the community as a whole.

Third Sunday of Easter

María Teresa Dávila

ACTS 3:12–19
PSALM 4
1 JOHN 3:1–7
LUKE 24:36B–48

The resurrection experiences and the experiences of the earliest Christian communities point to two paradoxes of Christian living that have both obsessed and shaped us for centuries. First, the resurrection narratives make clear that the disciples' joy in seeing the resurrected Christ is balanced with the sobering presence of the wounds of the cross on our Savior's flesh (Luke 24:38–48; cf. John 20:27). Why did the resurrection, such an important salvific act of divine love, not erase the marks of a foul and violent death? The second paradox is related to the first. How were the nascent Christian communities to deal with the many ways people were excluded from free and full standings as human beings in the Roman Empire, exclusions that are often based on the marks with which we brand others and which keep them "outside the gates"?[1] The readings for this Third Sunday of Easter struggle with these two related tensions in Christianity.

Often our building of the beloved community and our work for justice are overcome by a deep desire for an antiseptic and pure version of our faith and its practices; so we forget that a resurrection community must bear the marks of the cross and that inclusion cannot be at the cost of erasing the histories of those we frequently keep outside the gate. Today's reading from the Acts of the Apostles, as well as the resurrection appearance of Jesus in Luke, pushes these early communities to struggle with the bodily histories we bear, and with whether our whole selves are accepted in emerging redemptive communities. These readings warn against engaging in the work of justice and inclusion

---

1. The phrase "outside the gates" is commonly used in Christian theology. I am most familiar with its discussion in Orlando Costas, *Christ outside the Gate: Mission beyond Christendom* (Eugene, OR: Wipf & Stock, 2005).

inside our communities of faith in ways that gloss over the historical and very incarnate pain that is the result of the sin we do to each other. Indeed, the reading from 1 John 3 epitomizes the challenging task of Christian imagination in balancing the tensions inherent in our resurrection tradition by clearly relating Christian love to knowing and doing the truth.

Luke 24:36b–48

The disciples gathered together are only beginning to digest the news from the two returning from their journey to Emmaus—the story of an intimate encounter with the resurrected Jesus that ended in the breaking of the bread—when they too encounter the same vision among them, the presence of their Savior greeting them with the words "Peace be with you" (v. 36b). This particular passage is highlighted by an emphasis on the corporeal presence of the risen Christ. The troubled disciples until this time have collapsed under the weight of the hopelessness of a movement for liberation and justice dashed by the execution of its leader. Now they have to come to terms with the return of their leader and its meaning for their own future and the future of the movement.

Two things are troubling here, both for the disciples and for today's congregation that seeks to be faithful. First, Jesus' victory over death energizes his followers for a specific kind of ministry. While his trial and execution were marked with the dramatic back and forth of the powers (both government and religious authorities), his victory over death is described as a more personal victory, apart from the drama and fanfare of the public struggle that had occurred just a few days before. Much as Jesus' own ministry was initiated among the people, gaining public attention as his message spread and gained influence, the ministry of that initial community begins in an intimate way with experiences of the resurrected Christ in bodily form, standing among them, eating with them.

Second, Jesus' proof that he is in fact their teacher, risen from the dead, is his own mutilated body. The witness of his suffering is the mark of his victory. He does not say, "I have conquered death, so that the marks of death have been overcome and erased." Instead, Jesus says, "Look at my hands and my feet; see that it is I myself. Touch me and see; for a ghost does not have flesh and bones as you see that I have" (v. 39). Truly the marks of his martyrdom are a sign of his suffering *and* his victory over the injustice of his death.

This narrative of the disciples' experience with the resurrected Christ is the recollection of all historical bodily suffering and a reminder that reconciliation and victory over injustice must take place within the context of the real and concrete injuries that have marked the human form throughout history, particularly that of the poor and the racialized other. Jesus' invitation to the disciples to see and feel his wounds has a sobering effect on the joy of the disciples upon encountering their risen and victorious leader. A nation or society that claims to have overcome a particular injustice or evil—or that is still working through structural and concrete suffering—must reckon with the wounds that remain unaltered by the establishment of human rights, or the return of lands wrongfully taken, or the restoration of human relationships torn by inequality and sin. Most truth and reconciliation commissions in different countries trying to correct their histories of racial oppression and violence acknowledge that real transformation for justice cannot take hold unless the wounds, personal and corporate, are acknowledged as present in the everyday lives of those who have been wronged.

This Gospel passage is critical for the work of justice because it provides a faithful and liberating place for our memories of concrete and historical suffering. Jesus' invitation to the disciples to look and feel his wounds is not meant to incite their thirst for revenge and violence, or to inspire pity. Rather, it is meant to highlight the greatness of God's salvific act through Christ in history, a salvation that did not require the decimation of opposing armies or the spilling of blood in a political coup. God's salvific activity in the resurrection embraces and transforms unjust suffering so that the work of building the realm within history can continue among those commissioned to preach love and repentance (v. 47). The work of building the beloved community takes place within history and within our wounded bodies. Negating the marks of the suffering of the oppressed among us is to make Jesus' resurrection a ghostly appearance, unrelated to salvation in history.

Acts 3:12–19

Peter and the other leaders find themselves with the bodily presence of a man crippled from birth, whom they cured in the name of Jesus Christ (3:2–8). But much as Jesus' bodily wounds remind us of his status as a political prisoner before his death, this man's very presence remind all in the temple that he had not previously been healed. While he is no longer crippled, he is still marked with his history prior to being healed. Peter's speech reminds the audience that God's work through Jesus Christ has given this person renewed health. The man's presence is a witness of God's love and God's power to restore.

A religious community's faithfulness is to be measured by its concrete inclusion or exclusion of those persons whom society deems disposable or outside of history. In order for inclusion to witness to God's glory and salvific love, it must take the form of admitting personal and corporate histories of suffering. Precisely those characteristics that make particular groups sit as beggars outside the doors of our congregations—migrants and the racial other, the poor and the physically challenged, those the church excludes because of their sexual orientation or their gender—are the characteristics of the histories on which salvation is wrought. To work for inclusion and justice in our religious communities means that we—like the disciples welcoming the resurrected Christ with his wounds and Peter reaching out to the man at the gate—embrace the whole persons in our midst, with their particular stories of suffering, corporate experiences of injustice, and universal desire for love and inclusion.

Psalm 4 and 1 John 3:1–7

The Christian paradox of a risen Christ still with the wounds of the cross, and of the cured cripple still with the wounds of exclusion, can be addressed only with the imagination brought about by deep faithfulness in God's loving peace. Important to both the psalm for this Sunday and the reading from John's epistle is the emphasis on truth as part of the liberative activity of God. Psalm 4 asks, "How long . . . shall my honor suffer shame? How long will you love vain words, and seek after lies?" (v. 2). The First Letter of John warns, "Let no one deceive you. Everyone who does what is right is righteous, just as he is righteous" (1 John 3:7).

At the heart of becoming faithful is the pursuit of truth, one of the most important elements of the task of justice. Only in truth can we come to experience God's love and peace. The epistle's message for this Sunday, centered on the love of God and becoming like Christ, demands truth and knowledge as requirements of love. As loving communities of faith, we must acknowledge the wounds that we bear and the wounds that we cause in truth and in love. With the psalmist, we must confront those who would rather gloss over the suffering of those in our midst or those outside the gate with the way such deception mocks God's true salvific love. With John, we must demand that our community of love and faithfulness, of christification and living in the hope of the risen Christ, be honest to the legacy of the cross and the burdens of history, lest we are marked to repeat our violent forms of religious, social, and political exclusion and domination.

All the readings for this Sunday convey a deep hope seated in the radical demand for truth telling in charity. The heart of the task of truth telling is not to reengage in the violence that occasioned our original hurt and sins against one another. Rather, the heart of truth telling is to witness to the God of truth, justice, peace, and love who commissions us, along with the first disciples, to be witnesses to the love that brought Jesus back from the dead and that saves the crippled and excluded—a witnessing that can occur only with our concrete acts of inclusion and love, recalling the wounds of history as part of our transformative contribution to the realm of God in history.

Earth Day (April 22)

John Hart

LEVITICUS 25:18–24
PSALM 65:5–13
COLOSSIANS 1:11–20
MARK 12:1–12

The Revised Common Lectionary does not contain a season or a Sunday that focuses on the natural world. Earth Day (April 22) can help fill this void. Organizers began Earth Day in 1970 to call attention to the growing ecological crisis, by focusing on such things as pollution, using up nonrenewable resources, and creating waste that threatens the survival of the environment. Earth Day gives the minister an opportunity to help the congregation think about a theology of the natural world, about how to become better stewards of Earth, and about honoring the integrity of all created things.[1] Since Earth Day often takes place in the season of Easter, the preacher could suggest that from the apocalyptic point of view, the resurrection of Jesus pointed to the regeneration of Earth as well as the whole cosmos.

> The women we worked with recounted that unlike in the past, they were unable to meet their basic needs. This was due to the degradation of their immediate environment as well as the introduction of commercial farming, which replaced the growing of household food crops. But international trade controlled the price of the exports from these small-scale farmers and a reasonable and just income could not be guaranteed. I came to understand that when the environment is destroyed, plundered or mismanaged, we undermine our quality of life and that of future generations.[2]
>
> *Wangari Maathai*

1. Contemporary Christian eco-theology/ethics writers often capitalize planet Earth. This practice promotes respect for our planet, aligns capitalization with other planets, and distinguishes planet Earth from earth, the soil of Earth.
2. Wangari Mutta Maathai, "Nobel Lecture," in *Lex Prix Nobel: The Nobel Prizes, 2004*, ed. Tore Frängsmyr (Privately published: Nobel Foundation, 2004), 312.

In 1970, a group of U.S. environmentalists decided to promote a day annually to care for planet Earth. They believed that if people would celebrate Earth each year, attempt to reverse the human production processes that pollute Earth, and promote practices to protect Earth, over time Earth would be restored, species would be conserved, and people would have happier, healthier lives. While this original Earth Day was a secular holiday, for the person of faith it can be transformed into a sacred holy day.

On Earth Day, Christians are called to reflect on how God expects us to treat creation and to use Earth's natural goods responsibly and carefully. "Natural goods" are those natural benefits of creation that fulfill a purpose that might or might not provide for human needs. The customary term used for such natural benefits, "resources," is misleading: It implies something waiting to be extracted by humans for human purposes. However, these goods do quite nicely as found in nature through interrelated, integrated, and interdependent interaction among Earth's living and nonliving beings. Humans view them as "good" because they also can help people to provide for human needs and well-being. God's good creation, then, is present to us as a sacred, even sacramental, commons—a place both revelatory of divine presence and available to provide for human *needs* (not every human *want*). In the presence of the Creator, we are to help each other and to promote our well-being in relationship to the well-being of all biota—the living creatures with whom humans share their Earth home.

The Scripture readings for today remind us that Christians are called to fulfill a twofold socioecological responsibility: to care for people and for planet. While socially and ecologically disruptive corporations declare that "employment and environment" or "economics and ecology" are contradictory concepts, thoughtful Christians realize that these are *complementary*. Sabbath year and jubilee year teachings, among others, weave community and individual responsibility to God's creation and creatures, with responsibility to those whom Jesus would call, centuries later, "the least of these" (Matt. 25:31–46).

Leviticus 25:18–24

Leviticus 25:1–7 describes the three requirements for the *sabbath* year (every seven years): rest for the land (enabling Earth's regeneration, and allowing domestic and wild creatures to eat Earth's fruits undisturbed by a private "owner" of part of God's land); release of slaves (providing personal and familial liberty); and remission of debts (facilitating economic renewal). The *jubilee* year, a "Sabbath of Sabbaths" (seven times seven years, often rounded to "fifty years"), described in Leviticus 25:8–17, adds a fourth requirement:

redistributing the land to its original, post-exodus Hebrew inhabitants or their descendants.

Today's text teaches people that if they faithfully observe the sabbath year and jubilee year, they will be secure on the land, and the land will provide for their needs. Observing these would mean that the harvest gathered in the sixth year would have to sustain the people not only for the seventh year, but also, since neither planting nor harvesting was allowed in year seven, for the eighth year, and even into the ninth year. People are advised to be confident that God, who knows their needs, will provide food for them, as God did in the wilderness during the exodus.

Leviticus states a fundamental biblical principle: Earth and all Earth contains are God's. Therefore, despite any laws they might develop, people have no perennial right to private property or what it produces: "The land shall not be sold in perpetuity, for the land is mine; with me you are but aliens and tenants" (25:23). This principle, of course, contradicts individual, family, and corporate "rights" to perpetual ownership, which are legally absolutized in many countries. Principles contrary to biblical teachings state that Earth and what Earth produces through biological or geological processes are "private property" to be used, abused, and disposed of according to the "property owner." Biblical teachings prioritize community rights over private rights: The flow of power is from God through community to individual: God → community → individual. Current property policies and practices that privatize land not only have reversed the biblical order, but have eliminated divine consideration entirely: private → community → [God].

Christians should have greater respect for God's Earth and ensure that Earth's natural goods are distributed to meet the common good. In the first Genesis creation story, God calls all creatures "very good"; before the flood God instructs Noah to save all species, and after the flood God makes a covenant not only with people but with Earth and all life.

God loves all creatures. Evolutionary processes in biological development reveal God's creativity, the ongoing nature of "creation," and the ongoing creation of "nature." Similarly, planetary integrity and equilibrium are maintained through natural geological or meteorological dynamics (even when such might cause what are, for humans, "natural catastrophes"). Humankind disrupts these processes through irresponsible mining practices, overconsumption of Earth goods, excessive emissions of carbon and sulfur that alter Earth's climate, and releases of effluents that poison water. By contrast, when "natural goods" are acknowledged to be provided by God, they become available to sustain life and to ensure planetary equilibrium and stability, and might be extracted or altered to meet community needs.

Psalm 65:5–13

Psalm 65:5–13 celebrates God's creativity, power, and solicitude for all creation. God visits Earth through the falling rain, thereby providing water needed for agriculture and abundant harvest. Not only humanity benefits from rain. The wilderness, hills, meadows, and valleys all shout for joy, revealing their fruitfulness in beautiful flora or grain and pasture for livestock. All Earth is productive when its rhythms flow freely, and when people are integrated responsibly with Earth's processes. The psalm prompts the hearer to be grateful for what God has created and to use the natural goods of creation to provide responsibly for human needs.

Colossians 1:11–20

Colossians 1:11–20 instructs the Christian community that Jesus is the "image of the invisible God" (v. 15) and that in Jesus "all things in heaven and on earth were created" (v. 16) and "hold together" (v. 17). Through Jesus too, "God was pleased to reconcile to [God] all things, whether on earth or in heaven" (v. 20).

The epistle presents points to ponder on Earth Day. Since Christians, who are "followers of Christ," are also "images of God" in creation, how might they reveal God in their care for creation and for each other? How might they respect all creatures, and enable them to "hold together" in interrelated, integrated, and interdependent creation, rather than selfishly disrupt creation, polluting air, land, and water, and promoting adverse impacts on Earth's climate? How might they too "reconcile all things" in ecological, meteorological, and geological balance, by negating their past conduct and conserving or renewing evolutionary and dynamic processes that result from divine creativity?

Mark 12:1–12

Earth Day themes are present too in Mark 12:1–12. Jesus' parable describes what God will do if people do not use God's Earth in ways God intended, but rather reserve for themselves the natural goods that Earth produces for all. In the parable, a landowner develops property into a vineyard and leases it to tenants. The tenants were supposed to use the vineyard as the owner had intended, to provide for themselves and others as they made their livelihood, and to return some of its fruits to the owner for his use and disposition. However, the rebellious tenants kill the owner's servants and his son when the servants and son try to collect from the tenants what they owe the owner.

The parable teaches that people owe God gratitude and praise for what they have received, and should responsibly use God's vineyard as its owner intended. The vineyard's fruits are not just for the immediate tenants, but for other people and purposes. From an Earth Day perspective, the parable teaches that God wants the vineyard's produce to provide for the needs of the poor and for other creatures. If the "tenants"—who include all rural and urban people in succeeding generations—do not use the land *entrusted* (not *given*) for the purposes God intends, then God can displace current occupants and give other residents the opportunity to care for God's Earth and to use its fruits as God intends them to be used.[3]

Wangari Maathai, the 2004 Nobel Peace laureate, illustrates today's themes in her life and work; she has directly implemented the biblical themes cited earlier. In her native Kenya, she saw that women were unable to meet their basic needs because of environmental degradation and export-oriented commercial agricultural operations that were controlled by transnational corporations and their corrupt local allies. Such practices harmed communities in the present and jeopardized future generations. Maathai responded to women's needs from her core religious convictions, her living faith, and through her compassion—her love for the poor and socially oppressed. In the spirit of James 2 and 1 John 3, she saw her sisters (and the poor in general) in need, and helped them overcome their societally stipulated social status. She confronted directly the political institutions and economic structures that allowed corporations and individuals to abuse Earth and extract natural goods as "resources" for personal benefit, rather than as benefits for planetary and community well-being. Politically powerful individuals enriched themselves, put profits above people, caused environmental destruction, and deprived ordinary citizens, especially the poor, of beautiful and safe places to live and natural goods to earn their livelihood.

Maathai organized local common people, particularly women, to plant and protect trees. Restored forests became a community benefit under community control. Maathai and members of her Green Belt organization planted more than a million trees. A Billion Tree campaign followed, which stimulated responsible arboriculture throughout the world. As a result of Maathai's innovative work with local communities, throughout Africa recently restored forests today provide extensive habitat for animals, protective cover and shade for all biota, aesthetic beauty for people, and, when used responsibly and equitably, wood for housing, cooking, and heating—all of which sustain life and provide work for local communities.

3. The interpretation of the parable offered here avoids the trap of supersessionism with which Christians so often read Mark 12:1–12 and its parallels.

Preachers might ask, how can Wangari Maathai's work prompt the congregation to look around their neighborhood or community and develop projects that address the needs of the poor while promoting careful use of Earth's natural goods? Preachers might question, who are the urban or rural people suffering from economic or social hardship, and what are the "trees" they need to provide for themselves, their families, and their communities? These "trees" might have different forms in different community settings, such as houses, health care, jobs with just wages and safe working conditions, child care, meaningful education, care for elders. Christians should explore how they might identify these kinds of "trees," and work together to meet their neighbors' spiritual, social, and sustenance needs.

Whether or not its founders intended, Earth Day is a celebration of creation—and an expression of thanksgiving to the Creator. On Earth Day, Christians acknowledge that creation as a whole, from distant stars to seashore starfish, is localized in the sacramental commons, the historical context for contact with God. In this commons, compassionate Christians fulfill their responsibilities to Creator, creation, and community.

Earth Day should be every day. Christians should strive daily to care for creation and care for community, to be solicitous of planet and people. Christians should be caretakers of creation and compassionate toward the biotic community of its living members, sustaining thereby the basic principles of an unending sabbath year. People in an ongoing way can express faith in God; embody fidelity to God's instructions to serve and conserve Earth, all biota, and human communities; and ensure that all people live with dignity and justice, and have a sufficiency of Earth's goods to meet their daily needs.

Fourth Sunday of Easter

Scott C. Williamson

ACTS 4:5–12
PSALM 23
1 JOHN 3:16–24
JOHN 10:11–18

The lectionary readings for this week raise a number of interrelated themes around the duty to love on both religious and moral grounds. Theologically, we model fidelity to God as we follow Christ's example of love. The love that we share with our brothers and sisters in Christ's name is God's love. But love can get us into moral hot water. To share God's love in the name of Jesus Christ is to participate in a new political reality that challenges and threatens religious leadership, even as it does good deeds for people in distress. To love in the name of Jesus is a faithful response to salvation. It is cause for celebration. Conversely, to love in the name of Jesus is a dangerous political act that undermines the systemic power structures of the old age with the power of the Holy Spirit. It is cause for arrest and trial. Christians are not free to divorce their love of God from the moral obligation to love their brothers and sisters. The love of Christ compels a more complex witness.

Acts 4:5–12

Peter and John have just been brought before a council of religious leaders. The setting of Acts 4:5–12 is before the council. Immediately preceding today's text, Acts 3 details the miraculous healing of a lame man the day before, an act that occasioned Peter's preaching at the temple and brought the apostles before the council. Peter healed the man in Jesus' name and then urged the amazed crowd to repent and receive baptism in the name of Jesus Christ. Invoking the name of Christ in this way set off the controversy and presented the council with a dilemma. In addition to the matter of heresy, the council had a political problem on their hands. The message was spreading.[1] The authorities could not deny that a man lame from birth had been healed, or argue that such a miraculous healing was wrong. Instead, the council inquired about the authority for the healing. Verse 7 raises the important question, "By what power or by what name did you do this?" By framing their religious and political concerns about Christian preaching around the issue of authority, the council was careful to question the ethics of the arrested men without disavowing the good of the healing.

In verse 9 Peter refers to the "healing" of the lame man as a "good deed." The word for "healed" carries the double meaning of "saved."[2] The man was healed from his physical infirmity. Moreover, he was saved from God's judgment. This understanding of the essential relatedness between physical healing and salvation is important to the work of social justice, because it resists any attempt to bracket the spiritual dimension of salvation from the material implications of what it means to be saved in the name of Jesus Christ.

In the nineteenth century, Frederick Douglass chastised the antebellum church in the South for caring about white souls but not black bodies. "We have men sold to build churches, women sold to support the gospel, and babes sold to purchase Bibles for the poor heathen! All for the glory of God and the good of souls."[3] Douglass argued that slaveholders who were saved by God should become agents of healing for slaves. God's amazing grace not only opened their eyes to the injustice of slavery, but also changed slaveholders into abolitionists. The rest was merely a sham religion that worshiped the cross with a whip alongside.

Psalm 23

Psalm 23 celebrates God's exceeding goodness and steadfast love. The first line of this beloved hymn paints a portrait of God as the good shepherd who leads followers to abundance and protects them from evil. For the psalmist, following God means that all of one's material needs for sustenance and security will be met. No matter how turbulent the times, no matter how many enemies or obstacles appear on the horizon, no matter how many times the supplicant has strayed down wrong paths, the good shepherd calls and comforts the sheep with green pastures and still waters. Though our enemies wait for us, they wait in vain, because God ultimately watches over us. God prepares a table for us and sends goodness and mercy to accompany us on our

---

1. Acts 4:4.
2. The verb translated "healed" in v. 9 (Gk. *sōzein*) is translated "saved" in v. 12.
3. Frederick Douglass, Appendix to *Narrative of the Life of Frederick Douglass, an American Slave* (1845; repr., New York: Soho Books, 2010), 1.

journey to Zion. We have only to trust, follow, and accept the provisions that God has for us.

In the context of the accompanying lectionary readings for this Sunday, the psalm can inspire new ways to understand love. Following are two such prophetic allusions. Whatever else the love of Christ entails, it means trust in God. The psalmist writes with conviction, "I shall not want." To accept God as the good shepherd means to trust in God's love with a single-minded loyalty. The relationship to God that God intends for us is not possible if we hedge our bets about the sufficiency of God's love or the depth of her mercy. We cannot keep Mammon on speed dial, fearful that God might fail to deliver.

Further, the psalmist writes, "I fear no evil" (v. 4). Whatever else the love of Christ entails, it energizes us to resist runaway fear, that panic for self-preservation that is often an immediate reaction to an experience of evil. Evil-doers incite fear to invoke our compliance, to direct our behavior, and even to steal our worship. To accept God as the good shepherd means to live in the presence of evildoers, mindful of the life-destroying harm they can unleash against us and our loved ones, and determined to keep our fear in check. The relationship to God that God intends for us is not possible if we are constantly soul sick in fear of evil. To be constantly soul sick in fear is a paralyzing moral disorder that prevents our participation in the work of social justice.

Examples of persons and groups who manifested such lack of fear in the face of threat are numerous. When black demonstrators filled the jails for justice in the 1960s, they did so knowing that there was not a more dangerous place for a black person to be than behind the bars of a southern jail. To fear no evil is both a catalyst for social justice and a major reward. God motivates us to resist injustice, and encourages us to stay the course. More than this, God creates community in the most unlikely places and can turn even dark, squalid jail cells into sacred space.

1 John 3:16–24

In this passage, John rails against the spirit of separation that is threatening a community of followers. He addresses a community that is in danger of allowing its disagreements to supersede its unity, in effect fracturing the body of Christ and giving a false image of love to the world. Separatists might have good reason to believe as they do, but they lack faith if they allow that reason to trump the mutual love that is foundational to the community of believers. Further, they lack faith, because the love that they share belongs not to them but to God. Our love is nothing more than an instance or manifestation of the love of God that lives in us. We falsely claim divine love as a personal possession when we withhold it from anyone for any reason. Surely love has failed where disunity triumphs.

A particularly thorny problem for social justice is how to balance unity under God with civil disobedience. The act of resisting injustice can fan the flames of disunity and thereby threaten the fellowship that God intends for us. The Civil Rights Movement was grounded in the belief that civil disobedience and unity are both authorized by God. These activists trusted in God to resist inequality and to invite adversaries to join in a new fellowship of racial equality.

Rosa Parks broke a law in 1955 when she refused to give up her bus seat to a white man. When the police arrived to arrest her, she did not know whether her act of civil disobedience would occasion any positive result. She believed nonetheless that God was able to transform the disunity of segregation and the noncooperation of civil disobedience into the unity of a reconciled community. By refusing to stand, Parks stood for a broader, deeper, and more authentic national community. Civil disobedience is effective when it galvanizes resistance to injustice, but it is just only when it intends a larger and better unity, inclusive of its opponents.

John 10:11–18

The main message of this passage can be summarized in the expression "one flock, one shepherd." Echoing themes from the Psalm 23,[4] John 10:11–16 addresses in fuller measure how the good shepherd is known and the constitution of the flock. Verses 17 and 18 abandon the shepherd metaphor and address the meaning of Jesus' sacrifice in the context of his relationship with God.

Jesus Christ is the good shepherd. The good shepherd lays his life down willingly and has power to take it up again. The "hired hand" (vv. 12–13) stands in contrast to the good shepherd. The hired hand manages the sheep and thus exercises some authority over them; but when wolves attack, the hired hand will abandon the sheep and seek personal safety. The hired hand is powerless to protect the sheep. More troubling, the hired hand does not truly care for the sheep.

The constitution of the flock is taken up in verse 16. The flock is not all of one fold. On the contrary, Jesus has sheep that do not belong to the same fold. Though these sheep from outside John's congregation do not belong to the same fold, they still hear Jesus' voice and belong nonetheless to the one flock.

The idea that Jesus brings diverse folds into one flock has rich implications for social justice. The image of one universal and united flock, however, is as

4. See also Ezek. 34:11–16.

challenging as it is comforting. When we fail to distinguish our particular fold from the universal flock, we are tempted to confuse the two. How easy it is to act as if our fold is the prototype for the flock. At stake is how far mutual love requires us to bend and change in order to be united to our *other* brothers and sisters, those outside our fold. What new languages must we learn to love them?

The United States now has more Latino and Hispanic residents than African Americans. Do our religious communities truly celebrate this milestone in diversity and its possibilities for becoming a more inclusive church? Should we require our clergy to speak Spanish? Some, however, think we should build walls on the border, so that our fold is not overrun by outsiders. The times require us to hear the good news again, and that changes our identity and creates a new political reality. The love of Christ compels us to listen for Jesus' voice as it is heard by our brothers and sisters outside our fold. Then and only then will we be able to share in God's love for them.

Holocaust Remembrance Day: Yom haShoah (Late April to Early May)

Clark M. Williamson

Ecclesiastes 1:1–11
Psalm 102:1–17
1 John 3:11–24
Matthew 23:29–35

Yom haShoah (Heb. for "Day [*yom*] of Catastrophe [*shoah*]") is sometimes known colloquially as "the Shoah" or as Holocaust Remembrance Day. According to the Jewish calendar, the date is the 27th of Nisan (a date that varies from late April through early May). Holocaust Memorial Day could help congregations mourn the murder of six million Jewish people and repent of anti-Judaism and anti-Semitism. While honoring the particularity of the Holocaust, this remembrance can also encourage synagogue and church to join in mutual resistance to all forms of genocide and racial and ethnic oppression.

> No statement, theological or otherwise, should be made that would not be credible in the presence of the burning children. . . . The Holocaust reveals that Christianity has the stark choice of contrition, repentance, and self-purification, or the continual temptation to participate in genocide or pave the way for it. If Christianity has barely survived the first Holocaust, I do not believe that it can survive a second with any real moral capital at all.[1]
>
> *Irving Greenberg*

The reality of evil is the great test of faith and of our inherited theology. To remember the Holocaust is to make ourselves vulnerable to Ecclesiastes' claim that "all is vanity" and to Psalm 102, with its prayer for the oppression

---

1. Irving Greenberg, "Cloud of Smoke: Pillar of Fire: Judaism, Christianity, and Modernity after the Holocaust," in *Auschwitz: Beginning of a New Era*, ed. Eva Fleischner (New York: KTAV, 1977), 41.

222

of the weak and its hope for a new time of compassionate justice. To remember the Holocaust is to face Matthew's diatribe against scribes and Pharisees and our oldest bias against Jews as essentially hypocritical, and to let 1 John's claim that the love of the neighbor is the test of our faith be taken to heart.

Ecclesiastes 1:1–11

Ecclesiastes stands in the tradition of Wisdom literature. In Proverbs, Wisdom literature gave advice to those seeking to improve their lot in life in the context of a well-functioning state in a time when things were going well. Job introduced a discordant note. Things were not going well with Job. Instead of prosperity and in spite of his faithfulness, he lost everything. His experience contradicted conventional wisdom. In Ecclesiastes, things are going badly for everybody, not just one person. Written after 250 BCE and before the Maccabean rebellion, when Judea was under the control of the emperor Antiochus IV Epiphanes, Ecclesiastes reflects a time of turmoil, economic deprivation, and oppression, when God was not delivering the people from injustice and when hard work did not produce dividends.

That Job was included in the canon testifies to the love of the Jewish tradition for questions. Giving voice to a distinctive theological viewpoint, Ecclesiastes' point of view is based in his experience and that of his society as a whole. He challenges the fundamental principles of biblical faith. For him, God is uninvolved and, at best, distant. Revelation is of no help. Wisdom is futile. His is an audacious book.

There were various Jewish theological responses to the Holocaust. Emil Fackenheim in *To Mend the World* made the point that the proper response to evil was to repair the world by deeds of loving-kindness, thus "mending the world."[2] Richard L. Rubenstein argued that the God of traditional theism was dead. A God who is unqualifiedly omnipotent and omniscient had allowed Auschwitz. Rubenstein could no longer trust such a God. "We have turned away from the God of history to share the tragic fatalities of the God of nature."[3] Elie Wiesel wrote, "The God of love, of gentleness, of comfort, the God of Abraham, of Isaac, of Jacob has vanished forevermore . . . in the smoke of a human holocaust exacted by Race, the most voracious of all idols."[4]

"Vanity of vanities, says the Teacher, vanity of vanities! All is vanity" (v. 2). There are times that seem Godforsaken. How can we find it possible to trust God, other people, or even ourselves after some of our experiences? Some Jews came through the Holocaust with their faith intact. Some lost it in the

2. Emil L. Fackenheim, *To Mend the World* (New York: Schocken Books, 1982).
3. Richard L. Rubenstein, *After Auschwitz* (Indianapolis: Bobbs-Merrill, 1966), 68.
4. Elie Wiesel, *Night* (New York: Avon Books, 1969), 9.

camps. Ecclesiastes bears witness to his profound sense of the meaningless-ness of life: "A generation goes, and a generation comes, but the earth remains forever" (v. 4). And we forget the people of long ago, as we will be forgotten (v. 11). "What has been done is what will be done" (v. 9), says Ecclesiastes. Genocide happened. People said, "Never again!" and it still happens.

There are no easy answers to Ecclesiastes' challenge to us. Christians, whose story includes the crucifixion, know the monstrosity of evil, its sheer destructiveness, and its capacity to wipe out hope, trust, and love. We can lament with our Jewish brothers and sisters the pain of the Holocaust, and let ourselves be burned by it. With them, as in the synagogues today, we can come through the pain to a deeper awareness that in God we have a compan-ion who suffers with us.

Psalm 102:1–17

Ideal for Holocaust Remembrance Sunday, this psalm is a prayer for the weak. It is theologically significant that we do not know if it was written for those in exile or those enduring the impoverished situation in Judea after the return. It is a prayer for those suffering affliction at any time. Its language is evocative of the Holocaust: "I eat ashes like bread, and mingle tears with my drink" (v. 9). After the Nazis' gruesome hanging of a child in Auschwitz, said Elie Wiesel: "That night the soup tasted of corpses."[5] Psalm 102 is an appropriate prayer that the church, aware of its sinfulness, can offer to God to ask for grace.

Significantly the psalm contains two threads: one focusing on an individu-al's personal affliction, scorn of enemies, and abandonment by God, and the other on the whole people Israel and the reestablishment of Jerusalem. Indi-viduals are individuals-in-community, a key idea in the biblical understanding of human beings, and we pray in solidarity with the predicaments and hopes of all people, including the people Israel.

Pastors should consider the whole psalm. Its fundamental theological con-cern is the role of God in bestowing meaning upon the weak, who are con-fronted with the predicament of time. "My days are like an evening shadow; I wither away like grass" (v. 11). "Do not take me away at the midpoint of my life" (v. 24). The question of faith, according to Paul Tillich, has to do with our awareness of our own finitude, an awareness particularly keen with regard to time.[6] We delude ourselves by thinking that we can be in command of time, but more deeply we are aware that this is a chimera. The psalmist knows that the human situation would be unbearable, were God thought of

---

5. Ibid., 76.
6. Paul Tillich, *Systematic Theology* (Chicago: University of Chicago Press, 1951), 1:192–98.

only as infinite, unchangeable, and eternal. We can bear our situation only in the knowledge that we are known and cherished by God, warmly embraced by God's love that bestows ultimate meaning upon our transient days.

That is why the weak one knows that God will "hear the groans of the prisoners [and] . . . set free those who were doomed to die" (v. 20). That is why God will reestablish Jerusalem, where God's name will be declared and God will be praised (v. 21). The hope is that there will be a time when compassion and justice will reign and the people will be restored, as Israel was after the Holocaust. The church should not only remember the Holocaust; it should celebrate the restoration of Israel and pray and act for peace in Jerusalem and all the world.

Matthew 23:29–35

Matthew's diatribe against "the scribes and the Pharisees" is a difficult text. Its language of slander and vilification typified many groups in the ancient world. Name-calling can be found in Paul (Phil. 3:2), the dialogues of Plato, and the literature of Qumran. Matthew's expansion on material found in Mark 12:38–40 and Luke 11:37–52 produces a lengthy polemic. We do not know that this language was uttered by Jesus. We do know that Paul speaks no word critical of Pharisees or scribes. It is clear from a comparison of the Synoptics that the intensity of conflict rises as we get further from the time of Jesus.

One problem with the passage is that it opens with praise for the teachings of the scribes and Pharisees: they "sit on Moses' seat; therefore do whatever they teach you and follow it" (23:1). Yet elsewhere in Matthew, Jesus defends the written Torah as opposed to the new teachings of the Pharisees. Another problem is that scribes were a professional class, not a group. Scribes were educated people who knew how to read and write. Many organizations and groups needed scribes. Even Matthew was written by a scribe (13:52). A third problem is that the diatribe leaves unmentioned the chief priests and elders, who are Jesus' main opponents in Jerusalem (26:14).

The major problem is its relentless name-calling and character assassination. In its anti-Jewish ideology the later church expanded upon Matthew and called all Jews "hypocrites" except when it called them "works-righteous."[7] They are hypocrites if they fail to adhere perfectly to Torah teachings, works-righteous and legalistic if they do. It is all too easy to accuse someone of hypocrisy, and quite impossible to defend oneself against the charge. In truth, none of us lives up to our professions of faith and morality. In Paul's view, the line between saint and sinner runs right through the middle of everyone;

7. See Clark M. Williamson, *Has God Rejected His People?* (Nashville: Abingdon Press, 1982), 89–105; Rosemary Radford Ruether, *Faith and Fratricide* (New York: Seabury Press, 1974), 117–82.

saints and sinners are not two groups. Hence, we should never accuse "them" of hypocrisy.

A further problem is that sociological studies of prejudice against Jews shows that Christians learn this bigotry in church. The more Christians believe the negative images of Jews found in Scripture and heard in church, the more they project those images upon Jews today.[8] Feminists have argued that language featuring negative images of women or making them invisible is harmful to real human beings. The same point holds for how we deal with negative images and stories about Jews in the Second Testament.

This kind of language in Matthew and elsewhere in early Christian literature is often explained in one of two ways. Either the target is not the Jewish people as such, but only the religious authorities; or the language is typical of that used by the prophets in criticizing the people Israel. Neither explanation provides much help. Are we to think that "the Pharisees," all Pharisees, were hypocrites? Were none faithful? How do we know? Are all contemporary rabbis hypocrites? When a preacher, fancying that he or she is being prophetic, lacerates the congregation as modern-day Pharisees, how effectively prophetic will such a preacher be?

Christians should develop ways of articulating the Christian faith that do not entail the use of an alienated other. Historically, Jews have played three roles in Christian discourse: prologue, antithesis, and scapegoat. As prologue they are currently invisible; as antithesis, the alienated other; and as scapegoat, responsible for all terrible events, beginning with the crucifixion. Preachers should replace Matthew's teaching of contempt with a teaching of respect for Jews and Judaism. Congregants cannot love neighbors whom they hold in contempt.

1 John 3:11–24

Although John's letter shares the Christology of the Gospel of John, it never mentions Jews, nor is there in it any hint of antagonism with advocates of the Torah or between Jew and Gentile. There are opponents in 1 John, whom the letter refers to as "antichrists," and of whom it says, "They went out from us, but they did not belong to us" (2:19). Since 1 John lays considerable stress on the Christology of the Gospel of John, "that Jesus Christ has come in the flesh" (4:2), we may assume that these opponents disagreed with John's Christology, but we do not know how they disagreed.

---

8. Rodney Stark, *Wayward Shepherds* (New York: Harper & Row, 1971). For an excellent study of how this learning takes place in Sunday schools, see Bernhard E. Olson, *Faith and Prejudice* (New Haven, CT: Yale University Press, 1963).

Our passage focuses first on the contradiction between love and hate. The command that we are to "love one another" recalls Jesus' command to his followers in John 13:34. John contrasts this command with the example of Cain, who killed his brother Abel (3:12; see Gen. 4:1–16). Jewish writers also used Cain to symbolize the impious and those who do not keep the teachings of Torah. John then shifts to a different point: "Do not be astonished, brothers and sisters, that the world hates you" (v. 13). John has already defined the world as "the desire of the flesh, the desire of the eyes, the pride in riches" (2:16). His community had a strong sense of alienation from society. That its world was religiously saturated with pagan shrines and ruled by "divine" Caesars should not be forgotten.

John's point is that loving our brothers and sisters is a test. Murdering is not only a physical crime; hating is also a form of murder (v. 15). So is having the world's goods and not helping the destitute (v. 17). The Greek speaks of "closing off our compassion" (v. 17; NRSV "refuses help"). Love shows that we have passed from death to life; its absence shows the opposite (v. 14). This is a test that the opponents failed when they walked out of the community. The passage is a test for those remaining in the community, by pressing them to consider whether they love those who walk out. Later John utters the commandment to think critically: "Do not believe every spirit, but test the spirits to see whether they are from God" (4:1). That we love one another is a test of our knowledge of God's love for us; it is not a condition placed on God's freedom to love.

John's next step is to reassure his readers of God's love for them (vv. 19–22). By loving one another we will know that we are from the truth and "will reassure our hearts before [God]" (v. 19). Our love tests whether we have received God's gracious gift. Sometimes our hearts "condemn us." But our anxious hearts can be put at ease by remembering who God is, "greater than our hearts, and [one who] knows everything" (v. 20). God's grace calms our self-accusation and permits us to approach God in prayer, knowing that what we do in love "pleases [God]." We do not appease God, but we may please God.

The passage closes by affirming God's commandment "that we should believe in the name of his Son Jesus Christ and love one another" (v. 23). The name "Jesus" means "God saves." Jesus describes his mission in the Gospel of John: "I have made your name known to those whom you gave me from the world" (John 17:6). By loving one another, we abide in Christ and he in us.

Perhaps on Holocaust Remembrance Sunday the church can be urged not to continue the long habit of closing off our compassion to the people Israel, but to become aware that they too are the sisters and brothers whom God has given us to love.

Fifth Sunday of Easter

Simone Sunghae Kim

ACTS 8:26–40
PSALMS 22:25–31
1 JOHN 4:7–21
JOHN 15:1–8

This week's lectionary readings invite us to examine more closely God's justice, rule, and lordship over all things and all people throughout generations. God's encompassing power and zeal to bring people and nations to salvation, life, and transformation are made possible and being culminated in the ministry and atoning work of Jesus Christ through the Holy Spirit.

We investigate similarities between the suffering of the psalmist in Psalm 22:25–31 and the suffering of the Korean people. Acts 8:26–40 reveals how God through the Holy Spirit takes charge and oversees bringing all people to the knowledge of God. God's seriousness about and invitation to the practice of love in 1 John 4:7–21 are discussed in light of God's own demonstration through the atoning sacrifice of Jesus Christ. John 15:1–8 illustrates God's justice and transformation that manifest themselves and result in the bearing of fruit, especially the fruit of love. This is made possible only when we steadfastly abide in the true vine, Christ Jesus, who is love.

To illustrate God's justice, restoration, and love in action, I use the example of Han-Il-Hap-Bang or Han-Il-Byeong-Hap (the annexation treaty), which took place August 22, 1910, between Korea and Japan as a forced treaty resulting in Japan's annexation of Korea. Indigenous Korean concepts, such as *han* (한/lamentation), *jungeui* (정의/justice), and *sarang* (사랑/love), weave in and out of the major themes and characteristics of God's justice, transformation, and love in this week's lectionary readings.

Psalm 22:25–31

Psalm 22 contains lament, justice, praise, and thanksgiving. Although an individual psalm of lament, it takes place in the larger context of the community, and thus the text has a communal dimension. After crying out to God for help and rescue from debasement (vv. 6–8), threat, and persecution (vv. 12–18) by the enemies, the psalmist finally declares that God's justice, rule, and deliverance will come in due time.

The notions of affliction, injustice, and suffering are of great significance, especially for Korean people, who commemorated on August 22, 2010, the 100th anniversary of Han-Il-Hap-Bang, which began the thirty-five-year Japanese rule over Korea. Much like the psalmist, Koreans felt as though they were worms (v. 6) who were surrounded and threatened by many strong bulls (v. 12) and dogs (v. 16).

Han-Il-Hap-Bang contributed and caused in Koreans much *han* (한/ lamentation).[1] The cries of the psalmist because of persecution and threat from enemies in Psalm 22 are much like those of Koreans oppressed and abused during the thirty-five-year rule. The unique Korean concept of *han* (한/lamentation), etched deep in the hearts and souls of Korean men and women, has passed down through generations, and haunts Koreans to this day.

One salient component of this psalm is the depiction of the psalmist as the suffering servant who cries out, "My God, my God, why have you forsaken me?" (v. 1). This cry parallels Christ's own cry on the cross (Matt. 27:46; Mark 15:34). Likewise, God is personally and deeply involved in the life and experience of the sufferer.

God finally rescues the psalmist from *han* (한/lamentation) and grants *jungeui* (정의/justice) in the life of the sufferer. Others, then, who are in similar predicaments, such as the poor, are given the opportunity to join the feast of which the sufferer is a part (v. 26). They all participate in a communal meal that symbolizes fellowship with God.[2]

What followed after the Liberation Day, August 15, 1945, that ended the thirty-five–year Japanese rule, is nothing but the abundance of God's grace.[3] However, Koreans must remember that they are called to celebrate and act out God's justice and grace with the oppressed and the poor. Koreans, who experienced firsthand such dire and painful unjust political, social, economic,

1. *Han* is an aching and sharp feeling of deep sorrow and lamentation that comes from much abuse and unjust treatment over a long period of time.
2. Peter C. Craigie, *Psalms 1–50*, Word Biblical Commentary (Waco, TX: Word Books, 1983), 1:201.
3. Korea has experienced a remarkable rate of economic growth and development that has brought blessing to many Koreans.

and cultural oppression by the Japanese government, must always extend and share God's *jungeui* (정의/justice) and sovereignty that were granted to them with other *han* (한/lamentation)-ridden individuals and nations.

The church in Korea is quite strong. Korea sends missionaries all around the world, not only spreading the good news but also building schools, hospitals, and other social, economic, and agricultural facilities, especially in developing countries. Like the psalmist in today's lectionary reading, those who tasted God's *jungeui* (정의/justice) and true freedom are to praise and glorify God and to feast in the communal meal with the oppressed and the poor. This is true not only in Korea, but wherever people have tasted that grace throughout the world.

Acts 8:26–40

This segment of Acts records God leading Philip, an evangelist, to preach Christ to an Ethiopian eunuch, a possible God-fearer, who embraces Christianity through the Suffering Servant passage in Isaiah 53. This is an example of God's initiating and taking charge through the Holy Spirit in bringing people and nations under God's sovereignty. It is noteworthy that the Ethiopian eunuch, though a high government officer who had come to God, would have been excluded from the assembly in the temple (Deut. 23:1).[4] God's calling of a eunuch into the family of God is of a great significance in that God induces *jungeui* (정의/justice) for those with limited lives. But what is most potent about the eunuch's situation is that the Suffering Servant's being deprived of justice in humiliation (v. 33) made it possible for this Ethiopian eunuch to take part in the divine assembly.

The passage ends in verses 39–40 with a striking occurrence when the Spirit suddenly takes Philip away and miraculously transports him to Azotus, where he continues preaching. In this instance, God through the Holy Spirit plans, initiates, orchestrates, enables, and executes the entire work of God's justice and reign.

Likewise, the sufferer cannot help but to thank God and God alone for deliverance and justice. Even as Koreans celebrated the 100th anniversary of Han-Il-Hap-Bang on August 22, 2010, they brought their focus and attention to the almighty and just God who eventually freed them from Japanese oppression.

4. G. H. C. Maggregor, "The Acts of the Apostles: Exposition," *The Interpreter's Bible*, ed. George L. Buttrick et al. (Nashville: Abingdon Press, 1954), 6:114.

1 John 4:7–21

This passage in a nutshell unfolds knowing and seeing God through *sarang* (사랑/love), and how we, like God through Jesus, ought to demonstrate love for one another. The author of the First Epistle of John tries to warn against the false teachers by pointing out the evidence of true faith which is *sarang* (사랑/love).[5] The seriousness of the text lies in the fact that living and being in God are directly tied to our actions and activities of love toward others. God's *jungeui* (정의/justice) ultimately is brought about through *sarang* (사랑/love) and transforms people into acting *sarang* (사랑/love).

As God delivers and frees us from bondage and oppression, and thus brings God's *jungeui* (정의/justice) in the world, it is our responsibility to love others, including those who persecute and unjustly treat us. As God is love (v. 8) and demonstrates to us that love through Jesus (v. 9), we now become responsible to act likewise and to love others as God's beloved children.

Through God's sacrificial and unselfish *sarang* (사랑/love) shown in the atoning sacrifice of Jesus Christ for our sins, God identifies and sympathizes with the *han* (한/lamentation) that Koreans suffered under the Japanese government. God's sympathy or rather interpathy[6] comforts and gives courage to Koreans so they can now continue to move toward love for the Japanese people. After all, the love with which we love is not our own. Rather, it is God's love through Jesus that is being activated in us and poured upon us by God. It is "not that we loved God but that [God] loved us" (v. 10).

John 15:1–8

This particular text goes well with John's main concern and focus: to reveal the words and works of Jesus. As this text puts forward the seventh and the last "I am" (vv. 1, 5) in this Gospel, it claims that it is essential for Christians to abide in Jesus, the true vine, and to bear much fruit. While fruit bearing can mean the general Christian lifestyle, it points here specifically to the act of loving one another as God loves us (v. 12). While 1 John 4:7–21 demonstrates that true believers are to exhibit love as God loves us in Christ Jesus with

---

5. Korean *sarang* (사랑/love) here is more appropriate than the English "love." Like Greek agape, *sarang* (사랑/love) denotes self-giving love. Moreover, as it embodies *jung* (정/affection), a sticky, undetachable, affectionate and relational bond, *sarang* (사랑/love) transcends one's emotional preference (such as like or dislike, or love or hate) toward its object. As such, it better describes Johannine love, especially in light of the concept of community of love.

6. Interpathy denotes a feeling that a person encounters as she willingly, deliberately, but temporarily, abandons her own worldview to enter into the affective world of the other for a deeper level of understanding. See David S. Augsburger, *Pastoral Counseling Across Cultures* (Philadelphia: Westminster Press, 1986), 27–35.

sacrificial love, the current text urges us to abide in Jesus, the true vine, which enables us to bear the fruit of love.

Pruning of every branch that bears fruit for even greater fruit bearing in verse 2 reminds us of the Suffering Servant in a figurative sense. Pruning as "God's painful discipline for [the] true servant"[7] allows us to join in the wounds, pain, and suffering of Jesus on the cross, which demonstrated and resulted in the greatest act of fruit bearing, the ultimate expression of love.

The true vine (v. 1) implies that there is a false vine. Isaiah 5:1–7 describes the unfruitful vine that brought forth wild grapes instead of good grapes. The unfruitful vine was the house of Israel that failed to produce good fruit (Isa. 5:7).[8] But in John 15 Jesus becomes the true vine, and believers must remain in Jesus to bear much fruit.

Thus bearing the fruit of *sarang* (사랑/love) totally depends on Jesus and our abiding in him. Sufferers, including Koreans, are to love even those who caused them to suffer, with the love that resulted in their steadfastly remaining in Jesus, the true vine. God's *jungeui* (정의/justice) and God's *sarang* (사랑/love) are embodied as the freed sufferer turns around and shows the perpetrator what God has given those who suffer.

One of the many cruel and unjust acts that the Japanese army committed during the thirty-five–year rule over Korea was forcing many Korean women to become "comfort women," that is, sex slaves for the Japanese imperial army. While some officials in the Japanese government since the early 1990s have apologized for the Japanese exploitation of the comfort women, official Japanese policy does not recognize the Japanese government to be legally liable for what happened to the comfort women. The government itself has not attempted to make reparations to women who served in the comfort stations, although a private fund now seeks to do so in a limited way.[9]

---

7. J. H. Bernard and A. H. McNeile, *A Critical and Exegetical Commentary on the Gospel according to St. John*, International Critical Commentary (Edinburgh: T. & T. Clark, 1953), 2:480.

8. The congregation to which John wrote was likely in tension with some Jewish leaders (whom John calls "the Jews"). One purpose of the Gospel of John was to justify the separation of the Johannine community from a nearby synagogue or synagogues and its leadership. One of John's strategies to justify this separation was to contrast the true vine (Jesus) and the good fruit (those who believe in him and who follow his commandments) with the bad vine (the members of the synagogue who do not believe in him). The preacher needs to help the congregation recognize that John's condemnation of the Jewish leaders and their followers is caricature that has had heinous consequences. Indeed, today's congregation should repudiate this way of thinking and speaking.

9. A summary and critical analysis of the controversy surrounding the limitations of Japanese apologies and reparations can be found at Tessa Morris Suzuki, "Japan's Comfort Women: It's Time for the Truth (in the ordinary, everyday sense of the word)"; http://japanfocus.org/ -Tessa-Morris_Suzuki/2373 (accessed September 26, 2010).

Believing that the apologies so far have been inadequate, and believing that justice requires concrete acts of remembrance and contrition, eleven Korean American high-school students took the lead in establishing a public memorial in Bergen County, New Jersey, in memory of the Korean comfort women. On April 20, 2010, the Bergen County government also agreed to pass a resolution calling for an adequate apology from the Japanese government. As of the time of the unveiling of the memorial in October 2010, no apology had been forthcoming in response to the county government's request. While the Japanese government was silent on this occasion, this small yet significant act is one way of manifesting God's *jungeui* (정의/justice) on the face of the denying perpetrator. God's *jungeui* (정의/justice) and *sarang* (사랑/love) are extended not only to Koreans but to all individuals, communities, and nations who have experienced any form of oppression, injustice, and mistreatment and thus bleed with much *han* (한/lamentation).

God's act of *jungeui* (정의/justice) may be quite different from the way we think of justice. For instance, God's way of *jungeui* (정의/justice) may come in the form of consolation through commemorating the victims of the oppressed rather than retaliating or revenge. This does not mean that the oppressor can or should get away without being punished or facing up to his or her wrong doings. God is the judge (Ps. 75:7) who is and will bring about the ultimate justice to all. But by bringing *jungeui* (정의/justice) through the Suffering Servant who is the originator and enabler of *sarang* (사랑/love), God rules and reigns over both the sufferers and the oppressors.

Sixth Sunday of Easter

Choi Hee An

ACTS 10:44–48
PSALM 98
1 JOHN 5:1–6
JOHN 15:9–17

This week's lectionary readings lead us to love one another and abide in the love of God together. God's commandment that we love one another as God has loved us permeates these readings. The ultimate fulfillment of this commandment is found through the sharing of God's justice and love. The gift of the Holy Spirit has been poured out on Jesus' disciples, on the Gentiles, the world, all nations, and the earth so that they may be united with one another and may abide in God. These readings urge us to extend our love and faith beyond our Christian sisters and brothers and to establish friendship with God in honoring one another.

John 15:9–17

In verse 9, before Jesus' farewell, he declares his love to his beloved people and asks them to abide in him. "Abide in my love" is the definitive form of Jesus' hope and wish for his people. This message is repeated over and over in John 14 and 15. Jesus wants his people to know that he will be with them and live in them even after his departure. In order for his beloved people to be with Jesus and in order for Jesus to be with them, there is one condition; his beloved people have to keep his commandments.

"Abiding in Jesus" is not easy work. It brings responsibility and requires accepting consequences. Keeping Jesus' commandment requires hard work, even suffering, for what is right. We need patience and care until we bear fruit. At the same time, "abide in my love" is a necessary human condition for having the ability to love. It brings joy that is possible only from love.

In verse 13, Jesus invites his beloved people, his beloved community, to be friends with him. The word "friend" (*philos, philē*) in verses 13–15 is from the verb "to love" (*phileō*). To be a friend with Jesus is to love Jesus. To love Jesus is to be a friend with Jesus. Friendship is the symbol of his genuine love.

The invitation of friendship with Jesus had a significant meaning in the hierarchical society of antiquity. As described in verse 15, Jesus brings a horizontal dimension to his relationship with his beloved people. This relationship denies hierarchical control and power. It does not allow some people to possess oppressive authority, and it opens the full possibility of sharing mutual responsibility and interdependency.[1] It requires equal interdependence with Jesus. As Jesus establishes this relationship with his beloved people, so his beloved people must establish this relationship with one another, accepting each other's difficulties and differences based on love when they keep Jesus' commandments.

The concept of friendship with Jesus is a new paradigm for his relation with all people and all the earth. It obliges us to form a new vision and creates a new power within the world and beyond. Jesus' order invited people to participate with their own will and power. In verse 16, this relationship is initiated by Jesus' choice. Jesus chooses people and invites them to be his friends. However, in this relationship, people still have a choice to accept or reject this offer. Jesus opens this mutual interdependent relationship and accepts the consequence. He lays down his life for his friends and is resurrected from death for his friends. In order to be his friends, we must follow the example of Jesus' love for his friends and keep his commandments. By Jesus' prior choice to be their friend, his friends can accept the invitation from Jesus and bear mutual responsibility with him.

1 John 5:1–6

This text centers in a confession of one's faith in God, Jesus, and the Spirit. In verse 1, the author of First John confesses Jesus as the Christ (*Christos*). To believe (*pisteuō*) in Jesus as the Christ (v. 1) and as the Son of God (v. 5) is the basic belief of the author's faith and has been the most essential belief of Christian confession. While Jesus is Christ and the Son of God, First John describes believers as being "begotten of God" (v. 1, NRSV "born of God"). Being "begotten of God" (Gk. *gegennētai*) can be translated as children of God and/or as beings originated from God, not from human generation. It means

---

1. Choi Hee An, *Korean Women and God: Experiencing God in a Multi-Religious Colonial Context* (Maryknoll, NY: Orbis Books, 2005), 126–27.

that whoever confesses Jesus as the Christ and the Son of God bears God's origin, love. In this logic, love has its origin in God, is passed on to the Son of God, and permeates those who are begotten of God. Dwelling in God's love (John 14–15) is natural for human beings because it is in their flesh and souls. They are originally created from God and from God's essence. It is their *habitus*.[2] In order to return this love to God or in order to be in God, those beings begotten of God must keep Jesus' commandments. As beings "begotten of God," God's beloved children should know each other and love one another.

In verses 3b–4, his commandments are not burdensome. This passage reminds us that love is neither a burden nor something overwhelming. Actually, the commandment "love one another" gives the begotten of God power to overcome the world. Love gives them a final victory and restores God's justice over the world.

Acts 10:44–48

The work of the Spirit and baptism in the name of Christ are the important themes in this passage. The Spirit urges Peter to extend his limits and opens a new horizon. The love of Jesus and his commandments are extended, not only among Jesus' disciples or within Peter's known boundaries, but also beyond his knowledge.

In Acts 10:1–43, Peter has seen the vision from God and has been sent by God to Cornelius's house. He argues with God for what he knows is right, but he is challenged by God to do what is right for God. Peter has to cross over his traditions and boundaries to accomplish God's commandments. The one God has chosen for salvation has been revealed to Peter. God asks Peter to carry out God's commandments, which is to become an agent whereby God welcomes Gentiles as Gentiles into the church.

We need to explore one important movement in verse 44. From Peter's point of view, his speech is interrupted twice (10:44, 11:15) by the Spirit. However, from the Spirit's point of view, these are not interruptions. The Spirit has worked through Peter continuously and has poured out the gift of God on people through him. His speech is not interrupted but empowered by the Spirit's manifestation. His work is endorsed by God in the Spirit's movement. God's interruption is not really an interruption but an interaction with Peter.

---

2. As Pierre Bourdieu uses *habitus* as presence of inherited structures of thought and action, I define *habitus* in this context as presence of inherited love from God. It is a human condition of ability to love God and others inherited by Jesus though the Spirit. See Pierre Bourdieu, *Outline of a Theory of Practice*, trans. Richard Nice, Cambridge Studies in Social and Cultural Anthropology (Cambridge: Cambridge University Press, 1977).

God's salvation interacts with Peter's work and is the gift of the Spirit. The Holy Spirit falls upon all who hear the word, not because of Peter's speech, but with his speech and in his speech. God does not work alone, and people do not believe in God only because of a vision from God. In the interaction between God and people, people proclaim God's word, and people who hear the proclamation witness God's work and experience God's presence. The gift of the Spirit pours out "even" on the Gentiles in this interaction and gives an equal opportunity for them to become God's beloved children. Gentiles are also beings "begotten of God" and bear the origin of God. They share the same gift of God as they equally bear the same responsibility for following God's commandment to love one another.

In verse 47, after Peter becomes a witness not only of Jesus and his work but also of the Spirit and the Spirit's manifestation, he baptizes Cornelius and his household. Peter sees what they have. He recognizes that these people "have received the Holy Spirit just as we have." The meaning of baptism, then, is "sharing what we have." Whoever is baptized in the name of Jesus Christ shares the same *whatever we have and they have* together. By baptism, they have what we had first, and then we receive what they have next. After we share what we have and what they have, we become them and they become us. Our individual cultures are not erased, but we and they become one, in the sense of living with one another in mutual respect and support. By baptism, we become the one body of Christ. They are in us and we are in them. There are no more circumcised believers and uncircumcised Gentiles. There are no more others. This is a new thing that Peter and his disciples have never seen before. This is an astonishing thing that they witness now. This is a marvelous thing that God has done.

Psalm 98

This passage praises a marvelous thing that God has done. It recalls an astonishing moment that God's people have witnessed especially in the exodus from Egypt and the new exodus from Babylon. The ultimate purpose of this salvation is manifestation of God's justice and righteousness for Israel and for all the earth. This universal demonstration brings forth a new song. This is God's victory.

In verse 3, because of this salvation, God reveals God's steadfast love and faithfulness to the house of Israel and pours out these gifts "even" on the Gentiles and all the earth. God has not forgotten God's creatures but has remembered God's steadfast love and faithfulness for all God's creation. God has made them witnesses of God's victory. God has re-membered Jesus' disciples, Gentiles, nations, and all the earth in God's steadfast love and faithfulness through Jesus' life, death, and resurrection. The whole creation and "the begotten of God" have responded in remembrance and re-membrance of God's steadfast love and justice. There are no more we and others. There are no more I and It. All the earth and the whole creations of God have become one and have seen the victory of God together. This is holistic union with God. Now all of creation can rejoice in God's salvation.

In verses 4–8, after God's salvation, people have new eyes to see how the sea roars, how the floods clap their hands, and how the hills sing together for joy and praise to God. The whole creation is excited to be a witness of God's justice and righteousness. It rejoices in God's coming and God's judgment. Through Jesus' life, death, and resurrection, God restores justice and righteousness and reminds us of God's steadfast love and faithfulness. Jesus comes to judge the earth and reinstates righteousness in the world. His resurrection completes God's justice and steadfast love and brings God's victory. At the presence of God, Jesus, and the Spirit, people are now able to see what God has done and how God's righteousness prevails in this universe. Jesus came and will come again, and we will sing our new song together.

Abiding in God's love is a radical act. It asks us to cross over our boundaries, our differences, and our standards. It requires us to have new eyes to see people, nations, and the whole creation. Abiding in God's love leads us to build a new relationship among us. As the begotten of God, we have a responsibility to build this new relationship with our neighbors, foreigners, the immigrant, the poor, the powerless, the oppressed, the marginalized, nature, any living and nonliving creatures, and the whole of God's creation. The union with these is the union with God. In other words, the union with God is the union with neighbors, foreigners, the immigrant—the whole creation and the universe. It is a way of living and sharing together as "us" beyond our imagination. It is possible now because of God's love though Jesus with the Spirit.

Peace in the Home: Shalom Bayit (Second Sunday in May)

Marie M. Fortune

RUTH 2:4–12
PSALM 15
2 CORINTHIANS 8:8–15
JOHN 14:18–24

The new Peace in the Home: Shalom Bayit replaces Mother's Day and Father's Day, which often tend to sentimentality, can promote stereotypes of women and men, sometimes idealize family relationships, and exclude persons who are not parents. The purpose of preaching on Peace in the Home is to call the congregation to help all people live in settings of security, love, and justice. It affirms the diversity of family lifestyles common in our churches and cultures, including traditional households, the single life, gay and lesbian families, and biologically unrelated people who live as family. The preacher can make connections to Sexual Assault and Abuse Awareness Month (April) and Domestic Violence Awareness Month (October).

Getting the "overview" of Jesus' and Paul's perception of the family enables you and me to see to it that the component parts of the whole human community as a living system of face-to-face relationships are mobilized around the nurture and the enlargement of children's life. They are not shut up to the suffocation of an unventilated nuclear family. God has other faces and forms in addition to those of mother, father, brother and sister. Basic sources of hope are not shut up to these significant persons alone.[1]

Wayne E. Oates

---

1. Wayne E. Oates, "The Extended Family," in *When Children Suffer: A Sourcebook for Ministry with Children in Crisis*, ed. Andrew D. Lester (Philadelphia: Westminster Press, 1987), 195.

Shalom Bayit is the foundation of the Jewish family. It establishes the family as a place of peace and harmony where each family member is respected and loved. It does not suggest that "peace" means silence and secrets about what goes on in the family.

For Christians, these values also underlie our understanding of family: Jesus identifies "family" as those persons who seek to do God's will (Mark 3:31–35).

In my comments about preaching on peace in the home, I will frequently remind the reader that every Sunday you are preaching to victims, survivors, and perpetrators of abuse within the family. One in three people (at least) sitting in the pews has had personal experience themselves or with someone in their immediate family of physical, verbal, or sexual violence. They are listening very carefully for any word that speaks to them and to their memories or current experiences.

You are also preaching to the bystanders, that is, those who surround victims, survivors, and perpetrators, who see and hear the abuse but don't want to get involved. However, the bystander could be an enormous resource in this situation.

In these passages, we are challenged because none of these passages would traditionally be considered texts about home and family. Yet when we study them together, they do in fact offer us a rich context in which not only to consider home and family, but also to ask, what does "peace" really look like?

It perhaps goes without saying that "peace in the home" certainly stands in stark contrast to domestic violence and terror. But it cannot be said too often: remember who is sitting in the pews. So as you go deeper and wider in considering home, family, and peace, do not hesitate to make it plain.

For better or for worse, religious teachings, doctrines, and sacred texts are always relevant for Christians facing sexual or domestic violence. Too often in the past (and present), teachings, doctrines, and texts have been roadblocks to ending the abuse and bringing healing and safety. For example, "Wives be subject to their husbands" and "God hates divorce" can easily be misinterpreted to silence victims of abuse and justify the actions of abusers.

But teachings, doctrines, and texts may also be very powerful resources. In Scripture, the prophets, Psalms, and Gospels especially speak to the experiences of the vulnerable and oppressed and call the powerful to account. This needed approach requires a critique (or deconstruction) of the roadblocks that can be created by patriarchal interpretations of religious teachings and a development (or reconstruction) of useful resources that empower victims and survivors to address their experiences.

So I will be cautioning the reader regularly to remember carefully who is listening to your preaching here. There will be some who are allowed out of their homes only to come to church; some who as adults remember clearly the abuse of one parent by the other; some who as teens may be in an abusive dating relationship; some who as children were sexually abused by an adult or teen. There will also be those who have abused or are currently abusing a family member, some of whom are struggling with guilt and shame but don't know where to turn.

As the preacher and pastor, you are a generalist and not a specialist. You don't have to have all the answers. But you can be a resource rather than a roadblock and begin by opening the door and giving your congregation permission to come to you. Then you will have the opportunity to connect an individual or family to the community resource they need, while continuing to walk with them pastorally.

Ruth 2:4–12

It is ironic that Ruth 1:16–17, which is so often used in heterosexual marriage ceremonies, is actually about the faithfulness of a daughter-in-law for her mother-in-law.

> Where you go, I will go;
>   where you lodge, I will lodge;
> your people shall be my people,
>   and your God my God.
> Where you die, I will die—
>   there will I be buried.

This passage is Ruth's speech to her mother-in-law, Naomi, after both have been widowed. Ruth follows her mother-in-law into a foreign land and cares for her. As two single women together, they should have been under public protection (Deut. 10:18; 24:17–22; Isa. 1:17; Jer. 49:11); but the system of protection did not work for them. They become protectors of one another. In chapter 2, Ruth is attempting to gather wheat that is left behind by the reapers. Boaz, the landowner, approaches her, realizing who she is. He gives her permission to gather the wheat and tells her she will be safe from the reapers and may drink water that the reapers draw.

Ruth is surprised that she has found favor and questions why Boaz is providing for her and protecting her. She is vulnerable. Boaz says that he knows how she has cared for Naomi and that God is rewarding her. Then he concludes by naming "the God of Israel, under whose wings you have come for refuge!" (v. 12).

This God is not Ruth's God, but Boaz manifests God's blessing by providing for her and Naomi and lifts up this powerful image of the God whose wings provide a place of refuge and safety, the mother hen or eagle.

Ruth manifests *shalom bayit* by her care of her mother-in-law. This family value is not only about one's attitude toward other family members. It is also about the basics of food and safe shelter.

Psalm 15

The psalmist asks God, Who may live in your house? Who will you welcome into your home? The short answer here is that God welcomes those who practice *shalom bayit*. Verses 2–5 make very clear and concrete what God expects from us: to be honest and do the right thing, emotionally, verbally, and financially. This is what Jesus means in Mark 3:31–35, and it stretches our understanding of family beyond our biological relatives.

Specifically, verse 4, "who stand by their oath even to their hurt," is a good description of fiduciary duty. This is the expectation of helping professionals in relation to clients, patients, congregants, and so forth: that we promise to act in their best interest, even if it is not in our own best interest; that we will be faithful to one another, even to our own disadvantage. This is what Ruth does for Naomi.

John 14:18–24

"I will not leave or abandon you even after I am gone. I will not leave you without resources even after I die." The image here is one of the parental God who, through Jesus, promises to continue to be present even when absent. This is the faithfulness that we see in Ruth's commitment to Naomi. What a powerful promise, then, Jesus makes to his followers prior to his death: "I will not leave you orphaned" (v. 18).

But this promise is conditional: "Those who love me will keep my word, and my [Creator] will love them, and we will come to them and make our home with them" (v. 23). Jesus' followers are called to love and follow God. If they do, they will not be abandoned. "We will . . . make our home with them." This is the home the psalmist describes in Psalm 15.

2 Corinthians 8:8–15

In Paul's second letter to Corinth, he is attempting to address issues of conflict in the Corinthian church, some challenges to leadership and to him, and the concern for the financial support for the collection for Jerusalem.

This particular passage addresses economics in a very concrete fashion. Paul is urging the Corinthian church to fulfill its financial pledge. He does not hesitate openly to discuss money and the organization of the church. In our time, we do not always follow Paul's lead in these matters. But Paul is not simply try-ing to collect this debt owed to the Jerusalem church. He is making this appeal in terms of the relationship they share as brothers and sisters in Christ.

In the context of Jesus' generosity in becoming poor for us, Paul appeals for the Corinthians to fulfill their commitment because they desire to be faithful to their relationships with other Christians and with him.

Paul also applies a fundamental gospel economic principle: "a fair balance between your present abundance and their need" (vv. 13–14). Clearly this is also a moral principle: the responsibility to provide economically for those who have less. I am reminded here of Jesus' teaching in Luke 12:48: "From everyone to whom much has been given, much will be required; and from the one to whom much has been entrusted, even more will be demanded." Jesus is not even calling for sacrificial giving, but for a "fair balance."

Paul then refers to Exodus 16:18: "The one who had much did not have too much, and the one who had little did not have too little" (2 Cor. 8:15). Again the appeal is to fair balance, that each one might have sufficient for his or her need.

And what does all of this have to do with peace in the home? These four passages taken together push us to expand our understanding of peace and of home. We are challenged to understand the values of peace as it relates to safety, protection, food, shelter, love, and support, all of which contribute not only to the well-being of our sisters and brothers but also to harmony among us. "Home" is also expanded far beyond the structure in which we sleep at night (for those of us lucky enough to have one). We are invited into God's home; we are accepted into God's home. But . . . we are also called to love God and follow Jesus' teachings.

Ruth and Naomi create a home together and are blessed because they fol-low God's leading. This is a picture of *shalom bayit*. The psalm, the John pas-sage, and the Corinthian passage all help to make it plain to us what it means to follow Jesus in the most concrete ways possible.

Peace in the home is about the quality of relationships we share with fam-ily and neighbors, relatives and strangers, natives and immigrants. In God's home, justice and equality define our relationships with one another. If we do our best to follow Jesus, we will know peace in its fullest sense. But this peace is not passive; it requires action every day. These passages give us insight into the action that is called for. Paul is being very clear with the Corinthians: this is what you need to *do* because you are in fellowship with other Christians. This is how we find our home in God.

Ascension of Jesus

R. Mark Giuliano

PSALM 47
EPHESIANS 1:15–23
LUKE 24:44–53
ACTS 1:1–11

The story of the ascension in Luke and Acts pictures Jesus ascending to the right hand of God. While Ephesians does not narrate that vision, that letter too sees Jesus at the right hand of God. In antiquity the right hand was the hand of power. The ascension thus affirms that the ascended Jesus is at God's right hand to rule the rulers of the earth. At its core, the ascension is political and social, for it asserts that all rulers and their realms are fully accountable to God, and that God wills for all realms to reflect the values and practices of the realm of God. Psalm 47 does not mention Jesus, but it makes a similar theo-centric point: God is sovereign over all nations and rulers. In the comments that follow, we reflect on how these texts help us consider different aspects of God's sovereignty.

Psalm 47

In worship, we affirm one of our most essential beliefs: there is a God and we are not God. As the psalmist draws our attention heavenward, our focus is lifted from ourselves and our own worldly distractions and recentered on God enthroned above all the earth. In worship, our busy and often anxious preoccupation with self-centered pursuits finds peace in God. Just as Psalm 46:10 asks us to "be still and know that I am God," so Psalm 47 calls us to be loud with praise and know that it is God, "the Most High" (v. 2), who is above all, and not ourselves.

Both individuals and congregations, no matter how righteous in their good works, find it difficult to be full of themselves when their mouths are filled with praise to God. How can we boast in our personal or congregational achievements when we are called to "rise and shine and give *God* the glory, glory"? The psalmist's call to praise God can act as a corrective to the dark spirit of smug, self–centered piety that sometimes pervades and even consumes the justice-focused church.

John Wesley directed worshipers to sing "lustily" and "with good courage" and yet to sing "modestly" and not to "bawl so as to be heard above the rest of the congregation." For Wesley, as for the psalmist, the goal of worshipful singing is to "have an eye to God in every word you sing. Aim at pleasing [God] more than yourself, or any other creature."[1] By blowing the trumpet (shofar) to God (v. 5), we are less likely to blow our own horn.

The same can be said for the hands: as our hands are wonderfully preoccupied with the rhythmic clapping in worship, we are reminded that we are saved not by our own strength or works, no matter how good or just, but only by the grace of the One who is "[ruler] of all the earth" (v. 7). No matter how many homes for Habitat we build, or how many meals we share with the hungry, *God* "chose our heritage for us" (v. 4). In other words, there is a God, and we are not God. Hallelujah! Amen!

Ephesians 1:15–23

My twenty-two-year-old son, Dylan, has a degenerative eye disease called retinitis pigmentosa, which leaves him with severe tunnel vision during the day and virtually sightless at night. He is legally blind. A few months back he had trouble sleeping because of the early-hour noise in his apartment. Dylan's mother suggested that he use earplugs at night. Dylan responded with his usual humor: "Mom, I can't wear earplugs; my ears are my eyes."

For the writer of the letter to the Ephesians, our hearts are our eyes too. Through his prayerful words, this writer introduces a new metaphor. He asks that through the "eyes of [the] heart enlightened" (v. 18) believers might discern their hope in Christ, the riches of the inheritance of the faith community, and the "immeasurable greatness" of power in Christ "for [those] who believe" (v. 19). For Paul, hope, inheritance, and power in Christ are accessed through the special lens of the enlightened heart, which is granted by God through a "spirit of wisdom and revelation" as believers come to know God (v. 17). In his 1995 novel *Blindness*, the Portuguese author José Saramago imagines the breakdown of society when all of its citizens lose their sense of sight. Perhaps for Paul the reordering of the world comes as we learn to see God and God's plan through the new eyes of the heart.[2]

---

1. John Wesley, *Directions for Singing, Select Hymns*, 1761, as published in *Voices United: The Hymn and Worship Book of the United Church of Canada* (Toronto: United Church Press, 1996).
2. José Saramago, *Blindness*, trans. Giovanni Pantiero (New York: Harcourt, 1999).

For Paul the heart (Gk. *kardia*) is not a romantic notion; it is the spiritual and moral center of our being. Paul challenges readers to see through heart to the center of faith.

Although Paul never writes about the temporary blindness that Luke atrributes to him in Acts 9:8–9, some writers surmise that during that time Paul learned a new way to trust God and others, such as the ones who "led him by the hand and brought him into Damascus" (Acts 9:8). However, the author of Ephesians, steeped in Pauline theology, does exhort believers to transcend the limitedness of physical sight and the outer world that it perceives and to be guided by the inner self (*esō anthrōpon*, 3:16).

My son maneuvers the big city of Toronto, Canada, where he lives, without full use of his eyes. His other senses have not mysteriously become greater, but he has learned to use them. He has learned to trust those other senses as his new eyes. As in the old Ray Charles shtick, my son jokes that he can even tell if a woman is good looking by feeling her wrist.

Research confirms that when sight is impaired, hearing is strengthened slightly, particularly pitch and depth perception.[3] The same studies reveal, however, that these sensitivities increase only moderately when sight is lost at younger ages and insignificantly when lost after age ten. While not exaggerating the research and unwittingly perpetuating a stereotype, preachers might embrace Ephesians as an opportunity to explore the sixth sense of the heart and how it may increase as we learn to walk not by sight but by faith (2 Cor. 5:7).

The eyes of the heart see those who ache from hunger and poverty with compassion, where too often the eyes in our heads view others with fear and suspicion. By juxtaposing the dialectic lenses of scathing honesty and unwavering hope, the eyes of faith see the broken communities in which we live, not only for what they are, but also for what they could be. For Ascension Sunday, preachers and teachers might consider inviting congregations to rub their world-weary vision and to refocus through the eyes of the heart, to see the world as God does. Imagine Christ sitting at God's right hand (v. 20), saying, "Wow! You should see the hopeful view from here!"

In the fall of 2009, when all but one of the eleven mass-murder victims from Imperial Street in Cleveland had been identified, an elder in our congregation suggested that we donate a cemetery plot and provide a memorial

3. Frédéric Gougoux, Robert J. Zatorre, Maryse Lassonde, Patrice Voss, Franco Lepore, "A Functional Neuroimaging Study of Sound Localization: Visual Cortex Activity Predicts Performance in Early-Blind Individuals," research article, published Jan. 25, 2005 | doi:10.1371/journal.pbio.0030027; http://www.plosbiology.org/article/info%3Adoi%2F10.1371%2Fjournal.pbio.0030027 (accessed February 23, 2010).

service for the one remaining "Jane Doe." He reminded us that while her family and friends may have forgotten her, God had not. He challenged us to view the so-called forgotten woman through the eyes of the heart.

I notice an irony. Often our son sees aspects of the world better than I do. He perceives stumbling blocks and opportunities that I miss. Often, a so-called disability can be an advantage that allows those without sight to perceive more clearly than others. The preacher can help enlighten the heart of the congregation by listening to the prophetic witness of such individuals and communities.

Luke 24:44–53

In our age of megachurches and Senate Finance Committee hearings that investigate megawealth ministries, one wonders if our religious leaders have confused Jesus' ascension to the right hand of God with their own. Jesus never called the church to be successful; he called us to be faithful. So just what is our relationship to the ascension of Jesus? Quite simply, we are witnesses. Literally speaking, we are those who "remember."

We remember the living story of Jesus by what we say (or do not say), what we do (or do not do), and by who we are—new beings continually transformed by sacred Word and Presence. We stand below, along with the first disciples, looking upward toward heaven with amazement, and our trembling fingers point as our quaking voices proclaim, "Behold!"

We belong to a great cloudy chain of witnesses, beginning with the "two men in dazzling clothes" at the open tomb (Luke 24:4) who announced, "He is not here, but has risen" (Luke 24:5), and including the first preachers, "Mary Magdalene, Joanna, Mary the mother of James, and the other women" (Luke 24:9), who dared to tell the story, and the two men "in white robes" who stood by to witness the ascension (Acts 1:10). Luke assures us that both Jesus' resurrection and his ascension have been verified, according to Deuteronomy, by "two or three witnesses" (Deut. 19:15). According to Luke, the early church is part of that chain of witnesses, and so are we.

While we know whom we remember, we might ask how we remember. Does our buildup of megawealth or megachurch truly bear witness to the one who surrendered his entirety? Does a success model emulate a cross-centered faith? Perhaps we bear witness to the Jesus story most profoundly by our worshipful presence and our just activity in the community by refusing to abandon old urban neighborhoods in search of new suburban members, and by standing with those who stand alone in the fight for justice, rather than driving by in our SUV.

Acts 1:1–11

Theophilus gets honorable mention twice from Luke. First, he is addressed as the "most excellent Theophilus" in Luke 1:3. Luke mentions him again at the opening of Acts (1:1), where Luke writes like a professor reviewing the first unit of a course before continuing with the second. Luke assumes Theophilus remembers what he has been taught, but underscores the main points as he builds the foundation for the rest of the story.

Is Theophilus a real name? Given that he is called "most excellent," conjecture is more likely that it is an honorary title for one of Luke's patrons. Lending weight to this argument is the translation of his name: "Friend of God."

Those who are engaged in ministries of justice and social transformation often find themselves being supported by friends, gracious souls both within and beyond the community of faith, who finance mission projects and underwrite special programs. Many of us who remain in the city core are able to do so only because of a previous generation's generous endowments. The old buildings that house our shelters, meals for the hungry, schools for single mothers, and gathering space for worship are funded by the descendants of Theophilus. Can we overlook the fact that endowments sometimes come attached with the condition that a decorative plaque be placed to commemorate the name of the one who gave the endowment? Of course we can; after all, Luke wrote two whole books dedicated to his benefactor, Theophilus.

On Ascension Sunday, as we look to our Jesus in the sky, perhaps we can honor those who stand quietly beside the community of faith with their gifts, the business and community leaders that are poised, ready, and willing to donate from their abundance so that the church can continue in its ministry. At the same time, preachers might use this time to challenge the church to follow Theophilus in ministries of justice and compassion.

Seventh Sunday of Easter

Luke A. Powery

ACTS 1:15–17, 21–26
PSALM 1
1 JOHN 5:9–13
JOHN 17:6–19

The relationship between the faithful and the unfaithful in communities of faith is a theme in the readings for today. The reading from Acts invites us to ponder the evil that may reside within the church. While Psalm 1 distinguishes between the righteous and the wicked, that distinction is not always so clear in life. John reminds us that real lives hang in the balance when we testify. The Gospel lesson calls the church to think about how congregations under pressure can maintain a vital community, while experiencing "us and them" dynamics.

Acts 1:15–17, 21–26

This book is addressed to Theophilus (1:1), who may be an individual or any "lover of God" (the meaning of "Theophilus"). If the latter, this message is for a wider audience, any lovers of God, including us. Jesus has ascended and his followers await the promised Holy Spirit (1:5, 8). His disciples and others are in a "room upstairs" praying (1:13). Prayer pervades this passage (v. 24) yet spiritual disciplines cannot hide the truth of the state of the church. Even the stress on Scripture and its fulfillment (vv. 16, 20) cannot erase the shortcomings of the followers of Jesus.

The church of Christ has a mixed history. Though the disciples are to witness (1:8, 22), they are imperfect. "The church meets no failure or deceit in the world that it has not first encountered in itself—even among those who founded and led the very first congregation."[1] The most obvious imperfect

1. William H. Willimon, *Acts*, Interpretation series (Atlanta: John Knox Press, 1988), 25.

249

witness is Judas, a "guide for those who arrested Jesus" (v. 16). Yes, Judas "was numbered among [the disciples] and was allotted his share in this ministry" (v. 17), but in the end he decided to "go to his own place" (v. 25). He received his due "reward" (v. 18), revealing that leaders are not immune from the temptation of evil. Even Peter has a tainted history with Christ (Luke 22:31–34, 54–62). But Peter remains a believer (Acts 15), while Judas "[falls] headlong" (v. 18).

Both of these disciples, but especially Judas, reveal that evil is not always outside the church, but may occur within. Outsiders are sometimes not as threatening as insiders. There is no room for conceit, as if the wicked or the unjust are always "out there," when they may be "right here" in the pew or the pulpit. Throughout the history of the church, Christians have perpetuated evil. One of the most hideous genocides was propelled by so-called Christians: the enslavement of African peoples in the United States and other parts of the world.

David Walker in his 1829 *Appeal* says, "The white Americans having reduced us to the wretched state of slavery, treat us in that condition more cruel (they being an enlightened and Christian people), than any heathen nation did any people whom it had reduced to our condition."[2] Many Christians viewed other people as objects to be dominated. African American slave Christians were martyrs who "bore witness to the Christian gospel despite the threat of punishment and even death at the hands, not of 'pagans,' but of fellow Christians."[3] Many white Christians refused baptism to many slaves, so that the slaves might not be deemed equal. They beat slaves when the slaves worshiped, because worship threatened the social order. Whites used Jesus to bless injustice. Like Judas, the church has innocent blood on its hands.

Sometimes it is easier to attempt to wash the blood from church history than to face tortured history. It is easier to ignore the blood of the martyrs than to listen to their Christian witness. Unfortunately, Judas's death is downplayed in the lectionary. The lectionary excludes Acts 1:18–19, which tells of Judas's bloody demise. The gory "reward of his wickedness" (bowels gushing) is omitted. The exact details of his death may not be clear (cf. Matt. 27:3–10), but what is clear is that Judas is easily replaceable. The disciples quickly choose another apostle through casting lots (vv. 24–26). Judas is easily forgotten.

Is it enough to justify Judas's death (v. 19) by saying "the scripture had to be fulfilled" (v. 16) or "for it is written" (v. 20)? It is too easy to move on

---

2. David Walker, *Appeal to the Coloured Citizens of the World, but in Particular, and Very Expressly, to Those of the United States of America* (1829; repr., New York: Hill & Wang, 1965), 7.

3. Albert J. Raboteau, "'The Blood of the Martyrs Is the Seed of Faith': Suffering in the Christianity of American Slaves," in *The Courage to Hope: From Black Suffering to Human Redemption*, ed. Quinton Hosford Dixie and Cornel West (Boston: Beacon Press, 1999), 23.

because "the word tells me so," but what about human beings? What about the life of Judas, who had shared in the ministry? African American religious leaders have sometimes ignored biblical texts or read against them or moved beyond them in a hermeneutically free manner. For instance, Howard Thurman's grandmother refused to listen to Paul's letters, except 1 Corinthians 13, because during the time of slavery white preachers used Paul to justify slavery.[4] What is at stake is human life. Human life is more important than a human-created religious text or its interpretation. Judas unjustly betrayed Jesus, but where is the compassion of God for those who stray? The contemporary church often forgets fallen leaders who betrayed loved ones or their congregations or God. Likewise, the church seldom embraces Judas's humanity. Are those we think of as wicked not worthy to be affirmed as human? The church should affirm the equality and kinship of all people, including Judases.

It may be easy to forget fallen disciples and evildoers, even so-called terrorists, by wiping away traces of their blood from a lectionary, but doing so raises the question of the degree to which we are willing to love enemies (see Luke 6:27, 35). Instead of cursing "traitors," we are to love them. Grace is not cheap, but neither is human life.

Psalm 1

In Psalm 1, the destiny of the wicked is also clear: "The way of the wicked will perish" (v. 6). Happy or blessed are those who do not "take the path that sinners tread" or "follow the advice of the wicked" (v. 1) because their way leads to destruction. The path toward life is obvious. "No partly righteous, no a-little-bit-wicked."[5] There is no wiggle room except for the chafflike wicked to blow away (v. 4). The disobedient will not flourish but die. Those who do not follow the law (torah), God's way, will not prosper.

On the other hand, the "righteous" (v. 6) are happy, because "their delight is in the law of the LORD" on which they "meditate day and night" (v. 2). Because of obedience, they are firmly planted trees by "streams of water," yielding "fruit in its season" (v. 3). The psalm thus sets up an antithesis between those who follow God and those who do not. The righteous prosper; the wicked perish.

In fact, however, followers of God do not always prosper. Many times, it seems as if the evil prosper. As evidence, simply remember slavery in the United States and around the world, the Jewish Holocaust, and the Rwandan

---

4. Howard Thurman, *Jesus and the Disinherited* (Nashville: Abingdon Press, 1949), 30–31.
5. James L. Mays, *Psalms*, Interpretation series (Louisville, KY: John Knox Press, 1994), 42.

genocide. Contrary to the psalm, these events suggest that the way of the wicked prospered at moments when humans were dehumanized. Another psalmist agrees with this critique by noting that the wicked prosper (Ps. 73). Thus the perspective of Psalm 1 should not be so cut and dried. Perhaps the psalm is forward looking when it asserts that "sinners" will not stand in "the congregation of the righteous," but the present reality is that "sinners" are always members of churches.

But we know whose side God is on. "[For] the LORD watches over the way of the righteous" (v. 6). The demise of the wicked may not always occur in the present, but this text points us toward a future when the wicked way is no more, while the righteous followers of God are planted by holy streams.

1 John 5:9–13

This passage stresses testimony, not human testimony, but God's testifying to Jesus, a divine testimony declaring that eternal life comes through Jesus (v. 12). Again, a follower of God will live, whereas those "who do not believe" (v. 10) will die. By believing in Jesus, individuals "have the testimony in their hearts" (v. 10), so they can witness to what God has done in Christ. Consequently, the writer encourages readers to make this testimony their own. Otherwise, they make God a "liar" (v. 10) and they will not live.

In this discussion about Jesus, the lectionary reading does not include the water and blood, which is how Jesus "came" (v. 6). The lectionary skips the earthly, nitty-gritty life of Jesus. We thus lose the humanity of Jesus with the stress on divinity and eternality. Yet a part of John's testimony is the blood (v. 8), which reminds us that the life the Son provides came through an earthly death; the writer assures the reader that "we have seen [it] and heard [it]" (1:3). This blood is the seed of Christian faith.

This testimony is a matter of life and death. In our contemporary environment of commercialized and casual Christianity, nothing seems to be at stake; in fact, real lives hang in the balance. One only has to remember the witness that led to the deaths of Dietrich Bonhoeffer in Germany, Archbishop Oscar Romero of El Salvador, Dr. Martin Luther King Jr., and the many other women and men from the civil rights movement and other freedom struggles.

John 17:6–19

Ongoing struggle in the world for followers of Jesus Christ is also implied by this prayer. Jesus prays to God for "those whom you gave me" (v. 9), a notion repeated several times here. He prays that they would be protected

(vv. 11, 12, 15) "from the evil one" (v. 15) "so that they may be one, as we are one" (v. 11). Forces press on the followers of Christ, perhaps because of their minority status. So-called minorities, even in the United States, deal with daily hostility just because minorities are different. Yet the clear embrace of their own cultural identity as affirmation of who God has made them, and the communal development of safe spaces for cultural expression, keep minority groups together—African Americans, Asian Americans, Hispanic Americans, Native Americans, and others. Outside forces try to destroy the oneness of these groups, but they have continued to declare, "I feel like goin' on." The church as minority can also "go on" as a safe space, if it embraces its identity as the body of Christ and does not succumb to evil external pressures. Evil forces are real and threaten Christian unity, resulting in Jesus' prayer for oneness. Jesus says, "Not one of them was lost except the one destined to be lost, so that the scripture might be fulfilled" (v. 12), referring to Judas. But was not Judas's life worthy to be saved also?

The others had "kept [God's] word" (vv. 6, 8, 14), and this made the difference in their destiny, such that Jesus can say to the Father, "They are yours" (vv. 6, 9), and they "do not belong to the world" (vv. 14, 16). John makes a clear distinction between "us and them," "the world" and those who are "yours." Indeed, Jesus makes certain not to ask "on behalf of the world" (v. 9). The dichotomy between the followers of Jesus and others is even sharper as Jesus prays, "Sanctify them in the truth" (v. 17). They are to be set apart from the world as they seek a common purpose of following Christ with a faith that holds "to God's unchanging hand."

The division between "us" and "them" is clear in the Fourth Gospel, doubtless in part because of the animosity of many in ancient society toward the church. Yet what John presents as lucid is murky today. What do we do when the divide between the church and world is not clear? What happens when those who are non-Christian act more Christian than Christians? What do we do when Christians are in control of the worldly systems of empire that keep the poor poor and help the rich get richer? Who is "the world" then? Who is the perpetuator of evil, and who needs to be protected from the evil ones? These questions point to the fact that we live in an ambiguous reality of gray. Those who are "yours" may not be so clear, however, because even though "your word is truth" (v. 17), not every embodiment of that word is. In other words, "Everybody talking about heaven is not going there."

Day of Pentecost

John S. McClure

EZEKIEL 37:1–14
PSALM 104:24–34, 35B
ROMANS 8:22–27
JOHN 15:26–27; 16:4B–15

Pentecost is a season of hope. The breath of God's creating Spirit blows anew, reminding us that death and despair do not have the last word. The story of dry bones in Ezekiel 37:1–14 urges us boldly to claim the power of God's Spirit, and to "prophesy" to the dry bones of injustice and death-dealing violence around us, in the confidence that injustice and violence will end and that our social world can live in the way God wants. In Romans 8:22–27, Paul reminds us that we are people of the Spirit, who always seek new possibilities for human flourishing, never caving in to the body of death and decay around us. John 15:26–27 and 16:4b–15 encourage us to take heart and to follow the Spirit, Christ's Advocate, who will lead us into all truth.

Ezekiel 37:1–14

Contemplating a nation in ruins, Ezekiel is led by the Spirit into a valley full of dry bones where he has a vision of God's life-giving Spirit resurrecting an entire nation. The question is "Can these bones live?" (v. 3). Instead of Ezekiel asking this question of God, it is God who asks this question of Ezekiel. The answer relies on Ezekiel's willingness to trust in the power of God. Ezekiel answers: "O Lord GOD, *you* know!" (v. 3).

In today's context, in which nations point nuclear warheads at one another, toxic waste is poisoning ground water, and many go without health care and food, we are often quick to ask *God*, "Can these bones live? Is there hope?" Yet God asks this question of *us*. Do we place our trust in God's power to save us at this moment in history? If we do, then God has one very simple instruction: "Prophesy to these bones, and say to them: 'O dry bones, hear the word

254

of the LORD'" (v. 4). God instructs us to speak God's word directly to the dry bones of death all around us, trusting that through our ministries the Spirit can bring life to the dead bones in our social worlds.

For years Charles Campbell taught a course at Columbia Theological Seminary in Atlanta on "street preaching." Students left the classroom and went onto the streets of Atlanta to places where the "principalities and powers" were plying their wares. Some students situated themselves on street corners between enormous buildings where power brokers were making decisions that would have a direct impact on who could afford health care, food, utilities, and other resources. Other students went to places where people were homeless or living in poverty, or to graveyards such as the one to which Ezekiel was led. They made their way to any place where they could find dry bones of death, and the students preached. They prophesied, not to a congregation in the usual sense, but to the principalities and powers, confronting the forces of injustice and despair, trusting that God would make good on the preached Word. When they preached, they believed that a new nation could be born from the dry bones.

The story of dry bones takes place at the intersection of human weakness and divine power. It reminds us that God's power is made great in our weakness, and that the power the church wields is not the power of the sword, but the power of God's Spirit working through the Word proclaimed. It seems foolish to many that the church would confront the principalities and powers of this world with these seemingly little words of prophecy. And yet, according to Scripture, this is precisely how the seeds of resurrection are sown: through words spoken in the face of death and in the power of the Holy Spirit.

In February of 2009, a small group of people gathered outside the state penitentiary near Nashville. Earlier, all of those gathered had received a phone call from TCASK (Tennessee Coalition to Abolish State Killing), letting them know that a vigil would take place that night in solidarity with Steve Henley, who was to be executed shortly after midnight. They made their way on the coldest night of the year to a grassy area just outside the prison walls. They gathered, hugged one another, sang, and spoke brief messages of hope over a crackling megaphone. A television reporter arrived and asked one of the witnesses why she was there. She said: "Because we have hope! We do not believe this is the way God wants us to treat each other! We believe that our voices can make a difference."

This little group prophesied to dry bones, claiming God's resurrection power in spite of, and in the face of, despair and death. When word came that the execution was done, tears were shed, more songs were sung, and then everyone went home. Was it foolishness? Was it worthless? Not according to those gathered. All those who work for social transformation know what this is about. Every time someone makes a phone call, writes a letter to a senator or representative, paints a homemade sign and shows up on a street corner, or otherwise speaks out against injustice, they prophesy with an emphatic trust in the God of resurrection (vv. 8–10).

Romans 8:22–27 and Psalm 104:24–34, 35b

In Romans 8, Paul "ups the ante" on the story of the dry bones in Ezekiel 37. Paul expands the theme of hope beyond the nation to the entire creation, which has been "groaning in labor pains until now" (v. 22). This is the same creation praised by the psalmist in Psalm 104 as utterly dependent on the breath of God (Ps. 104:30). God has designed creation to provide for every living thing "in due season" (Ps. 104:27). Yet, according to Paul, this creation suffers under the weight of human sin and groans for new life. According to Paul, a decisive cosmic shift is underway, in which the resurrection power of the Spirit has come upon the community as "first fruits" of a new creation (Rom. 8:23). This has created heightened anticipation that the reign of God has begun and is in their midst. Three things bear testimony to this new world: the groaning of creation, the hope that Christians have in Christ, and the presence of the Holy Spirit interceding on the world's behalf.

From the perspective of social justice and transformation, one notable thing in this text is the materiality of the hope. The *material* creation is groaning and in labor, and hopes for nothing short of the "redemption of our bodies" (v. 23). Embodied, physical existence is not pushed aside as irrelevant, but is transformed in the eschatological reign of God. Christians participate in God's redeeming of the human body and the body of creation. This is the work of the second humanity (Adam), those who no longer serve that which destroys created bodies, but live to represent the new creation.

To put it bluntly, Christians are those who do not adapt well, if adaptation means accepting death, decay, and the body of death (despair, sin, futility, and hopelessness) as inescapable. Instead of adapting to these realities, Christians sense the firstfruits of the Spirit and hope for things that are not seen (v. 24). In short, Christians adapt to the experience of the Holy Spirit, which brings them into significant conflict with the biological, political, and social systems of death. The Spirit brings a profound hope in future possibilities in the face of current discouragement.

The portrait of this Spirit interceding "with sighs too deep for words" (v. 26) provides us with an image of the Spirit *within us*, seeking out new possibilities of life, freedom, and community all of the time, whether we know it or not. With this Spirit deep in our hearts, we can never adapt to a world of injustice, violence, and hopelessness. We adapt only to the Spirit's prayer of resurrection hope for every living being. That is our "natural" environment as Christians.

John 15:26–27; 16:4b–15

The lection presses forward with the theme of the Holy Spirit as a profound purveyor of future possibilities. The disciples at the Last Supper are sad that Jesus is leaving. And for John's church, the resurrection appearances are a long way in the past. With Jesus leaving, and memory likely to dry up, Jesus gives the promise that, through the Spirit, the risen Christ will continue to encounter the disciples and lead them into all truth. Although Jesus has gone ahead of them to prepare them a place (14:2–3), he promises that a future with him will make its way from the future into the present through the work of the Holy Spirit. Although the Spirit's leadership will mean many things, these texts indicate that the Spirit will clarify the kind of world in which they live and show them the things they must resist on their journey home to Christ.

From the perspective of social justice and transformation, it is helpful to think more deeply about the three things that the Spirit will clarify. First, the Spirit will "prove the world wrong about sin" (16:8). Although Jesus identifies this sin as not believing in him, the meaning of this disbelief is filled out when we think about what Jesus represented: self-giving love and mercy, even to death. What is condemned, then, are patterns of disbelief that turn away from love and justice and cleave to violence, ambition, greed, and self-securing power.

Second, the Spirit will prove the world wrong "about righteousness" (v. 10). A better translation is "justice." The Spirit's proof about justice wears two faces. (a) The Spirit will prove that the real justice meted out at the crucifixion was divine justice, which destroyed the power of sin. (b) The Spirit will prove that the cross renders a divine verdict of no to violence toward others as a way of life. The Spirit helps the disciples see that Jesus is the justice of God in *every* respect—a plumb line for measuring what is just and merciful. This perspective helps the church avoid caving in to false views of what is just, right, or suitable.

Third, the Spirit will prove the world wrong "about judgment, because the ruler of this world has been condemned" (v. 11). The crucifixion was not a victory for Satan (the forces of evil), but the overcoming of Satan. The Spirit reminds Jesus' followers that the power of evil has been broken in Christ and that the power they have within themselves as Christ's followers is unstoppable. The Spirit will not let the disciples be ruled by despair in the face of the violence, injustice, and fear that seem often to be in control of the world.

The final theme is that of witness. Jesus tells the disciples, "The Advocate . . . will testify on my behalf" (15:26). The disciples also are to testify "because you have been with me from the beginning" (v. 27). Witnessing means standing firm for one's convictions in situations fraught with fear, ambiguity, and instability. Like the disciples, we are to follow the leadership of the Spirit through the world, plowing our way through uncharted territory where truth is contested.

Rhetoric about "truth" blares from television sets and politically polarized radio stations. Self-interest and party interest seem more important than human welfare. At the same time, we live in a nation of pension funds and investments, of automobiles that guzzle gas, and we consume more than our fair share of Earth's resources. Our situation is saturated with moral ambiguity, and we can easily be tempted to leave the path charted by the Spirit and seek our own security at the expense of others. In this situation, John's Gospel provides a powerful antidote, reminding us that we are never alone; we have come from the cross, and we are on our way to a home already prepared for us. The way is not easy, but the Spirit will show us what is true and just, and will not let us fall into despair.

First Sunday after Pentecost (Trinity Sunday)

Kee Boem So

ISAIAH 6:1–8
PSALM 29
ROMANS 8:12–17
JOHN 3:1–17

This week's readings for Trinity Sunday invite us to reflect on transformation initiated by life in the Trinitarian relationship. The heart of the doctrine of the Trinity is participating in the life of the intimate relationship of the triune God. When we experience Trinity at work in our life, this leads us to transformation. The Trinity is not an abstract doctrine but a practical reality with implications for Christian life. We see a vital implication of the Trinity for transformation in Christian life when we encounter the mystery of the Trinity in our life. The questions we will ask in this week's readings are, How does the triune God transform us? What are the social implications of that transformation?

In these remarks, the life of the Trinitarian relationship will become clear. What we experience in the life of the three persons of the Trinity is a life of perfect community, a call to transform our communities by following the model of the Trinitarian relationship, and an invitation to participate in the Trinitarian life as a community by embodying God's peace, love, and justice as God's responsible agents.

John 3:1–17

The reading from John shows the theme of personal transformation. The text is divided into two parts: the dialogue between Jesus and Nicodemus (vv. 1–10) and the discourse of Jesus (vv. 11–17). Nicodemus, "a leader of the Jews," comes to Jesus by night (v. 1) The Gospel of John is full of symbolism. Here night symbolizes the sphere of existence that does not understand

God. We will see whether or not Nicodemus will be able to see God's glory manifested in Jesus as he gets out of his own darkness.

Jesus challenges Nicodemus by saying, "Very truly, I tell you, no one can see the [realm] of God without being born from above" (v. 3). Another symbol is at work: the Greek word *anōthen* means either "again" or "from above." Jesus plays on the double meaning of the word, but the intention is actually the same: "to be born 'again/anew' is to be born 'from above,' that is, to be born of the Spirit."[1] Jesus wants Nicodemus to get out of his darkness by his encounter with Jesus, through whom he can see God's reign in the world through being born of the Spirit.

Because Nicodemus does not understand Jesus' words but takes them literally (v. 4, "Can one enter a second time into the mother's womb and be born?"), Jesus clarifies: "Very truly, I tell you, no one can enter the [realm] of God without being born of water and Spirit" (v. 5). The text indicates two types of birth: by water and by the Spirit. Here we encounter another symbol, water. Water also has a double meaning: the mother's amniotic fluid, which represents physical birth, and the water of baptism, through which believers experience spiritual birth. John plays on these two meanings: even if "one is born 'of water,' 'of the flesh,' one must also be born 'of the Spirit'—that is, anew and from above."[2] The message is clear: One should enter the life of the Spirit (a new way of life centered on the Spirit), leaving the life of the flesh behind. This is a provocative invitation to a personal transformation.

Nicodemus responds from the perspective of his old way of life: "How can these things be?" (v. 9). However, we see later that the transformation begun in this dialogue is continued when Nicodemus defends Jesus to the Jewish authorities opposed to Jesus (7:50–51) and when Nicodemus appears with "a mixture of myrrh and aloes" at Jesus' burial (19:39). John thus pictures Nicodemus as one who grows in personal transformation.

However, his transformation does not remain in the personal realm only. Nicodemus's two other appearances in the Gospel of John show that he develops a critical stance, both defending Jesus before his fellow Jews who question Jesus and objecting to Roman imperialism. In the Fourth Gospel, when Jesus explains his identity and mission he implicitly confronts Roman imperialism by criticizing "the world," the domain in which Caesar rules. Nicodemus's personal transformation gets him into a similar position, which is critical of the powers of the status quo.

The second part of the text explains another aspect of personal transformation: one should accept the revelation of "heavenly things" (3:12) so that

---

1. Marcus J. Borg, *The Heart of Christianity: How We Can Be Passionate Believers Today* (New York: HarperSanFrancisco, 2003), 106.
2. Ibid.

one may have "eternal life" (vv. 16–17). John later reveals the essence of eternal life: "And this is eternal life, that they may know you, the only true God, and Jesus Christ whom you have sent" (17:3). The nature of this "knowing" is participating in the Trinitarian relationship, as Jesus continues in 17:21, "[I ask] that they may all be one. As you, Father, are in me and I am in you, may they also be in us, so that the world may believe that you have sent me." The personal transformation initiated by the encounter with the Trinity leads to building up community in the model of the Trinitarian relationship of mutual support.

The first reading is an invitation to the life of the Trinitarian relationship: entering the reign of God through being born of the Spirit, and enjoying eternal life in the present through accepting God's revelation in Jesus. This personal spiritual transformation includes social dimensions, as it changes our views of society and community, reflecting the Trinitarian relationship. This transformation is not a one-time experience but an ongoing process as in the case of Nicodemus. A definitive moment in this process is baptism, which leads us to the second reading.

Romans 8:12–17

According to this text, as God enjoys intimate communion among the three persons of God, we are invited to participate in the Trinitarian relationship in our relationship with God and with others. The theme of being born of the Spirit is discerned here again: "So then, brothers and sisters, we are debtors, not to the flesh, to live according to the flesh—for if you live according to the flesh, you will die; but if by the Spirit you put to death the deeds of the body, you will live" (vv. 12–13). The new life is centered on the Spirit rather than on the flesh. Again, the new life does not remain on the personal level but also includes social life: living out the values of the life in the Spirit by striving to manifest the realm of God in this world.

This new life in the Spirit is based on community: "For all who are led by the Spirit of God are children of God" (v. 14). According to Paul, children of God are those who cry, "Abba! Father!" (v. 15) so that we become "heirs of God" (v. 17). This communal aspect of transformation is manifest in life "led by the Spirit," which "unites us to one another and to Christ."[3] Therefore, new life in the Spirit leads to transformation in community, which manifests the life of the Trinitarian relationship. Baptism is the definitive moment of transformation to this new community.

3. David L. Bartlett, *Romans*, Westminster Bible Companion (Louisville, KY: Westminster John Knox Press, 1995), 75.

For Paul, to be united to Christ by the Spirit also means "we suffer with him so that we may also be glorified with him" (v. 17b), which is the true meaning of baptism. Previously in Romans, Paul said of baptism, "Do you not know that all of us who have been baptized into Christ Jesus were baptized into his death? Therefore we have been buried with him by baptism into death, so that, just as Christ was raised from the dead by the glory of the Father, so we too might walk in newness of life" (6:3–4). Baptism is dying to one's old way of life and rising again in "newness of life."[4] Therefore baptism is the moment of one's transformation in which the new life of the Spirit is enacted. This transformation is also a moment of entering into a new community and a new social order modeling Trinitarian relationship to embody the love and justice of the realm of God in this world.

Psalm 29

The theme of social transformation emerges in this "enthronement psalm" (v. 10) that has "glory" as its key word (vv. 1–3, 9).[5] All creatures and even "heavenly beings" ascribe to God glory and strength. This cosmic exaltation of God derives from God's reign in heaven and earth (vv. 3–9b). Then the psalmist turns to the transformation that all people experience when they encounter the reign of God: "May the LORD give strength to [God's own] people! May the LORD bless [God's own] people with peace!" (v. 11). God gives God's strength to God's people, who, in turn, become the vessel through which divine peace can be delivered.

This transformation has many implications for human society. When one encounters the triune God, ascribes to God glory and strength, and joins in the temple with others in praising God (v. 9c), one is also invited to manifest God's peace in the world. This call to spread God's peace involves community. The praising community will experience the peace manifest in the life of the Trinity in its own community first, and then will manifest the peace in its active involvement in society as the agent of peace. The next reading further develops this theme as it particularly combines personal spiritual transformation and social transformation.

Isaiah 6:1–8

In this famous passage Isaiah receives the call from the triune God. The references to the Trinity are found in the triple use of "holy" (v. 3) and in God's

---

4. Borg, *The Heart of Christianity*, 109–11.
5. J. Clinton McCann Jr., "Psalms," in *The New Interpreter's Bible*, ed. Leander Keck et al. (Nashville: Abingdon Press, 1996), 4:792.

self-reference in the plural (v. 8). Isaiah encounters the triune God whose glory fills the whole earth (v. 3).

In the midst of this holy encounter with the Trinity, Isaiah acknowledges his uncleanness: "Woe is me! I am lost, for I am a [person] of unclean lips, and I live among a people of unclean lips; yet my eyes have seen the [Sovereign], the LORD of hosts!" (v. 5). We experience this phenomenon when we encounter the mystery of God. This is a moment of *tremendum mysterium*, tremendous mystery, as Rudolf Otto calls it.[6] When humans encounter the triune God, feelings of guilt and shame arise in front of the holy mystery.

This awareness moves Isaiah to personal spiritual transformation: repentance and restoration. Upon hearing Isaiah's sighs, one of the seraphs takes a coal from the altar, touches the prophet's mouth, and says, "Your guilt has departed and your sin is blotted out" (v. 7). Now the prophet possesses a cleansed mouth, with which he speaks on behalf of God. This personal transformation leads to the second transformation, which moves the prophet to call for social transformation.

God does not speak to Isaiah directly. Isaiah overhears God's commission and responds immediately: "Then I heard the voice of the Lord saying, 'Whom shall I send, and who will go for us?' And I said, 'Here am I; send me!'" (v. 8). Isaiah's personal transformation makes him sensitive to God's call, which in turn leads him to respond to that call with no hesitation. This second transformation is accepting one's social responsibility toward the world as God's agent or coworker.

These two transformations, the personal and social, are inherently related. This is the true nature of spirituality, what Jon Sobrino calls "political holiness." Sobrino says, "Spirituality today in the absence of the practice of liberation is purely generic, evangelically impossible, and historically alienating. Liberation practice without spirit is generically good, but concretely threatened with degeneration, diminution, and sin."[7] Hence, our prophetic response to contemporary issues should come out of our deep experiences of holy mystery. And our encounter with the triune God leads us to our responsibility in the world: To enact the love and justice of the life of the Trinitarian relationship and to spread God's peace to the world in our striving to model the community of the Trinity.

As we meditate on this week's readings for Trinity Sunday, we are invited by the mystery of the Trinity to participate in the life of the Trinitarian relationship as a transformed community to enact the love, peace, justice of the realm of God here and now.

6. Rudolf Otto, *The Idea of the Holy* (New York: Oxford University Press, 1958).
7. Jon Sobrino, *Spirituality of Liberation: Toward Political Holiness* (Maryknoll, NY: Orbis Books, 1988), 29.

Proper 3 [8]

Safiyah Fosua

HOSEA 2:14–20
PSALM 103:1–13, 22
2 CORINTHIANS 3:1–6
MARK 2:13–22

Jesus said, "I have come to call not the righteous but sinners" (Mark 2:17b). This week's theme, *acceptance*, presents a steep challenge to the Christian church. Are we capable of receiving those whom God has forgiven? Did the Israelites ever accept Hosea's Gomer? Why did the apostle Paul have so much trouble being accepted—even in light of his tremendous ministry? Is it possible for a present-day traitor, like Mark's tax collector or others that society despises, to find a home among today's faithful? The ultimate question: Are our congregations ready for the changes required truly to accept the needy and the notorious into our fellowship?

Hosea 2:14–20

The eighth-century prophet Hosea was known for his passion for religious purity at a time when Israel was known for repeated apostasy. Hosea spoke truth, even when it was painful to hear. Once, Hosea even criticized Israel's king for an unwise alliance with Assyria (Hos. 7).

Ironically, Hosea's own household was riddled with controversy: this passionate defender of the faith was married to a woman known for her unfaithfulness. Gomer's embarrassing actions undoubtedly made Hosea the object of much gossip. The names of his children—Lo-ruhamah ("no mercy"), Lo-ammi ("not my people"), and the eldest, Jezreel (recalling a painful site in Israel's history)—shouted a distress call from a home that was out of sync.

This second chapter of Hosea drops us into a turning point in the prophet's narrative. We find ourselves like late-arriving theatergoers trying to decipher the plot of a fast-paced movie. Is Hosea's wife a harlot or a religious infidel? Is this marriage real, or does it stand for something else? Will they stay together? And just what did Gomer do?

Recent scholarship leans toward the interpretation that Hosea's marriage was real, not symbolic. Traditional interpretations insist that Gomer was sexually unfaithful to Hosea: Speculations over the nature of her sexual infidelity range from streetwalker to adulteress to temple prostitute. But at least one reliable scholar asserts that the Hebrew phrase *eshet zenunim* indicates not that Gomer was a woman of depraved character but that she was a woman who took part in Canaanite rites.[1] Either way, harlot or idolater, Hosea's lived metaphor holds together. Israel was repeatedly guilty of worshiping foreign gods, and God felt betrayed. Yet, in spite of Israel's grievous sin, God would eventually take her back, forgive her, and love her as before.

On a contextual note, Hosea's life story forces us to look in the mirror at our own households and how we respond to similar disappointments. Hosea's struggles are instructive for families that experience tension because of the Christian faith or because of varying *levels of faith commitment*. The story also models restoration for congregational systems who often do not know what to do when a faithful church member or a close member of their family is found guilty of something worthy of jail time, like selling, making, or using illegal street drugs. As hurtful as Gomer's lifestyle was to Hosea, he remained committed to his relationship with her. Hosea's continued love and commitment provided an opening for God's grace to be available to Gomer, his wife.

The good news of the passage and a recurring theme of this day may be found in this snippet from Hosea's story. God has plans to woo Israel and win her back. They will go back to places where they once made memories together, like the wilderness. She will receive vineyards to remind her of the good things they have shared. She will surely remember the miracles when she sees the desolate Valley of Achor become a place of hope (v. 15). Struggles with the environment, with the animals and birds with which we share this planet, and the struggle of war will give way to peace. The idolatrous name of the Baals will be removed from her mouth and replaced with a term of endearment—"My husband" (v. 16). God does not give up on people when they sin. God looks for ways to restore them.

1. Gerhard von Rad, *Old Testament Theology*, trans. D. M. G. Stalker (Louisville, KY: Westminster John Knox Press, 2001), 2:141.

Psalm 103:1–13, 22

Psalm 103 is from Book IV of the Psalms. Royalty and martyrs, songwriters and Bible commentators, saints and penitents have found comfort in this psalm. In the psalm, God is good to both individuals and the community. The psalm's repeated exhortations to bless the Lord from the depths of the soul move the reader and the hearer into the realm of appreciating a God who is beyond anything we had expected or imagined.[2]

One line of the psalm—"forgives all your iniquity, who heals all your diseases" (v. 3)—hints that it was written as a psalm of thanksgiving and possibly refers to the psalmist's recovery from a major illness or to David's spiritual restoration after his sin with Bathsheba. Others call it a psalm of praise when they look at its hymnlike qualities, its reminder that we are all mere mortals and sinners, and its refrainlike exhortation to bless the Lord. It has been difficult to tie this psalm to a specific event because the psalmist calls us to praise that goes beyond thanksgiving for a specific event. This week, we are drawn to its assurance that God forgives and heals on an individual level (v. 3) and that God "works vindication and justice for all who are oppressed" (v. 6).

Psalm 103 has been treasured by those who are acutely aware of their need for the grace of God. The metaphor that God removes our sins as far from us "as the east is from the west" (v. 12) is a reminder that the guilt of sin need not be a barrier between us and God. What a conundrum—that the same God that works justice is also slow to punish and forgets about the sins of the ones who fear God (vv. 8–10)!

God is not the Hebrews' or the Christians' tribal god who desires the well-being only of the well behaved. God does not remove only polite sins, and God's love is not reserved for polite sinners. God continues to love those considered the dregs of society's barrel and the people we consider beyond redemption. God loved a person like Gomer, who was accused of sexual taboos or idolatry.

God's grace is available to both pimps that oppress and the prostitutes they exploit. The grace of God is able to reach prisoners. Ask prison chaplains about the newly found faith of men or women jailed for anything from murder to back-alley theft. Then, contrast this snapshot of grace with the lack of grace that ex-offenders frequently experience when they attempt to become part of a congregation. Such actions suggest that we do not believe what we preach. But the first-century church fiercely believed in forgiveness

---

2. Walter Brueggemann, *The Psalms and the Life of Faith*, ed. Patrick D. Miller (Minneapolis: Augsburg Fortress Press, 1995), 50–51.

and transformation. No wonder Paul and Silas sang their hymns of praise within earshot of both jailed and jailors (Acts 16:25).

2 Corinthians 3:1–6

The apostle Paul needed the kind of acceptance described in Hosea 2 and Psalm 103. Before being called to witness to the Gentiles, Paul had the kind of credentials that he eschews in 3:1. He had done all things Hebrew according to the rule book. He was well read, well connected, well regarded, and headed for high places (Phil. 3:5–6). Though he had done everything *by the book*, Paul still found himself on the wrong track. His zeal for persecuting Christians and hauling them to jail became known throughout Israel. According to Luke, on the day that Christ arrested him on the road to Damascus, he had come with letters from the high priest authorizing him to take Christians as prisoners to Jerusalem (Acts 9).

Paul's encounter with Christ changed him. He was no longer the one who persecuted that new "wrongheaded" sect of the Jews; he was now a member of the despised group! It came as no surprise that the Christians who had known him as a persecutor were slow to embrace him as a genuine member of their group; according to Luke, some of his contemporaries branded him as a traitor and made trouble for him (Acts 14:19, 17:13). In Galatians, Paul states that he was called to preach to the Gentiles (Gal. 1:15–16). While Paul does preach to Jewish people in Acts (e.g., Acts 28:17–22), his ministry in Acts is focused primarily on Gentiles (Acts 9:15–16; 18:1–6).

Paul, who had once been highly credentialed, found himself with few credentials but those that come from God. He was loosely connected to the emerging Christian leadership group. Who was able to vouch for him? Paul's response: the ministry in Corinth was his letter of commendation. They were his letter, written with the Spirit of the Living God (3:3) not on tablets of stone, but written on human hearts just as Jeremiah had promised (31:33). If we wish to know who Paul is, if we want to know about any others of the redeemed, look at the fruit of our labors in the Lord.

Mark 2:13–22

The call of Levi is one of a series of controversy stories that raise a critical question: how do people of the family of faith respond when the unfathomable grace of God is extended to those we consider sinners or enemies? We are quick to applaud for ourselves when we hear the words of the psalmist reminding us that God removes our sins as far as the east is from the west. But see how uncomfortable we become when the same grace of God is offered to Gomer (whether harlot or idolater) or to Paul in spite of his past. Here in Mark 2 God is at it again with yet another example of uncomfortable grace!

We are so accustomed to reading the call narratives that we often miss the scandal that having a *Jewish* collector of *Roman* taxes added to Jesus' motley crew. In Moses' time the tribe of Levi was set aside to tend temple worship and to handle holy things (Num. 3:5–9). This Levi has betrayed his calling by collecting taxes for an occupying government, Rome, and was likely guilty of collecting extra money for himself. He was a traitor and perhaps a thief! Tax collectors were such a threat to the community that they were mentioned separately as if they were a special class of sinners (vv. 15–16).

What scandal when Jesus called this extraordinary sinner to follow him! Seemingly worse, Jesus did not shrink from being seen in public with him. In fact, they broke bread together—along with others like him. This was quite different from being in the company of the poor or the indigent; this was banqueting with the bad![3] Nevertheless, we may presume that Levi repented, since Jesus said that repentance was one of the fundamental steps to joining the movement toward the realm of God (Mark 1:15).

In the final verses of this week's Gospel (vv. 18–22) the Pharisees move from their objections to Rabbi Jesus sitting at table with sinners and tax collectors to a different question about standard religious practices. The pious fasted frequently. Even John the Baptist's followers fasted frequently. Jesus' group did not. The Pharisees want to know why. Jesus' reply: "Fresh skins for new wine!" (NEB, TEV).

All of this week's readings challenge us on this two-thousand-year-old point: Jesus came not to call the righteous, but sinners to repentance (v. 17). In this respect, the Markan Jesus is truly Jewish, for calling sinners to repent was central to Judaism. Furthermore, Judaism provided means for forgiveness. Mark believed that the risen Jesus would return so soon that Gentiles need not convert fully to Judaism in order to be fully forgiven and prepared for the apocalypse. As the Jesus movement evolved, its distinctive mission became that of calling Gentiles to repent (13:10). The new wine was Mark's congregation welcoming Gentiles into the community of the last days. A lasting contribution of the Gospel of Mark, then, is to assure Gentiles who repent that their sins are forgiven and that they are full members of God's family alongside the Jewish community.

---

3. Ben Witherington III, *The Gospel of Mark, A Socio-Rhetorical Commentary* (Grand Rapids: Eerdmans, 2001), 121.

Proper 4 [9]

Diane G. Chen

1 SAMUEL 3:1–10 (11–20)   DEUTERONOMY 5:12–15
PSALM 139:1–6, 13–18   PSALM 81:1–10
                                  2 CORINTHIANS 4:5–12
                                          MARK 2:23–3:6

Doing justice is both noble and difficult. While it is at the heart of God's agenda for the world, it requires courage, obedience, and sacrifice. In this set of readings, God's unconditional response to Israel's cry for help becomes the blueprint for Israel's treatment of the oppressed (Ps. 81). This modus operandi underlies the Sabbath law, in which even slaves are entitled to God's gift of rest (Deut. 5). Jesus radicalizes the practice of divine justice by prioritizing all life-giving actions. Similarly, Paul preaches the gospel despite unmentionable sufferings at every turn. Because he subscribes to God's agenda, he embraces the message of salvation as "treasure in clay jars" and presses on in faith and doggedness (2 Cor. 4). God, the all-knowing and all-seeing one, continues to call people to implement the divine agenda in spite of personal cost (Ps. 139). The young Samuel responds openly and readily (1 Sam. 3). What about us?

Psalm 81:1–10

Psalm 81 summons worshipers to celebrate the goodness of the God of Jacob. The mention of a full moon and God's ordaining of these festivities point to the feasts of Passover and Tabernacles as possible settings. Passover commemorates Israel's hasty escape from Egypt, and Tabernacles remembers the time of desert wandering during which the Israelites dwelt in tents.

The exodus was God's paradigmatic act of justice on Israel's behalf. God responded to the cries of Jacob's descendants, crushed by their Egyptian taskmasters (Ps. 81:7a; see Exod. 1:13–14; 5:6–19). The Israelites did not need to qualify for aid, nor were they required to stand in line. God heard their cry of raw despair, even though some of them did not even know who God was (Ps. 81:5).

In the wilderness, God instructed Israel to live as his people. "The secret place of thunder" recalls the theophany at Sinai, where thunder and lightning both preceded and followed the giving of the law (Ps. 81:7b; see Exod. 19:16–20:18). Yet at Meribah, Israel failed to believe that the One who warded off Pharaoh's pursuers would keep them alive.

To exhort the worshipers not to repeat the sins of their forebears, the psalmist appeals to God's absolute claim over Israel: "I am the LORD your God, who brought you up out of the land of Egypt" (v. 10a). On the basis of this claim, Israel "shall not bow down to a foreign god" (v. 9). God's exclusive authority was neither malevolent nor self-aggrandizing. Had it not been for God, Israel would not exist. The Israelites' skepticism was unwarranted and shortsighted. Yet in response to their complaints God offered grace: "Open your mouth wide and I will fill it" (v. 10b)—with water, manna, quail, and ultimately with the produce of a land flowing with milk and honey.

As God delivered Israel, God delivers us, from enslavement to freedom, from exploitation to redemption, and from lack to plenty. God continues to liberate us from such things as abuse in the home, economic oppression, colonialism, racism, sexism, and violence. Even when we fail to keep covenant, God does not abandon us. If we commit ourselves to seeking after God wholeheartedly, divine help will flow generously: freedom, justice, and grace will permeate the fabric of our society. The abuser will have an opportunity to repent and rehabilitate, economic justice and sharing resources will yield security for all, and different racial and ethnic communities will live together in mutual respect.

Deuteronomy 5:12–15

Standing at the receiving end of God's grace and justice, we are called to extend the same to others, especially those over whom we exercise power. This dual emphasis, of taking what we learn from the vertical dimension of our life with God, and then expressing it in the horizontal dimension of our life in the community, lies behind the rationales for the command to observe the Sabbath.

The recordings of the Fourth Commandment in Exodus and Deuteronomy both speak of keeping the Sabbath day holy, doing all the work on six days and none at all on the seventh (cf. Exod. 20:8–11). This cessation of work applies to all Israelite households, including male and female slaves, livestock, and resident aliens.

In Exodus, the command is justified by the precedent set by God in creation. God worked for six days and rested on the seventh, so God's people must follow suit and keep the day consecrated by desisting from work. An alternate rationale with communal implications is provided in Deuteronomy. Here male and female slaves are twice mentioned, emphasizing that observing the Sabbath will allow them to "rest as well as you" (v. 14). In the stratified society of the ancient world, slaves and livestock were their owner's property. Work, especially menial labor, belonged to those on the lowest rungs of the social ladder. Rest was a luxury that only the well-to-do could afford. Seen in this light, the Fourth Commandment is counterculturally egalitarian. All in Israel—people regardless of rank or status, resident aliens, and even animals—are to enjoy God's gift of rest. The Sabbath becomes a weekly reminder that all are equally valued in God's economy. Sabbath observance thus provides an opportunity for the privileged to exercise justice in a concrete way.

Deuteronomy reminds Israel of her humble beginnings: "Remember that you were a slave in the land of Egypt, and the LORD your God brought you out from there with a mighty hand and an outstretched arm" (v. 15). Precisely because they once were numbered among the oppressed, but are no longer, they should not do to others what they would never again want done to them.

This is a word of challenge to employers and supervisors and, indeed, to all who have power among us. Supervisors must provide adequate Sabbath. Furthermore, in biblical Israel, Sabbath was a communal experience. Everyone rested at the same time, so that the community system itself had a time of renewal, to regain energy for the coming week and to recover perspective and see difficult issues afresh. By comparison, the United States today is increasingly frenetic. People constantly live under pressure, confusing busyness with a sense of self-worth. The biblical Sabbath both sits in judgment over this restlessness and offers us a model for renewal. Congregations could take a lead here by practicing real Sabbath as a demonstration to the larger culture of the clarity of purpose and regeneration that can result. In so doing, the seeming inefficiency of the Sabbath is transformed to effective life-giving action for all.

Mark 2:23–3:6

The connection between the Sabbath and God's justice is embodied by Jesus, who shows us the true spirit of the Sabbath through his life-giving actions. In the first of the two vignettes, the story of the disciples picking grain, technically the disciples (not Jesus) break the Sabbath law. But Jesus, the rabbi, is responsible for his disciples' actions. While it is illegal neither to pluck the heads of grain as one traverses a farmer's field nor to eat on the Sabbath (Deut. 23:25), rubbing the grains between the hands to get rid of the husks might have been reaping, a violation of Sabbath life (*m. Shabbat* 7.2).

Jesus turns to David's story as rebuttal. His appeal to David anticipates his pronouncement in 2:27–28: "The sabbath was made for [people] and not [people] for the sabbath; so the Son of Man is [ruler] even of the sabbath." Judaism, of course, already held that the purpose of the Sabbath was to help people (e.g., *m. Yoma* 8:6; *b. Yoma* 85b). The point in today's text lies beyond a casuistic argument. The point is not "If David could do it—forget about the minor details—I could do it too." Rather, the text strikes a christological note: Jesus is greater than David; he is the sovereign Messiah and the Danielic Son of Man (Dan. 7:13–14). By calling himself "[ruler] of the sabbath," Jesus is making a bold claim, aligning himself with the creator of the Sabbath.

God's original day of rest precedes the law that regulates its observance. The Sabbath is God's gift to serve people; people are not to serve the Sabbath. The issue is therefore one of priority, not whether Jesus is playing fast and loose with God's commandments by claiming to be ruler of the Sabbath. In Jesus' view, if assuaging his disciples' hunger brings restoration, then the prohibition against reaping is overridden. To do otherwise actually undercuts the true purpose of the Sabbath.

A similar point is made in the next story, in which Jesus on the Sabbath heals a man with a withered hand. Even though some rabbinic circles grant exception to the Sabbath law when life is in danger, a withered hand does not qualify. Just as the disciples could have missed a meal for a day, Jesus could have waited until the Sabbath was over to heal the man.

Since Jesus' opponents are watching his every move, they inadvertently give him the perfect stage to explain what doing good and saving life really mean, especially on the Sabbath. The man's handicap is not only physical; it also has social and economic dimensions. His ability to earn a living is hampered by his physical limitations, and his standing in the community is diminished. Jesus wastes no time in healing the man, because even a few hours to the end of Sabbath is too long a wait to restore a person to wholeness.

The Pharisees fail to interpret the man's healing as God's approval of Jesus' Sabbath "work." Yet God's heart is inclined toward giving life—to oppressed Israel, male and female slaves, hungry disciples, and this man with a withered hand. For the sake of bringing a person to physical, communal, and spiritual wholeness, Jesus' actions adhere to the Sabbath law at its very best. Jesus makes a critical analysis on the practice of Sabbath in his own time from the perspective of the purpose of Sabbath.

Because we above looked specifically at Sabbath issues in connection with Deuteronomy 5, I offer an analogy that shows the principle of making a critical analysis of a contemporary practice on the basis of the deeper value that it is supposed to support. One purpose of government and laws is to create a safe environment for citizens. At times, however, law-enforcement agents cross the line from taking actions that promote safety to brutality. Police brutality can actually make communities more unsafe by inciting disenfranchised residents toward violent attitudes and behaviors.

2 Corinthians 4:5–12

Paul frequently introduces himself as the slave of Jesus Christ (Rom. 1:1; Phil. 1:1), but to call himself and his coworkers slaves of the Corinthian Christians, in verse 5 he recalls Jesus' statement that he "came not to be served but to serve, and to give his life a ransom for many" (Mark 10:45). Paul serves his church as Jesus serves his disciples. This reversal of hierarchy has integrity when both see themselves first as God's servants, sent not to lord over their subordinates, but to serve the people.

The paradox lies not only in Paul's self-understanding but also in the content and execution of his mission. The gospel that he preaches—a crucified Christ, a stumbling block to Jews and foolishness to the Greeks (1 Cor. 1:23)—is a "treasure in clay jars" (2 Cor. 4:7). Carried by the ordinariness, fragility, and disposability of the messengers, the gospel is a treasure beyond measure.

Outwardly, Paul's predicaments spell powerlessness. Yet, like the toy in the 1970s for which the slogan was "Weebles wobble but they don't fall down," Paul's tenacity testifies that God's power overcomes the worst of attacks on God's servants. Even as Paul and his coworkers find themselves on the verge of death, they are "not crushed, . . . not driven to despair, . . . not forsaken, . . . not destroyed" (2 Cor. 4:8–9). Paul, the human clay jar in all his frailty, is sustained by the Potter who shapes the vessel.

As Paul encounters deadly perils in his mission, God injects the life of Jesus into him. In God's economy, things are not what they appear on the outside. Life emerges from death, gain from losses, God's power from human weakness (2 Cor. 12:9). Suffering and powerlessness are the givens if we choose to embrace God's cause for social justice in a world that rewards the rich and strong at the expense of the poor and weak. Yet God continues to work through fragile vessels such as Dorothy Day, Mother Teresa, César Chávez, and so many others who appear to be powerless but through whom God makes a mighty witness. The call is still extended today. How should we respond?

1 Samuel 3:1–10 (11–20); Psalm 139:1–6, 13–18

In these alternate readings, the last point concerning God's call may be further developed. On the one hand, Samuel's call is unmistakable, even spectacular. On the other hand, since every human being is under the intense and loving gaze of his or her Maker from conception to grave, every life has a unique call to the service of God.

Samuel's call comes at a time when prophetic words and visions are rare; thus nobody expects to hear God's voice. Moreover, Samuel is still a lad. He has yet to enter the special relationship with God that he will later experience as a prophet. Not surprisingly, he mistakes God's voice for that of the priest Eli. Even so, whether or not he fully realizes it, Samuel is already living in the locus of God's presence: he ministers in the temple by day and sleeps next to the ark by night.

After three calls, Eli realizes what is happening and instructs Samuel to respond to God: "Speak, for your servant is listening" (v. 10). In obedience Samuel attends to God's voice even before he appropriates his calling. His open posture invites God to take the next step. While God's message of judgment is against Eli and his sons, its delivery through Samuel anticipates his appointment to the prophetic office. This encounter inaugurates a special relationship between God and Samuel. In due time the boy's initial response to Eli, "Here I am," will become his lifelong response to God.

God calls Samuel to be a judge to lead the community in living in covenant with God and with one another. The covenant involves social justice—purging the community of forces that undermine covenantal living (such as Eli's sons) and seeing that all in the community live together in mutual support.

God knows Samuel more than the boy realizes. This knowledge, however, is not lost to the poet of Psalm 139, who petitions the all-seeing and omnipresent God who judges rightly to vouch for his innocence before his accusers. In the first and third strophes (vv. 1–6 and 13–18), the psalmist marvels at God's knowledge of him. Because God's scrutiny stems from love, God's penetrating gaze—from outward action to inward thought, at all times, in all places—evokes a sense of security rather than fear. God is ever present and ever supportive.

The God who examines is also the God who delivers and vindicates. God is the One who calls and sends out his servants: Israel, Jesus, Paul, Samuel, and this psalmist. We are next. God's agenda has not changed. God calls us to be instruments of God's peace and justice. Do you have the courage to say, "Here I am, Lord. Speak, for your servant is listening"?

Proper 5 [10]

Song Bok Jon

1 SAMUEL 8:4–11 (12–15),
16–20 (11:14–15)
PSALM 138

GENESIS 3:8–15
PSALM 130
2 CORINTHIANS 4:13–5:1
MARK 3:20–35

Today's lectionary readings invite us to discern God's justice for both *outsiders* and *insiders*, asking how we would respond when we transgress our covenantal relationship with God and God's creation. When God asked Adam and Eve why they ate the fruits from the tree, they each tried to deflect the blame. The elders of Israel asked Samuel to give them a monarch, even though they knew that they, especially the marginalized, would suffer exploitation. The religious leaders of Israel condemned Jesus as possessed with the demons. And Paul urged the believers in Corinth to endure their afflictions with the assurance of eternal glory. Although we often respond to injustice with anger, denial, or frustration, God, who is steadfast in love and abundant in mercy, always calls us to struggle with God to discern justice through the eyes of God.

Genesis 3:8–15

Upon eating the fruit from the tree, Adam and Eve realize they are naked and hide themselves from God; they feel shamed. This text describes God as a judge who inquires why they have committed this violation. God asks Adam, "Who told you that you were naked? Have you eaten from the tree of which I commanded you not to eat?" (v. 11). Adam, however, blames Eve, whom he dearly calls "bone of my bones" (2:23), as the one who made him eat the fruit from the tree. Eve acts similarly, in that she also blames the serpent as the one who caused her to disobey God (3:13). At the onset of creation, when questioned about their disobedience, human beings waste no time in evading responsibility and blaming one another.

Speaking justice is sometimes narrowly misunderstood only as holding others responsible for injustice. A looming risk of such a constricted perception lies in ill-conceived schemes to declare ourselves innocent. Since the Deepwater Horizon oil spill on April 20, 2010, there has been ongoing debate around who is responsible for this largest oil-spill accident in history. The U.S. government held the BP corporation accountable for this accident, while the attorneys representing BP blamed the engineers of Transocean and Halliburton (the companies who did the actual drilling). Some media and laboratories argue that the environment can dissipate the harm. In the meantime, sea creatures and seafarers deluged with oil in the Gulf of Mexico bellow, "Who will be responsible to both God and creation? Who will hide? Who will actually tarry long enough to answer the call?"

Although this text traditionally has been preached to explain how sin and death came to this world, Walter Brueggemann argues that this text is rather a story about "the struggle God has in responding to the facts of human life."[1] When encountering the injustice perpetrated by Adam and Eve, God could have destroyed them. However, God speaks justice by preserving their lives. Speaking justice in the pulpit, therefore, is a way of claiming *life* for everyone by proclaiming the jubilee, not only to us when oppressed, but also to us when we are the oppressors, whether exposed or hiding.

1 Samuel 8:4–11 (12–15), 16–20 (11:14–15)

The elders of Israel are not pleased with the current political and religious system and say to Samuel, "You are old and your sons do not follow in your ways" (8:5). They ask Samuel to give them a monarch to rule over Israel. They believe such a ruler will make them "like other nations" in that he will "go out before [them] and fight [their] battles" (v. 20). While Samuel is displeased with their request, God reminds Samuel that the elders of Israel are actually requesting to replace God as their sovereign leader with a human ruler: "For they have not rejected you, but they have rejected me from [ruling] over them" (v. 7). In Deuteronomy 20:4, God is clearly described as a warrior who fights for Israel: "For it is the LORD your God who goes with you, to fight for you against your enemies, to give you victory."

In the clash between the reign of God and that of a human leader, God orders Samuel to tell the Israelites the consequences of having a monarch to rule over them. Samuel tells them that such a leader will demand their sons and daughters for battle and service in the royal house. The monarch will take

---

1. Walter Brueggemann, *Genesis*, Interpretation series (Atlanta: John Knox Press, 1982), 50.

one-tenth of their grain and flocks. He will enslave them to work for him. However, the most frightening consequence will be when they will cry out in despair over their choice, God will ignore their plea: "And in that day you will cry out because of your [ruler], whom you have chosen for yourselves; but the LORD will not answer you in that day" (v. 18).

The elders of Israel initially came to Samuel seeking justice in their current political and religious system. This justice they sought, however, was perverted still in ways that would perpetuate, even multiply, the injustices among them. Bruce C. Birch insists that these "seekers" were not concerned about the consequences of leadership, which leads him to believe that "this gathering represents the more influential and wealthy in Israel, who were most likely to gain from the move to [monarchy]."[2] How often do our leaders claim to speak in the voice of the people and yet pursue those means that reinforce privilege? Whether we are in the positions of leadership or stand in need of leadership, we must learn to question, "Who stands to gain or retain power by this action?" Even discerning democracies vote in self-interest. Hence we may need to question also the voice of the populace. How do we discern the right path of our nation? To what ends? By what means? When and how then do we call upon God to lead us?

This text challenges our society to ask, "Does our claim of acting justly bring injustice to others? Does God see our justice as just?" In Portsmouth, New Hampshire, September 5 is celebrated as the day when the Treaty of Portsmouth was signed that ended the Russo-Japanese War in 1905. The churches ring their bells and the children on the streets ring their small bells to commemorate this "treaty of peace." Theodore Roosevelt, president of the United States, led the negotiation for this treaty and won the 1906 Nobel Peace Prize. However, one of the provisions in this treaty was to endorse Japanese occupation of Korea in return for American dominance in the Philippines. Koreans consequently lived under Japanese oppression for thirty-six years: They were forced to abandon their own language and culture. They lost their sons in a draft for the Pacific war, and their daughters were seized as "comfort women"—sexual slaves for Japanese soldiers. Their properties were controlled by the Japanese government. They were forced to worship the emperor of Japan. A question regarding this treaty arises, "Peace for whom?"

Contemporary Christians live in relationship with the civic government, with electing the president as one of our most cherished rights. We want our political system to pursue justice and to guarantee freedom and peace.

2. Bruce C. Birch, "The First and Second Book of Samuel," in *The New Interpreter's Bible*, ed. Leander Keck et al. (Nashville: Abingdon Press, 1998), 2:1027.

However, do our political choices benefit specific groups in our society while oppressing others? Are our ways of understanding and doing justice always just before the eyes of God?

Psalm 130 and Psalm 138

In Psalm 130 the poet asks for God's deliverance from trouble. The psalmist asks God to hear supplications because the poet believes that God is the God of forgiveness (v. 4), steadfast love (v. 7), and power to redeem (v. 7). The psalmist acknowledges that there is no one who can stand blameless before God. However, God, who is abundant in mercy and forgiveness, tunes God's ears to God's children and hears their supplications. Therefore, Psalm 130 is not only a song of God's deliverance but also a song of hope in God, who never ignores God's children. In verse 7 the song expands to encourage all Israel to hope in God, who "will redeem Israel from all its iniquities" (v. 8). The individual prayer in the beginning becomes communal in seeking deliverance of the whole nation.

Psalm 138 is a song of thanksgiving and praise for God's deliverance. While it is difficult to date Psalm 130, many scholars believe Psalm 138 is from the postexilic period.[3] In Psalm 137, the poet expresses sorrow and agony because of being mocked by enemies and not being able to sing the song of Zion. However, in Psalm 138 the tears and sorrow of the poet turn to joy and thanksgiving for the steadfast love and faithfulness of God, who brought the captives to their homeland.

Although both Psalm 130 and Psalm 138 speak in the first person singular, the supplications and thanksgiving in the psalms are grounded in the pain and joy of their community. While the driving forces behind the supplications to God in Psalm 130 are not clear, the praise in Psalm 138 indicates thanksgiving for liberation, returning home, and restoring one's country. Attention to the communal contexts of these songs and the emotions attached to them offer great ways to experience these psalms in preaching.

After losing the country to Japan for thirty-six years, Korea gained independence in 1945. The Rev. Kyung-Jik Han, pastor of Young Rak Church in Korea, captured in his sermon the emotions of the psalmist upon the news of the independence of Korea. Sharing the moments in which he heard a radio announcement on August 15 that Japan accepted the Potsdam Declaration,

---

3. J. Clinton McCann Jr., "The Psalms," in *The New Interpreter's Bible*, 4:1231, points us to James Luther Mays's conclusion that Psalm 138 "can be understood as a general song of praise by the restored community in the postexilic period, written under the influence of the prophets whose words are gathered in Isaiah 40–66." See James Luther Mays, *Psalms*, Interpretation series (Louisville, KY: John Knox Press, 1994), 424.

which set the terms for the Japanese surrender, Rev. Han described the joyful weeping of teachers, the gathering of persons in hours of embrace and thankful tears, "so deeply touched and . . . thankful that they were just filled with thankfulness wondering how they could repay . . . this grace."[4] Rev. Han's sermons in those days joined the chorus of Psalm 138 in thanksgiving for justice long sought in prayer.

Psalms of thanksgiving build upon the psalms of prayer for deliverance. They build upon psalms of prayer rooted in God's steadfast love. Preachers may need to join with Psalm 130 in prayer to God, who is merciful and abundant in steadfast love, who hears the cries of mourners. God never passes by our supplications but preserves our lives against the torment. When held together, Psalms 130 and 138 bridge the chasm between our prayers in seeking justice and our thanksgiving for God's enduring love and faithfulness in the prospect of deliverance.

Mark 3:20–35

Jesus proclaimed the good news of God: "The time is fulfilled, and the [realm] of God has come near; repent, and believe in the good news" (Mark 1:15). He not only proclaimed the reign of God, but also lived into it by driving out demons, healing the sick, forgiving sins, and eating with tax collectors and sinners. Mark pictures Jesus challenging some of the practices of traditional religious leaders. For example, when Jesus forgave the sins of the paralytic, the scribes grumbled, "It is blasphemy! Who can forgive sins but God alone?" (2:7). In our text today, when Jesus overpowered the unclean spirits and drove them out, he was accused of being possessed by demons and of belonging himself to the household of Beelzebul (3:22). Jesus, however, pointed out that those who accused him of being possessed were themselves possessed by unclean spirits.

The dynamic between Jesus and his accusers encourages us to question whether political or religious groups today who behave like Jesus' accusers are actually acting as unclean spirits when they harrass those who seek justice. For example, as September 11, 2010, approached, a pastor in Florida threatened to burn copies of the Qu'ran to protest building a Muslim community center near Ground Zero, where terrorists flew planes into the World Trade Center in New York City. Many homosexuals in the United States still live with the pains of rejections from their families, religious communities, and society. In the midst of such confrontations, preachers must ask questions: "Why do we

4. Kyung-Jik Han, "The Mind of the First 8.15 (Independence)," in *The Preaching Series of Rev. Kyung-Chik Han*, 12 vols., Sunday evening worship (August 14, 1955). Author's translation from a manuscript in his possession.

feel threatened? How does justice become distorted in our very own claims of faith or righteousness?"

Upon hearing that his mothers and brothers were waiting for him, Jesus redefines family: "Whoever does the will of God is my brother and sister and mother" (v. 35). Doing the will of God must be understood in terms of what it means to live the values of the reign of God. In his own ministry, Jesus invites the marginalized, heals the sick, and shares table with sinners. Jesus teaches us likewise to embrace the diversity of our communities and our global society; hence we must ask, "Who are our brothers and sisters in Christ? Are we their brothers and sisters and mothers?"

2 Corinthians 4:13–5:1

In this text, Paul encourages the believers in Corinth to hope for the final victory, when God who "raised the Lord Jesus will raise us also with Jesus and will bring us . . . into his presence" (v. 14). Paul employs a dualistic rhetorical structure—"what can be seen" and "what cannot be seen," "temporary" and "eternal," "outer nature" and "inner nature," and "earthly tent" and "building from God"—urging the believers to strive beyond the former, in the assurance of the latter. Although our bodies may be temporarily afflicted, Paul redirects our sight to see the signs of God, preparing us for eternal glory in God (v. 17). Those who follow the *way* of Christ, though afflicted, perplexed, persecuted, and struck down while living on the earth, do not live ultimately in despair (4:8–9).

This text must be approached with some caution, considering the different historical and social contexts of the church in Paul's time and the church in the United States of the twenty-first century. For Paul, being a Christian in the Roman world meant that one inevitably faced hardships, persecution, and sometimes martyrdom for one's faith in Christ. Similarly, within several countries today, practice of religion is prohibited. For example, in North Korea many Christians must gather in underground churches to avoid the eyes of their government. For them, Paul's counsel is immediately pastoral.

In most democratic countries, however, believers seldom experience real persecution. The First Amendment to the U.S. Constitution guarantees freedom for every religion. In principle, each person in the United States is constitutionally protected from being persecuted for his or her faith in God and the practice of religion. The different contexts of Paul's church and ours, therefore, raise a caution with which we as twenty-first-century Christians must wrestle. The church itself must be careful not to become complicit in oppression. Many have argued that the hand of God in human history has blessed Christianity in the United States with power and privilege, even while

persecution persists in other places. Yet Christians in the United States sometimes distort our faith into forms of persecution and violence to others.

Indeed, in our context of North American power, the very notion that we
bear afflictions with eyes on eternal glory may perpetuate abuse by telling the
marginalized to endure unjust affliction "in faith." In many faith communities,
current afflictions are taught as the necessary passage through which we can
attain eternal glory. Battered spouses are sometimes forced to maintain their
marriages for the sake of Christ. Eurocentric leaders sometimes urge racial/
ethnic minorities to persevere in silence, for the sake of peace and unity in
our churches and society. The church should not encourage battered spouses
or oppressed racial/ethnic communities to interpret their hardships as something to be endured for the sake of being faithful. Instead, in the language
of our text, the preacher should encourage them to recognize that God is at
work in the call to social justice to renew their situations. Present liberation
is a foreshadowing of living in the "house not made with hands, eternal in the
heavens" (5:1).

Proper 6 [11]

Carolynne Hitter Brown

1 SAMUEL 15:34–16:13   EZEKIEL 17:22–24
PSALM 20   PSALM 92:1–4, 12–15
                              2 CORINTHIANS 5:6–10 (11–13), 14–17
                                                    MARK 4:26–34

Today's readings tell about the person God uses. God surprises the world by using unlikely candidates to bring about divine purposes. The one whom God uses literally shocks the world with her humility, other-centeredness, self-sacrifice, and efforts to please God. Ultimately, this is so that glory goes to God alone. The preacher should discuss what a socially just world is, but even more, what the heart of a social justice seeker looks like. Paul summed up God's order when he wrote, "God chose what is foolish in the world to shame the wise; God chose what is weak in the world to shame the strong; God chose what is low and despised in the world, things that are not, to reduce to nothing things that are, so that no one might boast in the presence of God" (1 Cor. 1:27–29). Power, earthly wisdom, physical strength, fame, fortune—all that the world treasures—are not treasured by those striving for a fair and peaceful world. Instead, they strive to turn the world's values upside down by honoring the weak, the poor, and the downhearted. In short, they respect the "foolish things of the world." They shine brightly in a world of darkness, glorifying God in the process.

1 Samuel 15:34–16:13

God's selection of David as king of Israel is a poignant example of God's unexpected reversal of the world's values. The pivotal verse for today is 1 Samuel 16:7, "The LORD does not see as mortals see; they look on the outward appearance, but the LORD looks on the heart." The specific nature of David's heart is not discussed here, but Scripture indicates David stood out as a man whose heart was humble and true to God's desires. God told Jeroboam,

282

"My servant David . . . kept my commandments and followed me with all his heart, doing only that which was right in my sight" (1 Kgs. 14:8). No one expected a man like David to be God's choice to lead Israel. Even Samuel, God's appointed prophet, saw David's brother Eliab and thought, "Surely the LORD's anointed is now before the LORD" (1 Sam. 16:6). Verse 7 shows that Samuel's reaction was based on Eliab's appearance. Indeed, David "was ruddy . . . and was handsome" (16:12), but he was a lowly shepherd, the youngest of eight brothers, whose own father did not deem him appropriate for Samuel's consideration (16:10–11).

God raises leaders from unexpected places. What better example is there than the quiet, middle-aged seamstress named Rosa Parks? Parks's refusal to relinquish her bus seat to a Eurocentric person was the spark that led to the Montgomery bus boycott. Later she was deemed the "mother of the civil rights movement." Her resolve to maintain dignity and resist unjust treatment set off a chain of events that altered race relations permanently.

Evangelist Everett Swanson traveled to South Korea in 1952 to preach to American troops. Just before he left Korea, a missionary asked Swanson how he was going to respond to the needs of the Korean orphans he met, once he was home. The missionary's question prompted Swanson to start a ministry called Compassion International to secure medical supplies and funds to purchase rice and fuel for Korean children. Today, Compassion addresses the effects of poverty on more than one million children in twenty-five countries, sponsoring early intervention programs, AIDS initiatives, disease prevention, education and vocational training, leadership development, and numerous other programs mitigating the lack of resources children in developing countries contend with every day.

Parks and Swanson are examples of modern Davids. Seemingly from nowhere, God used them to make an indelible mark on humanity. Although neither had any particular training or authority, they experienced a moment when righteousness called them to do something. Outside of God's realm, the far-reaching results of their actions could never be guessed. Their lives demonstrate how God uses men and women the world never notices.

Ezekiel 17:22–24

Like 1 Samuel 15, the reading in Ezekiel portrays the realm God envisions. Ezekiel is prophesying about a future realm. "A sprig from the lofty top of a cedar" refers to the restoration, or rebirth, of God's design for the world and creation. God will establish this realm like a tender sprig planted on a "high and lofty mountain," making it to "produce boughs and bear fruit" (vv. 22–23). Overturning human structures of power, God alone establishes this realm and demonstrates that God is all-powerful and just. God shows preference for the lowly, saying, "I am the LORD. I bring low the high tree, I make high the low tree. I dry up the green tree and make the dry tree flourish" (v. 24).

Today's world is in desperate need of people who live out God's holy premise of exalting the oppressed and the poor over the powerful and prosperous. One need think only a moment to name a multitude of unjust social conditions that exist as a result of powerful entities lording it over the weak. One of the most obvious instances is Eurocenteric racism. Before this injustice can end, members of the privileged class must work with great energy and creativity to tear down the structures of power that ensure the status quo. Only when African Americans and other racial/ethnic communities have equal access to every opportunity, as well as respect for their qualities and preferences, will racism cease to be a problem. Affirmative action is one measure that could offer change, if broadly enacted.

Martin Luther King Jr. said, "A society that has done something special *against* the Negro for hundreds of years must now do something special *for* him, in order to equip him to compete on a just and equal basis." King argued that justice for African Americans meant whites must surrender long-held beliefs and act on behalf of the practical needs of African Americans. According to King, whites

> must see that the Negro needs not only love but also justice. It is not enough to say, "We love Negroes, we have many Negro friends." They must demand justice for Negroes. Love that does not satisfy justice is no love at all. . . . absolute justice for the Negro simply means, in the Aristotelian sense, that the Negro must have "his due." There is nothing abstract about this. It is as concrete as having a good job, a good education, a decent house and a share of power. It is, however, important to understand that giving a man his due may often mean giving him special treatment. I am aware of the fact that this has been a troublesome concept for many liberals, since it conflicts with their traditional ideal of equal opportunity and equal treatment of people according to their individual merits. But this is a day which demands new thinking and the reevaluation of old concepts.[1]

King was right on with the Ezekiel 17 concept of elevating the low tree or giving it "special treatment," so it might grow tall. The world God planned is one in which people live together peaceably and freely.

Perhaps the first step the privileged might make in learning to elevate the low tree is to walk a mile in the low tree's shoes, so to speak. Scott Harrison

---

1. Martin Luther King Jr., *Where Do We Go from Here: Chaos or Community?* introd. Vincent Harding (Boston: Beacon Press, 2010), 95.

lived a plush life in New York City; he was promoting nightclubs and fashion events until personal dissatisfaction led him to ask, "What would the opposite of my life look like?" To answer the question, Harrison volunteered as a photojournalist for "Mercy Ships," floating hospitals that bring medical services to the world's poorest places. Harrison's experience with Mercy Ships permanently changed his perspective. He explains, "Spending time in a leper colony and many remote villages, I put a face to the world's 1.2 billion living in poverty."[2] When Harrison stepped down from the lofty branch of prosperity, it led him to found Charity: Water, a nonprofit organization that brings clean drinking water to people in developing nations.

Harrison's choice may seem extreme, but there are countless close-to-home ways the privileged can bless and lift up those who suffer. Business owners can hire workers of different backgrounds and experience; medical professionals are always needed in low-income areas or in developing countries; teachers and others with special skills can tutor and offer training to those who otherwise could not afford educational advantages; lawyers can join equal justice organizations and offer counsel to the poor and marginalized; and the list goes on. Purchasing fair-trade items to support fair wages and safe working conditions, or participating in community organizations like the Boston Faith and Justice Network, "in which people support each other in spending less, buying justly, and giving collectively," can make a difference. In God's rule, there should not be distinctions like tall and low, green and dry. One day, God will judge the tall and green trees, and raise up the low and dry trees. Today, congregations must be honest and ask themselves, "What are we doing to water the dry tree so it may flourish?"

Psalm 20 and Psalm 92:1–4, 12–15

David wrote Psalm 20 as a song of blessing for the congregation to sing to him. Verses 1–5 may at first appear a bit self-centered, but they actually reflect David's confidence in himself as God's "anointed" (v. 6). His confidence rested in the fact that he knew God's presence ("from his holy heaven," v. 6; see also Heb. 9:24) was with him and that God would answer him "with mighty victories by his right hand" (v. 6). Because David was a righteous and just king, God honored him. He wrote, "Some take pride in chariots, and some in horses, but our pride is in the name of the LORD our God" (v. 7). Chariots and horses are the powers David's enemies trusted, but David followed the Lord's way.

---

2. Scott Harrison, quoted on http://sebas13.wordpress.com/2010/07/21/scotts-story-truly-inspiring/ (accessed August 5, 2010).

What powers do rulers, nations, or those who oppress others trust in today? So often the answer is money—and, with it, power and control. Consumerism is rampant, with people who are wealthy buying more and more "stuff" at the expense of people who are poor. Wealthy nations are depleting the world's natural resources, and in North America, people buy bigger homes and line their bank accounts in order to feel secure. The accumulation of material goods brings a sense of security, but this passage makes it clear that security like this is fleeting. Trust in God means emptying our possessions of emotional power, thereby freeing us to give and serve according to God's plan.

When God's people see God's hand at work, they give praise (Ps. 92:1, 3–4). God is faithful and loving and continues to be visible and active in the world (v. 2). "The house of the LORD" and "the courts of our God" represent God's presence on earth, and those who abide in covenantal relationship with God will flourish and live abundantly (v. 13). Again we see the metaphor of the flourishing tree, but here it refers specifically to "the righteous" (v. 12). The contrast between the green tree and the low tree in Ezekiel 17 is a contrast between the powerful and the weak; in this psalm the tree God causes "in old age . . . [to] produce fruit" and to stay "green and full of sap" (v. 14) is the one who is righteous, abides with God, and continually gives God glory. Pastors can use this verse to expand on what the low or dry tree is—the one God causes to flourish. The low tree may literally represent one who is poor or weak but also the one who makes herself low.

2 Corinthians 5:6–10 (11–13), 14–17

If only one nugget of truth for social justice could emerge from this passage, it might be "Christ's love compels us" (v. 14 NIV; NRSV "the love of Christ urges us on"). In his letter to Corinth, Paul explains that Christ's realm is for all people and teaches the church that in response, they should "live no longer for themselves" (v. 15). It is because of Christ's love that we "try to persuade others" of the coming of Christ's realm (v. 11), and in Paul's case, to the point of great personal sacrifice. Living sacrificially for the sake of others is induced by what is "in the heart" (v. 12). The righteous, those who are "a new creation" (v. 17) through Jesus, strive to convince those of the world to join in fulfilling God's covenantal plan, even if others think the faithful are out of their minds (vv. 13, 17).

They are willing to make themselves lowly because it is their goal to please God, and they understand that God uses the foolish things of the world to bring about peace. Nelson Mandela's life is a wonderful example of this realm principle. After twenty-seven years in prison, Mandela forgave his captors and became a model of reconciliation for South Africa and the world. His

Truth and Reconciliation Commission, formed when apartheid ended, has been replicated in other locations to resolve issues related to past wrongs.

Mark 4:26–34

The first parable in this passage reveals God and people working together to bring about God's design for creation. The farmer scatters, and God makes the seed sprout and grow. In a natural progression, God brings the plant to full fruition, and then men and women do the work of harvesting what God has produced (vv. 26–29). In God's realm, God and people work in mutuality to bring about God's desired plan. God performs the mystical work of growing the seed, so that glory is God's alone.

The parable of the Mustard Seed parallels the other readings in its portrayal of God's realm. God causes the smallest seed to grow so much so that it becomes the tallest tree in the garden. God takes the mostly unlikely choice, plants it, and then nurtures it into a lush bower so that every bird "can make nests in its shade" (v. 32). The tall tree is a symbol for God's realm—God's community of love that gives life and refreshment to all who gather near it.

Vivien Morris, a Boston nutritionist, realized that the poor of Mattapan, her community, lacked access to fresh foods and nutritious choices. According to Morris, low-income, urban communities are often "food deserts," since community members are financially and physically limited to less healthy options. To address this concern, she and her colleagues formed a coalition to begin a farmers' market cohosted by two churches. Morris's efforts continue to bring new opportunities and choices to her neighborhood. Like the farmer in Mark 4, Morris planted in her community a small life-bringing seed of change that now thrives and nourishes those who gather near.[3]

3. The story of Vivien Morris and the Mattapan Farmers' Market can be found in *Special Places*, 16.2 (Summer 2008): 12–14.

Juneteenth: Let Freedom Ring (June 19)

James Henry Harris

JONAH 4:1–5
PSALM 17:1–7
1 CORINTHIANS 7:17–24
MATTHEW 25:1–13

Slavery ended in most of the United States at the conclusion of fighting between the Union and Confederate armies in April and May of 1865. However, slavery continued in Texas until June 19, 1865, when a Union army arrived in Galveston and announced freedom for slaves. That date (Juneteenth) celebrates the actual end of slavery and sometimes includes the reading of the Emancipation Proclamation and an abundant outdoor meal. A Juneteenth sermon might reflect critically on the degree to which people of color in the United States are still in need of emancipation from racism and other systems of injustice.

All persons born or naturalized in the United States, and subject to the jurisdiction thereof, are citizens of the United States and the State wherein they reside. No State shall make or enforce any law which shall abridge the privileges or immunities of citizens of the United States; nor shall any State deprive any person of life, liberty, or property, without due process of law; nor deny to any person within its jurisdiction the equal protection of the laws.
Fourteenth Amendment to the U.S. Constitution, 1868

Juneteenth remembers the situation of slaves in Texas, who had been legally emancipated in 1863 but who did not know about their freedom until 1865. The biblical texts today invite the congregation to help get the news about God's liberating actions to persons and communities who have still not experienced liberation. Jonah calls us to carry the good news to the other. The psalm remembers *all* who are affected by injustice. The parable of the Ten Bridesmaids urges the church to invite everyone into the movement toward the realm of God. The church today should reject the teaching on slavery in 1 Corinthians.

Jonah 4:1–5

There is an absurdity permeating these opening verses. This prayer is as absurd and helpless as the opening lines of Albert Camus' award-winning novel *The Stranger*: "Mama died today. Or yesterday, maybe; I don't know."[1] The puzzling dismissiveness by the novel's protagonist, Meursault, is more understandable than Jonah's inability to correlate God's mercy toward him with God's forgiveness and mercy toward others. God has not done any more for others than for him.

Jonah has been elected by God to preach to the Ninevites, and this is the last thing that Jonah wants. Maybe Jonah understands better than others that to be elected is to be chosen to suffer pain and death. Professor of modern Judaic studies Peter Ochs states emphatically that no one in his right mind wants to be elected by God. To be elected is to suffer and be rejected and persecuted.[2] This perspective allows me to understand Jonah's action from a different angle—knowledge and fear of suffering experienced by the Hebrews during their 400 years of captivity and bondage. In the twenty-first century, the Holocaust continues to loom large in any discussion of modern atrocities and tragedies.

Jonah's anger appears to be grounded in a selfish egoism devoid of compassion. God's grace and mercy upon the Ninevites is met with a vehement cry of disdain by Jonah, a prayer grounded in selfishness and disinterest toward the other (vv. 2–3).[3]

Initially, I wanted to believe that Jonah flees in the opposite direction—contrary to the directive of the word of God—because of fear, youthful rebellion, or lack of clarity regarding his call. Now we learn that Jonah's rebellion

---

1. Albert Camus, *The Stranger* (New York: Alfred A. Knopf, 1946), 1.
2. This perspective is from my seminar notes in a graduate theology course at the University of Virginia cotaught by Gene Rogers and Peter Ochs, Election and Incarnation, fall 2001. See also James Henry Harris, *The Courage to Lead: Leadership in the African American Urban Church* (Lanham, MD: Rowman & Littlefield, 2002), 33–52.
3. In this story both "YHWH" and "Elohim" are used to refer to God. For Jonah, YHWH is God and for the Ninevites, Elohim is God. The detailed distinctions are less critical to me than they are to some Bible scholars and theologians. For an excellent explication of this story and these distinctions, see R. Kendal Soulen, "The Sign of Jonah: A Christian Perspective on the Relation of the Abrahamic Faiths," in *Crisis, Call, and Leadership in the Abrahamic Tradition*, ed. Peter Ochs and William Johnson (New York: Palgrave MacMillan, 2009), 15–30.

is generated by an egocentrism unbecoming of a prophet. God halts his flight and allows him grace and mercy as he is swallowed by a fish and lives to be given a second chance. Yet he seems to learn no lesson from his near-death experience or from the sermon he finally preaches to the Ninevites. Because the Ninevites "turn from their evil ways and from the violence" (3:8b), God changes God's mind and does not do what God has said God will do (3:10). Now Jonah is unhappy and angry (4:1) and prays, acknowledging God's nature as one of changeableness and compassion as a result of the Ninevites' repentance.

In this text God is not the unmoved mover of Aristotle, but God is moved to change according to people's actions. God's compassion toward the other is met by Jonah, not with prophetic understanding, but with disdain and anger. Instead of being angry, Jonah should smile as he recognizes God's providence at work in front of him. When God does good for others, it should make us happy.

An African American folk song rings out in my own consciousness: "It's me, it's me, it's me, O Lord, standing in the need of prayer."[4] Jonah, the beneficiary of God's mercy and grace, acts as if his character is flawless. His previous disobedience and prophetic miscalculations did not cause God to turn God's back on him. God's wrath is mediated by love and compassion, and Jonah has benefited from God's love while escaping completely God's wrath. Yet he remains selfish and preoccupied with his own ego, and he does not understand that God is sovereign Lord and can do whatever God pleases for whomever God wants. God is God!

In the Black church, the congregation would respond in a call-and-response fashion to the preacher's assertion about the autonomy and sovereignty of God by saying, "All the time," that is, "God is God, all the time!" Like Jonah we are still in the process of becoming what God wants us to be. In the language of the Black church, the lesson from the book of Jonah is "I ain't what I oughta be, but thank God, I ain't what I used to be."

Jonah is called by God to preach a message of warning to the Ninevites but he runs in the opposite direction. Jonah pays for his rebellion by being swallowed by a huge fish. In the face of this self-imposed catastrophe, Jonah prays for God's deliverance, and his life is spared. In response to God's second call to preach a message of warning to the city of Nineveh, Jonah adheres to the call and travels to the city to share his message. He preaches a short, but effectual message; as a result of his message and the monarch's proclamation, the entire city believes in God, fasts, and puts on sackcloth, and God changes

4. Traditional African American song, "It's Me, O Lord," http://www.gospelsonglyrics.org/songs/its_me_o_lord_standing_in_the_need_of_prayer.html (accessed May 10, 2010).

God's mind as a result of their turn from "their evil ways." Jonah is infuriated because God is being God. God extends mercy toward the Ninevites, but Jonah would rather die than see them delivered.

God asks Jonah a very important question: "Is it right for you to be angry?" (4:4). The suggestion is that Jonah may not be correct in his understanding of God, himself, or the Ninevites.

God has blessed us, but if God blesses those of whom we do not approve, we often become unhappy. What do we fear when God shows mercy and grace to those of whom society does not approve? We are to realize that intolerance of others is a "going in the opposite direction" from God's way. God is free to show mercy, grace, and love unbound by our narrow human limitations and understandings.

Psalm 17:1–7

The opening verses of this psalm speak of the prima facie self-confidence of a righteous person, almost to the point of self-righteousness. The focus on the self could not be more blatant: "Hear a just cause, O LORD; . . . give ear to my prayer from lips free of deceit" (v. 1). This language is the antithesis of what we see in the prophet Jonah fleeing from God. Unlike Jonah, the psalmist here calls for God to elect him—to test him, as we soon see.

The psalmist's goodness, expressed in language of innocence that beckons God to examine and test, is an expression of the psalmist's confidence regarding the justice of God (vv. 1–2, 8). This type of confidence seems to me to defy human weakness and to invite God to administer a test. All humans are prone to fail without God's mercy and grace. The language of the psalmist comes frighteningly close to saying, "Elect me because I am righteous." I shudder to think that any human being can be so holy and guiltless—so righteous. Yet there is a clear recognition of the need for God to intervene and deliver from enemies.

The psalmist confirms that the psalmist has neither spoken ill of others nor acted violently toward others (vv. 3–5). To be sure, there is something good here. Human beings need to avoid acting violently toward one another. African American males in particular need to avoid violence, especially toward their own brothers and sisters. Black-on-Black crime grieves my heart and soul. Avoidance of violence or gangstas who rob and murder without blinking an eye is of paramount importance to the advancement of the Black community.[5] Violent gangstas are also seen in white-collar America on Wall Street

---

5. Willem A. Vangerem, "Psalms," in *Zondervan NIV Bible Commentary: Old Testament,* ed. Kenneth Baker and John Kohlenberger III (Grand Rapids: Zondervan, 1994), 1:812–13.

and in corporate behemoths that are deemed "too big to fail" while little people continue to suffer. Our prayer, like that of the psalmist, is that God's justice may prevail.

The psalmist brims with self-confidence: "You will find no wickedness in me" (v. 3). Yet, no matter how rightly the psalmist *thinks* the psalmist acts, there is a possibility that God will see something in the psalmist that the psalmist is incapable of seeing in himself.

As we read this psalmist's plea, we find another flaw in this theology. As he solicits protection from God, his prayer becomes more egocentric: "Keep *me* as the apple of your eye; hide *me* in the shadow of your wings" (v. 8 NIV). Is he concerned only for himself? Is he the only one in his town who is suffering from injustice?

There is nothing inherently wrong with praying for oneself. But there is something wrong with not praying for the other. Martin Luther King Jr. spoke of our interdependence. The nexus between self and other is the mark of the beloved community. In his "Letter from Birmingham City Jail," King said, "Injustice anywhere is a threat to justice everywhere."[6] We are all affected by injustice, whenever and wherever it occurs.

Matthew 25:1–13

When we first see the maidens, some are wise and some foolish. They were called to meet the bridegroom at a wedding in which all were participating. Upon arriving with their oil lamps, they found the bridegroom would be delayed. All of them fell asleep until the coming of the bridegroom was announced; then some found that they did not have enough oil for their lamps.

The maidens were not judged wise or foolish because some were asleep and others were not. They *all* slumbered. The difference was preparation: some came prepared for the long wait, while others were equipped for only a short wait. Are we prepared for the long haul or not? Is it possible for us to be always ready? What does such readiness look like in real life?

There is a final moment of accountability and judgment: the door will be open, or the door will be shut. Everyone has the opportunity to come to the wedding celebration prepared for the long wait; however, not everyone is prepared to endure delay. Since everyone has the opportunity to come prepared, everyone must always be ready. In this parable about the joy of coming to God in the form of a wedding, every person has an equal opportunity to

6. In *A Testament of Hope: The Essential Writings of Martin Luther King, Jr.*, ed. James M. Washington (San Francisco: Harper & Row, 1986), 290.

prepare for the realm of God. For Matthew, a key element in preparing for the realm is supporting others.

1 Corinthians 7:17–24

There are several issues in this text, but none is more difficult than slavery. Many Eurocentric scholars continue to try to explain away the sting of slavery in this passage.[7] However, I find these explications unacceptable and even offensive to African Americans.[8] Slavery is a violation of the humanity of the other and is antithetical to God, Jesus, and the Holy Spirit. God has called me to work for freedom, justice, and liberation of the oppressed, not to urge people simply to endure the existential condition of slavery in its many forms, past and present.

Growing up in rural central Virginia, I heard a lot of quartet music and "old school" gospel songs in church and at home as my uncles, cousins, and I would sing around the potbelly stove. One of these songs declared, "My soul just couldn't be contented, until I found the Lord."[9] This lack of contentment in the deep consciousness of the soul reminds me of one of the central tenets of Augustine: "My heart is restless until it finds rest [peace] in thee."[10] Both Augustine and the spiritual songs of the Negro church express a certain yearning for peace vis-à-vis *discontent* with existential distancing seen in the real-life situation of so many folk.

This dyadic dilemma engulfs me as I read this 1 Corinthians text. I am repulsed by the fact that it assumes that slavery would continue until Jesus returns. Because of that repulsion, I experience the Jonah syndrome, that is, going in another direction, every time I read it. It makes me angry. I don't want to be assigned a scriptural text that does not condemn slavery, because I still feel the pain and suffering of American chattel slavery. Even amidst the forms of slavery that continue today, I have also found the Lord. However, finding the Lord has only intensified my opposition to slavery. I assert, without trepidation, that I do not subscribe to the "free in Christ" theology that Paul advocates in this text. Freedom is a bodily function, and "spiritual freedom" does not suffice as long as the body is enslaved.

---

7. For example, Craig S. Keener, *1–2 Corinthians: The New Cambridge Bible Commentary* (New York: Cambridge University Press, 2005), 65–67.

8. African American New Testament scholars have often shunned this part of 1 Corinthians 7. See Boykin Sanders, " First Corinthians," in *True to Our Native Land: An African American New Testament Commentary*, ed. Brian Blount, Cain Hope Felder, Clarice Martin, and Emerson Powery (Minneapolis: Fortress Press, 2007), 288–90.

9. Clara Ward, "Until I Found the Lord," *African American Heritage Hymnal* (Chicago: GIA Publications, 2001), 454.

10. See Augustine, *The City of God* (New York: Doubleday Dell, 1958), 1.

Proper 7 [12]

Edward L. Wheeler

1 SAMUEL 17:(1A, 4–11, 19–23) 32–49
PSALM 9:9–20

JOB 38:1–11
PSALM 107:1–3, 23–32
2 CORINTHIANS 6:1–13
MARK 4:35–41

These readings focus on God's ultimate authority over all creation and God's protection of the helpless and oppressed. Even the reading from 2 Corinthians focuses on the availability of salvation through God's mercy and the great sacrifices Paul and others made to bring the gospel to the Corinthians.

1 Samuel 17:(1a, 4–11, 19–23) 32–49

The story of David and Goliath is one of the best known in the Bible. Verses 32–49 tell a consistent story that provides several sets of contrasts that are instructive for those concerned about the fight for justice against oppressive forces. The first contrast is David's confidence with Saul's doubts (vv. 32–39). Saul sees David as only a youth who cannot defeat Goliath. David, however, is confident that his experience as a shepherd has given him skills to win the battle. Despite the persistence of injustice in the world, those who would dare right the wrongs must be confident that right can defeat might.

A second contrast is that of David's courage over against the fear of Saul and the Israelite army (v. 11). David said to Saul; "Let no one lose heart on account of this Philistine; your servant will go and fight him" (v. 32 NIV). Such courage is a prerequisite to fighting the forces of oppression.

The third contrast is the most significant. Saul and Goliath both trusted in the armor of war. Saul sought to dress David in his own armor (vv. 38–39). Goliath was fully armed (vv. 5–7, 41) and despised David's apparent unreadiness (vv. 42–44). Unlike both Saul and Goliath, David trusted God, claiming that God would fight for him and that his victory would affirm there is "a God in Israel" (vv. 45–46). "All those gathered here will know that it is not by sword or spear that the LORD saves; for the battle is the LORD's, and he will give all of you into our hands" (v. 47 NIV). The struggle for justice will not be won by force of arms. Justice, freedom, and equality are God's struggles, and God's justice will prevail.

Job 38:1–11

God's first reply to Job begins in 38:1 and continues through 40:5. Throughout the book, Job has sought to defend himself against the accusations leveled against him by his friends (e.g., chaps. 9, 13, and 18). Within today's passage, God speaks out of the whirlwind. That imagery reinforces the idea that God is in control of nature. In verse 2 God chides Job for speaking "words without knowledge." Job has made comments about the will of God, without knowing or understanding the divine will. God then challenges Job: "Brace yourself . . . I will question you, and you shall answer me" (v. 3 NIV). God turns the tables on Job. But by speaking to Job, God dispels Job's contention that God is distant, unapproachable, and unconcerned.

The words "Where were you?" (vv. 4–7) indicate God's careful creation of the earth's foundation, much as a builder laying out the dimensions before setting the cornerstone. What did Job know about God's creative work? The passage culminates with a celestial celebration.

In verses 8–11, God focues on the sea. The sea, in ancient writings, was often the seat of chaos. However, these verses articulate the idea that God has limited the chaos. The sea serves a purpose in the created order, and God has set boundaries beyond which it cannot go.

While this pericope does not speak directly to the injustice about which Job has argued previously, it puts Job's experience within a broader context. First, the passage places Job's mortality over against God's eternality. Job's lifetime and perspective are brief when compared to God's. Second, the passage indicates that, while God's purposes are beyond Job's ability to comprehend fully, God's purpose is consistent with the order in creation. Finally, God controls even the chaos and limits its destructive ability.

The struggle against the structures of injustice is rarely won in one lifetime. Whether against racism in America, apartheid in South Africa, the treatment of Aboriginal peoples in Australia or ethnic minorities in China, the struggle goes on for generations. According to the book of Job, God's ultimate purpose is for all creation to be in harmony and for the chaos to be limited. We do not often think of the elements of nature as allies in the fight against oppression, but for the book of Job, the continued existence of nature is a powerful witness to God's eternal intention to end injustice and to bring all things into supportive relationship.

Psalm 9:9–20

Psalms 9 and 10 were originally one psalm. Nevertheless, as Psalm 9 is now arranged, verses 9 and 10 proclaim that God is concerned about the oppressed. God will be "a stronghold in times of trouble" (v. 9 NASB). This is a powerful affirmation for those suffering oppression: God has been faithful to them in the past and can be trusted to protect them in the future.

In verse 11 the psalmist invites the people to join in the celebration of God. However, verse 12 foreshadows the challenges both the psalmist and the nation face in verse 13. While the psalmist is afflicted by "those who hate me," God is at work lifting "me up from the gates of death." This is a powerful affirmation for the oppressed: even in our difficulty, God is present and supporting.

Verses 15–16 indicate that God judges the nations by allowing them to be caught in the traps they make for others. God is sovereign over all nations and holds them accountable for oppression. The preacher might reflect on the ways that nations (and other political entities) today get caught in the traps they make for others; for example, nations that seek to bring about peace through warfare typically find that they increase violence.

The closing verses (vv. 17–20) anticipate what God will do on behalf of the needy. Verse 17 starts with an unfulfilled expectation, "The wicked will depart to Sheol," followed by the conviction that "the needy shall not always be forgotten" (v. 18) and by the plea that God will take action, so that the nations will know that they are "only human" (v. 20).

Despite the existence of injustice, the psalmist is convinced that God vindicates the oppressed and punishes those responsible for injustice. Those who believe Jesus is Lord and fight injustice should be encouraged, for the God of the universe is on our side. Those who afflict and oppress are only human and can never defeat God.

Psalm 107:1–3, 23–32

While there is a scholarly debate over the unity of this psalm, neither side is conclusive; therefore, it is fair to accept the unity of this psalm. Verse 3 suggests a postexilic setting. A psalm of thanksgiving, its focus is on God's steadfast love.

The psalmist identifies four distinct groups who should offer thanks for God's deliverance. Our pericope (vv. 23–32) focuses on seafarers. Verses 25–27 presuppose the traditional idea that the sea is a symbol of disorder. The description of a storm (v. 25) is both dramatic and embellished, but the danger is not to be underestimated. In the midst of the storm and the tumultuous sea, those in danger cried to God (v. 28a). Those on the ship realized their helplessness and saw God as the only source of salvation. God responded out of steadfast love and delivered them (vv. 28–32).

The psalmist sees God as master over nature, responding to the cries of the helpless and delivering them from destruction. The psalm calls the hearers to give thanks to God for God's loving-kindness or steadfast love. For those who feel overwhelmed by injustice and chaos, the psalmist's conviction about the steadfast love of God is hopeful. God's power extends over all creation, and those who call on God in trouble will find that God responds and delivers. So let us "thank the LORD for [God's] steadfast love" (v. 31).

2 Corinthians 6:1–13

Continuing the idea developed in 2 Corinthians 5:20–21, Paul opens with a claim that he and those with him are working with God in urging the Corinthians "not to accept the grace of God in vain" (6:1). Paul pleads with the Corinthians to accept the gift of God in Christ immediately because "now is the acceptable time; see, now is the day of salvation" (v. 2). For Paul, the day of salvation is the cosmic coming of the realm of God, when all things will be together in love, peace, justice, joy, and abundance. *Now* is the time to want to be a part of that age and to begin living toward it. *Now* is the day to act boldly for justice.

Paul claims in verse 3 that the behavior and attitude he and others have exhibited provide no basis for the congregation to reject the gospel message. The missionaries carried themelves in a manner consistent with the gospel. This noble behavior stands in stark contrast to the unjust way the Corinthians treated the missionaries. Paul asks for respect. The preacher today might identify contemporary groups yearning for respect.

Verses 4–10 mix the trials of Paul and his companions with a list of the sources that provided strength to persevere. In verse 5 Paul identifies injustices: beatings, imprisonment, and being in tumult. In verse 6 he recognizes the Corinthians' godly response: "by purity, knowledge, patience, kindness, holiness of spirit, genuine love." For Paul, their response to injustice affirms the power of the gospel to transform perpetrators of injustice into agents of justice.

Paul's ministry of reconciliation is based on God's making Godself known in Christ Jesus. Through Christ, humanity is reconciled to God, because God risked Christ on behalf of the effort to bring humanity back into fellowship. In this passage, reconciliation means reconciliation not only with God but with one another. Paul urges the Corinthians to participate in that reconciliation. The preacher needs to urge the congregation today toward the same actions. The preacher can add specificity to the sermon by naming specific groups with whom the congregation needs to be reconciled.

Mark 4:35–41

The boat on which Jesus sailed was crowded and riding low, making it susceptible to high waves when the sudden storm swept across the lake: "the waves beat into the boat, so that the boat was already being swamped" (v. 37b). The situation recalls the ancient depiction of the sea as chaotic. However, despite the danger, Jesus sleeps.

In response to Jesus soundly sleeping, the disciples react harshly: "Teacher, do you not care that we are perishing?" (v. 38). While the disciples' reaction might initially seem to be the understandable panic response of frightened people, the accusation that Jesus does not care is unjust. The disciples' question assumes that Jesus does not care about them. It also ignores the fact that Jesus is in the boat with them and facing the same danger. This passage reminds today's reader to be fair when criticizing others.

Jesus' response forms a wonderful pairing (vv. 39–40). First, Jesus rebukes the wind and the waves: "Peace! Be still!" (v. 39). Jesus' ability to control nature reminds the reader of God's setting limits to the sea (Job 38:8–11; Ps. 107:23–29). This dramatic message is to all who are threatened by chaos, including the chaos of injustice. No matter how threatening a situation, Jesus can restore order.

Jesus turns to the disciples. "Why are you afraid? Have you still no faith?" (v. 40). Jesus' question trumps the disciples' earlier harsh assessment of his sleeping. Jesus was asleep because he had complete trust in God. Jesus identified the disciples' fearful response as a lack of faith. The congregation to whom Mark wrote was in its own chaos and was in danger of being timid and losing faith. Mark does not record the question in verse 40 to excoriate the congregation but to urge them to learn from the disciples' negative example. Mark wants readers to have a faith that breeds confident witness, even in the face of situations that could cause panic. The preacher can urge today's community to such witness in the face of social chaos.

The disciples "were filled with great awe" (v. 41) and asked, "Who then is this?" People often fear persons who appear unafraid in dangerous situations. An absolute trust in God is still disconcerting, especially when that trust is exhibited at a time and place when death is a possibility. Not to fear death is unusual, unless you have found a cause in life that is greater than the fear of death. Martin Luther King Jr. affirmed that the cause of justice was more powerful than the fear of death when he preached his last sermon in Memphis in April 1968. Jesus reaffirmed his faith by being obedient to God, even to death. The preacher might ask the congregation, "Have you found a just cause that overshadows death for you?"

Seeking to respond to God's call for justice, the institution I serve, Christian Theological Seminary, traditionally a predominantly Eurocentric school, began a community-wide antiracism program in 2005.[1] The goals of this program are to dismantle Eurocentric privilege, to make Eurocentric people accountable to people of color, to create an environment in which all live together in respect, and to become a community in which power is shared and decisions are made with mutual consent. In Paul's language, the seminary seeks to become a community of eschatological reconciliation in the present.

Each member of the staff and faculty must undergo an intense three-day seminar exposing them to the history of racism, how racism destroys both people of color and people of European origin, and what must happen at both personal and systemic levels to move towards becoming an antiracist community. The entire staff and faculty meet twice each semester for continuing antiracism training. Students take a course centered in antiracism.

These efforts are gradually awakening an antiracist sentiment in the seminary. At the same time, this emphasis creates stresses that can be uncomfortable, especially for people of European origin. In public meetings, we have had moments so tense that you could literally feel the distress.

As president of the Seminary and initiator of the antiracism emphasis, I work hard not to take the criticism personally. At times, I walk the halls and greet persons in their offices. On Wednesday mornings, I also take time for prayer and meditation. At such times, today's readings from Job and Psalms remind me that God is still at work in the midst of chaos and change. A walk down the halls or time in prayer is not an escape from leadership but a reminder that God's will for justice endures long after the unhappy phone call, the angry e-mail, the confrontation in the office. The ship of my life may be in chaos at the moment, but I am part of a process that will lead to eschatological calm.

---

1. The program follows the philosophy of Crossroads Anti-Racism and Training, P.O. Box 309, Matteson IL 60443-0309. See http://crossroadsantiracism.org/ (accessed June 7, 2010). The underlying principles of the Crossroads approach are available in Joseph Barndt, *Understanding and Dismantling Racism: The Twenty-first-Century Challenge to White America* (Minneapolis: Fortress Press, 2007).

Gifts of Sexuality and Gender
(June 29)

Valerie Bridgeman

ISAIAH 49:1–6
PSALM 16:8–11
ROMANS 14:13–22
MATTHEW 5:3–16

This new feast, Gifts of Sexuality and Gender, envisioned for late June, assumes that sexuality and gender are gifts of God through which people embody covenantal relationship. While the church has often held that relationships between people of different genders are the norm, many people believe that sexuality can be expressed in other modes, including relationships between people of the same gender, as well as those with multiple sexual identities and those who are asexual and questioning. In connection with this feast, the preacher could help the congregation explore ways that it could deepen its understanding of sexual identity and expression.

A gracious, liberating church will teach us to claim our right to a pleasurable and good eroticism. It may also impassion us to invest ourselves in creating a more just and equitable church and world. Desire for pleasure can authentically include a desire for community and for a more ethical world. Contrary to many voices inside and outside the church, sex and desire are not necessarily dangerous, selfish, or self-indulgent. Rather, erotic power can be an indispensable spiritual resource for engaging joyfully in creating justice.[1]

Marvin M. Ellison

---

1. Marvin M. Ellison, "Common Decency: A New Christian Sexual Ethics," in *Sexuality and the Sacred: Sources for Theological Reflection*, ed. James B. Nelson and Sandra P. Longfellow (Louisville, KY: Westminster John Knox Press, 1994), 241.

These texts have been chosen to aid us in thinking deeply about "gifts of sexuality and gender." Usually "gifts of human sexuality" gets reduced to discussions about lesbian, gay, bisexual, transgendered, and questioning/queer peoples, but rarely about heterosexual people. Such discussions uncover the biases and beliefs that heterosexuality is the only "normal" way to be in the world. But what does it mean when being human—in the many ways humans are humans—gets demeaned and denigrated? When women, whatever their expressions of sexuality, are not valued simply because they lack a penis? When men who are not considered "manly" are labeled "gay" as a pejorative term? When gay men and lesbian women are considered some alien life form because they are not heterosexual? Add the variegation of transgendered, intersexual, questioning/queer, and bisexual people, and what it means to be human, and sexual becomes more complex than many people dare admit.

Sexualities are complicated. We like to think of our being human as a straightforward enterprise, but it is not. Often in the church, the act of having sex or making love is equated with one's sexual identity—that is, how one perceives oneself in the world. This sometimes leads some of us to think of ourselves as flawed at our core identity. If we could be honest, we often resist the psalmist's insistence that we are "fearfully and wonderfully made" (Ps. 139:14).

Many groups of Christians baptize people shortly after birth, long before there is any expression of their sexuality. At baptism, the Christian minister has no way (at present) of knowing whether the child she holds will be "straight" or "queer." These terms are foreign to the child who looks up at her and holds the finger of the one blessing as if it were the finger of God. If, as many Christians believe, baptism seals us for the work of God in the earth, then at baptism a child is sent and commissioned, irrespective of his or her expression of sexualities.

These texts help us rethink our relationships with ourselves, with our neighbors, and with our God.

Isaiah 49:1–6

The NRSV calls this section of Isaiah "the Servant's mission." It is the testimony of one who knows himself or herself to be "called" before birth and named while in utero. The Servant testifies that the call requires and demands an embodied, fully present person: a mouth "like a sharp sword," a body like a "polished arrow," a hide-and-seek presence until the time that God chooses to reveal the mission to the Servant.

God echoes the Servant's personal testimony, agreeing with every part of it—from womb to voice to catalyst. The double witness between God and

Servant reinforces the before-birth nature of call. And this witness also makes me wonder about the gifts of human sexuality and gender, embodied in the midst of call.

As with Isaiah's Servant, any God-called mission takes strength. That strength must be a God-given and God-infused strength. Despair and discouragement lurk in the face of calling God's people to place and purpose. The Servant believes that all his or her efforts are useless and that the labor and the struggle have been for nothing; but in an act of allegiance, the Servant notes that looking for rewards among mortals is futile. Those who work for God's cause must put their cause in God's hand and trust God to reward their faithfulness. Even this yielding to God's hand is physical, embodied.

This embodied yielding happens in the confines of a body that feels, yearns, desires, and wants other human contact, creative and procreative contact. The call of God is always in this human context. How will we help people bear the weight in their bodies—fully expressed and fully incarnated?

Psalm 16:8–11

How do we help people bear the weight of the embodied call? How do we hold our place on the planet, refusing to be moved? Certainly not without acknowledging the need for counsel, protection, and care. In that regard, the psalm's praise gives testimony to the same presence found in Isaiah 49. People often are able to endure ridicule and degradation when they are assured that God is with them. According to the psalmist, God is with him or her, giving counseling, standing before and beside, "before me" and "at my right hand" (v. 8). What an odd combination of the Deity's location, before and beside. Does the psalmist imagine a God who goes before to prepare the way, or a God who is a shield to protect from arrows and enemies? Is the Deity at the right hand as a sign of power and energizing force to embolden the psalmist? I believe these readings are satisfying. The Deity looms larger than life, larger than any circumstance. For people who face daily assault on their personhood because of their embodiment, the psalmist's praise could offer some comfort.

How do I help people bear the weight of the embodied call? Part of the answer, I believe, is that we can't, unless we acknowledge the fear and danger that sometimes the embodied self faces. The context especially for "out" LGBTQA (lesbian, gay, bixsexual, transgender, questioning, asexual) persons often is not safe. For some people, the notion that God loves bodies is itself scary.

Like the Isaiah passage, this section of Psalm 16 gives homage to an embodied dependence and relationship with God. The hand of God as protection and covering is in both passages as proof that ancient Israel often reflected on God as a hovering, protecting presence. This presence allows for the body to rest, the heart to be glad, and the soul to rejoice. The heart and soul are deeply connected to a body that rests secure. The psalmist is talking not about ethereal practices, but about the assuredness that God meets people in the flesh. This rest often is in the face of real fear and danger. It is not imaginary harm; the psalmist always faced the danger of wild animals and war.

How do we experience being shown "the path of life" (v. 11), when our way is strewn with the debris of pain inflicted by people and circumstances that despise our very existence? For the psalmist, bodily awareness of God's faithfulness happens in the face of death, represented by "Sheol" and "the Pit" (v. 10). This "forming-in-the-womb" God (Isa. 49:1) is "always before" the psalmist, continuing the bodily journey through life. It is a particular presence for a particular, distinct body. The psalmist enjoys the presence by exclaiming there is joy and pleasure when the psalmist is with God. Joy and pleasure, like fear of death, are bodily experiences.

It is easy to miss the attention to the body in these texts, since many of us are trained to read the text as philosophy and not as relational and conversational. We suffer too from the fear of the flesh, inculcated by the Platonic reading of the Bible. Many humans are trapped by established categories of "ways to be human or sexual," for example, the married woman who does not want children, the heterosexual man who cannot father a child, the transgendered person who feels encaged in the wrong body. Wherever a person may find the challenge of his or her sexuality and gender, fear is a way of not being able even to explore one's own life—the fear of being mislabeled, the fear of being "found out," for example. The promise the psalmist declares is in the midst of just such a climate. Wherever you find yourself being challenged, fear is a way of not even exploring one's own life. Much like the Barbra Streisand character in the movie *Yentl*, people wrestle with unsafe experiences, with being exposed as something "not normative," like a woman studying Torah. The psalmist declares even these persons can find "fullness of joy" in God's presence (v. 11).

Matthew 5:3–16

A former colleague and her husband decided to attend a Metropolitan Community Church (MCC) congregation, where she presumed their sexual selves would be markedly in the minority, since the MCC denomination was founded expressly to minister to people whose sexualities were not heterosexual. Surrounded by the LGBTQA community of faith, she described her time in the MCC as rich, mournful, and powerful. "Nothing is more powerful than worshiping with people who are oppressed and who still find a hope in God," she declared.

These are the blessed: those who struggle. The Beatitudes do not make light of nor minimize the hardship and struggle, hurt and grief of being human. They are not put together in a "serene" or syrupy way, in spite of the way they often are read. These sayings acknowledge the horror of being persecuted, of being sorrowful or poor in spirit, of seeking God or something that satisfies hunger and thirst.

I will never forget a young man who in the early 1990s died of HIV/AIDS. I was his chaplain. He languished in a bed, mourning the fact that his father, a minister, had rejected him and forbade his siblings or mother to contact him, for fear of their being ostracized. I remember him because one night I held him for three hours as he wailed into my chest. I held him without wearing the appropriate universal precautions, because I knew instinctively that he needed to be touched—skin on skin. When he was able to speak, I learned he had not been touched without latex gloves in four years. He had been abandoned not only by his family, but also by his created family of friends and a lover. He was the mourning one, the poor in spirit, the one who hungered and thirsted for righteousness. And I was the witness to his struggle to find dignity and God in that moment.

There are countless stories like his—of being ostracized or abandoned, considered a scourge in the earth. Reviled and persecuted, many LGBTQA persons find it hard to consider a "reward in heaven" (v. 12), but when they choose to live fully their lives, or when a heterosexual woman chooses not to "play by the rules," such people become "cities on a hill," a light to the world.

No one chooses rejection. Rejection often is the consequence of choosing oneself, as the person knows herself or himself internally. There is a cost in choosing one's truth. That cost sometimes comes as persecution, as it did for Matthew Shepard. And yet the Teacher here juxtaposes God's particularly kind attention (blessings) toward people who persevere and still choose God's life.

Romans 14:13–22

If what I have said about the previous passages rings true, then Romans 14:13–22 becomes instructive about how to continue to be in relationship with people. It is easy to say the words, "stop passing judgment" (v. 13 NIV), but we live in a world where we must make judgments daily about interactions with others. For people with minority sexual expressions, the writer's call to "not allow what you consider good be spoken of as evil" (v. 16 NIV) is the writer's call to choose to stop what you consider "good" if someone can call it evil. LGBTQA communities have closeted themselves for years in order to avoid this accusation. I think of people snarling at same-gender loving people who hold hands in public or show other signs of affection, who follow the snarling with "Keep it indoors!" but do not hold the same standard for heterosexual couples.

There is not equivalency in the text, of course, between expressions of one's sexuality or gender identity and matters of food and drink. The only question is how to "stop passing judgment" and how not to "cause someone else to stumble" (v. 20 NIV). Those who are privileged will use the text to say, "Your 'lifestyle' offends me, and therefore, you ought to stop, since you could cause me to stumble." Unfortunately, this sentence is not hypothetical; many a person faces just such marginalizing and silencing behavior or words.

What if the marginalized or silenced person said, "You offend me"? Would those in privileged and "normative" positions be willing to keep their belief "between [themselves] and God" (v. 22 NIV)? If so, what would that look like? What if all persons made up their minds "not to put any stumbling block or obstacle" (v. 13 NIV) in another's way? What would that look like?

At what point does the person "distressed" by the behavior of another take responsibility for his or her own emotional, theological, and ethical world and not expect someone else to keep him or her from feeling "uncomfortable"? At what point does the heterosexual yelling at the LGBTQA community members take at their word their commitments to Christ, to ethical living, and to faithful loving? In other words, how do we save our judgments for ourselves, or as Augustine once said, "give others a wide berth, and yourself a narrow way"?

Perhaps as we celebrate the gifts of gender and sexuality, the above reflections will help us move the conversation beyond contentious thinking of persons whose expressions of sexuality are not the dominant expressions. Perhaps we will remember that we all are called in a body that feels, wants, longs, and desires; that creativity and eros are kin gifts from God; and that all who we are and will be begins in a womb infused by God's grace.

Proper 8 [13]

Pablo A. Jiménez

2 SAMUEL 1:1, 17–27	LAMENTATIONS 3:23–33
PSALM 130	PSALM 30
	2 CORINTHIANS 8:7–15
	MARK 5:21–43

The lections for today bring an array of issues of justice into the presence of the preacher and the congregation. The readings from 2 Samuel and Lamentations lead us to think about the social consequences of war. The psalms provide points of identification with those whose suffering leads them to feel that God has abandoned them. While calling the Corinthians to contribute to the offering for the saints, Paul opens the door for us to consider the injustices when a few households have great wealth while most households have great needs. The passage from Mark asks us to consider the relationship between justice and the situations of women today.

2 Samuel 1:1, 17–27

The saga of David's ascent to Israel's throne is riveting. To understand it properly, it must be placed in context. The previous lessons from the Hebrew Bible in the lectionary address diverse topics, such as Israel's unfaithfulness (1 Sam. 3:1–10), Israel's demand for a king (1 Sam. 8:4–11), the anointing of David as future king (1 Sam. 15:34–16:13), and David's battle with Goliath (1 Sam. 17). The lectionary does not address David's relationship with Saul or with Jonathan. Without this background, today's lesson may be incomprehensible to many parishioners.

Second Samuel 1:17–27 is an elegy or funeral poem. It is characterized by the use of the phrase "How the mighty have fallen!" as a refrain (vv. 19, 25, and 27). Apparently, the text is placing on David's lips a traditional elegy, "The Song of the Bow" (v. 18). This song blends national and personal elements, remembering both the prowess as a warrior of Saul, the fallen king (v. 22), and David's close relation with Jonathan (v. 26).

I suggest a narrative approach to a sermon on this text. Such a sermon could begin with a summary of David's relationship with Saul and Jonathan. It is important to illustrate how Saul deteriorates, struggling to maintain both mental and spiritual health. Sadly, Saul loses the battle for his sanity, losing also his rule.

Another option is to focus on Jonathan. The Bible portrays his relationship with David in epic terms. Although some commentators have tried to read their relation as a romantic one, I do not think that this is accurate. Jonathan is a man of integrity, trapped between his loyalty to his father and his loyalty to his friend. Ultimately he sacrifices his life fighting a losing battle at his father's side. Jonathan thus evokes another young man who loved his friends to the point of sacrifice, hanging on a cross.

A sermon on this poignant lesson should use the refrain that characterizes this elegy. Use the refrain at the introduction and at the conclusion of the sermon. You may also use it to introduce each section of your sermon.

This text is full of topics related to issues of peace and justice. The first one, of course, is war. The consequences of war are devastating, particularly when the technological gap gives an unfair advantage to one side (the Philistines, in this case). The second one is human rights, particularly the rights of those trapped in the losing side of a battle. Saul commits suicide to avoid torture at the hands of his enemies, who would have exposed him publicly before murdering him. So the text leads us to ponder topics such as torture, political assassination, and even suicide. Third, we cannot disregard a troubling element of this elegy: the glorification of war. Can we honor those fallen in war as heroes without romanticizing war?

Lamentations 3:23–33

If the previous lesson glorifies war, this one confronts us with the terrible consequences of war, military occupation, and even genocide. The book of Lamentations is a collection of five poems about the aftermath of the fall of Jerusalem at the hands of the Babylonian army around 586 BCE.

The literary structure of these poems is unique. They closely resemble the community psalms of lament; at the same time, they evoke the funeral poem or elegy. However, they are crafted as acrostics. This literary pattern is intensified in the third poem, where each strophe has three lines that begin with the same letter of the Hebrew alphabet (three with *aleph*, three with *bet*, three with *gimel*, etc.).

We can only speculate about the reason for this particular structure. Maybe it was a memorization technique, intended to facilitate the oral transmission of the poem and its use in liturgy. Maybe it is intended to highlight the magnitude of grief. In any case, the literary structure challenges preachers who want to design sermons that follow the moves and structures of the text.

These literary compositions employ four different "voices" to convey their message. The first one is the poet, who is the implied author. The second one is a feminine voice, called the "daughter Zion," who personifies the destroyed city (1:6, 12–22). The third one is a masculine voice, which declaims the third poem. Finally, a fourth voice provides a vehicle for the community (5:1–22).

The third chapter is mainly declaimed by the masculine voice. The central position of the poem in the book, the particular masculine voice, and its brief positive theological assertions highlight the importance of this section. The poem mimics the structure of a psalm of lament, traveling from grief to hope.

The hopeful section begins on verse 21, which is outside the suggested reading. However, verses 21 and 22 are crucial for the interpretation of the lesson. Verse 21 announces a change of the focus of the poem, making an intentional move to hope. Verse 22 announces the main topic of the brief section that ends with verse 33: a celebration of God's *hesed*, a complex Hebrew theological concept that can be translated as mercy, steadfast love, or covenant love.

The poem asserts that God's *hesed* is eternal (v. 22), that it is always new (v. 23), and that it is our spiritual inheritance (v. 24). God's loving mercy satisfies the human soul (v. 24), demonstrating that God is good (v. 25). The faithful, who discern God's many blessings, know that it is good to be faithful to God (vv. 26–28), even in the midst of persecution and even torture (vv. 29–30).

The poet affirms that current tribulations, which may be misunderstood as divine rejection, are transitory: "The Lord will not reject forever" (v. 31). Tribulations end, but God's *hesed* endures forever. Even if God allows the current tribulations, the faithful know that God will ultimately have compassion and show mercy (v. 32). Why? Because inflicting pain is not part of the divine nature. God "does not willingly afflict or grieve anyone" (v. 33).

Ultimately, preaching about social justice is preaching about suffering. In this sense, Lamentations 3 provides a perfect vehicle to address myriad issues, at both personal and community levels. In historical perspective, the poem addressed mainly issues related to war and peace and military occupation. However, these issues today lead us to topics such as gentrification, the military and political use of rape as a weapon to terrorize women, and the social and psychological effects of disasters.

A sermon on Lamentations 3 must take seriously its literary structure. In particular, it should contrast the bleak tone of verses 1–20 with the hopeful note found in verses 21–33.

Psalm 130

This is one of the most beautiful poems in Scripture. Biblical scholars place Psalm 130 in three different collections. First, it is a Song of Ascents. Psalms 120 to 134 form the collection called Songs of Ascents because pilgrims who traveled to Jerusalem from different parts of the land probably used them. Israelites were required to worship at the temple of Jerusalem on the main religious festivities, particularly the Passover or Feast of Unleavened Bread, the Feast of the Weeks, and the Feast of the Booths. Although most inhabitants of the land did not attend all three feasts, many traveled to Jerusalem at least once a year. Later, those in the Diaspora tried to visit Jerusalem at least once in their lifetime.

Second, Psalm 130 is a song of individual lament. These psalms voice the trials, tribulations, and sufferings of a person in spiritual need, a person who is facing a crisis of faith. Combined with the community version, a third of all psalms can be classified as laments. These psalms begin with a cry for help and end with a statement of trust and faith in God. This movement from pain to hope is the characteristic trait of the laments.

Third, Christian interpreters have identified seven psalms that address human sin, begging for divine forgiveness. This collection, called the Penitential Psalms, includes Psalms 6, 32, 38, 51, 102, 130, and 143. Therefore, Psalm 130 is considered as the sixth Penitential Psalm. It is also popularly known as "De profundis," from the two first words of the psalm in Latin.

Psalm 130 begins with a heartrending cry: "Out of the depths I cry to you, O LORD. Lord, hear my voice!" (vv. 1–2a). This shocking opening is one of the main literary traits of the psalm. Therefore, it could be used both as an opening and as a refrain for a sermon on this text.

One of the main literary characteristics of this psalm is its ambiguity. The poet never describes the source of his emotional and spiritual pain. However, this ambiguity works to the psalmist's advantage, as it allows any reader in pain to identify with his cry.

Most people in crisis think that God is deaf to their plight. For this reason, anyone who prays with Psalm 130 can identify with the feelings expressed in verses 1–2. When in crisis, we cry out to God, seeking divine attention to our painful condition.

Verses 3 and 4, while identifying the source of the pain, are equally ambiguous. We simply learn that the psalmist has sinned and that such sin has provoked a crisis. The individual sin is not identified, opening infinite possibilities for interpretation. However, the psalmist does not dwell in the past. The poet simply acknowledges this sinful condition, stating that no human being can stand before God (v. 3). In short, the psalmist takes for granted that all human beings are sinners.

The turn toward good news of salvation begins in verse 4, which affirms that God forgives sinners. God's character is the source and motive for forgiveness. God is not moved to forgive us by our acts of repentance, but by the divine nature. Forgiveness exists in God, long before we repent. Acknowledging this theological truth should lead humanity to revere and worship God.

Verses 5 and 6 advance the psalm in an unexpected way. Instead of receiving an immediate divine act of mercy, the psalmist waits for God's intervention. The psalmist waits in hope, convinced that God will act in the near future (v. 5). However, this wait is not passive. The psalmist does not sleep while waiting (v. 6). On the contrary, the psalmist compares this wait with that of a soldier who guards the city during the night. The wait is active.

The psalm ends with a dual statement of faith, that God is the object of our hope and that God redeems and forgives humanity (vv. 7–8).

Anyone who has ever suffered can pray with Psalm 130, whatever the source of his or her emotional and spiritual pain.

Psalm 30

Much of what we have previously stated about Psalm 130 applies to Psalm 30. The main difference is that in this psalm the crisis is in the past. This is a psalm of thanksgiving in which the poet extols God, celebrating the divine intervention on his or her behalf. The psalmist, who was at the brink of death due to illness, is now in good health (vv. 2–3).

In response to God's mercy, the poet exults God's character, affirming that God is worthy of praise (v. 4). Like the poet of Lamentations 3, the psalmist contrasts the transitory nature of tribulation with God's eternal love (v. 5).

In verses 6–10 the poet details a spiritual journey, confessing that in arrogance the psalmist felt invulnerable (v. 6). The illness placed everything in perspective, forcing the psalmist to cry out to God (vv. 7–10).

The psalm ends with an image that illustrates the feelings of those who receive God's mercy: "You have turned my mourning into dancing" (v. 11). Although this phrase appears in a psalm of thanksgiving, it also summarizes the turn from pain to hope that characterizes the psalms of lament (vv. 11–12).

2 Corinthians 8:7–15

The reading from the epistle leads us to a new topic: stewardship. This is a meditation about the collection for the church in Jerusalem, raised by the apostle Paul in response to the agreements reached at the council of Jerusalem (Gal. 2:10).

In this text, Paul calls the Corinthians to fulfill promises made in the past. He begins by securing the audience's favor. The apostle states that the Corinthians, who "excel in everything" (v. 7), should also excel in generosity. Participating in the collection is not a command, but an opportunity to show how genuine is our love for others (v. 8). For the believer, Jesus Christ is the model of generosity (v. 9). In spite of being divine ("rich"), Jesus became human ("poor") in order to save humanity.

Against this theological backdrop, Paul encourages the Corinthians to finish what they have begun during the previous year (vv. 10–11). It is clear that the Corinthians have pledged a given amount of money and that Paul is simply asking them to fulfill their pledge. To those who doubt or resist, Paul says helping the poor is a matter of justice, procuring a "fair balance between your present abundance and their need" (vv. 13–14).

On the surface, this text raises several issues related to the life of the church, such as stewardship and administration. However, on a deeper level this text raises the issue of justice: the wealth of the few implies the poverty of many. In order to live in a better society, it is necessary to seek a social balance between abundance and need. This balance is achieved by the redistribution of wealth. Paul's advice may lead us to fashion sermons that delve into topics such as taxes, philanthropy, and affirmative action.

Mark 5:21–43

In this text, Mark tells two stories about women: the resurrection of a girl and the healing of an adult woman. They share a common trait, uncleanness. Judaism considered the dead ritually impure. Also, women were considered impure during their menstrual cycle. Therefore, these are stories about women rendered impure by disease or death.

The story of the woman who suffered a (presumably vaginal) hemorrhage is inserted or intercalated into the story of the young girl. This is a literary technique common in Mark (e.g., 11:12–25). As Jesus returns to Jewish territory, Jairus, a leader of a synagogue, asks him to heal his daughter (vv. 21–23). The plea is surprising, given that most synagogues were led by Pharisees.

As Jesus walks to Jairus's house, a crowd follows him. While Jesus is opening a way through the crowd, a woman touches his clothes and is healed immediately (vv. 24–34). Jesus stops to recognize the miracle and demands to know who has touched him. After Peter's customary gaffe (Peter is named in Luke 8:45, but not in Mark), given that in Mark the disciples do not fully understand Jesus' identity and mission until his death, the woman reveals herself as the object of God's mercy (v. 33). Jesus commends the woman for her deep faith (v. 34).

When Jesus reaches the girl, she is dead (vv. 35–43). However, the healing of the impure woman assures us that Jesus will also "heal" the now-impure dead girl. Overcoming fear and even mockery, Jesus raises the girl from the dead.

From the standpoint of social justice, these stories may serve as the basis for sermons that highlight the plight of women. Even today, woman are discriminated against at the workplace and financially oppressed. Even today, Jesus calls women who suffer to "get up" (v. 41) and enjoy the liberation provided by the loving God.

Fourth of July: Seeking Liberty and Justice for All

Ronald J. Allen

HABAKKUK 1:1–17
PSALM 50
2 PETER 2:1–3, 17–22
LUKE 6:17–26

Many churches join the larger culture in the United States by celebrating Fourth of July as Independence Day.[1] However, reflective Christians note that independence from Great Britain in 1776 did not bring freedom to slaves. Moreover, people at Fourth of July events sometimes uncritically wave the flag and celebrate the nation (and national policies that deny God's purposes). However, the preacher can take advantage of the interest in public life generated by the Fourth of July to help the Christian community think critically about the degree to which the United States (or any nation) is truly an environment of liberty and justice for all. What needs to happen for all in this nation to live in liberty and justice?

The obvious characters in [Israel's conquest of the land of Canaan] for Native Americans to identify with are the Canaanites, the people who already lived in the promised land. As a member of the Osage Nation of American Indians who stands in solidarity with other tribal people around the world, I read the Exodus stories with Canaanite eyes. And it is the Canaanite side of the story that has been overlooked by those seeking to articulate theologies of liberation. Especially ignored are those parts of the story that

---

1. While these comments focus on the Fourth of July as Independence Day in the United States, they could be calibrated for similar days in other nations. Canada, for instance, celebrates July 1 as Canada Day, in honor of Canada's being officially united as a single country on July 1, 1867.

describe [God]'s command to mercilessly annihilate the indigenous population.[2]

Robert Allen Warrior

The story of Israel's entry into the promised land as a great gift is one of the formative stories of Israel. However, Robert Allen Warrior, a Native American theologian, points out that to the Canaanites the same story is one of being conquered and killed. Warrior thus reminds us to consider the formative narratives of every community from the perspectives of all who are affected by the story. Many people in the United States—especially persons of European origin—think of the Fourth of July as a celebration of liberty and justice for all residents of this land. Yet Eurocentric males brutally denied liberty and justice to Native Americans, to people of African, Asian, and Hispanic origins, and to women of European origin. The sermon today can lead the church to work for liberty and justice for *all*. The Scripture texts assigned for the Fourth of July are intended to promote such reflection.

Habakkuk 1:1–17

The book of Habakkuk is protest literature. Prior to Habakkuk, Assyria had ruled the Middle East with an iron hand, repressing Judah (a small, defenseless nation). But by the time of Habakkuk (late seventh and early sixth centuries BCE), Babylon was overrunning the Assyrian Empire. Habakkuk prophesied at a time when Assyria and Babylonia were in conflict and when the internal life of Judah violated God's covenant with Judah. The local monarchs in Judah (especially Jehoiakim) suppressed internal opposition, conspired with the wealthy to exploit the poor, perverted the legal system, and ruled by violence.

Habakkuk, like other prophets, had believed that God would punish Judah for its sin. However, using the form of a lament, Habakkuk 1:2–4 protests to God that the social injustice in Judah has gone unpunished. Habakkuk expected that God would use the Chaldean (Babylonian) invasion as the means to enact judgment (vv. 5–11). However, Chaldean rule had only intensified injustice and violence in Judah as the Chaldeans were more corrupt than their predecessors (vv. 12–17). At one level, Habakkuk protests the brutal way in which the Chaldeans colonized Judah (note esp. vv. 13–14). At another level, the prophet protests that God has not acted justly (vv. 2, 17).

---

2. Robert Allen Warrior, "Canaanites, Cowboys, and Indians," *Christianity and Crisis* 49, no. 12 (1995): 263.

One possibility for preaching is to help today's congregations—especially those of European origin—recognize how we violate God's purpose in ways analogous to those of Judah during Habakkuk's day. The preacher can call attention to ways we deny liberty and justice for all. How does our culture promote violence? Habakkuk believed that God punished Judah by sending the Chaldeans to overrun the land. While contemporary Chaldeans may not be about to overrun the borders of North America, the preacher can warn the congregation that continued unfaithfulness creates conditions within the nation that bring about collapse. We must repent.

Another possibility for preaching is to invite the congregation to look at the world from the perspective of groups who are in situations similar to that of Judah—nations who are effectively colonized by other nations, and less powerful groups who must live under the heels of more powerful ones.

Habakkuk protests that God has acted unjustly by allowing evil to continue. While the preacher should encourage today's community to cry out to God regarding injustice, the preacher could also encourage the community to recognize that we cannot wait passively for God to act. The church must be an active agent in creating communities that are more just.

Psalm 50

Psalm 50, presented as a covenantal lawsuit in which God brings the community to trial, has four parts. (1) In verses 7–15 the community does not understand the purpose of sacrifice, as is evident when the community claims that sacrifices are to feed God. God does not need food (vv. 8–13). (2) The aim of sacrifice is for the community to give thanks to God and to renew their vows to live in covenant (v. 14). (3) According to verses 16–20, the community violates the commandments that are core to living in covenant community. These commandments maintain covenantal community so that all can live in blessing. (4) God wants the people to live faithfully so they can go the "right way" to salvation (v. 23). If the people do not repent, the community will collapse (v. 22).

On the Fourth of July, the preacher can invite the congregation to consider whether our worship leads to covenantal living. The sermon can call attention to the fact that all communities and nations have their own myths, rituals, and behaviors. Do the myths of the United States serve covenantal community among all peoples, or do they privilege some groups at the expense of others? If the latter, the preacher needs to help the community recognize that such behavior will ultimately tear the community apart, leaving all people in jeopardy (v. 22).

Luke 6:17–26

The Gospel of Luke and the book of Acts assume that history is divided into two eras—the present fractured world that is about to end, and the realm of God that is already being revealed through Jesus but will not arrive in fullness until the second coming. God seeks for all to repent and to join the movement toward the realm (e.g., Acts 2:38). Since Luke and Acts tell one story, the preacher should follow the themes of a passage from the Gospel into Acts.

This passage presents four blessings and four woes as if they are stark and unchangeable polarities. The preacher who focuses only on this passage will declare that those who are poor, hungry, weeping, and defamed because of their witness to the realm are already blessed, that is, they have a place in the realm. On the other hand, those who are rich, full, laughing, and well regarded are cursed, that is, they await perdition.

Viewed from the larger perspective of Luke–Acts, the passage has a double function. It assures those who are poor, hungry, weeping, and defamed that they have a place in the realm. The passage is also designed to shock those who are rich, full, laughing, and well regarded into repenting of their complicity in the old age and into sharing their resources so that (a) they will avoid destruction and (b) all in the community will be blessed. Through such sharing, the church in Acts was a community of blessing for all (e.g., Acts 2:42–47; 4:32–37). The unrepentant wealthy were condemned (e.g., Acts 5:1–11).[3]

The Fourth of July could prompt the pastor to reflect on this passage on three levels. First, with respect to the church, the passage provokes those who have resources and power to share with those who do not, so that there would not be a needy person in the church. Second, with respect to the United States, the passage calls for making power and resources available to all in the nation, and to resist the impulse to consolidate power and resources in the hands of a few. Third, with respect to the larger world, the passage pushes the congregation to consider how many people in the United States are rich, full, laughing, and well regarded, in contrast to nations that are poor, empty, weeping, and disregarded. God is already working toward an egalitarian world community in which all are blessed with resources. The United States can willingly join this movement or prepare for the fact that continued nation-centrism will lead to a genuine reversal of roles as other nations (swelling in population, manufacturing power, and military might) eventually turn the United States into a land that is poor, empty, weeping, and disregarded.

---

3. This perspective is developed further in Ronald J. Allen, *Preaching Luke–Acts*, Preaching Classic Texts (St. Louis: Chalice Press, 2000), 123–40.

2 Peter 2:1–3, 17–22

Second Peter was written in the form of a last will and testament. People in antiquity considered the last words of a person especially important. According to 2 Peter 2:1–3, false teachers taught that Christ would not return to judge the world. Consequently, Christians were free from moral limitation. The behaviors promoted by the false teachers destroyed community through secretly bringing into the community destructive teaching (v. 1), deceptive words (v. 3), slander (v. 10b), reveling in the daytime, dissipation (v. 13), adultery, enticing unsteady souls to join the false behavior (v. 14), speaking bombastic nonsense, acting on the desires of the flesh (v. 18), promising freedom but making people slaves to corruption (v. 19). It is not clear whether the author of 2 Peter believed these accusations to be true or was using invective that was commonplace at the time.

The author replies that Christ will return to judge the world. The false teachers and their followers will be condemned (2:4–10, 17–22). The letter pleads with the congregation to be faithful so they can enjoy community as God intends, both now and forever.

On the Fourth of July, the preacher can ask whether false teachers today promote policies that undermine community as God intends, in areas such as international relations, social welfare, and the distribution of wealth. Can the sermon name teachers who promote their false views through means such as talk shows, newspapers, and Internet columns?

The testament form of 2 Peter prompts today's preacher and congregation to ask, what legacy would we like to leave to the world? True teaching seeks to leave a world of openness instead of secrecy, generosity instead of greed, support instead of slander, freedom instead of slavery, and accountability to God and community.

The Fourth of July indirectly raises a broader issue: the inadequacy of the nation-state as the organizing principle for the world population. The world today is organized according to nations. For many people, national identity is an idol. Moreover, nations compete for power, land, natural resources, and wealth. Within nations, people compete for control of the populace, and such competition is often murderous. Indeed, many national boundaries are arbitrary and even misbegotten. Almost every nation maintains a military to protect national sovereignty, thereby not only fostering a culture of violence but wasting billions of dollars that could be used to improve the quality of life of all peoples. While democracies are typically less coercive than totalitarian states, winners often punish losers in ways that are disrespectful, belittling, and injurious.

The realm of God is an implicit criticism of the very idea of national sovereignty. In the realm, people of different cultures live together in mutual support, peace, justice, love, respect, and abundance. To be sure, the realm is not here in its fullness, but until it comes, the church can urge the peoples of the world to live toward the realm by replacing national interest (and other forms of self-centeredness) with the vision of all communities living together in realmlike ways.

Proper 9 [14]

Marjorie Hewitt Suchocki

2 SAMUEL 5:1–5, 9–10   EZEKIEL 2:1–5
PSALM 48   PSALM 123
                              2 CORINTHIANS 12:2–10
                                          MARK 6:1–13

The first two passages suggest that the way toward just and safe community is through identification with the enemy and through loving-kindness. The readings from Ezekiel, Paul, Psalm 123, and Mark all deal with the difficult issue of the leader whose initiatives prompt other people to respond negatively. How does one persevere when members of the community are indifferent or even hostile?

2 Samuel 5:1–5, 9–10

Insofar as Year B gives us the stories of the monarchs in Israel, this text tells of the final ascent of David to the throne of all Israel. It is preceded by chapters of intrigue, murder, revenge, and civil war. David is the anointed king of Judah, and Saul's son Ishbosheth rules Israel; each struggles to absorb the domain of the other. The final triumph of David is not through battle but through affirming his opponents. When Ishbosheth's captain, Abner, appears to come over to David's side, David sends him away in peace—but Abner is murdered by followers of David, without David's knowledge. David publicly mourns Abner, an act of civility noted by the people. When Ishbosheth's people learn that Abner is dead, they become dispirited, and two decide they will win favor with David by killing Ishbosheth, bringing his head to David. But David punishes them for murder. The people, seeing David act justly, acclaim David as the rightful sovereign of both Judah and Israel. David then captures the city of Jerusalem and proclaims it the city of David. He is thirty years old when his reign begins, and it lasts forty years.

319

To seek signs of justice in these internecine struggles plunges us into issues of political, military, and civil leadership. David shares in bloodshed; he is a warrior, first against the neighbors of Israel in the effort to expand Israel's territory, and then as ruler of Judah against his counterpart in Israel. In some ways the ancient tale of strife in Israel seems all too vivid against the backdrop of today's Israel in constant struggle with its neighbors. The small clue in the text is that the final victory is gained not through battle but through mercy. David publicly mourns the deaths of those who had opposed him. This public mourning gains him an identity with those who have been his foes, and they are enemies no longer. Today's conflict seems far different. But is there yet some role for identity with the foe, and consequent acts of mercy?

Psalm 48

The psalm is continuous with the text from 2 Samuel, beginning by celebrating Jerusalem, now the city of David, and weaving together the themes of military might and mercy. It does so by presenting three locations: outside the city, inside the temple, and inside the city.

Those located outside the city are rulers of other lands, and in happy hyperbole the psalmist speaks of them quaking at the beauty and strength of the unassailable city (vv. 4–7). Indeed, God sends strong winds that break apart the enemies' ships, so there is no point in sending in the marines! God has made the city a stronghold; God will guard forever this city, and the land it represents.

But then the psalmist shifts from militaristic language. We are no longer quaking with the alien rulers outside the city, but suddenly we are in the midst of the city in the temple, which rings with the praise of God (vv. 9–11). The panic of the would-be enemy gives way to the security of the insider: loving-kindness, righteousness, and gladness pervade the temple. We rejoice in the judgments of God, for they are righteous altogether.

From this center of security and serenity we are invited to walk about the city, admiring its beauty, its ramparts, its palaces (vv. 12–14). There is no fear, only safety and satisfaction. There is but one injunction: We are to tell our children, and they their children, for all generations, of this city and this temple that God has given us, secure in the knowledge that God will guide us all our life long, until death. For God is God, forever and ever.

The image presented in the psalm is of a center of safety and joy amidst the possible terrors of life. This center is righteousness, loving-kindness. If this is central in our lives and in our hearts, will we not also walk in safety in cities built to exhibit such qualities?

Ezekiel 2:1–5, Psalm 123, 2 Corinthians 12:2–10

These three lectionary texts can be read as a triptych, offering parallels with each other that yield parallels with our own situation and encouragement for our own journeys toward justice.

In Ezekiel's day, the people of Judah are in trouble. It is many a long year since the triumphs of King David; the two nations of Israel and Judah, united under David, were separated again under David's successors. The people of Israel have been taken captive by the Assyrians, and now, in Ezekiel's time, the people of Judah suffer a similar fate. Nebuchadnezzar of Babylon, warring with Egypt for dominance in the region, takes Judah as a vassal. The rebelliousness of the Judeans against this imposition leads Nebuchadnezzar to a wholesale exile of the upper classes and artisans to Babylon; only the poorest Judeans are left in the land. Five years into this exile we meet the prophet Ezekiel, by the river Chebar, in Babylon among the exiles.

Our lectionary text gives the story of Ezekiel's call by God to be a prophet. The call is preceded by the extraordinary vision of Ezekiel 1, where the Lord is presented as coming to Ezekiel out of a storm, surrounded by strange four-faced creatures and four wheels inside wheels, flashing with eyes and lights all around. Ezekiel takes all this as a witness to the glory of God; stunned, he falls on his face—and then God speaks to him.

First, God commands Ezekiel to stand (Ezek. 2:1). God does not require Ezekiel's abject subjection, nor does God lift him. Ezekiel is one of a captive people; inferiority and subjection are expected of a captive, are they not? God refers Ezekiel to Ezekiel's own power to rise and stand before God. If Ezekiel can rise and stand before God, cannot he rise and stand before his captors? God's call is liberating. When we see and experience injustice in our community, is there not a liberating call to stand?

Second, God's Spirit enters Ezekiel (v. 2). He is called to rise on his own; having done so, God's Spirit fills him, conjoining the strength of God with the strength of Ezekiel even in the midst of oppression. "We Shall Overcome" was the rallying song against oppression in our own United States. A people, rising against oppression, receive the strength of God's Spirit to speak against oppression. Isn't that still the case? When we name injustice of whatever sort, doesn't God's Spirit strengthen us in speaking and acting against it?

Third, even though the consequences of speaking do not lead to immediate repentance and reform, Ezekiel is to persist courageously no matter what the obstacles. Indeed, there is a sweetness to the word of justice that is to be savored, even in the midst of persecution and anguish. Is this not still so? We speak and act with passion against the injustices so apparent—death penalty, walls against "aliens," torture, discrimination, greed, callous indifference to the poor. In God's name and in God's strength we speak against the evils, and despite overwhelming obstacles, we find the courage to continue to speak. The call to the prophet Ezekiel, centuries ago, echoes still.

And now we turn to the psalm: "To you I lift up my eyes, O you who are enthroned in the heavens! As the eyes of servants look to the hand of their master, as the eyes of a maid to the hand of her mistress, so our eyes look to the LORD our God, until [God] has mercy upon us" (Ps. 123:1–2).

This psalm is one of several Songs of Ascents, to be sung by pilgrims as they approached the temple in Jerusalem, but to read it in the immediate lectionary context of Ezekiel's call to stand and to preach courageously against all obstacles is to find suggestive interpretive meanings. What if we read it as a "call-and-response" text relative to Ezekiel? God has told Ezekiel that his message will not be well received—it will be like preaching while sitting on a mess of scorpions (Ezek. 2:6)! Hardly an encouraging call! But we know that eventually Ezekiel's word is heard, and he becomes a prophet of encouragement: captivity will not be forever, the people will return to the land. He persists in his call despite initial discouragement. So now look to the words of this brief psalm. No longer is there a ruler on the throne of David—but God is the ultimate ruler, everlastingly enthroned in the heavens. Over against the contempt and scoffing of the captor Babylonians, there is One beyond them whose word is gracious and righteous. We are called by that Ruler over all rulers, so that we need no longer be subservient to the contemptuous and the scoffing. God is the one to whom we turn, the one we obey. In turning, we claim the promise of a land, a land no longer subject to contempt, but a land empowered by God to stand proud in the ways of justice.

If Ezekiel is a prophet called to prophesy despite the discouragements of a people who will not listen and whose work involves him in physical pain, the passage in 2 Corinthians shows that Paul is in some ways Ezekiel's counterpart. Ezekiel's call includes a vision of God; Paul, likewise, receives a vision that inaugurates his call. According to Luke in Acts 9, the vision is one of Christ appearing to him on the road to Damascus; in 2 Corinthians the apostle himself speaks of a vision, of being caught up into a sense of the immediacy of God's presence, and of hearing words that cannot be spoken. Ezekiel is told he will encounter hardship in his preaching ministry; Paul has just told the Corinthians of the countless beatings, stonings, shipwrecks, and other disasters he has incurred on his missionary journeys. Ezekiel also endures physical hardship, not through what others have done to him, but through the pressure and stress of the very message he is bound to give. And here Paul speaks of a physical torment, not imposed from what has been done to him, but arising just from who he is. Three times, he says, he has asked God to remove this "thorn in the flesh," but it is not to be. Instead, God says: "My grace is sufficient for you, for power is made perfect in weakness" (2 Cor. 12:9).

In essence, was not this the message to Ezekiel as well as to Paul? Perhaps it is simply the case that to be a prophet, insistently exposing unrighteousness, injustice, and greed, involves "disputes without and fears within" (2 Cor. 7:5). The power of Christ dwelling within us does not magically erase our conflicts or our fears. Rather, it creates within us the power to persist, knowing that even our weaknesses and troubles can be used by God for the accomplishment of good.

Ezekiel and Paul, two prophets in two very different times and in very different circumstances, are called and empowered by God. Their physical and psychic journeys are strewn with hardship. Nonetheless, the strength of God gives endurance and joy. All these centuries later we who read of their struggles and, more importantly, of their message know that, for all the difficulties, the words that God gave them to speak were effective, for we hear them still today.

If this was the case with Ezekiel and with Paul, why should it be different for us? We are called to speak words of justice, to do deeds of justice, and to inspire others to join us in the words and the deeds. Difficulties need not be discouraging: God calls us to stand, empowers us to speak, and will bring our message to fruition.

Mark 6:1–13

If the passage from Ezekiel speaks of resistance to the message from God, and the psalmist speaks of the contempt the righteous receive, and Paul speaks of the hardships of the journey, this passage from Mark shows Jesus to be no stranger to these problems. It is the Sabbath; Jesus and his disciples go to Jesus' hometown to speak the words of God. The passage does not give us the message of Jesus—nor does it need to. All the Gospels speak that message of a realm—a kin-dom—in which love, exhibited in justice and mercy, draws a people into *being* a people, united in a passion for common well-being.

Hear the response to Jesus as he gives the message in his hometown: "Who does he think he is?" (See vv. 2–3.) The contempt spoken of in the psalm is here poured on Jesus. On the one hand, the people recognize Jesus' wisdom in word and deed; on the other, these qualities are dismissed. After all, the people say, he's just the carpenter; we know his family; who is he, to come among us as if he were somebody?

He *is* Somebody. He is a Somebody who can make us all into Somebodies who can stand together before God in commitment to God's own kin-dom of caring and love, strengthened by God's grace toward implementation of that kin-dom. But the message is rejected by those who hear it in his hometown, dismissed because of what? Jealousy? Incredulity, that someone they have always known dares to speak things to them as if they had to learn? Who knows what prompted this rejection?

In response, Jesus calls his disciples together in order to send them to do good and to preach the message of God's kin-dom. They are to go in pairs, taking nothing for their journey except a staff for the road, a single tunic for clothing, and a single pair of sandals for their feet. To travel in such a way is to invoke the rule of hospitality; it is, in itself, a call to kin-dom, a call to caring, responsive love. If you are accepted, says Jesus, stay and do your work; if not, then your very rejection is a witness against those who refuse the goodness of hospitality. And so the disciples go, and they preach a message of repentance for our refusals of God's call, offering healing of body and spirit to all who receive them.

There is a promise in this text, especially in its joining with the other texts of the lectionary. Are we rejected in our work? So was Jesus. Are we treated with contempt? Jesus—and Paul and Ezekiel—knew something of that. If we seem to fail now, shall we take that as an ultimate discouragement? No! We know the ultimate outcome; we have experienced the life-giving resurrection from deeds of death to deeds of life; we know that the seemingly rejected words of the prophets continue to ring to this day. Even in the midst of rejection and contempt, Jesus sends us out. And so we preach, cast out the demons of injustice, and pour healing oil on the sick. The kin-dom of God is with us to this day and always, and the strength of Christ perfects us even in the midst of weakness.

Proper 10 [15]

Cláudio Carvalhaes

2 SAMUEL 6:1–5, 12B–19
PSALM 24

AMOS 7:7–15
PSALM 85:8–13
EPHESIANS 1:3–14
MARK 6:14–29

We are living in what the Christian liturgical calendar calls Ordinary Time (see below). What are we to do with these Ordinary Time texts? Based on what liberation theologians in Latin America do with Bible readings in base communities, we will interpret the Bible passages for Proper 10 for each year in the lectionary from the social location of a different, specific community. Instead of Bible commentaries, I have the voices of people reading the texts and giving input from their current religious/social/political/economic/historical situations. I hear the burning questions, the biblical, theological, and general life accounts that arise at a crossroads between a community and a pastor. The pastor here is someone who, like you and me, wants to learn about the Bible, not from Bible commentaries like this one, but from the lives of people who engage the Bible from their own social location.

At a community meeting, the preacher offers commentary on what Ordinary Time means in the liturgical calendar and asks the community to read the Scriptures for the day and to talk about each text, drawing connections to their own lives. In this process, the biblical texts and the story of the community combine in the thick hermeneutical accent of each specific community. This exercise in interpretation hopefully leads the preacher to material for the sermon. For the preacher can usually figure out how the community understands these texts and how the people's insights shed light on what the preacher needs to say.

For our lessons today, the pastor is living near the wall in Nogales, in the north of Mexico in the Sonora desert. The United States has built two thousand miles of wall across its border with Mexico to keep immigrants from crossing. On the wall, many people use art to make statements and white crosses to show their frustration, including frustration over how this wall has created more death but not solved the immigration problem. This wall affects millions of people and communities.

The pastor says the following to the small gathering of thirty people: "Friends, we are here to read the Bible and figure out what these texts have to do with us and our community in Nogales. What is God telling us to consider, to do, to change, to move, to engage, or to transform here today?"

Ordinary Time is related to the normative, the standard, the expected in life. In a sense the ordinary is the daily stuff of life fueled with extraordinary encounters with God. At this crossroads between the ordinary and extraordinary lies what we might believe in regard to God's presence, God's miraculous works, and our (extra)ordinary lives.

We are between the seasons of Pentecost and Advent, that is, between the time when the Holy Spirit descended on the disciples to prepare them to live in the world, and the advent of God in Jesus to live among us. Immanuel! So what are we to do with these texts?

The numbers in parentheses below indicate statements that participants made in the conversation about the text. Each number indicates a different statement.

2 Samuel 6:1–5, 12b–19

(1) Compañeros [companions, partners], David dancing! Andale! (2) Claro! What is strange is that David danced but we cannot dance in church today. (3) Como no? [why not?] Mexicans are always dancing. (4) Not in churches. The missionaries told us we could not dance. (5) They said dancing was the devil's way to lead us to hell, I still remember Sr. Stanley telling us that! (6) Pero no [But no], now we read this text from *our* cultural perspective. Look: Israel is like us when we gather together: we bring our symbols (like they had an ark), we have songs, music, and instruments (songs and lyres and harps and tambourines and castanets and cymbals), and we all eat together before we leave the church (to each a cake of bread, a portion of meat, and a cake of raisins). If David were here he would dance with the mariachis, filled with the Spirit!

(7) No! esto no es el evangelio de Jesucriso! [This is not the gospel of Jesus Christ!] (8) Why is it not the gospel? (9) He is right; it is not! Mariachis do not belong in the church! (10) Why not? (11) They do not belong to Jesus but to the devil. (12) No, no, no! It is our culture, hermanos [brothers], and we must not demonize our culture. God placed us in our own culture, and we must honor it. Mariachis, dancing, tortillas, all belong to God! (13) Demonizing what gives us life and has sustained our culture is not right. The missionaries understood the message of God from their own U.S. culture and brought

both culture and gospel to us. Don't you sing Mexican songs at home? (14) At home yes, not in church. There are proper places for proper things. (15) But aren't we Pentecost people? (16) Wait a minute, are we not also like the people in this passage when they looked at each other with hatred? We have to find a way to rejoice together. (17) If we are a Pentecost people, we must find a way to worship God and eat together.

Psalm 24

(1) Mira! [Look!] Everything belongs to God! Everything was created by God! This psalm sees everything connected—very different from what we hear from some people who demonize some things and respect others according to their cultural view. (2) It is like the song we sing all the time: *Pues si vivimos, para El vivimos y si morimos para El morimos. Sea que vivamos o que muramos, Somos del Señor, somos del Señor. "Pues Si Vivimos,"* "When we are living, it is in Christ Jesus, and when we're dying, it is in the Lord. Both in our living and in our dying, we belong to God, we belong to God. We belong to God, we belong to God."[1] (3) Mira, the heart of things lies in what the text says: "And who shall stand in his holy place? Those who have clean hands and pure hearts, who do not lift up their souls to what is false." Whatever we do, we must do with sincere and pure hearts! Our mariachis and dances can be an offering to God, our bodies a location for God's revelation! (4) Ordinary bodies made extraordinary through the incarnation of our faith in God! (5) Vea cómo somos hermosos! [See, we are all beautiful!] (6) God made us beautiful, and we will not accept anything that judges our bodies and culture as inferior to other cultures!

(7) But don't we detract from the gospel with these dances and songs? (8) No, hermano, no! Mira, God has given the Mexican culture to us! Dances, food, language, art, revolution, history, fight against the conquistadores, pride, honor, dia de los muertos—we will cherish everything that God has given us! And we will not accept any judgment in the name of God that says "Gospel=civilization=U.S. culture." (9) Pero [But] we cannot close ourselves to others. (10) Right, we cannot. Our doors will be open and even if others think we are exotic, this is *our* way of worshiping. This text has a demand for us: "Lift up your heads, O gates! and be lifted up, O ancient doors! that the [Ruler] of glory may come in." Let us open the doors of our churches and houses and dance in Tehuana dresses amidst the chaos and order of our cultures! Gracias sea dada a Dios [Let us give thanks to God].

---

1. Traditional authorship, based on Rom. 14:8, "Pues Si Vivimos" ("When We Are Living"), in *Chalice Hymnal* (St. Louis: Chalice Press, 1995), 536.

(11) Let us not forget those who are living in United States right now. For our hermanas y hermanos [sisters and brothers] who are living in El Norte, we can bless them by sending them this little prayer-like saying from our own artist Frida Kahlo: "I may be in America but only my dress hangs there . . . my life is in Mexico."[2] (12) Alabado sea el Señor! Praise the Lord!

Amos 7:7–15

(1) Mira! El Muro! [Look! The wall!] God is standing beside the wall! But why a plumb line? (2) Aiaiai this is terrible! God is saying to Amos that God will never pass in their midst! (3) This is tragic! (4) The plumb line shows the proper measure of God against this evil wall! "The high places of Isaac shall be made desolate, and the sanctuaries of Israel shall be laid waste." This is the result of this wall! (5) Yes, this wall next to us is a cruel and inhuman sin against God! This is the shadow of a country which says: "We don't want your people; we are sufficient to ourselves! We hate/fear you; to show that, we construct a wall so that we cannot even see you!" (6) Me recuerdo que [I remember that] President Vicente Fox denounced this project as "disgraceful and shameful." (7) Porqué? [Why?] The U.S. stole our lands and now treats those who cross the desert as terrorists!

(8) What do we see? This is the question God asked Amos and is asking us now! (9) We see this wall as evil! We are to prophesy against this wall day in and day out until the wall comes tumbling down like the walls of Jericho, like the wall in Germany not long ago! (10) Destruction will come upon all who think they own the earth! (11) We feel in exile in our own country. See, we depend on these *maquilas* for our salaries but they exploit us![3] Our brothers and sisters cannot plant corn because the U.S. government subsidizes the corn, and our government signed NAFTA. (12) NAFTA protects the products of the U.S. and Canada, and we must agree with them so we can receive their peanut money to help our economy. (13) Es terrible porque [It is terrible because] our government has agreed with it.

(14) What are we to do? Keep asking what God asked Amos: "What do you see?" (15) We must organize ourselves and fight against it! And if we don't feel like we can do much because we are peasants, let us remember what Amos said and what God responded to him: "Then Amos answered Amaziah, 'I am

---

2. Frida Kahlo, www.fridakahlofans.com/c0120.html (accessed April 27, 2010).
3. *Maquilas* are factories owned by people in the United States and other countries, but located on the Mexican side of the border. These factories import materials and equipment into Mexico without having to pay taxes to Mexico. With very low salaries and almost no rights for workers, these manufacturing companies not only profit greatly but they also produce vast amounts of trash that they leave on the Mexican side.

no prophet, nor a prophet's son; but I am a herdsman, and a dresser of syca-more trees, and the LORD took me from following the flock, and the LORD said to me, 'Go, prophesy to my people Israel.'" (16) Don't forget, hermanos y hermanas, el Espíritu Santo de Pentecoste is with us making the impossible possible, and empowering us to prophesy! (17) Amen!

Psalm 85:8–13

(1) We have to preach peace not hatred! (2) You are right! But there is no peace where there is no justice. Martin Luther King Jr. del Norte said: "Injus-tice anywhere is a threat to justice everywhere."[4] (3) Our salvation is in God! (4) Turning our hearts to God is to turn our hearts to peace and justice. (5) God's glory can dwell in our land only when "Steadfast love and faithful-ness will meet; righteousness and peace will kiss each other." (6) Que bonito! [How beautiful!] (7) When we use the land in God's ways, preserving and distributing it, we will see that "faithfulness will spring up from the ground, and righteousness will look down from the sky." (8) Our God will only give what is good if we honor the land, justice, peace, and a fair life for all. Alabado sea el Señor. [Praise the Lord.]

Ephesians 1:3–14

(1) Mira vos! We gain power by claiming to be children of God through Jesus Christ! (2) Otra vez [Again] we see that everything belongs to God, including the good and the bad of our culture. (3) We can do now what Christ will do later: connecting earthly things with heavenly things, that is, our ways of liv-ing with God's hope for our lives. (4) Not everything is good in our culture! (5) But we live to praise God in everything we do, be it at work, on the streets, raising our children, fighting against injustice, prophesying. (6) Telling God's truth to the world, announcing the salvation of God in Christ. (7) Mira! We are marked with the seal of the Holy Spirit!! (8) Do any of you know Manoel Scorza's novel *La Danza Inmovil*? He points to the struggle between mobility and immobility in Latin America, the wrestling between options, decisions, and taking positions! It is always a struggle to choose, to feel that we can opt, that we have the power to decide.[5] (9) Shall we start moving and choosing by moving and dancing as we sing this Mexican corito [song] with mariachis? Shall we try all together just to see how it goes?

4. Martin Luther King Jr., "Letter from Birmingham City Jail," in *A Testament of Hope: The Essential Writings of Martin Luther King, Jr.*, ed. James M. Washington (San Francisco: Harper & Row, 1986), 290.
5. Manoel Scorza, *La Danza Inmovil* (Buenos Aires: Plaza & Janes, 1983).

Mark 6:14–29

(1) We have so many John the Baptists who died in the desert announcing the way of the Lord. (2) Our people in the desert tried to find support for their families, searching for a life with dignity: They are the John the Baptists dying in the Sonora desert! (3) Remember José: He lost his job at the *maquila* because they cut the budget and he had no work for three years? He decided to go to Estados Unidos but fearing being captured by the border patrol got lost and died in the desert. I believe the Spirit was leading him to find a new life, but the situation that *we* created didn't allow the Spirit to fulfill God's desire. (4) Maria left Nogales with her three kids, four, seven, and eleven years old, to go to Arizona to meet her husband, When the helicopter of the border patrol came down to scare immigrants, she lost her two older kids in the desert. Her youngest died in her arms. She is in prison now, and nobody has told her the whereabouts of her two older kids. (5) Or Jorge whose wife fell ill when he had no money to pay for her treatment and to feed his kids and decided to venture into the desert. When he was deep into the desert, he realized he wouldn't be able to make it because he was not fit enough, and he had no food or water. However, he didn't want to come back and be a shame to his family. This Indian who was placing water in the desert met him and demanded that Jorge go back to his family. Jorge has never made it. (6) Was the Holy Spirit moving in those people who went into the desert to find life? (7) So many of our people are John the Baptist figures seeking lives of justice, salvation, and transformation for their families and their communities by distributing wealth and possibilities. (8) And yet, they are killed by the Herods of our time, who protect only those who are in the system. (9) The crosses on the wall, here in our church, and in the desert remember those who fight against unjust systems like John the Baptist. (10) Hermanos y hermanas, let us choose to fight and to never let their memories die. 11) We also must be like John the Baptist, announcing the kin-dom of justice, love, and peace of Jesus Christ.

Proper 11 [16]

Joni S. Sancken

2 Samuel 7:1–14a	Jeremiah 23:1–6
Psalm 89:20–37	Psalm 23
	Ephesians 2:11–22
	Mark 6:30–34, 53–56

This week's texts balance elements of God's surprising and dynamic (but not arbitrary) freedom to respond to changing circumstances with God's stead-fast faithfulness and abiding presence among God's people, which is stronger and more trustworthy than any earthly monarchy or political strength. God freely moves with Israel and resists David's suggestion that he build God a house of cedar, declaring to David that God "will make you a house." Jeremiah looks forward to a day when God will gather God's scattered people so that they might live without fear in a land of justice and righteousness. The psalm speaks of God's covenant faithfulness even in the most challenging circumstances. Ephesians recasts the church as a fitting dwelling place for God with Christ Jesus as the cornerstone, and Mark bears witness to Jesus' compassion for the crowd, even at cost to his own need for rest in the midst of a busy schedule. Regardless of the challenging circumstances we may face, we can count on God to be present with us as we too are built into a fitting dwelling place that bears witness to the reconciliation and peace to which Christ bears witness.

2 Samuel 7:1–14a, Psalm 89:20–37, Ephesians 2:11–22

The events leading up to these verses in 2 Samuel describe victory and security for the roaming warrior David, who is finally named ruler over all of Israel in chapter 5. He makes the city of Jerusalem the capital of Israel and moves the ark of God into the city with dancing and offerings (2 Sam. 6:13–15). David, now experiencing peace and comfort in his own house, desires that the ark of God, the presence of God among God's people, should also have a fine and comfortable house. David is a three-dimensional, very human figure who at times shows great empathy—as seen by his grief and lament over the deaths of Saul and Jonathan in 2 Samuel 1 and the kindness he shows to Jonathan's son Mephibosheth in chapter 9. At other times David is thoughtless concerning the well-being of others, as in having an affair with Bathsheba and orchestrating the death in battle of her husband Uriah in chapter 11. Initially, the prophet Nathan responds favorably to David's empathetic impulse to build a house for God, but Nathan gets a surprising word from the Lord later than night.

God does not want David to build a house for the divine presence. It is not within David's power to house God. God has moved with Israel from the time of the exodus. This divine freedom has allowed God to move in surprising ways, including calling forth David "from following sheep to be [ruler] over my people Israel" (2 Sam. 7:8). In this same freedom, God will build David a "house," not supported by beams of cedar but by God's everlasting covenant that will allow a future generation of David's line to build a temple to the Lord.

God is both free and faithful. The lectionary selection from Psalm 89, starting in verse 19, offers a vision that attests to and celebrates God's promise to David and God's faithfulness to that promise, even when subsequent generations forsake God's law and do not keep God's commandments (Ps. 89:30–31). Though these unfaithful members of David's line will be punished, God will still be faithful (Ps. 89:34–35). The broad context of this lengthy royal psalm moves from praise of God's faithfulness, exemplified by God's relationship with David, to despair in the experience of God's absence, expressed in the verses immediately following the lection, which address the military defeat of one of David's descendants, where the enemy is seen to be supported by divine power over against David's line. Speaking to God, the psalmist cries out, "You have exalted the right hand of his foes; you have made all his enemies rejoice. Moreover, you have turned back the edge of his sword, and you have not supported him in battle" (Ps. 89:42–43). The author calls upon God to be faithful, to uphold the covenant established with God's anointed, "Lord, where is your steadfast love of old, which by your faithfulness you swore to David?" (89:49). The psalm closes with a short doxology in verse 52 that serves to close out not just this psalm, but Book III of the Psalter.[1]

We understand David's desire in 2 Samuel to build a house for God. God's choice to stay homeless, however, surprises us. When given a choice, people

---

1. James H. Waltner, *Psalms*, Believers Church Bible Commentary (Scottdale, PA: Herald Press, 2006), 437.

choose security and safety, but many people have no choice. The pejorative term "homeless" implies that people without addresses do not belong anywhere, that they are rootless and without worth. People rushing to work do not notice the woman with her belongings under the overpass. Without fixed addresses, many "urban sojourners" struggle with invisibility, with feeling like "nobody."[2] Like the psalmist, they struggle with rejection and loss. They have become part of our landscape.

God's word in 2 Samuel challenges us. God chooses to remain free so that God can be near to God's people. As Christians, we believe that God's promise to build a house for David has found fulfillment in Jesus Christ as God incarnate. The church, as Christ's body here and now, is called to be a dwelling place for God and to acknowledge all of God's people. Our congregations must work to be spaces where everyone can be "someone" and all can feel at home—even those whom society renders invisible.

Writing to a Gentile audience, the author of Ephesians envisions God's expanding community as building on the faithfulness of God to Israel and extended in Christ, who has brought "those who were once far off" into relationship with God (Eph. 2:12–13). This passage features interplay between a number of dualities: uncircumcision and circumcision; far off and near; peace and hostility; strangers and aliens and citizens and members of God's household, with verses 14–16 likely a hymn or adaptation.[3] Verse 15 is bold in its declaration that "[Christ Jesus] has abolished the law with its commandments and ordinances, that he might create in himself one new humanity in place of the two, thus making peace." We should not take this to mean that Jesus is against the law, but that he makes it possible for believing Gentiles to join Israel in witnessing to God's purposes for all peoples. Israel's set-apartness is not abolished in Christ. Israel's distinctiveness—through such things as diet, circumcision, Sabbath and festival observance, use of Hebrew—is still in place. Israel's own culture is not rejected in favor of a Gentile universalism, but through Christ, faithful Gentiles stand alongside Israel in serving and witnessing to the one sovereign and gracious God. Through Christ, congregations today also have hope that God is still building on the covenantal foundations laid in the apostles and prophets, still healing divisions between humanity, and knitting us together into the household of God (Eph. 2:20–22).

2. A congregation of which I was privileged to be a part, primarily serving a community of persons with no fixed address, preferred the term "urban sojourners" to "homeless persons." While the latter draws distinctions between those with or without a home, the former reminds us of our common humanity, as everyone sojourns through life.
3. Thomas Yoder Neufeld, *Ephesians*, Believers Church Bible Commentary (Scottdale, PA: Herald Press, 2002), 106–7.

Jeremiah 23:1–6, Psalm 23

Jeremiah 23 begins with God's word of "woe" directed at David's unfaithful descendants, "the shepherds who destroy and scatter the sheep of my pasture!" Family history compounds Jeremiah's critique of the covenant violations of the monarchs. Jeremiah is a descendant of a Levitical priest, Abiathar, who supported Adonijah, Solomon's rival to David's throne, and who was subsequently banished to Anathoth (1 Kgs. 1:5–7; 2:26–27).[4] The words in Jeremiah 23 conclude a section started in Jeremiah 21, where the monarchs are judged and the cities threatened with horrible calamities. It is because of the unfaithful actions of these leaders that Israel suffers, but the text becomes hopeful with the promise that God shall attend to God's own flock and raise up "a righteous Branch" from David who shall "execute justice and righteousness in the land" (Jer. 23:5). Here too, God remains both free and faithful. God is free to punish those who violate covenant but promises to raise up future "shepherds" to care for God's people in safety. While God has granted them power, the rulers are still accountable to God, and when they lift up themselves and do not care for the poor and needy, God's judgment falls upon them. In particular, Jeremiah calls attention to the opulent home built by Shallum, son of Josiah, with forced labor for no wages (Jer. 22:13–14). Woe to those who lift up self at the expense of others! As earthly shepherds, we too are called to use the gifts God grants us to care for all of God's flock.

In Psalm 23, the voice of the psalmist bears witness to God's faithful provision. This is the image of a righteous shepherd who cares for the flock. In contrast to Jeremiah's unfaithful shepherds, God provides for the flock, leading them down right paths and providing protection even through the darkest valley. Rather than scattering Israel and handing them over to their enemies, the great shepherd becomes banquet host, providing a table of plenty and overflowing cup in the presence of enemies. Unlike those who pursue and seek to harm the psalmist, God pursues with goodness and mercy.

This psalm's intimate and concrete language has made it a favorite for many believers, but this can sometimes impede our ability to enter into the text in new ways. Envisioning oneself as a sheep or goat, animals not known for their intelligence or self-sufficiency, can help us to recognize our utter dependence upon God. Read in the context of the Psalter, Psalm 23 follows Psalm 22, perhaps most familiar to Christians for containing the agonized words of Jesus uttered on the cross, "My God, my God, why have you forsaken me?" (Ps. 22:1, Matt. 27:46, Mark 15:34). Psalm 22 expresses deep distress and lament

---

4. Leo G. Perdue, "Jeremiah," in *The HarperCollins Study Bible*, ed. Wayne Meeks (New York: HarperCollins, 1993), 1110.

before God. The psalmist cries, "I am a worm, and not human. . . . Many bulls encircle me . . . they open wide their mouths at me, like a ravening and roaring lion. I am poured out like water, all my bones are out of joint; my heart is like wax; it is melted within my breast" (22:6, 12a, 13–14). While dependency on God in Psalm 23 is pictured as secure resting and trust, the voice of dependency in Psalm 22 is one of desperation: only God can help. While Psalm 22 ultimately moves to praise for God's rescuing action and proclamation of God's sovereignty (22:21b–31, the agony expressed in moments of terror and darkness is starkly contrasted to the pastoral peace of Psalm 23. Juxtaposing these two psalms may help those who are deeply familiar with Psalm 23 to see it in fresh ways that acknowledge our own dependency in times of distress and security.

Mark 6:30–34, 53–56

Mark 6:30–34 picks up from the disciples' mission set out in 6:7–13 and provides the background and setting for the miracles of the feeding of the five thousand in 6:35–44 and Jesus' walking on the water and calming the wind on the Sea of Galilee in verses 45–52. The action pauses in verses 14–29 so that Mark can explain the circumstances of John the Baptist's execution at the hands of Herod.

In verse 7, the disciples are sent out in pairs to cast out demons and heal the sick, but verse 30 has them returning to reconnect with Jesus, eager to tell him about their experiences. The activity level was high, "for many were coming and going, and they had no leisure even to eat" (v. 31). As Jesus often retreats to be by himself and pray, Jesus also encourages his disciples to find a deserted place to rest; and so they "went away in the boat to a deserted place by themselves" (v. 32). The frenetic pace in Mark, highlighted by the repeated use of the qualifier "immediately" to describe the actions, is contrasted by these intentional pauses (1:35; 6:46; 9:2; 14:32). However, because of the traveling and the powerful acts of healing and exorcism, their fame had spread so that a crowd was waiting to meet the boat. Even though he has been busy and expending himself to engage with the crowds, Jesus is moved more by compassion than by his desire to take a break. The crowd is described as being "like sheep without a shepherd" (v. 34). In this way, Jesus is fulfilling the role of righteous shepherd from Jeremiah 23 and Psalm 23.

Verse 53 picks up after Jesus and the disciples, whom he joined midcourse on their Bethsaida-bound boat, have arrived onshore. We have just been informed that the disciples have been frightened and then astounded by Jesus' walking on the water and that they are still feeling confused about the loaves from the feeding miracle in verses 41–44 due to "hardened" hearts (v. 52).

As soon as they arrive on shore, the frenetic pace picks up again. The crowd recognizes Jesus "at once" and rushes to bring the sick to him (vv. 54–55). In contrast to the beginning of chapter 6, where Jesus' power is possibly affected by the unbelief of the people in Nazareth (vv. 5–6), now people can be healed by even touching the "fringe of his cloak" (v. 56).[5] Jesus' power is exercised in ways that extend compassion and care toward those in need. In the spirit of discipleship, we too should consider how we can exercise our power in compassionate ways.

It is interesting to note in verse 34 that the compassionate action of Jesus, the Good Shepherd, is that of teaching. One hundred years ago, the social gospel movement sought to address social ills and aid the poor in part through education. Our education system today remains uneven, despite the efforts of programs funded by the No Child Left Behind Act and the fact that affirmative action provides additional support for underrepresented groups in colleges and universities. There is a huge range in the quality of education a student receives, depending on the socioeconomic standing of her or his school district. In wealthy suburbs a child may receive a first-class education, while inner-city schools may not have basic supplies or even be safe environments for students and teachers. Such imbalances can set out life trajectories that are difficult to reverse without intervention.

Our churches are participants in communities with varied educational needs. This should be a concern even for aging congregations with a small population of children or college-aged students. At the systemic level, the church should call for quality educational opportunities for all students. At the congregational or personal level, Christians can offer tutoring in the church building or by being a reading partner in a local school. Moreover, education does not have to be only a secular concern; almost any action of the church gathered and scattered can be framed broadly as Christian education and can serve the purposes of learning about the Bible and church doctrine, forming of Christian character and habits, offering service to others, building social connectedness, and otherwise witnessing to the realm of God.

5. Dawn Ottoni-Wilhelm, *Preaching the Gospel of Mark: Proclaiming the Power of God* (Louisville, KY: Westminster John Knox, 2008), 116.

Proper 12 [17]

Wilma Ann Bailey

2 SAMUEL 11:1–15
PSALM 14

2 KINGS 4:42–44
PSALM 145:10–18
EPHESIANS 3:14–21
JOHN 6:1–21

The Bible moves back and forth from the universal to the particular. When readers become too focused on the particular (e.g., the family of Abraham and Sarah or the early church), they can forget the universal dimension. God is God of everyone, whether readers realize it or not, as the selection from Ephesians reminds us. These texts demonstrate that God is concerned about the physical lives and well-being of people, as well as the spiritual dimension of human life. There are stories from both Testaments about meeting the very basic human need of food. There are stories about the abuse of power, for instance, when David takes the wife of another man and uses her to satisfy his base desires. The other man in this case is a Hittite, not an Israelite, but the offense is an offense, regardless of whom it hurt. A Hittite is also a child of God. The injustice is exposed, and punishment ensues. The psalms remind us that God shelters the poor and that God will reverse current socioeconomic statuses. The poor will enjoy the bounties of God's reign. The psalms also remind us of the importance of attending to the structure of a text. In Psalm 14, such attention helps the reader comprehend how to distinguish between statements about the wicked and statements referring to all people. God has not given up on all people, but God does distinguish between those who do wrong and those who seek God.

2 Samuel 11:1–15

Second Samuel 11:1–15 tells of abuse of power, betrayal, deception, and murder on the part of David, Israel's second ruler. This incident does not occur at the beginning of David's reign, when he is preoccupied with establishing

337

the integrity of Israel vis-à-vis the other nations, nor at the end, when he has grown tired. It occurs when he reaches the height of his power. In this text, he takes advantage of a perk of his position. Ancient monarchs usually had multiple wives and concubines who represented wealth, status, and political alliances. In the ancient Near East, sovereigns functioned outside of the laws and customs that applied to ordinary people. But this was not to be true in Israel. The ruler of Israel was subject to Torah (God's instructions), just like any other Israelite. One function of the Israelite prophets was to keep the monarch in line.

Bathsheba's bathing is not an act of seduction. The prophet, Nathan, does not treat it as such. Bathsheba is not blamed. David has been told from the beginning that she is married. David is supposed to be on the battlefield with Joab and the other warriors, not enjoying a vacation at home. The language in verse 4 is explicit: "David sent messengers and he took her" (my trans.). In the parable that follows in 12:1–4, the lamb (Bathsheba) is the victim. Bathsheba expected David to be with her husband on the battlefield. David uses his power as ruler to take the wife of one of his most loyal subjects. When deception does not work, he has Uriah murdered. Uriah is a Hittite. David is an Israelite. Uriah, the foreigner who has dedicated his life to the protection of Israel, behaves as an Israelite ought to behave. He displays loyalty, integrity, and dignity, in contrast to a slimy, unfaithful David.

Blaming the victim, as is typical in the reading of this story, is perhaps the result of interpretation from a position of power, in which the interpreter identifies with the powerful person, or interpretation from a position of weakness, in which the interpreter thinks that by avoiding certain behavior she will not become a victim. The Hebrew Bible does not present its heroes as flawless. To do so would be idolatry. People who are given power must use it to protect and enhance the lives of those in their charge. The particular role of monarchs and their counterparts in modern society is to protect those who are least able to protect themselves and to help them to lead the fullest lives possible.

2 Kings 4:42–44

Many people know stories of the feeding of the multitudes from the Gospels. This precedent in 2 Kings 4:42–44 is relatively unknown. The man brings a gift of food representing the firstfruits of the harvest to Elisha the prophet. Elisha does not keep it for himself. He does not build barns to store it as a hedge against future need. He tells the man to give it to the people. The man balks. The food is not enough for a hundred people. Elisha, who is presented in other stories as a man who cares deeply about the physical well-being of people, tells him that God says that they will eat and have leftovers from the twenty loaves. He gives it to the people, and indeed food is left over.

The story does not say that the loaves were multiplied. That could have been the intended meaning, but the story may also suggest that each person took just a little, to make sure that his or her neighbor also had a little. Hunger is avoided for all. The resources are given to Elisha, but he chooses to share them with others. Many of us live with an excess of everything that we need. So when we read this story, we assume that everyone was sated. But for us the miracle may have been that everyone took just a little, so that all could be satisfied. This is the real-life situation in places in the world where hunger is an everyday reality.

Psalm 14

Psalm 14 is part wisdom psalm and part lament. As is typical of wisdom psalms, the wicked who do bad things are contrasted with the righteous who seek God. A complaint component places it in the category of lament. In order to understand the psalm, it is important to follow the structure. According to verse 1, the wicked have certain characteristics. They deny the existence of God (or gods). They destroy. They do abhorrent things. None of them does what is good. Verse 2 looks at humankind from the point of view of God. God looks to see whether there is any human who is prudent, who is seeking the Divine. Verse 3 is not a reflection on all human beings but, rather, a return to a description of the evil ones. Clearly, there are some righteous (v. 5), and God's people are distinct from the evil ones (v. 4) in the psalm. They have all become corrupt. None of them does good, not even one. Verse 4 returns to God and God's reflections on the evildoers. God asks whether these workers of iniquity who devour God's people and do not cry out to God know that they should be afraid because God is with the righteous. Using direct address to the wicked, verse 6 reads, "You shame ["confound," NRSV] the plan of the poor but God is their shelter" (my trans.). The wicked try to prevent the poor from progressing, but God will take care of the poor. The final verse reveals that the target of the wicked is Israel. The "poor" is a reference to God's vulnerable people. The affirmation is that God will deliver Israel and restore it, and there will be great rejoicing.

Many areas in the world that have experienced violent conflict, such as Congo and Afghanistan, are rich in material resources. These resources, however, almost never benefit the poor. When the poor speak up, demanding a share of the pie, they are quickly crushed by a global economic system that functions to benefit the few and the political structures that support the few.

God, however, is on the side of the poor and will restore what belongs to them. This is not a matter of charity but a matter of justice.

Psalm 145:10–18

Psalm 145 is a psalm of praise to God. In this psalm, the structure is also significant. The psalm is structured as an alphabetic acrostic. Each verse begins with a successive letter of the Hebrew alphabet. The psalm begins marveling about God's magnificence, mercy, and graciousness. It lists attributes of God. The selection for these readings begins with the tenth letter of the Hebrew alphabet, *yod*, which is similar to the English *y*. As in English acrostics, the writer sometimes chooses a word that fits the structure but requires some skill to fit with the thought. The English translations of verses 17 and 18 begin with the same phrase, "the LORD." However, in Hebrew, they do not. (The typical word order of Hebrew sentences is different from that of English.) After describing the attributes of God, as in Hannah's song in 1 Samuel 2 and the Magnificat, this poem speaks of reversals in society when God's justice is meted out. Those who are cared for by God are described as those who are falling, are oppressed (or bowed down), are calling to God, are in awe of God, and love God. God lifts them up and meets their needs. These are contrasted with the wicked (people? deeds?) that are destined for destruction. The psalm stresses that God is not indifferent. God is just.

In our world, those who are falling may be those who lose their jobs or housing or medical care or support system, or youth who commit minor crimes and get caught up in a criminal justice system that functions better as a school for crime than a rehabilitation center. We might add those who are so poorly educated in the school systems that they can barely read and write. God's justice demands the destruction of systems of wickedness. The challenge for Christians who want to be on God's side is to recognize, denounce, and work to dismantle systems that consistently perpetrate injustice and maltreatment of the most vulnerable in our society, in our world.

Ephesians 3:14–21

This selection contains a petition and a benediction. The petition is preceded by a statement of the posture of the author, bowing the knees. In the Bible, there are many postures of prayer: standing, prostrating, sitting, and here kneeling. Kneeling is a posture of vulnerability. In a kneeling position, one cannot protect oneself against attack.

God in this text is referred to as "father." The Greek word is *patēr*. This is significant because the next statement refers to every *patria* (family). The extended family in a patriarchal system is envisioned as carrying the name of the *patēr* (God). The statement that every family on earth "takes its name" (v. 15) from God is reminiscent of the Genesis claim that every person is created in the image of God. Here the affirmation is communal. God connects by name, not just with individuals, but also with family groups. This spiritual genealogy suggests that every family is part of God's family.

The author's prayer is expressed in second-person-singular language that is used as a collective "you." God is able to accomplish what needs to be done—not the Ephesians. The "fullness of God" can be recognized only by those who "know the love of Christ" which "surpasses knowledge" (v. 19). The reference to knowing and surpassing knowledge may be a reference to proto-gnostics, whose religion stressed the need to know a body of knowledge not readily available to all. The knowing in this text refers to a kind of knowing that is akin to the Hebrew notion of knowing in relationship, because the knowing is realized in an experience of love. That experiential knowing goes far beyond what one can know in an intellectual sense, and it is available to all.

The doxology that comprises the last two verses assures the church that it is God who accomplishes what needs to be done, not humans. God works within us (the community of faith), but it is not we who are ultimately responsible for the work. We need only to be willing to open ourselves to the power of God to work.

John 6:1–21

The story of feeding, told in all of the Synoptic Gospels as well as in John, is reminiscent of the feeding of the hundred in the Elisha story (2 Kgs. 4:42–44). In the latter text, a person brings the firstfruits of the barley harvest to Elisha. Initially there is not enough barley for everyone in the community, but God works through Elisha to multiply the barley so that everyone gets something to eat and there are leftovers. But the text does not suggest that the quantity of leftovers exceeds the original amount, as does the story in the Synoptic Gospels. The location of the story in John is the eastern side of the Sea of Galilee, Gentile territory.

A large crowd comes toward Jesus, and he asks a question. He wants to know where they can get enough food to feed the crowd. The question is, why should he care? It is not his responsibility to feed a group of people because they chose to follow him. But Jesus knows that they must be hungry. The narrator says that Jesus asks the question knowing already what he intended to do. Jesus is testing Philip. Andrew has identified a boy who has loaves of bread and fish to sell or donate. But that is not enough for so many people. Jesus asks the people to sit down. They do. Then Jesus gives thanks and has the food distributed among the people. After everyone had eaten, twelve baskets of excess bread were gathered up. Nothing is said of leftover fish. The people recognize this as a sign of the prophet that they were expecting. The prophet is one who understands the physical needs of people and responds to those needs. The people, however, try to force Jesus to be a monarch. He refuses. To rule as a monarch is to enter a secular political realm. This is not what Jesus chooses to do. He goes away to a place where he is alone.

At night, the disciples decide to cross the Sea of Galilee to Capernaum, a Jewish town. The sea is rough. In this telling of the story, the disciples are not afraid of the stormy sea. They row to control the direction of the boat. But when Jesus comes to them, walking on the water, they are afraid, until Jesus assures them that it is he. Ironically, they are afraid of the one of whom they least need to be afraid. When he gets into the boat, it is immediately at their destination, Capernaum. The movement—from land to sea to mountain to a grassy place, back to the sea, and finally to land again in twenty-one verses—is dizzying. Further, the movement is paralleled by Jesus' engaging with disciples and other people and withdrawing to be alone. Engagement and withdrawal are both needed to accomplish the work of God.

The church today is divided. Some Christians see themselves as activists, while others see themselves as oriented toward the spiritual. Such divisions should not exist. Those on the front lines of social justice must be spiritually empowered to do that work, lest they begin to limit themselves to what appears humanly possible. Those who are spiritually focused need to remember that Jesus commands his disciples actively to "follow." The political authorities saw Jesus as a threat. That is why they crucified him. To follow Jesus means that sooner or later you will bump into the status quo as you point toward a more just way.

Proper 13 [18]

Grace Ji-Sun Kim

2 SAMUEL 11:26–12:13A
PSALM 51:1–12

EXODUS 16:2–4, 9–15
PSALM 78:23–29
EPHESIANS 4:1–16
JOHN 6:24–35

The lectionary passages for today deal with power, leadership, and authority. In 2 Samuel, David misuses power for his own pleasure. The Exodus and Psalm passages remind us that whether we are alone, sharing bread, or committing sin, God is always in our midst. We cannot hide from God. God is with us when we sin and when we are doing good. Following acts of sin, we should not turn away from God but must turn to God and repent. Ephesians points to unity to overcome boundaries within our lives. We need to become one in the body of Christ. As all things come from God, we need to rejoice and be thankful for all things, especially for the bread from heaven (Jesus).

2 Samuel 11:26–12:13a

In this reading, we see an illustration of the consolidation of power and the misuse of one's power to dominate those who are powerless, weak, and vulnerable. The passage plays on the dynamics between the rich and poor, the powerful and the powerless, and the intimacy of husband and wife versus sexual domination by a powerful man.

Various responses reflect a multifaceted corruption of power: David's betrayal and murder of Uriah, his marriage to Bathsheba, and the silence of David's conspirators and those who knew what happened. Silence reigned until Nathan, a court prophet, confronted David in the name of the God of justice. The saga of David's career from slingshot and harp to international ruler alerts us to the danger of the lust for power changing leaders as they try to excuse their own greed and injustice.

343

The dynamics of power need to be carefully understood and negotiated. Postcolonial discourse encourages negotiating and disbursing power so that it is equalized rather than being held by one entity. Strategies need to be found that distribute power to avoid its misuse and empower the powerless. When power is not shared and distributed, hoarding power can lead to corruption and misuse at any level—from the world or nation to the organization, congregation, and family.

In this reading, men have a voice and are active, while women are silent and passive. The reader can only speculate how Bathsheba feels about becoming David's wife. As monarch, David orders her to his place. She obeys, perhaps out of fear, perhaps out of obedience. In a patriarchal society men have more power than women, who are sometimes viewed as little more than sexual objects. Throughout history, countless women have been sexually molested or raped; this increases during times of war, such as World War I, World War II, and the wars in Bosnia, Darfur, the Congo, Iraq, and Afghanistan. During World War II, many Korean women were kidnapped to become "comfort women" for Japanese soldiers. These comfort women were raped repeatedly by approximately fifty men a day. Many comfort women contracted diseases, and when deemed useless, they were killed. Sexual sins against women continue worldwide, and congregations and denominations need to bring these issues to public awareness so that they can be addressed. A preacher should not think these incidents are absent in the women (or men) in the congregation. Our call is to work for social justice by empowering women (and men) who are silenced, manipulated, and sexually abused.

Exodus 16:2–4, 9–15

In contrast to David, Moses and Aaron are faithful leaders. God and Moses are challenged by the Israelites who complain about the risks of freedom and who long for the "security" of bondage. The Exodus passage features leaders who are pressured by their people to change their perception of what the leaders know is God's will. Those who have the responsibility and power to move their communities forward are called to resist pressures, complaints, and insults. Those leaders are to present themselves, their people, and the tough situations before God, and follow where God leads them.

Moses and Aaron had already faced grumbling that bordered on open revolt, and found their lives threatened by 250 organized plotters (Num. 16). The presenting cause of the complaints in Exodus 16 is hunger. Underneath it, however, is fear. Those who demand food in the wilderness remember not the burdens and hopelessness of forced labor and degradation. Instead, they recall, and exaggerate, the full pots and plates, the security of being controlled (even though oppressed). Moses names the deepest issue: The people do not trust the God who brought them through the Red Sea and provided fresh water. The quail-based cookout met an immediate need but was not sufficient for their journey, so God provided for a long-term supply of strange but sustaining manna. The Lord provided "bread from heaven" one day at a time to sustain this people on their journey. This method of supply called for radical trust in God.

As Christianity continues to move to the global South, a growing number of Christians are poor. Those who are poor teach us that we need to trust God, because whatever we have is from God. Those who are rich easily forget this and believe that we have worked so hard and such long hours that we deserve all the wealth and riches of the world. The rich often think that we earned our wealth and that God had nothing to do with it. We live with a sense of entitlement. Instead of becoming stewards of the earth, we become dominators. We go to poor countries and take whatever resources we want or think we need. We colonize other people so that we can live more comfortably at the risk of hurting them. However, now is the time to ask ourselves how we in the global North (the rich) can use our resources to alleviate the suffering of those who are poor. Are we willing to give away our money and possessions to the point that we, ourselves, like those who are poor and without recourse, must live depending on manna from heaven?

Psalm 51:1–12

In this psalm, David is shamed and burdened with guilt, and so he humbles himself and seeks and receives forgiveness from God. He asks God to cleanse his heart and restore him. Oftentimes, we focus on what we think are our sins against God, but forget those against our brothers and sisters. While our reading says, "Against you, you alone, have I sinned" (v. 4), that perception fails to recognize our horizontal relationships, how often we sin against our neighbors. David sinned against God but also against his neighbor. The sin committed horizontally is just as important as the sin committed against God; therefore, we need to seek forgiveness for all our sins against God and, insofar as it is possible, seek forgiveness from our brothers and sisters, both near and far away.

Our sins are very personal at times. We cause our brothers and sisters great pain. The sin of David was against the others who were weak and subordinate. As we know from the reading from 2 Samuel, David sinned against the one without any power. When we sin against our neighbor and against those who are weak and powerless, it causes *han*.[1] *Han* is a Korean term that names the

---

1. For more discussion of *han*, see Grace Ji-Sun Kim, *The Grace of Sophia: A Korean North American Women's Christology* (Cleveland: Pilgrim Press, 2002).

pain and suffering of another, often caused by one's own actions. *Han* is the extreme agony experienced by those who are sinned against. *Han* reminds us of the suffering our sin causes. We need to capture this concept of *han* and remember the pain that we cause those who are poor and powerless.

The transgressions against our neighbor are committed in many ways, but not necessarily the way that David did. In a globalized world, we commit sin against those who are poor by our way of living. The nations of the North consume more than we need, thereby robbing both resources and wealth from the poorer countries. Our life of consumption is causing much *han* to those who are poor and to the world in which we live.

The psalmist recognizes that all sin is sin against God. The issue in confession and repentance is not cosmetic. The psalmist uses many verbs in the plea: "blot out" (v. 1); "wash" and "cleanse" (v. 2); "teach," "purge," and "wash" (vv. 6–7); leading to "create in me a clean heart . . . put a new and right spirit within me" (v. 10). True repentance calls for a *clean* heart and a *new* spirit. The verb "create" reminds us of God's act of creation in Genesis. As God created the heavens and earth, God can also create a clean heart and a new beginning.

Psalm 78:23–29

Apart from points concerning the need for leaders to seek the will of God, to maintain their course through wilderness times and the fear of the unknown, Psalm 78 indicates that the God whose name means Life-Giver-Sustainer knows both praises and complaints, blessings and even curses directed toward Godself, from those who claim to follow God's ways.

The Israelites were to work together to gather manna, and they were not to hoard it. There was enough to go around. They were to trust the Giver that they would always have enough to share. Today, we also need to think about the world as a community, whose members need to share resources and not hoard them. However, we live in a consumer society, in which our way of life is the way of consumption. With large refrigerators and freezers, we stock food. Our pantries overflow with foods that we cannot begin to consume. We gather more than we can eat and often throw much away. A preacher can help the congregation see connections between the foregoing aspects and both local and world hunger.

God cares for the hungry and weak. God provides for those who are powerless and downtrodden. When we cry out, God listens and provides for our needs. Latin American liberation theologians say that there is a "preferential option for the poor." God is with those who are poor and loves them. We in the rich Western world need to live with an active concern for those who have so little. This is an essential element of the good news. The rich in the Western world, with more than enough, need to share our possessions and live simply, so that the poor can simply live. There is enough food in the world for all; hunger is a combination of economic-political decisions, distribution logistics, and indifference on the part of the "haves" who exert power over the "have-nots." We need to love those who are poor, feed them, and take care of them, just as God did for the Israelites.

Ephesians 4:1–16

This reading also raises the issues of power and leadership in the context of faithfulness. The writer addresses one or more congregations that experienced factionalism over who is a more genuine believer than others. Some in the community believed that those who transitioned from Judaism into Christianity were superior and therefore should have more power than those who entered from other religions. Another debate focused on which positions in the church were more authoritative than others, with the result that the community failed to recognize the essential value of the various gifts.

The author holds that God in Jesus is the power who unites all believers and empowers them through the Spirit to be of one faith. This is a revolutionary way to shape and sustain a community, in the first century and today. Whatever their ethnicity, religious origins, or gender, everyone in the community is being drawn to become like Christ. Christ gives gifts to all members. Here we have a model of power being shared, rather than rulers grabbing it for themselves. While the author cites a series of offices, the power of these offices is to be expressed in the service-ministry of the one God for the building up of the one body. Each office is a leader-office and a service-office, and each is empowered by the Spirit.

This passage is helpful at all times in congregations, especially those experiencing power struggles among laity or clergy. The sense of being called into Christian fellowship for the sake of peace can be particularly meaningful in conflicted contexts. The church is the body of Christ (1 Cor. 12:27), and Christ seeks a new type of hierarchy in which we are all equal in God's eyes and in which each of us has an essential role.

There is one body and one Spirit. This has great implications for the worldwide church. The body of Christ is growing, and it is moving south to the poorer countries. As Christianity becomes less European and Western, we need to learn how to embrace, love, accept, and learn from those who are different from us. We need to live out the openness of God and seek ways to live as one. Hence we need to work toward eliminating hatred, discrimination, prejudice, and racism, all of which denigrate both recipient and abuser.

We need to speak the truth in love, and we must grow up in every way into the one who is the head (v. 15).

John 6:24–35

The Gospel of John is a tapestry of themes woven around Jesus, to lead people to "believe" Jesus is the Christ, the Son of God (20:31). This complex passage is part of the lengthy "bread of life" discourse (John 6:1–71). The chapter includes the sign of Jesus' popularity, the attempt to make him monarch (v. 15), some followers dropping out, and others realizing that Jesus has the words of eternal life. The last line of the reading sums up the passage: "I am the bread of life. Whoever comes to me will never be hungry, and whoever believes in me will never be thirsty" (v. 35).

A risk working with this Gospel is the possibility of presenting Jesus as a totally otherworldly visitor whose bread, water, and life are in a superearthly realm from which he has descended and to which he ascends. We must remember that the Word became flesh (1:14), that Jesus was at times tired and troubled and that he wept, bled, and died.

One exchange that may be explored is 6:28–29: "Then they said to him, 'What must we do to perform the works of God?' Jesus answered them, 'This is the work of God, that you believe in him whom he has sent.'" "Belief" in this gospel is always linked to seeing, seeking, following, doing, and being. Belief involves learning, being disciplined, gaining insight about the presence of God and God's will, becoming one of the children of God, being a friend of Jesus. And one of the culminating points is doing works greater than that which Jesus did (14:12). Believing in Jesus involves being alive in and through him for the sake of the world God loves (3:16).

How does Jesus' being the bread of life translate to large portions of the world's population who do not eat bread but rather rice? How easily one group can be excluded with the use of this image, which is immediately accessible to Western and Middle Eastern cultures but is foreign within other cultures. Awareness of these sorts of differences constitutes the first step toward inclusion and embrace. As we live in a multireligious and multicultural world, we need to be aware of our context and how even images that seem obvious to us can confuse and exclude others. We need to be mindful of people who do not have a Western background, accepting and rejoicing in them, recognizing that the differences can be places of love and not separation, where people come together in peace, love, and harmony.

Proper 14 [19]

Arthur Van Seters

2 SAMUEL 18:5–9, 15, 31–33   1 KINGS 19:4–8
PSALM 130   PSALM 34:1–8
                                                            EPHESIANS 4:25–5:2
                                                            JOHN 6:35, 41–51

According to John 6, Jesus presents himself as life-giving because he has come from God (the source of life). The implication is clear: through him God continues to be active in history. The brief vignette about Elijah in 1 Kings 19 provides a similar perspective on God as provider. Both Psalm 34 and Ephesians 4 remind us that the people of God experience the ways of God as blessing them as a community when they live out their faith. A sense of dependence on God leads to interrelationships that nurture communal hope. In a culture that seems so often centered on self and so vague about God's involvement in the world, the theology in these texts encourages the kind of hope that our world desperately needs.

The alternate texts from the Hebrew Scriptures point in a different direction. The death of Absalom and the grief of David (2 Sam. 18) call attention to the terrible internal suffering that military conflict creates: a suffering that families grieving the loss of loved ones continue to endure long after the conflict ends. Many who survive the battlefield suffer its debilitating trauma year after year. The cry of the sufferer in Psalm 130 points to the depths of the inner spiritual crisis experienced by so many affected by war.

John 6:35, 41–51

Feeding those who are hungry and providing clean, drinkable water to those who are thirsty is not to be underestimated. At the time of the exodus, the Hebrew people, faced with a fiercely hostile desert, cried out for sustenance (Exod. 16:1–17:7). Centuries later Jesus responded repeatedly to the physical needs of the masses but wanted them to know that God's view of human need goes even deeper. So, in John, Jesus speaks of himself as "the bread of life" (John 6:35). The people fail to grasp the metaphor when he goes on to speak of coming down from heaven (like the manna in the wilderness). They know that this is symbolic language suggesting divine origin, but it does not fit with their perception of him as "Joseph's boy." Jesus adds that the food he offers is his own flesh, a reference to what we have come to call the Lord's Supper. His listeners are aghast when he mentions eating his very flesh (vv. 41–51). Eating human flesh was and is revolting!

In order to avoid any impression of anti-Semitism in these verses, preachers need to point out that "the Jews" (v. 41) does not refer to all Jewish people but to some Jewish groups who did not recognize the validity of Jesus' ministry. It is important to remember that Jesus and the initial disciples were themselves faithful Jews.

This multilayered text, with its references back to the exodus and forward to the cross and "the last day," does not travel easily to our own time. The metaphors of manna, bread, and flesh no longer evoke fresh insights. So we have to recover the inner significance of this narrative for the first-century church and then translate this for today's world.

The Gospel writer is inviting the Johannine community to wrestle with the nature of faith for troubled times. The God they need is not distant but tangibly among them, through the continuing presence of Jesus as the bread of life, especially as they partake of what we now call the Lord's Supper. Indeed, that meal reminds them that Jesus was willing to suffer to give them genuine hope. In Jesus the presence of God concretely touches them in the depth of their lives. The Spirit of God enables seeing Jesus for who he really is—not just a Galilean but the Sent One, Messiah. Those who are open to the Spirit see that Jesus as "the bread of heaven" responds both to their present physical needs and to their ultimate spiritual ones.

Our secular culture faces a crisis of hope. It has lost a sense that God is engaged in our world. Much contemporary spirituality is so abstract that it does not reach us in our humanness. We are stuck in the present because we have dismissed the power of God's ultimate future breaking into the now through the coming of Jesus. The cancer patient so acutely aware of assaults on the body looks for more than some vague hope of immortality. The spark of the Divine within is hardly adequate to grapple with the radical brokenness of many countries in armed conflict. The social consequences of this mindset are that efforts to meet human hunger are woefully inadequate and many who try experience burnout. The realities of suffering cry out for a deeper response, one that is energized and sustained by the God who came in suffering love as the bread of life.

1 Kings 19:4–8

The theme of 1 Kings 19:4–8 overlaps with the John 6 passage. One expects that the prophet Elijah after his triumphant victory over the prophets of Baal would have a deep awareness of God's engagement in human history. But here he is in despair, frightened by threats of retaliation from Queen Jezebel. He prays for death. Even prophets have their limits!

Instead of dying, Elijah is fed by an angel (lit. a messenger) and urged to keep on taking nourishment, because God has intended a long journey for him. Again, God's offer is more than food; it is also an invitation to hope, to trust God's purposes. As the psalmist notes, "the angel of the LORD encamps around those who fear [God] and delivers them" (Ps. 34:7).

In a success-oriented culture like ours, Elijah's cringing response to threat is a timely reminder that victories can easily ring hollow. Winning a contract, being promoted to a higher position, or reaping unexpected profits may not translate into well-being. The experience of weakness within the context of faith, however, can become an opportunity for faith to mature. When the apostle Paul became acutely aware of his own weakness, he discovered the strength of God's grace (2 Cor. 12:7–10). Human failure is not an adequate reason to end one's life, because the Giver of life has purposes for our living that transcend even our sense of failure. The "right to die" movement views life without reference to *God's* purposes, shrouded as they may be in mystery. We are not isolated individuals but interconnected with family, friends, and many others. Wanting to die can be an acceptance of one's mortality, but this is very different from wanting to kill one's self or be assisted to die by others. The "final journey" is a sacred event that even prophets should not take unto themselves.

Ephesians 4:25–5:2 and Psalm 34:1–8

God's engagement with human life (the focus of the two previous readings) has ethical implications. In Ephesians 4 the writer points to the corporate nature of the church. The metaphor of the body implies a community of people "joined and knit together by every ligament with which it is equipped" (Eph. 4:16). This contrasts sharply with much of our contemporary aggregate way of thinking about God's people as merely a voluntary association, a gathering of individuals. Our obsession with polling numbers only exacerbates a quantifying tendency that obscures deeper dimensions of meaningful sociality.

Ephesians 4:25–5:2 sketches the broad lines of how the members of the body should relate to one another in community. Speaking truthfully arises from an awareness that church members belong to each other. This, in turn, fosters transparent honesty (4:25). Anger is divisive and can reflect external forces that undermine the fellowship (4:26). We may no longer use the symbolic language of Satan or the devil (4:27), but there are force fields of evil in our world that challenge the positive influences of the Spirit. One thinks of global economic systems, the military use of devastating weapons, and the deceptiveness of secularity.

We need a profound infusion of God's presence to overcome sinful tendencies toward divisive behavior and misrepresenting one another with a desire to hurt (4:28–31). The church, enabled by the Spirit, moves toward gentleness, forgiveness, and reconciliation (4:30). This implies a community of the baptized called to be genuinely open to God, in contrast to our society's emphasis on self-responsibility, as though it is all up to us.

This corporate and spiritual direction is crucial if the church is to engage in social issues, because the world needs bondedness in order to move toward wholeness. A people bonded by imitating God's love and generosity revealed in the Trinity has a profound capacity for reaching out (4:32–5:2). Congregations are not changed by moralistic sermons. They are remolded through collective reflection on the Gospel story in such passages as John 6, where Jesus speaks of his own willingness to sacrifice himself for the sake of the world.

The lectionary's selection of Psalm 34 encourages the very disposition needed by Elijah in his discouragement, by those of Jesus' contemporaries who resisted his invitation to faith, and by the early church in its struggle under persecution to be a Christian community. The cry for help emerges after the psalmist contemplates gratitude to God. Would that Jesus' listeners had begun with a similar disposition! As a result, the psalmist prays within a theological framework of humble trust. But this is not just an individual relationship with God. Others are to join in opening themselves to the majesty of God.

A culture like ours that overemphasizes individuality often results in people feeling as if they are alone in their suffering. It is part of the very nature of Hebrew worship as reflected in the Psalter to interweave the one and the many. Worship is a communal act. Sometimes our suffering overwhelms us, and we need the faith of others to feel sustained by God. So the gathered people of God are encouraged by the psalmist to "taste and see" that God is good, by recognizing that we are not alone but are supported by the faith of others—an admonition that was later given to the church (1 Pet. 2:3). The move to taste is a small step of faith that can lead to a new way of seeing.

2 Samuel 18:5–9, 15, 31–33 and Psalm 130

King David's lament for Absalom is not at all straightforward story. The politics of power feeds a frenzied struggle for succession. Again, as in the story of Joseph, the favored son (in this case Absalom) is at the heart of a family's internal turmoil. David comes across as someone conflicted between public responsibilities as king and a private life as a father who has abdicated his parental role. This is further complicated by a dynastic political system, so that family conflicts have immense public consequences.

David's generals are commissioned to put down Absalom's rebellion against his father, one likely prompted by the king's own incompetence in establishing justice. Many have rallied behind Absalom, even though he had previously murdered his own brother. Joab, however, is specifically instructed not to allow harm to come to Absalom. As the battle unfolds, Absalom finds himself hanging in a tree, perhaps because his long hair becomes entangled in the lower branches and his mule leaves him dangling "between heaven and earth" (an evocative phrase). His death comes not on the field of battle but in an act of assassination orchestrated by a defiant Joab.

When the deed is done, Joab has to get word to David. But he arranges matters so that Ahimaaz, the son of the high-ranking priest, Zadok, is protected, while a Cushite foreigner becomes a possible victim, since David had previously put a messenger to death for bringing bad news. Joab once again seems to be exercising divine prerogatives as a man of war.

It is hard to assess the lament of David over the death of Absalom. Is this the storyteller's attempt at a partial rehabilitation of David? The idealization of David, after all, became a persistent theme in ancient Israel. Do we make too much of the description of his outpouring of grief over his recalcitrant son, and forget the twenty thousand soldiers who lost their lives in this conflict? In the following chapter, Joab calls the ruler back to his responsibilities as head of state and military commander-in-chief (2 Sam. 19:5–8).

Here is the classic conflict between being both a parent and a monarch (or any other public person with significant responsibilities). But through the lens of the narrator, David comes off badly. In the overall story David is a leader of war; domestically he is a disaster. His family is conflicted, and his treatment of women is mostly dismissive. The narrator appears to have included this particular episode of David's grief over his rebellious son to point out how pathetic David is as a leader, even if he does have residual compassion for his beloved Absalom.

Here is the dilemma for a preacher. Does one give the narrator's perspective of a leader who has failed to be what he was called to be, or the domestic perspective of a persistent parental love even for a wayward offspring? This is precisely where the gospel of another heir of David transcends this choice, for in Jesus we see a prodigal's father, the man of sorrows who speaks forgiveness to the condemned man hanging next to him on a cross (Luke 15:11–32 and 23:39–43). But in this we also see the Prince of Peace who gives his life to transcend violence. Had David, the ancient king, loved his son appropriately, he would have received Absalom back as a son and not a possible future successor. The injustices of the father are replicated in the duplicitous behavior of the son. True leadership is all about trust and integrity. Where this fails in the intimacy of family, it is bound to be reflected publicly.

But there is the further challenge of preaching this text in a time of an increasing use of military force in the world to settle disputes. The Gospels signal the coming of the realm—a world of peace—through the way of the cross. This perspective is consistent with that of the ancient prophets, who confronted the bellicose ways of the throne of David and promised a coming child who would be called the Prince of Peace (Isa. 9:6–7).

When Psalm 130 is set next to the wrenching grief of David, the reader is drawn into another dimension of David's moment of acute despair. David is then seen as crying out to God from the depths. The psalm goes well beyond the story in 2 Samuel. But it may nevertheless be possible to imagine that a father, in such profound brokenness that he cannot yet look up to God, still bows before the One whose judgment shapes the nation's life (Ps. 130:3–4). The psalm helps us to be aware that cries from the depths are the beginning of hope, even when that hope still seems far beyond reach. Nelson Mandela was certainly in the depths of Robben Island prison before his amazing walk to freedom and the South African presidency.

When we look at this psalm through the lens of Gethsemane and the cross, through the ultimate experience of dereliction, we know that God is one who hears cries from the depths and hears them out of *hesed*, a steadfast covenantal love that persists, no matter what. Poet Julia Esquivel sees beyond the suffering of her people in Guatemala when she invites them

> To dream awake,
> to keep watch asleep,
> to live while dying
> and to know ourselves already
> resurrected![1]

Sojourner Truth Day (August 18)

JoAnne Marie Terrell

JEREMIAH 3:19–25
PSALM 106:1–5, 40–48
2 CORINTHIANS 3:12–4:2
LUKE 1:26–38

Born into slavery about 1797 in Ulster County, New York, Isabella Baumfree experienced a religious conversion and call to public ministry in 1843.[1] New York, like other northern states, had "gradual" emancipation laws, but Isabella knew in her heart that God had already set her free. So she "told Jesus it would be all right if he changed [her] name" because when she left the state of bondage she wanted "nothin' of Egypt" left on her account. According to her story, the name Sojourner was given to her in a vision, for she understood that she was to walk about the country preaching and doing God's will. To this name she added Truth, becoming a great advocate in the cause of freedom from oppression for African Americans and women.

An extraordinary orator, Sojourner followed her call to lecture and preach for the rights of women and the abolition of slavery. Her work included advocating for black soldiers during the Civil War, opposing the death penalty, and calling for other civic liberties. Her speech "Ain't I a Woman?" addressed to the Ohio Women's Rights Convention in 1851, is among the most persuasive, moving, and timeless testimonies to the God-given rights of women. On this Holy Day for Justice, when we celebrate women's suffrage in the United States, we remember Sojourner Truth's powerful and enduring civil rights ministry on behalf of women, African Americans, and all God's people.

Then that little man . . . says, "Women can't have as much rights as men, because Christ was not a woman." Where did your Christ

---

1. Since the birth date of Sojourner Truth is not known, we observe Sojourner Truth Day on the anniversary of an event that fulfilled a deep desire of her heart—the ratification of the Nineteenth Amendment in the United States (August 18, 1920) granting women the right to vote.

come from? . . . From God and a woman. Man had nothing to do
with him.[2]

Sojourner Truth

In the above quotation, Sojourner Truth demonstrates both her knowledge of
Scripture, especially the narrative of the annunciation in Luke 1:26–38, and a
deft interpretive framework that argued the centrality of woman in the Christian salvation story. She thereby empowered her own inclusion therein as a
woman who was formerly enslaved. Her experience of race, class, and gender
oppression made her a prime candidate for the freedom-granting tenets of
Christianity, of John Wesley's brand of Methodism, and particularly of the
African Methodist Episcopal Zion Church (est. 1796), to which she belonged.
Although Wesley himself had opposed slavery, the African American Meth-
odists in New York opposed *discrimination* within the (predominantly European) John Street Methodist Episcopal Church. The life of Sojourner Truth,
in dialogue with the biblical texts for today, helps us consider the ways in
which God's power and love continue to be liberating for women and others
in oppressive circumstances. Her witness teaches oppressed women and men,
and those in solidarity with them, to become channels through which God's
love and justice can reshape our society and world.

The unifying motif of the texts for today is "prophetic messianiasm"
(Reinhold Niebuhr's phrase).[3] In prophetic messianism, God is God of all
nations, yet identifies with the physical and spiritual descendants of Israel
as a covenant people, chosen to be "a light to the nations" and harbinger
of justice, of peace, and of a great salvation that embraces all people. The
texts speak severally through the voice of the prophet, the poet, the angel,
the virgin, and the apostle of God, proclaiming the need for exemplary
moral uprightness among the chosen people. The texts celebrate the faithfulness of God, despite our faithlessness, rebelliousness, unbelief, willful
blindness, capacity to enslave and oppress others, and the myriad other
ways human beings try to interdict God's intention and promise to bless
the whole world. The texts empower us to do in our times and places and
circumstances what Sojourner Truth did in hers: to be courageous, faithful, boundary-crossing advocates of God's will for justice and love among
all people.

2. Sojourner Truth, *Narrative of Sojourner Truth* (1850; repr. New York: Arno Press, 1968),
134–35.
3. Reinhold Niebuhr, *The Nature and Destiny of Man* (New York: Charles Scribner's
Sons, 1943), 2:23–24.

Jeremiah 3:19–25

The setting reflects the situation of a prophet and a people in exile, the community's leaders torn from the land they believed they had divine authority and assistance to inhabit, as their sacred story holds. The text begins with God's lament and admission to the failure of God's own plan for Israel to live as "the most beautiful heritage of all the nations" (v. 19b). Through idolatry, exploitation, and other forms of injustice, Israel had become, instead, a "faithless wife" (v. 20). Israel had the opportunity to return to repent and return to God (vv. 22–23) but they did not and must now "lie down in [their] shame" (v. 25) in exile until they become obedient and God returns them to their homeland.

On Sojourner Truth Day, the congregation's encounter with this text can help the congregation lament and repent of the horrors of slavery in the United States prior to the Civil War, as well as the lingering effects of racism, in its virulent, systemic, latent, sometimes *unconscious* forms. Moreover, the preacher could help the congregation recognize forms of slavery that exist today in the United States, especially in the sex industry and in industries making use of immigrant labor. Indeed, more than 1,000 slaves have been freed in Florida alone since 1997.[4] The sermon could help the congregation reclaim and remove the stigma of sin from those sisters and brothers engaged in the sex industry and mobilize the congregation for acts of solidarity with immigrant workers.

Given Sojourner Truth's emphasis upon the liberation of women, the preacher could further use this text to call attention to themes that have been used to oppress women. Because the text represents God with the masculine designation "My Father" (v. 19) and Israel with the feminine expression "faithless wife" (v. 20), and because of the pervasive power and persuasive rhetoric of sexism in this and other places throughout the Bible, it would be easy to take this imagery as blaming womankind for all the suffering humankind has endured and to justify the abuse of women. The preacher needs to help the congregation recognize that men share equal responsibility with women for injustice. In our world, the philandering husband is no less guilty than the philandering wife. It is vitally important to remember that (a) the Bible contains metaphors for God that are feminine in nature (e.g., Deut. 32:18; Ps. 131:2; Isa. 46:3–4); (b) masculine images of God are metaphorical;

---

4. http://en.wikipedia.org/wiki/Slavery_in_the_United_States (accessed September 13, 2010); see further "Slavery in the Twenty-First Century: Over 1,000 Freed Since 1997" (http://crooks andliars.com/karoli/slavery-21st-century-over-1000-freed-1997) and John Bowe, *Nobodies: Modern American Slavery and the Dark Side of the New Global Economy* (New York: Random House, 2008).

(c) all language about God is approximation for what otherwise cannot be described and cannot be circumscribed by an image; and, finally, (d) even in this passage, all the people, sons and daughters of God, are implicated in the dishonor of disobedience.

Psalm 106:1–5, 40–48

The poet echoes the language of covenant central to Israel's self-understanding: "chosen ones," "your [God's] nation," "your [God's] heritage," "his [God's] people" (vv. 4–5, 40). The author also invokes the tone of Deuteronomy, which asserts that God punishes the nation with oppression or rewards the nation with justice, deliverance, and compassion, in accordance with their unwillingness or willingness to adhere to divine law. Psalm 106:6–39 describes various ways that Israel in the past and in real time rebelled against God by violating divine law. Deuteronomic law asserted that Israel was called to worship God only and practice justice throughout the community, giving special attention to those who were poor. Yet Israel had worshiped other deities (even sacrificing their children to these deities) and had wantonly practiced injustice, disregarding the stranger and disenfranchising the poor. As a result, God became angry and sent them into exile.

But a more nuanced picture of God emerges as the poet more deeply reflects on the history and experience of the people with their God. Israel's God had not simply given a knee-jerk response to the nation's rebelliousness, but upon hearing their cries remembered the covenant God initiated and, further, showed "compassion according to the abundance of [God's] steadfast love" (v. 45). The poet wants the congregation to face fully and unflinchingly the fact of their sin. But even more, the poet wants the people to recognize that God did not (and does not) abandon the community to the consequences of its past sins. As God was repeatedly present to help Israel in its past, so God is present now to help restore the community by reaffirming their covenanted status and reestablishing for them their holy purpose in the world. The community needs to do its part by turning to God.

Sojourner Truth Day is observed on the day the Nineteenth Amendment to the U.S. Constitution was ratified, granting women the right to vote, a cause to which Sojourner Truth was deeply committed. The confluence of Sojourner Truth Day and the theme of women's liberation represented by suffrage could prompt the preacher to lament ways that women of color in North America continue to face race, class, and gender oppression. The preacher can further help the congregation recognize ways that North American culture as a whole continues to pay for the sin of violating God's intention of egalitarianism in human community. Nonetheless, in the spirit of the poet and the prophet, the sermon could also invite the congregation to join womanist theologians and others in working with God for the great era of equality toward which Sojourner Truth pointed us.

Luke 1:26–38

The annunciation set in motion the fulfillment of the high promise of prophetic messianism—that God would in the fullness of time send a Messiah who would lead the world to conform in all ways to God's desire for people to live together in justice, peace, love, and abundance. The word "messiah" (*Christos* in Greek) means "anointed one," so that *the* Messiah/Christ would be God's anointed instrument, who would fully and finally establish the justice, peace, and salvation that God intends for the world God created and loves.

This text makes a striking claim. Some Christians become greatly exercised over the question of whether Mary was truly a "virgin" or merely a "young maiden" when Jesus was conceived. However, the technical virginity of Mary is not necessary for such an incarnation. In any event, another aspect of the text is more important. The prophetic Messiah/Christ is conceived in an unlikely woman: unmarried, not a member of the circles of power, modest in income, and living in an out-of-the-way place. The prophetic Messiah/Christ therefore does not operate with conventional displays of raw power amid great social acclamation but, rather, works for social renewal through unlikely people and settings.

An heir of Jewish faith in God's promise, Mary is initially perplexed, interestingly, not by the fact that the angel has come but by Gabriel's salutation: "Greetings, favored one! The Lord is with you" (v. 28). Not only are angels assumed in her cosmology; there lingers in her unconscious—or, better, in her *sub*conscious—*expectation*, expressed theologically as *hope*, a theme that her conscious, workaday experience would suggest a need for, as a citizen of an occupied land. Almost immediately she accepts God's invitation to bear the prophetic Messiah/Christ. For the Gospel writer Luke, the virgin's response to the angel is a model for all who receive the news that "God was in Christ" Jesus, working to bring about a renewed world.

In her setting, Sojourner Truth was, like Mary, an unlikely vessel through whom God was working for abolition, gender equality, and other elements of a renewed world. Yet, like Mary, Sojourner Truth embraced God's invitation to be an instrument of justice. In the sermon, the preacher could help the community identify unlikely women today who join Mary and Sojourner Truth in pointing us toward God's renewing purposes.

Moreover, this text is pertinent to a particular issue facing women today. In some communities, fully 70 percent of children are born to single women.

This story is a marvelous illustration of God-with-us in every way! Every woman of childbearing age, ability, and desire should understand what Mary was given to know and with which she fully complied: that at conception the Holy Spirit can and will be upon you, that every child who is born is holy and is a son or daughter of God, capable of contributing to the coming reign of peace and justice.

2 Corinthians 3:12–4:2

Although this passage has been used in facile ways to certify Christianity as the successor religion to a failed Judaism, this is not Paul's point here. Paul does not reject Judaism as a worn-out religion or an old covenant whose adherents are inherently veiled, that is, who are unable to perceive God's purposes of love for all. Rather, the veil that Paul describes lying over Jewish minds is the refusal of some in that community to recognize Christ Jesus as God's means of fulfilling God's purpose to bless the Gentiles. This intent was present at the beginning of the old covenant (e.g., Gen. 12:1–3). Some Jewish people in Paul's day did convert to Christianity. To Paul, those who did not had "veiled minds," because they did not recognize that, through Christ Jesus, God was bringing other nations into covenant relationship as well. Paul wants Jewish people and all others to honor each other as members of God's beloved community. Thus the clause "all of us, with unveiled faces" (v. 18) can be broadly, even universally construed as referring to the fact that both Jewish and Christian people should recognize the ongoing work of the genuinely inclusive, loving, truth-telling, prophetic Spirit of Messiah/Christ in the unfolding new world.

When relieved of anti-Jewish sentiment, the motif of the veil can be a powerful symbol for today's congregation. In Sojourner Truth's era, many people of European origin had veiled faces, in that they did not see the injustice of uprooting people from Africa and enslaving them in the Americas. Many men likewise had veiled faces, not seeing the injustice of oppressing women, denying them the right to vote, and limiting their social roles. The preacher can join the apostle and Sojourner Truth, leading the congregation to recognize the veils blithely hanging across people's minds today regarding race, ethnicity, gender, and other matters. The preacher can help the congregation discover how life lived prophetically, in the Spirit of Christ, helps to remove those veils that blind us to God's good purposes.

Proper 15 [20]

Kah-Jin Jeffrey Kuan

1 KINGS 2:10–12; 3:3–14
PSALM 111

PROVERBS 9:1–6
PSALM 34:9–14
EPHESIANS 5:15–20
JOHN 6:51–58

"A single conversation with a wise man is better than ten years of study." So says an old Chinese proverb. In this week's lectionary texts, we find enough food for thought for multiple conversations on the way of wisdom—a way that involves grueling discernment between "good" and "evil" and relentless pursuit of what is "right" and "just." We have a royal narrative of a "wise" monarch; psalms of praise of divine covenantal promises; proverbial warnings against foolishness; and didactic missives about "bread of life" for "children of light."

1 Kings 2:10–12; 3:3–14

This text relates the transition of royal political leadership. David has died, and Solomon sits enthroned. The mention of David is a means to get to the story of Solomon. The Deuteronomistic Historian makes it clear that Solomon's rule (*malkût*) is now firmly established (2:12).

The lectionary skips to 3:3 with the Deuteronomist presenting an episode at the beginning of Solomon's reign stressing his religious devotion in the footsteps of his father (3:3a). Yet that affirmation is quickly mitigated by the Deuteronomist's comment that Solomon unfortunately "sacrificed and offered incense at the high places [*bāmôt*]" (3:3b). This statement foreshadows Solomon's future: at these high places the Israelites turn away from God.

Solomon sacrifices at Gibeon, the "principal high place" (3:4). Ironically, Solomon chose to perform his religious duties at a high place, rather than in Jerusalem where the ark, the symbol of the Lord's presence, is located (3:15). Solomon's decision to go to Gibeon serves a subtle theological purpose for

361

the Deuteronomistic Historian, who sanctions the monarch for his failure
to keep the nation together because of his propensity to worship other gods
(1 Kgs. 11:33).

In spite of Solomon's choice of venue for worship, God takes the initiative
to offer Solomon whatever the latter asks (3:5). Solomon petitions for the
ability to "discern between good and evil" (3:9), and this request is pleasing
to God, who agrees to grant him "a wise [chākām] and discerning [nābôn]
mind" (3:12). Furthermore, God throws in several things that Solomon does
not request—riches, honor, and longevity. In sapiential tradition, these things
come as a result of wisdom (Prov. 3:13–18). Here the Deuteronomic theologian offers a different perspective: such human desires for longevity, riches,
and honor come not from human wisdom, but are gifts from God, just as
wisdom itself is.

On the basis of the lectionary selection, it would be easy to focus on Solomon's piety, humility, and God-pleasing request for wisdom. However, a
preacher should consider the narrative in between 1 Kings 2:12 and 3:3, for
this section portrays a different side of Solomon. Solomon orders the execution of his brother Adonijah when the latter requests to have as wife Abishag
the Shunammite, the young virgin sent to keep David warm (1:1–4). Solomon
banishes Abiathar and orders the killing of Joab, the commander of David's
army, as well as Shimei, whose life David had promised to spare (2:8). Thus,
though Solomon's rule is already secure (2:12), he brutally kills off his enemies. The greater irony is that David told Solomon that it will take "wisdom"
on Solomon's part to dispose of Joab and Shimei (2:6, 9).

While Solomon's request for wisdom is admirable, justice-seeking preaching requires that we do not ignore the dark side of this monarch. Subtly the
Deuteronomistic Historian inserts details that make us wonder how a divinely
blessed monarch practices his divinely given gift. The double-sidedness of
human nature found in this story echoes in the poem by the Zen master Thich
Nhat Hanh, "Please Call Me by My True Names":

> I am the twelve-year-old girl,
> refugee on a small boat,
> who throws herself into the ocean after being raped by a sea pirate,
> and I am the pirate, my heart not yet capable of seeing and loving.[1]

Another interesting detail is the location of divine appearance. While the
high place of Gibeon may signal Solomon's propensity for "other gods," at
this very place God comes to the monarch in a dream. What does it mean that

1. Thich Nhat Hanh, *Peace Is Every Step: The Path of Mindfulness in Everyday Life* (New York: Bantam Press, 1992), 124.

Solomon receives a gift that seals his rulership at a holy site that is *not* dedicated to the worship of Israel's God? Such holy ambiguity could not be more profound, given the disputes over "sacred space" in our time. In the biblical witness God has a propensity to show up at unexpected places.

Proverbs 9:1–6

Proverbs 9 is easily broken down into three parts: verses 1–6, verses 7–12, verses 13–18. There is a clear parallel between the description of *chokmôt*, Lady Wisdom (vv. 1–6), and the description of *'ešet kĕsîlût*, Dame Folly (vv. 13–18). The juxtaposition of Wisdom and Folly is interrupted by the writer's judgment against the "scoffers" and the "wicked," who despise and dismiss wise counsel (vv. 7–12). We find here the well-known admonition "The fear of the LORD is the beginning of wisdom" (v. 10a).

The chapter begins with Lady Wisdom building her house. Likely, the house in this text alludes to the cosmos.[2] In Proverbs 3:19–20, God founded the earth by *wisdom*, established the heavens by *understanding*, and split the depths by *knowledge*. Similarly, Proverbs 24:3–4 speaks of a house being built by wisdom, being established by understanding, and having its rooms filled by knowledge.

While the text alludes to cosmos building, the notion of "house" occurs metaphorically here for a "way of life." Both Lady Wisdom and Dame Folly extend an invitation to others to turn toward their "house," their way of life. While Lady Wisdom goes out of her way to prepare a feast (vv. 2–3), Dame Folly just sits at the door of her house waiting to catch those who pass by (vv. 14–15). The contrast is stark. The choice is between life and death. Those who come into Wisdom's house feast and enter into life (vv. 5–6). Those who come into Folly's house find death awaiting (v. 18).

However, just as the way of wisdom scrutinizes assumptions of "good" and "evil," we must scrutinize the jarring portraiture of the two "feminine" characters here: Lady Wisdom, the resourceful mistress of the house, and Dame Folly, the seductress who entices passersby into shady activities. "Just preaching" questions such reification of "feminine virtues" and "feminine wiles" in the lives of real women. After all, how many capable women can live up to the standards of Proverbs 31, and how many are deemed "wicked" for refusing to bear the cosmos on their backs?

---

2. Raymond C. Van Leeuwen, "The Book of Proverbs: Introduction, Commentary, and Reflection," in *The New Interpreter's Bible*, ed. Leander E. Keck et al. (Nashville: Abingdon Press, 1997), 5:101.

Nevertheless, we do not want to lose sight of the divine image in Lady Wisdom. With hysteric generosity, the Holy One sets the table and invites humanity to eat and rest, so that we may live and walk in the way of insight.

Psalm 111

Psalm 111 is a song of praise beginning with *hallelujah* and is an alphabetic acrostic, meaning that each half verse begins with a consecutive letter of the Hebrew alphabet. This mnemonic device, unfortunately, is lost in translation.

The psalm begins with an imperative, *hallelujah*: praise God. The psalmist gives thanks to God with "my whole heart." The Hebrew *lēbāb* (heart) is not the seat of emotion, but rather the seat of intellect. Hence, the psalmist has in mind mindful, thoughtful, and intellectual praise rather than simple emotion. Such praise is most appropriately done in the company of those who seek to do what is right.

The psalm speaks of God's works in terms of greatness, honor, majesty (vv. 2–3), faithfulness, and justice (v. 7). The wonder and power of God is tempered with a description of God as gracious and merciful (or compassionate), doing the most basic things: providing food as well as giving the heritage of other nations to Israel (vv. 5–6), a reference to the exodus and possession of the land of Canaan. God does such deeds to keep the covenant God makes with the people (vv. 5, 9). In verse 7, "works" is paralleled by "precepts." Those who are wise and have understanding take delight in God's works and should therefore not only study God's precepts (v. 2) but also practice them (v. 10).

The psalm is interspersed with justice-related language: righteousness (*sedaqa*), gracious (*hanun*), merciful/compassionate (*rahûm*), faithful/truth ('*ĕmet*), just/justice (*mišpāt*), and covenant (*běrît*). *Sedaqa* connotes a relational quality of covenant obedience, that is, someone does for another who is incapable of doing but only of receiving. *Rahum* is related to the Hebrew word *rehem*, "womb," thus conjuring up the feminine image of the mother's womb protecting the child inside. '*Ĕmet* suggests the reliablity of God or humans in upholding covenantal relationship. *Mišpāt* is a word that can refer to both justice and judgment: it seeks the full integrity of the life of every person. In the sense of justice, *mišpāt* is used to advocate for those in need of support; in the sense of judgment, *mišpāt* confronts those who exploit others. *Běrît* initiates a relationship that is based on mutually assured obligations. Humanity, then, is called to reflect God's works and precepts, most of which have implications for social justice.

A justice-oriented preacher may want to pick up the theme of God's graciousness and compassion. Out of these things, God provides for basic needs.

In a world of striking disparity between the wealthy and the poor, it is a matter of justice that people of faith take seriously what it means to be gracious and compassionate, what it means to be advocates of providing for the most basic needs of all. Failure to do so makes a mockery of the covenantal relationship.

Psalm 34:9–14

Psalm 34 is also an alphabetic acrostic (see comments on Ps. 111 above). It is a song of thanksgiving on account of some unspecified deliverance (vv. 4, 6, 15, 17–18). Its link to this week's wisdom theme comes by way of the phrase "the fear of the LORD" (v. 11) and the affirmation of life.

Opening with praise of God (vv. 1–3), the psalmist speaks about a personal experience of being delivered and encourages others to "look to [God]" (v. 5) so that they may share in this experience. Verse 9 admonishes the community to "fear the LORD." The word "fear" (yārē') connotes not only reverence or awe but even more the notion of being afraid. Often fear leads one to seek God and to do what is right (see Job 1:1–5). This text also implies that wisdom and the desire to choose life come out of this fear of God.

The one who fears the Lord stays away from evil and deceit and does good (vv. 13–14). Such a person will seek peace (šālôm). The Hebrew verb šālēm means "to be complete, to be finished, to be sound." Hence, the noun šālôm connotes "wholeness, health, well-being, completeness, soundness, peace." Peace is, therefore, primarily used as a positive notion—wholeness, health, well-being, completeness—and not simply a negative, namely, the absence of war. To have šālôm is to have the resources—physical, spiritual, emotional, economic—for a community's well-being. Working for such peace requires a deep commitment to justice.

This understanding is founded on the concept of bĕrît šālôm, "a covenant of peace." A covenant binds two parties in a relationship based on mutually agreed obligations. Humans in a covenantal relationship with God are implicitly bound by ethical values. Thus the psalmist says, "Righteousness and peace will kiss each other" (Ps. 85:10).

Ephesians 5:15–20

This chapter begins with an admonition to live wisely by calling the congregation to imitate God (vv. 1–2), an important idea in the Hellenistic world. By imitating God, the congregation become "children of light" (v. 8). Hence, their speech and conduct must differ from those of the children of darkness, who are involved in fornication, impurity, greed, and obscene and vulgar speech.

Verses 15–20, introduced by the Greek conjunction *oun*, "therefore," indicate that the congregation is called to wisdom living because "the days are evil" (vv. 15–16). They are to live as the wise and not as fools–echoes of sapiential teaching. The juxtaposition of the wise people and the fools recalls the comparison and contrast of Lady Wisdom and Dame Folly. Dame Folly, personified as a loose woman (Prov. 7:5), seduces those who are unwise into a life of the flesh (Prov. 7:6–27). Lady Wisdom calls those who are wise to a life of prudence, intelligence, righteousness, and justice (Prov. 8:1–21). Indeed "the fear of the LORD is hatred of evil. Pride and arrogance and the way of evil and perverted speech I hate" (Prov. 8:13).

Similarly, to be wise in Ephesians means dissociating from evil. Moreover, wisdom living entails refraining from excessive drinking (and eating) and being filled with the Spirit. The writer makes this contrast because drunkenness and being Spirit filled manifest themselves in the loss of some physical faculties. Excessive drinking and eating are a matter of justice because such forms of debauchery have little regard for others. Wise living, finally, finds expression in thanksgiving to God because the wise life is a gift of God.

Justice seekers must be cautious about speaking too casually about the polarities of good and evil. Seeking to live wisely is a constant process of discerning. Yet few things in life can be defined as purely good or evil. While it is important to name evil, one must recognize the danger of naming something evil, because such an action can easily but inappropriately demonize the other. For example, some Christians claim that "Islam is of the devil," thus categorically demonizing all Muslims.

John 6:51–58

This text belongs to the "bread of life" discourse that begins in 6:35 and ends in 6:58. The chapter opens with Jesus by the Sea of Galilee and the crowd following him because of his signs and wonders (v. 1). Jesus raises the necessity of feeding the hungry crowd, thus leading to the discovery of a boy with five barley loaves and two fish and the miraculous feeding of the five thousand (vv. 4–13). The theme of bread continues with the crowd's mention of manna in the wilderness, the "bread from heaven" according to their religious heritage (v. 31). The appeal to ancestral memory elicits a teaching response from Jesus, who instructs the crowd that the bread from heaven was given by God and not Moses (v. 32).

The request of the crowd for the "premium" bread leads to this discourse about the "bread of life." In a double twist, Jesus turns the conversation about bread types into a self-identifying act with the declaration that he is "the bread of life" (v. 35), the "true bread from heaven" (vv. 32, 38, 41), sent by God

(vv. 44–46). *This* bread gives "eternal life." This section of the discourse contains a sapiential theme in the close connection between teaching and bread and life.[3] Raymond Brown finds "a clear reference to the sapiential symbolism of the bread" in 6:45, where Jesus cites from the prophets, "And they shall all be taught by God," to show what is taking place among the crowd that has come to him and hears him.[4] They who heed the way of insight (Prov. 9) will be "fed."

In our text, the language "bread of life" switches to "living bread." The switch is subtle, perhaps denoting a switch to a eucharistic theme through the subsequent language of flesh, eating, drinking, and living. In John's sense, participating in the Eucharist is participating in Jesus, which is participating in *life* itself, a way of life that derives from source of life, God. As Andrea Bieler and Luise Schottroff note, the "sacramental permeability" of the eucharistic act make possible the joining of that which is ordinary and mundane with what is holy and extraordinary, a state conducive for the ways of justice and ways of peace.[5]

3. Raymond E. Brown, *The Gospel according to John (i–xii)*, Anchor Bible (Garden City, NY: Doubleday, 1966), 272–74.
4. Ibid., 273.
5. See Andrea Bieler and Luise Schottroff, *The Eucharist: Bodies, Bread, and Resurrection* (Minneapolis: Fortress Press, 2007).

Proper 16 [21]

Mary Alice Mulligan

1 KINGS 8:(1, 6, 10–11), 22–30, 41–43

PSALM 84

JOSHUA 24:1–2A, 14–18

PSALM 34:15–22

EPHESIANS 6:10–20

JOHN 6:56–69

Several of the texts for today center around the theme of worship and community. These materials call the church to ponder whether the setting in which our worship takes place is a genuine community in which members perceive themselves bound to one another or simply a collection of individuals. This collective identity is important in the readings from 1 Kings, Ephesians, and John; reflecting on Psalm 34 helps us feel the encouragement of God necessary for continuing the struggle for justice, while reflecting on Psalm 84 leads to the conclusion that the religious community must be radically inclusive. The passage from Joshua raises enervating questions about the God-of-Wiping-Out-the-Canaanites.

1 Kings 8:(1, 6, 10–11) 22–30, 41–43

First and Second Kings rarely get much play in regular church study groups or preaching, stretching as they do from the end of David's life, through the construction of the temple, through a series of hereditary monarchs involved in intrigue, murder, and unfaithfulness to God (excepting Josiah), finally to the destruction of the temple and life in exile. The books of the Kings offer us a liminal position for theological contemplation as the monarchy surges and fails, as the sustaining challenge of the prophets arises. Just as we easily forget the grandmothers on whose shoulders today's prophets stand, so might we neglect the events that give rise to a new era of public calls for righteousness and justice for the poor.

In the eighth chapter of 1 Kings, the writer details the dedication of the temple. We might hear Solomon's prayer echoed in our own weekly worship.

He asks for divine awareness and forgiveness. He acknowledges our inability to contain God or to have all the answers. For modern justice and transformation interests, this text calls us to worship.

In corporate worship, as this passage vividly portrays, we remember the vastness of God. The human energy we forge against injustice and oppression, no matter how passionate, has a limit. On our own, we weaken and fail. The power of evil trumps human will. Good-hearted religious people can overcommit to good causes. In our peace and justice efforts, we must remind the congregation never to forget the necessity of divine companionship. Regular worship remediates our forgetfulness.

God initiates worship, and in our worship we become more than we were. When we pray for "a right spirit within us," we open ourselves to being shaped into a community of righteous power, better able to overcome the evils of injustice and oppression. Worship reenergizes us with Holy Spirit power, reminding us that we belong to God, to whose purposes we have committed our lives.

Psalm 84

In this pilgrimage psalm, we sense the psalmist's intense desire to arrive at the temple to rest in the presence of God. Whether speaking of a specific pilgrimage or a yearning to return from exile or the general desire to be closer than humanly possible to God, this hymn resonates within those who long for a world closer to God and God's purposes. The song paints an image of a glowing life possible only in the presence of the Holy One. In God's house, people live in safety, holiness, and justice. No wonder this picture arouses tremendous yearning in the listener. This psalm gave rise to Marchiene Vroon Rienstra's daily prayer book of feminist readings using psalms. She admits, "As I have written its pages, I have felt like the swallow of the psalms, building a nest of prayer on God's altar, where the feminine in me and other women— and also in men—may find a home."[1] Vroon Rienstra's translation of the psalm overflows with joy at the generous glory of God, with a shift to the feminine for both God and psalmist. Like a tiny swallow, the psalmist may rest secure at God's altar.

Others hear a different reading. S. Tamar Kamionkowski claims Psalm 84 reveals a strong erotic element in the yearning for God. Assuming a masculine worldview, a male psalmist, and a decidedly male God (a virile warrior), the LBGTQA community may welcome this psalm as confirmation of the

---

1. Marchiene Vroon Rienstra, *Swallow's Nest: A Feminist Reading of the Psalms* (Grand Rapids: Eerdmans, 1992), xviii. For worship, I suggest her translation, 9.

appropriateness of male-to-male longing as metaphor for one's yearning for God. "Read in this light, we have a beautiful example of a man's longing with all his body and soul to gaze upon the love of his life."[2]

If people are made in God's image, then God is simultaneously beyond gender (not having physical attributes) and omnigendered,[3] for the entire gender spectrum reflects God's image. Religious authorities have often spurned or maligned the physical body. Yet various Scriptures (including Psalm 84) reveal our legitimate longing for God with our whole being (including our physical selves). We yearn for completeness in and connection to the Holy. This psalm may be interpreted in familiar ways, while affirming our complete humanity. It also presents an opportunity to stretch a congregation's comfort zone about the feminine and erotic features of God.

Joshua 24:1–2a, 14–18

What a difficult book! We revel in Joshua's firm language in claiming the necessity of allegiance to God as the essential ingredient of Israelite identity, yet we shudder to consider the Israelites' readiness to annihilate all Canaanites. What should people of religious conscience make of this muddle? Our congregants must daily choose God, even as other forces are all around demanding allegiance (e.g., patriotic, economic, familial). Almost moment by moment we are required to choose one god or another, so this passage strengthens our commitment. Yet Joshua's language hides the violence. Notice his praise of God, who "drove out before us all the peoples, the Amorites who lived in the land" (v. 18). The original inhabitants of the land did not just catch God's vision and move away. They were driven out. They were slaughtered en masse.[4]

What shall we make of the apparent divine blessing on such killing? As we look around at our world, full of refugees who have fled from slaughter (the photos of machine guns and men swinging machetes come to mind), we know such stealing of people's homelands is wrong. Those who "escape" the initial slaughter are often "slaughtered" by hunger, lack of basic resources, broken lives filled with terror, and even vicious abuses in camps set up to serve or contain them.

2. S. Tamar Kamionkowski, "Psalms," in *The Queer Bible Commentary*, ed. Deryn Guest, Robert Goss, Mona West, and Thomas Bohache (London: SCM Press, 2006), 316.
3. See Virginia Ramey Mollenkott, *Omnigender: A Trans-religious Approach* (Cleveland: Pilgrim Press, 2001), chapter 3.
4. For a North American parallel, see Robert Allen Warrior, "Canaanites, Cowboys, and Indians," in *Ethics in the Present Tense: Readings from Christianity and Crisis 1966–1991*, ed. Leon Howell and Vivian Lindermayer (New York: Friendship Press, 1991), 45–51.

If images of people treated as disposable are not distressing enough, we can remember humanity's slaughter of the earth: centuries-old trees clear cut for factory farming, oceans overfished, and mountaintops removed for coal. How are we to reconcile our commitment to God with such slaughter?

Perhaps the most helpful sermon is preached from the disjunction. The preacher must probably spend time pacing the floor in contemplation on this one and rereading theology textbooks. How do we commit to the God-of-Wiping-Out-the-Canaanites? Some may want to argue the problem away by saying, "That was an ancient understanding, and this is now." But we must be cautious. Do we just cast off ideas from Scripture that do not seem to fit contemporary sensibility? On what then do we base retaining the things that do fit? A sermon from this passage might offer several possible solutions that are applicable, not just to this issue, but to the question of how we appropriately read, interpret, and apply difficult biblical texts in general. The preacher could particularly highlight various options in the Jewish tradition. In addition to being generally informative, this approach would discourage the congregation from thinking that the God-of-Wiping-Out-the-Canannites is the only—or even normative—picture of God in Judaism.

Psalm 34:15–22

This anthropomorphic deity has ears, eyes, and a face, and receives servants into protective refuge. The psalmist paints a comforting figure for those who are beaten down and need rescue, promising that the refugees will not have their bones broken or be condemned. Such words of safety and security are heartening, especially for those who feel vulnerable or needy. But what does this psalm mean in light of brutalities against the innocent (and the guilty, e.g., capital punishment)? We only have to recollect struggles through time and around the world to prove that seekers of justice often *do* have their bones broken and worse. How do we interpret biblical texts that go against our experience of how God interacts in the world? Such questions fit into the issues raised from the Joshua text.

Yet something about this psalm comforts us in spite of the reality of evil. We cling to the promise that regardless of enemies and circumstances against us, God always protects the righteous. Focusing on these divine promises articulates the difference between justice and injustice, between righteousness and evil. We need to keep these distinctions before us, reminding ourselves that even when we are brokenhearted, crushed in spirit, and even physically hurt, righteousness is still righteous and evil is still wrong. Sometimes it is almost enough to know the injustices against us are wrong and that the Holy One is aware.

Marchiene Vroon Rienstra offers a feminist interpretation, explaining her preferred designation for God:

> Frequently I use the name "El Shaddai" for God, which is found often in the Old Testament and which can be translated from the Hebrew as "breasted God," since the root word in Shaddai means "female breast." This is a clearly feminine name for God that supports the female images for God which are present in Scripture.[5]

When we are beaten up or brokenhearted, being nestled in our Mother God's lap is wonderful comfort. In spite of our frailties and failures to bring about justice, when we seek refuge in El Shaddai, we may find ourselves strengthened and recommitted to the struggle.

Ephesians 6:10–20

In keeping with the theme of worship raised earlier, we might connect with the importance of being divinely attired for battle. Remember David's refusing to wear armor that did not fit for the battle he waged against Goliath? Here we are called to don the whole armor of God—attire beyond human traits. We need such materials because those who focus on justice and social transformation often get exhausted, because they have depleted their spiritual reservoirs. Thus the importance of the Ephesian epistle in reminding us of our need to be strengthened by divine power, not mere human willpower. We are called to communal worship as well as communal action. Although we often ignore the reality of "cosmic powers,"[6] the forces we oppose are stronger than human effort can destroy. We need the communal power of the whole body of Christ, which includes divine power filling the church through Christ. The arming of the body is communal. Sze-kar Wan concludes: "To mature as a body of Christ, the earthly representatives of Christ need not just an inward gaze but also an activist spirit of call to Christ's headship, to engage as Christ does the principalities and powers of the world (6:10–20)."[7]

Preaching on the importance of worship reminds the congregation of both their need of God in their justice work and the divine elements at work in worship, for worship is more than liturgy (the work of the people). Worship

5. Rienstra, *Swallow's Nest*, xvi.

6. See Hendrikus Berkhof, *Christ and the Powers*, trans. John Howard Yoder (Scottdale, PA: Mennonite Publishing House, and Kitchener, ON: Herald Press, 1962, 1977); Charles Campbell, *The Word before the Powers: An Ethic of Preaching* (Louisville, KY: Westminster John Knox Press, 2002); Walter Wink, *The Powers That Be: Theology for a New Millennium* (Minneapolis: Augsburg Fortress Press, 1998).

7. Sze-kar Wan, "Ephesians," in *Theological Bible Commentary*, ed. Gail O'Day and David Petersen (Louisville, KY: Westminster John Knox Press, 2009), 413.

includes the Word of God contained in Scripture and preaching (remember, the Reformers claimed preaching *is* Word of God).[8]

In stressing our need for worship to prepare us for justice work, we must not ignore the need for justice and transformation in the church itself. For instance, we must strive for full inclusion of gay men and lesbians in the life and ministry of the church. We cannot put on God's full armor if we continue to deny to the church the gifts of a significant portion of the body. When by the power of God's Word and Spirit we are shaped into God's own people in worship, we are more likely to remain in godly shape as we scatter into the world on Monday morning.

John 6:56–69

This is a multifaceted passage, although it certainly continues the thinking about the power of communal worship raised previously. Not quite seven chapters into the Gospel of John the evangelist already has Jesus speaking eucharistically loaded words. Then painfully this teaching results in the turning away of followers. Simon Peter's words might even seem almost defeatist, "Lord, to whom can we go?" (v. 68). In other words, as attractive as leaving is, we recognize that we are chosen of God, so we have to stay.

How familiar such thinking may be. The teachings of Jesus crack open new possibilities in the congregation, yet some people resist them. Following the line of thinking raised in the Ephesians 6 commentary above, consider the idea that God has created a variety of sexual orientations and gender identities in humanity and pronounced them good. Rather than reflect and struggle with these ideas, some folks prefer to leave for a congregation that speaks in proof-text fashion against such diversity. (Such experiences perhaps should give rise to congregational discussions about what makes a legitimate church.)

The Eucharist imagery in the passage supports both the importance of unity (Comm-union) and the possibility of division (even disciples turn away). If sharing bread and cup make us one with Christ and one with the whole body of Christ (as various theologies claim), we must wonder how divisions are possible. Rafael Avila concurs:

> A community celebration of the Eucharist solemnly commits all Christians to struggle actively against everything that discriminates against and disintegrates humanity. It is a sacrilege, according to St. Paul, when a Christian community, after having received the same bread and the same wine, continues to maintain social, economic, and

---

8. See David Buttrick's discussion in *A Captive Voice: The Liberation of Preaching* (Louisville, KY: Westminster John Knox Press, 1994), 21–23 (43–46).

cultural differences under the pretext that a mystical unity has been established.[9]

Although the spiritual or mystical unity in Christ is an important aspect of the meal, physical unity matters as well. Something spiritual happens that forms us into a body united in more ways than mystically. "We share the bread not because we are one body, but we are one body because we share the bread."[10] We who have broken bread together damage the body if we bicker and divide.

For those who work for social justice, staying together is often most difficult when church members who seem to have held the congregation hostage (e.g., forbidding the ordination of gay men and lesbians, restricting marriage to opposite-sex couples, casting all abortions into the category of murder) stay. How do we witness to the unity of the body when communicants severely disagree about issues of justice and social transformation?

9. Rafael Avila, *Worship and Politics*, trans. Alan Neely (Maryknoll, NY: Orbis Books, 1981), 100.
10. Ibid., 57.

Proper 17 [22]

David Frenchak

Song of Solomon 2:8–13
Psalm 45:1–2, 6–9

Deuteronomy 4:1–2, 6–9
Psalm 15
James 1:17–27
Mark 7:1–8, 14–15, 21–23

The readings for today prompt us to think about the relationship of hypocrisy to social life. Mark warns about the dangers of social hypocrisy. James offers an antidote to such hypocrisy: living out the social values of Jesus, which are also the social values of Israel. The psalms emphasize that the holy God calls for holy living that eschews hypocrisy and includes justice in social relationships. The readings from both the Song of Solomon and Deuteronomy stress that faithful and just relationships exclude hypocrisy.

Mark 7:1–8, 14–15, 21–23

Social justice is necessarily a matter of distribution, and there may not be a better organizing theme for social justice than food. Social justice defines the framework within which particular applications of distributive justice arise. The question of who gets to eat and who does not get to eat, surfaces an abundance of social-justice issues.

This story is centered between the two mass feedings by Christ: the feeding of the five thousand and that of the four thousand (Mark 6:30–44 and 8:1–9). Eating, for those who are not starving, is a universal symbol of gathered community, and ritual and ceremony are natural components around food. Those who follow accepted ritual are blessed to eat, and those who do not are impugned. When these rituals carry religious meaning, what often emerges is social hypocrisy.

Hypocrisy occurs when people publicly subscribe to a moral value that gives them credibility and power, but privately behave in ways that are in sharp contrast to the credibility and power they have attained. Hypocrisy is easily identified with individuals, such as politicians who cheat on their spouses, but it may also be ascribed to whole groups of people who on appearance look as if they are practicing a moral and ethical code, but whose appearance is deceiving. This occurs because there is an assumed benefit to the group. When hypocrisy is ascribed to an identified group, we have social hypocrisy. Social hypocrisy is almost always a formative dynamic and power in issues of social justice.

Social hypocrisy is all around us today and is so prevalent that usually we ignore it. Practically all institutions, businesses, corporations, and political groups practice social hypocrisy. Our North American culture has become so accustomed to social hypocrisy that we have dumbed down our social conscience. There is an almost hypnotic quality to social hypocrisy. Being "two-faced" has become an acceptable way of life in many circles.

In this Gospel text, however, hypocrisy is a sin. This is true at the individual and the group level, but it is often more destructive at the collective level. The hypocritical group wishes to enjoy the approval of the social environment by appearing outwardly moral when functionally they are not. A good example is advertisements that suggest a particular company is committed to a sustainable environment, but where and how the company makes and spends money tell a totally different story. Budgets are, after all, moral documents.

Religious institutions are in particular danger of social hypocrisy, because they are value based and value driven. Social hypocrisy occurs when groups choose not to pay the price of commitment to their values. We do well to be aware of and inform our religious institutions and our congregations of the ever-present danger of this sin.

For more than thirty years, in my work in preparing pastors for urban ministry, I have been privileged to work with many denominations and seminaries (both evangelical and progressive), as well as a variety of churches and racial/ethnic groups. I testify that social hypocrisy can, all too easily, become a way of life in the culture of religious institutions. When religious social hypocrites rise to power, they bring religion and the gospel itself into disrepute.

In today's Gospel, Mark does not criticize the eating practices particular to Judaism. Jewish eating customs intend to help the community remember the One who fed them and to sanctify the body. Jewish food practices are intended to strengthen Jewish identity and therefore to help the community resist assimilation. Each time Jewish people eat, they are reminded that they serve the one, true, sovereign God and that their mission is to live according to God's values, so that all peoples (i.e., Jewish and Gentile communities) can live in love, peace, and justice. Mark does not reject these values and practices.

Instead, Mark criticizes people who do not live up to the best of their own tradition.

In a polemical effort to cast the Pharisees and the scribes in a bad light, Mark pictures them as looking askance at Jesus' disciples who were eating with "common" (*koinē*) hands (v. 2). Here Mark caricatures the Pharisees and the scribes and paints Jesus as a prophet confronting the sin of social hypocrisy.

Jesus was neither hypnotized by social hypocrisy, nor did he dumb down his prophetic word. Jesus calls social hypocrisy what it is: sin. Jesus names the hypocrisy. The Pharisees and the scribes ask him, "Why do your disciples not walk about according to the tradition of the elders, but (with) common hands they eat the bread?"[1] But he said to them, "Beautifully did Isaiah prophesy concerning you hypocrites, as it has been written, 'This people values me with the lips, but their heart they keep far from me. But idly they worship me, teaching as doctrines commandments of people. They let go the commandment of God to hold the tradition of people.'"[2]

Mark's basic message in this passage does not depend upon caricaturing the Pharisees and scribes. Any person or community can manifest hypocrisy. "Hear me all, and understand: There is nothing outside the person coming into that person which is able to defile that one, . . . but the things out of the person, coming out, are the things defiling a person. For from within, out of the heart of people, come out the evil thoughts, unlawful sex, thefts, murders, adulteries, covetous thoughts, iniquities, deceit, excess, an evil eye, blasphemies, pride, foolishness—all these evil things come out from within, and they defile a person."[3] Mark's essential point is that behaviors disrupt community and consequently have social consequences. Gentiles can manifest these misbehaviors.

The larger social context is instructive. This story is preceded by the feeding of the five thousand on the Jewish side of the Sea of Galilee, and the calming of the sea as they go over to "the other side"—the Gentile side—of the sea. Jesus' goal is the integration of both Jews and Gentiles into the community of the realm. The first feeding was among Jews. The Gentile feeding will come in chapter 8 with the feeding of the four thousand. This text assures readers that Gentiles can join Jewish people in the community of the realm, because what comes out of Gentiles can manifest the values of the realm.

1. Mark 7:5 as translated by John Petty, "Lectionary Blogging: Mark 7:1–8, 14–15, 21–23," Progressive Involvement, http://www.progressiveinvolvement.com/progressive_involvement/2009/08/lectionary-blogging-mark-7-18-1415-2123.html (accessed August 27, 2010).
2. Mark 7:6–7 as translated by ibid.
3. Mark 7:18, 20–23 as translated by ibid.

James 1:17–27

This text is an excellent companion to the Gospel reading. James wrote to a community of believers, people entirely aware of Jesus. The letter was written not to bring its readers to faith, but to instruct its readers on how to live out the faith they already had.

These eleven verses move in a logical progression. Verses 17–18 ground all that follows, stating unambiguously that all that is good comes from God, the source of lights, "with whom there is no variation or shadow due to change." James poetically acknowledges God's creative works and God's consistent faithfulness and then reminds us of our call to be the "first fruits."

The verses that follow offer concrete instruction on what it means to be firstfruits. Verses 19–21 provide instruction for receiving and internalizing the "implanted word that has the power to save your souls." A forceful call to action comes next in verses 22–27. The command to be "doers" of that word rather than only "hearers" leaves little room for compromise. The phrase "orphans and widows" (v. 27) represents all oppressed peoples—those about whom God is particularly concerned (see Isa. 1:16–17)—and, therefore, those for whom we are challenged to show particular concern.

James's emphasis on being "doers" has created dissonance among some theologians regarding this epistle. Some see James's message as conflicting with "faith only." This passage has made others uncomfortable because it can ignite flames of Christian commitment to social justice. Martin Luther famously referred to it as "an epistle of straw," with "nothing of the nature of the gospel about it."[4]

Contrary to these denunciations, James lays out not only the nature of the gospel but also what the gospel looks like when it is lived. The epistle lays out the practice of faith in the social community. James calls into question the role of anger, "righteous indignation," as a way of functioning and of honoring the word of truth. People in James's congregation were being hypocritical regarding that word. In our setting, however, righteous indignation is often accompanied by unfortunate arrogance and superiority.

The word of truth was something to which they listened with their heads, but it made no difference in the way they acted. The word of truth became doctrine about which they could argue, but it was not translated into a spirit of love or a behavior of service. Thus they were guilty of the sin of hypocrisy. James is clear: the issue is not how we declare the word of truth, but whether the word of truth is reflected outwardly by our spirit and our action.

---

4. Martin Luther, *Works of Martin Luther* trans. C. M. Jacobs (Philadelphia: Muhlenberg Press, 1932), 444.

I once heard a sermon preached from this text. After the passage was read, the pastor summarily told the worshipers that they were the sermon that morning. The preacher then dismissed the congregation on the spot and told them to go into their community and "look after the distressed." This was a way of putting into practice the genius of the text.

Psalm 45:1–2, 6–9 and Psalm 15

Separation of church and state was a foreign concept to the ancient Israelites. Their political leader was also their spiritual leader, and the expectation of the virtues and qualities exemplified by the monarch were in line with how they understood God.

Psalm 45 celebrates those virtues. Most scholars understand that this psalm lifts up the ruler of Israel on the wedding day and is thus referred to as a royal psalm. The sovereign is said to be most excellent, blessed forever, and clothed with splendor and majesty. The ruler will ride victoriously in the name of truth, humility, and righteousness. The scepter of the ruler will be one of justice, characterizing this reign as equitable, fair, and honoring God. The sovereign who loves righteousness and hates wickedness is anointed by God to a place of special privilege (v. 7; cf. Ps. 2 and 2 Sam. 7:8–16). This ruler is also known among the nations as indicated in the reference to the "daughters of [rulers]" (v. 9) and "the richest of the people" (v. 12). The result is that his name will be perpetuated throughout all generations as his children take up political offices (v. 16–17). Thus the Israelite monarch is pictured as exalted above all, possessing an eternal throne, much like God (v. 6). Indeed, the universal sweep of verse 17 indicates that all nations will praise this heir to David. Further, like God, he too blesses righteousness and punishes wickedness. While this was truly a deeply felt and believed image, it was not fulfilled by David, and thus this description is in search of the anointed one.

While none of us would ascribe these divine attributes to any of our immediate leaders, one cannot help but imagine what our society would look like if we raised our expectations of our political rulers to these standards, particularly in the understanding of the political leaders' role and responsibility related to social justice.

Psalm 15 connects holiness and social justice. While our society, including the church, seems to have lost the idea of holiness, it was a key concept to Israel, and we would be served well if we wrestled with the importance of the focus on holiness and its connection to social justice, clearly spelled out in this text.

God is holy. So what is required of human beings who are not holy to approach the Holy? Verse 2 lays out the character requirements: the way people are on the inside. We should be blameless (i.e., not guilty), because we know, to the best of our ability, we do what is right and because we speak the truth. One might easily understand this to mean that people of God are not hypocritical, they are not two faced, and they have a pure heart. This understanding appropriately fits individuals and systems, institutions and nations.

Then follows a descriptive list of outer behaviors not unlike those lifted up in the epistle of James. People of God do not slander others. They treat their neighbors justly. They do not talk about friends behind their backs; they do not enjoy associating with evil people but enjoy associating with those who are servants of God; people of God are honest about real losses in all financial transactions and do not try to make money from the losses of others, but instead keep their promises (financial) even when doing so costs them. Finally, people of God do not profit from schemes that are unjust or unfair. Social justice almost always has an economic factor, and people who want to be free to be in the sacred places of life on earth are individuals who operate ethically in their use of money.

Song of Solomon 2:8–13 and Deuteronomy 4:1–2, 6–9

When religion is anthropocentric, it has very little to tell us that is good news about passion and desire. When this happens, culture secularizes sexuality and misuses it. Pornography substitutes for mystery. There is, however, mystery at the core of this beautiful and passionate expression of erotic love. Here passionate love becomes sacred as an expression of beauty: the loving couple's longing becomes devotion, and lovemaking becomes worship. Here the cup of love overflows.

While many have tried to allegorize the Song of Solomon, one cannot escape the fact that the author actually was doing what he or she appeared to be doing: celebrating human love with poetry, reveling in romance and sexuality.

Those who are aware of the ways our culture makes an idol of romantic love and celebrates lust (which is romance's cruder expression) may be uncomfortable with the Song of Solomon. Were it not for the Song of Solomon, we might conclude that we have to choose between a culture that understands only myopic romance and a faith that leaves no room for romance. The presence of the Song of Solomon in the Bible reminds us that we can have God, fidelity, all the higher expressions of love, and still have our romance too.

The Song of Solomon reminds us that to be in love with someone is to find your whole being tied up with the beloved, to want to be wherever the lover is, to want good things for the lover. You can no more forget the one you love than you could forget your own name. You want to share all of yourself with the lover, and you want all of him or her in return. True love is experienced only when there is no hypocrisy. Without taking anything away from the beauty of this human expression and understanding of romantic love, it can be a life-changing experience when one seriously entertains the idea of God as our lover.

The Deuteronomy text can be read and understood as God's injunction to the freed slaves about the importance of keeping faith in word and action with what God has taught them if they want to enter the promised land. They must not be hypocritical by taking God's blessing of freedom but not living by God's word. Their faithfulness will be a remarkable witness to all nations about what it means to serve justice and a God of justice. The other peoples of the world will see that faithfulness leads to true and lasting blessing.

Proper 18 [23]

Barbara K. Lundblad

PROVERBS 22:1–2, 8–9, 22–23   ISAIAH 35:4–7A
PSALM 125   PSALM 146
JAMES 2:1–10 (11–13), 14–17
MARK 7:24–37

There's no need to twist this Sunday's readings into justice texts—each one speaks or shouts justice. Readings from Proverbs and James focus on justice for the poor. Isaiah and Psalm 146 echo the Gospel's focus on healing. Yet some who hear these readings may not experience justice for themselves or their loved ones. What do we say to people who live with disabilities when everyone in these texts is cured? How will women feel about Jesus' demeaning treatment of the Syrophoenician woman? Should any desperate mother be treated like this? More than a few people will be troubled by this picture of Jesus. Will the preacher try to defend Jesus, or was Jesus the one who needed to be healed?

Mark 7:24–37

Listen to her! There are only two places in Mark where women have speaking parts.[1] One happens at the very end of this Gospel: "Who will roll away the stone for us from the entrance to the tomb?" In today's Gospel we hear the voice of a particular Syrophoenician woman. She stands out in the Gospel as a feisty woman who dared to argue with Jesus. Listen to her! Or, to quote Jesus in the second story: " 'Ephphatha,' that is, 'Be opened.' "

But what do we make of Jesus in this story? Jesus has come into the region of Tyre, a Gentile region where he will remain through the beginning of the next chapter. Whose house he entered the narrator doesn't tell us, but in

---

1. Joan L. Mitchell, *Beyond Fear and Silence: A Feminist-Literary Reading of Mark* (New York: Continuum, 2001), 108. Mitchell draws from Joanna Dewey, "Women in the Synoptic Gospels: Seen but Not Heard?" *Biblical Theology Bulletin* 27, no. 2 (1997):59.

typical Markan fashion, Jesus wanted his presence to be a secret. Yet a woman somehow got inside that house and bowed down at Jesus' feet. Though we don't know her name, her cultural identity is not a secret: "Now the woman was a Gentile, of Syrophoenician origin" (v. 26). Should Jesus be surprised to encounter a Gentile woman in a Gentile region? He was the outsider inside the house.

This unnamed woman was a desperate mother, willing to do anything to find a cure for her daughter. She bowed down at Jesus' feet and begged—just as Jairus, the leader of the synagogue, had done in Mark 5:21–43. Jesus went with him without asking any questions. But here Jesus' response is different: "Let the children be fed first, for it is not fair to take the children's food and throw it to the dogs" (v. 27). Because the word "dog" here is uncompliment-ary, it is worth noting that Jewish people in antiquity typically spoke respect-fully of Gentiles, and, indeed, that many Jewish people anticipated that God would save Gentiles. While some Christians think that Jewish people com-monly referred to Gentiles as "dogs," that was not so.

Was Jesus exhausted? Was he upset that his place inside the house had been discovered? Jesus had already healed a Gentile—the Geresene demoniac (5:1–20), who didn't even ask for healing! Why is Jesus so harsh with this pleading mother? Our temptation is to prettify Jesus by saying he was testing the woman's faith, but there is no indication of that motivation in the text.

The woman becomes the primary actor. She takes Jesus' words and gives them new meaning:

> She counters Jesus' closed word with a transformative word from her own experience and social location. . . . She speaks the truth of her experience in her Gentile household, where dogs have a place and eat the crumbs children let fall beneath the table. She models an active, transformative receiving of the gospel that emancipates its word from socially and culturally constructed biases and boundaries.[2]

Her transformative word transforms Jesus, and her daughter is restored to health. This woman marks a turning point between two stories about feeding and crumbs. In chapter 6 Jesus feeds five thousand people on the Jewish side of Galilee. In chapter 8 Jesus will feed four thousand in Gentile territory. As they row back home and the disciples realize they've forgotten to bring bread, Jesus reminds them of these two stories. He asks them how many baskets were left over in the first story. "They said to him, 'Twelve'" (8:19). Then, he asked the same question about the leftovers in the other story. "And they said to him, 'Seven'" (8:20).

---

2. Mitchell, *Beyond Fear*, 108.

"Then Jesus said to them, 'Do you not yet understand?'" (8:21). He wants the disciples (and us) to remember what has happened in these feeding stories. There was food in abundance, with leftovers (crumbs)—twelve baskets for the people of Israel and seven for the Gentiles. Jesus is teaching his disciples the lesson he learned from the Syrophoenician woman. Listen to her! Her story is bigger than one Gentile woman, and the story of the deaf man with a speech impediment is bigger than he is. The word Jesus spoke to that man in private is a word he speaks to the readers of this Gospel: "Ephphatha! Be opened" (7:34). Be open to a word that crosses boundaries and confronts us with truth we haven't seen or heard before.

James 2:1–10

This is the second week in the book of James, and the preacher may have decided to preach a five-week series on this letter. James's words in today's reading can be heard as chastising Jesus' behavior in the Gospel text: "But if you show partiality, you commit sin and are convicted by the law as transgressors" (v. 9). While the Gospel text points to partiality toward one cultural/religious group over another, James focuses on partiality of economic realities that favor wealthy people over those who are poor. The language of this passage is enlivened by the dialogue inside the sanctuary. "Have a seat here, please," we say to the one with fine clothes. "Stand there," or "Sit at my feet," we command the one whose clothes are dirty. No polite "please" for *those* people.

Would we really say such things to people who are poor? We might not even have to decide, because people who are poor are often missing in our congregations. They may come to the soup kitchen or the food pantry during the week but may assume they are not welcome on Sunday. They may not have the right clothes or may fear they can't read the bulletin or sing the songs. No one has put up a sign telling poor people not to come, but the intentionality to bridge economic gaps is often missing. Of course, those who are poor may be in the congregation, but sitting by themselves. Or they may be more comfortable in other congregations and stay away from a middle-class congregation because they do not want the pressure of being asked to attend services (as if in response to the economic benefits they receive).

We might want to ask James how congregations can do what he urges here. Suburbs, cities, and towns are often divided by economics. Pastor Heidi Neumark talks about the day she went from the congregation she served in the South Bronx to a meeting of the Nehemiah Housing Trust on Fifth Avenue. She saw two very different economic pictures of New York City when she rode the subway from one neighborhood to the other and back again. When she got home, she was struck with how rare it is to see both communities:

> My guess is that there weren't many people gazing into the windows of Tiffany's and Illusions 99¢ Store on the same morning. That's too bad, because it does a lot for the renewal of the mind. Will we ever bridge the distance between Mi Jesus Fruits and Vegetables and Cartier? Mercedes-Benz and Pop's Candy Store? . . . Between those who shop there?[3]

There doesn't seem to be as much distance between rich people and poor people in James's letter. Both might show up in the assembly. But James isn't writing an etiquette manual. How people are treated isn't about good manners. It is a test of belief: "Do you with your acts of favoritism really believe in our glorious Lord Jesus Christ?" (v. 1).

Isaiah 35:4–7a and Psalm 146

This text is paired with the healing stories in Luke, affirming that what Isaiah prophesied is fulfilled in the ministry of Jesus: those who are deaf hear and those who are mute speak—in this case within one man. In many ways, Isaiah 35 does not belong here with the destruction and doom of the preceding chapter. Some scholars say these verses come from a later writer known as Second Isaiah. Others argue for a date later still—sixth century BCE or later—surely after the exile. Who moved it? Some things even our best scholarship cannot explain. Our wisdom falls short. The Spirit hovered over the text and over the scribes: "Put it here," breathed the Spirit, "before anyone is ready. Interrupt the narrative of despair."

The poem presents a glorious vision of transformation and wholeness. But how will people with disabilities hear this text? How will they hear the Gospel and Psalm 146? In almost every biblical text about disability, the person with the disability is cured. Yet congregations include someone in a wheelchair, another whose eyesight is failing, and someone whose son or daughter is mentally ill. There are no texts about a person who remains disabled and bears witness to God's power and grace.

To hear such texts, preachers must turn to people who are disabled. Nancy Eiseland died too soon after teaching for several years at Emory University. She was born with a disability that made it difficult and sometimes impossible to walk. In her book *The Disabled God* she writes:

---

3. Heidi Neumark, unpublished Bible study, Evangelical Lutheran Church in America (Consultation on Women and Children Living in Poverty, Chicago, June 26, 1999).

Who is the one we remember in the Eucharist? This is the disabled God who is present at the Eucharist table—God who was physically tortured, arose from the dead and is present in heaven and on earth, disabled and whole. . . . Christ's resurrection offers hope that our non-conventional, and sometimes difficult, bodies participate fully in the imago Dei. . . . God is changed by the experience of being a disabled body.[4]

This is a different picture from Isaiah's vision. Eiseland's writing affirms that the person with the disability is in the image of God without being cured. Another Nancy—Nancy Mairs—writes of her own experience with multiple sclerosis in her book *Waist-High in the World*. Rather than expecting to be cured, she longs for a world that will make room for her as she is. She knows it's impossible to prophesy the contours of her life in the days ahead, but she wants to make a map: "Maps render foreign territory, however dark and wide, fathomable. I mean to make a map. My infinitely harder task is to conceptualize not merely a habitable body but a habitable world: a world that wants me in it."[5]

Perhaps the preacher or worship leader will claim the role of prophet and rewrite the words of Isaiah:

Then the blind woman and her dog
    shall process with the choir;
and the deaf man shall paint the text
    on the sanctuary wall;
the veteran in the wheelchair
    shall serve communion,
and the deaf girl who cannot speak
    shall sign hymns that dance in space.

Psalm 146 echoes the Isaiah text and the Gospel's theme of healing: "The LORD sets the prisoners free; the LORD opens the eyes of the blind. . . . The LORD watches over the strangers" (vv. 7–9). How wonderful God's promise to strangers would sound to the Syrophoenician woman! This psalm begins the finale of praise that ends the Psalter. The four final psalms all repeat the opening words: "Praise the LORD!" This psalm also lifts up other themes of justice. The God of Jacob not only made heaven and earth, not only keeps faith forever, but is the one who "executes justice for the oppressed; who gives food to the hungry" (v. 7). Those themes connect to themes so prominent in James and in Proverbs. Congregations that chant the Psalms during worship

4. Nancy Eiseland, *The Disabled God: Toward a Liberatory Theology of Disability* (Nashville: Abingdon Press, 1994), 107.
5. Nancy Mairs, *Waist-High in the World: A Life among the Disabled* (Boston: Beacon Press, 1997), 6.

will hopefully find tunes that match the celebratory nature of this hymn of praise. In other congregations this psalm could be read responsively as the call to worship. Children can be invited to play instruments for verse 1 that can be used as a refrain: "Praise the LORD! Praise the LORD, O my soul!" People with disabilities—including someone signing the words—would provide another lens to the images of healing.

Proverbs 22:1–2, 8–9, 22–23 and Psalm 125

The lectionary selection jumps around in this chapter of Proverbs, marked by the commas. All of the verses focus on justice for people who are poor, and fit well with the themes of the reading from James. Worship planners could craft these proverbs into a litany or response to the sermon. These verses sound like wise sayings of Ben Franklin or perhaps religious fortune cookies! But these sayings are radically different from the popular prayer of Jabez, which appeared a few years ago on coffee mugs and motivational posters. These proverbs do not pray that God would "enlarge our territory," a phrase that can mean anything from gaining new members to gaining a bigger farm to making more money. Rather, these proverbs challenge hearers to do justice for the poor. How would individuals and congregations be changed if coffee hour mugs said: "Those who are generous are blessed, for they share their bread with the poor" (v. 9)? Or if name tags worn by members and visitors on Sunday morning didn't say, "Hello, my name is . . ." but included the first part of verse 1: "A good name is to be chosen rather than great riches"? Perhaps these ideas seem out of place today, but people can be encouraged to memorize Bible passages or to take verses with them during the week. The Rev. Jacqueline Lewis, senior minister at Middle Collegiate Church in New York City, often speaks about "story-ing a people." What biblical texts will "story" the congregation? These proverbs could help shape the congregation's story toward concern for the common good.

Psalm 125 echoes themes of justice laid out in the Proverbs reading, but those themes may be easy to miss. This is one of several Songs of Ascents traditionally sung or spoken as people went up to the temple in Jerusalem. Mount Zion is a destination, but also a metaphor for those who trust in God. Like the mountain, they cannot be moved. Consider singing the freedom movement song "We Shall Not Be Moved" alongside the psalm:

> We're marching on for justice, we shall not be moved!
> We're marching on for justice, we shall not be moved!
> Just like a tree that's planted by the water:
> We shall not be moved!

That freedom song picks up a central concern of this psalm: justice in the land: "The scepter of wickedness shall not rest on the land allotted to the righteous" (v. 3a). At first glance this might appear to be a promise that wicked foreign powers will not rule the land. A closer look reveals that the psalmist is concerned with how God's people live in "the land allotted to the righteous." The psalmist is talking about their land and their leaders, not somebody else. This land shall be governed with fairness and justice "so that the righteous might not stretch out their hands to do wrong" (v. 3b). Whether this is a warning to the king or to all the people, the psalmist says that going up to Jerusalem is not enough. God is calling people not only to worship but to govern the land with justice.

Perhaps another freedom song would bring that message home:

> Ain't gonna let nobody turn me around,
> Turn me around, turn me around . . .
> I'm gonna keep on a-walkin',
> Keep on a-talkin'
> Marchin' on to freedom land![6]

6. http://www.songsforteaching.com/folk/aintgonnaletnobodyturnmearound.php (accessed June 5, 2010).

Simchat Torah: Joy of the Torah (Mid-September to Early October)

Esther J. Hamori

DEUTERONOMY 34:1–5
GENESIS 2:1–9
2 KINGS 22:8–20
PSALM 119:73–80

Simchat Torah (pronounced sim-khat tor-ah) is a Jewish holiday celebrating the joy that comes with the gift of the Torah (the five books of Moses). In the synagogue, the Torah scrolls are taken from the ark into the congregation, often accompanied by dancing. Simchat Torah comes after Sukkot in the month of Tishrei (between mid-September and early October). The lectionary readings listed above reflect the practice of reading from Deuteronomy and Genesis in succession, honoring the Jewish practice of turning from the end of the Torah to its beginning. These readings (along with readings from the rabbinic tradition) remind us that interpretation involves ongoing conversation with the fullness of Scripture's many visions.

This is Torah's blessing: it gives life to those who study it. That is why the blessing [over reading Torah] says: "God implanted eternal life within us." This is the oral Torah . . . [it] gives forth blessing in the heart and bears fruit. This too, is a gift from God, as it says, "from Me does your fruit come forth" (Hos. 14:9). Even . . . the new interpretations of the sages, are a gift of God. This is the power that Moses left to the entirety of Israel through all generations, to the end of time.[1]

Rabbi Yehuda Leib

1. Rabbi Yehuda Leib Alter, *The Torah of the Sefat Emet*, trans. Arthur Green (Philadelphia: Jewish Publication Society, 1998), 374.

389

The biblical texts for today help the congregation recognize that the joy brought by Torah includes the gift of becoming aware of justice and injustice, so that we can respond accordingly. The reading from Deuteronomy reminds us that the people we exclude and marginalize are also people of God, and urges us to have eyes to see the justice and injustice all around us. The creation stories (Genesis 2:1–9) prompt us to reflect on what it means to be part of the natural environment, and to consider how then to relate to the rest of creation, including one another. The passage from 2 Kings recalls the reform that occurred when a version of Deuteronomy was found during the time of King Josiah, and calls attention to Huldah's role as prophet in that reform. Psalm 119 celebrates the life-giving Torah; the selection for today reminds us that love, mercy, and justice are inseparable.

Deuteronomy 34:1–5

Was it not enough that Moses was not allowed to enter the promised land? Moab was just about the worst place a self-respecting Israelite leader could end up. That is to say, several biblical authors assign a particularly negative role to Moab, from the story of its origin (incest between Lot and his daughters) to that of its exclusion from the worshiping assembly (as punishment for not helping the Israelites during their days in the wilderness). Moses did not simply stop short of entering the promised land; he died and was buried in Moab, the land of those who are excluded.

This text, in which Moses dies among the biblical epitome of the excluded, might prompt us to consider who the excluded are in our society, and what it could mean to be so fully among them. Moreover, we might think about the implications of the fact that this was no accident: God had specifically planned that Moses would die and be buried among the Moabites, as we see already in Numbers 27:12–14 and Deuteronomy 32:48–52. What could it mean for God to choose an "other" land, among an excluded people? Perhaps we could see here that Moab too is God's, that God's plan includes Moab—this other place, these excluded people (as we see most famously in the story of Ruth).

However, God does show Moses the land, saying, "I have let you see it *with your eyes*" (v. 4). Since this is how people generally see, and not a particularly necessary additional phrase, it should be taken as an emphasis: "I have let you see it with your *own* eyes." And here is what Moses saw: he saw the whole land, Gilead as far as Dan, he saw Naphtali, the land of Ephraim and Manasseh, Judah all the way to the Western Sea, he saw all the way down to the Negev, and across the Jordan Valley as far as Zoar (vv. 2–3). God shows Moses everything—the land of the patriarchs, where this happened and that happened, good and bad, and where the reader knows many other things are yet to happen, both good and bad.

The medieval Jewish commentator Rashi said of this passage that God showed Moses the whole land at peace, and also the oppressors who were destined to oppress it. Rashi considered each place that God showed Moses, in light of other biblical texts: God showed Moses the Danites practicing idolatry, but also showed him Samson, the hero who came from Dan. God showed Moses the land of Naphtali in peace, but also showed him Deborah and Barak of Kedesh-Naphtali at war with Sisera and his army. God showed Moses the land of Ephraim and Manasseh at peace, and also showed him Joshua, descended from Ephraim, at war with kings of Canaan, and Gideon, descended from Manasseh, at war with Midian and Amalek. God showed Moses all the land of Judah, at peace and in destruction, and showed him the reign of David and its victories.

According to this tradition, Moses saw all of the peace and all of the war that had happened and would happen in these places. Rashi continued with a play on words in his interpretation of "until the western sea." He suggested as one possibility that instead of reading *hayyam ha'aharon*, "the western sea," we read *ha'aharon hayyom*, "until the last day," to indicate that God showed Moses everything that would happen to Israel "until the last day."[2] Moses saw everything, the good and the bad, the just and the unjust. The prophet who left the legacy of the Torah, the instructions in justice, was able to see all of this. This tradition can remind us that we too should be endeavoring all the time to have eyes to see the justice and injustice in our midst.

Genesis 2:1–9

On Simchat Torah, we go back to the beginning, or, more accurately, we continue the circle from an end to a new beginning. We finish reading the Torah, remember the death of Moses, and then read about the creation of the first humans again. In fact, even in this passage from Genesis 2, we finish and begin again, almost without noticing. The first few verses of the chapter tell the end of one creation story: God has made the earth, greenery, buzzing things, and so on, and finally human beings on the sixth day, and now on the seventh day, God creates the Sabbath (*shabbat*), because on that day God ceased (*vayyishbot*, from the root *sh-b-t*) from the work of creation. This is explicitly the end of the story. Then another voice chimes in with another creation story in 2:4b: "In the day that the LORD God made the earth and the

---

2. *Rashi: The Commentary of Solomon B. Isaac on the Torah*, 2nd ed. (Frankfurt: J. Kauffmann, 1905), Deuteronomy 34:1–2.

heavens," when there were not yet any plants or greenery, and when God had not yet made it rain, at that point, this new creation story says, God made the first human. So even within a Simchat Torah reading, we go from already created back to the beginning.

While these two voices highlight some different ideas (in addition simply to having different perspectives, as in the order of creation), it is enlightening to read them together. The first voice tells us about the Sabbath. In Jewish tradition, one meaning of resting on Shabbat is that although we work and build and create on the other six days, we remember that we are part of creation, and not the Creator. This can prompt us to reflect on how we interact with the rest of the natural environment. The traditional practice of keeping the Sabbath entails not only resting on that day, though; it also involves preparing for it (cooking in advance, for example). We might combine these two ideas and contemplate here how one prepares to be part of creation, to plan ahead in regard to the natural environment of which we are a part.

We also see equality in the Torah's view of the Sabbath: it is a day of rest not only for the employer, but also for the employee; not only for the privileged, but also for the poor. The Torah goes so far as to say that even the animals should be entitled to rest on this day (e.g., Exod. 23:12). How might we act upon an understanding of ourselves as part of creation, equal to other parts? How might we plan ahead for our natural environment in a way that reflects both ecological care and the equality of all peoples? We hear more about global warming, for instance, than about specific issues of environmental racism (i.e., ways in which our society treats wealthy areas and poor areas differently in regard to pollution of various kinds).[3] What actions can we take to combat this kind of environmental injustice?

The second voice offering a creation story directly addresses the centrality of the natural environment that sustains humankind. In this story, the first person created is a man, which in Hebrew is the noun *adam*. While all sorts of damaging traditions have arisen regarding why the first person created was a man, it may simply be for the sake of the theologically significant wordplay: the *adam* is created from the *adamah* (ground, soil); the "earthling" is from the earth, the "human" from the humus. The link between humankind and the earth is established here and runs through the entire Bible.

---

3. See, for example, Robert D. Bullard, *Dumping in Dixie: Race, Class, and Environmental Quality* (Boulder, CO: Westview Press, 2000).

2 Kings 22:8–20

This text tells the story of when "the book of the law" was found, after having been lost for so long that its contents were unknown. This book was some form of Deuteronomy, as we see from Josiah's reaction. He initiates religious reforms in response to reading the contents of the book of the law, and the description of these reforms closely matches instructions in Deuteronomy. These standards were not easy to meet, and the reforms were rough. We do not have the same standards today, but we know all too well that it is not easy to live up to our own standards.

There were many people to whom Josiah's officials could have turned in response to the king's instructions, "Go, inquire of the LORD for me, for the people, and for all Judah" (v. 13). The prophet Jeremiah was active at this time, as was the prophet Zephaniah. Instead of "inquiring of the LORD" through one of these prophets, however, Josiah's officials turn to the prophetess Huldah. Her first words in verse 15 imply that this was Josiah's own choice. We see another surprising element in that verse as well. Huldah initially refers to Josiah as "the man who sent you to me" (v. 15). She knows that he is the ruler, as is clear from the following lines, but she refers only to his actions in seeking her out, not to his title or his power.

Modern readers might be surprised by either or both of these elements. However, there is nothing in the biblical texts to indicate that there was anything unusual in Josiah seeking out a female prophet, even with Jeremiah active, or that there was anything amiss in Huldah's language regarding the monarch. Even in the hierarchical society portrayed in many biblical texts, we see glimmers of the equality of all creation.

Psalm 119:73–80

This stanza of Psalm 119 begins with a poetic remembering of what it means to be a created person: "Your hands have made me and fashioned me; give me understanding that I may learn your commandments." As we saw in Genesis 2, speaking of creation does not only reflect something about our views of God; it also reflects our view of ourselves as part of God's creation, that is, part of nature. In this stanza, however, we see a different emphasis. In verse 73, God's hands bring life. As the psalmist continues, we see an expansion of this praise. In verse 77, it is not only God's hands, but God's mercy that brings life: "Let your mercy come to me, that I may live; for your law [*torah*] is my delight."

What kind of mercy brings life? Mercy is not merely an attitude. The psalmist is not referring to a feeling, but to the Torah. This stanza and the whole psalm are peppered with references to God's commandments, words, judgments, precepts, decrees, and so on. In verses 75–77, the psalmist begins each line with thoughts about how God delivers: "Your *judgments* are right. . . . Let your *steadfast love* become my comfort. . . . Let your *mercy* come to me, that I may live." As we see throughout the Torah, God's justice, love, and mercy are all intertwined. When we rejoice on Simchat Torah, we are not only rejoicing in a book; we are celebrating God's justice, love, and mercy, which together bring life.

There is a Hasidic saying: "On Simchat Torah, we rejoice in the Torah, and the Torah rejoices in us; the Torah, too, wants to dance, so we become the Torah's dancing feet." We do not just study the Torah, the book of justice. We become its dancing feet.

Proper 19 [24]

J. B. Blue

PROVERBS 1:20–33
PSALM 19

ISAIAH 50:4–9A
PSALM 116:1–9
JAMES 3:1–12
MARK 8:27–38

During these middle weeks of Ordinary Time, the bustle of the high holy days is either behind or in front of us. Things are relatively quiet, so much so that the rigor with which we normally reflect upon our relationship with God and others is becoming too relaxed. The readings for Proper 19 give us an opportunity to think about whether the church might be becoming too relaxed. In Proverbs, Wisdom instructs us in the transformed life that relies on God in all things. In the psalms, God reveals care for us in creation, in the law, and in our very testimonies. James stresses that we have the power and charge to speak blessing, and Mark reminds us that discipleship calls us relentlessly.

Proverbs 1:20–33

The first chapter of Proverbs bursts with a loud shout at which Wisdom makes her grand entrance. This entrance is so profound that it demands a setting suitable for her ensuing announcement. Therefore, she takes her place in the street, public squares, busiest corners, and the entrances of the city gates (vv. 20–21). Wisdom has but one question: how long will you continue on your current path toward destruction? This question cuts to the hearts of those to whom she speaks.

To the simple Wisdom asks, "How long will you continue to be naive and open to influences that work against God's purposes?" To the scorners Wisdom asks, "How long will you treat wise counsel with contempt?" To the fools, Wisdom asks, "How long will you remain conceited and opinionated and refuse instruction in God's ways?"[1] Wisdom demands a response to these questions. We can choose to go along with the simple, scorners, and fools; or we can heed Wisdom's call to live in cooperation with God's purposes. Justice demands just actions and a sense of fair play; more importantly, it requires just persons to provoke such actions. This is the purpose of Wisdom's call—the formation and transformation of humankind for the care and creation of a just society in which all can prosper in opportunity and abundance with mutual respect and dignity.

Although Wisdom calls, and calls, and calls, she will not do so forever (vv. 23–25). For those who do not attend to Wisdom, the consequences are clear: trouble and disaster, brought about by our own hands (vv. 26–27). This is the judgment for those who hear, but fail to heed Wisdom's call. Even when distress or calamities waken us from our complacency to seek Wisdom, she will not always spare us from the results of the foolishness of our prior choices. Wisdom refuses to ignore how we insolently ignore the unremitting call to live in the counsel of God (vv. 28–30). However, some listen, and for them Wisdom promises peace and safety (v. 33).

The preacher of today can join the preacher of Proverbs in reminding the reader that life is filled with choices. Life is lived in community, and we who seek to live wisely bear responsibility to consider the consequences of personal and social choices. The preacher could invite the congregation to listen for Wisdom's call in every situation in life: in personal relationships, in the life of the congregation, in the workplace, in school, in recreation, in the life of city, state, and nation. Which choices are wise, and which are foolish?

Isaiah 50:4–9a

This pericope extends our conversation with Proverbs by concentrating on the person who adheres to Wisdom's instruction. That person is called Servant. A servant is one who accepts instruction (wisdom) and lives out that instruction for the benefit of others, even in the face of hostile critics.

Punctuated by the refrain "the Lord GOD," who gives, opens, and helps, the Servant relies on and trusts in God (vv. 4a, 5a, 7a, 9a). Servants witness to the benefit of the instruction they have received from God and the impact that instruction has upon their behavior toward others (v. 4). Building on previously received instruction, the Servant continues to submit to additional learning and is not rebellious (v. 5). The result of accepting this godly instruction and due diligence is a transformed life: one that has the ability to stand in

---

1. Arthur Farstad and William MacDonald, *Believer's Bible Commentary: Old and New Testaments* (Nashville: Thomas Nelson Publishers, 1995), 793.

opposition to the standards of the unjust world. The Servant stands faithfully, even in the face of those who may harm him or her (v. 6). Servants know that if they follow God's instruction, they will not be put to shame, but will be vindicated by God's faithfulness (v. 7).

It is important that the preacher carefully consider the implication of suffering in this text. The text does not call for people to bear all suffering silently, that is, to be "not rebellious" (v. 5). The text refers not to suffering in general but to suffering caused by hostility to a Servant's witness for justice. Preachers need to prepare congregations for the possibility of such suffering in response to our own witness. Such suffering, although seldom discussed, is real. The text urges the congregation to consider ways that our suffering for justice can itself become a part of the struggle for justice. The Servant continued to witness for justice even when reviled. In a similar passage elsewhere, Isaiah points out that suffering witness for justice in the face of opposition has the power to prompt onlookers to contemplate that God may be acting through such resolve (Isa. 52:10, 13).

Psalm 19

Psalm 19 discloses the power of words in both written and verbal forms through three distinct voices: creation, God, and humankind. Creation speaks in the form of praise as it makes known the glory of God (v. 4). Daily we hear creation's voice as the seas roar and the waves break, as the wind whistles and the trees crackle, and as birds chirp and dogs howl. The power in their praise is that it never ceases. Day after day and night after night, creation continually reveals the glory of God (vv. 1–4). Highlighting one of the magnificent wonders of creation, the sun, the psalmist reflects upon its rising, its setting, its circuits, and the fact that nothing is hid from it (vv. 5–6). In all its magnificence it is yet one of God's creations and points us to God rather than itself. Creation speaks and its message is clear: that glory and honor belong to God alone.

Secondly, God demonstrates even the beauty and power of written words through the law (instruction). The instruction consists of decrees, precepts, commandments, and ordinances, all of which appear restrictive and punitive to the myopic eye, resulting in a lackluster life. However, the nature of the law (instruction) is "perfect, . . . sure, . . . right, . . . clear, . . . pure, . . . [and] true" (vv. 7–9). The law points not to a limited or dull life, but one of abundance and joy. The character of divine instruction reveals the depth of love that God has for us and God's steadfast commitment to us. The good news is the benefit of the law (instruction). The law has the power to revive the soul, make wise the simple, enlighten the eyes, and make one righteous (vv. 7–9). These enduring qualities, more than temporary pleasures or worldly measures of success, are to be desired (v. 10).

Laws are enacted for the good order and discipline of a society. When applied justly, societies flourish because all citizens are viewed as valuable and contributing members. When applied unjustly, divisions are created in which some members hoard more and others struggle with less. The issue at stake, where the nature of the law is concerned, is the heart and hands of those enacting them. When the person has a heart steeped in the character of God's will—just care for all—the law liberates the soul and the society. A few of the areas that have been impacted by just laws are those supporting human rights, environmental protection, academic access, and equal pay for equal work.

Finally, the voice of humankind speaks in a powerful recognition of self. With a confessional tone, the servant acknowledges these benefits of the law (instruction) by also acknowledging their warning. The psalmist confesses the burden of even unintended failure to uphold the standards set forth in the law and asks for forgiveness and continued protection from sin with a word of solemn prayer (vv. 11–14).

Psalm 116:1–9

This psalm, like Psalm 19, also discloses the power of words. In vivid details, the psalmist tells of a deeply personal experience and invites the reader to come alongside the psalmist to experience it as well. Verse 1 testifies to the psalmist's love for God. The depth of emotion expressed in love seemingly parallels both the depth of despair and the dramatic deliverance the psalmist has experienced. However, this psalm should not be viewed as repayment for goods received, but rather as a new direction in the life of the psalmist, a life of worship and praise. Like the psalmist's love for the Lord in critical times in life, when death seemed imminent, hell laying hold on us, with distress and anguish lingering like a long lost friend, we too may call upon the "name" of the Lord in prayer (vv. 2–4). The Lord, who first loved us, responds with grace, righteousness, and mercy in the midst of calamity (v. 5).

In the aftermath of this experience, the psalm speaks to one's own soul, calling the soul to rest in the bountiful blessings received from the Lord (vv. 7–8). The blessings are threefold in deliverance: deliverance of the soul, of the eyes from tears, and of the feet from stumbling (v. 8). In essence, the psalmist has been fully restored. In restoration, the psalmist will walk in the land of the living, but does so by informing others of the goodness of the Lord.

There is an old gospel song that begins with the words: "Said I wasn't gonna tell nobody, but I couldn't keep it to myself . . . what da Lord has done for me."[2] Psalm 116 echoes this sentiment by challenging the notion that one's relationship with God is personal and private. Testimony has the power to change and transform lives, if we would only share our story. Too often, we concentrate on the negative aspects of the events, rather than seeing God in the midst of them. When we testify to God working in the midst of our despair, regardless of how deep, we may begin also to see our neighbors living still in the despair of isolation and reach out to them with restoring relationship. Knowing, understanding, and trusting that we are never alone is a story worth telling with the power to transform.

James 3:1–12

This chapter opens with a warning to teachers about the greater standard to which they are held because of the power and authority of their speech (vv. 1–2). As teachers, they are public figures, in public places, with implicit and explicit authority over others. This authority is a breeding ground for sin. The text calls our attention to the power of influence and reminds us to handle it justly. This influence is located in a "small member" of the human body, the tongue, which although small, has great power (v. 5). Therefore, James urges us to control the tongue and the types of speech that come from it.

James believes that no one has the power to refrain thoroughly from misguided speech, for no one is perfect (v. 2). Living in a society in which freedom of speech is protected by law, the ability to say anything that one pleases moves beyond the requirements for a just society. For example, consider the half-truths told by the news media in efforts to sway viewers to one side of an argument or the half-truths of political campaigns in which lying and slandering are norms.[3] In these examples and others like them, no one comes out on top. The ones who win the races or sway viewers to their point of view do so at the destruction of others. Deplorably, the destruction of others is rarely considered, as long as the race is won, the ratings are high, and the reach of one's influence is extended. The tragic irony is reflected in verses 9–10 when the anointed tongue curses those whom God seeks to restore or bless.

James forces the questions, "Could the same results been obtained without the destruction of others? And if so, why do speak destructively? Indeed, can destruction serve God's desires for humanity?" These questions reach beyond the scope of speech, deep into the heart of the individual. Therein James shines a light upon motives and values. For we speak from the center

2. For the full lyrics, see http://lyricsplayground.com/alpha/songs/s/saidiwasntgonna tellnobody.shtml (accessed September 14, 2010).
3. Luke Timothy Johnson, "The Letter of James," in *The New Interpreter's Bible Commentary*, ed. Leander E. Keck et al. (Nashville: Abingdon Press, 1998), 12:206.

of our most important motives and values. Here James urges us to consider whether we speak blessing and cursing (vv. 9–10). They proceed out of the same mouth, but they lead to different social worlds. To mitigate the tragedy of speaking against God's purposes, the community can turn to the discipline and instruction described in Proverbs and Psalms.

Mark 8:27–38

The themes expressed throughout the preceding readings culminate here in attention to discipleship. This Gospel passage opens with a discussion on the identity of Jesus (vv. 27–29). The disciples appear enraptured by their own position with Jesus. Confident that they know their mentor and teacher, the disciples confuse their discovery of sight with insight. To what extent do they really—or do we really—understand the consequences of following Christ?

Immediately after Peter's bold role reversal, Jesus begins to teach them (vv. 31–33). What begins as revelation, on the nature of Christ's identity and ministry, suddenly becomes lessons on the challenges or costs of discipleship more broadly drawn. Jesus will soon suffer, but now in the spirit of Isaiah 50:4–9, he teaches that discipleship can lead to suffering. The cost of discipleship is largely determined by the choices we make. Jesus plainly states that we make a choice between a life that is complicit with the old age (and that will lead to one's losing a place in the realm, "forfeit their life," v. 36b; cf. v. 35a) and a life that witnesses to the realm (and that leads to salvation, v. 35b). If we are willing to deny our immediate personal security and suffer for the gospel and its call for justice now, we will ultimately be saved and restored by being joined with God in the coming of the realm.

Discipleship means daily attempting to serve others in solidarity to move toward the realm. Disciples recognize that we have responsibilities to love intently and to pursue justice. Discipleship defines our understanding of divine instruction throughout the preceding lectionary texts today. Discipleship orders our lives and our grasp of divine instruction toward transformation. This is evident as we come to know the Savior in a real and personal way, submit to the instruction daily, speak or act publicly against injustice, confess our failures, and tell of God's glory.

Preaching on these texts in light of social justice and transformation calls to remembrance the determined resolve of those stalwart servants among the Little Rock Nine, the Greensboro Four, or those who lost their lives at the site of the Orangeburg Massacre.[4] Indeed, the preacher might tell one or

---

4. On the Little Rock Nine, see http://en.wikipedia.org/wiki/Little_Rock_Nine; on the Greensboro Four, see http://en.wikipedia.org/wiki/Greensboro_sit-ins; on the Orangeburg

more of these stories in the sermon to inspire the congregation. In the face of opposition, the Nine, the Four, and those in Orangeburg persevered. They paid heavy prices, but their witness contributed to national transformation.

Preaching on these texts further calls to remembrance those who have stood and still stand for equitable lending practices and fair housing, even when powerful voices would restrict loans (or overcharge for them) and sanction concealed segregation of housing. It calls to remembrance those who tend to those who are hungry, homeless, and abused, even when misguided tongues dismiss such problems as drags on the larger society. These are just a few of those who set their faces like flint and press forward in their insistence on justice, even when they face resistance (Isa. 50:7). These texts call *us* too to stand in the face of injustice and to persevere as the conscience of a nation to account for its sins.

Massacre, see http://en.wikipedia.org/wiki/Orangeburg_massacre (all accessed on September 14, 2010).

International Day of Prayer and Witness for Peace (September 21)

Willard Swartley

DEUTERONOMY 10:12–22
PSALM 122
ROMANS 15:1–3
MATTHEW 5:38–48

In 1981, the United Nations established Peace Day for individuals and communities to take practical steps toward peace, e.g. lighting candles, organizing public events, observing a Day of Ceasefire, and making peace in personal and political relationships. In 2002, the UN set September 21 as the permanent Peace Day. In 2004, the World Council of Churches designated September 21 (or the closest Sunday) as International Day for Prayer for Peace. We enlarge the title to International Day of Prayer and Witness for Peace to encourage churches to repent of our complicity in violence, to pray for peace, and to take other actions that witness for shalom.

When I pray for peace, I pray . . . above all that my own country will cease to do the things that make war inevitable. . . . So instead of loving what you think is peace, love other [people] and love God above all. And instead of hating the people you think are warmakers, hate the appetites and the disorder in your own soul, which are the causes of war. If you love peace, then hate injustice, hate tyranny, hate greed—but hate these things in yourself, not in another.[1]

Thomas Merton

These texts blend four themes: justice for those who are vulnerable in society; peace of the city; love of enemy; and inclusive hospitality. These themes

---

1. Thomas Merton, *New Seeds of Contemplation* (New York: New Directions Books, 1972), 121–22.

are pillars for Christian ethics and moral living. When practiced together, they point toward a world of peace.

Deuteronomy 10:12–22

The mandate of justice to those who are vulnerable is not some secular notion of "each receiving one's due," but a sacred covenant obligation. This text is rooted in covenant consciousness of whose we are: people of "the LORD your God"—a phrase occurring eight times in this passage, with "LORD" and "God" occurring separately also. The text begins with theological foundations: "What does the LORD your God require of you?" (v. 12). Four verbs frame the obligation: fear, walk, love, and serve. The latter verb includes worship, elaborated in verse 20. Verses 13–17 describe God's initiative and the people's response in the covenant, implying a mandate for social justice, a theme punctuating the Hebrew Bible (Exod. 22:21–23; 23:9; Lev. 19:9–16, 34; Deut. 24:19; 26:12–13; cf. Prov. 31:8–9; Isa. 1:16–17; 3:13–15; Amos 2:6–7; 4:1–3).

Justice for the orphan, widow, and stranger is not a utopian eschatological vision, but a concrete mandate for daily life. The book of Ruth illustrates how this prescription works in social community. Naomi included Ruth—widow, stranger, and perhaps orphan—into Naomi's family, into full integration into the community, and this inclusion led to Ruth's inclusion in Israel's messianic genealogy.

The final frame of the text is praise and memory. Verse 21 invites praise to the God who has done awesome wonders on behalf of the people, and verse 22 recounts essential history, how God blessed those few in number who went into Egypt, so that now they are "as numerous as the stars in heaven." Social justice is not freestanding but is encased within religious reality, historical experience, and vital covenant relationship. Social justice is not an add-on to religion but is the heart of what it means to be God's people. Obedience to this mandate is the precondition of entering the promised land (10:12–11:12).

This text speaks to Christians today on several issues, especially immigration reform and health-care reform. With verse 22 we rehearse the immigration story of our ancestors, naming the country and circumstances of their journey. Knowing that story, we must welcome those who now want to immigrate to our country. On health care, we must provide for those who are most vulnerable (including widows, aliens, and orphans), who cannot afford health insurance. Health care should not be the pawn of market profit, and reform dare not be hamstrung by party politics. Both obstacles hinder worship of God. Indeed, the prophets denounce worship without justice and care for the poor (Amos 5:21–24; Mic. 6:1–8).

Psalm 122

Psalm 122 is oriented to worship in the temple in Jerusalem. Children in church school today often memorize verse 1. "Going to church" should be an occasion for joy, celebration, and prayer for the peace (*shalom*) of the city. The word "peace" occurs three times in the text. The term has a range of meaning; in this context its two connotations are well-being and security. What are the conditions that make such peace possible? I recall a tourist bus chugging up the mountain toward Jerusalem, and the Israeli guide repeating verses 6–8. But he did not speak of conditions necessary to achieve peace. Since I rode on that bus, Israel has begun to build a wall dividing Israelis from Palestinians. This is Israel's security insurance from suicide bombers and other acts of terrorism, but it separates the two peoples and produces its own insecurity and violence. Rather, community built on trust and sharing of the land's resources are the means toward the city's—and every city's—welfare and security.[2]

Matthew 5:38–48

In this text Jesus blazes a trail to living peace. His word is not only a technique that shocks and surprises, but a radical turning from the Roman Empire's understanding of peace (prosperity that follows war) to formation of loving community. Placing Matthew's version alongside its parallel in Luke 6:27–36 shows that Luke's version is framed with the "love of enemy" command. Not resisting evil is in the service of loving the enemy, meaning that nonretaliation seeks the transformation of enmity into friendship.

Walter Wink interprets Matthew's five examples of *not resisting* as "focal instances" that throw the enemy off guard and thus may disarm the enmity.[3] Wink holds that "do not resist" (*antistēnai*, v. 39) means "do not resist violently." The five examples here show a form of nonviolent resistance whereby those who are poor or oppressed claim their dignity and open the door to a new relationship between the oppressor and those who are oppressed. The enemy is disarmed by a surprise response: turn the other (left) cheek to one who insultingly slaps you with the back of his right hand on your right cheek;

2. Editor's note. Relationships among Palestinian and Jewish peoples are complex, thus making preaching on peace in that sphere a complicated matter. Many people in both Palestinian and Jewish communities seek peace. Two groups in the Jewish community who, with different accents, exemplify finding ways toward peace that respect the various sensitivities involved, are Americans for Peace (http://peacenow.org) and Jewish Voices for Peace (www.jewishvoicesfor peace.org) (accessed August 10, 2010).

3. Walter Wink, "Neither Passivity nor Violence: Jesus' Third Way," in *The Love of Enemy and Nonretaliation in the New Testament*, ed. Willard M. Swartley (Louisville, KY: Westminster/John Knox Press, 1992), 104–11.

when sued for your coat in court give your undergarment also, and thus stand there naked—shocking and shaming everyone; and offer to go a second mile when required to carry a Roman soldier's load one mile (*angareia*). Such response throws the opponent off balance, introducing a third way besides flight and fight; the situation is radically redefined.

This approach of nonviolent resistance does not guarantee that the other side will refrain from violence. It rather creates a new paradigm by using "moral jujitsu" to disarm the enemy. Wink's interpretation has been criticized as too tactical: Jesus is not prescribing some tactical "win" over the one doing evil. My response: If the "tactic" leads to transformation of enmity into friendship, it fits. But if it intensifies enmity, then clearly this is not what Jesus meant. Luise Schottroff links Jesus' teaching on nonretaliation and loving the enemy to the tradition of prophetic judgment. God vindicates the righteous against the evildoer. Further, "this behavioral ensemble consisting of refusal to pay retribution, expecting prophetic judgment, and loving the enemy has its reason or its goal in the justice of God or in the sovereignty of God."[4]

This refusal to repay in kind (evil for evil) is appropriately amended by Paul's injunction to "overcome evil with good" (Rom. 12:21). Paul's command fits hand in glove with loving the enemy. Moreover this moral practice identifies those who are "children of your Father in heaven" (Matt. 5:45), which links to Matthew 5:9, "Blessed are the peacemakers, for they will be called children of God."

This way to peace earmarks identity and is foundational for Christian ethics. But this is not natural human response. It does not come instinctively. We are wired to fight back and to do one better than the last blow from the opponent. The way to win is to crush the opponent, so that the opponent surrenders or dies. Even the best politicians think and act that way. That is why defense spending is so big in national budgets, especially in the United States of America. But if Jesus is right, then this thinking is wrong. There is a better way, and Greg Mortensen has shown that way in Afghanistan.[5] Multiply Greg Mortensen's type of work by a million people dotting the globe with such efforts, and we have the Jesus ethic that overcomes evil with good through loving initiatives. With the many church and NGO efforts worldwide, there

---

4. Luise Schottroff, "'Give to Caesar What Belongs to Caesar and to God What Belongs to God': A Theological Response of the Early Christian Church to Its Social and Political Environment," in Swartley, ed., *Love of Enemy*, 236.

5. Two of his books point the way: Greg Mortensen, *Stones into Schools: Promoting Peace with Books, Not Bombs, in Afghanistan and Pakistan* (London: Penguin Books, 2009), and *Three Cups of Tea: One Man's Journey to Change the World One Child at a Time* (London: Penguin Books, 2007).

are likely already one million, but we lack the creative, long-term sustainable Mortensen-type models.

Romans 15:1–3

Romans 15 begins by reminding the Christians in Rome in house churches composed of Jewish and Gentile Christians that those who are strong should be considerate toward the needs of those who are weak. The heart of Christian community beats with the blood of those who do not seek to please themselves but seek to serve the neighbor and thus fortify the community's health. Christ is the model (v. 3; cf. Phil. 2:5–8). This other-oriented attitude is willing to suffer insults (vv. 3–4) for the sake of building up one another and living in harmony with one another (vv. 5–6). In Rome, the "strong" and the "weak" are calling each other names, and Paul seeks to nip this arrogance in the bud, by appealing to the self-deferring mind of Christ.

After this prologue, Paul bursts forth: "Welcome one another . . . as Christ has welcomed you" (v. 7). Again, Christ is the model who willingly became "a servant of the circumcised" to fulfill God's "promises given to the patriarchs, in order that the Gentiles might glorify God for [God's] mercy" (vv. 8–9). Then follow four quotations from the Septuagint, each with Gentiles as the end goal of God's election of and promises to Israel. This makes the point incontestable: those with election credentials are to welcome those whom God intends to include within God's salvation.

Romans 15:1–13 is prologue for Paul's appeal to the wealthier Gentile believers to provide material assistance for the poor Jewish Christians in Jerusalem (vv. 25–26). This relief gift manifests the solidarity of Jews and Gentiles in Christ. This is health care within the church, mutual aid for those in need. As Paul says in appealing to the Corinthians to respond to this material need, response is a matter of justice—"a fair balance between your present abundance and their need" (2 Cor. 8:13–14). Paul's principle is mutuality, and it goes both ways: "If the Gentiles have come to share in their [the Jews'] spiritual blessings, they ought also to be of service to them in material things" (Rom. 15:27).

Paul's plea for the Jews to welcome the Gentiles in the early part of Romans 15 has its reverse complement in the latter part of the chapter. This is hospitality in attitude and action. Paul confronts us with prophetic power to grasp anew the diversity of the Christian body and its demand upon us to live truly as brothers and sisters.

These four lectionary texts provide the criteria for measuring the genuine Christian health of our congregation(s). Stirring our conscience and imagination in several related dimensions of peace and justice, they challenge us toward the goal of Paul's benediction in 15:13: "May the God of hope fill you with all joy and peace in believing, so that you may abound in hope by the power of the Holy Spirit." Paul was a hope-filled, joy-filled, Holy Spirit–empowered apostle of the gospel, and we are called to follow his path, just as he followed in the steps of Jesus Christ. He knew God as "God of peace," a unique title heading seven of his benedictions, Romans 15:33 and 16:20 among them.

Proper 20 [25]

Catherine Gunsalus González and Justo L. González

PROVERBS 31:10–31
PSALM 1

JEREMIAH 11:18–20
PSALM 54
JAMES 3:13–4:3, 7–8a
MARK 9:30–37

All the readings for today except the Gospel lesson reflect typical Wisdom literature: the way of God is wise, and those who travel this path will be rewarded with a good life. This life is both personal and communal. God takes the side of the wise and defeats their enemies. The Gospel lesson reminds us to look beyond the surface, however, for here the wise one is defeated by the enemies, and God's vindication comes only after the wise one suffers death. Social justice themes permeate both the Wisdom literature proper and its use by the Gospel writer.

Proverbs 31:10–31

This passage is probably the most familiar of all of Proverbs. It is often read on Mother's Day. We can approach it in two ways: (1) what it teaches us about the role of women and (2) what it says about a righteous person regardless of gender. In regard to women, there is no reason to try to force ancient patterns of marriage on contemporary society, but in a culture that, assumed by much of the Bible, often makes it appear a wife should leave most important economic decisions to her husband, this passage shows a very different point of view. In these verses, the wife decides what land to buy, what goods to make in the home, how to sell them. She takes charge of a great deal of the household's governing, especially in economic matters. Her husband is a respected member of Jewish society and spends his days seated at the gate of the city with other important men, deciding matters of justice in cases that are brought to them. The wife's activities make it possible for him to do this. It is also important to note, of course, that women engage in matters of justice (v. 20) and that the home is to be a place of justice.

In terms of justice, it is clear that the household is organized so that the wider issues of justice in the community can be dealt with by the husband. He has the support of his family so that his time can be used in this fashion. We might wish that the tables had been turned, so that the husband supported the wife, who then was able to be such an elder. In Judges we do have the story of Deborah, who was a judge, evidently supported by her husband Lappidoth (Judg. 4:1–10). In this Proverbs passage, the wife also has a concern for justice in the way she organizes the household.

Regardless of the culture, households should be so organized that members can answer the call to be involved in wider community issues of justice. Surely the family of the wise woman in Proverbs 31 could have had more money flowing into the household if the husband had been as gainfully employed as the wife. Yet he spent his time in service to the wider community, probably without compensation. A modern equivalent could be a household that has less money flowing in because one or more of its members is involved in unpaid or low-paying work that leads to justice. Indeed, in some households headed by a single adult, the adult engages in low-paying work that leads to justice.

The passage gives a good description of the righteous person, regardless of gender. Even more, it shows a righteous household, a whole family that seeks justice. The husband and wife trust each other and are faithful. The children grow up in this atmosphere and learn to recognize righteousness and participate in it. They all work hard and provide not only for the family, but also for all others who work with the family. They also provide for the poor. They supply what is necessary for the household to face winter and other hardships without fear. Evidently they do not waste their money on things that are not useful. They are provident and do not run up debt. There is much here that is helpful for families seeking to live wisely. Bringing all the possible money into the household is not the greatest goal. Having what is necessary and then serving the wider community in pursuing justice is a greater goal.

Psalm 1

This psalm emphasizes much of the wisdom already seen in the Proverbs passage. The wise person seeks to do what is right according to the law of God. But there is more. As is typical of Wisdom literature, those who seek righteousness are told they will do well. They will prosper, just as the righteous household in Proverbs prospered. The wicked will not do well. There is truth in the fact that someone who is profligate, who wastes both time and money, who does not take advantage of opportunities to learn and grow in goodness, probably will not do well. In our own day, they may wreck their credit and be in debt, living from one day to the next without a sustainable future. As we know from recent history, when banks, insurance companies, and other large financial institutions engage in irresponsible financial dealings, they can wreck the financial life of whole nations.

However, justice demands that we say clearly that not all those who end up in difficult economic straits are there because of their own recklessness. There is no simple straight line between pursuing righteousness and "succeeding" in life. The psalm has great truth, but other psalms will point to the unjust who seem to prosper and the just ones who are in difficulties (e.g., Ps. 73). The reverse is also true: those who prosper are not necessarily the righteous and wise ones. This caveat, however, should not prevent us from seeing the truth that following the path of justice and righteousness does help to keep us from some of the problems the foolish face.

The psalm points to the fact that if we associate with people who see no point in pursuing justice, we will eventually be affected by them. If we are to remain faithful to the path of righteousness, we need solidarity with others who live by God's law of justice. In a society in which getting to know "the right people"—those who can help our careers or our social standing—is important, this psalm is a call to associate with those working for justice. They may not be high on the social scale, and they may even hinder furthering our own careers, but they will keep us on the right track.

Jeremiah 11:18–20

This brief passage is about a moment in the life of Jeremiah. He is warned by God that there is a plot against his life. He has had no idea he was in danger, and now he discovers that he has almost walked into a trap. He could have lost his life. In these few verses Jeremiah shows that he now knows the danger he is in. At the same time, he is sure that God will rescue him, that the plot against him will fail. He looks forward to the time when he will be vindicated and his enemies will be punished.

Jeremiah uses the same imagery that is found in Isaiah 53:7—the lamb led to the slaughter—that early Christian writers use to interpret the death of Jesus. This is probably the reason for the choice of this passage for today.

Jeremiah's words are very much in line with the Wisdom literature we saw in the previous psalm. Those who do what is just and right will be protected by God. They may be in difficulties for a while, but ultimately God will rescue them, and those who want to destroy the righteous will be defeated. Jeremiah commits his life and work to God, trusting that God will ultimately vindicate him and he will be victorious over the enemies who now seek his life.

These are clearly words to those who seek justice. Jeremiah is able to be faithful in following God's difficult way because he trusts in God's faithfulness. His enemies assume they are following the more prudent way to save their lives in the face of danger to the nation. But God's way, although foolishness to the faithless, is the road to the greater security God gives.

Psalm 54

This psalm picks up the theme of the Jeremiah passage, that God's faithfulness is the source of security in the face of enemies. God and God's law cannot be separated. The law, which seeks justice, is the will of God. More than that, the law describes the kind of society God created human beings to live in. If we seek justice, then we help society reach the goal God has for it. If we are content to live in injustice, then we are willing to live in a dysfunctional society, one that denies the intent of its creator. God is on the side of those who wish to help society become what God wants. Those who are content with an unjust world cannot expect help from God.

In our work for justice in our society, we need to be sure we are following God's intent: that we "set God before" us (v. 3). God's intentions and not ours will triumph. If we expect to be vindicated in the future, it is because God's plans cannot ultimately be thwarted.

Just as Jeremiah expects to see the defeat of his persecutors, so the psalmist anticipates a time when he or she will experience triumph over the insolent ones who now trouble the psalmist. The theme of vindication may sound very negative, as though we are told to be vindictive. That is not the case. We are not to seek our own vindication. Rather, God is the one who can be vindictive, and there is no danger there, since God's wrath is tempered with God's mercy in a way that human vindictiveness cannot be. We are told to leave the matter of our own vindication in God's hands—to commit our cause to God—and then to go about acting justly. We can count on God's faithfulness to us and on God's own intentions for the future.

James 3:13–4:3, 7–8a

These verses from James sound very much like the Wisdom literature we saw in Psalms 1 and 54. Here there is great emphasis not only on the particular actions that lead to greater justice, but also on the attitudes that lead to these actions. The stress is on gentleness. Righteousness is to be pursued with gentleness. The same act in the cause of justice can be taken either because of ambition or because of a sincere wish to follow God. The act may be the same, but the motivation is different. In the church, much so-called prophetic ministry is accompanied with anger and pride in one's own righteousness. True wisdom is gentle, peaceable, and merciful. That is a difficult standard to uphold in our pursuit of justice.

James continues by saying that when our intentions for justice are informed by our own ambitions, we are cut off from asking support from God, because we seek something for ourselves. We often ignore the fact that ambition and pride are often combined with work for justice. We may seek to be recognized as a leader in just causes. We may even seek to have enemies, because we wish to be seen as martyrs in our pursuit of justice. These hidden attitudes compromise our work.

Our goal must be the single-minded pursuit of God's will. James 4:8 is the basis of Søren Kierkegaard's book *Purity of Heart Is to Will One Thing*.[1] In that writing Kierkegaard goes through all the ways in which a good action can be accompanied by evil desires, thus warping our intent to do what is right. The solution is to draw nearer to God, to put aside our own personal goals, which are temptations, and seek only what God wishes.

Mark 9:30–37

The Gospel lesson includes two pericopes. The first, Jesus' words to his disciples about his coming betrayal, death, and resurrection, confuse the disciples. The second, the disciples' argument about who will be the greatest in the realm, shows how far they are from understanding what Jesus is about. The first section goes well with the passage from Jeremiah. The Epistle deals with the same concerns as the second section of the Gospel.

The parallels between Jeremiah and Jesus are obvious. Both pursue the way of God. Both are surrounded by opponents who believe they themselves are wiser than the prophet or Jesus. Both are betrayed. Both commit their causes to God. Both are firm in their belief that God will vindicate them. The great difference is that Jeremiah expects his vindication to be in his lifetime, and rightly so. That is what God intends. Jesus, on the other hand, is sure that his vindication will come after death—vindication by resurrection! That also is what God intends.

What about us? In our search for justice, do we expect to see our cause win, or are we able to pursue goals that may need time far beyond our lives? Do we believe in the resurrection so strongly that we know we shall see the justice of

---

1. Søren Kierkegaard, *Purity of Heart Is to Will One Thing*, trans. Douglas V. Steere (New York: Harper & Row, 1956).

God triumph even after our death? Do we judge success in matters of justice only by clear victories that the world can see, or are we able to work for justice when true victory is so far off that it seems useless to strive for it?

The second pericope is quite similar to the words in James. Here the disciples are double-minded. They wish both for the realm to succeed and for their own positions of authority to be guaranteed. They want both justice and a reward for pursuing justice. If they had to choose—justice and anonymity, or injustice and fame—which would they choose? Many of us would hesitate to choose the pursuit of justice if we were sure it would lead to opprobrium by our family and friends. But if such a pursuit can be combined with social approval or at least good press, then we are quite willing to put up with some discomfort.

The words of Jesus are final: only those who forget about themselves and seek justice with a pure heart will be great in the realm. In this world they seem to be last, because their work for justice is not mixed with their own personal motives. In the realm, these last ones shall be first.

Jesus uses the example of a child, one who can do nothing in return for those who minister to him or her. Those who welcome such a child, welcome Jesus himself. Their motives cannot be to gain anything that the child can give them. Those who minister to such a child—those who pursue justice for its own sake without mixed motives—find that they are serving not only Jesus but also the God who sent him. We either serve justice and God or serve justice and ourselves. If it is the former, we may well be last now, or the way we are pursuing may lead to our losing social status in the future. If it is the latter, we may well be first now, but we will be last in the world to come.

Proper 21 [26]

Noelle Damico

ESTHER 7:1–6, 9–10; 9:20–22   NUMBERS 11:4–6, 10–16, 24–29
PSALM 124   PSALM 19:7–14
                                                         JAMES 5:13–20
                                                         MARK 9:38–50

The lectionary readings for Proper 21 offer preachers an opportunity to explore how God's intended well-being is established through the exercise of power. Esther's savvy navigation of the king of Persia's authority, court protocol, and weakness, saves the Jewish people from genocide. In the wilderness, God demands that Moses and the people share power and curb their desire for excess. Psalm 124 extols God for being on the people's side when they were attacked, while Psalm 19 declares that God's law guides the faithful into practices of justice mirroring God's own acts of justice. James counsels practices of prayer that promote dignity and equality among assembly members. And Jesus insists the disciples align themselves with his most vulnerable followers and make extreme choices in order to ensure communal well-being.

Esther 7:1–6, 9–10; 9:20–22 and Numbers 11:4–6, 10–16, 24–29

The passages from Esther and Numbers seem, at first, to present contrasting visions of how faithful people should exercise power. Esther is the savior of her people, while seventy elders share in the spirit that once solely rested on Moses. God is not mentioned once in the book of Esther, while in the book of Numbers, God is not only an interlocutor with Moses but also a primary actor challenging the community's own understanding of power and its limits.

But the two readings also have much in common. Both passages struggle with how best to wield power in order to survive—in Persia as a minority community and in the wilderness fleeing slavery for still-unknown promised land. Both texts describe communities living contingently—under threat from powerful people or in the desert living only at God's behest. Both texts recount stories of how the Hebrew community survives against the odds—the one escaping genocide, the other learning more properly to envision God's desire for life together.

The book of Esther recounts how a Jewish orphan, living in Persia during the fifth century BCE, rises to prominence as the nation's queen and uses her power to protect the minority Jewish population from annihilation. This fictional tale is the foundation for the Jewish celebration of Purim. The book of Esther resists easy moralizing. It forces readers, tellers, and hearers to enter into the narrative not simply as a story, but as experiment for living that questions, tests, and deploys the power God has entrusted to us.

The lectionary passages describe how Esther outmaneuvers the king and his advisor Haman. The king has granted Esther a petition (ask anything—even up to half my dominion) because he is pleased with a banquet she has thrown for him and Haman (5:6). Esther uses this opening as a foothold. She lubricates the king with wine and then reveals that if the king orders that all Jews be killed, she will be among them (7:1–4). Esther is savvy. She cloaks her petition with the honor of the king, explaining that the king's reputation will be damaged if she and her people are destroyed. Indeed if she and her people had *simply* been sold into slavery, well, she would have held her peace. But annihilation is a step too far. No enemy could possibly compensate the king for such damage, she asserts, alluding to the ten thousand talents Haman paid the king to cover royal expenses related to genocide (3:9).

Esther weaves together the fate of the Jews and the good name of the monarch while simultaneously establishing Haman's culpability. Esther is far more than your average diplomat; she's a veritable expert of political jujitsu. Look how deftly and completely she ties the ruler's hands. If he disagrees with her, he will impugn his own honor. Esther sets the stage: the monarch and Haman become players in her theatre. In 9:20 we're told that Mordecai, Esther's uncle, "record[s] these things" and enjoins the Jews throughout Persia to set this date aside to celebrate how the "Jews gained relief from their enemies" (9:22).

What lessons might be drawn from such a tale? One lesson might be to learn how dominating power works—what its modi operandi is and where its weaknesses lie. The ruler had the absolute power of life and death over his subjects. But he also had his honor to protect (consider the fate of Queen Vashti, 1:19). Further, this sovereign had three weaknesses—drink, beautiful women, and making decisions on the recommendations of advisors. Esther uses all three to gain a royal audience and stake her claim.

Another lesson from this tale might be that one of the *anawim* (poor and powerless people), not a powerful Jew by birth, was the means of the people's salvation. Esther began life as an orphan. It is significant that Mordecai instructs the Jewish people to mark this celebration not only by sending gifts to one another but also by sending "presents to the poor" (9:22).

The book of Esther features vulnerable characters who are unafraid to handle power and who view their future as something for which *they*, not a monarch or even God, are responsible. Esther is not a simple hero; she stands for vulnerable people, exemplifying the intelligence, resourcefulness, and fidelity that are necessary for dominated people to survive in dangerous times. In our own day it's not only political leaders that hold the fate of whole peoples in their hand, but corporations and international agreements as well as economic, political, and social systems. How is the church working together with vulnerable people to analyze and alter those forces that treat people as expendable?

The selections from Numbers 11 recount how the people's desire for meat in the desert causes Moses and God to square off, resulting in God's division of the spirit among seventy elders of the camp. Moses is angry at God's displeasure toward the complaining people and for saddling him with leadership of this difficult community. "If this is the way you are going to treat me," Moses yells, "put me to death at once" (v. 15). Now all leaders at one time or another have reached the end of their rope with God and with their communities. We can sympathize with Moses. And we can appreciate the way that Moses later affirms both the prophesying of the elders who responded to his call to gather and that of those two elders who remained in the camp but were prophesying nonetheless.

A facile read of the story could lead preachers to opine on the importance of sharing the burden of leadership among many leaders within the community of faith. And while the lectionary passages suggest this reading, it is not unambiguous. For example verse 25b explains that while the seventy elders once prophesied, "they did not do so again." We do not know why. But it certainly does not bode well for shared leadership over the long haul.

When we read the passage assigned for today in the context of the whole chapter, the story begins to look less like a lesson in power sharing and more like a lesson in curbing excess. Moses overhears the people's complaints for meat and assumes that he is supposed to produce meat for them . . . somehow. Moses does not become angry with them, but instead he becomes angry with God. He's not exercising good judgment, and he needs to get over himself. Moses isn't the only leader; he never has been. Remember Miriam, Aaron, Jethro? And God helps him to a better sense of his own importance by distributing the spirit among the seventy elders—even if it's only for a time.

In stark contrast to Moses, God most certainly doesn't presume that the people's complaint for meat is justified. In fact, if we read beyond the confines of the lectionary, the narrative describes God angrily and retributively killing those people who complained that they wanted meat (11:1, 33–34). Reading the whole chapter, God's people appear to be under as much threat from God as they are from their own desires and the challenges of the wilderness.[1]

The craving for meat (by the people) and the desire to produce meat for them (by Moses) anger God, the same God who has liberated the people from slavery and preserved them in the wilderness. God cries, "Enough," through word and deed and viciously reorders the community by cutting off those who desired more than was reasonable and distributing power of the spirit, at least for the moment, far beyond Moses. Here we have a foreshadowing of Jesus' teaching to his disciples in Mark 9. The path to freedom and the formation of a just community appears harsh when compared with the priorities and practices of the world. The people last ate meat when they were slaves in Egypt. God requires them to divest themselves of this comfort and to trust in God's provision of manna in the wilderness.

It is often said that what you see depends on where you stand. These two texts from Esther and Numbers invite preachers to imagine life as a dominated, minority community, striving against the odds for survival, but bearing witness to God's faithfulness and God's vision of well-being amidst that very struggle.

Psalm 124 and Psalm 19:7–14

In Psalm 124 the Israelites give thanks that God was on their side (vv. 1, 2). The psalmist imagines a series of calamities, had not God been Israel's defender. Unspecified enemies attacked the Hebrew people but they were able to escape. God did not give them over "as prey" to their enemies (v. 6), though presumably God could have. The degree of God's intervention is not clear; either God broke the snare or allowed it to be broken. Either way, without God, the psalmist and the congregation that sings this psalm assert that the people would have been swept away. The psalm confesses that the people's help is in the name of God "who made heaven and earth" (v. 8). Their fate was in God's hands, the same powerful hands that formed the universe.

Too often texts of dominated people have become texts of domination, when they are uncritically appropriated by powerful interests or when people who were once oppressed become powerful and forget that it was in their vulnerability, not their strength, that they sensed God on their side. This psalm is the confession of a people who have been attacked and who, against the

---

1. We will set aside the theological question of whether God actually acts in this way. What is the important notation for our current exploration is that the narrative attributes the fire and plague to God.

odds, have been saved. The psalm does not make the triumphal or imperial claim, "God is always on our side," but rather expresses the particular gratitude of the vulnerable, "If it had not been the LORD who was on our side . . . then they would have swallowed us up alive" (vv. 1a, 3).

Psalm 124 is complemented by the verses from Psalm 19—a song that describes the splendor and justice God's law displays and intends for the world. How does God's law revive the soul? Not simply by existing, but by reversing expectations (the simple are made wise), by energizing the heart, and by helping the faithful see clearly how they are to live. An alternative translation of "God's ordinances" (v. 9) is "God's deeds of justice."[2] God's deeds of justice are true (v. 9), valuable (v. 10a), and delectable (v. 10b). In short, both the Torah and God's acts bring justice to life!

James 5:13–20

These beloved verses on prayer have given encouragement to struggling Christians across the millennia. In many ways they are universal words, intended for all Christians in all times and places who are facing difficulty, encouraging believers to pray fervently, confess to one another our shortcomings, and trust that God will hear and respond. But these words do not exist in a vacuum; they are the culmination of an epistle written to an assembly constituted predominantly if not exclusively of poor people, living in a dominated world (1:9). These words, and the epistle as a whole, counsel an ordering of the church's life and practice that prizes equality over preference or deference (2:1–7), and trust in God, who is able to bring about well-being even under the worst personal or social conditions (5:15–17).

James never minces words, castigating the rich for their treatment of the poor and their ostentatious display of wealth, while chastising those in the assembly who would emulate or pander to them. Indeed this final chapter begins, "Come now, you rich people, weep and wail for the miseries that are coming to you" (5:1). So we should understand James's counsel on prayer as a continuation of his critiques of injustice as well as a concrete practice through which the assembly and its members can reorient themselves as "friends of God" (4:4–12). Through prayer, the community orders and reorders itself as an assembly of equals, both in fundamental critique of the wider world and in loving support of one another as we seek God's guidance for how to live.

"Don't talk about us; talk with us" is the motto of Picture the Homeless, a grassroots organization founded and led by homeless people in New York

---

2. Clint McCann, "The Psalms," in *The Discipleship Study Bible*, ed. Bruce C. Birch et al. (Louisville, KY: Westminster John Knox Press, 2008), 752.

City. The group organizes for social justice around issues like housing, police violence, and the shelter-industrial complex. "Our name is about challenging images, stigma, media (mis) representation—as well as putting forward an alternative vision of community," they explain.[3] Picture the Homeless worked with area clergy to gain access to potter's field on Hart Island, where more than 750,000 poor and indigent New Yorkers are buried, to hold interfaith memorial services. At a recent service a member of Picture the Homeless stood with clergy and students and said, "We recognize that in God's name these are our brothers and sisters. That's what calls us to be here."[4]

As we read James from varied social locations in the twenty-first century, the epistle exhorts the church to be identified with those who have been made poor and vulnerable in our world—not in the sense of charity, but as sisters and brothers, one to another, acknowledging the faithfulness of God, the defender of the vulnerable (Ps. 124). In prayer and in all aspects of its life together, the church demonstrates God's inbreaking reign when it fosters relationships of dignity and equality among people.

Mark 9:38–50

The Gospel reading for this week echoes the passage of Numbers in sharing power more widely and cutting off anything that endangers life in community. Jesus warns his disciples to care most about how they treat "the little ones," those followers of Jesus who have been made vulnerable or poor. Jesus insists there be no barriers between them and these "little ones," even if they need to "amputate limbs." The community is like a person in recovery from the powers of this world. And what looks strange from the outside brings life and health to one who has sobered up.

Jesus continues claiming that when the disciples endeavor to live in relationship with "the little ones," they will be "salted with fire" (v. 49). But they should value this wounding, which distinguishes them from the world, for it is through this "salting with fire" that the community will be shaped into God's provocative, peaceful witness in the world.

---

3. Picture the Homeless Web site: http://picturethehomeless.org (accessed June 1, 2010).
4. Eileen Markey, "Homeless, Nameless—and Honored," *City Limits*, March 25, 2010, http://www.citylimits.org/news/articles/3911/homeless-nameless-and-honored (accessed May 29, 2010).

Peoples Native to the Americas Day
(Fourth Friday in September)

Martin Brokenleg

LAMENTATIONS 5:1–22
PSALM 130
JAMES 4:1–10
MATTHEW 18:15–22

Native American Day is often observed on the fourth Friday of September in the United States and National Aboriginal Day on June 21 in Canada. Peoples native to North America celebrate their identities, histories, and cultures, and also demonstrate for justice. The preacher could help Eurocentric communities repent of the atrocities they have perpetrated against Native Americans and First Nations or First Peoples (as they are known in Canada) and could also help the congregation become more informed about the culture, practices, and religious beliefs and practices of indigenous communities, especially those shared by original inhabitants and later comers.

In 1969, a group of Native Americans occupied Alcatraz Island and its abandoned prison, in the middle of San Francisco Bay. They said, "We, the native Americans reclaim . . . Alcatraz Island. . . . [T]his island is more than suited for an Indian Reservation, as determined by [Eurocentric] standards. [For] this place resembles most Indian Reservations in that it is: isolated from modern facilities. It has no fresh running water . . . inadequate sanitation . . . no oil or mineral rights . . . no industry . . . no health care facilities . . . rocky and unproductive soil . . the population has always exceeded the land base . . . [and the people have] always been held as prisoners."[1]

"Proclamation to the Great White Father and All His People"

1. "Proclamation to the Great White Father and All His People," in T. C. McLuhan, ed., *Touch the Earth: A Self-Portrait of Indian Existence* (New York: Simon & Schuster/Touchstone Books, 1971), 164–65.

This commentary begins with a comparison and contrast between the cultures of First Nations and Euro-American peoples. It then sets the biblical texts for today in that discussion.

During the racial tensions in the 1960s, some progressive Christians seemed to relish being accused of wrongs so they could feel guilty. African American and Native American speakers were invited to churches to accuse Eurocentric congregations of historical offenses. Euro-American Christians were ordered to make reparations for past injustices and to experience intense guilt for the past. This activity did little to advance community between these groups. In the twenty-first century, First Nations are interested in what needs to happen for radical justice to occur, rather than inducing guilt over past experiences.

A real relationship presumes accurate mutual understanding, particularly of the inner worlds of one another. First Nations are not a homogenous group but are made up of distinctive culture groups. Certainly Native peoples share some physical traits, such as general lactose intolerance and a recent epidemic of diabetes, but none of these physical conditions is enough to make First Nations a distinctive race. Since intermarriage has occurred many times, Native peoples are not so much a racial group as a cultural group. As will become clear, both the inner and social worlds of First Nations are quite different from those of Christians of European descent.

Probably the greatest difference between Natives and newcomers in the Americas is the communal life of Native peoples and the individualism of Western culture. From the first moments of life through the end of life in this world and beyond, First Nations live in communal relationships. A Native child is born into a family of 250 to 300 people spread over five generations. Parents and siblings constitute a household that is only a small part of the family.

The child has a biological mother and a biological father. The brothers and sisters of those parents are also the child's parents. They are not aunts, uncles, or first cousins once removed. They are real mothers and fathers. A typical First Nations child nurses from several mothers and is cared for by many fathers. In most First Nations, a child below age five cannot identify the biological parents, because all parents love and cherish the child. In the generation above one's parents, the adults are all grandparents. In the child's generation, one has brothers and sisters. There are no cousins, since each child is also the child of the other parents. Down one generation from the child, every person is a child of that person. Of course, one would identify one's own children as one's children, but there are no nieces or nephews since they are all one's children. Moving down one more generation, a person has grandchildren everywhere. Within such a large family, one must have high social intelligence and know how to live communally.

In a communal culture, not only is one's own identity subordinate to that of the family, but also one's sole motivation is the family and its well-being. Reward comes only from successful family relationships, not from monetary or prestigious outcomes. A communal person's ethics assumes seeking the good of the group rather than that of the individual. One's behavior assumes communal relationship and sharing goods.

This communal life conflicts with the individualism of the dominant cultures of the Americas. The dominant cultures assume an individualistic paradigm for education, professional development, and housing. Individualist culture assumes that everyone wants the individual version of these things. Many Eurocentric North Americans are shocked that Native people do not want all that the dominant society has to offer. First Nations typically will accept only certain aspects of Western culture. Beyond those basics, Native people prefer our own ways.

Deep misunderstandings exist when Christians from an individualistic culture make assumptions about the world of Christians from a communal culture and vice versa. North American Christianity inculturates Western European values and practices. Over many centuries, Europeans have altered the original Middle Eastern cultural expression of Christianity to fit Western culture. Native Americans mistakenly see Christianity as "the White person's religion" when Christianity is not in its original form but in its European adaptation. In its European form, Christianity uses the arts, ceremonial formats, symbol systems, language, and mentality of Western culture.

People of European background have laid patterns of individualism over Christianity as though individualism is foundational to the teaching of Jesus when it is not. The phrase "your *personal* Lord and Savior" is commonplace in many Eurocentric churches, as though faith is an individual affair. For First Nations and other communal cultures, faith is a communal experience and the entire community sees its teachings belonging to the group.

Individualism also leads people in the dominant culture to try to achieve security by accumulating wealth. Some Christians say that individual wealth is a sign of God's blessing. For First Nations, sharing what one has is a higher value, and possessing things for one's self is contrary to human nature.

European peoples also promote a gospel of progress, the idea that the world is getting better and better. When Native peoples see the world as already in a state of wholeness, Eurocentric people often see this viewpoint as backward. Native Americans value cultural tradition and social customs from ancestral times.

First Nations have a history of theologizing successfully. Aboriginal languages have a nuanced vocabulary for spiritual dynamics that is missing in

English. For example, Christian First Nations understand their cultural and spiritual traditions to be sacred, to be a part of their "Old Testament." Those traditions embody the history of God's relationship with the Native community from creation to the present. People of European origin have sometimes tried to tell First Nations that the "First Covenant" implies that God knew only one people on the face of the earth and that God knew no Native Americans. This absurdity is countered by Native American traditions and by the Bible, whose First Testament asserts that God knew all peoples of the earth (e.g., Pss. 65:9–13; 67:1–7).

Contemporary Native Christians can understand their tribal cultures as lenses through which to hear the Bible, including the teachings of Jesus. The Lakota, called Sioux by the governments, understand Jesus to be a medicine person. Such a person embodies a special relationship with the sacred, teaches profound truths, heals all negative qualities, and guides others to the lives they were intended to have. Medicine persons are not the same as ordinary people, since they have unique qualities that mark them. All traditional Native peoples honor gay and lesbian persons since that quality is a sign of their sacredness. Only a severely acculturated Native person would reject gay men or lesbian women.

Among the Lakota, Jesus is a sun dancer who made his vow to suffer "so the people may live." By fulfilling his vow, he guarantees a full life for the community. While he suffers, he is in full relationship with all that is sacred, and he embodies the right relationship of all things.

A Christian community concerned for justice will self-evaluate its attitudes toward the culture in which it lives and its attitudes toward people of other cultures. If one knows even some of the rudimentary differences between Western cultures and Native American cultures, adjustments can be made in basic understandings of human nature. Cultural conflicts can create such dissonance that Native people cannot hear any of the teachings of Jesus. Actions based on cultural difference can create distance that cannot be bridged. Attitudes based on differing values can cause disagreements that cannot be resolved. How can love of God and of one another exist with such enormous inner differences?

On Peoples Native to the Americas Day the preacher can honor the love of God for all by helping create mutual understanding among peoples of different cultures. When approached sympathetically from the viewpoint of First Nations, the discussion of the Bible readings that follow can inspire sermons whose purposes include mutual understanding leading toward justice. These readings can help the church respect First Nations people, cultures, and religion. The comments can help the church understand how Native peoples listen to the Bible for its help in strengthening communal life.

Lamentations 5:1–22

This passage is a communal lament written after the Babylonians had captured Judah. The communal grief poem describes the fractured community under Babylonian occupation, including the loss of possessions, family relationships, and resources. The writer calls on God to act in behalf of the sad state of Judah.

Aspects of the contemporary lives of First Nations are similar to the situation of Judah under Babylonian oppression. Congregations of European origin could join First Nations in lamenting the losses that have beset First Peoples over the last centuries and the isolation and loneliness that are part of the individualistic European world.

Of course, there is a major difference between the situations of the people of Judah and of Aboriginal peoples. Judah had sinned and thereby invited destruction (vv. 5:1, 16b). First Peoples did not lose their lands because they sinned, but because people of European origin stole lands from First Peoples. As noted in connection with Psalm 130, First peoples do not assume a deity will singularly change their situation, but they look to communal cooperation to renew the life of the community. James 4:1–10 suggests that European repentance is one way that European people can participate in this renewal.

Psalm 130

This psalm is a song of trust that God will forgive the community and deliver it from distress. The psalmist calls to God from the ocean depths of difficulty. "Out of the depths I cry to you, O [God]." The psalmist points out that if God's willingness to redeem were based on the number of faults in a community, then God would never have to redeem. No one would deserve God's help. However, the psalm acknowledges that God's character is to forgive. Israel can be confident in God's salvation. The psalm ends on a note of hope, because "with [God] there is steadfast love" (v. 7).

Finding meaning in difficult circumstances is important. On the one hand, First Nations have felt, "Out of the depths, I cry." On the other hand, Native theology is broader than seeing a deity taking care of all things. First Nations turn to an understanding of the balanced relationships among all things to explain troubles and illness. When the balance is upset, troubles result. The task of healers and ceremony is to restore balance.

James 4:1–10

The Letter of James was written to a congregation divided into factions. This discord violated God's purpose. Some members of the community engaged in self-centered behavior and exploited others. Many people engaged (figuratively) in murder, violent disagreements, stealing, and adultery. The self-serving group used their gain from such behaviors on pleasures that had no lasting value. In so doing they were no longer friends of God but operated on unregenerate values (vv. 1–4).

James calls the self-serving people to repent (vv. 7–10). God has already given them grace to do so (vv. 5–6). Repentance is the way to reconstruct the community according to God's purposes.

Matthew 18:15–22

Matthew 18 is a manual of pastoral care for a congregation in which some members destroyed the sense of community. Matthew 18:15–22 intended to help the community deal with members who ruptured the congregation. Jesus explains that an offended person must point out to a fellow believer that the offense has happened, in the hope that the offending believer will repent and become a supporting member. If that does not work, additional witnesses are to confront the unrepentant offender. Jesus makes the striking statement that earthly offenses have consequences in heaven.

The purpose of this passage, like James 4:1–10, is not to punish wrongdoers but to help maintain a healthy communal life. Both James 4 and Matthew 18 presume that occasionally participants do things that disturb the life of the community. First Peoples see that behaviors are not simply individual misbehaviors but violate community. The congregation needs to address such indiscretions for the common good. When the offending member responds positively to healing suggestions, that person can be restored to full participation, which both strengthens the community and heals the injuring party.

Proper 22 [27]

William B. McClain

JOB 1:1; 2:1–10   GENESIS 2:18–24
PSALM 26   PSALM 8
                                        HEBREWS 1:1–4; 2:5–12
                                                MARK 10:2–16

The Hebrew Bible begins with one very basic assertion: the universal Creator God brought the world into existence and set forth its purpose. This was long before Israel would struggle to recognize that purpose. In their theological reflection on creation, the writers of Genesis make this assertion in almost confessional and doxological fashion: "In the beginning . . . God . . ." (Gen. 1:1). The Gospel of John reinforces this theme: "In the beginning was the Word" (John 1:1).

The creation story today establishes a relational model for creation and sets the tone, temper, and terms for preaching all of the lectionary texts for today (or any Sunday!). Indeed, the human being not being alone correlates with God not being alone. Immediately God moves to fix the problem, and thereby to establish God's purpose for creation: for human beings to be in relation with God and each other, responsible to God and each other, and thus the same for marriage and family, society and civilization.

The African American poet James Weldon Johnson caught the spirit and the beautiful imagination of the old Black folk preacher in trying to convey the narrative of creation to a congregation; he wrote in a sensitive and apt way about God's action and purpose in creation:

> And God stepped out on space,
> And He looked around and said,
> "I'm lonely—
> I'll make me a world."[1]

1. James Weldon Johnson, *God's Trombones: Seven Negro Sermons in Verse* (New York: Penguin Books, 1990), 17. This book offers seven sermons in this same literary/preaching style,

426

Genesis 2:18–24

This reading, from the second creation story, contains the key line: "It is not good that [the human being] should be alone" (v. 18). God then forms the woman and man. Ronald Allen and Clark M. Williamson point out in their *Preaching The Old Testament: A Lectionary Commentary* that "verse 7 gives no explicit indication that the first human being [*adam*] was a male; sexual orientation becomes explicit only in v. 23. . . . [Moreover] there is nothing in the symbolism of the rib in antiquity or in the narrative itself to suggest that the second human being is subordinate to the first."[2] The *adam* has no say in the creation of this partner as "helper." And, lest we miss it, none of the animals is called "helpers." Again, a careful reading of the text will indicate that *adam* was made from the dust of the earth, but the second human is made from the actual human being, and therefore, "They are of the same stuff, thus suggesting primeval equality."[3]

The New Revised Standard Version translates carefully to help readers see that the character of the relationship between the two persons is what is important in the expression "helper as his partner" (v. 20b). And in verse 24 we read, "They become one flesh," a phrase so very often used to try to prove that identity is lost in marriage. However, "one flesh" is simply the Semitic or biblical idiom for "one." I will discuss this further in connection with the Gospel. Let it suffice here to say that the passage simply means that the two work together jointly to fulfill their role by living together in covenant with each other and in harmony with the natural world. Identity is not surrendered, but rather used to enhance their work together—as any marriage between two persons ought to do. As Phyllis Trible so carefully points out, God recedes to the background, "not as the authoritarian controller of events but as the generous delegator of power who even forfeits the right to reverse human decisions."[4]

One is reminded of the popular gospel song "I Need You to Survive," by Hezekiah Walker.[5] Here the songwriter reminds us of our codependency in creation that we so often miss. We are intertwined with all of creation; we are made to be in community and should not even try to exist as islands unto ourselves.

---

along with a traditional African American prayer, "Listen, Lord."

2. Ronald J. Allen and Clark M. Williamson, *Preaching the Old Testament: A Lectionary Commentary* (Louisville, KY: Westminster John Knox Press, 2007), 192.

3. Ibid.

4. Phyllis Trible, *God and the Rhetoric of Sexuality*, Overtures to Biblical Theology (Philadelphia: Fortress Press, 1978), 173.

5. For the lyrics, see http://www.stlyrics.com/lyrics/gospel/ineedyoutosurvive.htm (accessed July 31, 2010).

Since we are not meant to be alone, in preaching this text, the preacher ought to ask: What changes do we need to make to live together with mutual dignity and integrity? What is required of us as individuals, as churches, and as a society to establish a just economic system, with health care for all; right treatment of immigrants; the protection, nurture, and care of children (see especially the Gospel section); the care of orphans and widows; the concern for persons infected and affected with HIV/AIDS and those who are rejected by our world? To work to establish a world where people can have peace with power, bread with dignity, and be valued as persons of worth ("a little lower than the angels," Ps. 8:5 KJV) without regard to race, gender, class, ethnicity, place of birth! Martin Luther King used the language of "the beloved community," but his whole notion of that goal for society was taught to him and embedded in his call to ministry and Jesus' call for the realm of God. Why else would he have ever written his "Letter from Birmingham City Jail"? He knew Jesus taught us to pray, "Thy [realm] come, . . . on earth as it is in heaven" (Matt. 6:10 RSV).

Job 1:1; 2:1–10 and Psalm 26

Why do bad things happen to good people? This is the question the book of Job raises. The book of Job is one of the oldest in Scripture and is written to help the Israelites understand what appeared to them great injustices in the world. Job's story begins with God bragging on Job and then giving Satan permission to strip Job of all that Job values. The text raises many questions; among the most important is, does God actually sanction bad outcomes for people?

The book offers us some resolution, although not a theological one that answers all of our questions. Reason and rational thinking have their proper work to do and can often lead us to important truths; they should always be used as tools to help understanding and clarity and coherence, but they do not have supreme authority. The book of Job reminds us that our ways are not God's ways, that bad things happen, not necessarily as the consequences of sin, but with God's permission. Sometimes only faith can help us move through terrible circumstances. In a society that decided that he must have deserved the fate that befell Job, the prayer of Psalm 26 might have been Job's prayer: "Vindicate me, O LORD, for I have walked in my integrity" (Ps. 26:1).

How often we make judgments about people based on the things that happen to them—much like Job's friends! Without looking at the problems of poor educational systems, classism, racism, sexism, nativism, racial profiling, and other systemic issues, many good practicing Christians judge that people who are poor or homeless, and persons from other nations seeking a better life for themselves and their families and called by some "illegal immigrants," are lazy, unmotivated, trifling, and "undesirable." With Job and the psalmist, these people too can pray, "Vindicate me, O LORD, for I have walked in my integrity."

Often preachers make an unnecessary and prolonged stop to pigeonhole and negatively profile women at Job 2:10: "You speak as any foolish woman would speak." The point is not the gender of the speaker, but the lack of wisdom in cursing God. A foolish male—of whom there are plenty—could have said the same! The old *Interpreter's Bible* has it right: "The insanity of human wisdom is opposed to the sanity of faith!"[6] Yes, "Vindicate me, O LORD . . . redeem me, and be merciful unto me" (my paraphrase of Ps. 26:1 and 11b). A contemporary version might be this: Vindicate those throngs of people who seek justice, freedom, liberation, and peace amidst a world bent on misjudgments, keeping the poor poor, and making the rich richer; a world that fails to seek peace, but instead builds economies out of the business of war and rumors of war. Please, Holy God, save the church from "weak resignation to the evils we deplore."[7]

Hebrews 1:1–4; 2:5–12

I am always amazed when I read this text. Written as a circular letter, the book of Hebrews is penned to encourage Christians who are losing faith while contending with a pluralistic society and wondering, "Is Christ ever coming back?" God holds us in such high esteem that our God puts our welfare above the angels and made redeeming us a priority. That's the message. If that is the case, then why do we not love one another? How do we justify mistreating children? How can we be careless about the needs of others?

The writer of Hebrews makes clear to those who are in danger of renouncing their faith that "God spoke *of old* to our fathers [and mothers, too, as in Miriam and Ruth and Elizabeth and Mary Magdalene] by the prophets" (1:1 RSV). God spoke to Isaiah to help us see that our God is the Lord of all life, and is honored by justice and will not accept empty ceremonies as substitutes. Amos called for justice to run like a river. Martin Luther King and the leaders of the civil rights movement of the 1960s—both Christian and Jews—quoted Amos often in their speeches and sermons. Rabbi Abraham Heschel often made the point: "Few are guilty, but all are responsible."[8]

---

6. Paul Scherer, "Job" (Exposition), in *The Interpreter's Bible*, ed. George A. Buttrick et al. (Nashville: Abingdon Press, 1954), 3:921.

7. A line from Harry Emerson Fosdick's hymn "God of Grace and God of Glory," written in 1930. See *The Chalice Hymnal* (St. Louis: Chalice Press, 1995), 464.

8. Abraham Joshua Heschel, *The Prophets* (New York: Harper & Row, 1962), 16.

The writer of Hebrews thought of the Psalms as prophetic literature and quoted them often. And, yes, God has spoken through the Son, whose priority was concern for the poor. The Gospels and Letters contain more than two thousand references to poverty and the poor, such as "The Spirit of the Lord is upon me . . . anointed me to bring good news to the poor . . . to proclaim release to the captives" (Luke 4:18). Jesus is harsh in judgment: "As you did it to one of the least of these . . . you did it to me" (Matt. 25:40). In today's Gospel lesson, Jesus is indignant about those who would abuse or hinder children. The reference to children is particularly important this month, when we honor children in connection with Children's Sabbath, as the National Children's Defense Fund urges us to do.

Mark 10:2–16

Roman society had little use for children. The precariousness of their lives made it easy to disregard them. And since they were not "productive" members of society, they were often ignored, abused, abandoned, or sold. Children were often required to be seen and not heard, and female children were often ignored. Jesus, however, not only says that children are important in the realm, but uses them as examples of citizenship in the realm. There was a similar attitude in the civil rights movement of the 1960s—especially in Birmingham, Alabama. After the children were allowed to come and participate in public demonstrations, the adults in the movement were much more prepared to face fire hoses, police dogs, cattle prods, and other instruments of cruelty and pain. The adults became more courageous *because the children came*—a fact of history often ignored. I know this to be true: I was there!

In the first part of the text, Jesus becomes the champion of the cause of women. He does so by transferring the discussion from the way the Pharisees put it ("Is it lawful?" v. 2) into the higher realm of the purposes of God, and the spiritual realities of marriage. As Jesus saw it, the purpose of God for creation is a stronger theological and biblical claim than any argument for particular cultural, civil, or legal practices. Jesus probes the deeper intentions of God's purposes and the law, as he does with food regulation and the Sabbath. He saw how human interpretation and tradition violated God's purpose in the marriage relationship. That is part of why ministers often include in traditional Christian ritual for marriage that Jesus "adorned and beautified it with his presence at Cana of Galilee."[9] Pheme Perkins, my former colleague at Boston College and an outstanding New Testament scholar, puts

---

9. See any of the regular rituals for Christian marriage of almost any Christian denomination.

the matter succinctly: "Jesus opposed substituting human traditions for the commandments of God."[10]

Jesus is even more emphatic about children being prevented from coming to him: "But when Jesus saw this, he was *indignant* and said to them, 'Let the children come to me; do not stop them'" (v. 14). In our world, in which we become so used to cruelties, so familiar with so many evils, we can easily become indifferent unless an injury happens directly to us or to those dearest to us. By comparison, it is humbling to compare the things about which Jesus became indignant: money changing in the temple; when the table crowd sought to discourage the woman who sought to anoint Jesus for burial and he cried, "Let her alone!'; indifference to human need; the callous attitude of his disciples and their officious blindness that would keep children away.

One can only wonder what he would be indignant about if he walked our streets and made his way to some of the back alleys of our cities, and maybe looked in the window at what goes on in our churches. Maybe this Sunday the preacher can help the people of the congregation to see some of the things that we too should be indignant about, and perhaps we can start on this October Sunday with how children are treated in our society. The Children's Defense Fund will gladly provide many facts and figures about the treatment of children.[11] And maybe the church can say again with Jesus: "Let the children come; do not stop them." I just wonder what would happen if the church of Jesus Christ followed his example, found its prophetic voice again, and *became indignant!*

---

10. Pheme Perkins, "Mark," in *The New Interpreter's Bible*, ed. Leander Keck et al. (Nashville: Abingdon Press, 1995), 8:643.
11. See www.childrensdefense.org.

World Communion Sunday
(First Sunday in October)

Joseph R. Jeter Jr.

DEUTERONOMY 8:1–10
PSALM 117
1 CORINTHIANS 11:17–34
JOHN 14:27–31

On World Communion Sunday (the first Sunday in October), congregations across the world partake of Communion. Someone has described the sacred table on this day as 25,000 miles long. In our fragmented world, in which groups often relate with suspicion and violence and even try to destroy one another, the churches of the world coming together to break the loaf and drink the cup is a sign of God's intention for all peoples to live together in love, peace, and justice. The sermon might help the congregation confess ways that it contributes to the fragmentation of the world and to resolve to witness to love, peace, and justice.

> In wine and grape juice, in wafer and tablet and loaf, in prayer rail and brass tray, in all the variations we find our many differences given concrete form. . . . These differences divide us, but the fact that we all continue together around communion tables . . . is an important expression of who we are—the one church of God. . . . Communion has the power to bring us back together at the one table of Jesus, even against our petty struggling for the positions that define our own righteousness.[1]
>
> *Jon L. Berquist*

---

1. Jon L. Berquist, *Ancient Wine, New Wineskins: The Lord's Supper in Old Testament Perspective* (St. Louis: Chalice Press, 1991), 2–3.

Deuteronomy 8:1–10

The book of Deuteronomy binds memory and faith for the children of Israel and all their heirs. The Israelites crossed over into the hot, arid Sinai. There was little food and water there, but God fed them with manna. Their survival was completely dependent upon God. Hundreds of years after the exodus, Deuteronomy instructs the people to remember how God led them through the wilderness, humbled them with hunger, and fed them. Remember. Then, right after these words, Deuteronomy 8:1–10 reminds them that God is now taking the people into a good and fruitful land, with abundant water, where they will lack for nothing. Remember. Your ancestors barely survived, but now you have everything. The reader, whether thousands of years ago or yesterday, knows the risk that the text makes clear. The people begged and pleaded with God, and God fed them; now God gives everything to them, and woe unto them if they have forgotten to thank, serve, and praise God.

The classic motion picture *Shenandoah* features a self-sufficient pacifist farmer, played by James Stewart, during the War between the States. He claims his family has no part in the war, although they are eventually dragged into it. But in one scene, the family is gathered around the table for dinner and Stewart offers this prayer:

> Lord, we cleared this land. We plowed and sowed it and harvested. We cooked the harvest. It wouldn't be here; we wouldn't be eatin' it if we hadn't done it all ourselves. We worked dog-bone hard for every crumb and morsel, but we thank you anyway, Lord, for this food we're about to eat. Amen.[2]

Few of us can claim such self-sufficiency, but unfortunately our nod to God is often similar. The Deuteronomist said, "Do not forget what God has done for you." The themes in Deuteronomy of remembrance, obedience, and humility are appropriate on World Communion Sunday. Let us take seriously these three calls: remember God's love, walk in God's ways, and share the bounty of God with those who need it.

The early church had trouble bringing together diverse cultures and approaches to the faith. Heresies were rampant. Hippolytus, martyred in the confusion and later sainted, wrote a manual of church order and worship about 197 CE containing the earliest order of the Eucharist we have. As churches today also become more diverse, a celebration of the Eucharist

---

2. *Shenandoah*, a Universal film, 1965. Written by James Lee Barrett, directed by Andrew V. McLaglen, produced by Robert Arthur.

on this special day based on the order of Hippolytus[3] could be a symbol of shared life. The service offers bread, cheese, and olives. Remember. Walk in God's ways. Share the bounty.

There are three cups in Hippolytus's service: water, milk and honey, and wine. Water symbolizes cleansing of the soul. Milk and honey represent the fathers and mothers blessed by God in the good, new land. Wine suggests the blood of Jesus, poured out for sin. Today these symbols are emphasized in different ways around the world. Tens of thousands die every day from contaminated water, especially in Africa. Not surprisingly, some churches in West Africa gather around a table loaded with clean, pure water, symbol of the purity of Jesus and his love. The pure water is to drink now and to carry home. Some feminist groups in the United States bring milk and honey to the table, not so much to honor those who made their way to the promised land, but to honor Mary, the mother of Jesus, who gave him the milk of life. In the first two millennia of the church, wine was almost the sole eucharistic drink. These days many churches use wine less because of alcoholism and poverty. There is, for example, much grape juice in North America and kava juice in the South Pacific. A World Communion Sunday service might have a variety of drinks set on the table, each representing a way that certain groups of Christians best understand and love Jesus. People could drink from the cup most familiar to them, drink from a cup strange to them, or drink from them all. Remember. Walk in God's ways. Share the bounty.

Psalm 117

This psalm has two claims to biblical fame: it is the smallest psalm and (some say) the very center of the Bible. But the theme of the two verses is seldom preached. The psalm is not written just for the Hebrews, but for "all you nations!" (plural) and for "all you peoples!" (plural). "When Christians say and sing this psalm they remind themselves that the praise of God is complete only when they intend to praise in concert with all people. . . . It is a psalm for any Lord's Day, but it is especially appropriate for the celebration of World Communion Sunday."[4]

"Praise in concert with all people." Christianity does not always receive a good grade in this matter. For example, Charlemagne baptized conquered peoples by driving them through a river, not exactly in concert. And it is chilling to stare at the photograph of Reich Bishop Ludwig Mueller, who has

---

3. "The Apostolic Tradition of Hippolytus," in *Liturgies of the Western Church*, ed. Bard Thompson (Philadelphia: Fortress Press, 1980), 20–24.
4. James Luther Mays, *Psalms* (Louisville, KY: John Knox Press, 1994), 373.

raised his arm in the Hitler salute, along with the storm troopers (SA) standing next to him.[5] Yes, many Christians have reached out to other denominations, religions, and cultures to praise God, finding ways to sing together. But there is much to do.

When we approach the table on this Sunday, let us pause for a moment, look out the window, and "see" how this table reaches around the world, with enough space to seat and serve more than a hundred nations, more than a billion people! Much more than twelve baskets full will be left over today. They will be needed.

John 14:27–31

Chapters 13 and 14 describe the Last Supper of Jesus and his disciples. John does not directly mention the institution of the Lord's Supper, but he does speak about foot washing; the dialogues between Jesus and Judas (betrayal), Peter (denial), and Philip (who Jesus is and what he leaves); and the promise of the Holy Spirit. Our text is about one of these. Jesus is about to be subjected to violence, crucifixion, and death. So what does he leave with his disciples? Does he encourage them to get even with his persecutors? No. He says, "Peace I leave with you; my peace I give to you" (v. 27). With this gift Jesus did not suggest there would be an absence of conflict in the world, but that God would carry Jesus' followers through the conflict to heaven.[6]

He continues his encouragement: "Do not let your hearts be troubled, and do not let them be afraid. . . . The ruler of this world . . . has no power over me" (vv. 27, 30). Trouble and fear were indigenous to the protochurch. Had not Jesus preached a gospel of peace, the church might have disintegrated through internecine squabbles. The Eucharist, which brought people from "every tribe and language and people and nation" (Rev. 5:9) to the same large table, may well have been the primary factor that held the church together.[7] We are Christians by the love of Jesus, manifest at that rough wooden table and on the rough wooden cross on the morrow.

Jesus concluded the Last Supper with the desire "that the world may know that I love the Father" (v. 31). As we gather worldwide around all manner of "tables," let us reaffirm that Jesus loved God and showed us how to love God and one another. Nothing is more important.

At a small evening Communion service, the group sat in a circle. We talked about what the Lord's Supper meant to us. Someone mentioned the film *Places*

5. *Betrayal: German Churches and the Holocaust*, ed. Robert Ericksen and Susannah Heschel (Minneapolis: Fortress Press, 1999), cover; photograph taken in 1933.
6. Correspondence with Ronald Allen.
7. From Revelation to John 14:6.

in the Heart, starring Sally Field. The movie ends with a Communion service. As the trays are passed, one person in the group is stunned to see everyone in the movie, living and dead, taking Communion. The brokenness among people in the movie is rectified in sharing the bread, the cup. I mentioned James Sanders's affirmation that whenever we gather for Communion, the whole church is present and "we are surrounded by so great a cloud of witnesses," living or at rest.[8]

When it came time for us to pass the bread and cup around the circle, I invited each person to take a piece of bread and to name someone dear to them who has gone before us and is part of the cloud of witnesses, and then, when the cup arrived, to name a living person they wish were here with us. By the time we were finished, the size of our little communion circle had tripled. We were surrounded by love.

1 Corinthians 11:17–34

Why do we celebrate the Lord's Supper?[9] First, because Jesus told us to, and second, because it has proved to be a powerful vehicle of the Spirit of Christ among us. The central text used as the warrant and authority for our service comes from 1 Corinthians 11:23–26. There are several key phrases here. Paul said, "I received from the Lord what I also handed on to you" (v. 23). He did not just make this up. "On the night when he was betrayed, [Jesus] took a loaf of bread" (v. 23). No one, in my opinion, has interpreted this better than James Sanders:

> It was on the night in which we betrayed him that he broke bread and gave it to us. . . . [God's grace is expressed] in the midst of our sin: we know that God comes to us in our [act of] betrayal.
>
> This was our night; the night the church was conceived. And we were all there, all twelve of us, seated about the table. . . . I know of a certainty that because Judas was there I am not excluded. What if he had not been present? Then that bread would not be for me.
>
> No excuse . . . could possibly increase the love which there surrounds us or the forgiveness which there indicts us. And then we realize . . . that salvation is also judgment, . . . the judgment of his grace: I do love you still.[10]

---

8. Paraphrased from James Sanders, *God Has a Story, Too* (Philadelphia: Fortress Press, 1979), 96.

9. This section on 1 Corinthians 11:17–34 is excerpted from a paper I read at the 2007 meeting of the Academy of Homiletics.

10. Sanders, *God Has a Story, Too*, 94, 96, 100. See also Joseph R. Jeter Jr., *Re/Membering: Meditations and Sermons for the Table of Jesus Christ* (St. Louis: Chalice, 1996), 58–59.

Then come the elements and the call to remembrance. We proclaim his death. This is hard. This is not happy. My mentor, Ronald Osborn, wept at the table when he remembered Jesus loved us this much. It is a time of spiritual focus. It is an intensely personal and yet communal experience. The table represents more than what Jesus did for us; it also represents what the church must do for God.

Communion is finally and strangely a social experience. I wrote a book once that included 141 Communion sermons and meditations, including extensive coverage of this text. But I always focused on verse 23 and following, never on verses 17–22. Why? Because I did not understand what in the world Paul was getting at in vv. 17–22. You come together to "humiliate those who have nothing" (v. 22)? That made no sense to me. But a recent book by Robert Garland[11] left me both stunned and more grateful than ever to Paul. Garland shows that participants at Greek and Roman banquets often derided deformed people. Romans in the imperial era developed derision into an art form of brutal sophistication. "In convivial settings hunchbacks, cripples, dwarfs, and obese women clumsily imitated acrobats, jugglers, and dancers"[12] while the diners laughed. Could Paul have seen that horrible practice moving toward the table of the Lord and stopped it cold? It is unlikely that the church in Corinth was involved in such doings, but Paul did say, "You . . . humiliate those who have nothing. . . . Should I commend you? . . . I do not commend you!" (v. 22). The Corinthians were at least mistreating those who "had nothing." I want to say we are different, but I cannot, once I realize that Paul is talking to us. Have mercy on us, O God. Everyone is welcome; everyone is important. This is an inclusive table. No one should leave the table with nothing.

11. Robert Garland, *The Eye of the Beholder: Deformity and Disability in the Graeco-Roman World* (Ithaca, NY: Cornell University Press, 1995).
12. Ibid., 84.

Proper 23 [28]

Miguel A. De La Torre

JOB 23:1–9, 16–17
PSALM 22:1–15

AMOS 5:6–7, 10–15
PSALM 90:12–17
HEBREWS 4:12–16
MARK 10:17–31

In 1977, Billy Joel sang that "only the good die young" in his pop-rock album *The Stranger*. Its popularity was due, in part, to the song being banned from many radio stations because of its perceived anti-Catholic lyrics. Billy Joel clearly states, "I'd rather laugh with the sinners than cry with the saints, the sinners are much more fun." Maybe not fun but, probably, they live a more profitable life. The good do die young, while the evil prosper.

Amos 5:6–7, 10–15

By contrast, the prophet Amos claims that those who seek God shall live, but trouble will befall those who "turn justice to wormwood" (v. 7). The prophet condemns those who fail to do justice, trampling instead on heads of the poor. They may build earthly palaces and plant precious vineyards, but they will never live in these mansions or drink the wine of their harvest (v. 11). Yet for those who seek good and not evil, they will live in the presence of God (v. 14). If we are honest with ourselves, the promise of life and God's company is a message that usually does not match reality. All around us we see that the faithful are crushed by oppressive structures that enrich those who live in fine manors and sip expensive wines. Those who choose evil can afford the finest health care, prolonging their iniquitous lives, while those who are trampled usually live short, brutal lives. To make matters worse, often it seems that in the midst of their sufferings, God is silent. It appears that Billy Joel might be right after all; only the good do die young, as well as the disenfranchised and dispossessed.

For many, if one is faithful to God, then God will bless that person; but if, instead, one does evil things, then God will curse that person with misfortune.

Obedience to God's command has as much to do with the desire for God's rich blessings as it does with the fear of God's wrath. This form of theology has been present since the earliest writings of the biblical text. Today such a perspective has become popular among many Christians. It has come to be called the prosperity gospel. Basically, it claims that we are children of the King, and the King wants to shower blessings (here understood as riches) upon us. All that is required from us is faith, to name and claim the blessings that are awaiting us. All we need to do is ask from a loving Father who wants to give us the desires of our heart, because, after all, our God loves us so much that God wants only the best for us. Believers can always be spotted, for they are the ones possessing health and wealth. For those who lack such blessings, this is an indication of a shortage of faith or, worse, the manifestation of disbelief.

Job 23:1–9, 16–17

And yet, we are confronted with the problem of Job, a book that has Satan raising a very legitimate question. Does Job (or, in fact, any of us) honor God only because we benefit from God's protection or suffer from God's punishment if we are disobedient? Is piety linked to prosperity? Do we continue to trust in God even in times of adversity, in times of want, in times of suffering? Satan, not the antithesis of God but a member of God's holy counsel, proposes that the real test of righteousness is continued faithfulness to God even during adversity, when no promise of retributive justice or hope for any reward is in sight. God accepts Satan's counsel and decides to test Job. In effect, God—not Satan—is responsible for the evil that befalls the faithful Job, including the loss of his wealth, the loss of health, and, more tragic, the loss of all his children. God sends this evil through Satan, for the text shows us that Satan is unable to act independently from God. The disturbing conclusion that the book of Job elucidates is that God does as God pleases, and who is humanity to question the ways of the Deity?

Holding on to the belief that the faithful are blessed by God and only the wicked are cursed and punished, Job makes his case—a case that does not want for arguments (v. 4). He recognizes that as an honest man, he would surely win his case before any judicial court (v. 7). It is God who is hard pressed to bring a legitimate charge against Job. Because Job has lived a righteous life, his lament contains a rebellious, accusative tone toward God for inflicting unwarranted suffering (v. 1). He has done no wrong deserving the darkness that now hides him and the gloom that veils God's presence from him (v. 17). But alas, he is unable to make his case directly to El Shaddai, for God cannot be found. Regardless of whether Job goes eastward or westward, God is not present (v. 8) or, worse, chooses not to be present.

Psalm 22:1–15 and Psalm 90:12–17

Along with the psalmist, as well as the future Messiah, Job cries out, *"Eli, Eli, lema sabachthani?"*—"My God, my God, why have thou forsaken me?" (Ps. 22:1; Matt. 27:46). The biblical text teaches that even those who are virtuous suffer. And while the burden of such suffering might be bearable if God's presence were known, Job, the psalmist, and even Jesus himself cry out all day to a God that does not answer (v. 2)—a God who appears to be absent. Yes, it is true that their forebears placed their trust in a God who rescued and saved them (vv. 4–5), but such past testimonies are insufficient when facing a jeering crowd that with the toss of their heads sneer, "You relied on God, then let God save you! You say God is your friend, then let God rescue you!" (paraphrase of v. 8). In the randomness of life's vicissitudes, in the hopelessness caused by oppressive structures, in the solitude of a silent God, those who place their trust in the Almighty can still be like those whose bones are all disjointed. A once courageous heart melts like wax as the tongue fastens itself to a dry palate (vv. 14–15).

In the midst of the human condition, the psalmist of Psalm 90 encourages us to seek God's pity; counting the few remaining days we have (Ps. 90:12–13). We should beseech God to make our future as happy as our past was sad (v. 15). The psalmist recognizes that any hope of morning filled with love and days of happy songs (v. 14) rests upon the mercies of God. While this may be true, it may not be enough. Regardless of whether the sweetness of God is with us or not (v. 17), we are still left wondering why our past had to be so sad.

Hebrews 4:12–16

More important, we must ask why those who follow God's precepts are usually the ones who end up crucified. Why do the good people seem to die young? In the midst of our suffering we demand to know where God is hiding. Maybe the answer to our query is that God is in the same place where God was while God's beloved Son was being lynched on a Roman tree. We may not understand God's ways, which honestly seem so unfair, but we do have a supreme high priest who is capable of feeling our weakness with us, a high priest who has been tempted in every way as we have been and yet emerged sinless (vv. 14–15). Jesus did not deserve all that befell him, specifically the agony of the cross; and yet he remained faithful to a silent God.

The cross exists not for us to figure out why it is there or why Jesus had to hang from it. Rather, the cross exists to show us how our undeserved sufferings, our rejection by those privileged by society, and our death become the suffering, rejection, and death of God. We can have faith in a God, even when this God appears absent, because, through Christ, God intimately knows our pain, since God experienced our pain, creating solidarity with all who continue to be crucified today so that the few can continue to have abundant life at the expense of the poor. Because our Lord has wounds upon his flesh, just as the righteous carry all manner of physical, emotional, and financial stigmata, we then can approach God's throne of grace in confidence, knowing we will receive mercy and find grace in our hour of need (v. 16).

Those being crucified today become Jesus Christ in the here and now. Their suffering has the potential of redeeming the powerful and privileged by providing them with an opportunity to interact with Christ manifested in the lives and struggles of those living on the margins of society. As those with power die to their privilege and seek solidarity with those who suffer under oppressive structures, they discover an opportunity to meet and know Christ. In a culture that privileges those who are male, those who are wealthy, and those who are white, solidarity with Christ, who forsook his own equality with God to take the form of a human, requires Christ's disciples also to "take up their crosses" and follow him. In short, it requires dying to whatever creates privilege and prevents solidarity with the crucified people of today. Salvation, as liberation, requires crucifying maleness, riches, and whiteness—in other words, the active dismantling of any social structure designed to privilege one group at the expense of another.

Mark 10:17–31

It is difficult to learn this lesson when "blessed" with riches, as was the case with the young man, a member of a leading family, who approached Jesus asking the question, "Good Master, what must I do to inherit eternal life?" (v. 17). For many Christians today, the answer to such a question is easy: accept Jesus as your *personal* Savior and Lord of your life, usually through the recitation of what has come to be known as "the sinner's prayer." In many churches, salvation is achieved by making a public profession (at times by walking down a church aisle), joining the church, renouncing drinking and carousing, and getting baptized. Depending on denominational association, this is how many ministers throughout the United States would come to answer the question posed by the young man in the Gospel of Mark.

Fortunately, Jesus does not provide the response commonly given in some portions of modern Christianity. Jesus does not invite the young aristocrat to repent of his sins and then allow Jesus to enter into his life in a personal relationship. Instead, Jesus tells him to keep the commandments, which the rich young man confesses he has kept since his earliest days (vv. 19–20). Then

Jesus does the unexpected. Rather than simply accepting the young man as a follower, Jesus, out of love for him, tells him to sell all that he owns and distribute the money to the poor to gain treasures in heaven. Only then can he follow Jesus. But when the rich young man hears Jesus' words, the price to pay is too high, so he leaves full of sadness (vv. 21–22).

As the rich young man walks away, Jesus makes a disturbing pronouncement to the disciples who remain: "How hard it will be for those who have wealth to enter the [reign] of God! . . . It is easier for a camel to go through the eye of a needle than for someone who is rich to enter the [reign] of God" (vv. 23, 25). A faith based solely on individual belief and disconnected from public responsibilities and actions allows the rich young rulers of our time to claim to be followers and disciples of Christ, but Jesus determines salvation by how the rich interact with the poor. Because such a reading is difficult to accept, readers of this passage are quick to spiritualize the text by claiming that the primary message of the story is that Jesus must be the center of every aspect of the life of the believer. All idols—whether they are riches or something else like status, family, a job, and so on—must be relinquished. In this particular story, wealth just happens to be the idol of this young man, and his downfall is his unwillingness to abandon this particular idol. The probable conclusion is that the wealthy of today must also be willing to give up everything for Jesus. But they don't really have to do it, or radically change their lifestyles; they just have to be willing.

Yet Jesus connects the salvation of the rich man with his response to the poor. Anyone who claims power and privilege, whether from maleness, whiteness, or economic class, forfeits his or her claim to God's eschatological promise, just like the rich young ruler. God's reign is not promised to those who are oppressors or benefit from oppressive structures. To insist on such a lifestyle forfeits any claim to God's hope. Believing in Jesus or even keeping the commandments is insufficient for obtaining salvation. Concentrating solely on personal faith divorced from praxis—actions of loving justice—encourages a cheap grace. Jesus attempts to force the rich young man, as well as us today, to move beyond an abstract belief in Christ to a material response to those who are hungry, thirsty, naked, alien, sick, and incarcerated. Jesus links salvation with our response to the least of these. The task for those seeking eternal life must go beyond an intellectual understanding of Jesus Christ to the actual doing of Christlike actions—not because salvation is achieved through those actions, but because they serve as witness to the empowering grace already given by God.

The Gospel of Mark fails to show how the rich young man is responsible for the plight of the poor, or even has enriched himself at their expense; but because he is rich, he automatically becomes linked to their poverty. Why?

Because to continue worshiping Christ apart from any commitment to those who are the least is tacit complicity with the overarching structures of oppression that exist, specifically along gender, race, and class lines. Simply stated, no one gets into heaven without a reference letter from those who are poor! To ignore the cry of those who are marginalized is to deny Christ's message, regardless of whether or not we confess our belief in Jesus and proclaim his name with our lips.

Night of Power (27th of Ramadan)

John Kaltner

GENESIS 15:1–6
PSALM 96
HEBREWS 6:13–20
MATTHEW 6:19–24

The Night of Power (*Laylat al-Qadr*) is important to the Islamic community because, according to Islamic tradition, that is the night that God revealed the Qur'an in its entirety to the prophet Muhammad through the angel Gabriel (Jibril). The Night of Power is observed on the 27th of Ramadan. Since Islam follows the lunar calendar (which is shorter than the solar calendar), it eventually occurs in all of the months of the solar calendar followed by Christians.[1] Given the tensions between some Christian and Islamic communities, the preacher could use the occasion of the Night of Power to consider relationships between these groups. What do we have in common? Where do we differ? How can Christians encourage respect between the two communities?

Say: "We believe in [God] and in what has been revealed to us and what was revealed to Abraham, Isma'il, Isaac, Jacob, and the Tribes, and in (the Books) given to Moses, Jesus, and the prophets from their Lord: We make no distinction between one and another among them, and to [God] do we bow our will (in Islam)."

Surah 3:84

O [humankind]! We created you from a single pair of a male and female, and made you into nations and tribes, that ye may know each other (not despise each other).[2]

Surah 49:13

1. From 2011 through 2020 the date of the Night of Power moves from September to August, July, June, May, and April.
2. Surah 3:84 and Surah 49:13 in Abdullah Yusef Ali, *The Meaning of the Holy Qur'an*, 9th ed., Arabic and English Texts (Brentwood, MD: Amana Corporation, 1997), 149, 1342–43.

On this Holy Day for Justice we are asked to put aside the false gods and idols we have created and to recognize God as the one true Creator of all that exists. In the Gospel reading Jesus draws a distinction between earthly and heavenly treasures and urges us to not be seduced by the former. In a similar way, God tells Abraham that the stars above him point beyond themselves and represent the many physical and spiritual offspring he will have.

The message of the Qur'an, whose revelation is celebrated today, brought Muslims into the family of Abraham. These readings remind us of how much we can learn from Islam, the religion of those relatives from whom so many of us remain estranged. Their belief system, although much like our own, is different enough that it allows us to explore new ways of thinking about God and God's relationship to us. In the process, Abraham's family is brought closer together and finds itself gazing into the sky in search of heavenly treasures. In our increasingly complex and diverse world, what do the stars represent for us?

Psalm 96

All of creation is invited to sing to God and to celebrate God's majesty. The universal dimension of the psalm is seen in its many references to the earth, the nations, all peoples, and families. The rich diversity present in the world means that each community recognizes and calls upon God in its own manner. One way Muslims do this is through the *Fatiha*, the opening chapter of the Qur'an, which serves as an introduction to the book and has much in common with Psalm 96:

> [1]In the name of God, the merciful One, the compassionate One! [2]Praise be to God, Lord of all creation, [3]the merciful One, the compassionate One, [4]king of judgment day. [5]We worship You; we ask You for help. [6]Guide us along the straight path, [7]the path of those You have favored, those who incur no anger and do not go astray.

The psalm and the *Fatiha* both begin with a reference to God's name, and they share an understanding of who God is—the ruler of all creation who, as sovereign, is worthy of all praise and worship. Both also stress the need to avoid sin, which the Qur'an describes as "going astray" and the psalm presents as worshiping false gods. These texts remind us that the works of creation are meant to worship God and should never be taken as objects of worship themselves. The *Fatiha* and Psalm 96 are two voices in the world's song of praise to God, and they create a magnificent harmony that extols the greatness of the merciful and compassionate One who created all the world's peoples.

Genesis 15:1–6 and Hebrews 6:13–20

These readings speak of the promise God made to Abraham that he would have many descendants (Gen. 15:5). That promise can be understood in two different ways, one literal and the other figurative. In the first sense, God is speaking to Abraham about his biological offspring—his children and his children's children, extending through successive generations. But if the promise is understood figuratively, God is describing Abraham's spiritual heirs, those who are related to him through faith as well as by blood.

The first Qur'an passage quoted above (3:84) captures well the second way of understanding God's promise to Abraham. It presents him as the first link in a chain of prophets and other believers who trace their roots back to Abraham, whom the Qur'an considers to be the quintessential monotheist. The family-like nature of relationships among Abraham's spiritual offspring is expressed in the often-repeated claim that Muslims have their origin in Ishmael while Jews and Christians are the descendants of Isaac.

The Qur'an verse calls for belief in what was revealed to Abraham and the other prophets throughout history, and it urges that no distinction be made among them. Abraham is the starting point, and the text from Genesis has a subtle way of communicating just how important he is. God speaks to Abraham prior to this in the book of Genesis, but this is the first time it is said the "word of the LORD came to him" (vv. 1, 4). This is an expression commonly used to describe when prophets and others receive a message from God, and this is its first appearance in the Hebrew Bible. The very first occurrence of this important phrase is found in the context of God's promise to Abraham of descendants, both biological and spiritual.

God assures Abraham, still known here as Abram, that his offspring will be a great multitude by comparing them to the stars in the heavens. Even in our world, with its scientific sophistication, the experience of standing in an open field and gazing up into a star-filled sky can be awe inspiring. We behold the vastness of creation; our relatively insignificant place in the cosmos comes sharp relief. If each of those stars represents one of Abraham's descendants, as God says, the diversity and complexity of his family is equally astounding. The second Qur'an reading (49:13) tells us that this is the case: humanity is a remarkable patchwork of different colors and shapes, all part of God's plan allowing the various members of Abraham's family to learn from and about one another.

A star plays an important role in Abraham's life in the Qur'an, but it teaches a different lesson. In 6:76–78 he observes a number of heavenly objects, and is tempted to reach the wrong conclusion. "When the night closed around him he saw a star and said, 'This is my Lord.' But when it waned, he said, 'I do not like things that wane.' Then when he saw the moon rising he said, '*This* is my Lord.' But when it set he said, 'If my Lord does not lead me, I will be one of the lost ones.' Then he saw the sun rising and he said, '*This* is my Lord! This is truly the greatest.' But when the sun set he said, 'My people, I disavow all that you worship beside God.'" This brief episode highlights Islam's rejection of idol worship and its radical monotheism. It also warns readers: if even Abraham can be tempted to worship something other than God, the rest of us must always be on guard against the idols we create and are drawn to.

This same theme occurs in the reading from Hebrews with its reference to God having no one greater by whom to swear (v. 13). This idea is in line with Muslim belief that nothing in creation—even the sun, as Abraham learns—should be placed above the Creator. This idea is encapsulated in one of the most frequently heard Arabic phrases throughout the world—*allahu akbar*, "God is greatest." The phrase is repeated four times in the Muslim call to prayer, which is announced five times a day from all mosques. It addition, the phrase is heard frequently in everyday speech and is often used for decorative purposes on buildings and works of art. It is a constant reminder of God's supremacy and, in the words of Hebrews, "unchangeable character" (v. 17).

The reference to Jesus in the last verse of the Hebrews reading abruptly changes the subject to reinterpret the Abraham story. It introduces a christological element that transforms the tradition about the promise to Abraham into a statement about Jesus' relationship to humanity. The Gospels and Letters often make similar use of material from the Torah, Prophets, and Writings, giving them a Christian "spin." The same thing occurs in the Qur'an, which often presents biblical themes and figures in ways that are in line with Islamic theology and beliefs. An example of this is seen in the story about Abraham and the star, mentioned above.

This phenomenon plays a significant role in Muslim-Christian relations. How should we respond to the way "our" stories are reimagined and reinterpreted in the Qur'an? Who owns them? Is it fair for Christians to criticize the Qur'an's reworking of biblical material when the Gospels and Letters make similar moves with the Torah, Prophets, and Writings? These are important questions to consider on this feast day that commemorates the revelation Ishmael's side of Abraham's family received from God.

Matthew 6:19–24

In a sense, Jesus is the biggest obstacle to Muslim-Christian relations. He is the elephant in the room when Christians and Muslims talk theology. The reason is simple, but hard for many Christians to hear: Muslims maintain that believing Jesus is God is a sin. In fact, the Qur'an teaches it is the one sin that

God will not forgive. The Arabic term for this offense is *shirk*, or "association," and it refers to any attempt to associate a created someone or something with the uncreated God. To do so, in Islam, is to violate the unity that is the core of God's essence. In the eyes of Muslims, the Christian doctrine of the incarnation is an example of *shirk*.

Christians need to understand why Muslims think this way. The Muslim view is not due to ingrained hostility toward Christianity. At the heart of their rejection is the deep veneration Muslims feel for the absolute oneness of God. It reflects their reverence toward God, not their contempt toward Christianity. Islam teaches that one should not confuse the tangible beauty and goodness of the world, as personified in the life of Jesus, with the transcendent beauty and goodness of its Creator.

Jesus makes a similar point in this reading from Matthew. He cautions against focusing so much on earthly treasures that we neglect heavenly ones. If this happens, he warns, one's heart will be in the wrong place. In effect, he speaks about the temptation to create idols. A false god can take many forms—it might be a person, an object, an idea, or a behavior. Jesus reminds us that we cannot serve both a god of our own making and the God who made us.

Islam's insistence on the oneness of God can be a check against the tendency to create and worship idols in our lives. In a certain sense, Muslims are more immune to the moths, rust, and thieves that can sometimes accompany belief in a God who takes human form. Like all human beings they are tempted, but Muslim faith tells them it is impossible for God to be fully present in something created.

That is not the case for Christians, and sometimes belief in the incarnation has led to statements like that of Saint Athanasius, bishop of Alexandria in the fourth century: "God became human so that humans might become divine."[3] That is simultaneously an exhilarating and a troubling thought. It privileges humanity and acknowledges our capacity to be like God. But, at the same time, it raises the prospect that we might come to think we *are* God.

Where is our treasure? Whom or what do we serve? All Abraham's spiritual offspring would do well to take their lead from Abraham, gazing up at a starry sky in the Qur'an, who came to realize that not all that glitters is God.

---

3. For a traditional formulation, see Athanasius, *The Incarnation of the Word of God*, trans. A Religious of CSMVSTh (New York: Macmillan Co., 1946), 93.

Proper 24 [29]

Henry H. Mitchell

JOB 38:1–7 (34–41)	ISAIAH 53:4–12
PSALM 104:1–9, 24, 35C	PSALM 91:9–16
	HEBREWS 5:1–10
	MARK 10:35–45

This week's meditations could be called a collection of possible responses to the injustices suffered by active believers. We encounter different responses to such suffering in the readings from Job, the Psalms, Hebrews, and Isaiah. The preacher today might help the congregation recognize various ways people can respond to their own experiences of injustice. Which ones are more faithful for the congregation in its present context?

Job 38:1–7 (34–41)

In my final year as a boy soprano, my best solo said, "Oh, that I knew where I might find him," sung with childlike warmth and urgency. Little did I dream that these words of Job (23:3) flowed out of his deep desire to argue with God. Most people would probably react the same way I did, by moving away from the verse's original meaning. We tend to feel that we are owed an explanation for the unfortunate encounters God allows to happen to us day after day.

The interesting angle to this situation is Job's desire to argue with God on a person-to-person basis, with an arbitrator in charge. This same position is more common today. Much of the theological topic called theodicy is in this same vein. Why does God allow injustices that we would not permit if we were in charge? Like Job, we want to know the rationale. However, the irony of our actual position is that we cry for God's explanation mostly when the injustice is against *us*, not others.

Yet when we treat others with obvious injustice, we offer explanations such as, "The federal funds that could have been used to reinforce the levee in New Orleans were used for more *important* projects, and in other places. God is just, and calls us to be just. God understands our good intentions, even if the dwellers of the low grounds do not." And, we say such things with a straight face. Any answers we propose to unjust suffering such as that experienced along the levees of New Orleans should be viable and practical, with budgets and blueprints, not wishful, abstract defenses of God's permissive will, assumed to favor the Army engineers. Nevertheless, every serious student of the Bible should be assured that God honors the pointed questions of the sincere seeker after truth.

Psalm 104:1–9, 24, 35c

Once one has overcome sympathy with Job's desire to bring his complaint before God, person to person, the next expression is likely to be, "Some nerve! How dare Job imagine challenging the Almighty, All-knowing, Omnipresent, and Just God?" I have heard many Christians make such statements.

The earliest human belief began with great awe before the higher being. This overwhelming wonder was and is the foundation of all great religions. Anthropological studies suggest that awe is the first known response of humanity to the great other. Western culture holds the defining feature of the human being to be thinking: *Homo sapiens* (Latin for human being, *homo*, and thinking, *sapiens*). But those same prehistoric tools that proved us to be thinkers were found in graves that also proved us to have primitive belief as early as we manifest thinking: *homo credens*; the human being as believer. Human worship is as old as human life.

Psalm 104 urges the sensitive soul to praise God for reasons in harmony with our best understanding of the natural world, as well as with the silent testimony of the prehistoric graves. "O LORD, how manifold are your works! In wisdom you have made them all" (v. 24) says it all. In other words, profound awe and praise are the natural response to awareness of the things God has made, a few of which are mentioned. They range, in the mind of the psalmist, from grass and trees to the entire cosmos of earth, clouds, and sky. The works include the providential watering and feeding of creatures from birds to wild donkeys. So the psalmist vows to praise God while still in possession of life (v. 33), and cries out in irrepressible praise, "Bless the LORD, O my soul!" (v. 35c).

Without such awe and praise of God at the beginning of human life, we would not have known ourselves to be human; we would have seen ourselves as just another animal. Praise of God is far more than mere religious exercise or a growing liturgical tradition of good manners before God. Jesus affirmed the primacy of praise by placing praise at the beginning of his prayer: "Hallowed be your name" (Matt. 6:9). While praise is at the heart of liturgy, praise did not arise out of liturgical concerns. Praise grew spontaneously out of primitive humanity's urge to relate to the Creator and Sustainer of human life. The early generations had a gut-level awareness that they were incapable of all these sustaining creations, and they sought to reach this Creator by praise.

This psalm recognizes that behind all of creation is awesome power, which suggests authority and sovereignty for its direction and purpose. God gives order to this vastness and the nature therein, appointing places and borders (v. 9), and setting times. This order and its beauty only add to the awe of it all, calling forth the praise that arises from human depths. To be sure, the creation can sometimes be dangerous to human life and even to its own order, as in the case of Hurricane Katrina discussed earlier.

An awestruck twelve-year-old soprano surveyed the scene from a very high point overlooking Yosemite Valley in Yosemite National Park. As she stopped for her adult companions to catch up, she burst forth with a powerful and sincere rendition: "Then sings my soul, my Savior God, to thee, how great thou art, how great thou art!" There was not a dry eye in the party (and this simple rerun in my memory is very nearly as deeply moving even now). Such reaction to God's handiwork motivated this psalm.

This kind of praise happens all too seldom, not that it has to happen in Yosemite. There are parks in every city, and the sky is everywhere. Even the design of a sanctuary can assist, as one senses the vastness of God's presence. Isaiah 6:1 records such a setting: "In the year that King Uzziah died, I saw the Lord, . . . high and lofty, and the hem of his robe filled the temple." All too many worship spaces sacrifice height for width and increased seating. Low ceilings lower the spiritual horizons that could loosen one's tight grip on life and deep concern about me and mine. An inadequate worship space robs one of the awe, wonder, and praise that melt self-centeredness and open the heart to gracious generosity and unwavering justice.

Praise also fulfills the self. I think of heaven as a place where everybody has a voice for praise, and everybody fits into one of the many vocal parts. People praising on earth are practicing for heaven, whatever the quality of their earthly vocal cords. Their praise is equal in the ears of God. All have equal access to the same presence and providence for which to offer praise.

Psalm 91:9–16

This passage is usually to the liking of the typical faithful as it is God's promise of care and safety. The popularity of this theme is due to our awareness of the cruelty and injustice in the world and of our desperate need for such protection. However, this preference for protection is probably matched by gladness over the fact that there is no direct statement of moral or ethical demand in the package—no point-blank call to justice and righteousness. This must not be misunderstood, to get us off the hook. Such obligations are in the package deal inescapably. We dare not assume that our statements of faith in God and loyalty to God are adequate, with the rest of the relationship being on our own terms. God's protection applies to all of life, but we should be aware of what we are asking God to protect, especially if we are requesting God to protect the evil ways in which we act as individuals, groups, and communities—to say nothing of whole nations—like a brief petition I heard: "Lord, bless this mess, please."

Today's worldwide economic recession is due in large measure to the audacious mishandling of the public's pensions and savings. Yet all too frequently we find people who teach Bible school on Sunday to be among the major perpetrators of mismanagement on Monday. They seem to think their safety was secured by God, freeing them to exploit honest citizens. The greatest surprise is that their churches have not declared enough truth to power for them to have a bad conscience. They know it is bad business, but the families of faith have said nothing about the moral dimension. Blessed are they who with clear conscience can claim the promise in verses 8–9: "Because you have made the Lord your refuge and security, no evil shall befall you" (my paraphrase).

Hebrews 5:1–10

In this passage, the purpose of the writer of Hebrews is to interpret Jesus' ministry by assigning him this role. The purpose of these remarks is to open up aspects of Jesus' priestly role as models for frequently underemphasized aspects of the service of today's laity and clergy. Most of these underemphasized ministries are clearly set forth in Jesus' statement in Luke 4:18–19. In other words, priestly ministry has a justice component.

Note that Jesus does not flee those suffering but, rather, grows up among them and identifies with them and their suffering. As a priest offers up sacrifice for the sin of the people, Jesus offers up his own life.

This sin is not solely personal, and the needs involve hunger and sickness on a wide scale, plus injustice and poverty. It is here that Jesus' priesthood model reaches back to the life and work of the ancient priest-king, "Melchizedek, the righteous." Melchizedek's government was ethically accountable, and the courts of the palace were places for service (Gen. 14:17–24). Those whose unselfish labors are in the service of Jesus are to be fundamentally concerned about those who suffer from injustice.

Progress in civil rights and justice has been built on the suffering and service of prayer and songs of servants, led by preachers. If we are to keep the gains and move on to abolish the evils that still exist, we need all Christians to embrace the models of Melchizedek and Jesus.

Mark 10:35–45

Underneath the concept of undeserved suffering is the assumption that such suffering should be avoided. In today's pericope, Jesus' disciples James and John asked him to promise them a special seat of honor at the end of their services as his faithful followers. They wanted to choose and guarantee their reward in advance.

Jesus' response makes it plain that we were given this life for the purpose of engaging in service, for which there would be no immediate or predictable recompense. "Whosoever wants to be considered great among you will get there by being an unremunerated servant of ordinary people—a slave" (my paraphrase of vv. 43, 44). We are not to undermine the economic system of work and wages, but rather we are to become available to the realm of God as part of a limitless labor force for justice and righteousness, aid for the hungry and homeless, healing for the sick, release for the imprisoned, and peace (my partial paraphrase of Luke 4:18).

When service is paid, it is ordered by and subordinate to the source of the remuneration. The laborer in behalf of the realm is free to seek the realm's unfettered justice and righteousness, and to minister to all human need. Jesus, the "boss," has no interests to protect other than those for which he was, and all of us are, anointed.

James and John were rightly criticized by the other disciples, for even heaven itself is not to be sought for self. According to Matthew, those who did the most labor for the most needy were surprised at their reward, which had never crossed their minds (Matt. 25:37).

Isaiah 53:4–12

The last and most demanding response suggested for Job's complaint is at the very heart of the gospel: the redemptive role of the Suffering Servant. Isaiah 53 is widely read at Christmas and Easter, partly because it is sung so often in Handel's *Messiah*. But the seasonal emphasis seldom includes the theme of vicarious, redemptive death and suffering. This may be charged to the truly celebrative themes of the holidays, like "Joy to the World" and "Christ the Lord Is Risen Today." Such hymns hardly fit with suffering servanthood. The cross symbolizes the efficacy and ultimate victory of vicarious suffering, but that victory is hardly comparable to the multitude of tangible materials with which the culture floods the minds of the masses at Christmastide and is not always connected to the victory at Easter.

How then does one make suffering servanthood real and engaging to any age, young or old? When attempted with words only, such a goal is all but impossible. Jesus did it with picture images and gripping stories. We call them parables. Instead of being dependent on such a verbal admonition as "Be a suffering servant," or "Be compassionate, whatever it may cost," Jesus told a story of a good Samaritan. He portrayed a person who risked being beaten himself, in order to help a man already beaten. The victim might have died otherwise. Hearers might not have identified with Jesus on a cross, but they did with the Samaritan.

The ordinary Christian needs to embrace suffering servanthood. It is easy to see a Mother Teresa without daring to identify with her. She was extraordinary, we say. However, we need to see ourselves as fully capable of such servanthood, and enjoying it.

Fifty or so years ago, there was a pioneering prime-time television show entitled *This Is Your Life*. Each week a person whose whole life was devoted to helping others was surprised with a program on which those who had been helped were brought back from all over, to tell what it had meant to them and to say, "Thank you." There were many tears, but they were tears of joy, among all: the honorees, the persons they had rescued, and the audiences. The honorees had risked and given their all, and every one of them was unspeakably glad they had been suffering servants. They did not think of it as suffering or sacrifice; they were personally fulfilled, because that was what they were born to do in the first place.

Today, there are thousands if not millions of people, throughout the world, who have found the secret of suffering servanthood. As I write, there is not enough space on the land, in the air, or on the water, to accommodate the people seeking to help the earthquake victims in Haiti. It may have taken the sight of literal heaps of dead and dying to stir so many, but once again, the helpers feel as if it is a blessing to be motivated to dig deep and give all.

What Jesus did, as Suffering Servant, for our sins, and what God provides for our every need, must be paralleled by our glad embrace of our own self-fulfilling and joyous servanthood. Call it suffering if you like, but do not omit the awesome fulfillment of the purpose for which you were born, including the joy.

World Food Day (October 16)

James L. McDonald

LEVITICUS 19:5–14
PSALM 136:23–26
COLOSSIANS 2:8–19
LUKE 14:12–14

World Food Day, which was first observed in 1981, takes place on October 16 in recognition of the founding of the United Nations Food and Agriculture Organization. The purpose of World Food Day is to arouse action against world hunger. From the perspective of World Food Day, the preacher can encourage the congregations to engage in comprehensive efforts to end hunger by directly providing food for hungry people, by pressing for patterns of growing and using food that benefit local communities, by activism designed to change systems of food production and distribution, and by advocating healthy and responsible eating.

> Our society's stated mantra to end hunger has grown tired and hollow. We know its cause—poverty; we know its solution—to end poverty. Yet we . . . treat hunger only as a symptom of poverty. We are disingenuous by continuing to tinker with the nation's complex, usually disconnected, network of food assistance programs . . . the expansion of food banks . . . will never get us any closer to a solution.[1]
>
> *Mark Winne*

Ending hunger is sacred work. Our passages for today help us understand why.

---

1. Mark Winne, *Closing the Food Gap: Resetting the Table in the Land of Plenty* (Boston: Beacon Press, 2008), 184.

Leviticus 19:5–14

Few Christians turn to the book of Leviticus for inspiration. Today's Christian who turns to Leviticus casually may think the book is technical, rule oriented, and anachronistic. The book is largely a set of instructions for priests (Levites) on worship. Our passage, from a section called the Holiness Code, prescribes ethical behavior not for priests but for ordinary people ("all the congregation," v. 2). To gain inspiration from Leviticus, it is necessary to consider not only its rules but its ultimate purposes: to bring us into a closer relationship with God and to make us holy.

Holiness has both tautological and mystical qualities. Only God is holy. God's being defines the holy. The sacred is whatever is of God. We and everything else become holy by encountering God. In *I and Thou*, Martin Buber divided the world into two parts—the holy (I-Thou) and the not-yet-holy (I-It).[2] In the not-yet-holy, people relate to each other and to things as objects.

But in the holy, our awareness of other people and of everyday inanimate objects becomes an opportunity for encountering something new and distinct. Relationships become the place where we meet at the level of feeling and sensing, where barriers fall, and where we experience deeper connections. In the realm of the holy, the whole becomes greater than the sum of its parts, and life itself is transformed. In our encounter with the other, we experience the unexpected, we discover that which had been hidden, we hear music as if for the first time. These are I-Thou relationships and God is in the midst of them. God appears in the I-Thou relationship itself.

Leviticus 19:5–14 prescribes mostly "You shall nots": Do not be greedy, swindle, or steal; refrain from lying, do business honestly, do not swear falsely in God's name; renounce your tendency to despise those who are deaf or trip those who are blind. Note what punctuates these proscriptions: "I am the LORD." Herein lies the connection to holiness. Each of these forbidden acts entails someone viewing another person as an object to serve one's own interests. But God will not have it, not because God wants to restrict human action, but because these acts desecrate the human spirit of both the actor and the victim. To put it more bluntly, if you steal from people who are poor, you are stealing from God.

Jewish interpreters have generated voluminous midrashim on these passages.[3] The rabbis who comment on the gleaning rules in verses 9–10 add to the requirements set out in the Bible. It is important, Maimonides notes, that

---

2. Martin Buber, *I and Thou: A New Translation with a Prologue and Notes*, trans. Walter Kaufman (New York: Touchstone Books, 1970).
3. E.g., *m. Peah* 1:2, 4; 8:7; *b. Baba Bathra* 8b.

the corner of the field left for the poor to harvest should be at the far end of the farmer's property, out of sight to both the farmer and others, so that even the farmer would not know who had harvested from the fields.[4] This arrangement protected the anonymity of the poor person and that person's dignity. By knowing for certain where she or he could harvest, a poor person would be spared the shame of having to hunt publicly. In this way, Jews help the poor, or practice *tzedakah*, which is often translated from Hebrew as "charity." However, the Hebrew root *tzedek* is more closely translated as "justice" or "fairness."

My friend Rabbi Lennard Thal observes: "One obvious question is why it was deemed necessary to repeat this passage a few chapters later. Some say for emphasis; others point out the context: it falls in the midst of a description of the High Holy Days and three major pilgrimage festivals. In either case it reminds us that while ritual and holy day observance is important, we should never forget ethical demands."

Maimonides, a celebrated twelfth-century Jewish scholar, philosopher, and physician who wrote a code of Jewish law, the *Mishneh Torah* (*The Code of Maimonides*) delineated eight levels of *tzedakah*. The highest is achieved when one takes the hand of another and gives that one a gift or a loan, engages in a partnership, or finds work by which that person can live.[5] The highest form of assistance one can give to poor people is to help them become self-sufficient.

This is Mike Winne's argument in his book, cited at the opening of this comment. As a country we are not addressing the root causes of hunger. Rather, we are putting a bandage on a wound that requires a more sustained response. Healing the scourge of hunger requires transformation, both of us and of those who struggle to feed themselves.

People are hungry because they do not have enough income to feed themselves and their families. In the United States, 40 percent of the people who come to food banks are working families whose wages do not pay them enough. The 2009 U.S. Census Bureau report showed that 40 million Americans live at or below the official federal poverty line of $21,834 for a family of four. By the time all factors are taken into account, 100 million people, almost one-third of the U.S. population, live on the edge of poverty. Poverty rates are nearly double among African Americans and Latinos. The unemployment rate among young African American men ages eighteen to thirty-five hovers around 50 percent at all times.

---

4. Moses ben Maimon, *The Code of Maimonides, The Book of Agriculture*, trans. Isaac Klein, Yale Judaica Series 21 (New Haven, CT: Yale University Press, 1979), 2.2.12 (54–55); cf. the translator's note 12 (421).
5. Moses ben Maimon, *The Code of Maimonides*, 2.10.7–14 (57–58).

Many U.S. congregations and their members are involved in feeding programs: food pantries, soup kitchens, food banks. But the actions of governments far outweigh those of churches and charities. The burgeoning food bank movement in the United States came in the early 1980s, when deep cuts were made in U.S. antipoverty programs. If Christians are going to address the problem of hunger, we must help people stand on their own two feet.

Psalm 136:23–26

Psalm 136 extols the steadfast love of God, the creator and redeemer. Verses 4–9 recount the creation and verses 10–22 recite the exodus story. Verses 23–26 sum it up: God remembered, rescued, and fed us. God's remembering is astounding because God remembered the people of Israel "in [their] low estate" (v. 23).

The word "estate" as it is used in this context refers to social class, an assignation based on one's relationship to the land. The highest estate belonged to those who had large amounts of productive land and who employed or owned others who did the work. Those in the lowest estate were landless: peasants, indentured servants, and slaves.

In the political realm, the higher one's estate or social class, the more privileges were conferred. The highest estate was the ruling class, for example, monarchs and barons. They made the decisions, collected the taxes, controlled the army, and ran the economy.

Israel recognized that when God remembered them, they were at the bottom of the social and political ladder. They were slaves; they had nothing; they owned no land; they had no political cachet. Yet God did not ignore Israel. God took notice, heard their cry, and had compassion. God delivered Israel from their enemies, brought them safely into the promised land, and gave them food to eat. God liberated Israel from slavery (which increased their estate), gave them land (which increased their estate), and fed them, which gave them the strength to establish themselves on the land and develop as a nation. For this, the psalmist urges the people to remember and give thanks to this most amazing God.

In terms of ending hunger, the exodus story reminds us that simply feeding people, without liberating them from oppressive social systems and providing them with the resources to establish themselves and their communities in sustainable ways, is a terrible distortion of God's liberating work. God not only liberated Israel from oppression; God empowered Israel to become a great nation. Today, the exodus of people from hunger and poverty requires their empowerment.

Luke 14:12–14

Luke 14:12–14 is part of a longer story about a dinner that Jesus attends at the house of a religious leader one Sabbath. Over the course of the dinner, Jesus heals a man, upbraids the guests for their social-climbing proclivities, counsels humility, chastises the host for the character of his invitation list, and tells a parable about a great banquet where all of the original invitees were no-shows. In each case, Jesus demonstrates the nature of the reign of God.

Jesus' words to the guests and the host in our passage are two sides of the same coin. To the guests, Jesus says, "When someone invites you to dinner, don't take the place of honor." And to the host, Jesus says, "The next time you put on a dinner, don't just invite your friends and family and rich neighbors, the kind of people who will return the favor. Invite some people who never get invited out, the misfits from the wrong side of the tracks" (*The Message*). Sharing a meal with others should not be the occasion for reinforcing the advantages of wealth but, rather, an occasion for breaking down the social barriers that divide and alienate.

Jesus criticizes those whose social actions are designed to put others in their debt. If our social actions are calculated to generate a return on our investment of time, effort, and money, then we will always exclude poor people and others who could not return the favor. For Jesus, this is not the reign of God. If you want to be blessed, he says, act in ways that truly benefit others, not simply yourself, however artfully you may have learned to practice this conceit.

Colossians 2:8–19

Paul's appeal in Colossians 2 picks up the theme from Luke's Gospel. In Luke, Jesus urges his followers to do justice, so that they will become richly blessed at the resurrection. Likewise, Paul wants the church to participate in the new reality that was created by Christ through his death and resurrection. He exhorts the church in Colossae to root itself in Christ's redemptive power, a power that far exceeds any other in heaven or on earth.

In many ways, Paul's letter to the Colossians is his most mystical piece of writing. Paul tries to convey the deep meaning of Christ. Paul wants the Colossians to embrace and live that deep meaning. He worries they will fail to see the power of Christ that is available to them and will instead be captivated by frothy philosophies that excite the mind and stir the emotions but that ultimately leave their lives and the world itself unchanged.

Through Christ the fullness of God dwells in you, Paul says. Everything that Christ has to offer the world has been offered to you—forgiveness, a clean slate, a new lease on life, the freedom to be who God created you to be, an unbroken connection to the living God. Ground your life in Christ and live it, he urges.

On World Food Day, Paul's appeal echoes the words of Isaiah:

> If you remove the yoke from among you,
>   the pointing of the finger, the speaking of evil,
> if you offer your food to the hungry
>   and satisfy the needs of the afflicted,
> then your light shall arise in the darkness
>   and your gloom be like the noonday.
> (Isa. 58:9b–10)

Paul's appeal in Colossians, like Isaiah's, tells us that when communities of faith seek to address hunger at its root, God is with us. God's presence is assured when we do justice, not because our actions make us better people, but because doing justice changes our relationship to others and transforms the world in accord with God's purposes. This is why ending hunger is sacred work.

Proper 25 [30]

James Anthony Noel

JOB 42:1–6, 10–17   JEREMIAH 31:7–9
PSALM 34:1–8 (19–22)   PSALM 126
                                          HEBREWS 7:23–28
                                            MARK 10:46–52

The Babylonian captivity and return is the time period and context when most of the texts from the Torah, Prophets, and Writings were given much of their present form. Hence, the issue that these passages address is the despair, disappointment, and hopelessness of a people who have been defeated and forcibly removed from their homeland and politically subjugated in a foreign land where, distanced from the temple, they had no anchor to maintain their distinct religious identity. During Jesus' ministry the Jewish people were repressed under Roman rule. Although the temple had been restored and was in full operation, its viability was of little material benefit to Jews located in the lower rungs of an economically stratified society. The themes that dialectically emerge from today's texts taken together are two: (1) the contrast between the collective religious and emotional experiences of sorrow and joy—signified in the texts by the word "cry" and/or descriptions of individuals or people crying—and (2) the coordination of Jesus' roles as prophet and priest. These passages describe people who, in the midst of crying, experience a sudden reversal of their fortune through God's intervention and are able to shout for joy over their deliverance.

Who is crying now, and why? Can we say to them what Martin Luther King Jr. said in a sermon: "How long . . . not long"?[1] What is the church's proclamation to those who are suffering from racism, poverty, colonization, sexism, and other systemic oppressions? Let us think of people in our inner

---

1. Martin Luther King Jr., "Our God Is Marching On," in *A Testament of Hope: The Essential Writings of Martin Luther King, Jr.*, ed. James M. Washington (San Francisco: Harper & Row, 1986), 230.

cities, in the Sudan, as well in the suburban spiritual wastelands. A possible sermon title could come from a spiritual: "Someone's Crying, Lord: When Are You Coming?"

Job 42:1–6, 10–17

There is probably no literary figure who has more reason to cry than Job. He is meant to function as the personification of the exilic community, which was wondering whether continued faith in God was justified in light of its continued captivity. This book of poetic dialogue was written during the Babylonian exile and return sometime between 600 and 150 BCE. The figure of "the Satan" resembles the figure in Zechariah 3:1–2 who stands beside Joshua as his accuser before the heavenly council. In Job's case, his accusers are not only in heaven but on earth—his friends who articulate the conventional understanding of divine justice. If God's people break the covenant, then God will punish them until they repent and the covenant is restored. If God's people remain loyal and obedient to the covenant's requirements, they will enjoy God's protection from evil and misfortune. Job refuses to accept the logic of his friends, but for the wrong reason. Job bases his case upon his sense of his own righteousness and is admonished for this by God at the end of the book, right before God restores to Job all that he has lost during his ordeal. This reversal in Job's fortune gives him reason to rejoice. The book intends to show that although God is just, the workings of God's providence are beyond human calculation.

Psalm 34:1–8 (19–22) and Psalm 126

Psalm 34 is meant to encourage personal and corporate righteousness while reflecting on the conventional understanding discussed above. It reflects the concern of the exilic community for personal righteousness. Righteousness will be rewarded. The psalmist makes such guarantees (v. 9). Of course, this psalm can be interpreted only in the eschatological sense, because life teaches us that the righteous suffer. The exilic community grappled with this issue during their captivity.

Psalm 126 was written during or after the return to Jerusalem from captivity. After the long years of captivity and with the hope of deliverance fading into oblivion, when their liberation took place, the psalmist says, "we were like those who dream" (v. 1). It was almost unbelievable, but the psalmist recalls that when they realized their liberation was really occurring, "our mouth was filled with laughter, and our tongue with shouts of joy" (v. 2). Here, as in Job, is the experience of a radical reversal in one's circumstance of suffering, so that one's lamentation is transformed into praise.

Jeremiah 31:7–9

Jeremiah's career, from 627 BCE to about 580 BCE, comprised three periods: (1) the period from 627 to 605 BCE, when the southern kingdom of Judah was threatened by Assyria and Egypt; (2) the period from 605 to 586 BCE, when Judah was being attacked by Babylon and he prophesized God's judgment upon Judah; and (3) the period about 586–580 BCE, after Judah's defeat, when he ministered in Egypt and Jerusalem. Jeremiah proclaimed both judgment and redemption. Because of Judah's sins against God, the Babylonian captivity was inevitable and just. But Jeremiah also preached the necessity for repentance and forbearance from the exiled community, as he envisioned the promise of a remnant experience: God's deliverance in the future through a new covenant whose law would no longer be external but in their heart (31:33). In Jeremiah 31:7–9 God's deliverance has begun. The remnant is told to sing and shout over their deliverance from captivity (v. 7). God will "gather them from the farthest parts of the earth" and, furthermore, "among them are the blind and the lame" (v. 8). In v. 9 Jeremiah after having instructed the people to sing and shout says: "I will lead them back."

Mark 10:46–52 and Hebrews 7:23–28

Mark was the first Gospel to be written, about 70 CE, which is evidenced in its predictions about the destruction of the temple. Whereas during the exile and return the Jewish people were preoccupied with the rebuilding of the temple, the anchor and center of their religious identity and absolute necessity for covenant faithfulness, Mark has no use for the temple. As a part of Mark's polemic against certain Jewish leaders, we regard Mark's Gospel as being hostile to the temple. In Mark, Jesus' mission is tied up with its destruction. He goes to Jerusalem to confront the religious authorities connected with the temple, who are also complicit with the Roman Empire in oppression.

After his baptism and temptation in the wilderness, Jesus begins his ministry announcing, "The time is fulfilled, and the [realm] of God has come near; repent, and believe in the good news" (1:15). He then addresses and recruits his first disciples, who made their living fishing, Simon and Andrew, with the command, "Follow me" (1:17). Believing the gospel and following Jesus are the characteristics of discipleship. But where is Jesus headed? He is headed toward Jerusalem, to do battle with the religious authorities. En route Jesus does battle with the demons that hold human beings in bondage, by healing people and by announcing the good news. From Mark's point of view, the healings critique the temple, which could not cleanse lepers, feed the hungry, give sight to the blind, or raise the dead.

Whereas the concern of the postexilic writers was to encourage the Jewish community to maintain its efforts in rebuilding the temple to assure God's continued protective presence, Mark's theology is one that views Jesus' person and ministry as rendering the temple superfluous. Hence, the fig tree incident following the triumphant entry into Jerusalem that we celebrate on Palm Sunday (11:20–24). After finding the fig tree barren and cursing it, Jesus enters the temple and casts out the money changers. The fig tree incident is also a critique of empire—according to the research of New Testament Professor Annette Wissenrieder of San Francisco Theological Seminary—because its emblem is found on Roman coins of that period.[2] However, what is consistent and similar in all the texts we are considering is the outcome—especially for the poor and oppressed. The people singing "Hosanna!" as Jesus enters Jerusalem are a different class of people from those who are connected with the temple's operation. They are the people whose needs are not satisfied by its operation, who are expectantly waiting for God's intervention—deliverance—on their behalf, either through the Messiah's coming or the restoration of Jewish rule. They exclaim, "Blessed is the coming [realm] of our ancestor David!" (11:10), replicating blind Bartimaeus's "cry" in 10:47.

Mark is being ironic in reporting the titles by which blind Bartimaeus and the crowd address Jesus, because Jesus did not come to reestablish a sovereign Jewish state but to inaugurate the apocalyptic reality of the Son of Man spoken of in verse 45. This idea is elaborated upon and expanded in the Hebrews passage, which develops a Christology of Jesus as the high priest who offers the perfect sacrifice of his own blood, which renders the temple henceforth unnecessary. In this way Jesus' work is truly redemptive, because it paves a highway to God for those exiled from the divine presence.

The key, however, in overcoming one's exile and entering into God's presence through the work of Jesus is not just believing the gospel but acting on it by following Jesus. This is the point Mark makes when he reports at the end of the passage that Bartimaeus "regained his sight and followed him on the way" (10:52). Jesus has said to the blind man that it is his faith that has cured him. According to Theodore W. Jennings, "this faith is not right belief nor

2. Annette Wissenrieder, "The Didactics of Images: The Fig Tree in Mark 11:12–14 and 20–24," in *The Interface of Orality and Writing: Hearing, Seeing, Writing in New Genres,* ed. Annette Wissenrieder and Robert Coote, Wissenschaftliche Untersuchungen zum Neuen Testament 1 (Tübingen: Mohr Siebeck, 2010).

a pious resignation to inscrutable providence . . . it is demonstrated as the refusal to be silenced, as the refusal to wait for a better time, as the refusal to wait for an appointment. It is the rude insistence that the calamity be attended to now."[3]

Here we recall Martin Luther King Jr.'s "Letter from Birmingham City Jail," in which he states, "Freedom is never voluntarily given by the oppressor; it must be demanded by the oppressed."[4] But in making that demand and in doing what Bartimaeus did when he cast his cloak aside, "sprang up and came to Jesus" (v. 50), one assumes the risk of retaliation from the power structure. In other words, one risks martyrdom in following Jesus.

The above may explain the present paralysis of the church, which like the postexilic Jewish community is preoccupied with building its temples and its liturgical practices but does not utter a mumbling word against the oppressive and exploitative features of the American Empire. In this regard, the church suffers from a form of blindness; it enjoys a type of physical sight but lacks both vision and insight concerning its true mission and where Christ is seeking to lead it. Bartimaeus had insight and vision regarding Jesus before he received physical sight! The church has succumbed to and become captive to a distorted understanding of the priestly role of Christ, wherein it feels guaranteed of his heavenly intercession on its behalf as long as it goes through the ritualistic motions of faith. But Hebrews reminds us that although we (the church) are to "run with perseverance the race that is set before us, looking to Jesus. . . . in [our] struggle against sin [we] have not yet resisted to the point of shedding [our] blood" (Heb. 12:1–2, 4).

The theology or religion of the African American slave community, as articulated in its spirituals, made no distinction between Jesus' priestly, monarchial, and prophetic roles. In their abject condition of being brutalized by the seemingly invincible power their masters and the slave system in general imposed, they imagined God, Jesus, and the Holy Ghost operating as a force more powerful than the reality and agents of their oppression. Thus Jesus appeared in their minds as a king, as in the spiritual. "Ride on, King Jesus."

Ride on, King Jesus,
No man can a-hinder me.[5]

---

3. Theodore W. Jennings, *The Insurrection of the Crucified: The Gospel of Mark as Theological Manifesto* (Chicago: Exploration Press, 2003), 175.
4. Martin Luther King Jr., "Letter from Birmingham City Jail," in *A Testament of Hope*, 292.
5. "Ride On, King Jesus," in *The African American Heritage Hymnal*, ed. Delores Carpenter and Nolan Williams Jr. (Chicago: GIA Publications, 2001), 225.

Interestingly, in reference to the blind in the Jeremiah text and Bartimaeus in the Mark text, one verse goes:

> When I was blind and could not see,
> King Jesus brought that light to me.

One of the verses to a spiritual that John Lovell Jr. documents in his *Black Song: The Forge and the Flame* goes as follows:

> He is King of Kings, He is Lord of Lords,
> Jesus Christ the first and last, no man works like him.
>
> He built his throne up in the air, . . .
> And called his saints from everywhere.
>
> *He pitched his tents on Canaan's ground*
> *And broke the Roman kingdom down.*[6]

Although the African American slave community confidently expected God to intervene on their behalf, it did not sing these songs with the sense that it could wait passively for liberation to occur. They engaged in work stoppages, slave rebellions, escapes, and other acts of sabotage whenever the opportunity presented itself. Songs like "Walk Together, Children" and "Steal Away" testify to this attitude. At the same time, in other spirituals we perceive an awareness on the slave's part of freedom and deliverance from captivity being so close at hand that it can be celebrated in the now with ecstatic lyrical expression. During the Civil Rights Movement, Martin Luther King Jr. preached:

> I know you are asking today, "How long will it take?" Somebody's asking, "How long will prejudice blind the visions of [human beings], darken their understanding, and drive bright-eyed wisdom from her sacred throne? . . . How long will justice be crucified and truth bear it? . . . I come to say to you this afternoon, however difficult the moment, however frustrating the hour, it will not be long, because "Truth crushed to the earth will rise again." How long? Not long, because "No lie can live forever." How long? Not long, because "You shall reap what you sow." How long? Not long, because "The arc of the moral universe is long, but it bends toward justice."[7]

Any sermon preached today in the United States must identify—regardless of the congregation's race, ethnicity, or social class—the nature of its captivity to the forces of global capitalism, of which the United States is a major agent.

---

6. John Lovell Jr., *Black Song: The Forge and the Flame* (St. Paul: Paragon House, 1972), 231, my emphasis.

7. Martin Luther King Jr., "Our God Is Marching On," in *A Testament of Hope*, 230.

The sermon needs to identify that to which members of the congregation are being held captive. Although poverty is a form of captivity, so too is consumerism, which valorizes the commodity as God. It is probably a greater challenge to demonstrate to affluent folk ways in which they are enslaved, blind, uninformed, and ignorant regarding their true condition. In *The Protestant Ethic and the Spirit of Capitalism*, Max Weber diagnosed the West as being in an "iron cage" wherein there are "specialists without spirit, sensualists without heart [and] this nullity imagines that it has attained a level of civilization never before achieved."[8] Such will be the case until the church begins once again to follow Jesus into the pressing social issues and deprivations of our time to announce the gospel and deliver the captives. Meanwhile the captives are singing: "For I know a change is going to come."

8. Max Weber, *The Protestant Ethic and the Spirit of Capitalism*, trans. Talcott Parsons (New York: Charles Scribner's Sons, 1958), 182.

Children's Sabbath
(Third Weekend in October)

Shannon Daley-Harris

2 SAMUEL 9:9–13
PSALM 78
ACTS 16:16–24
LUKE 18:15–17

The National Observance of Children's Sabbaths® weekend was founded by the Children's Defense Fund in 1992 to encourage religious communities to honor children as sacred gifts and to nurture, protect, and advocate on behalf of children. Congregations focus worship, education programs, and activities on the urgent needs of children in our nation and on God's call to respond with justice and compassion. This event is designated for the third weekend of October. The sermon is a vital opportunity to give voice to the crises facing our nation's children—such as poverty, violence, lack of health care, abuse, and neglect—as well as opportunities for us to respond with justice and mercy to improve the quality of life for children in the local community and throughout our nation.

> Beyond the charity and justice all faiths demand, all children need for faith institutions to speak and stand up to those who treat them unjustly.[1]
>
> *Marian Wright Edelman*

The texts for the Children's Sabbath demonstrate how children and those who care for them are and are not welcomed in our midst—from one who was forgotten now finding a place at the table, to one who tends the mothers and young finding favor in God's sight, to those who were turned away find-

---

1. Marian Wright Edelman, *The Sea Is So Wide and My Boat Is So Small: Charting a Course for the Next Generation* (New York: Hyperion Books, 2008), 44.

ing a place in Jesus' embrace. Each passage invites us to consider how we will welcome children with the love and justice God intends.

2 Samuel 9:9–13

Mephibosheth was the son of Jonathan and grandson of the monarch Saul. When Saul was killed, Mephibosheth's caregiver picked up the child and fled (2 Sam. 4:4). Mephibosheth fell and became lame. The child returns to the narrative only after David has solidified his power and searches for survivors of Saul. David does not know about Mephibosheth, but when Ziba tells David about Mephibosheth, David promises Mephibosheth a place at his table, thus expressing loving-kindness (*hesed*). Mephibosheth is incredulous at such kindness (2 Sam. 9:1–8). David repeats these promises (2 Sam. 9:9–13). With Saul's land restored to him, Mephibosheth will have food, livelihood, and future. The text states four times that Mephibosheth will eat at David's table as one of David's children. The last line of the passage notes that Mephibosheth is lame in both feet.

Mephibosheth's story has much for Children's Sabbath. First, children, like Mephibosheth, may be in jeopardy because of political events. Moreover, children may be unintentionally injured by those who seek to help them.

Second, the text reminds us that we are called to help children as an expression of God's enduring, loyal, constant loving-kindness (*hesed*). Third, the passage encourages us to consider how we can act, as did David, to secure children's basic survival needs.

Fourth, as David welcomed this grandson of his former enemy at his table, we hear an invitation to enter into *relationship* with children. How might we not only meet basic needs of children but also ensure that *all* children, especially the forgotten and least likely ones, have a place at our national table of plenty, at the table of our communities, and even at our own tables? To treat children as part of the family means to want for *all* children what we want for our own children, or what our parents wanted for us. We must work for *all* children to have health coverage, not just our own; for *all* children to have rich educational opportunities, not just our own; for *all* children to have security and stability, a home and hope, and a future bright with promise. We who have a place at the table of Christ can hear the reminder to welcome children to a place at that table.

Finally, we hear words of caution. Even as Mephibosheth assumes a place at the king's table, a new future before him, the narrator defines him by his disability: "Now he was lame in both his feet" (v. 13). We often define children and adults by their disabilities, loss, and limitation. Instead, we should think of children's abilities, gifts, and possibilities.

Psalm 78

This psalm affirms the importance of memory and of sharing stories of God's actions from one generation to the next (v. 4). However, the psalm also cautions children not to become "like their ancestors, a stubborn and rebellious generation" (v. 8). In the final verses we move from those who were faithless to one who was faithful. God chose David to tend God's people as a shepherd (vv. 70–72). God's servant was not in a lofty position but was a humble shepherd. As shepherd, David did not use a rod to beat predators, or a staff to direct wayward rams, but gently tended the mothers and their young, watching out for the most vulnerable. This is the essence of ministry: watching out for the most vulnerable of the community—especially children.

Acts 16:16–24

This text focuses on the interactions of Paul and Silas with a "slave-girl who had a spirit of divination and brought her owners a great deal of money" (v. 16).[2] When Paul and Silas exorcised a demon from the young woman, her owners became enraged and took the missionaries to court for loss of income. The court flogged the missionaries.

On Children's Sabbath, the first concern raised by the text is the exploitation of children. In our day, many children experience exploitation or oppression. Poverty, gun violence, racism, abuse, gangs, and bullying all leave children at the mercy of those with power over them. Child exploitation today is as real as children in bonded labor around the globe, as close at hand as children treated as consumers worth billions to industry, and as pervasive as children in sexual servitude.

The encounter of Paul and Silas with the child occurs on their way to a place of prayer. The second insight from this passage is that we encounter the children for whom we are to be advocates in the community as well as in our congregations.

Third, we listen to the child's words. The child, a "slave-girl" serving greedy masters, speaks the truth when she refers to Paul and Silas as "slaves of the Most High God" (v. 17). Paul does not appreciate this truth telling. Instead, "so troubled" (NIV) or "very much annoyed" (NRSV), he silences her by commanding the "spirit" (a demon) to come out of her (v. 18). His response does not derive from a commitment to justice but from the desire to get rid of her annoying behavior. He "liberated" her from the demon, but he

---

2. On slavery in antiquity, see S. Scott Bartchy, "Slavery in the New Testament," in *HarperCollins Bible Dictionary*, ed. Paul J. Achtemeier (San Francisco: HarperSanFranciso, 1996), 1030.

did not even try to liberate her from slavery. We too are sometimes troubled or annoyed by the truth that children offer, and we try to silence them, rather than to celebrate their wisdom and insight. We often address symptoms of oppression but fail to address the root problem.

It is important to notice that the child essentially disappears from the text. Gail O'Day asks the haunting question, "What becomes of her life after Paul silences her divination? Is she returned to the slave market once her economic value to her owners disappears? The slave girl is only a commodity to her owners, and she is treated no better by Paul and the story itself. Luke shows no interest in the slave girl as a human being."[3]

Fourth, this text highlights the resistance of those who have exploited the child. They protest the end of their ability to make money from the child by using multiple threats: legal action, physical violence, defending the status quo. Those who oppress or exploit children continue to use such tactics.

When Paul and Silas intervene, they are accused in public, attacked, stripped, beaten, and imprisoned. Those who would intervene in the exploitation of children today are sometimes hesitant, fearing accusation and attack.

Although our text ends here, the story does not. When Paul and Silas are imprisoned, an earthquake opens the prison doors. Instead of slinking off, as their captors hoped, the missionaries stand their ground. Instead of fleeing the city as instructed, they go to Lydia's house to encourage others (Acts 16:25–38). Such encouragement is for all who would intervene on behalf of exploited children.

Luke 18:15–17

This passage is so familiar that it is tempting to jump to the punch line, "Whoever does not receive the [realm] of God as a little child will never enter it." But we do well to remember that, beginning with 17:20, Luke recounts questions about the reign of God with increasing frequency. Indeed, in Luke 17:20, Jesus points out that the realm "is not coming with things that can be observed." Even more important, "The [realm] of God *is among you*" (v. 21). Aspects of the realm are already present.

Parents were bringing infants to Jesus for blessing. Why? R. Alan Culpepper notes the high infant and child mortality rates of Jesus' day; 30 percent of children died in infancy, and of those who survived another third died by age six, and another 60 percent by age sixteen. No wonder these parents sought Jesus's blessing and his healing touch.[4]

---

3. Gail R. O'Day, "Acts," in *The Women's Bible Commentary*, ed. Carol A. Newsom and Sharon H. Ringe (Louisville, KY: Westminster John Knox Press, 1998), 400.

4. R. Alan Culpepper, "Luke," in *The New Interpreter's Bible*, ed. Leander Keck et al. (Nashville: Abingdon Press, 1995), 9:344.

The text does not say why the disciples turned away the little ones, but they may have shared their society's view of children. Judith Gundry-Volf writes about the two social and religious contexts in which children resided in Jesus' day, Hellenistic and Jewish. Both contexts evidenced parental love for and pleasure in children. Children were valued for the economic contribution they would make to the family and also for carrying on the family line. Nonetheless, children occupied the lowest rung on the social ladder, with no rights of their own, largely subject to the control of their fathers.[5] Children were vulnerable and dependent on their parents or, in the absence of parents, on the community.

Although Jewish people in Jesus' day did not idealize childhood, neither did they dismiss children. Indeed, one of the purposes of human life is to be fruitful and multiply (Gen. 1:26–28), and a child-filled home is a staple image of blessing (e.g., Ps. 128:3–4). Jesus' attitude toward children in our text is in this stream of thought.

Jesus responds compassionately to the presence of the children. Jesus calls for the children with an empathic double command: "Let the children come . . . do not stop them." He then teaches: *"It is to such as these that the [realm] of God belongs"* (v. 16). As in Luke 17:20, Jesus emphasizes that the reign of God already belongs to these children. There is nothing more these infants need do; the reign of God is theirs.

Then, with the solemn preface "Truly (*amen*)," Jesus continues, "I tell you, whoever does not receive the [realm] of God as a little child will never enter it." Here Jesus turns to the future: If the disciples want to live within the reign of God, they must manifest the same sense of vulnerability and dependence they witnessed in the children.

What does this text say to us on Children's Sabbath? First, we know that children—especially children in poverty and in racial/ethnic communities—face daunting odds that jeopardize their lives, health, development, and futures. Many parents seek healing, blessing, and hope for their children, yet all too often forbidding staff or agencies stand between them and help. How can the church embody the compassionate response of Jesus?

Second, we see the power of coupling action with teaching. Jesus stands up for the children in no uncertain terms. He not only takes action to welcome the children, but he also uses the opportunity to teach. How can we use our advocacy and hands-on service to children and families as opportunities to reflect on and share with others God's intention for justice and compassion?

---

5. Judith M. Gundry-Volf, "The Least and the Greatest: Children in the New Testament," in *The Child in Christian Thought*, ed. Marcia J. Bunge (Grand Rapids: Eerdmans, 2001), 31–36.

Third, we hear anew the affirmation that the reign of God *already* belongs to children. It is present reality and not just future promise. We must embody that news in a way that lights the heart of every child.

Finally, this passage invites us to examine our own hearts. Do we have the sense of humility, vulnerability, and dependence on God that will lead us to experience God's reign?

All Saints' Day

Gennifer Benjamin Brooks

ISAIAH 25:6–9
PSALM 24
REVELATION 21:1–6A
JOHN 11:32–44

All Saints' Day acknowledges the communion of all Christians—the great cloud of witnesses—with a motif of resurrection and new life, and holds before us a vision of the new world order that God intends as the ultimate destiny of the faithful. The texts for today invite us to see beyond the limitations of life in the present, beyond the death-dealing structures of social inequities and the ever-widening gap between the haves and the have-nots, to claim the promise of God's reign in and beyond the present into the eternal. Isaiah's vision and John's revelation intersect at the reality of Lazarus's delivery from death, an earthly resurrection that assures us of the promise of eternal life and invites us all to gather at the banquet table prepared for all peoples.

Isaiah 25:6–9

God is preparing a feast of divine riches for those who have labored in vain to experience the world's bounty. All around the world, people are hungry in body and spirit. The crises of physical hunger, starvation, and attendant ills are responsible for the death of thousands daily. Spiritual hunger leads others to suicide and addictive behaviors that bring certain death. For those caught in today's traps, as for those to whom Isaiah writes, the image of the apocalyptic feast offers a message of new life. The apocalyptic feast is set on the mountain of God; it is a feast of rich food and wines to which all are invited to celebrate the new life that represents God's unmerited favor. This text is both an assurance of the coming new world and an invitation to work toward that world in the present.

Isaiah's message was written to a people who were experiencing the destruction of their society and community. They were hungry for deliverance and new life. The text showcases God in action, a creative force at work to restore and make new those who have been victimized by the powers of the world, powers that have brought death and destruction, tears and disgrace to the children of God. In too much of the majority world today, children cry daily because of their life situations. They lack the resources that make life not only bearable but also worthy of celebrating. Their tears give voice to the anguish of their hearts and their empty bellies. Many, like Isaiah's exiles, see in their situation the absence of God. Many believe that God's eyes are closed to their plight. The certainty of their own deaths is a shroud that hides God and prevents them from seeing or living in the light of God.

The message of this text is to all peoples and nations and races, without consideration for status or cultural dividers. Isaiah's promise is meant to offer the assurance of God's visible presence to the children of God, even in the midst of their life-as-death situations. The text speaks volumes to those who exist in the shadow of death that has cast its pall over them. Isaiah speaks a word of hope to those who have been so beaten down by life that their existence is a living death. It offers hope to those who are hungry for a life they do not have, who struggle for life in the here and now, who can see nothing beyond the immediacy of their death and crave a foretaste of the divine feast.

Through Isaiah, God promises that God is aware of the difficult conditions of life and is actively present to transform those circumstances. This text is an assurance that death is not the end for those who wait on God. God knows the need to transform people, situations, and systems that breed injustice and cause hunger and death. God promises a great banquet that celebrates the end of hunger and the defeat of death. God offers all a place at God's table of grace and sets to rejoicing the new community in life forevermore.

Psalm 24

This psalm, connected with the procession of the ark into the temple, offers the opportunity to engage key questions in the relationship between God and human beings. The psalm is a reminder of the life of righteousness to which all the children of God are called. The definitive statement that begins this psalm asserts God as creator of all things and sets the scene for responding to questions of the divine-human relationship. Who is God? Who are the people of God? What is the substance of the divine-human relationship? How are human beings to relate to one another and the created world?

God is aware of all people because God is the creator of all things and worthy of praise. For the psalmist, purity of hands and heart are requisite for worship. God will vindicate and bless all who trust in God, who lift their souls to God in worship, who honor God as creator and seek to live in righteousness and bring about the reign of God on earth. These are key teachings of Judaism.

Revelation 21:1–6a

In John's vision of the new creation, the created order is completely gone—heaven and earth and sea are no more. The coming of the new Jerusalem, the holy city, is a direct contrast, not only to the original creation that began in chaos, but also to the present chaos of church and society, which is marked by corrupt leadership, war and violence, discrimination and prejudice, and oppressive systems that often punish the innocent and reward the guilty. In the new creation, chaos gives way to order, and perfection abounds.

Similar to the passage from Isaiah, this text offers both assurance and invitation. The perfection of the new heaven and earth is confirmed with the absence of mourning, crying, pain, and death (v. 4). The text further offers the assurance of God's abiding presence in the eternal realm. The image of the bride and her husband reprises the idea of the feast cited by Isaiah 25:6. Jerusalem the bride has overcome the violence of her captivity, and all are invited to celebrate her joining with the bridegroom at the wedding feast. The voice confirms it: "God is among mortals" (v. 3). This realm is a place of justice and peace, because God has not only created it with heavenly perfection, but God is present among the mortals who inhabit the perfect place that is the holy city.

In the new Jerusalem, all are made clean, inhabitants of the holy place with clean hands and hearts who have lived within and beyond the violence of the old world order, have withstood the injustices of life, have shed the tears of anger and sorrow and pain, have been disgraced and left for dead, and have triumphed through the deliverance of God. All creation, made new by God's re-creating presence and power and grace, sees the ending of sorrow and the beginning of a new and joyful life in the holy city. The holy city is the culmination of work of God. This city is a model for life in the present, a paradigm for the earthly city where all people experience a just world, with peace and plenty, joy and praise to the living God, who is Alpha and Omega, beginning and ending.

John 11:32–44

Mary's restatement (v. 32) of Martha's statement (v. 21) speaks for many who have stood in a similar place of grief and pain. This critical question addresses both the omnipresence of God and the nature of Christ. If Christ cannot be trusted to stand beside his disciples in the midst of trouble, who then is God, and what is the true relationship between Christ and his disciples? The world's hungry, those who are stricken with grief or torn apart by the death of loved ones lost to war and street violence, the living dead caught in addictions of body, mind, and spirit—all question the absence of God's redeeming grace in their life situations.

Jesus, "greatly disturbed in spirit and deeply moved" (v. 33b) to tears, goes to the place where Lazarus's body is entombed. He is ready to turn the situation from death to life, from human sorrow to the glory of God. Although he has already spoken words of assurance to Martha, both the response of the crowd and the grief of the sisters witness to the doubts that plague their hearts. Even today, such doubts push and pull with unremitting force into places of dis-ease where sickness and death, anger and tears, greed and violence are the accepted norms. Tombs of doubt and despair hide the glorious view of Christ's presence and power, and they deny fullness of life in Christ. The crowd's response to Jesus' tears is also the response of the oppressed and afflicted of the world, who seek the assurance of his presence and power in their time of trouble.

Mary and Martha in their sorrow might even have questioned whether they were considered of enough significance to warrant Jesus' attention. There are many people today who wonder the same thing, whether they matter enough to warrant the attention of the world or of Christ. People of color are often ignored or receive poor treatment from others because of their physical appearance; some who speak with an accent or language that is different from those in their present society are often considered illiterate; people who are poor often get short shrift from the systems that are intended to serve their needs. Generally, society has little regard for those who do not conform to the often-unreasonable criteria society has established for acceptance. This text offers the assurance that Jesus knows and values each person and will respond to the needs of all.

Jesus knows the impact their brother's death has had on Mary and Martha, and he also considers the impact his own death will have on the disciples. The invitation by the sisters to "come and see" (v. 34b) the place where the body had been placed may have impressed on Jesus the devastating impact that his death would have on the followers left behind. Similarly, this text says to the church and the world, "Come and see the impact of death on children and families victimized by war, natural disasters, and health crises such as the AIDS pandemic."

At the tomb Jesus' command to remove the stone, his prayer to God, his calling forth of the dead man, and the demand to loose Lazarus of the cloths that bound him offer both a word of assurance and an invitation. Heard by those who are bound by oppressive systems that cause their lives to be little more than death tombs in which hopes and dreams rot, his words serve as a reminder that Jesus has the power to release all who exist in any form of captivity, to enable them to experience freedom in and through Christ. They offer assurance of Christ's redeeming presence and invite all who are faced with the reality of life-and-death situations to trust his life-giving power.

Christ's resurrecting power is still at work in the midst of unmet dreams, entombed hopes, and deadly systems and structures of injustice and oppression. Jesus responds with new life to the situations of loss and death that hold us back from experiencing the fullness of life he offers. Christ calls us forth to live in newness of life, resurrection, and life everlasting. We are loosed by his command, through his love, and we live because he is the resurrection and he is life.

Proper 26 [31]

Elizabeth J. A. Siwo-Okundi

RUTH 1:1–18
PSALM 146

DEUTERONOMY 6:1–9
PSALM 119:1–8
HEBREWS 9:11–14
MARK 12:28–34

The lectionary readings for this week begin and end with commandments about love. We journey with Naomi, Orpah, and Ruth, who love God by caring for orphans, widows, and immigrants. We journey with the psalmist, who shows that when human help is unpredictable or nonexistent and shame overwhelms us, we still have a choice about how we interact with God and God's people. We also journey with Jesus, who combines commandments to uplift love as the ultimate sacrifice.

Deuteronomy 6:1–9

Deuteronomy 6:1–9 is concerned with the development of a loving, loyal, lifelong relationship with God. The commandment is concise: "You shall love the LORD your God with all your heart, and with all your soul, and with all your might" (v. 5). Love is not a flighty romantic feeling but an action-centered, complete commitment to God. The largest portion of this passage is dedicated to giving directions on how we can remember and practice this commandment. The author urges us to keep the words of the commandment in our hearts, recite them, talk about them, bind them, fix them, and write them on visible places (vv. 6–9). The ways in which we love God must be personal (in our hearts and at home), generational (for us, our children, and our children's children), public (written on our doorposts and gates), and consistent (when we lie down and when we rise). The more we learn and engage the commandment, the more we become accountable for acting upon it. This commandment must be so ingrained within us that our circumstances will not alter its significance nor deter us from loving God always, everywhere, and with everyone.

Ruth 1:1–18

Loving God means acting upon that love with the most vulnerable and forgotten of God's people. This passage introduces us to Naomi, who is married and has two sons. A severe famine interrupts the joys of their life and causes the family to relocate in hopes of finding food and better living conditions. Shortly after the move and perhaps as a result of the famine, Naomi's husband dies.[1] Naomi is left to care for her sons by herself and to do so in a foreign land. She is now an immigrant *and* a widow; and her children are orphans.

In ancient Near Eastern society, widows, orphans, and strangers (immigrants) are the most destitute people, because they do not have the care, protection, and security afforded by others.[2] Fatherless children are particularly vulnerable, given the centrality of fathers in supporting their families and guarding the inheritance of their sons. Naomi struggles to care for her fatherless sons, and they eventually marry kind, local women named Orpah and Ruth. After years of grief and uncertainty, Naomi can finally rest!

The rest is short lived. Within a mere ten years, Naomi's two sons die. Naomi and her daughters-in-law were initially linked by a shared love of Naomi's sons; now they are linked by a title that speaks of desperation and lack of security: widow. It is possible that her daughters-in-law have children who are now orphaned, just as their fathers were once orphaned.[3] Three widows, several orphans, no income, and deep grief—how will they survive? Surely the community and local leaders know of the widows' plight. But no one comes forward to help them.

Upon learning that the famine there has ended, Naomi decides to return to her homeland. Orpah and Ruth begin the journey with her, but Naomi pleads with them to return to the homes of their mothers. She shares with them two blessings: "May the LORD deal kindly with you, as you have dealt with the dead and with me" and "The LORD grant that you may find security" (vv. 8, 9). Then she kisses them, and they weep aloud. Despite Naomi's blessings,

---

1. A famine is large-scale shortage of food due to numerous factors. Famine increases the chance for starvation, malnutrition, disease, and death. If Naomi's husband died as a result of the famine, it is possible that Naomi and her sons were also sickly—making Naomi's situation all the more dire.

2. See Elizabeth J. A. Siwo-Okundi, "Listening to the Small Voice: Toward an Orphan Theology," *Harvard Divinity Bulletin* 37, nos. 2–3 (2009): 33–43.

3. Though commentators agree that Orpah and Ruth are childless, I suggest that Orpah likely has children. Her decision to return to her family may in part be due to her desire to support her children. It is possible, however, that Ruth's first child is not born until much later (Ruth 4:13–17).

Orpah and Ruth insist upon staying with her. Naomi pleads with them a second time, from a practical standpoint. Having been a widow for some time, she knows that a widow's life is one of instability and uncertainty. She could have remarried years ago, but now she declares, "I am too old to have a husband" (v. 12). Her daughters-in-law, however, are still young and can remarry easily. If Naomi could birth more sons for them to marry, she would do it, but doing so is not an option.

Naomi's second plea, ending with her feeling as though God has turned against her, leads the women to weep aloud again. Orpah thinks carefully about Naomi's proposal. In the midst of tears and kisses, Orpah makes the difficult decision to return to her family (vv. 14–15). Would her family receive her after all these years, and would they be willing or able to care for her and her children until she remarries? Many preachers and commentators view Orpah as a selfish and ungrateful woman who abandons her mother-in-law in the midst of tremendous grief. Those who do not condemn Orpah simply ignore her and focus on Ruth, the book's namesake. As Orpah leaves, Naomi pleads with Ruth a third time. But Ruth clings to Naomi and refuses to return to her mother's home. For her refusal she is applauded by those who focus on her poetic words of loyalty: "Where you go, I will go; . . . your people shall be my people, and your God my God" (v. 16).[4] Ruth's move would require many adjustments, for she would now be a widow and an immigrant. Would Naomi's family accept Ruth, and would Ruth find suitable opportunities for marriage?

This text is one of love, compassion, and difficult decisions. We cannot continue to condemn Orpah for deciding to return to her family when Naomi has made the same decision. Orpah's decision is encouraged and mirrored by Naomi. Ruth's decision is accepted by Naomi and offers both of them continued friendship. Naomi has admitted that Ruth *and* Orpah have been kind to her family. Three times, she refers to them as "my daughters" (vv. 11–13). Her blessing is for *both* of them. Both of them have come to know the God of Naomi by living with her. Though Naomi feels that God has turned against her, she acts upon God's command to care for orphans, widows, and immigrants and does so by supporting Orpah and Ruth. Naomi loves them so much that she wants for them to seek kindness and security—even if doing so means leaving her.

Psalm 146

Our love for God is often influenced by the circumstances in our lives. Psalm 146 gives two directions, each of which contains an element of hope. The first

4. Ruth's words—spoken at a time when she is a widow and prospects for marriage are unknown—ironically become incorporated into numerous present-day wedding ceremonies!

direction, "Praise the LORD," is a simple one. It invites us to insert our experiences alongside those assumed by the psalmist. The psalmist leads by example, proclaiming, "*I* will praise the LORD as long as *I* live; *I* will sing praises to *my* God all *my* life long" (v. 2, emphasis added). The psalmist's confession adds a personal level to praising God, while suggesting that praising God is a lifelong commitment. When our lives are chaotic and our world is in a mess, we still have control. We can *choose* to praise God. We may not agree with our circumstances or the circumstances around us, but each of us has the power to proclaim with the psalmist, "*I* will praise the LORD as long as *I* live; *I* will sing praises to *my* God all *my* life long." In making a personal declaration of praise, we do not dismiss the reality of our circumstances. Instead, we acknowledge them by praising our way through them.

The psalmist's second direction is a warning: "Do not put your trust in princes, in mortals, in whom there is no help" (v. 3). Then in whom should we put our trust? Quite simply, trust God. God has a history of being faithful. The psalmist contrasts the untrustworthy nature and mortality of human leaders with the trustworthy and infinite nature of God. When humans die, "their plans perish" (v. 4), but God is always present, was present at the very beginning of time, and "keeps faith forever" (v. 6). The continued existence of God's creation is a testimony to the everlasting presence and trustworthiness of God. When we are struggling or suffering and injustice is everywhere, it is easy to turn to princes, mortals, and those who have or represent leadership, money, power, and influence—each of which can help us. However, the psalmist warns that princes and other such mortals do not always provide help, even if some of them have the power to do so. Their love of neighbor is often limited and distracted by the benefits of their positions.

The psalmist's focus shifts from unhelpful, powerful leaders to those who are neglected in society. The psalmist names the people for whom the uncertainty of life would make it challenging to praise God (vv. 7b, 8). The list concludes with strangers, orphans, and widows (v. 9)—a group that is mentioned together throughout the Bible as needing special assistance.[5] For them and many others, God is the one who executes justice, gives food, sets people free, opens opportunities, uplifts, loves, and watches over the most vulnerable in society, *especially* when princes and those in positions to offer help have chosen not to do so. "Happy are those whose help is [God], whose hope is in the LORD their God" (v. 5)—the God who has a history of faithfulness and does not allow wickedness to prevail. We can *choose* to trust God. In trusting God, we are able to express love by helping those whom leaders have failed to help.

5. Psalm 146:9 is an opportunity to connect to the story of Naomi, Orpah, and Ruth's experience as and with orphans, widows, and immigrants.

Psalm 119:1–8

Many of us spend our lives searching for happiness. In our search, we conclude that friends and family do not understand us; intimate relationships and activities are unfulfilling; alcohol and drugs are harmful; shopping and gambling are expensive; and work and play are unsatisfactory. Everywhere we turn, our search is fruitless, leading us to declare constantly that we are unhappy! Perhaps sensing the human desire for happiness, the psalmist shares some observations: "Happy are those whose way is blameless, who walk in the law of the LORD. Happy are those who keep [God's] decrees, who seek [God] with their whole heart, who also do no wrong, but walk in [God's] ways" (vv. 1–3). The psalmist is showing us *how to be happy*, but the greatest contribution of the psalmist is that of giving us a clue as to *why many of us are unhappy.*

Much of our unhappiness is rooted in shame (v. 6). We are ashamed of the decisions that we have made in the past. We are ashamed of not being where we think we should be or of not having accomplished what we think we should have accomplished "by now." We are ashamed of the ways in which we have hurt others by our actions or lack of action and how others have hurt us. When the truth is before us and we do not like that truth, then our hearts are filled with shame rather than love. That very shame becomes our fixation, and our unhappiness is magnified. Instead of moving forward toward a resolution, we run away from life, hide, and push away people who are able to support us. Shame prevents us from progress and peace. Instead of focusing on our shame, the psalmist encourages us to fix ourselves completely on God's commandments. By seeking, learning, observing, and focusing upon God's commandments, we "shall not be put to shame" (v. 6). Our hearts will be released from the burden of shame so that we can fully praise God and experience true happiness. In so doing, we participate in our own healing and the healing of those around us.

Hebrews 9:11–14

This short passage includes complex metaphors and images reflecting on important historical aspects of sacrifice. In the coming of Christ, the focus shifts from external sacrifices that purify our flesh from defilement to internal sacrifices that purify our conscience "from dead works" (vv. 13–14). Dead works are those actions and activities that clutter our conscience, keep us bound in shame and guilt, and prevent us from offering ourselves to God in service. The importance of conscience cleansing is that we become internally and entirely free to serve and "worship the living God" (v. 14). To worship God is to love God and the people of God.

Mark 12:28–34

The text begins with a scribe asking Jesus the question, "Which commandment is the first of all?" (v. 28). Jesus is not perplexed by the question, nor does he hesitate to answer it. He immediately responds by sharing the words of Deuteronomy 6:5. Being part of the Jewish tradition, Jesus has done what the author of Deuteronomy directed—he has kept the words of the commandment, recited them, talked about them, and learned them in every way possible—so that when he is publicly tested, he is able to respond with great confidence. What is intriguing about Jesus' response is that he gives the scribe a longer answer than is required. He could have stopped by simply reciting the first commandment. Instead, he continues talking and says, "The second is this, 'You shall love your neighbor as yourself.' There is no other commandment greater than these" (v. 31). Jesus takes two commandments (Deut. 6:5 and Lev. 19:18) and makes them into one! The love of God cannot fully exist without the love of neighbor and self.

The scribe does not argue with Jesus or even press him to choose only one commandment, as originally requested. Instead, he accepts Jesus' answer. He publicly says, "You are right, Teacher; . . . this is much more important than all whole burnt offerings and sacrifices" (vv. 32–33). Jesus sees that the scribe has responded "wisely" (v. 34). The wisdom in the scribe's response is not that he agrees with Jesus, but that he is able to understand and engage Jesus' response in relation to sacrificial acts long valued by the community. The threefold love proposed by Jesus requires that we offer our internal selves to our neighbors. The exchange is so intense that "after that no one dared to ask [Jesus] any question" (v. 34). It is *this* combined love commandment that we must now keep in our hearts, recite, talk about, bind, fix, and write on places that are visible; and make that love personal, generational, public, and consistent. This commandment must be so ingrained within us that our circumstances will not alter its significance or deter us from loving God always, everywhere, and with everyone.

Proper 27 [32]

Bob Ekblad

RUTH 3:1–5; 4:13–17   1 KINGS 17:8–16
PSALM 127   PSALM 146
                                       HEBREWS 9:24–28
                                       MARK 12:38–44

This week's readings have certain things in common and many differences. We see key features of God's not-of-this-world-as-usual reign. Redemption comes to those who are poor, vulnerable, and excluded as religious insiders pay attention to divine instructions, cross borders, go into enemy territory— and are themselves saved in the process. Naomi adopts Ruth the Moabite and gets an offspring who becomes an ancestor of Jesus Christ. Elijah is sent to a Sidonian widow who provides for him out of the last of her supplies, and receives miraculous provision. A Jewish widow who gives all is elevated as the one who gives more than all the wealthy donors in Mark 12. We see how the economy of God's reign begins with surrender in total trust of all that one has—one's vulnerable self (Ruth), the last of one's flour and oil (1 Kgs. 17:8–16), one's praise and trust in the invisible God (Ps. 146), Jesus' offering of his life (Heb. 9), or a widow's two small coins (Mark 12).

Ruth 3:1–5; 4:13–17

In Ruth 3:1–5 and 4:13–17 Naomi offers exemplary care for her daughter-in-law Ruth—a person who represents "otherness" and difference on several levels. Ruth is from Moab, whose origin in the Hebrew Bible happens through the story of Lot's seduction by his two daughters, one of whom gave birth to a son Moab (Gen. 19:30–38). Moabites were viewed as relatives, tainted as they were by their incestuous origins from Lot, who was not directly called by God but brought along by Abram into his call (Gen. 12:4).

Moab was also often a national enemy of Israel (e.g., Exod. 15:15; Pss. 60:8; 83:6; 108:9). The Moabite king Balak called on Balaam to curse Israel (Num.

22–24) and the Benjaminite Ehud led an army in a dispute over the Jordan fords, and killed 10,000 Moabites (Judg. 3:12–30). The Moabites served other gods (Ruth 1:15). In spite of these differences, Naomi is an exemplary advocate who calls Ruth "my daughter" and seeks security for her (Ruth 3:1).

Prior to this, Naomi herself receives companionship and support from Ruth, her daughter-in-law and fellow widow, after the deaths of their husbands. Naomi's advocacy on Ruth's behalf with their relative Boaz reflects the Abrahamic vocation to be a blessing to every family on the earth (Gen. 12:3)—in spite of Joshua, Nehemiah, and other prohibitors of alliances with people of other faiths (Ezra 9:2; 10:2–3; Neh. 13:3, 25–27). Boaz invites Ruth to join his harvesters. Ruth humbly submits to Naomi's advocacy strategy, demonstrating radical obedience to the "elect": "All that you tell me I will do" (Ruth 3:5). Naomi urges typical approaches of the powerless before the powerful: stealth, trickery, cunning. She sends Ruth washed and perfumed to lie down at his feet at night after he has eaten and drunk.

Ruth humbles herself before Boaz, making herself vulnerable before him, asking him to take her as a wife in ways that once again show exemplary advocacy. Ruth advocates for Naomi's dead husband, Elimelech ("my God is king"), whose sons have died, leaving him without an heir to pass on his name. Ruth assures Elimelech and her own husband's genealogy—placing herself before the kinsman redeemer Boaz, who himself embraces a foreigner. According to Matthew's genealogy, Boaz is Rahab the prostitute's son (Matt. 1:5), showing that blood connections from Judah to Israel's Messiah pass through characters not viewed as pure according to religious criterion. And God himself is involved in this entire adoption process. While Boaz adopts Ruth, embracing her as his wife, God makes sure she conceives (4:13)—adding another level of divine advocacy. Finally, Naomi herself seals the adoption through embracing Ruth's child Obed, nursing him to such an extent that people say: "A son has been born to Naomi" (4:17).

How is God at work in the similar ups and downs of our lives? This text challenges us to align ourselves with God and to extend radical hospitality to strangers and even enemies.

1 Kings 17:8–16

This passage shows another religious and ethnic insider (Elijah) being cared for by an impoverished foreign woman outsider (the widow of Zarephath). It also shows the God of Israel using the insider to bless the outsider in the heart of enemy territory. In the process, the distinction between insider and outsider gives way to new possibilities for community.

The narrator has alerted the reader to King Ahab's doing "evil in the sight of the LORD" by marrying Jezebel, who served and worshiped Baal and persecuted God's prophets. Ahab even built an altar for Baal (1 Kgs. 16:29–34). Jezebel is the daughter of Ethbaal, ruler of the Sidonians, and may have been in power at the time of this story. The rulers of Sidon are described as destined for judgment in Jeremiah 25:22 and Ezekiel 28:21–22.

Elijah confronts Ahab with a word of the Lord: "There shall be neither dew nor rain these years, except by my word" (1 Kgs. 17:1)—a word that led to economic hardship. The Lord then sends Elijah east of the Jordan, where ravens bring him bread and meat and he drinks from the brook, until it dries up (1 Kgs. 17:2–7). God gives Elijah precise instructions regarding where to go next, reminiscent of God's missional instructions to Philip that touch the Ethiopian eunuch (Acts 8:26): "Go now to Zarephath, which belongs to Sidon" (1 Kgs. 17:8–9). God sends Elijah into the heart of Jezebel's turf—to Zarephath, a Phoenician city in Sidon near the Mediterranean coast.

Given the associations with Sidon cited above, the reader expects God's judgment in and on Sidon. But a more hidden "power encounter" is about to take place. "I have commanded a widow there to feed you," the Lord says (v. 9), subverting sacrifices to Baal's insatiable appetite by pointing to provision given by faith from the weakest of human agents. In the face of Ahab's powerful father-in-law, the Lord sends Elijah to receive provision from an impoverished widow who has only enough for a final meal for herself and her son. The widow points out that she has only "a handful of meal in a jar, and a little oil in a jug" (v. 12). However, Elijah urges the widow to exercise radical faith in the invisible God by preparing a meal. The widow does according to Elijah's word. The words are confirmed by the sign that follows: The jar of meal was not exhausted and the jug of oil did not become empty (v. 16).

In this story there is no hint that God has commanded a widow there to provide for Elijah. Elijah commands the widow. Elijah shows extreme obedience to God, and the widow equally extreme obedience to Elijah.

Provision comes from the least—the outsider, outcast, foreigner—as in the story of Ruth. Yet the insiders (Naomi, Elijah) have the role of receiving and protecting, as they too step out in faith. Are we willing and able to hear God's instructions leading to provision and mission?

Psalm 127

In this psalm the psalmist emphasizes the Lord as builder of the house and guard over the city. Indeed, God must be directly involved in a home or city, or those who build the home or watch over the city do so in vain (v. 1). While not referring directly to Ruth and Elijah, this psalm confirms that God acts in the providential ways described in those stories. The economy of God's rule invites rest and trust, living by gift and not by the sweat of the brow (v. 2). There is freedom from toil of life outside the garden, and God is depicted as giving even as people sleep (v. 2). Children are viewed not as a result of the curse, but as arrows in a man's quiver who will protect from enemies (vv. 3–4). How might this psalm challenge contemporary Christians to shift trust away from self, money, and powers and onto the Holy Spirit?

Psalm 146

Psalm 146 is a call to worship God, followed by a command not to look to powerful people for benefits. "Do not put your trust in princes, in mortal [human beings], in whom there is no help" (v. 3). Presidents, representatives, people with money, power, and influence are finite—and so are human mediators of the Divine like Naomi, Boaz, and Elijah (v. 4).

This psalm challenges normal human thinking and conventional orientations to the extreme. Happiness comes from the invisible God, who invites total allegiance and absolute trust. "Happy are those whose help is the God of Jacob, whose hope is in the LORD their God" (v. 5). In contrast to impermanent mortals, God is the maker of heaven, earth, sea, and "all that is in them" (v. 6).

The psalmist affirms the truths visible in the stories of Ruth and of Elijah's encounter with the widow of Zarephath: God executes justice for the oppressed. The psalmist echoes Isaiah's Servant poems and Isaiah 61, depicting God as setting prisoners free, opening the eyes of the blind, thwarting the way of the wicked, and on top of everything, reigning forever (Isa. 42:1–9; 49:1–6; 50:4–11; 52:13–53:12; cf. 61:1–7). The listing of God's actions here is especially wide ranging, offering hope to the most marginalized: foreigners, orphans, and widows. All of us need to join God in these endeavors.

Hebrews 9:24–28

This reading describes Jesus as the universal advocate par excellence. Jesus' high priestly role is not marked by the limits of a particular geographical place and annual liturgical calendar. Jesus' priestly intercession is cosmic and once for all. He does not intercede only for Israel's sins by entering into the holy place in the Jerusalem temple ("a sanctuary made by human hands, a mere copy of the true one"). Jesus enters heaven itself—appearing before God on our behalf (v. 24).

Jesus has been manifested "to remove sin by the sacrifice of himself." Here the text does not specify to whom Jesus sacrifices himself. Is this sacrifice to God—in the tradition of penal substitution? Is Jesus sacrificing himself to us, giving us his body and blood—suggested by the Synoptic Gospel accounts of the Last Supper? These verses do not answer these questions. The writer presents atonement as a mystery that defies reductionism. The discretion of the author not to specify who offers Christ to whom must be respected. At the same time, the good news that sin is carried away once for all must be announced, especially to those prone to carry their own sin, through self-blame or difficulties in forgiving themselves.

Jesus' universal priestly work breaks down the dividing wall between Jews and non-Jews, affirming that Gentiles—including widows, orphans, those who are poor and oppressed—have a place at God's table. The writer adds better news to good, describing Jesus' second coming as focusing not on judging sin—which has already been covered by his once and for all sacrifice—but "to save those who are eagerly waiting for him." Those who eagerly await Jesus' return can do so without fear.

I saw this dynamic at work during my prison ministry. "There aren't too many people who would eagerly wait for someone to come and punish them, are there?" I asked a group of jail inmates. "Well, in my case," said a middle-aged Caucasian inmate with a scraggly goatee, "My dad regularly used me for a punching bag whenever he came home. I would hide in the backyard, behind a tree, wherever I could. I was afraid of him because he was always drunk and he would beat me. I did eagerly await my mom's return. She was nice to me and would protect me from my dad." In the way that the inmate eagerly anticipated his mother's return, we can await Jesus.

Mark 12:38–44

In Mark 12:38–44 Jesus contrasts the leaders of the Jerusalem temple with impoverished widows. "Beware of the scribes," Jesus tells a large crowd (v. 38), and then launches into prophetic critique reminiscent of critiques of Israel's leaders by Isaiah (Isa. 1:10–17) and Ezekiel (Ezek. 34:1–10).

The scribes during Jesus' times were professional official scholars of the Bible and Jewish tradition—depicted throughout Mark as Jesus' enemies (2:6; 3:22; 11:18, 27) and those who plot to kill him (14:1, 43, 53; 15:1, 31). Jesus exposes and denounces religious posturing for power and influence, visible in their walking about in long robes, respectful greetings in public places, and special seats in synagogues and at banquets, which Jesus says they "like" (v. 38). According to Jesus, these social perks gained through professional religious status come at the expense of the weak and vulnerable—in this case, widows.

"What image of God would people have through observing these religious leaders?" I ask inmates dressed in red prison-issue uniforms. "Not a good one at all," one of them answers. Nobody could imagine going to these scribes for advice or comfort. People observing these scribes might see themselves as lesser in comparison, and could interpret religion as favoring a few—a mirror of widening economic gaps and growing class divisions in our world.

"Do we see this still today?" I ask. "Everywhere all the time," a man immediately answers. The men talk about their experiences in church, but also right there in the jail, where people brag about things they don't have and differentiate themselves from others through gang affiliations or crimes committed. Where do you see contemporary equivalents of these scribes and of widows in your community?

According to Jesus, this professional religious class was not observing Isaiah's teaching: "Learn to do good; seek justice, rescue the oppressed, defend the orphan, plead for the widow" (Isa. 1:17). Jesus sees them as devouring widows' houses (v. 40), which is best understood in reference to Jesus' words about the widow's offering in verses 41–44. Jesus' final rail against the scribes' long public prayer, designed to impress, includes a strong warning to avoid self-serving religious show: "they will receive the greater condemnation" (v. 40).

In the next scene, Jesus sits down opposite the treasury and observes people giving tithes. The narrator tells how Jesus was observing rich people who were putting in large amounts, and then describes him focusing in on a poor widow who gives two coins worth a cent. Jesus calls his disciples to him, enacting a lifting up of the lowly, after having brought down the haughty. "Truly I tell you, this poor widow has put in more than all those who are contributing to the treasury. For all of them have contributed out of their abundance, but she out of her poverty has put in everything she had, all she had to live on" (vv. 43–44).

In the economy of Jesus' realm the amount is less important than the faith. Jesus highlights the widow's act of giving everything she had, which represents total trust in God, much like the act of the widow of Zarephath. Unlike the Sidonian widow, an outsider who obeys Elijah's request, Mark's widow appears to be Jewish, contributing to the temple treasury freely.

In contrast to the scribes and possibly the rich, whose actions are intended to impress the people watching them, the widow is not doing anything to impress, nor is she ashamed to give so little. Through an act of bold faith, she gives rather than hoarding what little she has. "If Jesus reveals God in these stories, what is God like?" I ask the inmates.

"This story shows that the way things are, the injustices of this world, are not God's will," a man astutely observes. "Jesus denounces the way things are normally done, the religious leaders' attitudes, the ways the rich give from the excess of what they have, which shows these things are not Jesus' will. Jesus is against the injustice of the scribes' devouring the widow's house. It's not Jesus' will how our unjust legal system works."

Clearly Jesus sides with the vulnerable and weak, the underdog. How would it look to embody this way of Jesus in your life, community, and world?

Proper 28 [33]

L. Susan Bond

1 SAMUEL 1:4–20
1 SAMUEL 2:1–10

DANIEL 12:1–3
PSALM 16
HEBREWS 10:11–14
(15–18), 19–25
MARK 13:1–8

The texts for this Sunday begin to set the thematic and theological stage for Advent. While the texts vary in the degree of apocalyptic theology and imagery, they all participate in the apocalyptic language world of pregnancy, childbirth, generativity, and new life. The Daniel reading is one of only two or three in the Torah, Prophets, and Writings that talks directly of resurrection. The Markan Little Apocalypse hints at the birth pangs of "the suffering." The Hebrews text borrows from the primitive language world of the Gospels and Letters to discuss Christian access to "a new and life-giving way."

Mark 13:1–8

This text, the beginning of the Little Apocalypse, is set against the backdrop of the temple in Jerusalem, a construction project of Herod the Great that created controversy. Whether Mark's Gospel was written immediately before or immediately after the destruction of the temple in 70 CE, it is certainly written during the Jewish revolt against Rome.

The air in Jerusalem was full of apocalyptic fanaticism, indicative of the social upheaval in Jerusalem and one of the worst epochs of Jewish history. The poverty rate was escalating astronomically, and the tax burden gutted half of family incomes. People were losing their property and falling into destitution. Rome met Jewish resistance with violence and lined the highways to Jerusalem with crosses.

The text for today is only a portion of the full pericope, which extends through v. 13. Preachers, then, should read Mark 13:1–13. As the chapter begins, Jesus has just left the temple for the last time, after teaching inside the temple for the whole day and delivering the example story of the widow's mite, along with warnings about the scribes and the Pharisees. As they are leaving the temple, one of the Twelve exclaims over the grandeur of the temple (the Markan disciples are *never* portrayed as apt pupils), and Jesus' response comes almost as a rebuke (another typical Markan pattern): "Well, it won't last forever."

An abrupt change of venue finds Jesus on the Mount of Olives, "over against" (*katenanti*) the Temple Mount, which is apocalyptically significant, as the Mount was headquarters of God's fight against the enemies of Israel. From here Jesus speaks to Peter, James, John, and Andrew, who want to know (in disciple confusion) how to recognize the signs that the time is fulfilled and how to estimate the arrival time of the *basileia*, the realm.

In a lovely, clever response, Jesus tells them only how to recognize the beginning of the end, but not the end itself. Cosmological disaster is standard apocalyptic fare; when coupled with natural disaster, war, and international conflict, the total situation is pretty much the typical human condition. "It will start like this," he says. "There will be earthquakes and famines and wars and rumors of wars and false prophets and international conflict. But that's only the beginning of the birth pangs."

The Markan use of birth and delivery imagery is significant. Paul uses similar imagery to discuss the coming of the *basileia*, the new age, supporting Mark's perspective that the date of that coming cannot be predicted. The "birth pangs" precede the emergence of something entirely new. Paul uses the same word when he talks of the "whole creation . . . groaning in labor pains until now" (Rom. 8:22).[1]

Mark uses similar imagery when the veil of the temple is "torn in two" during the terrifying darkness at Golgotha (Mark 15:38); the Greek word *schizō* is used, which can describe a womb tearing open in childbirth. Mark thus accumulates major biblical allusions to birth and generativity into one overarching image. The coming of the realm is like giving birth and, like childbirth, comes in waves, with the pain of waves increasing as the birth nears. Awareness of the realm starts in pain and endures cycles of unpredictable pain and then painlessness and then hope, but its outcome is inescapable. So goes Christian witness and the approach to the *basileia*.

We must be careful with the temple imagery so that we do not invent a Jesus against Judaism. Jesus was not opposed to Jewish faith and practice. From Mark's point of view, like a biblical prophet Jesus critiqued his own house, which points preachers in the direction of questioning the entrenched interests of our own religious houses. For example, we can call into question

1. See also the birth pang imagery in Rev. 12:1–6.

those who align Christian faith with national security, national imperialism, manifest destiny, and prosperity gospels.

It is easy to grow weary and frustrated facing injustices on our own. Women fighting for gender equality or struggling to escape poverty will continue to suffer indignities. Gay and lesbian persons are still not afforded full civil rights as American citizens. People of color know that they are still in the struggle, as states attempt to resurrect Jim Crow laws that masquerade as immigration reform. We long to know, "How long, O Lord, how long?" To such folk, the preacher can take a Markan approach by assuring the congregation that the *basileia* will come. Jesus will return. We who live in the interim wait without fear or worry. "We wait with hands dirty from our work in this world; with hearts full of compassion for those who suffer."[2] We await the childbirth, not by being idle, but by actively engaging in the push.

Hebrews 10:11–14 (15–18), 19–25

The book of Hebrews is considered part of the Pauline corpus only in the most general way; almost no one accepts Pauline authorship. Some scholars have called it the most difficult book of the New Testament because of its unique christological claims about Jesus as both a divine Son and a high priest.

Interpreters sometimes read Hebrews' pre-Anselmian version of Christ's substitutionary sacrifice back into Paul's older *Christus Victor* model. While the substitutionary Christology of Hebrews is more typical of contemporary Christian communities, preachers should be wary of considering it legitimate *Pauline* salvation theology. Paul's *Christus Victor* approach was *not* a personal theory of substitution (Jesus died in our place for our personal sins), but a dramatic claim that the death and resurrection of Jesus reversed history and thwarted Satan's attempts to kill off our hopes for a better world.

Regardless of authorship and unusual Christology, many scholars argue that Hebrews was written as a sermon for Jewish Christians mourning the loss of Jerusalem, giving them a new and powerful theology of access to God. These two theological events, Good Friday and the loss of Jerusalem, provide symbolic connections to the Markan text. The symbolism of childbirth and the *basileia* dominate verses 19–20: "And so, dear brothers and sisters, we can boldly enter heaven's Most Holy Place because of the blood of Jesus. By his death, Jesus opened a new and life-giving way through the curtain into the Most Holy Place" (NLT).

The social-justice prompts for preaching from this text come from three related claims about how the community constitutes itself. (1) We draw near

2. Mary S. Hulst, "Strange Comfort," *Calvin Theological Journal* 41 (2006): 137.

to each other because of Christ. (2) We hold fast (without fear or faltering) to our faith. (3) We stir one another with acts of love. The communal hermeneutical approach is power in the hope and encouragement it offers, not just to individuals, but also to communities of faithful activity.

Reading beyond the assignment to the end of the chapter, we discover additional confirmation of this claim: We are bound to one another in God's grace, strengthened through fellowship, and sustained in risky public witness. The community can be confident in the face of opposition and hostility, and it can offer bold public witness, based on the assurance that God's future brings justice on earth.

1 Samuel 1:4–20 and 1 Samuel 2:1–10

The birth of Samuel, a watershed event in Israel's history, marked the end of the period of judges and the ushering in of the monarchy. Samuel's birth to a barren mother was accompanied by signs, miracles, and divine intervention. The church uses this reading, coming before Advent, as an interpretive lens for the birth of Jesus as another historical pivot point for Israel. Reverberating throughout this "birth of a hero" paradigm are echoes of Sarah, Hagar, Jochebed, Leah, Rachel, Naomi, Ruth, and ultimately Mary the mother of Jesus.[3]

These texts present the story of Hannah, a woman plagued by barrenness while her husband's second wife is blessed with fertility. Intertwined with Hannah's story is the narrative of Eli and his family dynasty. Eli, a priest of Shiloh, has two corrupt priestly sons. When Hannah comes to the sanctuary to pray silently, Eli misunderstands her prayer and accuses her of drunkenness. Eli's confusion over what he hears (he is also losing his sight) returns as a theme later in the Samuel cycle. To this point, Hannah is a barren woman, and Eli is the respected holy man. But then the narrative reverses. Hannah corrects Eli, a priest who cannot recognize prayer. Unfazed, Eli joins Hannah in prayer and asks God to bless her. The child for whom they both pray will ultimately supplant Eli's own dynasty.

Hannah conceives, gives birth to a son she names Samuel (which means "God has heard"), and cares for her child until he is old enough, per her promise, to be dedicated to God and given into Eli's responsibility.

As she hands Samuel over to Eli, she bursts into a prayer-song, declaring that God has lifted and blessed her and witnessing to the way God works to humble the proud and to vindicate the oppressed. We might be tempted to hear this

---

3. Athalya Brenner, "Female Social Behavior: Two Descriptive Patterns within the 'Birth of a Hero' Paradigm," *Vetus Testamentum* 36 (1986): 257–73.

simply as a song of thanksgiving, but there is also a note of her triumph over Eli and a foreshadowing of the fall of his own house full of wicked priest sons.

The Revised Common Lectionary splits the narrative into two parts, omitting Hannah's active role in making a sacrifice (1:24–28) and resuming with her great song of praise that marks the beginning of the second chapter. Hannah's song, along with Miriam's song at Pharaoh's defeat (Exod. 15:21), was seen by early Christian communities as a paradigm and antecedent for Mary's Magnificat (Luke 1:46–55). Preachers should include what the lectionary excludes (1:24–28). Smart preachers should always attend to what the lectionary omits and search for voices that have been silenced by such splitting and narrative chopping.

Also echoing throughout this reading are themes of sacrifice, hope, and a new beginning where it seems least likely. These themes support the homiletical interpretations for the other readings for today, whether or not they are apocalyptic. Hannah becomes a model for living in hope in the middle of a Godforsaken world. She expects God to reach beyond the present order of the world and to do a new thing, to bring something unexpected.

Hannah's song not only anticipates Mary's Magnificat with its social reversals, but also anticipates the parabolic nature of Jesus' parables and the parabolic reversals at the heart of apocalyptic theology. There are also hints of resurrection when verse 6 affirms that God "brings death and makes alive; [God] brings down to the grave and raises up" (NLT).

While many interpreters and preachers will be content to generalize and spiritualize Hannah's story, or to cast Hannah as a softly focused woman, this tendency depoliticizes and negates the theological claims of the texts. Hannah's story is a liberation text that anticipates a just world in which war weapons are broken, the hungry are full, the poor are lifted from the ashes, arrogant speech is judged by God, and corrupt religious dynasties fall. Hannah expects God to hear the marginalized and the oppressed and to transform the world.

Daniel 12:1–3

Readings from the book of Daniel surface only three times in the three-year lectionary: two readings for Year B (Propers 28 and 29) and one reading for Year C (All Saints' Day). Daniel is the most apocalyptic book in the Hebrew Bible. Since the Christian faith and its texts grew out of apocalyptic thought and imagery, we might expect to see more of Daniel.

The book of Daniel is narratively set during the Babylonian exile, between 540 and 530 BCE. But it was probably written long after the exile, during the Maccabean revolt against the Hellenistic ruler Antiochus Epiphanes IV, after he had taken the Jerusalem temple in 167 BCE and before it had been recaptured and rededicated by the Maccabeans in 164 BCE.

Today's brief reading comes at an odd point in the book of Daniel, after the most fantastic apocalyptic visions and images. It is set during a revolt against imperialist enemies. Like the words of Jesus in the Markan text for this week, this reading short-circuits idle speculation about signs and portents of the end times. Instead, Daniel 12:1–3 offers hope, the hope of resurrection. For Daniel, resurrection is not pie in the sky but part and parcel of the new social world that God fully puts in place after God intervenes in history in an apocalypse. Resurrection is God's way of being ultimately faithful to those who have suffered because of their own faithful witness.

For those who preach toward social justice and transformation, this is a good word. Our time of anguish should not be surprising to us; we do not suffer as those without hope (to paraphrase Paul in 1 Thess. 4:13), but we endure because we have hope in the resurrection, the ultimate reclamation of the dead, the ultimate "No!" to the forces that kill and crush.

Psalm 16

This psalm appears several times in the lectionary cycle, most notably during Easter with its resurrection and new birth themes, but also on a number of other liturgical occasions. Psalm 16 is an all-purpose psalm, since it acknowledges that the world is a horror of devastation and destruction, a place of fragility and deep sorrow.

Both testaments witness to the realities of sin and injustice, and both testaments unflinchingly recognize that the human spirit suffers the temptation to default and to allow injustice to overpower. We look around our own world and see that the powers of corporations have almost incapacitated democratic and justice-oriented ideals. Our planet suffers from devastations created and sustained by short-sighted human habits. Wars rage—not only the wars the United States pursues in Iraq and Afghanistan, but wars in countries already ravaged by poverty.

Yet, in spite of all evidence to the contrary, faith communities are called to trust the divine promises of a just world and to keep working toward those purposes. Our sense of futility, our fears of failure, and our own contemporary temptations to give up are not new. Martin Luther's hymn "A Mighty Fortress Is Our God" captured the timeless "battle" of Christian communities to endure in spite of overwhelming odds:

> And though this world, with devils filled, should threaten to undo us,
> we will not fear, for God hath willed his truth to triumph through us.[4]

4. Martin Luther, "A Mighty Fortress Is Our God," *Chalice Hymnal* (St. Louis: Chalice Press, 1995), 65.

Proper 29 [34] (Reign of Christ)

Jennifer L. Lord

2 SAMUEL 23:1–7
PSALM 132:1–12 (13–18)

DANIEL 7:9–10, 13–14
PSALM 93
REVELATION 1:4B–8
JOHN 18:33–37

Many preachers will recognize the words of Jesus in today's lesson as the words we hear on Good Friday. But here they are for the Reign of Christ, a Sunday some six months from Holy Week. Yet the Holy Week text also sets out the key issues for today: How is Jesus a ruler? What is his reign like? All the texts appointed for today in Year B show a canonical interest in this metaphor for God, from enthronement psalmody to apocalyptic visions. These themes are also in the semicontinuous first reading and accompanying readings. While these texts offer many ways to think about the regnant Christ, the main claim for today is clear: the reign of Christ surpasses the reign of any earthly ruler.

John 18:33–37

John's timeline of events for Jesus' arrest and death differs from that of the Synoptic Gospels. In the Synoptics, Jesus is killed on Passover. However, in John he is killed the day before Passover. Since the lambs slaughtered for Passover are actually killed the day before the Passover meal, in John Jesus is killed on the same day as the Passover lambs.

By placing the events of today's text on the day before Passover, the day the Passover lambs are slaughtered, John supercharges the concept of Jesus' monarchy. Jesus is a lamb set against imperial and religious rulers. Both Roman and Jewish powers oppose Jesus: the detachment of 200–600 soldiers at the garden who make the arrest, accompanied by Jewish leaders; both Annas and Caiaphas, former and current high priest; then the Roman governor of Judea, Pontius Pilate. This opposition of powers is echoed in Pilate's famous question, "Are you the [monarch] of the Jews?" (v. 33). Pilate again asks Jesus, "So you are a [monarch]?" (v. 37). In the middle of these questions Jesus says, "My [dominion] is not from this world. If my [dominion] were from this world, my followers would be fighting to keep me from being handed over to the Jews. But as it is, my [dominion] is not from here" (v. 36).

It would be a mistake for preachers to take these words from Jesus and use them to entrench an unsurpassable divide between God's dominion ways and our earthly ways. Because Jesus said that his reign is "not from this world," some preachers see no need to be concerned about God's *basileia* (reign) on earth, because we can just wait for it in the afterlife. Some preachers hold that the sole responsibility for bringing the realm belongs to God and that the realm has little to do with human effort. Some ministers conclude from these words that we do not have to love our neighbors in the present, because Jesus' rule applies to another (heavenly) world. But such ideas about the *basileia* misread. Jesus' comment is not about location of this reign but is about its origin, source, and strength. When Jesus says, "My dominion is not from here," it means, "My dominion has its origin in God." Jesus tells his followers that if they want to be a part of this dominion, they are to love one another (e.g., John 13:31–35).

Preachers could focus on the reign of God intended on earth now, and challenge us again to know that Jesus' life, death, and resurrection are not pleasant piety only for inside church walls but are for the world to know. This means that water turns to wine, systems break open, the dead rise. New life is not only possible but promised. The church can live this piety by protesting legislation that sanctions racial profiling in U.S. border states and elsewhere, teaching agricultural technology to peasants in southern Sudan, providing reproductive information for teachers to give to girls and boys and women and men. This piety responds faithfully to God and is, at times, at odds with the church.

Preachers could also focus on the origin of God's reign as separate from the church. This statement is important, as reports continue to abound of abuses of the young by clergy. It is also important when the church thinks about the crucifixion of Jesus. The church often tells the story of the death of Jesus in such a way as to encourage anti-Semitism. The preacher often contrasts Judaism (bad) with church (good). John's statement is a theological gift that keeps our human efforts in perspective: we must always ask if our work is consistent with the reign that God intends. When we are not consistent with God's intentions—for example, when clergy abuse children or when the church misrepresents Judaism—the door is open for repentance. Furthermore, the origin of God's reign is deeper than mere human awareness. Indeed, the Romans tried to kill Jesus. Over the centuries, people have repeatedly tried to kill the Jews. But God raised Jesus from the dead. And God continues to support the Jewish community.

Daniel 7:9–10, 13–14 and Psalm 93

If we want to know where Jesus gets his strength as he stands before Pilate, we only need to read these words from Daniel, a passage in back of the picture of Jesus in John. Daniel sets out the source and strength of the reign of which Jesus is part. We see thrones and a throne. There is the Ancient of Days (v. 13, NRSV "Ancient One), whose clothing is white, whose hair is like pure wool, and whose throne is fiery flames with wheels of burning fire. Thousands and ten thousands attend this presence. And the court is ready to record human deeds. This Ancient One adjudicates righteously.

These images of a powerful and revered judge are striking. To some they may be too hierarchical. For this image—God as old man—gives patriarchy a proof text. This combination of a throne and a court could license a dangerous hierarchy. But the text was authored during the Maccabean revolt, when the Jews lived under military occupation. The strange vision of this text, alongside the context of subjugation, speaks of hope and expanded possibilities for a people suffering ongoing tribulation. There is a source beyond the day-to-day realities. We who live without a monarch (and who on this liturgical day need to make connections between monarchial governments and other forms of governments) need to remember there are those who do live under despotic rulers.

We see this hope. In the lone person standing without guile before the army tank in Tiananmen Square. In women in Africa and Southeast Asia taking microloans to earn money to educate themselves and their children over against patriarchy and rogue governments. In politicians and scientists relentlessly educating about global warming in the face of global corporate resistance. In every action against the unjust nation-state.

The psalm functions as a response to Daniel's apocalyptic scene. In Psalm 93 we see again a throne and an enthroned One. This One is majestic and girded in strength. This rule is not capricious but is stabilizing. This enthronement psalm echoes the assertion of other ancient Near Eastern claims: the chaotic primordial waters are defeated, and here the floodwaters praise this monarch. The rulings of this ruler give good order and safety. But according to the enthronement psalms, God is no longer one god among gods. Now only this One is sovereign and provides security.

Revelation 1:4b–8

Like Daniel, this book is an apocalyptic writing born in a tumult. The book discloses God's deliverance and judgments and offers an alternative to the oppression Christians faced in Asia Minor about 90–95 CE. Whereas Daniel's story is set in the Babylonian exile, John of Patmos speaks of Rome as Babylon.

This text from Revelation echoes other texts. The salutation is a greeting from God, who is past, present, and also future (v. 4b). We are welcomed and enfolded into this One who is throughout all time. This passage resonates with Jesus' words to Pilate in that they speak of a strength that does not derive from earthly political powers but from One who is cosmic. The greeting of this text also calls to mind the Ancient One depicted by Daniel and the One enthroned in majesty (Ps. 93).

In verses 5–8 two more themes connect with the other texts that are important for Reign of Christ Sunday. The first is naming Jesus as a witness. This is an extension of the salutation: "And from the seven spirits who are before [God's] throne, and from Jesus Christ, the faithful witness, the firstborn of the dead, and the ruler of the [rulers] of the earth" (vv. 4b–5). A witness to the ways of God is costly and powerful, as Jesus points out: "For this I was born, and for this I came into the world, to testify to the truth" (John 18:37). Jesus is a testimonial in his very bodily existence. Here the preacher could connect the witness of Jesus before Pilate to this salutation in Revelation, which references Jesus' witness to the ways of God.

Christians today differ in how they think of Jesus, but most Christians seek to emulate him: as a model of One into whom we grow. This emulation is manifested in the young child who convinced her parents to downsize their home and share the wealth; in the group of retirees who do not cease volunteering and are paired with kindergarten children to buy winter coats and a choice toy; in the career woman who, confronting legislators, lobbies for the rights of persons with disabilities.

In this verse from Revelation, Jesus is both witness and the "ruler of the [rulers] of the earth" (v. 5). His rule is the standard by which to measure the rule of all other rulers. He rules their wealth, landholdings, global investments, and legislative deliberations. He rules the despot and the favored ones. All these aspects of leadership are subject to Jesus.

The preacher could make another move. The preacher could move to verse 6: "To him who loves us and freed us from our sins by his blood, and made us to be a [dominion], priests serving his God and Father, to him be glory and dominion forever and ever. Amen." The preacher could speak of the reign of God according to John, Daniel, and the psalm, and then make the interesting connection to this verse that asserts that *we* are a dominion. We who follow Christ are, in our very bodies, the reign of Christ. There is judgment and audacity in these words, because we know we do not always manifest the reign of God.

2 Samuel 23:1–7 and Psalm 132

The reading from 2 Samuel gives us the last words of David, indicating that God has ruled through David in a way similar to the way God rules through Jesus. "The God of Israel has spoken, the Rock of Israel has said to me: One who rules over people justly, ruling in the fear of God, is like the light of morning, like the sun rising on a cloudless morning, gleaming from the rain on the grassy land" (vv. 3–4). God is a rock (a protector) and God is the sun— an ancient image for a monarch. This is royal theology from the Deuteronomist, who lauds the Davidic line and sees Jerusalem as the center of Israelite worship. The psalm appointed for this reading reflects these ideals.

Yet there is tension. The Davidic kingship is to be marked by the justice of God through the earthly sovereign's care for the people. But such behavior is only part of David's story. His story includes manipulation, lying, and exploitation. Through David's behavior we are reminded that even a divinely appointed earthly ruler does not always keep covenant with God. *God's* steadfastness is the origin and source of any good that comes from earthly rule. From this perspective we are called not only to evaluate earthly leadership but to lean into what God calls leaders to be and do. It is not enough to critique what is in front of us; we must revise the practices of leadership for both church and state, to conform more fully to God's purposes of love and justice.

Psalm 132, appointed for this 2 Samuel reading, reiterates the themes of the Davidic monarchy and the centrality of Jerusalem. This is a psalm of Ascents—sung by those going up to Jerusalem. It tells the story of David finding a house for God. The psalm recounts the covenant between God and David and underscores God's choice of Zion: "'I will abundantly bless [Zion's] provisions; I will satisfy its poor with bread'" (v. 15).

These readings serve as both a good warning and a promise. They are a warning for us who live among rulers who claim forms of divine appointment. Church officials go through the rigors of preparation and elections, as do state politicians. But such leaders can succumb to lying, injustice, and misrule. Though God is the source and origin of our actions, we can fall away—through public and private failings, for example, sexual abuses, theft of church treasuries, taking leisure time when a minister should be helping a congregation through a merger or even a closure.

Some leaders are so keen on a personal vision that they ignore the parishioners in front of them, in order to build a name for themselves with a new program or by generating mismatched missions. The leader who does not have a healthy sense of self can make every congregational interaction the personal stage for glory. We fail when we do not confront such behaviors, when judicatories pass these leaders along unchecked, when we perpetuate networks and keep secrets about inglorious actions. In covenantal hope we keep watch for such departure from God's intentions and work to recall and revision the purposes of leadership.

These passages also promise that when failures occur in communities, God does not give up on leaders or communities. God promises to provide the resources we need to act faithfully. We may need to repent of our attitudes and actions. We may need to revise how we live. But God seeks to work with us so that all may live in blessed community.

Thanksgiving Day

Traci C. West

JOEL 2:21–27
PSALM 126
1 TIMOTHY 2:1–7
MATTHEW 6:25–33

Individuals who suffer abuse at the hands of family members may wonder why they should feel thankful to God. In particular, most heterosexual women[1] who have been emotionally and physically tormented by their husbands, boyfriends, or intimate partners would be grateful for empowering theological messages by church leaders that directly speak to their crisis situations. Unfortunately, in worship preachers usually avoid the subject of intimate violence (physical and sexual assaults) against adult women, or tacitly reinforce the sanctity of their victimization with theology about the virtue of suffering as Jesus did. A justice-oriented interpretation of this set of lectionary passages can constructively respond to the search for relevant, emboldening theologies of thanksgiving by women victim-survivors in our congregations. These texts provide an opportunity to give thanks for God's attention to their anguish and insistence on their entitlement to equality and well-being.

The passage from Joel offers reassurance about God's restoration after shaming, fearful experiences. Psalm 126 declares that joy shall follow weeping. Ironically, to accomplish the truth telling championed by 1 Timothy 2, we must reject the endangering lies about women (of all sexual orientations) found in 1 Timothy 2. Finally, with its emphasis on genuine fulfillment as a goal of faith-filled living, Matthew 6 addresses inevitable anxieties about

---

1. Intimate-partner abuse also occurs in same-gender relationships. I have chosen to emphasize heterosexual relationships because of (1) the numerous explicit messages in Christian tradition about female submissiveness to males in heterosexual intimate relationships, and (2) the fact that the overwhelming majority of violence in contemporary intimate-partner relationships is committed by heterosexual males. I do not want to convey inaccurately the idea that intimate violence in heterosexual relationships can be equated with its occurrence in same-gender relationships.

practical needs of victim-survivors, as well as of entire congregations when they make radical changes to end the violence.

Joel 2:21–27

In Joel, thanksgiving to God begins with reassurance for the fearful (v. 21). In abusive intimate relationships, abusers often employ an array of surveillance tactics to maintain a climate of fear and intimidation. With increasing frequency, some abusers now utilize technology to stalk and control their intimate partners. A woman's abusive partner might review the history on her computer to see if she has Googled any battered women's services, use "sniffer" programs to monitor her e-mail, and convert cellular telephones into listening devices or plant hidden cameras to monitor her contact with friends and family. The abuser maintains the woman's social isolation, fear, and anxiety in conjunction with his godlike, inescapable presence. Abusers also use more ordinary means of control, such as repeatedly telling the woman that she is ugly, stupid, a bad mother, sexually undesirable, untrustworthy, or flirtatious with other men. When these cruel strategies make the women feel "like dirt," thankfully Joel's proclamation, "Do not fear, O soil" (v. 21), provides an appropriate intervention from God. It changes the stigma of being treated like "dirt" by the abuser into recognition by God as "soil" that contains wondrous nutrients. With help from others and transformative nurturing (vindicating rain, v. 23) the capacity for new, abundant life can emerge.

Descriptive rather than prescriptive phrases in Joel are relevant metaphors here. Ironically, weekly (or monthly) Communion liturgies about a bloodied, beaten body that is not merely virtuous but celebrated as sacrament subtly encourage women to accept abuse. Attacks by God's armies of "locusts" and "destroyers" (v. 25) are apt analogies for the resulting emotional, spiritual, and physical torment the victim-survivors can experience. More literally, when armies (v. 25b) wage war, increased violence against women at home (domestic violence) and abroad (sexual assaults) often occurs. Sexual violence against women is sometimes perpetrated even by supposedly liberating armies allegedly sent by God, such as the egregious example of the gang rape and murder of a fourteen-year-old Iraqi girl by U.S. soldiers in Mahmoudia, south of Baghdad, in 2006.

For the victim-survivor of domestic violence, often the feelings of humiliation and shock after being assaulted by someone she trusts and loves dovetail with the shaming silence of her church—as if such things did not happen to good Christians. Thankfully, there is good news for her in Joel's reaffirmation from God: "My people will never again be put to shame" (vv. 26b, 27b). Instead of isolating her, God claims her as "my people." The stigmatizing consequences of her abuse are acknowledged by God. Most importantly, God declares an end to it.

Psalm 126

Similarly Psalm 126 offers thanksgiving for God's restoration (v. 1). The psalm lifts up those "who sow in tears" (v. 5). Within its original cultural setting, the toil of sowing referred to everyday agricultural chores to provide food for the community. Today, the tears shed in response to an intimate partner-abuser often become a hidden part of an abused church member's life as she toils in everyday work, such as care for her children or for elderly family members, as well as earning money to support herself and her family, and to place in the offering plate to support her church.

Moreover, the pain and anguish that cause her tears are not factored into the damage of domestic violence redressed in a criminal court prosecution of the abuser. Even civil courts seldom provide recourse for victim-survivors of domestic violence to seek compensation for emotional distress intentionally inflicted by batterers.[2] Thank God for the alternative moral reality provided by the theology in this psalm. Based on the vindication theme in Psalm 126, the church can celebrate God's restoration of an abused woman's full human dignity. Her tears matter to God. God counts the costliness of the anguish and torment she endured as significant harm that demands restitution.

1 Timothy 2:1–7

One important reason for someone victimized by physical or sexual violence to give thanks to God would be her discovery of a responsive local community that both provides reliable resources to address her victimization and attempts to prevent others from being harmed in the same way. First Timothy 2 addresses the entire faith community and urges them to offer supplications, prayers, intercessions, and thanksgivings for everyone (v. 1). This concern clearly extends beyond the faith community and specifically includes secular authorities (v. 2). Therefore, when developing the means for accountability and transformation in response to violence against women, the moral and spiritual focus of our congregations must include societal structures of power, such as the police, judges, legislators, governors, and other policy makers. Which ones need to be asked to change, and which ones should be

---

2. For an insightful discussion of legal issues, see Martha Chamallas and Jennifer B. Wriggins, *The Measure of Injury: Race, Gender, and Tort Law* (New York: New York University Press, 2010).

thanked for a demonstrated commitment to justice and freedom from violence for women victim-survivors? Who are the social workers, activists, and hotline staff working for women's right to lives with peace and quiet (v. 2b) that should be named in prayers of thanksgiving?

Truth telling is one of the central themes of this text and is always an issue in violence against women. Timothy voices a universal understanding of God's desire for everyone to be saved and have accurate knowledge (v. 4), together with the author's more personal insistence: "I am telling the truth, I am not lying" (v. 7). The text reiterates that he is a teacher of Gentiles "in faith and truth" (v. 7).

Black feminist Chandra Ford recalls struggling with her rapist, who wanted to teach her a lesson because she was a lesbian. The manipulation of truth and lies became one of his tools of torment: "Laughing at me, he would ask me questions like 'Are you a lesbian?' There was no right answer, for when I said 'Yes,' he physically assaulted me, and when I said 'No,' he sexualized the assault telling me I enjoyed what he was doing."[3] Perpetrators of male violence against women often replace the truth about their own crimes with lies that find the women they victimize blameworthy. Unfortunately, some Scriptures teach lies about the innate blameworthiness of women, lending credence to the manipulations by perpetrators.

In 1 Timothy 2, just after the lectionary passage ends, the author's view of appropriate gender roles directly mandates women's silence and submission to men's authority, identifying women as innately transgressors (because of Eve) who can be saved only through childbearing (vv. 11–15). The 1 Timothy 2 lectionary passage cannot be preached truthfully without pointing out these assertions later in the chapter and noting them as false ideas about women's worth. Preachers must declare our thankfulness to God for women's unconditional equality, autonomy, and entitlement to speak to and assert authority over men. This kind of affirmation matters to women victimized by male violence. As Chandra Ford describes after pursuing the successful criminal prosecution of her rapist,

> I won, not because M. went to jail, but because I spoke when he and others counted on my fear to silence me. I still feel empowered today when I recall what it felt like to look directly in his eyes in the courtroom as I pointed him out to the judge, and uttered my truth in his presence. I won then when I chose to embrace my identity as a lesbian of color.[4]

3. Chandra Ford, "Standing on *This* Bridge," in *This Bridge We Call Home: Radical Visions for Transformations*, ed. Gloria E. Anzaldua and Analouise Keating (New York: Routledge, 2002), 307.
4. Ibid., 312.

Thanksgiving to God is in order for truth telling that (1) reveals the attacker's deeds and culpability, (2) liberates women from silencing that keeps other women in danger of being attacked by unrestrained perpetrators, and (3) also fully embraces the godliness and human dignity (v. 2b) of women victim-survivors attested to by the God-human at the center of our faith, Jesus Christ (vv. 5b–6).

Matthew 6:25–33

The words of Jesus in Matthew 6 urge us to focus on building genuinely righteous relations that reflect God's kin-dom in our midst (v. 33). The passage realistically notes that concern for practicalities like what we will eat and drink or how we will find clothes to wear (vv. 25, 31) can interfere with following through on this kin-dom pursuit.

When a victim-survivor of domestic violence considers leaving her home to escape an abusive partner, it may be difficult for her to ignore the financial consequences, especially if she has children. Similarly, anxieties might surface in a pastor who considers declaring from the pulpit that lies about women's salvation (1 Tim. 2:15) are told in Scripture and then explaining how those verses can support abuse of women. The pastor may wonder if such an unequivocal declaration could alienate church leaders and threaten her continued employment, thereby placing in jeopardy her ability to buy food and clothing. Or a congregation might be plagued by worriers concerned about losing members and financial contributions if they decided to adopt a comprehensive prevention strategy with a range of activities that included required Sunday school lessons on gender equality for all ages, youth-produced antiviolence Christian music, and interfaith community speak-outs for men on antiviolence and masculinity.

But thanksgivings to God should replace such anxieties. The Gospel passage reminds us that we are to trust in God instead of worrying (vv. 30–31). God will supply the basic provisions we need if we, as people of faith, make the embodiment of kin-dom relations (v. 33) our first priority. This passage is part of a group of sayings that Jesus teaches to a large crowd. Therefore, neither the women surviving male violence nor preachers trying to address it are asked to make radical kin-dom building changes as lone individuals. Thankfully, the entire faith community is invited to join together to support each other in the difficult step of shedding anxieties about what we might lose or may not have in the future, and instead trust in God to provide, as we make the necessary, dramatic changes to live into God's *shalom*.

Contributors

Charles G. Adams, *Hartford Memorial Baptist Church, Detroit, Michigan*

Ronald J. Allen, *Christian Theological Seminary*

Dale P. Andrews, *The Divinity School, Vanderbilt University*

Randall C. Bailey, *Interdenominational Theological Center*

Wilma Ann Bailey, *Christian Theological Seminary*

Dianne Bergant, CSA, *Catholic Theological Union*

J. B. Blue, *Boston University School of Theology*

L. Susan Bond, *Lane College*

Alejandro F. Botta, *Boston University School of Theology*

Valerie Bridgeman, *Lancaster Theological Seminary*

Martin Brokenleg, *Vancouver School of Theology (Emeritus)*

Gennifer Benjamin Brooks, *Garrett-Evangelical Theological Seminary*

Carolynne Hitter Brown, *Southern Baptist Church, Cambridge, Massachusetts*

John M. Buchanan, *Fourth Presbyterian Church, Chicago, Illinois*

Randall K. Bush, *East Liberty Presbyterian Church, Pittsburgh, Pennsylvania*

Lee H. Butler Jr., *Chicago Theological Seminary*

Terriel R. Byrd, *School of Ministry, Palm Beach Atlantic University*

Charles L. Campbell, *The Divinity School, Duke University*

Cláudio Carvalhaes, *Louisville Presbyterian Theological Seminary*

Diane G. Chen, *Palmer Theological Seminary, Eastern University*

Choi Hee An, *Boston University School of Theology*

Monica A. Coleman, *Claremont School of Theology*

Elizabeth Conde-Frazier, *Esperanza College, Eastern University*

Shannon Daley-Harris, *Children's Defense Fund, Washington, D.C.*

Frederick John Dalton, *Bellarmine College Preparatory School, San Jose, California*

Noelle Damico, *Presbyterian Hunger Program, Presbyterian Church (U.S.A.)*

María Teresa Dávila, *Andover Newton Theological School*

Miguel A. De La Torre, *Iliff School of Theology*

Bob Ekblad, *Tierra Nueva and The People's Seminary, Burlington, Washington*

Joseph Evans, *Mt. Carmel Baptist Church, Washington, D.C.*

Marie M. Fortune, *FaithTrust Institute, Seattle, Washington*

Safiyah Fosua, *General Board of Discipleship, United Methodist Church*

David J. Frenchak, *Seminary Consortium for Urban Pastoral Education (SCUPE) (Emeritus)*

Lincoln E. Galloway, *Claremont School of Theology*

Kenyatta R. Gilbert, *The Divinity School, Howard University*

R. Mark Giuliano, *Old Stone Church, Cleveland, Ohio*

Chris Glaser, *Metropolitan Community Church, Atlanta, Georgia*

Catherine Gunsalus González, *Columbia Theological Seminary (Emerita)*

Justo L. González, *Asociación para la Educación Teológica Hispana (AETH), United Methodist Church (Retired)*

Esther J. Hamori, *Union Theological Seminary, New York*

James Henry Harris, *Samuel Dewitt Proctor School of Theology, Virginia Union University, and Second Baptist Church, Richmond, Virginia*

John Hart, *Boston University School of Theology*

Olive Elaine Hinnant, *United Church of Christ, Denver, Colorado*

Ruthanna B. Hooke, *Virginia Theological Seminary*

Rhashell Hunter, *Racial Ethnic and Women's Ministries, Presbyterian Church (U.S.A.)*

Ada María Isasi-Díaz, *The Theological School, Drew University (Emerita)*

Joseph R. Jeter Jr., *Brite Divinity School (Emeritus)*

Pablo A. Jiménez, *Espinosa Christian Church, Dorado, Puerto Rico, and Chalice Press*

Nicole L. Johnson, *University of Mount Union*

Song Bok Jon, *Boston University School of Theology*

Nyasha Junior, *The Divinity School, Howard University*

John Kaltner, *Rhodes College*

Grace Ji-Sun Kim, *Moravian Theological Seminary*

Simone Sunghae Kim, *Yonsei University, Wonju Campus, South Korea*

Kah-Jin Jeffrey Kuan, *The Theological School, Drew University*

Jennifer L. Lord, *Austin Presbyterian Theological Seminary*

Barbara K. Lundblad, *Union Theological Seminary, New York*

Fumitaka Matsuoka, *Pacific School of Religion (Emeritus)*

William B. McClain, *Wesley Theological Seminary*

John S. McClure, *The Divinity School, Vanderbilt University*

James L. McDonald, *Bread for the World, Washington, D.C.*

Alyce M. McKenzie, *Perkins School of Theology, Southern Methodist University*

Marvin A. McMickle, *Ashland Theological Seminary, and Antioch Baptist Church,
Cleveland, Ohio*

Henry H. Mitchell, *Interdenominational Theological Center (Emeritus)*

Mary Alice Mulligan, *Christian Theological Seminary*

Ched Myers, *Bartimaeus Cooperative Ministries, Oak View, California*

James Anthony Noel, *San Francisco Theological Seminary*

Dawn Ottoni-Wilhelm, *Bethany Theological Seminary*

Peter J. Paris, *Princeton Theological Seminary (Emeritus)*

Rebecca Todd Peters, *Elon University*

Luke A. Powery, *Princeton Theological Seminary*

Melinda A. Quivik, *Liturgical Scholar, Houghton, Michigan*

Stephen G. Ray Jr., *Garrett-Evangelical Theological Seminary*

Sharon H. Ringe, *Wesley Theological Seminary*

Joni S. Sancken, *Eastern Mennonite Seminary, Eastern Mennonite University*

Elizabeth J. A. Siwo-Okundi, *Boston University School of Theology*

Chandra Taylor Smith, *The Pell Institute, Washington, D.C.*

Christine Marie Smith, *United Theological Seminary of the Twin Cities*

Kee Boem So, *New York Presbyterian Theological Seminary (Korean Presbyterian
Church Abroad)*

Teresa Lockhart Stricklen, *Office of Theology and Worship, Presbyterian Church (U.S.A.)*

Marjorie Hewitt Suchocki, *Claremont School of Theology (Emerita)*

Willard Swartley, *Associated Mennonite Biblical Seminary (Emeritus)*

JoAnne Marie Terrell, *Chicago Theological Seminary*

Leonora Tubbs Tisdale, *The Divinity School, Yale University*

Jeffery L. Tribble Sr., *Columbia Theological Seminary*

Arthur Van Seters, *Knox College (Emeritus)*

Traci C. West, *The Theological School, Drew University*

Edward L. Wheeler, *Christian Theological Seminary (Emeritus)*

Clark M. Williamson, *Christian Theological Seminary (Emeritus)*

Scott C. Williamson, *Louisville Presbyterian Theological Seminary*

Scripture Index

513

516   Scripture Index